D0900930

Chess Stars
Openings

Technical Editor: IM Sergey Soloviov

Cover design by: Kalojan Nachev

Translation by: GM Evgeny Ermenkov

The publishers would like to thank Phil Adams for advice regarding the English translation.

Copyright © Konstantin Sakaev 2011

Printed in Bulgaria by "Chess Stars" Ltd. - Sofia
ISBN13: 978 954 8782 84-5

Konstantin Sakaev

The Petroff: an Expert Repertoire for Black

Chess Stars

Other CHESS STARS Books

Repertoire books:

Opening for White Acc. to Kramnik 1.♘f3 by A. Khalifman
Volume 1a: Old Indian, rare lines in the Classical Variation, 2006
Volume 1b: The Classical Variation, 2006
Volume 2: Anti-Nim-Ind, Anti-Queen's Indian, English, 2008
Volume 3: English (1...c5), English (four knights), 2011

Opening for White According to Anand 1.e4 by A. Khalifman
Volume 8: The Sicilian, Paulsen-Kan and rare lines, 2006
Volume 9: The Sicilian, Paulsen-Taimanov and other lines, 2007
Volume 10: The Sicilian, Sveshnikov, 2007
Volume 11; The Sicilian, Dragon, 2009
Volume 12: The Sicilian, Rauzer Attack, 2009
Volume 13: The Sicilian, English Attack, 2010

Opening for Black According to Karpov by Khalifman

Current theory and practice series:

An Expert's Guide to the 7.Bc4 Gruenfeld by Sakaev, 2006
The Sharpest Sicilian by Kiril Georgiev and At. Kolev, 2007
The Safest Sicilian by Delchev and Semkov, 2nd rev.ed. 2008
The Queen's Gambit Accepted by Sakaev and Semkov, 3rd. rev. ed., 2008
The Easiest Sicilian by Kolev and Nedev, 2008
The Petrosian System Against the QID by Beliavsky and Mikhalchishin, 2008
Kill K.I.D. by Semko Semkov, 2009
The King's Indian. A Complete Black Repertoire by Victor Bologan, 2009
The Scotch Game for White by Vladimir Barsky, 2009
The Modern Philidor Defence by Vladimir Barsky, 2010
The Moscow & Anti-Moscow Variations by Alexey Dreev, 2010
Squeezing the Gambits by Kiril Georgiev, 2010
The French Defence. A Complete Black Repertoire by Nikita Vitiugov, 2010
A Universal Weapon 1.d4 d6 by Vladimir Barsky, 2010
The Meran & Anti-Meran Variations by Alexey Dreev, 2011
The Safest Grunfeld by Alexander Delchev and Evgenij Agrest, 2011
Fighting the French: a New Concept by Denis Yevseev, 2011

More details at **www.chess-stars.com**

Contents

PREFACE

The Petroff Defence is an exceptionally reliable and almost indestructible opening, and a hard nut to crack, even for the strongest and most meticulously prepared grandmasters theoretically. It is no accident that the Petroff Defence, named after its inventor and also know as the Russian Game, has for many years been the main opening weapon of Vladimir Kramnik and Boris Gelfand and has also been played regularly by Vishy Anand and Alexey Shirov. Nowadays there are also several very young and talented grandmasters who play it, such as Wesley So and Anish Giri. Anatoly Karpov and Artur Yusupov have been using it as a part of their opening armoury throughout their chess careers... The list could go on and on.

The Petroff Defence is characterised by the fact that on his second move Black does not protect his e5-pawn, but instead counter attacks with 2...♘f6, proposing to the opponent the immediate exchange of a pair of pawns, thus slightly simplifying the position and quickly defining the future pawn-structure.

What are the pluses and minuses of an opening repertoire based on the Petroff Defence, such as we are recommending in this book? I think I can see only one drawback. If White is an experienced player with a good grasp of theory, and he is in the mood to draw, then he should be able to share the point without too much problem. Still, the same can also be said about almost every other opening, because in contemporary chess it is tremendously difficult to win with Black unless White makes a serious mistake. On the other hand, there is a great advantage to consider: you will not obtain bad positions from the opening. The Petroff Defence is particularly suitable for players with a positional style, since in a calm, quiet contest you can easily win the game if the opponent takes too many risks. You can see this illustrated in the Complete Games section.

I have endeavoured to present and explain to you all the finer points of this opening, as I understand them. In general, the critical positions have been treated thoroughly and I have also suggested and analyzed a great many new ideas in this book. Some variations which have amassed considerable tournament practice, but which, in my view, are less principled, have been covered only briefly. Otherwise, the book would have become too big, losing its essential purpose. Unfortunately, too many authors write chess books in that way; they offer no original analysis and often quote outdated games, some of which are very weakly played and almost useless.

I hope that you, the reader, will enjoy studying this book, and I wish you wonderful tournament results with this opening!

Konstantin Sakaev,
Saint Petersburg 2011

Part 1

1.e4 e5

All White Replies without 2.♘f3

I have discussed numerous times and I know, from my own experience, how difficult it is for White to combat the Petroff Defence. Whenever you are preparing at home against the possibility of facing this opening in a tournament game, even if you are a very strong player you have great problems.

In Chapter One of our book, we shall first analyse some very rarely played attempts for White to avoid the Petroff and ♗lack's reaction to all of them is fairly simple.

Later, we deal with the **Vienna Game**, in which White plays "incorrectly" on the kingside and Black should respond with a classical counter-attack in the centre, ending up with an excellent position.

As for the **King's Gambit**, this is a very complex opening with a long and rich history, but readers will find very reliable ways to combat this too.

Finally, the **Bishop's Opening** is a direct attempt to avoid the Petroff and to introduce themes which are similar to those of the Italian Game. White's plans are destined to fail, however, because after **2...♘f6 3.d3 c6,** there arises an immediate conflict in the centre, which is quite advantageous for Black.

Chapter 1 1.e4 e5

Seldom Played Moves

2.d4

It is difficult to take the move 2.♕h5 seriously. Black has many attractive options and I shall show you just one of these: 2...♘c6 3.♗c4 g6 4.♕f3 ♘f6 5.♘e2 ♗g7 6.♘bc3 d6 7.d3, Nakamura – Sasikiran, Copenhagen 2005. Here, I believe Black's most logical move is 7...♘a5∓, exchanging White's light-squared bishop for the knight and ending up with a slight edge for Black.

We shall briefly deal with the move 2.d3. We have no intention here of analyzing plans based on some passive set-up for White with a bishop or a queen on the e2-square, or with a knight on d2. In all these cases Black should develop his knights on c6 and f6 and advance d7-d5, seizing space and ensuring a very comfortable position. We shall limit ourselves to examining White's active possibility of trying to advance with f2-f4. It is quite obvious that this pawn advance is very risky, since it exposes White's king, especially in connection with the fact that his light-squared bishop will be restricted to the e2-square. 2...♘f6 (Black is preparing d7-d5. It is safer for him to play 2...♘c6 and here 3.f4 seems to be too adventurous for White owing to 3...d5!) 3.f4 (A better move for White is 3.♘f3, but Black can answer this with 3...♘c6, followed by d7-d5. It is also good to play symmetrically with 3...d6, followed by fianchettoing the bishop on g7. The position is closed and White's extra tempo is irrelevant, so the game is equal.)

(diagram)

and now:

3...♘c6 4.fxe5 ♘xe5 5.d4 ♘xe4!? (This is an interesting move. It is simpler for Black to opt for 5...♘c6 6.e5 ♘e4 7.♘f3 d5

8.♗d3 ♗e7 9.0–0 0–0 10.♘c3 ♗f5 11.♖e1 f6=, with equality.) 6.♕e2 d5 7.dxe5 ♕h4 8.g3 ♘xg3 9.hxg3 ♕xh1 10.♗e3 ♕e4 11.♗g2 ♕xe5 (The game is rather unclear after 11...♕g6!? 12.♕f2 c6 13.♘c3∞) 12. ♘f3 ♕e6 13.♘d4 ♕e5 14.♘f3 ♕e6= and after a repetition of moves the result will be a draw;

3...exf4 4.♗xf4 (4.e5? ♘d5∓) 4...♘c6 5.♗e2! (5.♘f3 d5 6.e5 ♘h5 7.♗d2 h6!∓, followed by g7-g5!) 5...♗c5 (5...♗d6!? 6.♗xd6 cxd6 7. c4 0–0 8.♘c3 a6 9.♘f3 b5⇄) 6. ♘c3 0–0 (6...d5 7.e5 ♘g4 8.♗xg4 ♕h4 9.♗g3 ♕xg4 10.♘xd5 ♕d7 11.c4 ♘b4⩱ – Black has good compensation for the pawn, sufficient for equality.) 7.e5 ♘e8 8.♘f3 d6 (8...f6 9.d4 fxe5 10.dxe5 ♖xf4 11. ♕d5±; 8...♘d4!? 9.♘e4 ♘e6∞) 9. ♗g5 ♕d7 10.d4 ♗b6 11.♘d5 h6∞ – Black's position is fine apart from the knight on e8, making the position difficult to evaluate.

2...exd4

(diagram)

First of all, we shall look at White's possible deviations from the Centre Game:

A) 3.c3, **B) 3.♘f3** and then at the Centre Game itself: **C) 3.♕xd4**.

It is simply bad for White to play 3.f4? ♘c6 4. ♘f3 ♗c5∓ – he will not regain his d4-pawn and has no compensation whatsoever.

The line 3.♗c4 ♘f6 transposes to the Bishop's Opening.

A) 3.c3

With this move White is offering the sharp Danish Gambit. However, Black is not forced to accept the sacrifice and he has a simple and reliable way of obtaining an excellent position.

3...d5 4.exd5

After 4.♕xd4 the best White can hope for is equality. His c3-pawn deprives his knight of that square and does not enhance his position. After 4...dxe4 5.♕xe4 ♗e7 6.♗g5 ♘d7 7.♘f3 ♘gf6 8.♕c2 0–0 9.♗e2 h6 10.♗h4 ♖e8 11.0–0 ♘h5∓ Black has an excellent position, Tomas Batet – Korneev, Malaga 2002.

4...♕xd5 5.cxd4

The move 5.♘f3 makes little sense at this point, because White will have to capture on d4 with his pawn anyway.

5...♘c6 6.♘f3 ♗g4

7.♘c3

For 7.♗e2 ♗b4 8.♘c3 – see 7. ♘c3.

7...♗b4 8.♗e2 ♗xf3 9.♗xf3 ♕c4 10.♕b3

The endgame is equal after 10.♗xc6 bxc6 11.♕e2 ♕xe2 12. ♔xe2=

10...♕xb3 11.axb3 ♘ge7 12. ♗e3 0–0–0 13.0–0

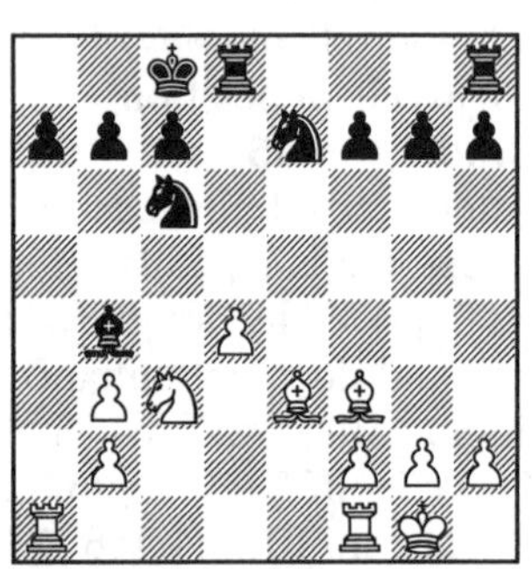

13...a5!

This move is better than 13... a6, which has been played much more often.

14.♖fd1, D.Mastrovasilis – Skembris, Greece 2001. Black should continue to play in the centre with **14...♖he8!=** and he solves all his opening problems.

B) 3.♘f3

With this move White is trying to transpose to the Scotch Game, which arises if Black replies with 3...♘c6. He is not obliged to do this however and has a very good alternative in

3...♗b4+

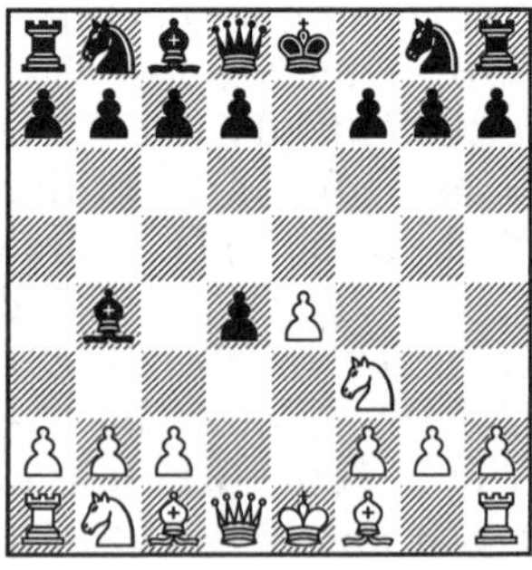

Now White can reply with: **B1) 4.c3** or **B2) 4.♗d2**.

B1) 4.c3 dxc3 5.♘xc3

After 5.bxc3, Black's safest move is 5...♗e7. The bishop is placed on a protected square and prevents the possible sortie of his opponent's knight to g5 (Even after 5...♗c5 6.♗c4 d6 7. 0–0 ♘c6 White can hardly prove sufficient compensation for the pawn.). 6.♗c4 d5! 7.exd5 ♘f6 8. 0–0 0–0 9.♗a3 (after 9.♗b3, Black has the resource 9...♘a6, with the idea of ♘a6-c5) 9...♘bd7 10.♗b3 ♗xa3 11. ♘xa3 ♘c5∓ and he is even slightly better, Zviaginsev – Motylev, Ubeda 2000.

5...♗xc3

If Black plays the immediate 5...♘e7, then White can reply with 6.♕d4 ♗xc3 7.♕xc3 0–0 8.b4!? d5 9.♗b2 f6 10.♗d3⩱, reaching a complicated position in which White has enough compensation for the pawn, Zviaginsev – Beliavsky, Portoroz 1999.

6.bxc3 ♘e7 7.e5

Or 7.♗c4 0–0 8.0–0 ♘bc6 9.e5 d5 10.exd6 ♕xd6 11.♕xd6 cxd6∓ and White must play precisely in order to fight for a draw, Velimirovic – Motylev, Herceg Novi 2000.

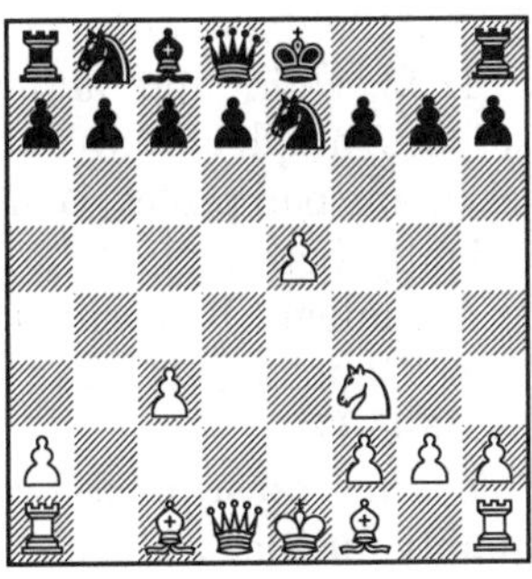

7...d5! 8.exd6 ♕xd6

After 8...cxd6 9.♗a3 ♘bc6 10. ♕xd6 ♕xd6 11.♗xd6 0–0= there is a transposition to the same endgame as in the main line.

9.♕xd6 cxd6 10.♗a3 ♘bc6

The priority in this position is quick development! If Black holds on to the extra pawn, then after 10...d5 11.0–0–0 ♘bc6 12.♗b5 ♗e6 13.♖he1± he runs into difficulties, Zezulkin – Karpov, Bastia 2002.

11.♗xd6 0–0

After 11...♗e6 White can play 12.♘g5 0–0–0 13.♗a3 ♘d5 14. ♘xe6±, so Black is reluctant to give up his second bishop for a knight.

12.0–0–0 ♗e6 13.♔b2

An attempt to play aggressively would not work for White: 13.♘g5 ♗xa2 14.♔b2 h6! 15. ♔xa2 hxg5 16.♗xe7 (otherwise White will be a pawn down without any compensation whatsoever) 16...♘xe7 17.♖d7 ♘g6 18. ♖xb7 ♖fd8= – Black's rook is ready to go to d2 and he is in no danger.

13...♖fd8=

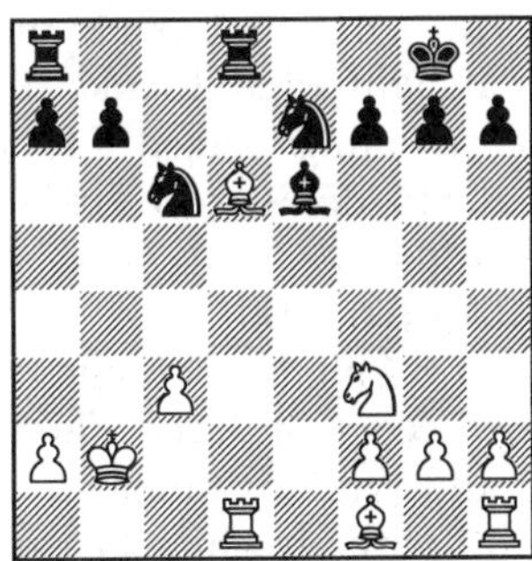

White cannot profit from the advantage of the bishop pair, since his pieces lack coordination, while Black has easy play on the light squares. He has the possibility of deploying his knight along the route e7-d5-b6 and later to a4 or c4, according to circumstances. White can hardly save his light-squared bishop from being exchanged, so the game is equal.

B2) 4.♗d2

4...♗xd2 5.♘bxd2

The position is completely equal after 5.♕xd2 c5 (If Black wishes to enter a more complicated struggle he can choose 5...♕e7 6.♕xd4 ♘f6 7.♘c3 ♘c6 8.♕e3 0–0 9.♗d3 d6±, but White maintains a slight edge, thanks to his space advantage.) 6.c3 ♘f6 7.e5 ♘e4 8.♕f4 d5 9.exd6 ♘xd6 10.cxd4 cxd4=

5...♘c6 6.♘b3

After 6.♗b5, Black replies with 6...a6! 7.♗xc6 (if 7.♗a4, then 7...♘ge7 and White is unable to play ♘d2-b3, without which he cannot regain his d4-pawn) 7...dxc6 8.♘b3 b6! 9.♕xd4 ♕xd4 10.♘fxd4 c5!=. Black has deployed his queenside pawns on dark squares and the endgame is excellent for him. On his next move he can continue with f7-f5!, liberating his bishop after an exchange of pawns, or obtaining the excellent blockading square e6 if White's e-pawn advances.

6...♘f6 7.♗d3 0–0 8.0–0 ♖e8

Here it appears to be almost equally strong for Black to play the immediate 8...d5!?

9.♖e1

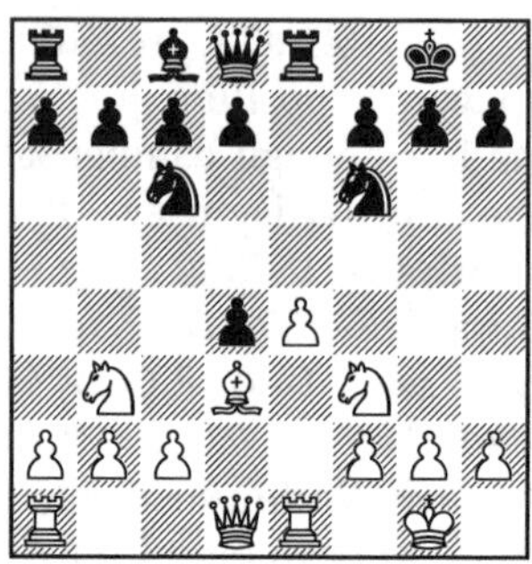

9...d5

It is a bit passive for him to opt for 9...d6 10.♘fxd4 ♗d7 11.♘xc6 ♗xc6 12.f3 ♕e7± and although Black does not have any weaknesses or any bad pieces, White is still slightly better thanks to his space advantage, B.Savchenko – Chadaev, Olginka 2011.

10.e5 ♘d7!

This is the most precise route to equality for Black. His alternatives are less convincing, for example: 10...♘g4 11.h3 ♘gxe5 12.♘xe5 ♘xe5 13.♗xh7 ♔xh7 14.♕h5 ♔g8 15.♖xe5 ♖xe5 16.♕xe5 f6 17.♕f4 b6 18.♘xd4 c5 19.♘b5 a6 20.♘d6 ♕e7 21.b4!±

There is also a way to reach a more complex but still approximately equal position: 10...♘e4!? 11.♘bxd4 ♘xd4 12.♘xd4 c5 13.♘b5 ♗d7=

11.♘bxd4 ♘xd4 12.♘xd4 ♘xe5 13.♗xh7 ♔xh7 14.♕h5 ♔g8 15.♖xe5 c5 16.♖xd5

16.♘f3 ♖xe5 17.♕xe5 f6=

16...♕f6 17.♘f3 ♕bx2 18.♖f1 ♕xc2 19.♖xc5 ♕e2= Black's king is a bit exposed, but White cannot exploit this effectively, so the position is equal.

C) 3.♕xd4 ♘c6

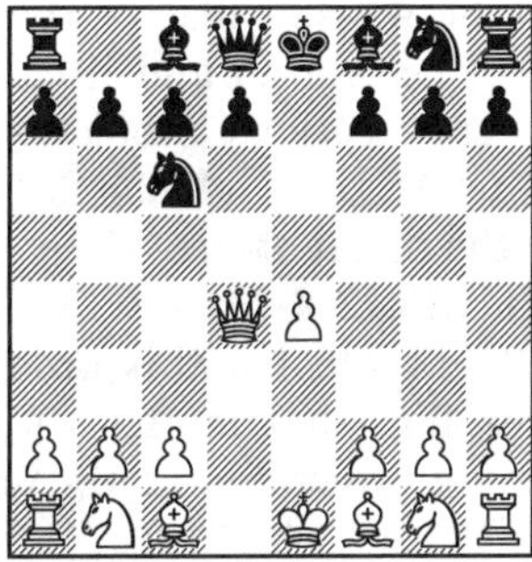

4.♕e3

The main idea of the Centre Game is to transfer the white queen to g3, exerting powerful pressure against the g7-square. Accordingly, retreating White's queen to a4 or d1 makes little sense. Black simply develops his knight on f6 and bishop on c5, obtaining a lead in development and seizing the initiative. After 4.♕d3, the best that White can hope for is to transpose to the main line: 4...♘f6 5.♘c3 ♗b4 (Black has another very promising alternative here in 5...♗c5!?) 6.♗d2 0–0 7.0–0–0 ♖e8 8.♕g3.

4...♘f6 5.♘c3

It is very important for White to continue with his development. After 5.e5? ♘g4 6.♕e2 (or 6.♕e4 ♕h4 followed by ♕h5 – White loses his e5-pawn) 6...d6 7.h3 ♘h6 (the piece-sacrifice 7...♘xe5!? looks very attractive too) 8.exd6 ♗e6 Black has a powerful initiative for Black.

After 5.♗d2?! Black's simplest reply is 5...♗e7 (Naturally he can also play 5...♗b4 and if White does not transpose to the main line with 6.♘c3, the game is equal.) 6.♘c3 d5! and after the exchange of the central pawns, Black's position seems more active.

It looks useless for White to play 5.♘f3?!, because he bars the way of his queen to the g3-square. After 5...♗b4 6.c3 (it is even worse for White to play 6.♗d2 0–0 and Black is threatening ♖e8) 6...♗a5 7.♗d3 0–0 8.0–0 d5!∓ Black is fighting for the initiative.

5...♗b4 6.♗d2 0–0 7. 0–0–0 ♖e8 8.♕g3

Or 8.♗c4 d6 9.f3 ♘e5 10.♗b3 c6∓ and White has no active prospects on the kingside, while Black is ready to withdraw his bishop to c5 with tempo and then begin an offensive with b7-b5 and a7-a5.

It would be disastrous for White to opt for 8.f3? d5∓ and his queen on e3 is exposed, becoming an easy target for Black's pieces.

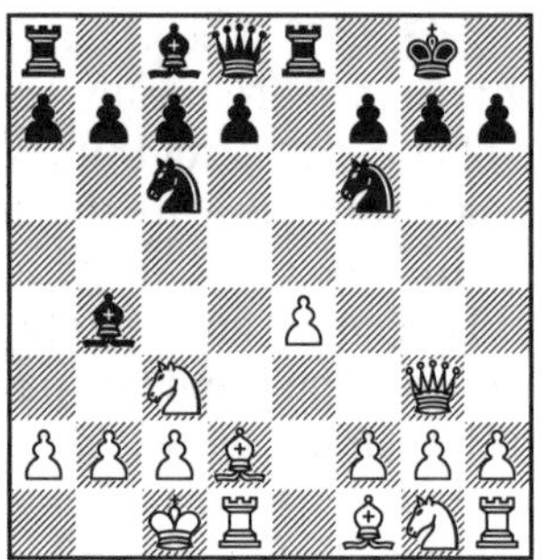

8...♘xe4

White does not have full compensation for the pawn after 8... ♖xe4, but the game becomes sharper and much more complex. A possible continuation is 9.a3 ♗a5 (9...♖g4!?) 10.f3 ♖e8 11.♘ge2 d6 12.h4, Shabalov – Martinovsky Chicago 1996. Black must play very precisely to neutralize White's kingside initiative, for example: 12...♔h8 (12...♘e7!?) 13. h5 h6 14.♘f4 ♗f5 15.♕h4 (White must try to advance his g-pawn; since he has no other reasonable plan) 15...♘e5 16.♗e2 ♕d7. Now, owing to some tactical nuances, it is bad for White to play 17.g4 ♗xc3 18.♗xc3 ♗xc2! 19.♖d2 ♗h7 20.g5 ♕f5–+. White might have some other interesting ideas, but if Black plays well he should be able to hold his own in all lines.

9.♘xe4 ♖xe4 10.c3

10.♗xb4 ♘xb4 (here it is also good for Black to play 10... ♖xb4!?∓) 11.a3 ♘c6 12.♗d3 ♖e8 13.♘f3 d6 14.♖he1 h6 15.♖xe8 ♕xe8 16.♖e1 ♕f8∓ and now Black just needs to play ♗c8-d7 and ♖a8-e8. White's initiative is insufficient to compensate for the sacrificed pawn.

10...♗e7! 11.f4

11.♘f3 d6 12.h3 ♘e5 13.♘xe5 ♖xe5 14.f4 ♖a5∓ Black's rook is well placed on a5 and it cannot cause any serious problems for him. Or 11.♗d3 ♗h4 12.♕f3 ♖e8∓ with the threat of ♘c6-e5.

11...d5 12.♗d3

12.♘f3 ♗f5 (In this order of moves, Black has another very interesting possibility in 12...♖a4!? 13. ♗d3 ♖xa2 14.♔b1 ♖a5 15.♖he1 d4∓, with very active play and some advantage.) 13.♗d3 ♕d7 14. ♗xe4 ♗xe4 – see 12.♗d3.

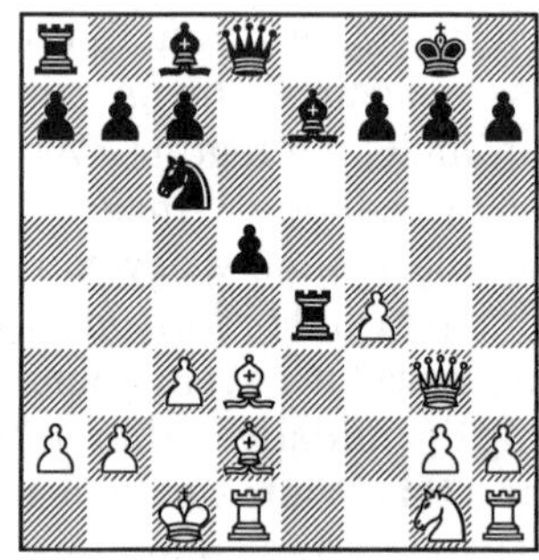

12...♗f5!

This is the right time to give back the extra material and seize the initiative!

More cautious play is less effective, for example: 12...♗h4 13. ♕f3 ♖e8 14.g4 ♗e7 15.♘e2 a5!∓, with the idea of a5-a4, continuing the attack on the queenside. The ensuing play will be rather sharp and White's compensation for the pawn will probably be insufficient.

13.♗xe4 ♗xe4 14.♘f3 ♕d7∓ White has a minimal material advantage, but Black's bishop on e4 is as good as a rook! There is no doubt that Black has a very powerful initiative, Rudd – Avrukh, London 2010 (**game 1**).

Conclusion

White moves pawns at the beginning of the game and develops his queen before his minor pieces, so he can hardly expect any advantage and must even think about equalizing. I believe that in all the rarely played lines analyzed in this chapter the best White can hope for is that his opponent is not well prepared to combat them. However, with solid, common-sense play in the centre, Black should be able to obtain excellent positions without any problems whatsoever.

Chapter 2 1.e4 e5 2.♘c3 ♘f6

Vienna Game

We shall analyze here **A) 3.♗c4**, **B) 3.g3** and **C) 3.f4**.

A) 3.♗c4 ♘xe4

4.♕h5

It is weaker for White to play 4.♗xf7+ ♔xf7 5.♘xe4 d5∓; Black occupies the centre and later he can castle artificially, since he has more than sufficient time for this.

White can continue his development, ignoring Black's knight for the time being, but that would only be sufficient for equality and no more: 4.♘f3 ♘xc3 (The other reliable way for Black here is: 4...♘f6 5.♘xe5 d5 6.♗b3 c6= White's bishop on b3 and the knight on c3 are severely restricted by Black's pawn-chain c6-d5, so Black has no opening problems whatsoever.) 5.dxc3

5...c6 (Black often plays here 5...f6, with the idea of holding on to the pawn. I do not like this move at all from the aesthetic point of view and would never play like this. Black falls behind in development and loses his right to castle comfortably; nevertheless, I have failed to find a direct refutation of it. Black wants to play d7-d6, followed by c7-c6 and d6-d5, while White can try to develop his initiative in various ways. He can play for example: 6.♗e3, keeping the option of ♕d1-e2 and 0–0–0, although he can also consider the simple possibility of 6.0–0 d6 7.♘h4 g6 8.♗e3, followed by f2-f4⩲ White has the initiative, but Black has considerable defensive resources.) 6.♘xe5 d5 7.0–0 ♗d6 8.♖e1 0–0 9.♗d3 ♘d7 10.♗f4 ♕f6 11.♘xd7 ♗xd7 12.♗xd6 ♕xd6=. The position is almost symmetrical and absolutely equal.

4...♘d6 5.♗b3

A rather dull endgame arises after 5.♕xe5 ♕e7 6.♕xe7 ♗xe7 7.♗b3 ♘f5 8.♘f3 (8.♘d5 ♗d8 9.♘f3 c6 10.♘e3 d5=) 8...c6=, followed by d7-d5.

5...♗e7 6.♘f3 ♘c6 7.♘xe5 g6 8.♕e2

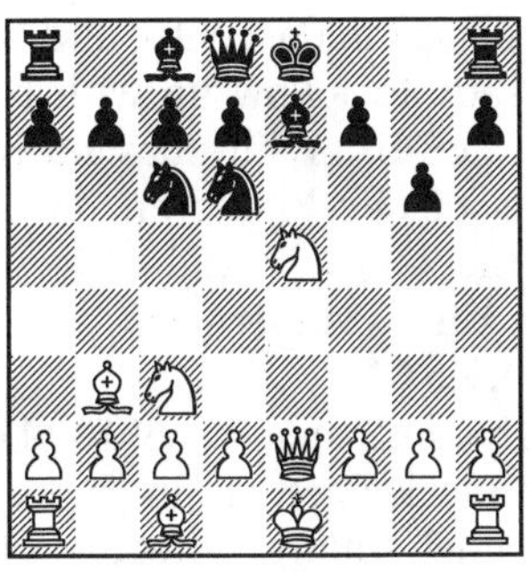

8...0–0

The game is more complex and approximately equal after 8...♘d4 9.♕d3 ♘xb3 10.axb3 ♘f5 11.0–0 d6 12.♘f3 c6= Anand – Ivanchuk, Monaco (rapid) 1992.

9.0–0 ♗f6 10.♘xc6

Black has an excellent position after 10.♘f3 ♖e8 11.♕d1 b6⩱

10...dxc6 11.d3 ♖e8 12.♕f3 a5 13.a4 ♗e6 14.♗xe6 ♖xe6⩱ and Black's position is even slightly preferable.

B) 3.g3

This move is not at all ambitious.

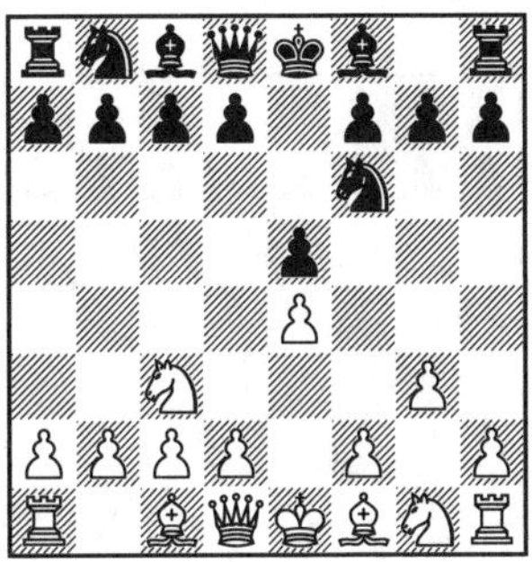

3...♗c5

I think this is Black's most logical reaction.

The line: 3...d5 4.exd5 ♘xd5 5.♗g2 ♘xc3 6.bxc3 ♗d6 7.♘f3 0–0 8.0–0 ♘c6 leads to the Glek variation (2.♘f3 ♘f6 3.♘c3 ♘f6 4.g3). Black has an alternative on his last move, which leads to original positions – 8...♘d7. His knight is more flexibly placed on d7, but it restricts the mobility of his own light-squared bishop. After 9.d4 h6 10.♖e1 exd4 11.cxd4 ♘b6 12.♕d3!± Zviaginsev – Avrukh, Ohrid 2009, depending on circumstances, White can squeeze his opponent's position by advancing his a- or c- pawns. He also has the possibility of increasing his piece-pressure with the move ♘f3-e5 and Black's play is not at all easy (it is weaker for White to opt for 12.♘e5 c6 13.c3 ♗e6=, with equality, Leko – Kramnik, Budapest 2001).

4.♗g2 0–0

Black should not be in a hurry to play 4...d6, since then his bishop has no retreat and White may soon try to exchange it by ♘c3-a4.

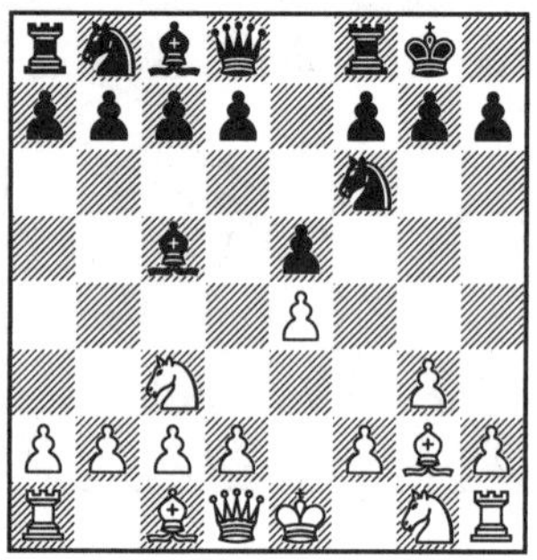

5.♘ge2

The move 5.♘f3 is simply bad here, owing to 5...d5!∓ and Black seizes the initiative.

5...♘c6

It would be premature for Black to immediately attack his opponent's centre with his knight still on b8: 5...c6 6.0–0 d5 7.exd5 cxd5 8.d4 exd4 9.♘xd4 ♗g4 10.♕d3 ♘c6, Stevic – Gdanski, Rijeka 2010. Here the move 11.♘b3! enables White to win his opponent's central pawn and Black's compensation will be insufficient.

6.0–0 ♖e8 7.d3

After 7.h3, Black continues with the same plan: 7...♘d4 8.♔h2 c6 9.f4 d5!, with the advantage.

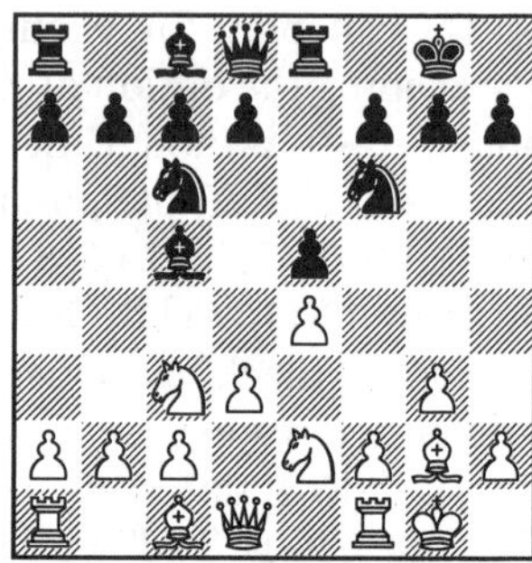

7...h6!

With this prophylactic move Black ensures long-term security of his knight on f6.

8.h3 ♘d4

After completing his prophylactic measures on the kingside Black is ready to open the centre.

It is also possible for him to play patiently with 8...a6 9.♔h2 d6 10.f4 ♘d4= when all his pieces are poised in the centre and Black is ready to follow up with b7-b5 and ♗c8-b7. White has no prospects of developing an initiative on the kingside and indeed his own king is vulnerable.

9.♘a4

If 9.♔h2 then 9...c6! 10.f4 d5!∓ and Black's activity in the centre is much more effective than White's play on the flanks, all in accordance with classic principles!

9...♗f8 10.f4

White can prevent the pawn-break d7-d5 by means of the somewhat artificial move 10.c4, but Black can counter this effectively with the line: 10...c6 11.♘ac3 ♗c5 12.♔h2 a6=, preparing b7-b5.

10...♘xe2 11.♕xe2 d5 12.fxe5 ♖xe5 13.♗f4

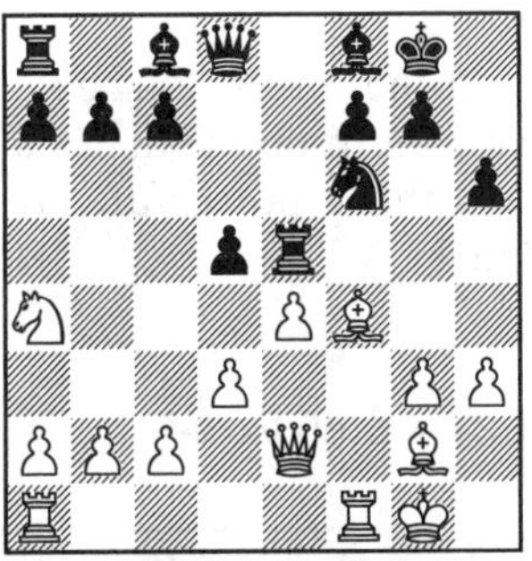

13...♖e8 (It is also interesting for Black to try 13...♖e6!? and in several variations Black's rook goes to the queenside, attacking White's pawns and pieces.) **14.e5 ♗d7 15.♘c3 d4 16. ♘d5 ♘xd5 17.♗xd5 ♗e6=.** Black has achieved safe equality.

C) 3.f4 d5

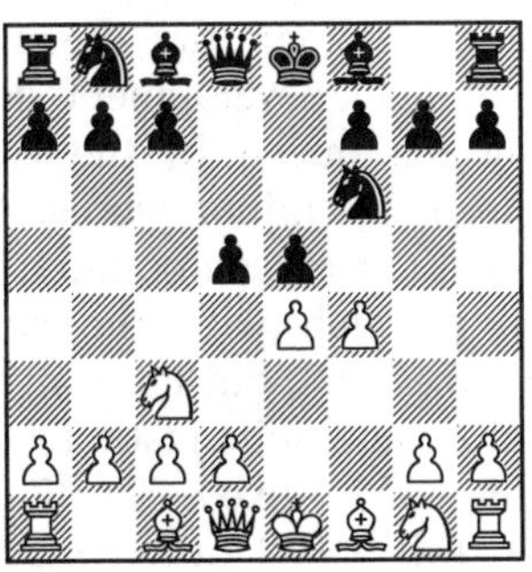

We shall now deal with the moves **C1) 4.exd5** and **C2) 4.fxe5**.

C1) 4.exd5

This move only helps Black's development, so it cannot be good.

4...♘xd5 5.fxe5 ♘xc3 6. bxc3 ♕h4 7.♔e2 ♗g4 8.♘f3 ♘c6 9.♕e1 ♕h5

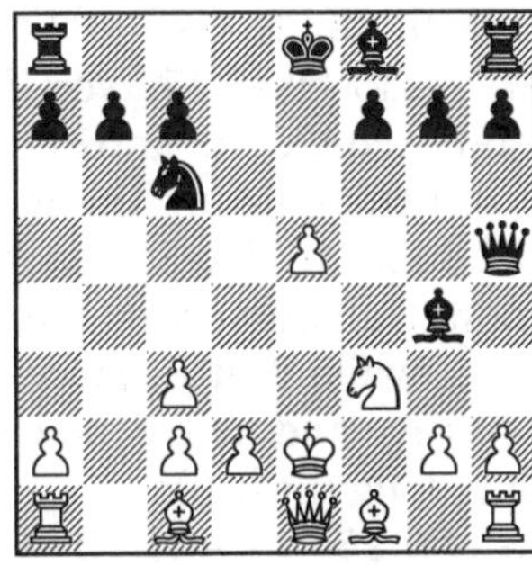

White's king is in front of his army, so he cannot even equalize, despite having an extra pawn.

10.♔d1

After 10.d4 0–0–0 11.♔f2 f6! the f-file is opened and White has some problems. 12.♗b5 fxe5 13.♗xc6 bxc6 14.♕xe5 ♕g6 15.♖e1 ♗d6 16.♕g5 (after 16.♕e4, Black can again play 16...♖df8!, with the idea of increasing his pressure along the f-file with the move ♖f8-f5!) 16...♖df8! 17.♖e2 ♖f5 18.♕xg6 hxg6∓. Black regains his pawn, maintaining the initiative in the process.

10...♗xf3 11.gxf3 ♕xf3 12. ♗e2 ♕d5

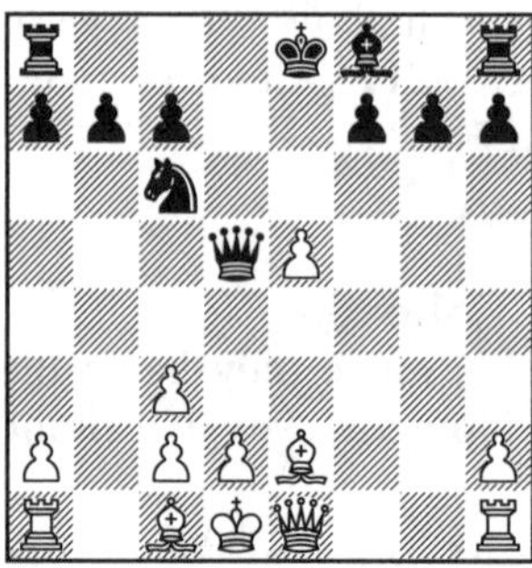

13.c4

White cannot achieve anything with 13.♖f1 0–0–0 14.♕f2 (after 14.♗f3 ♕xe5 15.♗xc6 ♕xe1 16.♔xe1 bxc6 17.♖xf7 ♗d6∓ he will have difficulty saving the game) 14...♔b8 15.♕xf7 ♕xe5∓. Black exerts powerful pressure on the central files, while White's pieces are very passive and he has no counterplay along the b-file.

13...♕xe5 14.♖b1 0–0–0 15.♗g4 f5

The position is double-edged after 15...♔b8!? 16.♗f3 ♕f6 17.♖f1 ♗c5⇄. Black has an extra pawn and active pieces while, as compensation, White exerts powerful pressure on the b-file and on the long diagonal.

16.♕xe5 ♘xe5 17.♗xf5 ♔b8 18.♗e6 ♗c5 19.d3 ♖he8 20.♗g5 ♖d6 21.♗d5 c6 22.♗e4 h6 23.♗f4 ♖f6 24.♗g3 ♔c7∓

(diagram)

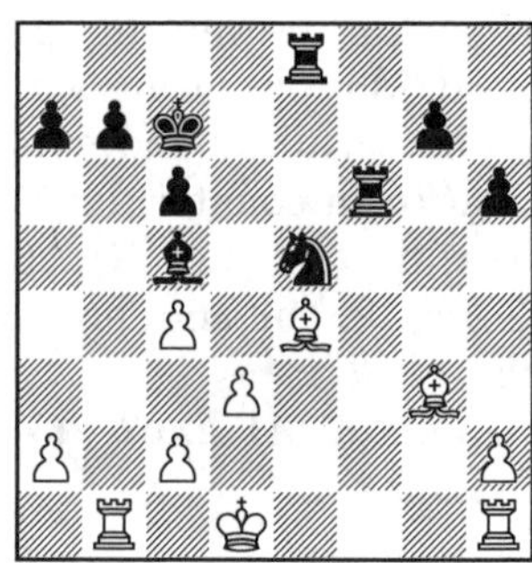

Black's next move will be ♗c5-f2, exchanging the enemy bishop on g3 and neutralizing the possible danger. White must play very precisely to salvage a draw, because his pawn-structure is inferior. If he plays 25.♔e2, then Black can reply with 25...♗d6, with the powerful threat ♘e5xc4.

C2) 4.fxe5 ♘xe4

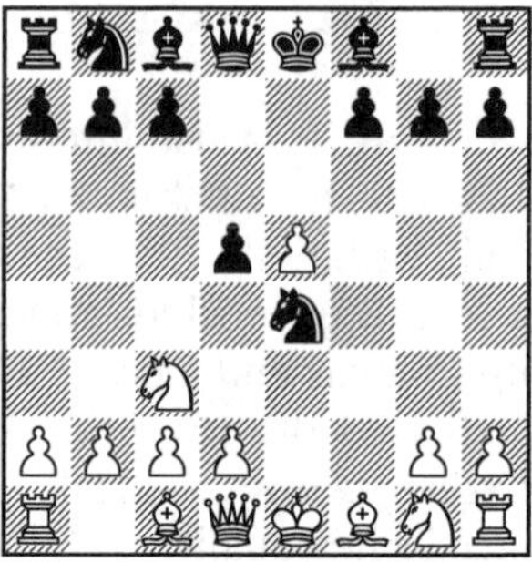

5.♘f3

It would be just crazy for White to play 5.♕f3, ignoring the principles of quick development, developing his queen in the centre ahead of his minor pieces. After 5...♘c6! (Black can obtain a very good position with the simple move 5...♘xc3, but he is striving for more and quite justifiably so.) 6.♗b5 ♘xc3 7.bxc3 ♕h4 (7...♗e7 8.d4 0–0 9.♗d3 (after 9.♘e2 f6

10.exf6 ♗xf6 11.♘f4 ♘e7∓ Black is also slightly better) 9...f6 10.♕h5 g6 11.♗xg6 hxg6 12.♕xg6 ♔h8 13.♕h6 ♔g8= it all ends in a draw by perpetual check) 8.g3 ♕e4 9.♕xe4 dxe4 10.♗xc6 bxc6 11.♘e2 ♖b8∓. Black has a strong bishop-pair and an advantage in the endgame.

Although Black's knight on e4 is very strong, attacking it with 5.d3 is too passive. White's bishop will remain on f1 and the pawn on e5 will be deprived of support. 5...♘xc3 6.bxc3

6...d4! Black destroys his opponent's pawn-chain with this move. 7.♘f3 ♘c6 8.♗e2 (it is no better for White to play here 8.cxd4 ♗b4 9.♗d2 ♗xd2 10.♕xd2 ♘xd4∓; his pawns are a sorry sight, while Black will soon castle, establishing a considerable lead in development in the process.) 8...♗c5 9.0–0 dxc3 10.♔h1 0–0 11.♕e1. Black already has an extra pawn and White can hardly create any meaningful threats on the kingside. Black has many good moves to choose from and I believe his best possibility is: 11...♘d4!

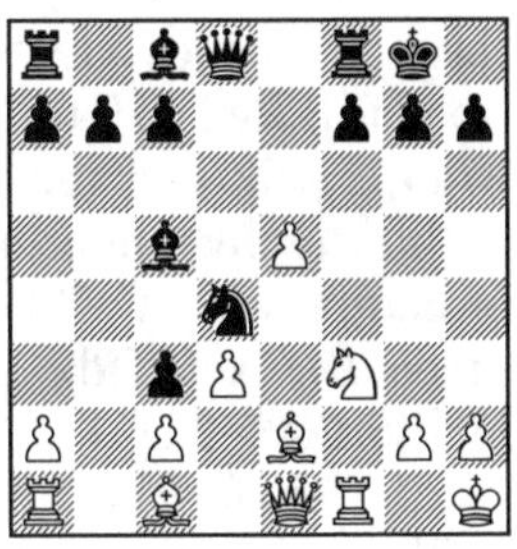

and now:

12.♗d1 ♖e8! 13.♕xc3 ♘xf3 14.♕xc5 ♖xe5 15.♕c3 (White loses after 15.♕f2 ♕d4 16.♕xf3 ♖f5–+) 15...♘d4 16.♗f4 ♖e7∓. White's compensation is far from sufficient;

12.♕xc3 – This attempt by White to restore the material balance is completely ineffective. 12...♗b6 (12...b6!?) 13.♕d2 ♘xf3 14.♗xf3 ♗d4 15.♖b1 ♗xe5 16.♖b5 ♗d4 (A very cautious player with Black, fearing the transfer of White's rook to the kingside, could choose 16...♖e8 17.♗d5 ♗f6 18.♗xb7 ♖b8 19.♗c6 ♖xb5 20.♗xb5 ♗d7∓, with a slight edge for Black.) 17.c3 (White cannot regain his sacrificed pawn, since after 17.♗xb7 ♗xb7 18.♖xb7 ♗b6 his rook on b7 is trapped.) 17...♗b6∓. Black has an extra pawn, while White cannot create any real threats on the kingside.

5...♗e7

If 5...♘c6 White can develop his bishop to an active position with the move 6.♗b5, preparing to castle.

6.♕e2

It is just a loss of a tempo for him to play 6.d3 ♘xc3 7.bxc3 0–0

8.d4 (here it is too passive for White to play 8.♗e2 c5 9.0–0 ♘c6 10.d4 ♕a5 11.♗d2 c4∓ and Black follows this up by undermining White's centre with f7-f6) 8...f6 9.♗d3 fxe5 10.♘xe5 ♘d7 11.♘f3 (11.♕h5 ♘f6 12.♕e2 c5 13.0–0 c4 14.♗f5 ♗xf5 15.♖xf5 ♕b6∓. Black's queen will go to e6 and his knight to e4) 11...c5 12.0–0 c4 13.♗e2 ♕c7∓ and later he will deploy his bishop on d6 and the knight on f6, with very promising play.

Compared with 6.d3, it is more logical for White to continue with 6.d4, but even then after 6...c5 7.♗d3 ♘xc3 8.bxc3 ♘c6 9.0–0 0–0 10.♗e3 c4 11.♗e2 b5= Black has excellent prospects on the queenside and his chances are by no means worse.

6...f5!

A double-edged position arises after 6...♘xc3 7.dxc3 0–0 8.♗f4 c5 9.0–0–0 ♘c6 10.c4 d4 11.♕e4∞ Janosevic – Gligoric, Belgrade 1964.

7.d3

Naturally, White cannot be happy with 7.exf6 ♘xf6∓, because all his pieces will be awkwardly placed.

7...♘xc3 8.bxc3 0–0 9.g3

This creates another attractive target for Black to attack, but it cannot be good for White to play 9.d4. After 9...c5 10.g3 ♘c6 11.♗g2 ♗e6 12.0–0 h6!∓ Black has an excellent blockading bishop on e6 and good prospects on the c-file.

9...c5 10.♗g2 ♘c6 11.0–0

It would be senseless for White to play 11.h4, with the idea of securing the g5-square for a knight-sortie. Black can simply counter it with 11...h6, since this move is an integral part of his plan in any case.

11...♗e6 12.♖b1 ♖b8 13.♔h1

It is difficult to suggest anything more active for White. Black has excellent control of all the squares in his half of the board, while the move 13.d4 will only create another target for Black, as we pointed out earlier.

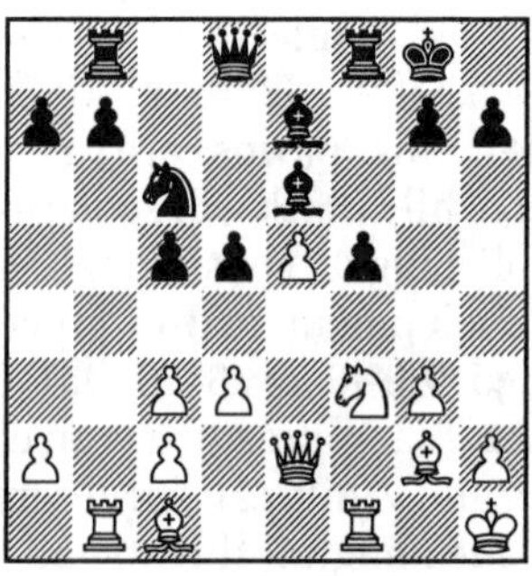

13...h6! 14.♗d2 b5∓ White's pawn on e5 is perfectly blockaded and Black has excellent prospects for a pawn-offensive on the queenside, as well as on the kingside by means of g7-g5!?, Meister – Timoschenko, Barnaul 1988.

Conclusion

The Vienna Game is an ancient opening which is more or less ignored by contemporary grandmasters. This is easily understandable. Black has demonstrated reliable ways of obtaining an excellent game and they are simple and easy to implement. It seems to me that White's most promising line is: 2.♘c3 ♘f6 3.g3, but Black should not have any problem countering that either.

Chapter 3 1.e4 e5 2.f4 exf4

King's Gambit

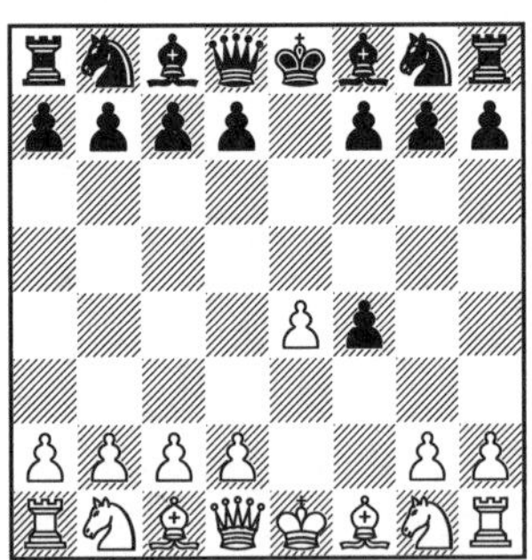

Of course, there are enormously complex and well-studied possibilities for both sides in this opening, since the King's Gambit possesses a tremendously rich history. But instead of analyzing the entire theory of this sharp opening I shall just try to show you one very good defence for Black,

We will deal here with **A) 3.♘c3?!**, **B) 3.♗c4** and the most important move for White – **C) 3.♘f3**.

A) 3.♘c3?!

I believe that to place the king in front of the bishop can never be good, "period"...

3...♕h4+ 4.♔e2 g5

The move 4...d5 is more popular, since it liberates the light-squared bishop, but it leads to an unclear position.

5.♘f3 ♕h5 6.d4 ♘e7

This is Black's most useful move. He develops his kingside, depriving White's knight of the d5-square in the process.

7.♔f2 d6

It is also good for Black to play 7...g4, forcing White to make an unpleasant decision. He must either sacrifice his knight on f3, or retreat it to a bad square. Still, Black does not need to sharpen the game so early, because he has a very good position anyway.

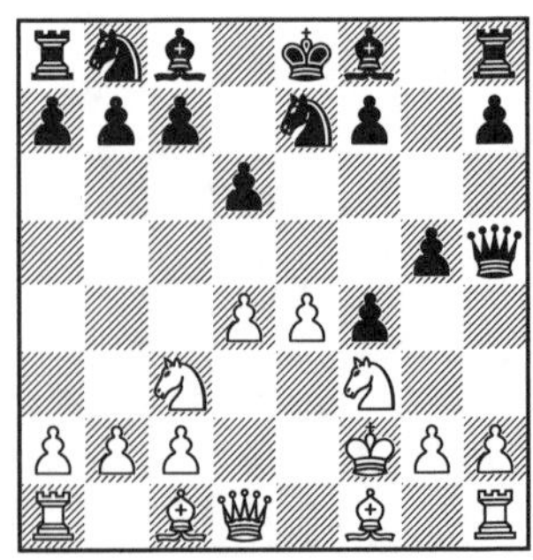

White has no compensation for the pawn and his king has no safe shelter, so Black has good

chances of soon organizing an attack against it.

B) 3.♗c4

3...d5!?

Black should refrain from depriving his opponent of the right to castle, since after 3...♕h4+ 4.♔f1, White's knight will be developed to f3 with tempo and his king's rook will later join in the action by means of the move h2-h4, undermining his opponent's pawn on g5.

Black can equalize safely and reliably by playing 3...♘f6 4.♘c3 c6 5.♗b3 d5 6.exd5 cxd5

and then:

the move 7.♘f3 allows 7...d4! 8.♘e2 (8.♕e2 ♗e7 9.♘e4 0–0 10.d3 ♘c6 11.♗xf4 ♘d5 12.♗d2 ♘a5 13.0–0 ♘xb3 14.axb3 f5 15.♘f2 ♗f6∓) 8...♘c6 (the position becomes very interesting after 8...d3, but Black does not need to sharpen the game so much) 9.d3 ♘d5! 10.♗xd5 (but not 10.♘xf4 ♗b4∓ and White loses his castling rights) 10...♕xd5 11.♘xf4 ♕c5 12.0–0 ♗e7∓;

7.d4 ♗b4 (the struggle is very complicated after 7...♗d6 8.♘f3 0–0 9.0–0∞) 8.♗xf4 (if 8.♘f3, Black has a very strong continuation in 8...a5! 9.a4 ♕e7! 10.♘e5 ♘c6 11.♗xf4 0–0 12.0–0 ♘xd4 13.♘xd5 ♘xd5 14.♗xd5 ♗e6∓) 8...♘e4 (the position offers chances for both sides after 8...0–0 9.♘f3 ♖e8 10.♘e5∞) 9.♘ge2 0–0 10.0–0 ♗xc3 (Black is intending an offensive on the light squares, so he gives up this bishop.) 11.♘xc3 ♘xc3 12.bxc3 ♗e6 13.♕f3 ♘c6 14.♖ae1 ♕d7= Ovetchkin – Sakaev, Serpukhov 2007.

4.♗xd5

Or 4.exd5 ♕h4 5.♔f1 ♗d6 6.♘f3 ♕h5 7.♘c3 ♘e7 8.d4 0–0 9.♔f2 ♘d7 10.♖e1 ♘b6 11.♗b3 ♘exd5 12.♘xd5 ♘xd5 13.c4 ♘e3 14.♗xe3 fxe3 15.♖xe3, Ju.Polgar – Topalov, Mexico 2010. In this position, Black could have struck a powerful strategical blow on the dark squares with the move 15...c5!, transforming the enemy bishop on b3 into a "big pawn". After 16.d5 g5! 17.h3 f5!∓, followed by g5-g4, Black's attack is crushing.

4...♘f6 5.♘c3 ♘xd5!

Black must capture this bishop

as soon as possible. It is inferior to play 5...♗b4 6.♘f3 0–0 7.0–0 ♖e8 8.♗b3± and White has the edge.

6.♘xd5 g5

In principle, all developing moves are good for Black here, for example: 6...♘c6, or 6...♗d6.

7.h4 c6 8.♘c3 ♖g8∓

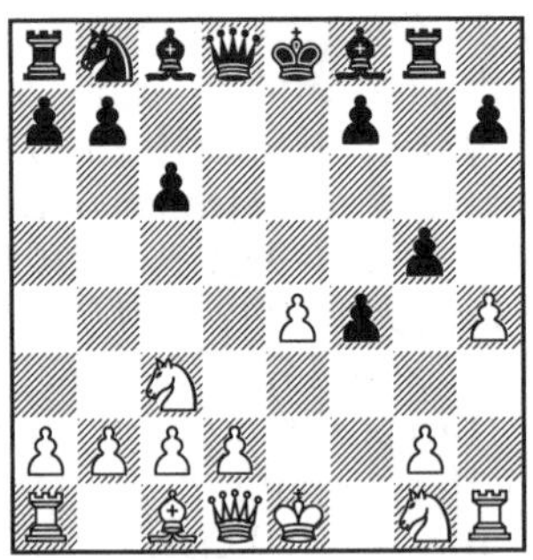

The position is quite sharp, but Black has very good prospects.

C) 3.♘f3

Here, just as on the previous move, I shall ignore all Black's possibilities apart from the most promising one.

3...g5!

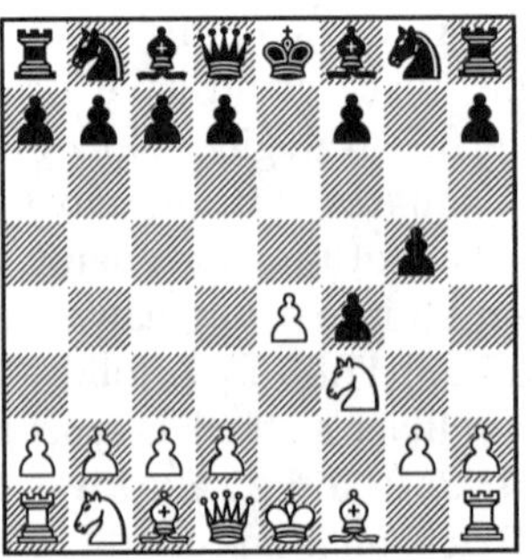

White has numerous alternatives here: **C1) 4.d4**, **C2) 4.♗c4**, **C3) 4.♘c3** and **C4) 4.h4**.

C1) 4.d4

This is a very dubious move.

4...g4!

In this precise position the knight-sacrifice on f3 is not as good for White as it is in many other lines. Black quickly attacks the d4-square and does not allow his opponent to obtain a big lead in development.

After 4...♗g7, an interesting try for White is the rarely played move 5.♘c3!?, since it is not as good for Black to win a piece with 5...g4 as it was on the previous move, because it is better for him to have developed his knight on c6 rather than his bishop on g7.

5.♗xf4 gxf3 6.♕xf3

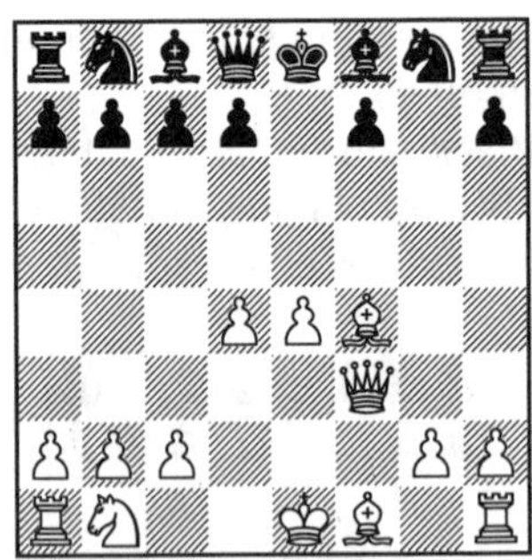

6...♘c6!

After 6...d6 7.♘c3 ♘c6 8. 0–0–0∞ White's compensation for the piece might still be insufficient, but the position remains extremely sharp.

7.♗c4

The move 7.d5 exposes the dark squares in general and the b2-pawn in particular. Black can exploit this immediately with 7...♕f6 8.dxc6 ♕xb2 and White loses material, since the line 9.♗c4 ♕xa1 10.♗xf7 ♔d8 11.0–0 ♕g7–+ does not work and the attack comes to a dead end.

7...d5 8.♗xd5 ♘xd4 9.♗xf7+ ♔xf7 10.♕h5 ♔g7 11.0–0

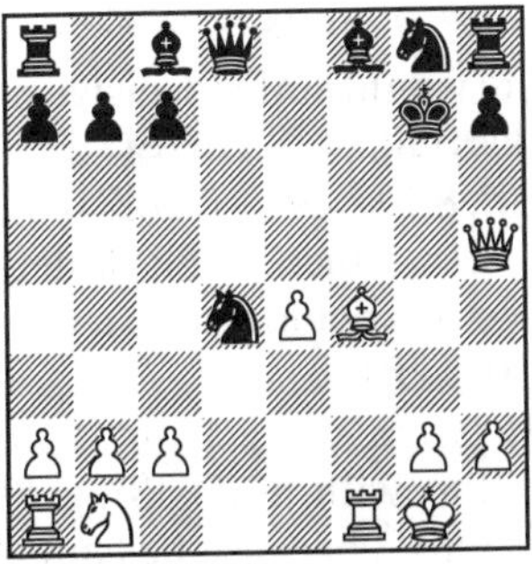

Now Black should not be greedy and try to hold on to the extra material. Instead he should be ready to return some of it in order to block the f-file.

11...♗f5!

The position remains quite unclear after 11...♗e7 12.♘c3 ♘f6 13.♕h6 ♔f7 14.♗e5∞

12.♗e5+ ♘f6 13.♘c3 ♗g6 14.♕h4

After 14.♕d1 ♗e7 15.♗xd4 c6 16.e5 ♘e8 17.♘e2 ♖f8 18.♖xf8 ♗xf8 19.♘f4 ♗f5∓ White's initiative is insufficient to compensate for the sacrificed piece.

Or 14.♕g5 ♗e7 15.♘d5 ♖f8 and here 16.♗xd4 loses to 16...c6–+

14...♘f3+! 15.♖xf3 ♗c5+ 16.♔h1 ♗d4 17.♗f4 h6 18.♖g3

After 18.♖d1 Black can simply bolster his bishop with the move 18...c5∓

18...h5 19.♗g5

Black was threatening ♘f6-g4.

19...♕e8 20.♖d1 ♗e5 21.♗f4 ♗xf4 22.♕xf4 ♖f8∓ Black's extra piece will be much more important than White's scattered extra pawns.

C2) 4.♗c4

4...♗g7

The line: 4...g4 5.0–0 gxf3 6.♕xf3∞ leads to a very sharp position; Black does not need to enter such complications.

5.d4

Or 5.h4 h6 6.d4 d6 7.c3 ♘c6 and the main line is reached by transposition.

5...d6 6.h4

If White does not break the pawn-chain g5-f4 he will have great problems, since the simple completion of his development is not very promising, for example: 6.0–0 ♘c6 7.c3 h6

and now:

for 8.h4 g4 – see 6.h4;

8.g3 ♗h3 9.gxf4 (9.♖f2 ♘f6 10. gxf4 ♘xe4∓ and Black later supports his knight with the move d6-d5) 9...♗xf1 10.♕xf1 g4 11.♕g2 gxf3 12.♕xg7 ♕f6 13.♕xf6 ♘xf6 14. ♘d2 ♖g8 15.♔f1, Kleinschroth – Scherer, Zell 1993 and now Black could have obtained a great advantage with 15...♖g4 16.e5 ♘h5∓;

after 8.♕b3, it is very strong for Black to continue with 8...♕d7!∓, creating the threat of ♘c6-a5;

8.♕a4 ♗d7 9.♕b3 ♘a5! 10. ♗xf7 ♔f8 11.♕a3 ♔xf7 12.♕xa5 c5∓ Zvjaginsev – Akopian, Rijeka (rapid) 2010.

6...h6 7.c3 ♘c6 8.0–0 g4 9.♘e1

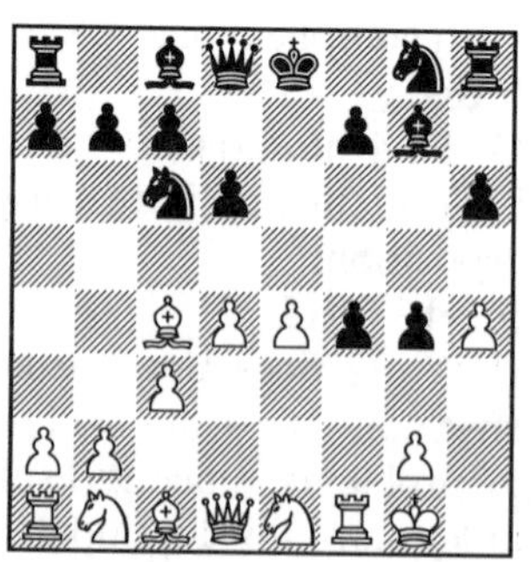

Here it is very promising for Black to expose the enemy king with the move

9...f3!

The game Nakamura – Ivanchuk, Cap d'Agde 2010, continued with 9...♕xh4 10.♗xf4 ♘f6 11. e5 dxe5 12.dxe5 g3 13.♗xg3 ♕xg3 14.exf6 ♗f8 15.♘d3 ♗d6 and White had the chance to enter a slightly better endgame with 16.♕e1 (instead, in the game he played the risky line: 16.♕h5 ♗g4 17.♗xf7 and here Black could have won with 17...♔d8! 18.♕d5 ♗e2–+ and White would suffer decisive material loss) 16...♔f8 17.♕xg3 ♗xg3 18. ♘d2 ♖g8 19.♘e4 ♘e5 20.♘xe5 ♗xe5 21.♖ad1±, which, if Black defends correctly, should end in a draw.

10.gxf3

It is not correct for White to continue with 10.♘xf3? gxf3 11. ♕xf3 ♘f6∓, because he cannot do anything worthwhile along the f-file and without that his attack comes to a dead end.

10...♕xh4

After 10...g3 11.♘g2 ♘f6∞, White's centre is beautiful, but his king is potentially vulnerable.

11.♘g2 ♕h3 12.fxg4 ♘f6∓

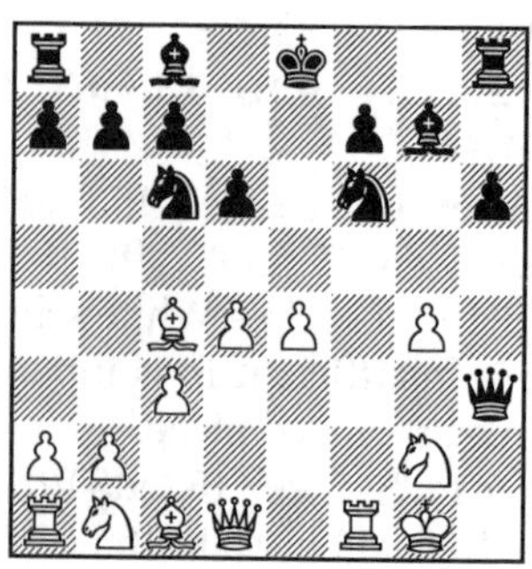

White's knight is awkwardly placed on g2 and destroys the harmony of his pieces, while Black has an excellent position.

C3) 4.♘c3

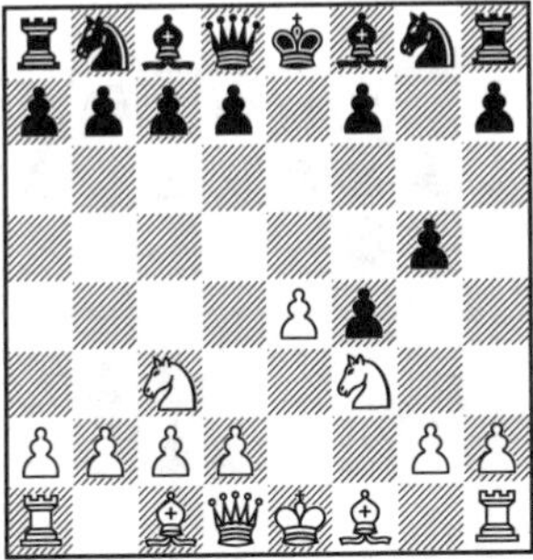

GM Vadim Zvjaginsev tried recently to resurrect this ancient move. In some variations White's knight is ready to go to d5, but the serious drawback of the placement of the knight on c3 is that his d4-pawn is insufficiently protected.

4...♘c6

It is less good for Black to play 4...g4 5.♘e5 ♘c6 (a very complicated endgame arises after 5...♕h4 6.g3 fxg3 7.♕xg4 ♕xg4 8.♘xg4) 6.♘xg4 ♕h4 7.♘f2 ♗c5 8.d4 ♗xd4 (White's initiative is very dangerous after 8...♘xd4?! 9.b4! ♗b6 10.♘d5↑) 9.♕f3∞ with a double-edged position.

(diagram)

5.g3!

This is the essence of GM Vadim Zvjaginsev's idea. White does not allow his opponent to capture

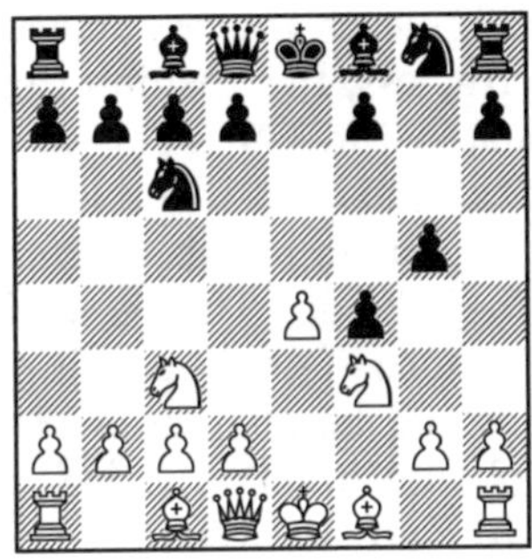

the knight with the move g5-g4 and destroys the pawn-wedge g5-f4 without having to make heavy sacrifices. Additionally he wishes to quickly develop his queenside pieces with the idea of eventually castling on the queenside.

Unfortunately for romantic players the ancient gambits are unsound:

5.d4 g4 6.♘e5 (6.♗c4 gxf3 7.0–0 leads by transposition to the position arising after 5.♗c4 g4 6.0–0 gxf3 7.d4) 6...♘xe5 7.dxe5 ♕h4 8.♔e2 ♗c5∓

After 5.♗c4, Black has the resolute response 5...g4! and White is forced to sacrifice his knight, but in many variations the fact that he has delayed the development of his kingside with his fourth move becomes important. 6.0–0 (6.d4 gxf3 7.♕xf3 ♕h4 8.g3 ♘xd4 9.♕f2 ♕f6 10.♘d5 ♕e5 11.0–0 ♗c5 12.♗xf4 ♘f3 13.♔g2 ♗xf2 14.♗xe5 ♘xe5 15.♘xc7 ♔d8 16.♘xa8 ♗c5–+ – White's knight on a8 is trapped and Black must win) 6...gxf3 7.♕xf3 (7.d4 ♘xd4 8.♕xd4 ♕g5 9.♖f2 ♗c5 10.♗xf4 ♕xg2 11.♖xg2 ♗xd4 12.♖f2 c6∓ –

White's pieces are very active but nevertheless, the position can be evaluated in Black's favour, thanks to his considerable material advantage in this endgame.) 7...♕h4! 8.♘d5! This is White's best chance. (Otherwise, his position would be terrible: 8.g3 ♗c5 9.♔g2 ♕h6 10.d3 d6 11.♗xf4 ♗h3 12.♔h1 ♕g6–+ – White is a piece down and his attack has been parried. No doubt, he cannot be happy with the immediate transition into an endgame in the following sample variation: 8.d3 ♘e5 9.♕xf4 ♕xf4 10.♗xf4 ♘xc4 11.dxc4 d6 12.♘d5 ♔d7 13.♖ad1 c6 14.♘e3 ♔e8 15.♗xd6 ♗xd6 16.♖xd6 ♗e6–+ and his chances of salvation are very problematic.) 8...♗c5 9.♔h1 ♘e5 10.♕e2 (White loses immediately after 10.♕c3 ♘g4 11.h3 ♘f2 12.♔h2 c6–+) 10...f3 11.gxf3 ♗b6∓ He has some positional pressure, but it cannot compensate fully for the missing piece, so Black is clearly better.

5...g4!

Black should play this move! He does not win the enemy knight, but he ensures a powerful pawn-wedge on f3.

He can also play more solidly, emphasizing development: 5...d6 6.d4 ♗g7 7.d5 ♘e5 8.gxf4 gxf4 9.♗xf4 ♗g4 10.♗b5 ♔f8 11.♗e2 ♗xf3 12.♗xf3 ♕f6 13.♗xe5 ♕xe5= the game is double-edged and approximately equal, Zvjaginsev – P.Smirnov, Novokuznetsk 2008.

6.♘h4 f3

The position becomes completely irrational after 6...♘d4 7.♘d5 fxg3 8.hxg3 ♘f6 9.c3 ♗d6 10.♕a4! ♗xg3 11.♔d1 c5 12.cxd4 ♗xh4 13.dxc5 ♘xd5 14.exd5 h5 15.d6 ♕f6∞, but Black does not need to engage in such adventurous experiments.

7.d4

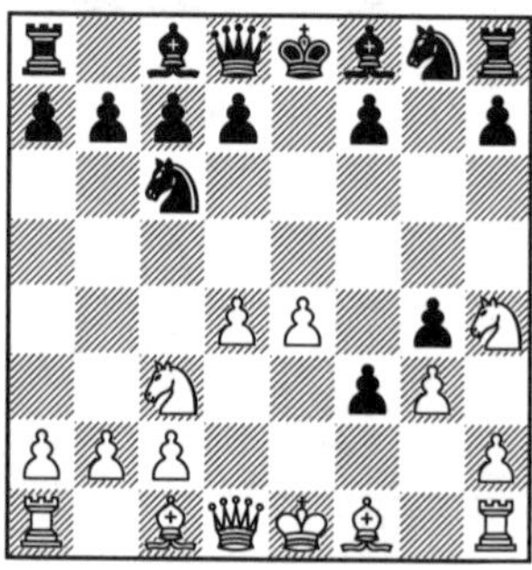

Now, under the cover of the bastion on f3, Black can strike a blow against the enemy centre:

7...♗b4!

After 7...♗e7, White should simply fortify his centre with the move 8.♗e3! and it will be bad for Black to give up his bishop even for the sake of winning a second pawn.

8.♗c4 d5!

It is rather passive and too slow for Black to continue with 8...d6 9.0–0 ♘xd4 10.♘d5 ♗c5 11.b4 ♘e2 12.♔h1 ♗d4 13.c3 ♗e5 14.♗xe2 fxe2 15.♕xe2 c6 16.♘e3↑ and White has a powerful initiative.

9.♗xd5 ♘f6! 10.♗xc6 bxc6 11.♕d3 c5!

11...♖b8 12.♗h6∞

12.dxc5 ♕xd3 13.cxd3 ♘d7

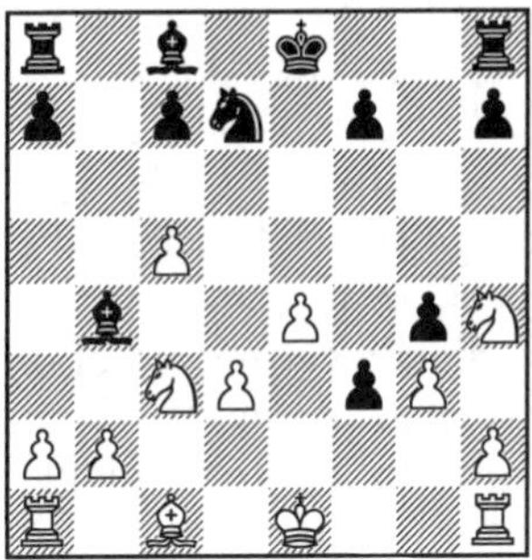

14.♔f2

Otherwise Black will comfortably pick up the enemy c5-pawn.

It is not good for White to play here 14.d4 ♘f6∓ since his light squares are tremendously vulnerable.

14...♘xc5 15.♘d5 ♘xd3 16.♔e3 c6 17.♘f6 ♔e7 18.♘xg4 ♗xg4 19.♔xd3 f2!∓ and White must think about salvation.

C4) 4.h4

4...g4 5.♘e5

It is bad for White to play 5.♘g5? h6 6.♘xf7 ♔xf7 7.♗c4 d5 8.♗xd5 ♔e8∓ and his compensation for the piece is insufficient.

5...d6 6.♘xg4 ♘f6

White has two possibilities here: **C4a)** 7.♘**f2?!** and **C4b)** 7.♘**xf6**.

C4a) 7.♘f2?!

It cannot be good for White to withdraw the knight to a defensive position, losing a tempo in the process.

7...♖g8 8.d4 ♗h6 9.♘c3 ♘c6

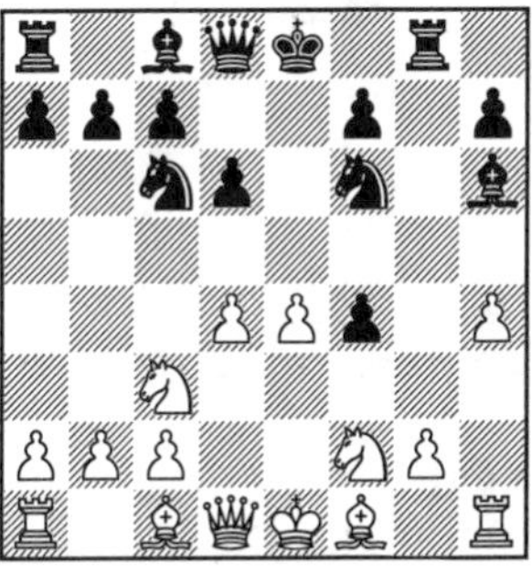

10.♘d5

After 10.♗b5, Black has numerous promising possibilities: 10...a6, 10...♗d7, but his most attractive is 10...♖xg2! 11.d5 a6 12.♗a4 (12.♗f1 ♖xf2 13.dxc6 ♖xf1 14.♔xf1 bxc6∓ and he obtains several pawns and an attack for the exchange.) 12...b5 13.♘xb5 axb5 14.♗xb5 ♗d7 15.♗xc6 (or 15.dxc6 ♗g4∓ and Black's initiative is crushing) 15...♗xc6 16.dxc6 ♕e7∓. White is undeveloped and his defence will be tremendously difficult.

10...♘xd5 11.exd5 ♕e7 12.♗e2 ♘b4 13.c4 ♗f5 14.♕a4 ♔f8 15.♕xb4 ♖e8 16.♕d2 ♖xg2 17.♔f1 ♖g3 18.♕d1 ♗e4 19.♖h2 f5–+ and White is helpless against the threat of ♕e7-g7, so Black wins, Fedorov – Shirov, Polanica Zdroj 2000.

C4b) 7.♘xf6 ♕xf6 8.♘c3 ♘c6

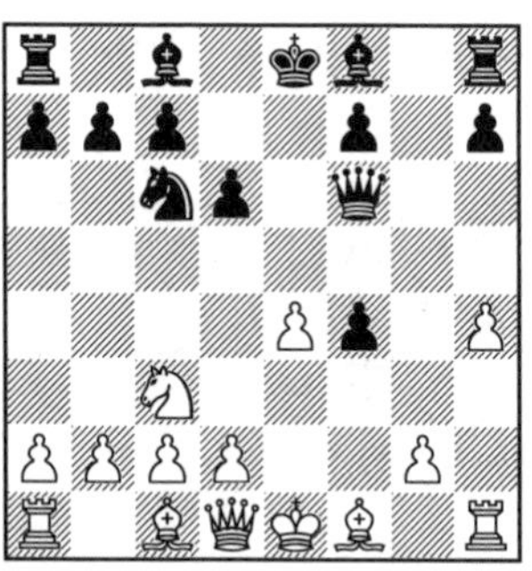

9.♘d5

After 9.♗b5, Black's best reply is 9...♔d8!, after which White must give up his bishop (otherwise Black will play ♘c6-d4) and Black's king will be completely safe on d8. So 10.♗xc6 bxc6 11.d3 (there is merely a transposition of moves after 11.♕f3 ♖g8 12.d3 ♗h6) 11...♖g8 12.♕f3 ♗h6 13.♕f2 ♖b8 14.♘e2 ♖xb2 (the position is equal after 14...f3 15.♕xf3 ♕xf3 16.gxf3 ♗xc1 17.♖xc1 ♖xb2=) 15.♗xb2 ♕xb2 16.0–0 ♕xc2 17.♘xf4 ♕xf2 18.♖xf2 ♗g7 19.♖c1 ♗d4 20.♖xc6 ♖g4 (Black has a good alternative here in the move 20...f5, immediately getting rid of one of his isolated pawns. His bishop is superior to White's knight in a struggle on both sides of the board, so Black is even slightly better. The material left on the board however, has been reduced considerably, so his winning chances are only minimal.) 21.♘d5 ♗b7 22.♖c4 ♗xf2 23.♔xf2 ♖xh4 24.♘xc7 ♖h5= Fier – Leitao, Guarulhos 2006.

9...♕g6 10.d3 ♕g3 11.♔d2

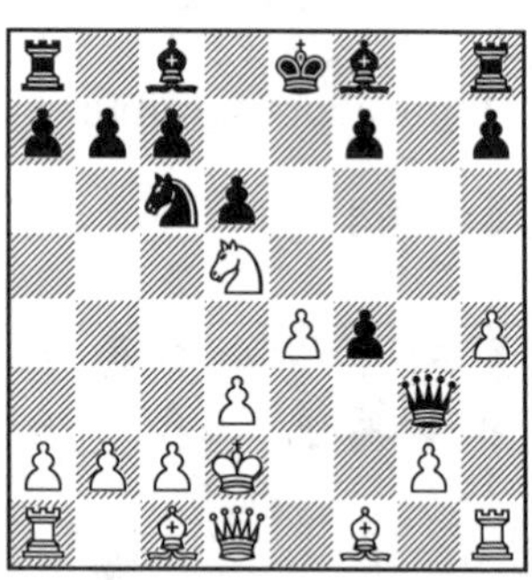

This position has been encountered in practice numerous times and Black has so many possibilities that an extensive analysis is just impossible. I think his best way of solving his problems is:

11...♘b4!

Both kings carry out rather strange sorties in the variation 11...♘d4 12.c3 c6 13.♘f6 ♔e7 14.

cxd4 ♔xf6 15.♔c2 ♔e7 16.♗e2±, but subsequently White will soon deploy his bishop on f3 and gain an edge.

It would be interesting for Black to try the move 11...♗h6!?

However, he cannot solve his problems with the line: 11...♘e7 12.♕e1 ♘xd5 13.exd5 ♗e7 14.♕xg3 fxg3, Fedorov – Anand, Wijk aan Zee 2001, since White can continue here with 15.♔c3! (in the above-mentioned game, he played 15.♗e2 ♖g8 16.♔d1 ♗g4=, with equality) 15...♖g8 16.d4!±, with the idea of ♗f1-b5! and Black will have some complicated problems to solve.

12.♕f3

It would be too risky for White to try here 12.♘xb4 ♕e3 13.♔c3 ♗g7 14.♔b3 ♕b6 15.♗xf4 (it would be even worse for him to opt for 15.c3 a5→ and he immediately comes under a crushing attack, Beck – Heimann, Pforzheim 2005) 15...a5 16.a3 c5 17.♗d2 ♗d7→; Black has created the threat of ♗d7-a4! and White has no comfortable defence against this.

12...♕xf3 13.gxf3 ♘xd5 14. exd5 ♖g8 15.♔c3 ♗h6 16.♗d2 ♗f5 17.♖e1 ♔d7=

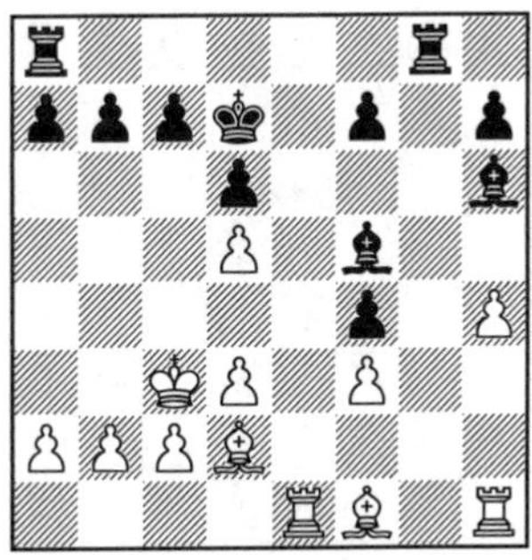

Black has a very good position in this endgame.

Conclusion

The King's Gambit is a very interesting opening with a rich and exciting history. We must admit that it contains numerous possibilities which have not been extensively analyzed at all. Some of the positions are so sharp and non-standard that often even the best computer programs fail to evaluate them correctly. Still, I believe that the lines for Black that I have suggested are quite reliable and our thorough analysis should help Black to play them with confidence.

Chapter 4 1.e4 e5 2.♗c4

Bishop's Opening

The Bishop's Opening is being played more and more often, just with the aim of avoiding the Petroff Defence. White hopes to transpose to the Italian Game, in which he can rely on a long positional battle, maintaining a minimal edge.

2...♘f6

We will analyze now **A) 3.d4** and **B) 3.d3**.

The move 3.♘c3 leads to the Vienna game 2.♘c3 ♘f6 3.♗c4.

After 3.f4 – the Greco Gambit, Black obtains a good game with the reply 3...d5.

A) 3.d4 exd4 4.♘f3

The Urusov Gambit arises after this move.

Black can counter 4.e5? with the typical response 4...d5! with advantage.

4...♘xe4

After 4...♘c6, there arises a well-known theoretical position, favourable for Black, but it is also good to capture the pawn.

5.♕xd4 ♘f6 6.♘c3

After 6.♗g5, Black can solve all his problems with 6...♘c6! (It is inferior for him to play instead 6...♗e7, because after 7.♘c3 c6 8.0–0–0 d5 9.♖he1 ♗e6 10.♕h4 ♘bd7 11.♘d4, unnecessary complications arise.) 7.♕e3 (after 7.♕h4, Black has the resource 7...d5 and White does not have any compensation for the pawn.) 7...

♕e7 8.♗xf6 gxf6 9.♘c3 ♕xe3 10. fxe3 ♗b4∓ and White must fight for a draw in a clearly worse endgame.

6...♘c6

It is too risky for Black to opt for 6...c6 7.♗g5 d5 8.0–0–0 ♗e7 9.♖he1 (9.♕h4!? Avrukh – Skripchenko, Linares 2001) 9...♗e6 10.♕h4 ♘bd7 11.♘d4 with complications.

7.♕h4

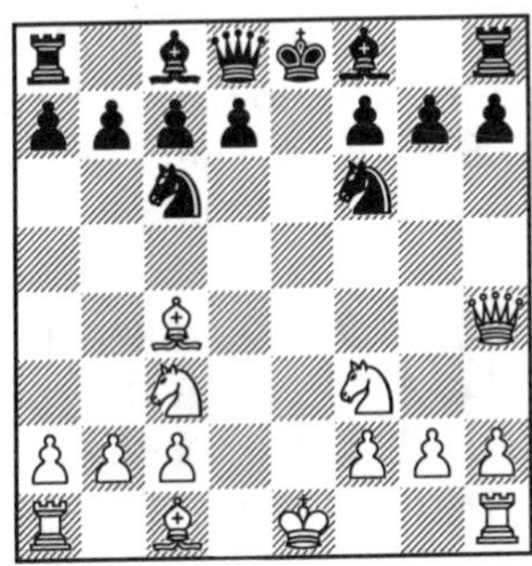

7...♗b4

After 7...♗e7 8.♗g5 d5 9.0–0–0 ♗e6 10.♘xd5 ♘xd5 11.♗xd5 ♗xd5 12.c4± White seizes the initiative.

8.♗g5

8.0–0 ♗xc3 9.bxc3 0–0 10. ♗d3 d5 11.♖e1 (but not 11.♗g5? h6 12.♖fe1? hxg5 13.♘xg5 g6–+) 11... ♘e4 12.♕f4 ♗e6 13.♖b1 ♖b8 14.c4 ♘c5 15.♖d1 ♘xd3 16.♖xd3 d4 17. ♘xd4 ♘xd4 18.♖xd4 ♕xd4 19. ♕xd4 ♖bd8 20.♕d3 ♖xd3 21.cxd3 b6= with a draw, although Black still has a symbolic edge.

8.♗d2 ♕e7! 9.♔d1 d5! 10.♘xd5 ♘xd5 11.♗xd5 ♕xh4 12.♗xc6 bxc6 13.♘xh4 ♗c5∓ and Black's position is preferable.

8...♗xc3

Here 8...♕e7!? is interesting; a possible continuation is 9.♔d1 ♗xc3 10.bxc3 d6 11.♘d4 ♘e5 12. ♖e1 c5 13.f4 cxd4 14.fxe5 dxe5 15.cxd4 ♗e6 16.♖xe5 0–0–0= with a very complicated and approximately equal position.

9.bxc3 0–0 10.0–0–0 h6

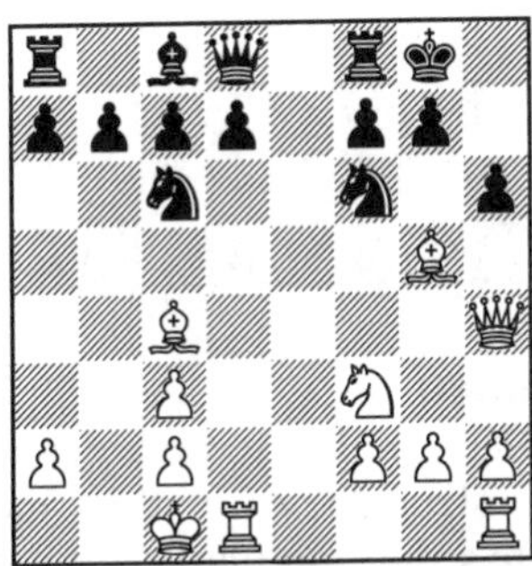

11.♗xh6! gxh6 12.♕xh6 d5!

Black loses after the passive move 12...d6 13.g4! ♗e6 14.♗d3 ♖e8 15.♖hg1! ♘d7 16.♗h7 ♔h8 17.g5!+–, with the deadly threat of g5-g6.

13.♗d3

After 13.g4, Black has the resource 13...♕d6!

White can force a draw immediately with the line: 13.♖xd5 ♘xd5 14.♗d3 f5 15.♕g6 ♔h8 16. ♕h6=

13...♕d6

Black has created the threat of ♘f6-e4, so White must take a draw by a perpetual check.

14.♕g5

The move 14.♘g5? can be countered with 14...♗f5 15.♗xf5 ♕f4–+

14...♔h8 15.♕h6 ♔g8= – Drawn by perpetual check.

B) 3.d3

3...c6

Black wishes to create a complex struggle with this move. White's development at the moment is not in harmony with the classical principles (it is accepted that knights should be developed before bishops), so Black is trying to seize the centre with his pawns. There is a good alternative in 3...♗c5, transposing to a type of Italian Game under very favourable circumstances, because Black's knight has not been developed to c6 yet and can be placed on d7, which is sometimes even more harmonious. 4.♘f3 0–0

5.0–0 (White has tried to exchange Black's bishop for his knight, but in the game McShane – Kramnik, London 2009 (**game 2**) this did not bring him any benefits: 5.♘c3 d6 6.♘a4 ♗b6 7.c3 ♗e6 8.♗b3 ♗xb3 9.axb3 ♘bd7=, with equality. The pin of the f6-knight is not dangerous for Black either, since it can be supported by the other knight on d7: 5.♗g5 d6 6.♘bd2 ♗e6 7.c3 ♘bd7 = and the position is approximately equal, Tiviakov – Ivanchuk, Merida 2004.) 5...d6 6.c3 ♗b6 7.♗b3 ♘bd7 8.♘bd2 c6 9.♖e1 ♖e8 10.♘f1 ♘f8 11.♘g3 ♘g6 12.h3 h6

Now the position is completely symmetrical. Both sides have deployed their forces harmoniously and White's opening advantage is practically nullified. Black can be quite happy with the results of the opening. The game Alekseev – Gelfand, Astrakhan 2010, continued with: 13.d4 ♗d7 14.♗c2 c5 15.dxe5 dxe5 16.♘f5 ♗e6 17.♕e2 ♕c7 18.♘h2 c4 19.♘g4 ♘xg4 20.♕xg4 ♕d8 21.♖d1 ♕f6 22.♕f3 ♘h4 23.♕g4 ♘g6 24.♕f3 ♘h4 25.♕g4 and the players agreed to a draw.

The line: 3...♘c6 4.♘f3 transposes to the classical Italian Game (We should also mention that White has the attractive move 4.♘c3, with the idea of developing the other knight to the e2-square.).

4.♘f3 d5 5.♗b3

After 5.exd5 cxd5 6.♗b3, Black has the interesting check – 6...♗b4+! He is able to complete his development in this way, while maintaining his pawn-centre. 7.c3. This square is important for the development of White's knight but now it has been occupied by a pawn, so Black's bishop retreats. 7...♗d6 8.0–0 0–0 9.♗g5 ♗e6= and Black has obtained a good game.

5...♗d6

Here Black tries to be tricky sometimes with a check 5...♗b4+, aimed at preventing the development of White's knight on c3, or he plays 5...a5, trying to make trouble for the enemy bishop. However, we shall analyze Black's most solid and, I believe, best move.

Now White can maintain the tension with the move **B1) 6.♘c3**, or he can give up the centre with **B2) 6.exd5**, in order to complete his development while attacking the enemy centre.

B1) 6.♘c3 dxe4

The move 6...d4!? has been played only rarely. It looks a bit risky, but shows fighting spirit. 7.♘e2 ♘a6 (He has a reasonable alternative here in fortifying his centre with 7...c5!? 8.♘g3 ♘c6) 8.a3 ♘c5 9.♗a2 0–0 (after 9...♗e6, White has the resource 10.b4!, doubling the enemy pawns on the e-file) 10.0–0 h6±. White is slightly better, but Black has his trumps as well. He has seized space and White will find it difficult to advance with f2-f4.

7.♘g5

It is senseless for White to leave his knight on c3. After 7.dxe4 ♘a6∓ Black's knight will go to the c5-square and he will even have the edge.

After the harmless-looking move 7.♘xe4 things are not at all simple and Black must play very precisely: 7...♘xe4 8.dxe4

8...♗g4! 9.h3 (White would not obtain much with 9.♗g5 f6 10.♗e3 ♘a6 11.♕e2 ♕e7 12.0–0–0 ♘c5=) 9...♗h5 10.♗g5 f6 11.♗e3 ♘a6 12.♕e2 ♕e7 13.0–0–0 ♘c5 14.♗xc5 ♗xc5=, with equality, Rogers – Tseshkovsky, Vrsac 1987.

If Black does not play 8...♗g4 he will have problems:

8...h6 9.♗e3↑ and later White develops his queen on d2 and castles queenside with tempo;

After Black's natural move 8...0–0, White again has the chance to develop his pieces with tempo: 9.♗g5! ♕c7 10.♕d2 ♗g4 11.0–0–0 ♗e7 12.♗xe7 ♕xe7 13.♕d6 ♕xd6 14.♖xd6± and his lead in development is considerable, Hou Yifan – Bu Xiangzhi, China 2010;

8...♗b4 9.♗d2! (White does not achieve much with 9.c3 ♕xd1 10.♔xd1 ♗d6, for example: 11.♔c2 ♔e7 12.♗e3 f6 13.♖ad1 ♘a6=; or 11.♗e3 ♘a6 12.♔e2 f6 13.♖ad1 ♔e7=; or 11.♔e2 f6 12.♖d1 ♔e7 13.♘d2 – after 13.♘h4, Black has the cold-blooded reply 13...g6 – 13...♘a6 14.a4 ♘c5 15.♗c4 a5 16.b3 ♖d8 17.f3, draw, Short – Westerinen, Brighton 1982) 9...♗xd2 10.♘xd2 0–0 11.♘c4± and White maintains an edge thanks to the vulnerable d6-square in the enemy camp.

7...0–0 8.♘gxe4

A transposition of moves arises after 8.♘cxe4 ♘xe4 9.♘xe4 ♗f5=

8...♘xe4 9.♘xe4 ♗f5

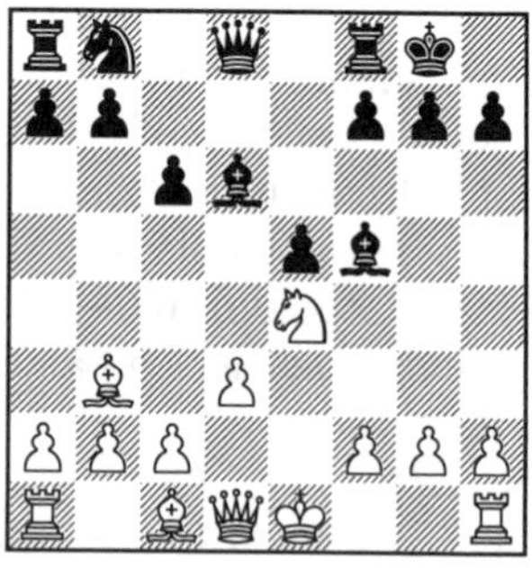

10.♕f3

The position is equal after 10.0–0 ♘a6 11.♘xd6 (11.♕f3 ♗xe4 12.dxe4 ♘c5 – see 10.♕f3 ♗xe4 11.dxe4 ♘d7 12.0–0 ♘c5) 11...♕xd6 12.♕f3 ♗e6= Anand – Kramnik, Frankfurt (rapid) 1998.

10...♗xe4 11.dxe4 ♘d7

12. a3

White has tried some other moves here with the idea of preserving his light-squared bishop from exchange.

In the game Movsesian – Bu Xiangzhi, China 2010 (**game 3**) White tried to place his bishop on c2, but after 12.c3 a5 13.0–0 a4 14.♗c2 ♕e7 15.♖d1 ♖fd8 16.h4 h6 17.g3 b5= he failed to obtain any advantage.

12.0–0 ♘c5 13.♗c4 b5 14.♗e2 ♕e7 (the move 14...♕h4 was tested in the game Tiviakov – Rozentalis, Kallithea 2009 and after 15.♗e3, it became clear that the e4-pawn was taboo, so Black had simply lost a tempo by not developing his queen to e7 immediately (it would be bad for him to play 15...♕xe4 16.♖fd1 ♗e7 17.♗xc5 ♕xf3 18.♗xf3 ♗xc5 19.♗xc6 since he would lose a pawn) 15.♖d1 ♖fd8 16.♕g4 ♘e6 17.c3 a5=

12...♘c5 13.♗a2 ♕e7 14.♗e3 ♘a4 15.♗b3 ♘c5 16.♗a2 ♘a4 17.♗b3 ♘c5 18.♗a2, draw, Rublevsky – Sakaev, Sochi 2008.

B2) 6.exd5

6...♘xd5

It is interesting, but very risky, for Black to opt for 6...cxd5!? 7.♗g5 (It is too slow for White to continue with 7.0–0 ♘c6 8.♗g5 ♗e6 9.♘c3 ♗c7 10.♘b5 ♗b6 11.♖e1 a6 12.♘c3 ♕d6 13.♗h4 0–0 14.♗xf6 gxf6 15.♕d2 ♔g7∓ and in the game Kamsky – Gelfand, Bazna 2009, Black obtained a very good position. White cannot achieve anything much with the line: 7.♘c3 d4 8.♘g5 0–0 9.♘ce4 ♗b4 10.c3 ♘xe4 11.♘xe4 ♗e7=) 7...♗e6 (it would be careless for Black to opt for 7...♘c6 in view of 8.♘c3 and after 8...♗e6, White has the tactical blow 9.♗xd5!) 8.♘c3

8...♕a5! (here, if 8...♗c7, White has the resource 9.d4! e4 10.♘d2 0–0 (after 10...♘c6, White can play 11.♗xf6 gxf6 12.♘dxe4±, while if 10...♗a5 11.f3!± and the opening of the game seems to be in White's favour) 11.♗xf6 gxf6 12.♕h5 ♗a5 13.♘xd5 ♗xd2 14.♔xd2 f5 15.♘f4 ♕xd4 16.♔c1±; Black's king is vulnerable and he is clearly worse) 9.0–0 ♘c6 10.♕e1 (The position is very difficult to evaluate after 10.a3 h6!? 11.♗h4 g5 12.♗g3 g4 13.♘d2

0–0–0 14.♗h4 ♗e7∞) 10...♕c5! (after 10...d4, White has the remarkable resource 11.♗xe6! dxc3 12.b4! ♘xb4 13.♗b3± and his offensive on the light squares is tremendously dangerous for Black).

It looks like the best for White here is the prophylactic move 11. a3!? (11.♗xf6 gxf6 12.d4 exd4 13. ♘xd5 0–0–0 14.♘xf6 ♗xb3 15. cxb3 ♕f5 16.♘e4 ♗f4 17.♘g3 ♕g6⩱ – Black's passed d-pawn is very powerful, so he has excellent compensation for the pawn). The b4-square is very important for his queen in numerous variations, since it does not have too many squares to go to. Meanwhile, in some lines, White retreats his bishop from b3 and his b-pawn can go forward. So it appears that if Black does not wish to defend an inferior position (which happens in all the variations in which he plays d5-d4 and his pawns are doubled on the e-file), then he must play 11...0–0–0!?∞. Positions with opposite sides castling are often sharp and double-edged and this is no exception, so there great complications will arise, with unpredictable consequences.

7.0–0 0–0 8.♖e1

We shall now analyze the risky pawn-sacrifice **B2a) 8...♗g4**, as well as the solid positional move **B2b) 8...♘d7!**, fortifying the centre.

It is not good for Black to opt for 8...♖e8, due to 9.♘g5! h6 (9... ♖e7 10.♘c3↑) 10.♘xf7! (in a game between junior players, the move 10.♘e4 was played, but that made White's previous knight-move senseless) 10...♔xf7 11.c4 ♗b4 12. ♖e4 ♘f6 13.c5 ♔f8 14.♖xb4 ♘a6 15.♖c4 ♗f5 (it is even worse for Black to play here 15...♗e6 16.♖c3 ♘d5 17.♗xd5 ♕xd5 18.♗e3± and White has a solid extra pawn) 16. ♗e3 ♕xd3 17.♘d2 ♖ad8 18.♕f3 ♗e6 19.♗c2 ♕d5 20.♕g3⩲ with an advantage to White.

B2a) 8...♗g4 9.h3 ♗h5 10. g4 ♗g6 11.♘xe5 ♗xe5 12.♖xe5 ♘d7 13.♖e1 ♕h4 14.♕f3

(diagram)

14...♖ae8

It is not an improvement for Black to continue with 14...♖fe8 15.♗d2 ♘e5 16.♕g2 ♘f4 17.♗xf4 ♘f3 18.♕xf3 ♖xe1 19.♔g2 ♕f6

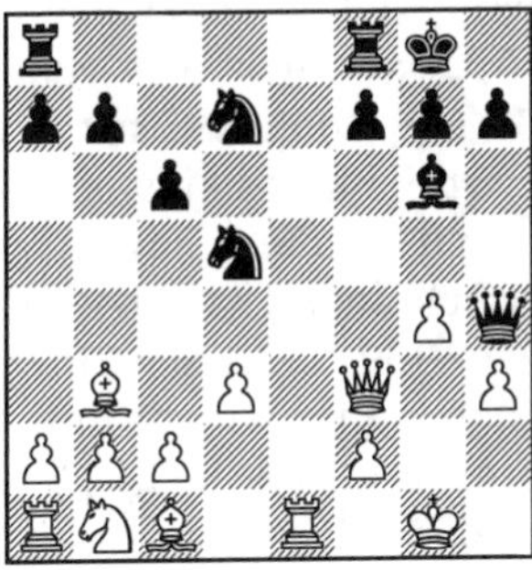

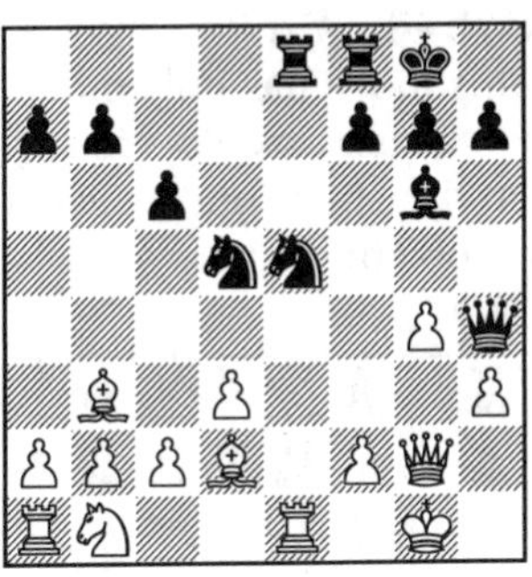

20.♕g3! ♕xb2 21.♗d2 ♕xa1 22.♗xe1 ♕xb1 23.♗c3 ♖e8 (it is even worse for him to choose 23...♔h8 24.h4+–: White will soon capture the bishop on g6, ending up in a technically winning position) 24.♕c7 – Black loses all his queenside pawns and White's pawns become unstoppable. It is also important that Black's bishop on g6 is completely out of play.

15.♗d2!

In the game Alekseev – Shirov, Germany 2007, there followed 15.♖f1 h5 (it was stronger for Black to play 15...♘c5!±, preserving some compensation for the pawn) 16.♘c3 ♘xc3 17.bxc3 ♔h7 and here after 18.♗a3 ♖h8 19.♔g2± White would maintain a great advantage.

15...♘e5

15...♖xe1 16.♗xe1 h5 (16...♘e5 17.♕g3 ♕f6 18.♘c3 ♘f3 19.♔f1±) 17.♗xd5 cxd5 18.♗c3 ♖e8 19.♘d2 ♖e6 20.♕g2 hxg4 21.hxg4±; White's knight will come to f3 and Black will have no compensation for the pawn.

16.♕g2

16...♕f6

The alternatives are inferior:

16...h5 17.♘c3 hxg4 18.hxg4 ♘xc3 19.♗xc3 ♘xg4 20.f3+–;

16...♘f4 17.♗xf4 ♘f3 18.♕xf3 ♖xe1 19.♔g2 ♕f6 20.♕g3 ♕xb2 (an attempt by Black to preserve by all means the pin along the first rank would not work: 20...♖fe8 21.♗d2 h5 (21...h6 22.♗xe1 ♖xe1 23.f4 ♕e7 24.f5 ♗xf5 25.gxf5 ♕e2 26.♕f2 ♕e5 27.♘c3 ♖xa1 28.♘e4+–; 21...♖1e2 22.♘c3 ♖xd2 23.♖e1 ♖f8 24.♕e3+–; 21...♖d1 22.c3+–) 22.♗c3 ♕g5 23.♗xe1 ♖xe1 24.f4 ♕e7 25.f5 ♗xf5 26.gxf5 ♕e2 27.♕f2 ♕e5 28.♘c3 ♖xa1 29.♘e4+–) 21.♗d2 ♕xa1 (21...♖fe8 22.♗xe1! ♕xa1 23.♗c3 ♕xb1 24.h4+–) 22.♗xe1 ♕xb1 23.♗c3 ♖e8 24.h4+– his bishop on g6 is trapped and Black loses.

17.♗xd5 cxd5 18.f4 ♘c4 19.dxc4 ♖xe1 20.♗xe1 ♕xb2 21.♗c3 ♕c1 22.♔h2 ♕xf4 23.♕g3 ♕xc4 24.♘d2 ♕e2 25.♔g1 ♖e8 26.♘b3 ♕xc2 27.♖e1± – Black's pawns are harmless and White has excellent chances of exploiting his extra piece.

B2b) 8...♘d7!

This move has only one drawback: Black blocks his light-squared bishop, but he can solve this problem later.

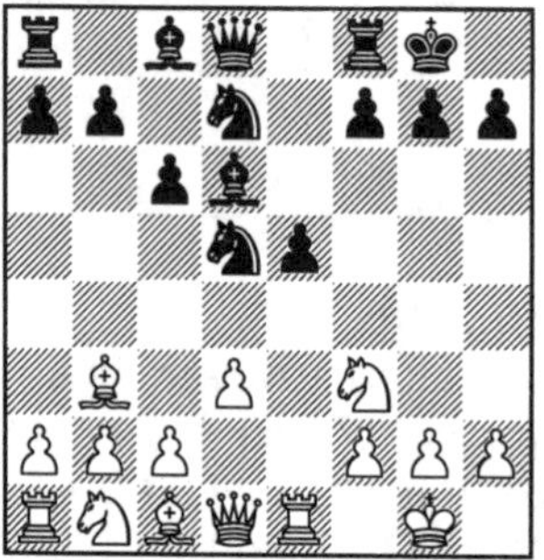

We shall now analyze the immediate opening of the centre **B2b1) 9.d4** as well as the calm completion of White's development **B2b2) 9.♘bd2**.

B2b1) 9.d4 exd4

It is just a loss of time for Black to play 9...♘5f6, because after 10.♘c3 exd4 11.♕xd4, White gains a lead in development. A possible continuation is 11...♘c5 12.♗g5 h6 13.♗h4 g5

14.♖ad1 ♗xh2 15.♔xh2 ♕xd4 16.♖xd4 gxh4 17.♖xh4 ♔g7 18.♗c4 ♗e6 19.♗xe6 (it is also good for White to continue here with 19.♘e5± – Black's king is vulnerable and White's advantage is overwhelming, Tiviakov – Hera, Budva 2009) 19...♘xe6 20. ♘e2!, transferring the knight to the f5-square: 20...♖ad8 21.♘g3 ♔h7 (21...♖d5? 22.c4 ♖a5 23.b4+–) 22.♖xe6 fxe6 23.♘g5 ♔g6 24. ♘xe6 ♖h8 25.♘xd8 ♖xd8 26.♘f1± – White has an extra pawn and excellent winning chances.

10.♗xd5 cxd5 11.♕xd4

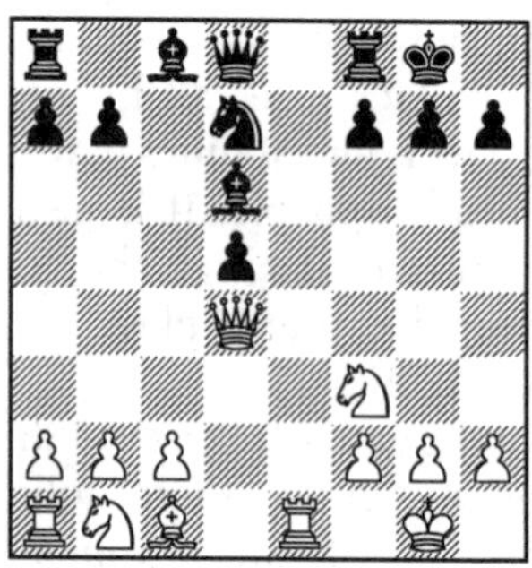

11...♗c5!

This is the right move for Black, because he must play actively! He should be ready to sacrifice a pawn in order to bring his pieces up to the firing line. After 11...♘b6 12.a4!± (if 12.♗f4 ♗f5⇄ Black has counterplay) Black's position is unpromising and White's permanent threat of a4-a5 dooms Black to completely passive defence. 12...♗e7 (it is even worse for him to opt for 12... ♗f5 13.a5 ♘c8 14.♘c3!±) 13.♗f4 ♗e6 (after 13...♗f5, White should play 14.♘c3, just as before) 14.♘c3± and Black is faced with a long and laborious defence.

12.♕d3

If White accepts the pawn-sacrifice Black obtains full compensation thanks to his bishop-pair and more active pieces: 12.♕xd5 ♕b6 13.♖e2 ♘f6 14.♕b3 ♕a6 15.♘c3 ♗e6 16.♕a4 ♕b6 17.♕h4, Tiviakov – Stefanova, Wijk aan Zee 2004.

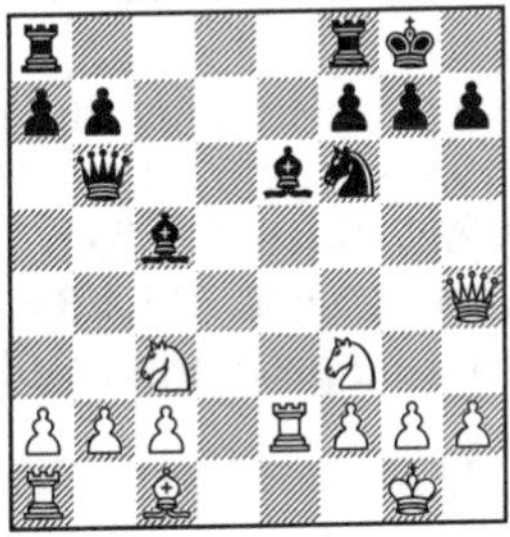

A possible continuation is 17...♖fe8 (Black can also hold the position in the variation 17...♗g4 18.♘a4 ♕a6 19.♖e5 ♗d6 20.♖g5 h5 21.♘c3! ♖fe8 22.♗e3 ♗xf3 23.gxf3 ♗e5=, but the main line of our variation is much more reliable; after 20...♗xf3 21.♖xg7 ♔h8 22.gxf3 ♖g8 23.♖g3 ♗xg3 24.hxg3, Black's dark squares are seriously endangered) 18.h3 (it amounts to more or less the same after 18.b3 ♗g4 19.♘a4 ♕c6 20.♖xe8 ♖xe8 21.♘xc5 ♗xf3 22.gxf3 ♕xc5 23.♗b2 ♕xc2 24.♗xf6 ♕g6 25.♗g5 h6=) 18...♘d5 19.♘a4 ♕b5 20.♖e1 ♗b4 21.c4 ♕xa4 22.cxd5 ♗xd5 23.♗d2 ♗xf3 24.♕xb4 ♕xb4 25.♗xb4 ♗c6=, with a draw.

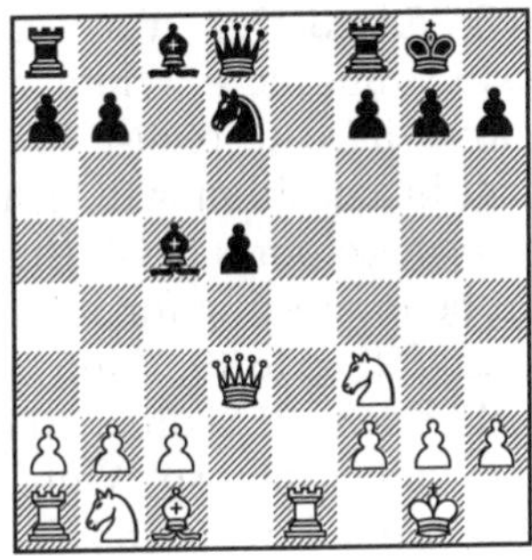

12...♕b6!

This is Black's most active move.

He cannot solve his problems with 12...♖e8 13.♖xe8 ♕xe8 14.♗f4! (14.♕xd5? ♕e2–+; 14.♗e3 ♗xe3 15.♕xe3 ♕xe3 16.fxe3 ♘b6=; 14.♘c3 ♘e5 15.♘xe5 ♕xe5=) 14...♕e4 15.♕d2

15...♘f6 (15...♗b4 16.♘c3 ♗xc3 17.bxc3 ♘b6 18.♖e1 ♕a4 19.♗e3±) 16.♘c3 ♕b4 17.♗e5 ♗f5 (17...♘e4 18.♘xe4 dxe4 19.♕d8 ♗f8 20.♘g5 e3 21.fxe3 ♕e7 22. ♕xe7 ♗xe7 23.♘f3±; 20...h6 21. ♗c3 ♕c4 22.♘h7 ♔xh7 23.♕xf8 f6 24.♖d1 ♕xa2 25.♗xf6! gxf6 26.b3 ♗g4 27.♕xa8 ♗xd1 28.♕xb7 – White picks up the enemy bishop on d1 with checks and wins. There is also a very attractive twin-variation:

24...e3 25.fxe3 ♕e2 26.♖e1 ♕xc2 27.♗xf6±, but here White must still work hard to realise his advantage in a position with bishops of opposite colours) 18.♖f1 (here it might be interesting for White to try 18.♗xf6!? gxf6 19. ♕xd5 ♕xb2 20.♖e1 ♕xc3 21.♕xf5±; Black's king is vulnerable, so White has the edge) 18...♘d7 19.♗d4± White has consolidated his position and is ready to start attacking his opponent's d5-pawn. Unfortunately for Black the move 19...♕xb2 is refuted with a simple but very effective series of moves: 20.♘a4! ♕a3 21.♘xc5 ♘xc5 22.♕g5 ♗g6 23.♕xd5 ♖c8 24.♖e1 b6 25.h4!→ and Black has suddenly come under an attack out of nowhere.

13.♖e2 ♘f6 14.♘c3

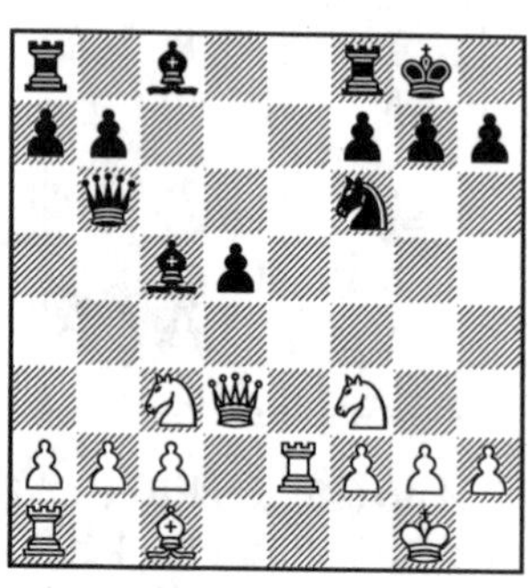

14...♗d7!

It is essential to deprive White's knight of the possibility of going to the a4-square with tempo.

In the game Morozevich – Gelfand, Biel 2009, Black allowed this and after 14...♗g4 15.♘a4 ♕c6 16.♘xc5 ♕xc5 17.♗e3 ♕c4 18. ♖d2!± he was forced to defend a slightly inferior position, a task which he failed to cope with.

15.♗e3

After 15.♘e5, Black follows with 15...♗g4! 16.♘xg4 ♘xg4 17. ♕f3 ♘xf2! 18.♖xf2 ♖ae8→ with an attack!

15...♗xe3 16.♕xe3

Or 16.♖xe3 ♖fe8 17.♖xe8 ♖xe8 18.b3 ♕c5, and Black has sufficient counterplay along the c-file.

16...♕xb2 17.♖b1 ♕a3 18. ♘xd5 ♕xa2

He can also play here 18... ♕xe3 19.♘xf6 gxf6 20.♖xe3 b6=

19.♘e7 ♔h8 20.♖xb7 ♖fb8 21.♖xb8 ♖xb8 22.h3=, and Black has no problems at all.

B2b2) 9.♘bd2

9...♗c7

After 9...♖e8, White has the powerful resource 10.♘e4! ♘7f6 (his pieces are also much more active after 10...♗f8 11.d4 exd4 12.♕xd4±) 11.♗g5 (here White could consider 11.♘xd6 ♕xd6 and now an interesting try is 12.c4!?

♘b4 13.d4, as is the immediate 12.d4!?) 11...♗f5 12.h3 ♗g6 13.♘h4 ♗e7 14.♘xg6 hxg6 15.♕f3±; White enjoys the advantage of a powerful bishop-pair.

The move 10.♘c4 (after 9...♖e8) would not be correct, because Black's e5-pawn is sufficiently protected and White should concentrate his forces on the kingside. After 10...♗c7 11.c3, in the game Vachier-Lagrave – Gelfand, Khanty-Mansyisk 2009, Black decided to oust the enemy knight from the c4-square, but weakened his queenside in the process: 11...b5 (it was correct for him to play 11... f6!= and Black would have no problems) 12.♘e3 ♘7f6 13.♘xd5 (Naturally it would be premature for White to play 13.a4, because of 13...♘f4↑) 13...♘xd5. Now White should choose 14.c4 (the move 14.a4 allows the unpleasant pin 14...♗g4; in the game White played rather impulsively 14.d4? and after 14...e4 15.♘g5 ♗f5∓ Black obtained an advantage) 14...♘f6 15.cxb5 cxb5 16.♘g5⩲ and after Black protects his pawn with the rook, White can continue with 17.♘e4, trying to reach an almost symmetrical pawn-structure with a minimal positional plus.

10.♘e4

(diagram)

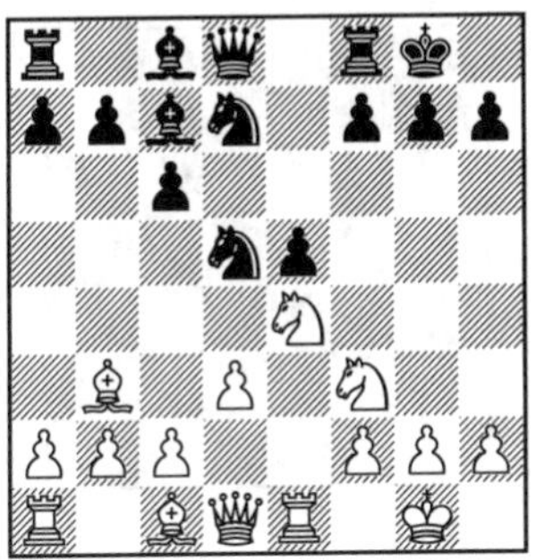

10...h6

It would again be premature for Black to move his rook to e8: 10...♖e8 11.♗g5! (11.h3 h6 12.♗d2 ♘f8 (12...♘7f6=) 13.♘h2 f5?! (13...a5 14.a3 ♘e6=) 14.♕h5↑ Nevednichy – Beliavsky, Plovdiv 2008) 11...f6 12.c4 ♘e7 13.♗d2 ♘f8 (13...c5 14.♗a4 ♘c6 15.h3 and Black will have problems freeing his knights from the pin; 13...b6 14.d4±) 14.d4 exd4 15.c5 ♘d5 16.♘xd4⩲ with a slight edge for White.

11.♗d2

We should consider the alternatives for White:

11.c4 ♘5f6 12.♘xf6 ♕xf6=;

11.♘g3 ♖e8=;

after 11.h3, Black can play 11...♖e8, fortifying his e5-pawn and preparing to transfer his knight on d7 to f8 or f6 (the game Nevednichy – Fridman, Plovdiv 2008, continued with 11...♔h8?! 12.♗d2 a5 13.a3 – 13.c4⩲ – 13...f5?! 14.♘c3 ♘xc3 15.♗xc3 ♕f6 16.♖e3± and White maintained a considerable advantage, since Black had difficulty completing his development);

11.d4 ♘5f6 12.♘xf6 ♕xf6 13.c3 exd4 14.♘xd4 (or 14.♕xd4 ♕xd4 15.♘xd4 ♘f6=, leading to complete symmetry and equality) 14...♘e5 15.f4

and here Black has two equally good possibilities:

15...♘g6 16.g3 c5 17.♘c2 (the endgame arising after 17.♘b5 ♗b6 18.♗e3 ♖e8 19.♗xf7+ ♕xf7 20.♘d6 ♕f8 21.♘xe8 ♕xe8 22.♕d6 ♕e6 23.♕xe6 ♗xe6∓ seems more pleasant for Black; or 19.♕d2 ♗h3↑ with ideas of capturing on e3, followed by c5-c4, as well as possible knight-sorties to f4 or h4, accodring to different circumstances) 17...b5 18.♗d5 ♖b8=, and the position is approximately equal;

15...♘g4!? – this seemingly reckless knight-move turns out to be correct. 16.h3 ♕h4 17.hxg4 (17.♖e2 ♘f6 18.♕d3 ♗d7 19.♗d2 ♖ad8=) 17...♗xg4 18.♕d2 ♗xf4 19.♕xf4 ♕xe1 20.♔h2 (20.♕f1 ♕xf1 21.♔xf1 ♖fe8 22.♗f4 g5 23.♗g3 c5, followed by ♖a8-d8) 20...♕h4=, with a draw by a perpetual check.

(diagram)

11...a5!

This is a very clever move with the idea of ... taking control of the b4-square!

Black has many other natural moves at his disposal:

White is better after 11...♘7f6?! 12.♘xf6! (12.♘g3 ♖e8 13.h3 a5 14.a3 a4 15.♗a2 ♗d7 16.♘h4? – 16.c3= – 16...e4 17.♘hf5, Efimenko – Paehtz, Dresden 2007, 17...exd3∓) 12...♕xf6 13.d4

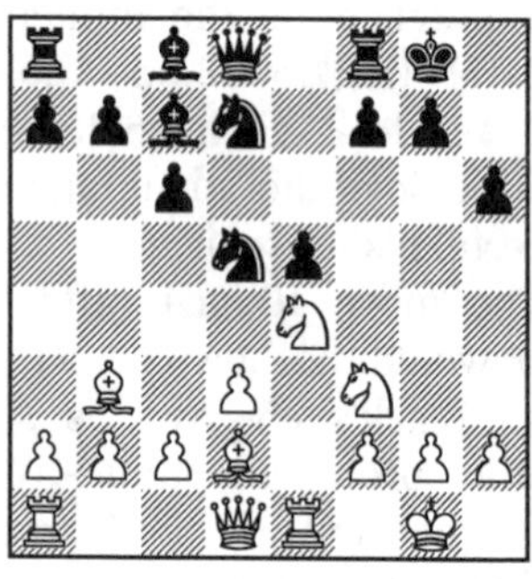

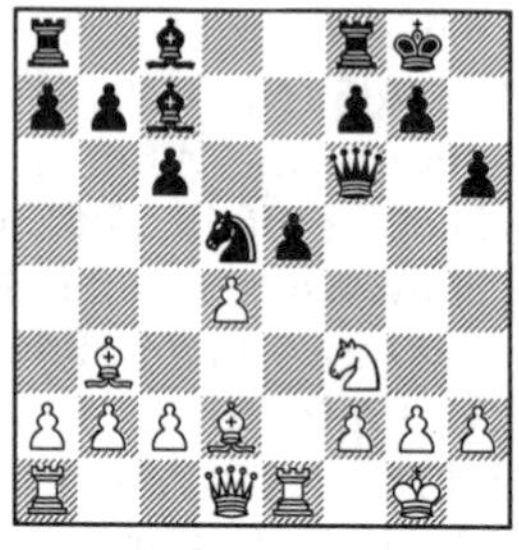

13...e4. This is an interesting attempt by Black to seize the initiative, in the spirit of the Marshall Attack, but it is unsound (13...♗g4 14.c4 ♘e7 15.dxe5 ♗xe5 16.♖xe5 ♗xf3 17.♕e1 ♘f5 18.♖xf5 ♕xf5 19.gxf3 ♖fe8 20.♗e3 ♕xf3 21.♕d1 ♕h3 22.♔h1 ♖ad8 23.♕e2±; 13...exd4 14.♗xd5 cxd5 15.♗b4±) 14.♖xe4 ♗f5 15.♖e1 ♖ae8 (15...♖fe8 16.c4 ♘f4 17.♗xf4 ♗xf4 18.♗c2) 16.c4 (16.♘e5 ♗xe5 17.dxe5 ♖xe5 18.c4) 16...♘f4 17.♗xf4 ♗xf4 18.♗c2 ♖xe1 19.♘xe1 ♗e6 20.♕d3 g6 21.h3±;

After 11...♔h8, White can concentrate on the target on h6 with the move 12.♕c1! (it is inferior to play 12.♘g3 a5 13.a3 f5, with a double-edged position, Kobalia – Motylev, Sochi 2007). Now it is not good for Black to play 12...f5, because of 13.♘c3± and he will have problems with the protection of his e5-pawn. Therefore, he must continue with 12...♔h7 but after 13.c4 ♘f4 14.♗c2↑ White seizes the initiative, because he exerts powerful piece-pressure against the central squares and has the undermining pawn-break d3-d4 up his sleeve.

However, Black has a reliable alternative in 11...♖e8 12.h3 ♘7f6 13.♘g3 ♗d7 14.a3= with a complicated middlegame and approximately equal chances. It would less convincing for Black to opt for 12...♘f8 (instead of 12...♘7f6) 13.c4 (13.d4 f5 14.♘g3 e4∞ or 14.♘c3 e4= with a complicated and approximately balanced position) 13...♘f6! (the move 13...♘e7 allows the line 14.♗xh6! gxh6 15.♘f6 ♔g7 16.♘xe8 ♕xe8 17.♘xe5↑; 14...f5 15.c5 ♗e6 16.♘d6↑ White has a dangerous initiative; 13...♘f4 14.♗xf4 exf4 15.d4 ♗f5 16.♗c2± White is slightly better, because Black will need time to bring his knight on f8 into play) 14.♕e2 (14.c5 ♗f5 15.♕c2 ♘d5=) 14...♘e6 15.♘xf6 ♕xf6 16.♕e3 ♘d4 (here it would be too risky for Black to play 16...♘f4 17.♕xf4 exf4 18.♖xe8 ♔h7 19.♖ae1±) 17.♘xd4 ♗b6 18.♗c3 ♗d7 19.♕f3 ♗xd4 20.♕xf6 gxf6 21.♗xd4 exd4= although he should manage to save this endgame)

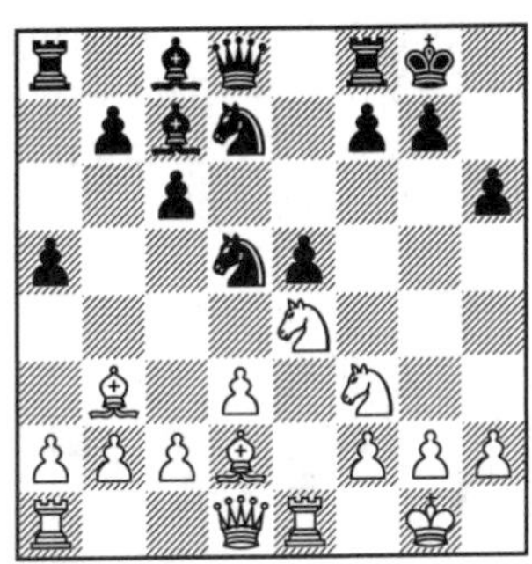

12.c4

If now 12.a3, Black can continue bravely with 12...♘7f6, making use of the circumstance that in the variation 13.♘xf6 (after calm developments along the lines of 13.h3 a4 14.♗a2 ♖e8 Black will have no problems whatsoever) 13...♕xf6 14.d4 exd4 15.♗xd5 cxd5, White will not have access to the b4-square for his bishop. This is where you can see the effect of the move 11...a5!

After 12.c3 it would be interesting for Black to play 12...f5!? (12...♘7f6= would be sufficient for equality) 13.♘g3 ♘c5 14.♗c2 f4 15.♘e4 ♘xe4 16.dxe4 ♘f6=, with an active position.

12...♘f4

It is less precise for Black to play here 12...♘b4, because of 13.♗c3! (White's alternatives cannot create any problems for Black: 13.♗xb4 axb4 14.c5 ♘f6 15.♘xf6 ♕xf6=; 13.c5 ♘xd3 14.♗g5 hxg5 15.♕xd3 ♘f6 16.♕xd8 ♖xd8 and after every capture of the g5-pawn, Black blocks White's bishop with the move 17...♘d5) 13...f5 (13...c5 14.♘g3 ♕f6 15.♗a4↑) 14. c5 (the play is very interesting after 14.♘g3!? ♘c5 15.d4 exd4 16. ♗xd4±) 14...♘d5 (It is inferior for Black to play 14...♔h8

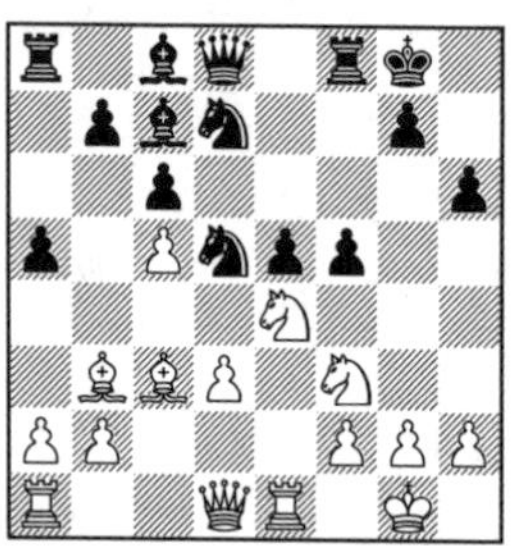

15.♘d6 ♘xc5 16.♘f7 ♖xf7 17. ♗xf7 ♘bxd3 18.♘xe5! ♘xe1 19. ♕xe1 ♔h7 20. ♗g6 ♔g8 21.♘f7 ♕f8 22.♕d1! ♗f4 (The idea of White's last move can best be seen in the variation 22...♗e6 23.♘xh6 gxh6 24.♕d4+– and Black gets mated.) 23.♕f3 ♗e6 24.♕xf4 ♗xf7 25.♗xf5± and White's bishop on c3 is so powerful that he has an overwhelming advantage.) 15. ♘d6 ♘xc5 16.♗xd5 cxd5 17.♘xc8 ♖xc8 18.♗xe5± White preserves a slight edge thanks to his domination of the e5-square.

13.♗xf4 exf4 14.d4 ♘f6=

White would have had some advantage with a pawn on c3 instead of c4. Now the weakness on d4 and his passive bishop make his position not at all attractive and the game is equal.

Conclusion

In playing the Bishop's Opening White is usually hoping to deviate from the well-known theoretical lines. He wishes to obtain a calm position with a slight edge, in the spirit of the Italian Game, and sometimes the game even transposes to that opening. However, if Black replies with 3...c6 the game is quite different from the usual developments in the Italian Game. Our analysis shows convincingly that there is not a single variation in which White can obtain even a minimal edge and Black has an excellent position in all lines.

Part 2

1.e4 e5 2.♘f3 ♘f6

All White Replies without 3.d4 and 3.♘xe5

I n the second part of our book we analyse some rarely played possibilities for White on move 3.

After 3.♘c3, Black can reply with 3...♗b4, acquiescing to a slightly worse, but very solid, position.

The symmetrical move 3...♘c6 is also simple and quite reliable. Of course, players with Black will need to memorize the main lines of the variations arising after 4.♗b5 ♘d4.

The move 4.d4 leads to a harmless version of the **Scotch Game**, while after 4.g3, Black obtains approximately equal chances in fighting positions of a non-forcing nature.

Chapter 5 1.e4 e5 2.♘f3 ♘f6

3.♘c3

The "amateur" variation 3.♗c4 ♘xe4 4.♘c3, is covered in Chapter 2 on the Vienna Game with 2.♘c3 ♘f6 3.♗c4 ♘xe4 4.♘f3.

White cannot obtain any advantage in the opening with the passive line: 3.d3 d6 (here 3...♘c6, followed by d7-d5, is also good for Black) 4.♗e2 g6 5.0–0 ♗g7 6.♘c3 0–0 7.♗g5 h6 8.♗e3 ♘c6 9.h3 d5 10.exd5 ♘xd5 11.♘xd5 ♕xd5 12.♖e1 ♖e8 13.c3 b6= Sedlak – Sakaev, Vrnjacka Banja 2010.

3...♗b4

This bishop-sortie is a reliable option for Black, although it is a bit passive. He presents his opponent with the advantage of the bishop-pair, but develops quickly, while keeping the position closed.

It is more ambitious and popular to continue with 3...♘c6, which presents White with a wide choice of systems (none of them very promising, however...) and we shall analyze these in the following chapters.

4.♘xe5

The position is equal after 4.♗c4 0–0 5.0–0 d6 6.d3 ♗xc3 7.bxc3 ♗e6.

4...0–0 5.♗e2 ♖e8 6.♘d3 ♗xc3 7.dxc3 ♘xe4

Now White can only create some problems for his opponent by making the most natural move in the position – castling.

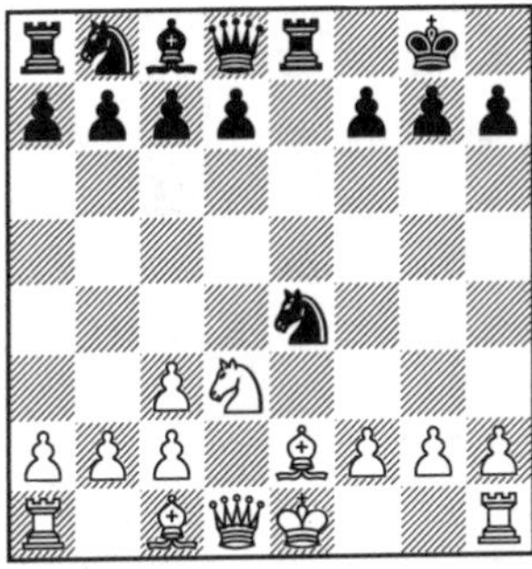

8.0–0!

Theory considers 8.♘f4 as the main line, but I think that this move, closing the diagonal of White's own bishop, loses the minimal edge that he has already acquired. 8...d6 9.0–0 ♘c6! (this is more active than the more popular choice for Black here: 9...♘d7) 10.a4!? This is an original way for White to bring his a1-rook into action.(He would not achieve much with the natural line: 10.c4 h6 11.♗e3 ♗f5 12.♖e1 ♘f6 and Black has no problems at all.). 10...h6 11.a5 a6 12.c4 ♗f5 13.♖a3 ♘f6 14.♖g3 ♘e4 15.♖e3 ♘f6, Sutovsky – Sakaev, Serbia 2009 (**game 4**). White's most prudent decision here would be to repeat moves.

8...d5!

Black must play actively if his opponent lets him. He has exchanged his dark-squared bishop, so it would be positionally justified to build his pawn-chain on the dark squares, keeping the position closed. In this particular case, however, there is a concrete reason why the move 8...d6 is not good. White has the opportunity of seizing additional space and then pinning the enemy knight on f6 with 9.f3! ♘f6 10.♗g5 ♘bd7 11.♖e1 b6 12.a4 (it also looks attractive to begin an offensive on the light squares with 12.♘b4!? ♗b7 13.c4 h6 14.♗h4 a5 15.♘d5 g5 16.♗f2 ♘xd5 17.cxd5 ♕f6 18.b3±) 12...a5 13.♘f2 h6 14.♗h4 ♘c5 (14...♘f8 15.♘e4 g5 16.♘xf6 ♕xf6 17.♗f2±. White maintains a slight edge, since Black's king is vulnerable, Howell – Giri, Wijk aan Zee 2009).

Now it is very good for White to continue with 15.f4!, preventing g7-g5 and thus maintaining the unpleasant pin on Black's f6-knight (it is inferior for White to play 15.b4: after 15...axb4 16.cxb4 ♖xa4 17.♗xf6 ♕xf6 18.♖b1 ♘b7 19.♗b5 ♖xe1 20.♕xe1 ♖a8 21.♕e8 ♔h7 22.♗d3 g6 23.♘e4 ♕d4 24.♔f1 ♔g7 25.♕c6 d5 26.♘c3 ♕e5 27.♘xd5 ♖a1 28.♖xa1 ♕xa1 29.♔e2 ♕e5 30.♔d2 ♘d8 31.♕c3 ♕xc3 32.♔xc3 ♘e6 33.♗c4 ♗b7 34.♘e3 ♘d8 35.♗d5 ♗c8 36. ♔d4 ♔f6= Black should be able to hold this position) 15...♗f5 16.g4! ♗d7 17.♗f3 ♖xe1 18.♕xe1 ♖b8 19. b3±

White's space advantage promises him a slight edge and Black is faced with a long defence.

9.♘f4

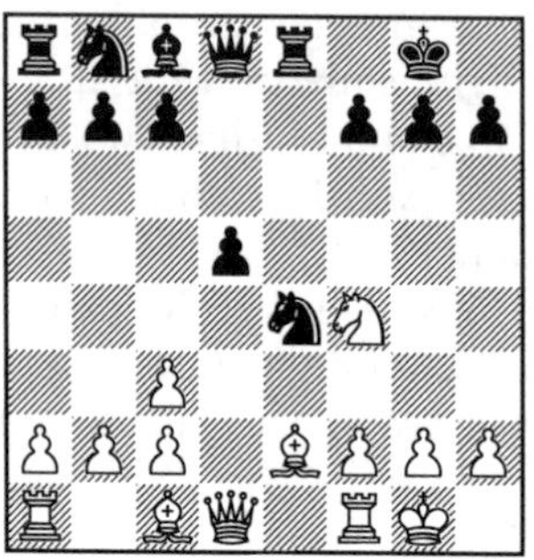

9...♘f6!

Black's knight on e4 is only pseudo-active, since it blocks the e-file and impedes Black's other pieces from occupying their best squares.

He usually continues with 9...c6 here, but after 10.c4! d4 11.♖e1± there arises an open position in which White's bishop-pair is very powerful.

10.♗e3

White cannot create problems for his opponent with 10.♗f3 c6=. Black's bishop goes to f5 and his knight on b8 is transferred effortlessly to e5 via the d7-square.

10...♗f5!N

After 10...♘c6 11.♗f3 ♗e6 12.♖e1± Black has difficulties.

11.g4 ♗e4!

(diagram)

12.g5

White can sacrifice a pawn with 12.♖e1 ♘c6 (it is weaker for Black to opt for 12...h6 13.♗f1 ♘c6

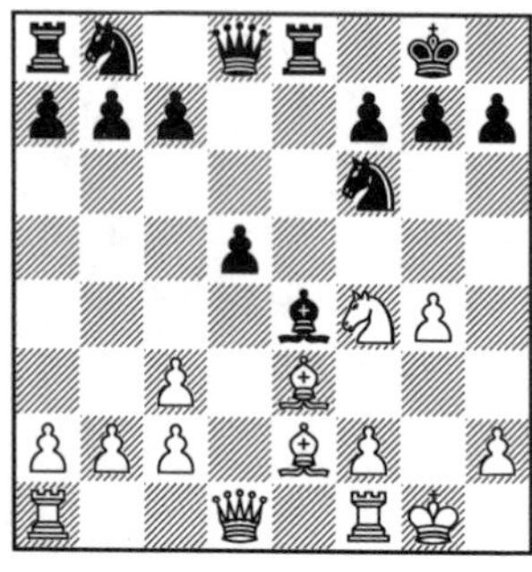

14.f3 ♗h7 15.♕d2 ♘e5 16.♕f2 ♕d6 17.♘d3±; 16...c6 17.♘d3 ♘fd7 18.♘xe5 ♘xe5 19.h3±; White has the edge, since he can advance his pawn with tempo from f3 to f5, forcing the enemy bishop out of play on h7)

13.f3 ♗xc2 14.♕d2, but after 14...h6 15.♗f2 ♗h7 16.♖ad1= White's compensation is only enough for equality.

Or 13.g5 ♘d7 14.♘xd5 (after 14.♘h5 ♘b6 15.♘g3 ♗g6 16.♕d2 ♘c4 17.♗xc4 dxc4∓ Black's position is even slightly preferable) 14...♖e5 (he can also solve his problems with 14...♘de5 15.c4 ♘xc4! 16.♗xc4 ♘e5 17.♗e2 ♗xd5=) 15.c4 ♖xg5 16.♗xg5 ♕xg5 17.♗g4 ♗xc2 18.♕xc2 ♕xg4= with a draw by perpetual check.

12...♘fd7 13.♘xd5 ♖e5 14.c4 ♖xg5 15.♗xg5 ♕xg5 16.♗g4 ♗xd5 17.h4

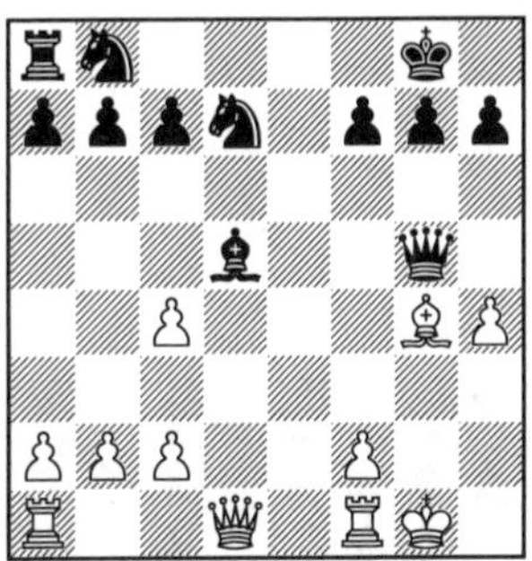

17...♕f4!

After all Black's other options his initiative is gradually neutralized and White's extra exchange should tell, for example: 17...♕xh4 18.cxd5 ♘f6 19.♗f3 ♘bd7 20.d6!±, and the opening of the central files is in his favour, or 17...♕g6 18.h5 ♕g5 19.f4 ♕h4 20.cxd5 ♘f6 21.♗f3 ♕g3 (21...♕xf4 22.♗g2 ♕e3 23.♖f2 ♘bd7 24.♕f3±) 22.♗g2 ♘g4 23.♖f3 ♕h2 24.♔f1 ♕h4 25.♗h3 ♘h2 26.♔g2 ♘xf3 27.♕xf3±; material equality has been restored, but White's pieces are much more active.

18.cxd5 ♘e5 19.♗e2 ♘bd7 20.♕c1 ♕xh4 21.♕e3

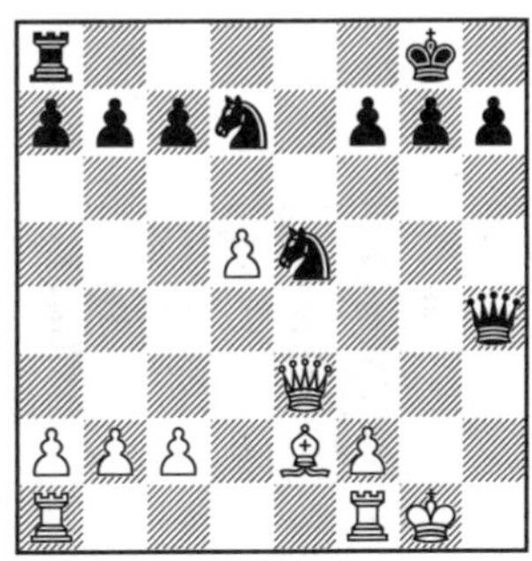

21...f5!

Black's pawn is ready to join in the attack.

22.♕g3 ♕f6 23.f4 ♘f7⩱. One of his knights will occupy the blockading square d6 and his other knight is headed for e4, so Black has excellent compensation for the exchange.

Conclusion

The move 3...♗b4 is not very popular but is reliable. Black obtains a solid position and avoids having to study long theoretical variations. The drawbacks are that the variation is a bit passive for Black and his opponent is presented with the advantage of the bishop-pair. Overall, the line is playable, of course, but I suspect that it will not be to everyone's taste, so in the following chapters we shall examine Black's more ambitious alternative: 3...♘c6.

Chapter 6 1.e4 e5 2.♘f3 ♘f6 3.♘c3 ♘c6

Scotch Four Knights Belgrade Gambit

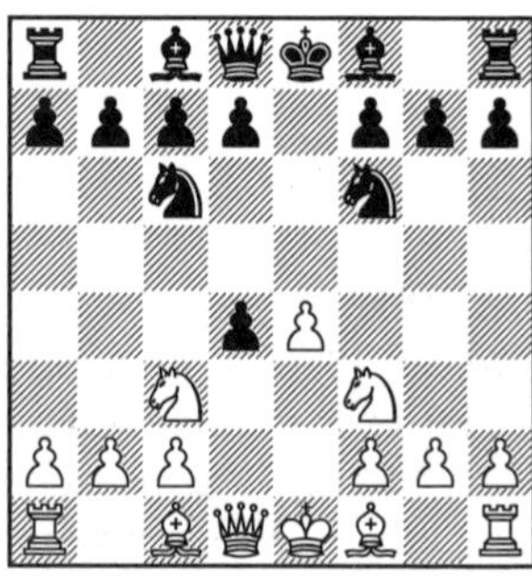

With his last move 3...♘c6 Black maintains the symmetry, but he still has good chances of avoiding a dull position with drawish tendencies. Instead, he can obtain a lively position with more than sufficient counter chances.

4.d4

With the white knight already developed to c3, the Scotch Game is not at all dangerous for Black.

White's other, more interesting alternatives will be analyzed in the following chapters.

4...exd4

(diagram)

5.♘xd4

The Belgrade Gambit is reached after the move 5.♘d5. What does Black need to know about it? The following variations are quite sufficient: 5...♗e7! 6.♗f4 (6.♘xd4 ♘xd5 7.exd5 ♘xd4 8.♕xd4 0–0=; 6.♗c4 0–0 7.0–0 d6 8.♘xd4 ♘xd4 9.♕xd4 ♘xd5 10.♕xd5 ♗e6 11.♕d3 ♕d7=) 6...d6 7.♘xd4 0–0 8.♘b5 ♘xd5 9.exd5 ♘e5=

5...♗b4 6.♘xc6 bxc6 7.♗d3 d5

8.exd5

After 8.0–0 ♗xc3 9.bxc3 dxe4∓ White has nothing to brag about.

8...cxd5 9.0–0 0–0 10.♗g5 c6 11.♕f3

If White plays 11.♘a4, he can end up in an inferior position, for example: 11...h6 12.♗h4 ♖e8 13.c4 ♗d6 14.cxd5 cxd5 15.♘c3 (Black's game seems better too after 15.♖c1 ♖b8 16.b3 ♗f4 17.♖c6 ♗e5.) 15...♖b8∓ and Black is better.

11...h6

If Black wishes to reach a position with more fighting possibilities, he should try 11...♗d6, with the idea of ♖a8-b8 and eventually ♖b8-b4.

12.♗xf6 ♕xf6 13.♕xf6 gxf6 14.♘e2 ♗d6 15.♘d4 c5 16.♘f5 ♗xf5 17.♗xf5=

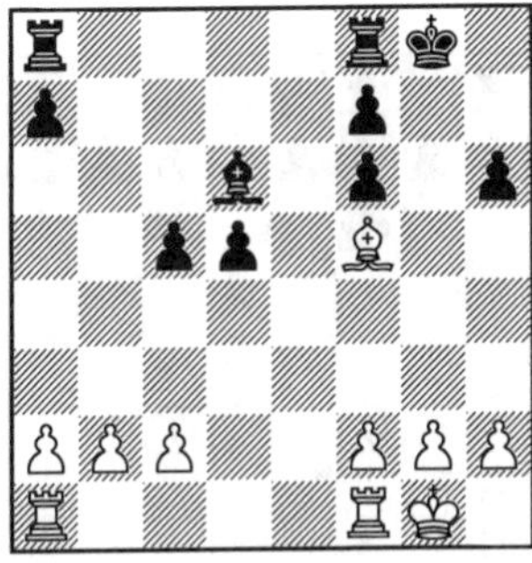

Here, the opponents can agree to a draw, as was done in numerous games.

Conclusion

White has developed his knight too early (in comparison with the Scotch Game) to the c3-square and he cannot claim any advantage whatsoever. Usually after 4.d4 the position quickly becomes simplified and the game is equal, so lately White players have more or less stopped playing this line.

Chapter 7 1.e4 e5 2.♘f3 ♘f6 3.♘c3 ♘c6 4.g3!?

Glek Variation

White sometimes plays this with the aim of reaching positions that have not been extensively analysed.

GM Igor Glek has contributed considerably to the development of this variation and has played numerous games with it.

4...♗c5

The position is about equal but much more open after 4...d5 5. exd5 ♘xd5 6.♗g2 ♘xc3 7.bxc3 ♗d6 8.0–0 0–0. A reasonable continuation is 9.♖b1 ♖b8 10.d4 ♖e8

(diagram)

and here White has two main possibilities:

11.♘g5 – this is the main theoretical line. After, for example,

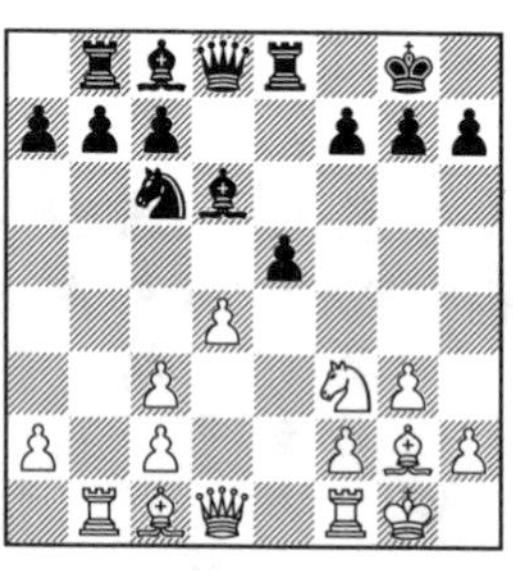

11...♗f5 12.♗d5 (it is harmless for White to play 12.♖xb7 ♖xb7 13. ♗xc6 ♖b1 14.♗xe8 ♕xe8⩱; Black has excellent compensation for the pawn) 12...♗g6 13.h4 ♗e7 14. ♗xc6 (14.dxe5 ♘xe5 15.♖e1 ♗f6 16.h5 ♗f5 17.♗f4 ♗xg5 18.♗xe5 ♗f6 19.♕d4 c6 20.♗xf6 ♕xf6∓ there arises an endgame in which Black is at no risk) 14...bxc6 15. ♖xb8 ♕xb8 16.dxe5 ♗xg5 (Black can try to seize the initiative here with 16...h6!? 17.♘f3 c5⩱, with sufficient compensation for the pawn) 17.hxg5 ♖xe5 18.♗f4 ♖e6= the position is completely equal;

11.♗g5!? – This is the only way for White to try to create any serious problems for Black. 11...f6! (The move 11...♕d7 blocks the bishop's diagonal and thus after

12.♗e3 exd4 13.cxd4 b6 14.c4± White ends up with a slight advantage.) 12.♗e3 b6! 13.♕d3 ♗b7! (after 13...e4, White is slightly better: 14.♕c4 ♔h8 15.♘g5 fxg5 16.♕xc6±) 14.♘d2 (Black's position is quite acceptable after 14.♘h4 ♘a5 15.d5 ♕d7 16.♘f5 ♖bd8=, followed by ♗d6-f8, exerting pressure against White's centre.) 14...♕d7 15.♖fd1 ♘a5 16.♗xb7 ♘xb7 17.♕a6 ♘a5 18.♘b3 exd4 19.cxd4 ♘c6=, with equality.

5.♗g2 d6 6.d3 a6

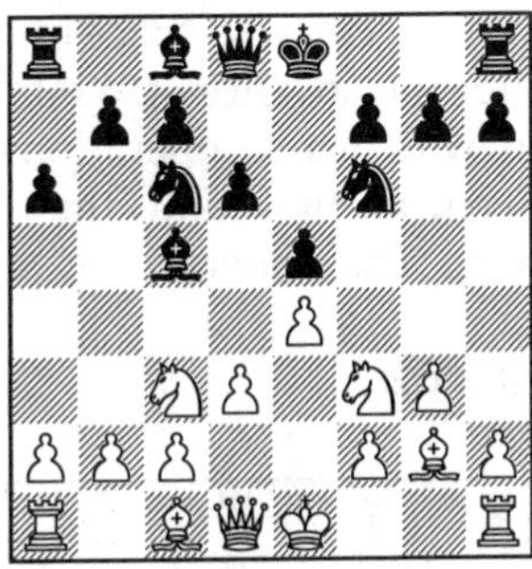

7.0–0

The move 7.♗e3!? was tried in one game by GM Vadim Zvjaginsev – a very inventive player who has made numerous opening discoveries. After 7...♗xe3 8.fxe3, the player with Black, GM Evgeniy Najer, played 8...♘e7. (After the automatic reply 8...0–0, Evgeny was possibly afraid of 9.♕d2!?, with the idea of castling queenside, when a very non-standard position would arise!) 9.♘h4 c6 10.♕d2 ♘g6 11.♘f5 ♗xf5 12.exf5 ♘f8 (it seems about equally strong for Black to play here 12...♘e7=) 13.0–0–0 d5= Zvjaginsev – Najer, Ohrid 2009 (**game 5**). In the subsequent complex manoeuvring struggle, the chances of both sides are approximately balanced, although in the game Black had the initiative.

7...0–0 8.♗e3

White can begin with the prophylactic move 8.h3, but that would not change the evaluation of the position. After for example: 8...♗e6 9.♔h2 h6 10.♗e3 ♗xe3 11.fxe3 d5 12.exd5 ♘xd5 13.♕e1 ♕d7 14.♖d1 ♖ad8 15.a3 ♘xc3 16.♕xc3 f6= the game is equal, Vorobiov – Sakaev, Novokuznetsk 2008.

8...♗xe3 9.fxe3 ♘e7 10.♘h4

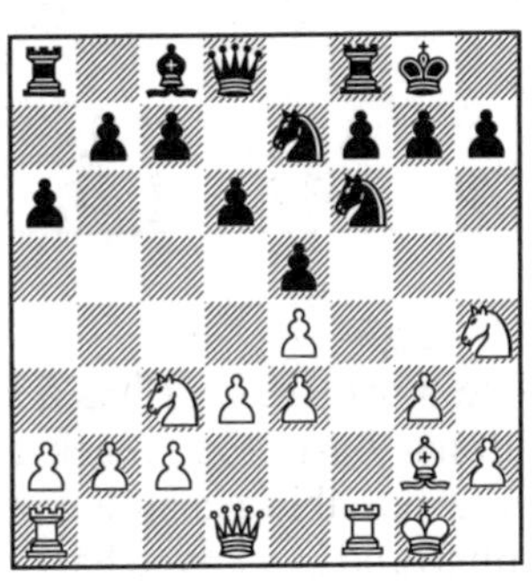

10...c6

An interesting position arises after 10...♗g4 11.♕d2 ♕d7

(diagram)

This move emphasizes the fact that White has not played h2-h3, restricting the mobility of Black's light-squared bishop. White has no constructive ideas

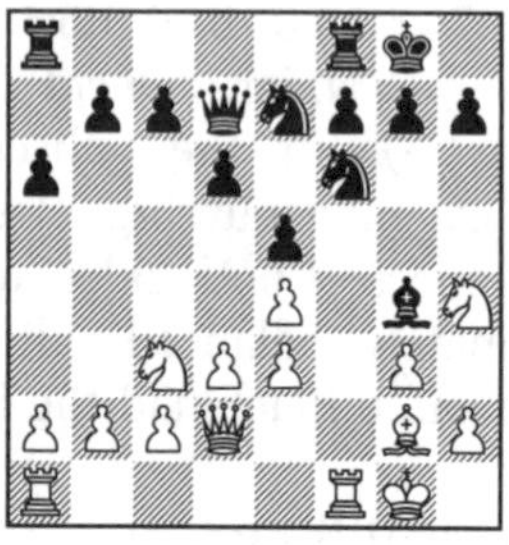

except for 12.d4 ♖ad8 13.♖xf6!? gxf6 14.♖f1 c6 15.♕f2!?≂ – there are no forcing lines, but White has sufficient compensation for the exchange.

11.d4

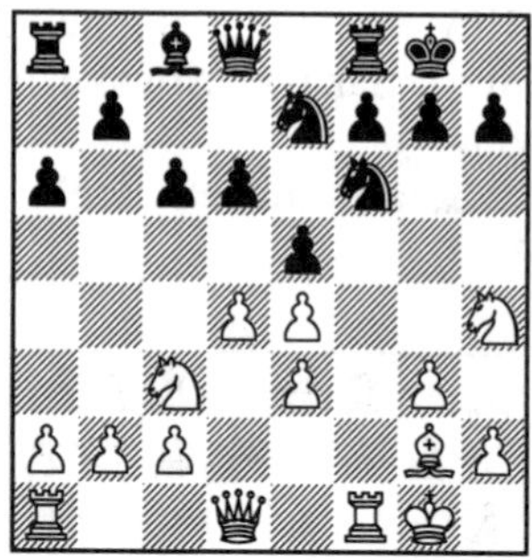

11...♘g6

The move 11...♘g4 has a solid positional basis too. Black rules out the possible exchange sacrifice on f6 and is ready to barricade the f-file with the move f7-f6. Still, this plan slows down his development and White can exploit this circumstance by energetic play: 12.♕d3! (In the game Shaked – Leko, Tilburg 1997 White played 12.♕d2, but Black was able to carry out all his plans and gain the advantage: 12...♘h6 13.♖ad1 ♗g4 14.♗f3 ♗e6 15.♕e2 b5 16.b3 ♕a5 17.♕d2 ♕c7 18.♔h1 ♖ad8 19.♗g2 f6∓) 12...♘h6 13.♘f5 ♘exf5 14. exf5 f6 15.dxe5! (this is stronger than the often-played move 15. h3=) 15...dxe5 16.♗e4 ♕xd3 17. ♗xd3±. Black's position is cramped and his b6-square is weak (White's knight is headed there), so the endgame is difficult for him.

12.♘f5 ♖e8

With his last move Black gives additional support to his e5-pawn, but he has an interesting alternative here: 12...♗xf5!? 13. exf5 ♘e7∞. He lacks space but can counter the advance of White's g-pawn with active operations on the central files and the dark squares. The chances are about equal.

13.♕d2

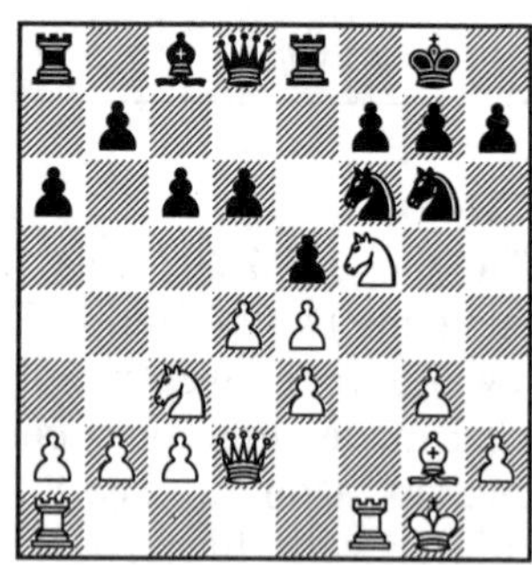

13...♗xf5!?

The move 13...d5 is sufficient for equality, but Black does not have to play this. After 14.♖ae1 (the position is also balanced after 14.exd5 cxd5 15.dxe5 ♖xe5 16. ♘d4 ♗d7=) 14...dxe4 15.♘xe4 ♘xe4 16.♗xe4 ♘e7 17.♘xe7 ♕xe7, the position is considerably simplified and the result should be a draw.

14.exf5 ♘e7 15.♖ad1 ♕c7 16.♘e4 ♘ed5=. Black will replace one blockading piece on f6 with another, so the prospects are approximately equal.

Conclusion

There was a time when you could surprise your opponent with a move like 4.g3 but those days are long gone. This variation has now even been tried a few times at top level, so sufficient material for analyses and conclusions has been amassed. Players who prefer more open positions can play 4...d5, but I prefer the move 4...♗c5. I believe this line to be more justified positionally and quite logical too, because it guarantees a strong Black presence in the centre and good prospects on the dark squares.

Chapter 8 1.e4 e5 2.♘f3 ♘f6 3.♘c3 ♘c6 4.♗b5

Four Knights Game

The Four Knights Game is, I believe, an opening taught in the first lessons of all children's chess classes. I am not planning to deal with this opening thoroughly. I shall just show you the basic theoretical lines which the player with Black should focus on.

4...♘d4

There is a mountain of theory on the symmetrical move 4...♗b4, and we shall ignore all of it. I will only mention that, according to the contemporary evaluation of this variation, White can claim a slight advantage.

White now has two possible bishop retreats: **A) 5.♗c4** and **B) 5.♗a4**.

It is a well-known draw after 5.♘xd4 exd4 6.e5 dxc3 7.exf6 ♕xf6 (but not 7...cxd2? 8.♗xd2 ♕xf6 9.0–0 and Black is dangerously behind in development) 8. dxc3 ♕e5 9.♕e2 ♕xe2 10.♗xe2 d5 11.♗f4 c6=

A) 5.♗c4

It may seem strange now, but this retreat of the bishop was the cause of great problems for Black for a long time.

5...♗c5!

This move is the correct solution of all the problems in this position. It is inconceivable now how White can create any difficulties for his opponent.

It is too risky for Black to opt for 5...♘xf3?! in view of 6.gxf3! ♗c5 7.♖g1± and White has a dangerous initiative along the g-file. However, the game is complicated but quite acceptable for Black after 5...d6 6.♘xd4 exd4 7.♘d5 ♘d7 8.0–0 g6∞

6.♘xe5

The position is equal after 6.d3 d6 7.♘xd4 ♗xd4 8.0–0 ♗e6 9.♗b3 0–0= Franzoni – Anand, Biel 1988.

6...♕e7

7.♘f3

It is rather dubious for White to play here 7.♘xf7?!, because of 7...d5! 8.♘xh8 dxc4∓

Black obtains an excellent position after 7.♘d3 d5 8.♘xd5 ♕xe4 9.♘e3 ♗d6 10.f3 ♕h4 11.♘f2 0–0↑

7...d5 8.♗xd5

White's position remains very passive after 8.♘xd5 ♕xe4 9.♘e3 ♗g4 10.♗e2 ♘xe2 11.♕xe2 0–0–0∓

8...♗g4 9.d3

(diagram)

9....0–0–0! 10.♗e3

If 10.♗g5, Sutovsky – Kram-

nik, Baku (rapid) 2010 (**game 6**), then besides the move that was played in the game – 10...♗h5!? – Black could have tried 10...h6 and after 11.♗e3 ♘xd5 12.♘xd5 ♖xd5 13.exd5 ♖e8 14.0–0 ♗xf3 15.gxf3 ♗d6 16.f4 ♕h4 there would be a transposition to the variation beginning with the move 10.♗e3, but with a pawn on h6 instead of h7. This cannot be harmful for Black at all.

10...♘xd5 11.♘xd5

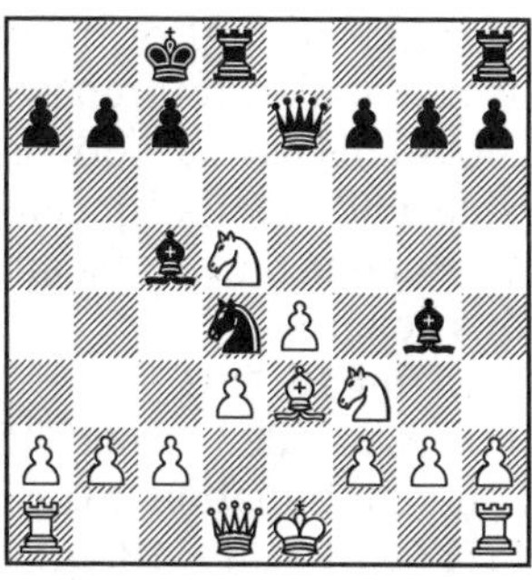

11...♖xd5! 12.exd5 ♖e8 13.0–0

Objectively speaking, White's most prudent move here is 13.c3, but it leads to a draw by force: 13...♘xf3 14.gxf3 ♕h4 15.♔d2

♖xe3 16.fxe3 ♕f2 17.♔c1 ♗xe3 18. ♔b1 ♗xf3 19.♕e1 ♗xh1 20.♕xh1 ♕e2 21.a4 ♕xd3 22.♔a2 ♕c4= with perpetual check.

13...♗xf3 14.gxf3 ♗d6

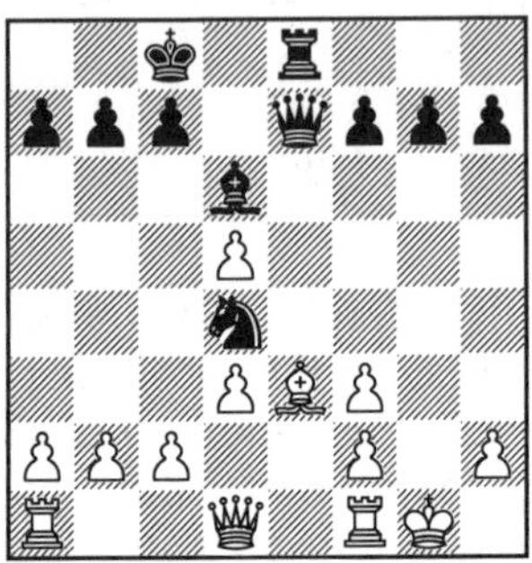

15.f4

Or 15.♔g2 ♕e5 16.♖h1 ♘f5 17. c3 ♕xd5 18.♕a4 ♖e6 19.♗g5 h6 20.c4 ♕xd3 21.♖he1 ♘d4 22.♕d1 ♕xc4 23.♖xe6 ♘xe6 24.b3 ♕b5 25.♗e3 ♕e5∓ – Now, in order to protect his h2-square White must make a rather awkward move with his queen to g1 or h1, when Black can patiently prepare the advance of his pawns, both on the kingside and on the queenside. White is doomed to a long and laborious defence.

15...♕h4 16.♔h1

Here it is safer to play 16.c3, with the continuation 16...g5 17. cxd4 (17.♔h1 ♕h3 18.♖g1 ♘f3 19.♖g2 gxf4 20.♕a4 c6 transposes to the main line of our analysis) 17...gxf4 18.♕f3 fxe3 19.h3 ♕xd4 20.fxe3 ♕xb2 21.♕f2 ♕g7 22.♔h1 ♕h6 23.♕f5 ♔b8=, and although Black has some initiative, White should be able to hold.

16...♕h3 17.♖g1 ♘f3 18.♖g2

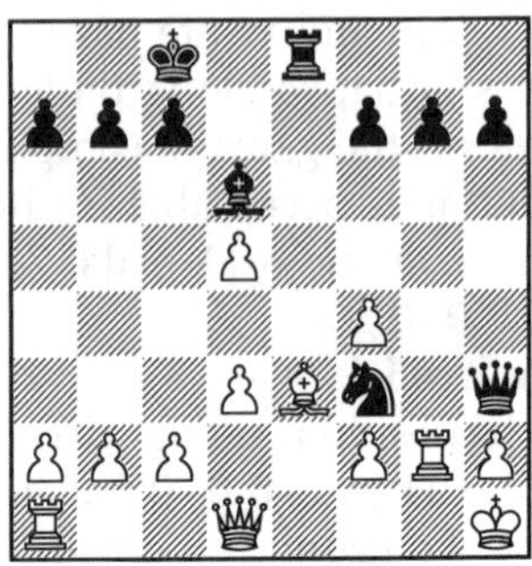

18...g5!

White has come under a dangerous attack. He will be happy if it all ends in perpetual check, but he might even get mated.

19.c4

The following variation is clearly in Black's favour: 19.c3 gxf4 20.♕a4 c6! 21.dxc6 fxe3 22.cxb7 ♔d8–+

19...gxf4 20.♕a4

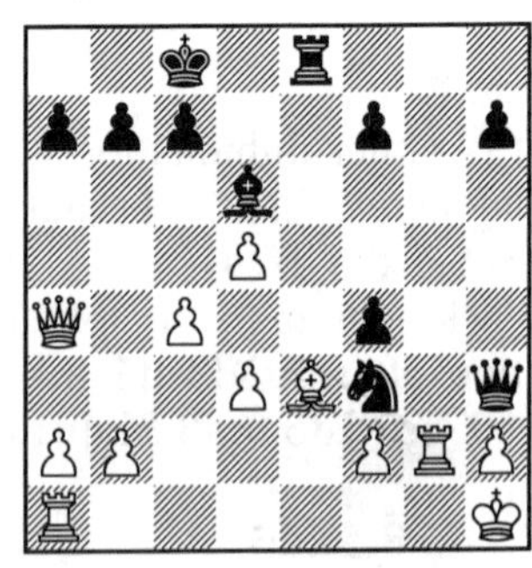

20...♔d8

It is worth considering the move 20...c6!? and after 21.dxc6 fxe3 22.cxb7 ♔d8 23.c5 ♗xh2 24. ♕g4 ♕xg4 25.♖xg4 e2 26.♔g2 e1=♕ 27.♖xe1 ♘xe1 28.♔xh2 ♔c7∓

there arises an endgame in which White must fight for a draw.

21.c5 ♘h4 22.♖ag1 ♗e5 23.♗xf4 ♘xg2 24.♖xg2 ♕f3, Motylev – Radjabov, Khanty-Mansyisk 2010.

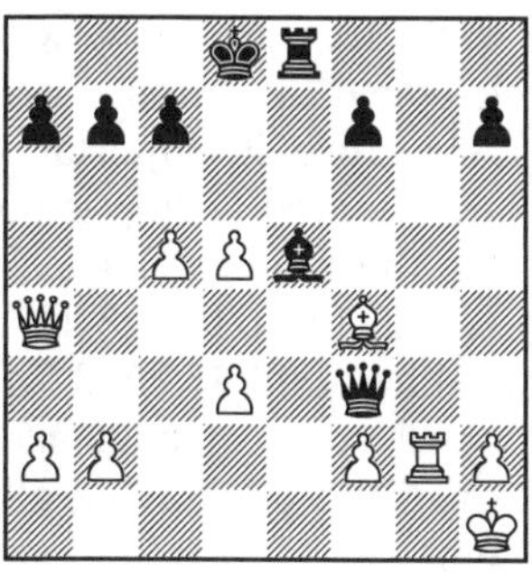

White can continue here with **25.♗g3! ♗xg3 26.hxg3 ♕xd5 27.♕c4**= and White has good chances of saving the game.

B) 5.♗a4

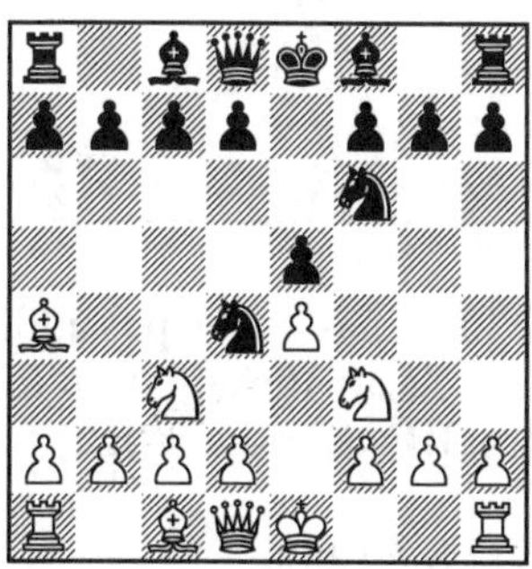

5...♗c5

It is too passive for Black to play 5...♘xf3 6.♕xf3 c6 7.0–0 d6 8.d3 ♗e7 9.♘d5±. White is slightly better, J.Polgar – Hammer, Kristiansund 2010.

An interesting position arises after 5...c6!?

and now:

the move 6.d3 enables Black to exchange his knight for the bishop and after 6...b5 7.♗b3 ♘xb3 8.axb3 d6= he obtains a very good game, since White takes two moves to advance his pawn to d4;

after 6.0–0, Black has a good reply in 6...♕a5, preventing the possible exchange on d4. There might follow: 7.d3 d6 8.h3 b5 (8...♗e7 can be answered with 9.♗e3, forcing the exchange of the knight on d4 under circumstances very favourable to White.) 9.♗b3 ♘xb3 10.cxb3 b4 (Black is not obliged to hurry with the advance of this pawn, since after 10...♗e7 11.d4 b4 12.♘a4 exd4 13.♘xd4 ♗d7, although it might seem at first sight that White is better, his knight on a4 is away from the centre and Black has more than sufficient counter-chances.) 11.♘b1 ♗e7 12.♘bd2 0–0 13.♘c4 ♕c7= – the position is approximately equal;

6.♘xe5 d5 7.d3 ♗d6 8.♘f3 ♗g4 9.♗e3 dxe4 (9...♘xf3 10.gxf3 ♗h5 11.exd5 – although Black has numerous attacking possibilities here, it was not so easy for him to prove their effectiveness in a practical competitive game, Ivanchuk – Caruana, Biel 2009) 10.dxe4 (10.♘xe4 ♘xe4 11.♗xd4 ♕a5 12.c3 ♘g5 13.♗e3 ♗xf3 14.gxf3 ♕f5∓ – Black's initiative is very powerful, Shanava – Khenkin, Drezden 2007; 10.♗xd4 exf3 11.gxf3 ♕e7⩱) 10...♘xf3 11.gxf3 ♗h5 12.♕e2 ♗e5 13.♗b3∞

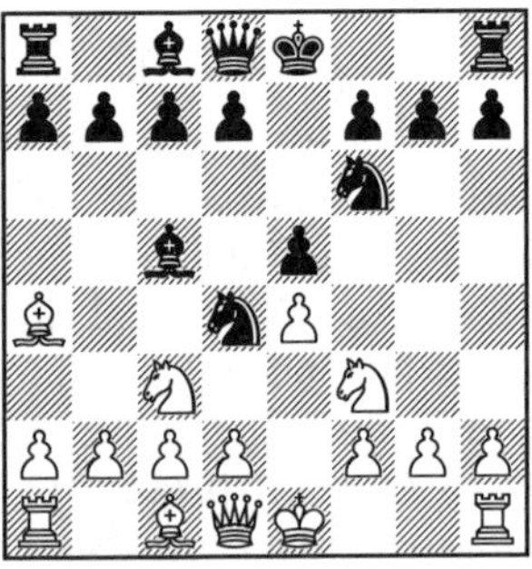

6.♘xe5

If White does not capture this pawn he will not achieve anything special out of the opening. Capturing after castling by both sides is simply bad: 6.0–0 0–0 7.♘xe5? (7.d3 d6 8.♘xd4 ♗xd4=) 7...d6 8.♘d3 ♗g4 9.♕e1 ♘f3 10.gxf3 ♗xf3 11.h3 (after 11.♘xc5, Black wins once again with the move 11...♘g4–+) 11...♘g4 12.♘f4 ♕h4 13.♘ce2 g5 14.♗d7 h5–+, mating..

6...0–0 7.♘d3

The move 7.d3 deprives White's knight of an important square and Black can obtain a very good position in the following manner: 7...d6 (here 7...c6!?, followed by d7-d5, is also good) 8.♘f3 ♗g4 9.♗e3 c6 10.♗xd4 (after 10.0–0 Black has the powerful continuation 10...♗xf3! 11.gxf3 ♘h5, followed by ♕d8-f6∓ and very good play on the dark squares; 10...b5 11.♗xd4 ♗xd4 12.♗b3 a5 13.a4 b4 14.♘e2 ♗xb2 15.♖b1 ♗xf3 16.gxf3 ♗a3∞ with a double-edged position. Black's pawn-structure is superior, but his dark-squared bishop is out of play for the moment.) 10...♗xd4 11.0–0 ♕a5 12.♗b3 ♗xc3 13.bxc3 ♕xc3 14.h3 ♗xf3 15.♕xf3 ♖fe8= Black will soon manage to advance with d6-d5, solving all his problems.

7...♗b6

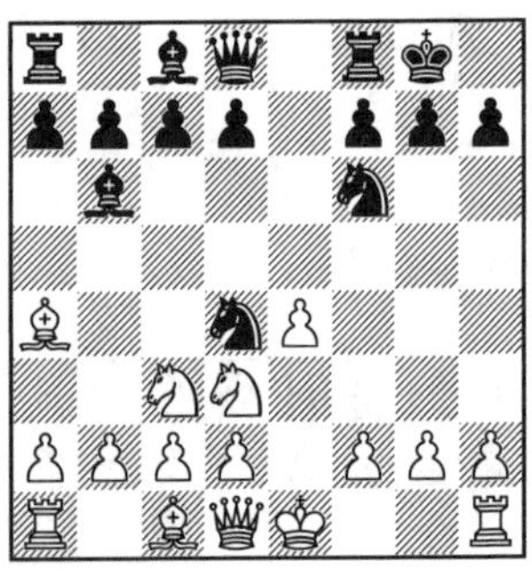

White has two possibilities here to clarify the situation in the centre: **B1) 8.♘f4** and **B2) 8.e5**.

B1) 8.♘f4 c6

It is also possible for Black to play immediately 8...d5

(diagram)

and now:

9.d3 dxe4 (9...c6 is also good, transposing to the variation with 8...c6 9.d3 d5) 10.dxe4 c6 11.0–0

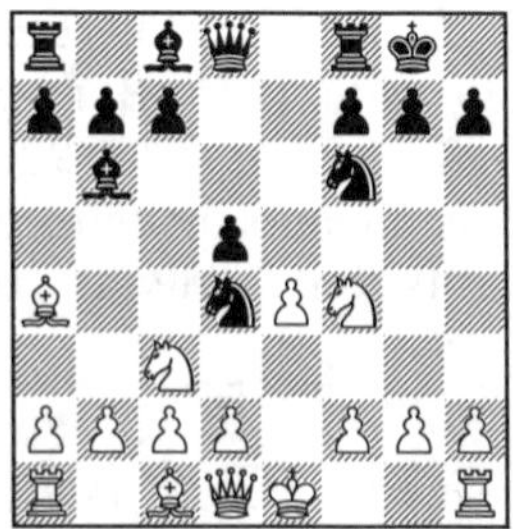

♖e8 12.♗e3 ♘xe4 13.♘xe4 ♖xe4 14.c3 ♘e6=;

9.♘cxd5 g5!? 10.♘xf6 ♕xf6 11.♘d3 ♕e7 12.0–0 ♕xe4 13.♔h1 ♘e2 14.b4 a5 15.♖b1 ♘xc1 16.♕xc1 ♗f5⩱ Black's compensation for the pawn is quite sufficient;

9.♘fxd5 ♘xe4 (An interesting option here is 9...♘xd5!? 10.♘xd5 ♕h4 11.♘e3 f5, Navara – Shirov, Prague 2004. White should continue with 12.c3!, when Black has to find some very creative ideas in order to prove that his compensation is sufficient.) 10.♘xb6 axb6 11.♘xe4 ♖xa4 12.0–0 ♘b3 13. cxb3 (it is worse for White to play 13.♖b1 ♘xc1 14.♘c3 ♖d4 15.♕xc1 ♖xd2 16.♖d1 ♖xd1 17.♕xd1 ♗f5∓ and Black is even better) 13...♖xe4 14.d3 ♖d4 15.♗e3 ♖xd3 16.♕f3=

9.d3 d5

10.0–0

Or 10.♗e3 dxe4 11.dxe4 ♘g4 12.♕d2 ♘xe3 13.fxe3 ♘e6∓ and Black has a clear advantage.

10...♗g4 11.♕d2 dxe4 12. dxe4

After 12.♘xe4, Black plays 12... ♘xe4 13.dxe4 ♕h4! 14.♕d3 (otherwise Black has the move 14... ♘f3) 14...♖ad8 15.♕g3 ♕xg3 16. hxg3 g5!∓

12...♗f3!

It is less convincing for Black to play here 12...♕e7 13.♖e1 ♖ad8 14.♘d3 ♗e6⩱, with compensation for the pawn.

13.♖e1 ♖e8 14.e5

The tactical justification of Black's idea is the variation 14. ♕d3 ♗xe4 15.♘xe4 ♘xe4

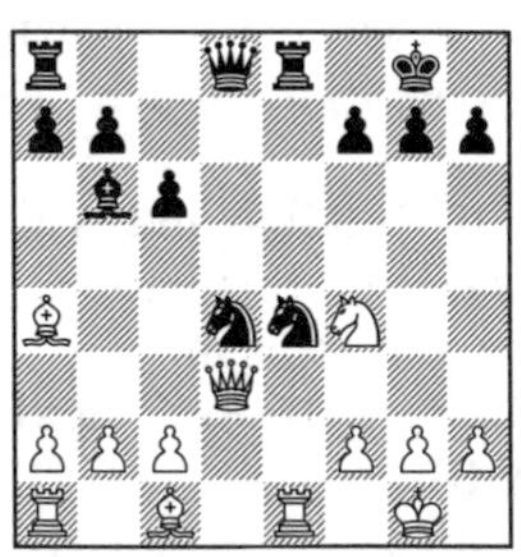

16.♖xe4 (16.♗e3 ♕g5 17.♗xd4 ♘xf2 18.♗xf2 ♗xf2 19.♔xf2 ♕xf4 20.♔g1 ♕xa4 21.♕d7 ♖ed8 22.♕xb7 ♕xc2∓) 16...♖xe4 17.♕xe4 ♘b3!∓, winning the exchange.

14...♘h5

The alternative is 14...♘g4 15.♘d3 ♕h4 16.♕f4 ♘xc2 (16...♖e6 17.♕g3 ♘f5 18.♕xh4 ♘xh4 19.gxf3 ♘xf3 20.♔g2 ♘xe1 21.♘xe1= and there arises an approximately equal but double-edged endgame, in which White's play is easier and more pleasant) 17.♗xc2 ♗xf2 18.♔h1 ♗xe1 19.gxf3 ♘f2 20.♘xf2 ♕xf2 21.♗e3 ♕xc2 22.♖xe1 ♕xb2 23.♗d4 c5 24.♖b1 ♕c2 25.♖c1 ♕b2=, with a repetition of moves.

15.e6

15.♘xh5 ♗xh5 16.♕f4 ♗c7 – White loses his e5-pawn and Black's pieces are much more active.

Or 15.♘d3 ♖e6 and White will not survive this attack once Black's rook joins in.

15...♕g5 16.exf7 ♔xf7 17.♗b3 ♔f8

A fantastic position arises after 17...♗d5 18.♘cxd5! (the line: 18.♗xd5 cxd5 19.♖xe8 ♖xe8 20.♔f1 ♔g8 21.♘cxd5 ♕f5 22.♘xb6 ♘xc2∓ is advantageous to Black) 18...♘f3 19.♔h1 ♘xd2 20.♗xd2

20...cxd5 21.♗xd5 ♔f6 22.♗c3 ♔f5 23. ♘e6 ♖xe6 24.♖xe6 (White has an excellent position, even though Black has an extra queen!) 24...♗c7 25.♖ae1 ♖d8 26.♖1e5 ♗xe5 27.♖xe5 ♔g6 28.♖xg5 ♔xg5 29.h4 ♔xh4 30.g3± – It is only White who might have winning chances.

18.♖f1 ♗xg2 19.♘e6 ♘xe6 20.♕xg5 ♘xg5 21.♔xg2 ♘e4 22.♘xe4 ♖xe4=

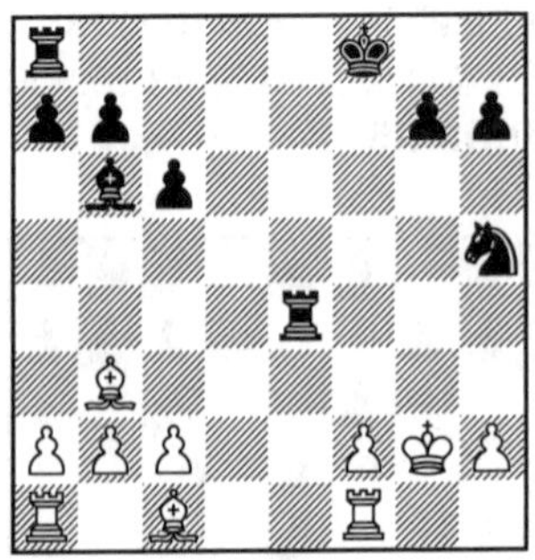

It is likely that there will soon arise an equal position with bishops of opposite colours.

B2) 8.e5

8...♘e8 9.♘d5 d6!

After 9...c6, Black is only trying to equalize and cannot hope for more. 10.♘e3 d5 11.c3 ♘f5 12.0–0 f6 13.♗b3!? White might advance c3-c4 at some point, destroying Black's solid pawn-structure. (It looks more natural for White to continue with 13.♗c2 ♗c7 14.f4 ♘xe3 15.dxe3 ♗f5, Motylev – Shomoev, Toljatti 2003. After 16.♗d2 ♗xd3 17.♗xd3 fxe5 18.c4 exf4 19.exf4 ♘f6 20.♕c2±, White would retain a slight edge.).

Black has two possibilities here, but neither of them is sufficient to equalize:

after 13...♔h8, White has the resource 14.♕h5! This surprising queen-sortie creates serious problems for Black. 14...♘h6, Vallejo Pons – Leko, Monaco 2005 (the move 14...g6 weakens the dark squares and after 15.♕e2 ♕e7 16. f4± White is clearly better) 15.♗c2 (In the game White tried the strange retreat 15.♘e1, after which Black obtained excellent compensation for the pawn.) 15... d4 16.♘c4 ♗c7 17.♖e1 b5 18.e6 ♗xe6 19.♖xe6 bxc4 20.♘c5± and White is better;

13...fxe5 14.♘xe5 ♘xe3 15.fxe3 (It is almost equally good for White to continue with 15.dxe3 ♘d6 16.f4± and he has the edge.) 15...♘f6 16.d4 ♗e6±

White's extra pawn, despite its being backward on e3, is quite useful. Black must fight for equality.

10.♘e3

After 10.c3, Black has 10... ♕g5! 11.♘e3 (it is not good for White to play 11.cxd4 ♕xg2 12. ♘e7 ♔h8 13.♖f1 ♗g4 14.f3 ♗h3 15.♕e2 ♕g5 16.♘d5 ♗xf1 17.♔xf1 ♗xd4→ and he comes under a dangerous attack) 11...♘f5 12.0–0 dxe5 13.♕f3 ♘xe3 14.dxe3 ♘d6 15.e4 ♕e7∓ and Black has a slight edge.

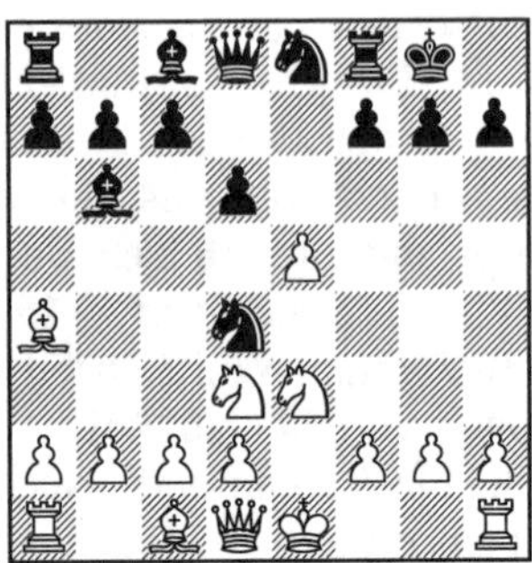

After 10.♘e3 Black has a pleasant choice between the calm and safe move **B2a) 10...c6** and the sharp **B2b) 10...c5!?**

However, we cannot recommend to Black the line: 10...dxe5 11.♘xe5 ♕g5 in view of 12.♘5c4! (better than 12.♘d7 ♗xd7 13.♗xd7 f5 14.c3 ♘f6∓) 12...f5 13.h4! ♕f6 (13...♕e7 14.c3 ♘c6 15.♗b3 ♔h8 16.f4±) 14.f4 ♘d6 15.c3 ♘xc4 (15...♕g6 16.♔f1 ♘e6 17.♘xd6 cxd6 18.♘d5± White consolidates his position, preserving his extra pawn) 16.♘xc4 ♕g6 17.♔f1 ♗e6 (here 17...♘c6± is a slight improvement, keeping some minimal compensation) 18.♘e5 ♕g3 19.cxd4+-. White has parried the attack and should win this position, Motylev – Shirov, Moscow 2001.

B2a) 10...c6 11.c3

11.0–0 dxe5 (the same position arises after 11...♗c7 12.f4 dxe5 13.♘xe5 f6; while 12.c3 ♘f5 transposes to the main line – 10... c6 11.c3 ♘f5 12.0–0 ♗c7) 12.♘xe5 ♗c7 13.f4 f6 14.♘5g4 (14.♘d3 b5 15.♗b3 ♔h8⩱∞ and White's knight on d3 impedes the completion of his development) 14...b5 15.♗b3 ♘xb3 16.axb3 ♘d6 17.d3 ♖e8⩱∞ Black has obtained excellent compensation for the pawn.

11...♘f5 12.0–0

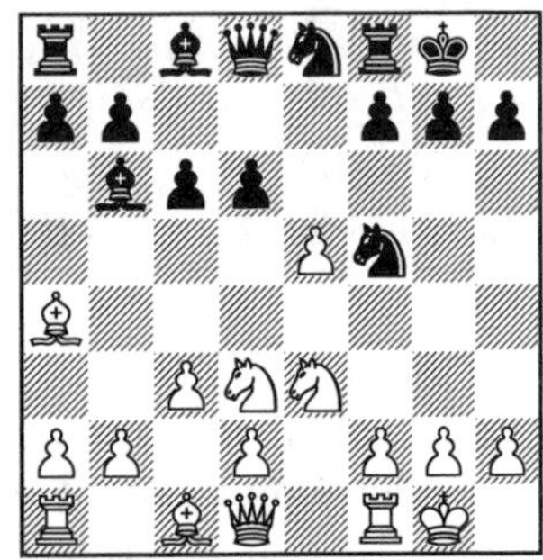

12...♗c7!

Black increases the pressure against the e5-pawn, forcing White either to allow Black's knight to go to the d6-square with tempo, or to give back the extra pawn. It is weaker for Black to continue with 12...♘xe3 13.dxe3 ♗f5 14.♗c2 ♕e7 15.exd6!? This is a very important decision, but it is the only way for White to fight for the initiative (it would be harmless for Black for White to try here 15.e4 ♗xe4 16.♖e1 d5=). 15...♘xd6 16.♔h1⩲; White wants to play f2-f3 and then e3-e4, when it would be very difficult for Black to prove that the activity of his pieces compensates for the sacrificed pawn.

13.♖e1

Or 13.♕e2 ♘xe3 14.dxe3 dxe5 15.e4 ♕e7 16.♗e3 ♘d6 17.f3 ♘c4 18.♗f2 ♗b6= and the position is equal.

After 13.f4 ♘xe3 14.dxe3 ♗f5 15.♗c2 (15.♘f2 dxe5 16.e4 ♗e6 17.f5 ♗c4∓; Black has a slight edge, Adhiban – Aleksandrov, Kolkata 2009) 15...dxe5 16.♘xe5 ♗xc2 17.♕xc2 ♗xe5 18.fxe5 ♕e7=

13...dxe5 14.♘xf5 ♕xd3 15.♘e7

15.♗c2 ♕d8=

15...♔h8 16.♗c2 ♕d6 17. ♘xc8 ♖xc8=

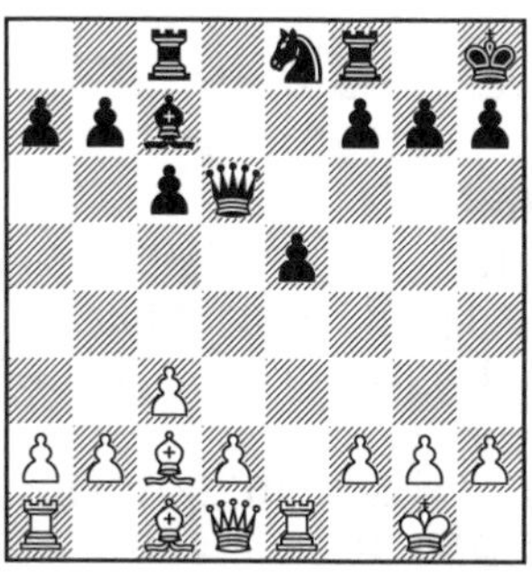

White has the bishop-pair, but Black has more space, so the game is equal.

B2b) 10...c5!?

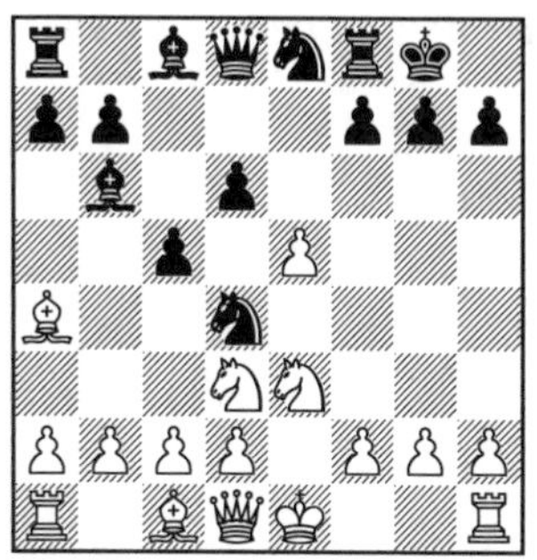

Now in some variations White must consider the possibility of Black advancing his b- and c-pawns.

11.c3

Black's idea can be best seen in the variation 11.0–0 dxe5 12.♘xe5 ♗c7 13.f4 b5 14.♗b3 c4 15.c3

and now:

a calm and safe continuation for Black is to play 15...♗xe5 16. fxe5 cxb3 17.cxd4 ♕xd4 18.♕xb3 (The natural move 18.axb3, opening the file for the rook with tempo, is weaker for White. After 18... ♕xe5 19.d4 ♕e4!∓ Black's queen on e4 is tremendously powerful.) 18...♕xe5 19.♕d5 ♕xd5 20.♘xd5 ♗e6 and the endgame looks like a dead draw;

it might be interesting for Black to try 15...cxb3!? 16.cxd4 ♘f6! (after 16...bxa2, White has the reply 17.♕f3± and Black will have problems with his rook on a8) 17.♕xb3 ♕xd4 18.♕c3 ♕d6⩱∞ Black has excellent compensation for the pawn.

11...♘f5 12.♗b3

12.0–0 ♘xe3 13.dxe3 c4 14. ♘b4 dxe5 15.♕h5, Sulskis – Neubauer, Vienna 2008, (15.♕xd8 ♗xd8=) 15...♘f6 16.♕xe5 ♗e6⩱∞

12.exd6 ♕xd6 13.♗c2 ♘f6 14. 0–0 ♗c7 15.g3. Now the best move for Black is the patient reply 15... ♖e8! (or 15...♘xe3 16.dxe3 ♕c6 17.f3 c4 18.♘f2± and White is well-prepared now for e3-e4; 15... b5 16.♘f4 ♘h4 17.d4 ♗b7 18.d5 ♖ad8, Acs – Khalifman, Hoogeveen 2002, 19.♘h5! ♘xd5 20. ♕g4 ♘f3 21.♕xf3 ♘xe3 22.♕xe3 ♕d5 23.♘f6 gxf6 24.f3±; Black's doubled pawns are a definite weakness in his set-up.) 16.♕f3 ♘xe3 17.dxe3 ♗g4 18.♕xb7 ♗e2 19.♘f4 (19.♖e1 ♖ab8 (here an interesting try is 19...♗xd3!? 20. ♗xd3 ♕xd3 21.♕xc7 ♘e4∓ with quite promising play on the light squares) 20.♕xb8 ♖xb8 21.♖xe2 ♕d5∓ Black's centralized queen is so powerful that White is faced with a difficult defence.) 19...♗xf1 20.♔xf1 ♖ab8 21.♕f3 ♖bd8 – Black's initiative is very dangerous.

12...♘xe3 13.dxe3 dxe5 14.♘xe5 ♕g5

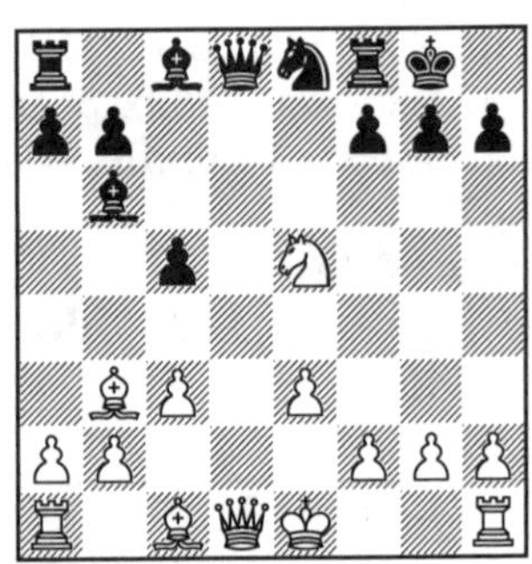

15.♘f3

After 15.♘d7 ♗xd7 16.♕xd7 ♕xg2 17.♕d5 ♕g6∓ White fails to complete the development of his queenside.

15...♕xg2 16.♖g1 ♕h3 17. ♖g3 ♕h5 18.♖g5 ♕h3 19.♖g3= – Drawn by repetition of moves.

Conclusion

I believe that in the system with 4...♘d4! in the Four Knights Game White cannot expect any advantage. This is because his bishop on c4 or a4 often remains cut off from the action by Black's strong pawn-barrier c6-d5. Furthermore, in several lines Black obtains excellent play on the dark squares, although sometimes he needs to sacrifice a pawn to achieve this.

Part 3

1.e4 e5 2.♘f3 ♘f6 3.d4

Petroff Defence 3.d4

The variation with 3.d4 has been analyzed extensively.

If play follows the main theoretical line: **3...♘xe4 4.♗d3 d5 5.♘xe5 ♘d7 6.♘xd7 ♗xd7 7.0–0 ♗d6**, the drawish tendencies are quite clear in most of the positions reached.

As for the other lines after 3.d4, it seems to me that Black always obtains very good positions and in the popular variation **5.dxe5 ♗e7 6.0–0 ♘c5** he even has excellent chances of seizing the initiative, because White's e5-pawn turns out to be cut off from the rest of his forces.

It is more or less the same after **4.dxe5 d5 5.♘d2** – the e5-pawn is too far away from White's camp and Black can either exchange on d2, or retreat with the knight to c5 and in both cases he ends up with a very good game.

Chapter 9 1.e4 e5 2.♘f3 ♘f6 3.d4

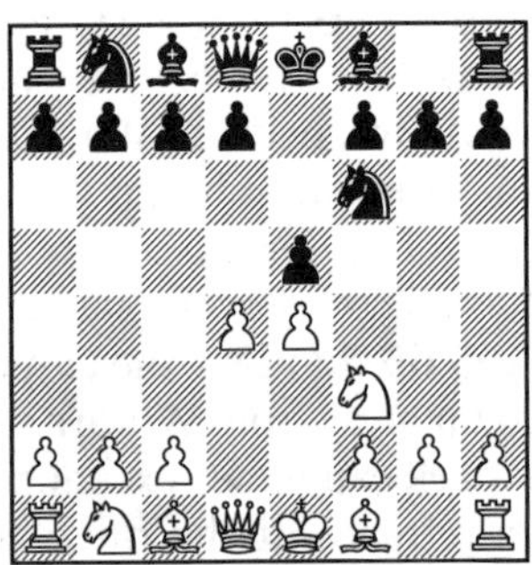

With this move White is trying to open some lines and develop rapidly. He plans to capture the e5-pawn one move later, with either his knight or his pawn.

3...♘xe4

The move 3...exd4 is well-known to theory. After 4.e5 ♘e4 5.♕xd4 d5 6.exd6 ♘xd6 7.♘c3±, despite the symmetrical pawn-structure, White maintains the initiative thanks to his more active pieces.

4.dxe5

We shall deal with the more popular move 4.♗d3 in the Chapters 10-15.

The line: 4.♘xe5 d6 5.♘f3 d5 transposes to the variation 3.♘xe5 d6 4.♘f3 ♘xe4 5.d4 d5 (see Chapter 19).

4...d5 5.♘bd2

This move has been played many times with White by GM Jan Nepomniachtchi.

5.♗d3 transposes to the variation 3.d4 ♘xe4 4.♗d3 d5 5.dxe5 (see Chapter 10).

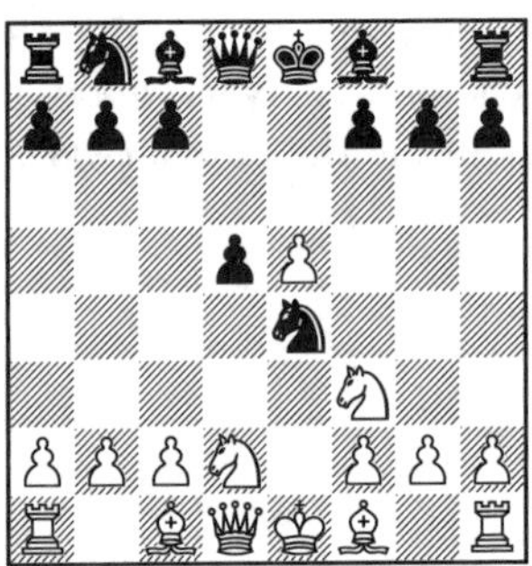

Black has two possibilities here and they both deserve attention: **A) 5...♘c5**, the knight is headed for the wonderful blockading square at e6, and **B) 5...♘xd2**, with the idea of not wasting any time on manoeuvring.

A) 5...♘c5 6.♘b3

White has also tried some less ambitious moves here:

6.♗e2 ♗e7 7.0–0 0–0 8.♘b3

♘xb3 9.axb3 c5 10.c3 ♘c6 11.♗f4 ♗f5 12.♗d3 ♕d7= Negi – Giri, Wijk aan Zee 2010;

6.a3 a5 (It is also good for Black to play 6...♗e7 7.b4 ♘e6 8. c4 0–0 9.cxd5 ♕xd5 10.♗c4 ♕c6= and Black's knight is headed for the f4-square with great effect, while his rook is ready to go to d8, occupying the open file.) 7.♗e2 ♗e7 8.0–0 0–0 9.♖e1

9...♘c6 (The position will be almost identical after 9...f6 10. exf6 ♗xf6= with very active play for Black, Shabalov – Motylev, Moscow 2010.) 10.♘f1 f6 (Here 10...♗f5 11.♘g3 ♗g6 12.♗e3± is less precise; White maintains a slight edge thanks to his control of the b5-square, Short – Kramnik, Wijk aan Zee 2010.) 11.exf6 ♗xf6 12.♘g3 g6 13.♗e3 ♕d6=

6...♘e6

Here 6...♘xb3± has been played many times and is by no means bad, but it improves White's pawn-structure, so it seems to me to be less logical.

(diagram)

7.♘bd4

We should examine White's alternatives:

7.h4 c5 8.c4 dxc4 9.♕xd8 ♘xd8 10.♘bd2 ♘bc6 11.♘xc4 ♘e6 12.♗d2 ♘ed4 13.♘xd4 ♘xd4 14. ♖c1 ♗e6 15.♗d3 0–0–0= Bauer – Giri, France 2010;

7.c4 dxc4 8.♗xc4 ♕xd1 9.♔xd1 ♘d7 10.♗xe6 fxe6 11.♘bd4 ♘b6 12.♘g5 ♔e7 13.b3 ♘d5 14.♗a3 ♔e8 15.♗b2 ♔e7 16.♗a3 ♔e8 17. ♗b2 ♔e7, draw, Vachier-Lagrave – Gelfand, Khanty-Mansyisk 2009;

7.g3 c5 8.♗g2 ♘c6 9.0–0 ♗e7 10.c3 0–0 11.h4? (or 11.♗e3 b6=, with equality) 11...c4 12.♘bd4 ♘exd4 13.cxd4 ♗g4 14.♕d2 f6→ and White comes under a dangerous attack, J.Polgar – Gelfand, Khanty-Mansyisk 2009.

7...♘xd4 8.♘xd4

White has also tried 8.♕xd4 h6 9.♗d2 ♗e6 10.h4 (This is not an attacking move; it is prophylaxis against the possibility of g7-g5.) 10...c5 11.♕f4 ♘c6 12.h5 ♕d7 (Black's queen is uncomfortable on the d-file, so the move 12...♕b6 is clearly better.) 13.c4?! (it is more prudent for White to continue here with 13.0–0–0=) 13...0–0–0 (Here it is at least as good for Black to play 13...♗e7∓, followed by castling kingside.) 14.0–0–0 ♗e7 15.♗c3 d4 16.♗d2 f6 17.exf6 ♗xf6 18.♗d3 ♖hf8 19.♖de1 ♗e7 20.♕g3 ♗d6 21.♕h4 ♗e7 (Black could have continued the fight here, for example with 21...♗g4 22.♗e4 ♖de8∓) 22.♕g3, draw, Nepomniachtchi – Alekseev, Havana 2010.

8...♗e7

It is rather dubious to play 8...c5?! 9.♗b5! ♘d7 10.e6 cxd4 11.exd7 ♗xd7 12.♗xd7 ♕xd7 13.♕xd4 ♗e7 14.♕xg7 ♕e6 15.♔d1 ♗f6 16.♕g3 0–0–0 17.♖e1 ♕b6, Jakovenko – Wang Yue, Nanjing 2009. White could have created problems for his opponent with: 18.♕b3! ♕c6 19.♗f4!±

9.♗d3

9.♗f4 c5 10.♘f3 ♘c6 11.c3 ♗e6 (instead, 11...g5! 12.♗g3 g4 13.♘d2 ♗f5↑ would be very strong) 12.♗d3 h6 13.h3 ♕d7 14.♕d2 0–0–0 15.0–0–0 d4! 16.c4. Here, in the game Gashimov – Li Chao, Khanty-Mansyisk 2009, the players agreed to a draw, although after 16...♘b4 17.b3 g5 18.♗g3 ♘xd3 19.♕xd3 ♗f5∓ Black would have an edge.

9...0–0!

It is inferior to continue with 9...c5 10.♘f5 ♗xf5 11.♗xf5 ♘c6 12.f4± and, thanks to the bishop-pair, White has the edge. In the game Gashimov – Gelfand, Lugo 2009, Black suddenly blundered with 10...0–0? and after 11.♘xg7! ♔xg7? (He could have defended more resiliently with 11...c4 12.♘f5 ♔h8 13.♘xe7 ♕xe7 14.♗e2 ♕xe5±) 12.♕h5+– White's attack proved to be decisive.

10.0–0 c5 11.♘f5 c4 12.♘xe7 ♕xe7 13.♗e2 ♖d8∓

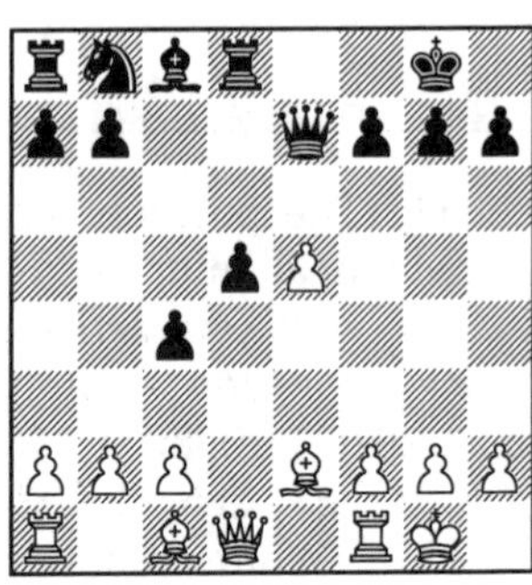

Black's bishop will go to f5 and his knight to c6, after which he will be ready to advance with d5-d4, with an excellent position.

B) 5...♘xd2 6.♗xd2 c5

It is less precise for him to play 6...♗e7, in view of 7.c4! 0–0 8.♕c2!±. White is ready to castle queenside, after which he will exert pressure along the d-file, with a lead in development.

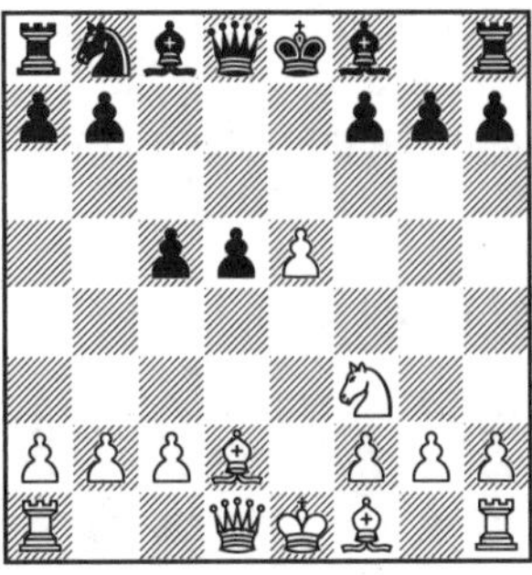

Now, White can either try piece-play with **B1) 7.♗g5**, or undermine Black's centre with **B2) 7.c4**.

B1) 7.♗g5 ♕a5 8.c3 ♗e6 9. ♗d3 ♘c6 10.0–0 h6

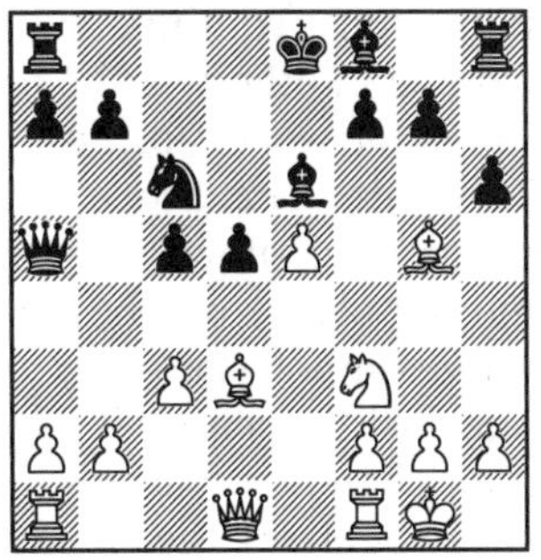

11.♗d2

It would be too risky for White to opt for 11.♗h4, since this bishop might become a target for Black's advancing pawns:

(diagram)

11...♕c7 – this move is a bit too cautious. 12.♖c1 ♗e7 (Here it is not so good for Black to play 12... g5 13.♗g3 0–0–0, because of 14. b4!∞) 13.♗g3 (the position would be approximately equal after 13.

♗xe7 ♕xe7 14.h3 0–0 15.♗c2 d4! 16.cxd4 ♖fd8!=) 13...♕d7 14.b4 cxb4 15.cxb4 ♘xb4 (15...♗xb4!?) 16.♘d4 ♘xd3 17.♕xd3 0–0 18.f4 f5 19.♗f2 ♖ac8 20.♖cd1 ♖cd8 (Here it would be much more interesting for Black to try 20...♖fd8 21.g4 g6∓) 21.♖c1 ♖c8 22.♖cd1 ♖cd8, draw, Svidler – Kasimdzhanov, Nalchik 2009;

11...g5! 12.♗g3 0–0–0!

13.♖e1 (It would be incorrect for White to play 13.b4?! cxb4 14.cxb4 ♗xb4 15.♖b1 d4, since his knight on f3 and bishop on g3 are cut off from the queenside.) 13... ♗e7∓ and in the impending sharp fight on both flanks Black's prospects are preferable.

11...♕c7 12.♖e1 ♗e7

Also playable, but not essential, is the aggressive option 12...g5!? 13.b4 (after 13.♕e2 it is very promising for Black to play 13...0–0–0!∓) 13...g4! Black should fight for the dark squares. (It is weaker for Black to opt for 13...c4 14.♗c2 ♗g7 15.♕e2 g4 16.♘d4 ♘xd4 17.cxd4 0–0–0±; 15.♗a4 0–0 16.♗xc6 bxc6, Gashimov – Fridman, Mainz (rapid) 2009. Now White should play 17.h4!, developing an initiative on the dark squares.) 14.b5 ♘a5! 15.♘h4 ♘c4∞

13.♖c1 ♕d7 14.a3 0–0 15.b4 ♖fd8=

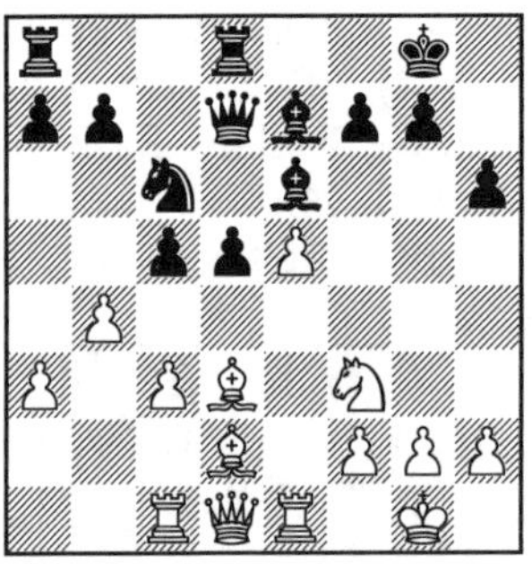

The position is about equal. Black can neutralize his opponent's potential threats along the b1-h7 diagonal with the move ♗e6-f5, while after **16.♗e3**, he has the wonderful possibility of: **16...d4! 17.cxd4 cxb4! 18.axb4 ♘xb4 19.♗b1 ♖ac8** (The immediate 19...a5!? is possibly even stronger for Black.) **20.♕e2 ♖xc1 21.♗xc1 ♗d5**∓. White's hopes are based on a possible kingside attack, since his bishops are aimed in that direction. Black's queenside pawns however, together with his excellent blockade on d5, appear to be more important and so he has the advantage, Nepomniachtchi – Bu, Sochi 2009 (**game** 7).

B2) 7.c4 ♘c6

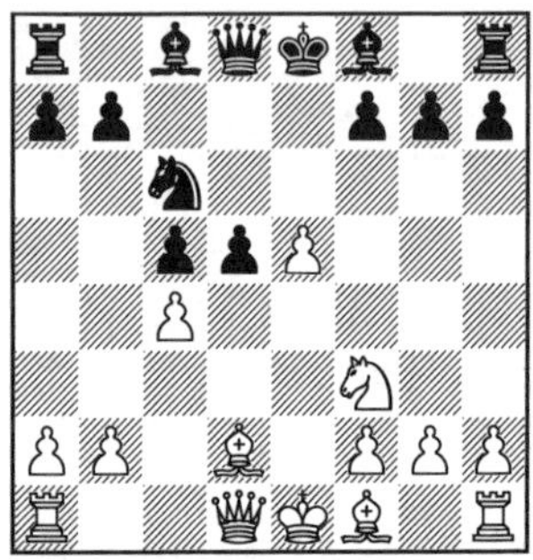

8.♗d3

White must continue with his development; otherwise he might end up in the worse position:

8.♕b3 d4. This move is very good because now the white queen is isolated on the queenside and cannot exert any pressure against the centre. 9.♗d3 g6! (9...♗e7 is inferior, since the bishop does not attack the enemy e5-pawn in that case. After 10.0–0 0–0 11.h3± White maintains a slight edge.) 10.0–0 ♗g7 11.♕b5 ♕b6 12.♖fe1 0–0 13.a4 ♖e8∓ and White cannot advance with 14.a5 because after the exchange of queens his e5-pawn will be hanging;

8.♕c2 ♗e6 9.cxd5 (It might be interesting, but very risky, for White to try 9.0–0–0!?, which Black should counter with the calm move 9...♗e7. After that he can choose between closing the centre with d5-d4, followed by preparations to castle queenside, or simply castling kingside. In the latter case, White's king might turn out to be in danger on the queenside.) 9...♕xd5 10.♗c3

10...♖d8! Black's concrete actions are very effective. (It is quite safe to calmly play 10...♗e7 11.♗d3 0–0–0! 12.♗e2 ♔b8 13.0–0 ♘b4 14.♗xb4 cxb4 15.b3 ♕c5=, with an approximately equal position; but it is inferior for Black to continue with 11...♖c8?! 12.0–0 ♘b4 13. ♗xb4 cxb4 14.♕e2 0–0 15.♖fd1± Nepomniachtchi – Fridman, Natanya (rapid) 2009). 11.♗e2 ♘d4! 12. ♘xd4 cxd4 13.♕a4 ♖d7 14. 0–0–0 ♗c5 15.♗xd4 0–0 16.♗f3

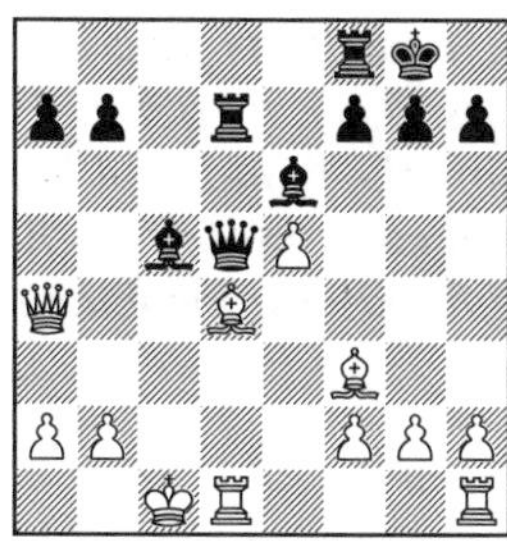

16...♕xd4! 17.♖xd4 ♖xd4 18. ♕b5 ♗b6 19.♗xb7 ♖fd8∓. Black's rook is ready to penetrate to the seventh rank and White is unable to counter this effectively, so Black is clearly better.

8...♗e7

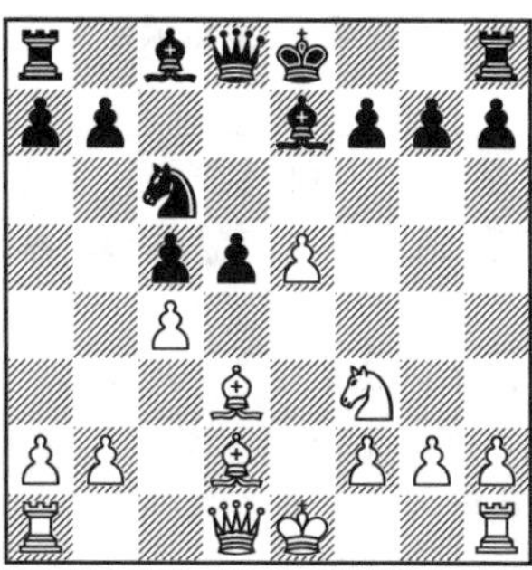

9.h3

With this move White prevents Black's bishop from being developed to a comfortable position on g4.

If 9.♕b3, then after 9...dxc4 10.♗xc4 White's bishop comes to the c4-square in two moves, having stopped at d3 on the way, and this tempo-loss should tell in the future. After 10...0–0 11.0–0–0 ♕b6 (It is even stronger for Black to play 11...♘d4 12.♘xd4 cxd4∓, with a slight advantage, because White's king is very uncomfortable on the c-file.) 12.e6 fxe6 13.♗xe6 ♔h8=, the position is balanced, Smirin – Alterman, Israel 1998.

9...♗e6

It is less precise for Black to play 9...0–0, since after 10.♕c2 he will have to lose a tempo with the move 10...h6, in order to remove the h7-pawn from attack.

10.♕c2

Here Black can counter 10.♕b3 with the standard reaction 10...♕b6∓ – his pieces are better coordinated and the possible endgames will be in his favour.

10...dxc4 11.♗xc4

11...0–0!

Black is able to maintain the tension in the centre, abstaining from any hasty action.

11...♗xc4 12.♕xc4 ♕d7 13.♕g4 (or 13.0–0–0 ♕e6! 14.♕xe6 fxe6∞ with a very complicated position) 13...0–0–0 14.♗c3 ♕xg4 15.hxg4 b5 16.b3 h6∞ with a double-edged endgame, Nepomniachtchi – Rakhmanov, Dagomys 2009.

12.♗xe6

But not 12.0–0 ♗xc4 13.♕xc4 ♘xe5!∓

Black has no reason to be afraid of 12.♗d3 g6 13.0–0 ♘b4 14.♗xb4 cxb4 15.♖fd1 ♖c8 16.♕e2 ♕b6=. His pieces are quite actively placed and this compensates for the minimal defect in his pawn-structure.

12...fxe6 13.♖d1 ♘d4 14.♘xd4 cxd4 15.♕b3 ♕b6=

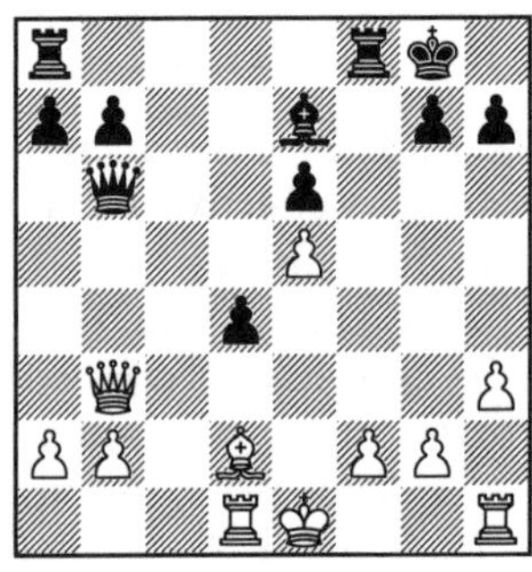

Black has nothing to worry about in this endgame.

Conclusion

White's e5-pawn is separated from the rest of his forces and although it cramps Black's position a little it is also a target and thus a potential liability. In addition, Black obtains the wonderful blockading square at e6 and his pieces are very well coordinated on the light squares. He thus reaches good positions without any problems after both 5...♘c5 and 5...♘xd2.

Chapter 10 1.e4 e5 2.♘f3 ♘f6 3.d4 ♘xe4 4.♗d3 d5 5.dxe5

This move has become very fashionable lately. At first, White was playing it just to reach fresh positions, but soon the theory of this line began to develop steadily. Although it leads to interesting positions, Black is fine in all cases.

We shall analyze the move 5.♘xe5 in Chapters 11-15.

5...♗e7

Here 5...♘c5 usually transposes to other variations and only rarely leads to independent positions. One interesting possibility is 6.♘c3 c6 7.♘d4!? g6!? (after 7...♗e7, Black has to take into account both 8.♗e2 and 8.♗f5!?) 8.0–0 ♗g7 9.f4 0–0 (9...♘xd3!? 10.♕xd3 0–0∞ Naiditsch – Kosteniuk, Moscow 2009) 10.♗e2, Nisipeanu – Sakaev, Kallithea 2008. Black can continue here with 10...f6! 11.exf6 ♕xf6 12.♗e3 ♖e8 13.♘xc6 bxc6 14.♗xc5 ♘a6 15.♗f2 ♕xf4=, obtaining a good position.

6.0–0

After 6.♘bd2, Black's best reply is the thematic move 6...♘c5, leaving White's knight on d2, where it stands in the way of his dark-squared bishop and completely rules out the possibility of making the undermining move c2-c4.

6...♘c5!

After 6...0–0 Black must reckon with the variation 7.c4 ♘c6 8.

♗c2! ♘b4 (8...♗e6 9.♕e2 ♘c5 10. ♖d1 d4 11.♘c3 ♗g4 12.♘d5±) 9. cxd5 ♘xc2 10.♕xc2 ♕xd5 11.♖d1 ♕c6 12.♕xc6 bxc6 13.♗e3 c5 14. ♘bd2 ♘xd2 15.♖xd2! (It is less precise for White to play 15.♘xd2 ♗e6 16.♖dc1 ♖fd8 17.♘b3 ♗xb3 18.axb3 ♖d5 19.f4 f6= Jakovenko – Harikrishna, Sochi 2008.) 15... ♖b8 16.♖c1 ♖b5 17.♗g5 f6 18.exf6 gxf6 19.♗f4 ♖b7 20.b3± and White maintains the advantage in the endgame.

Now White can try to exert piece-pressure against the centre with **A) 7.♘c3** or avoid the exchange of his bishop with **B) 7.♗e2**.

After any other moves by White, Black can continue with his development by castling, or (an even more promising idea) he can immediately exchange the bishop on d3, for example: 7.♗e3 ♘xd3 8.♕xd3 c5∓, or 7.h3 ♘xd3 8.♕xd3 0–0 9.♗f4 ♘a6∓, and in both cases Black has the more pleasant position, thanks to his bishop-pair and the successful blockade on the light squares.

A) 7.♘c3 ♘xd3

It is best for Black to capture this bishop immediately.

If 7...c6, then 8.♘d4 (It might be more precise for White to play here 8.♗e2 0–0 9.♘d4, preventing the exchange of his bishop.) 8...0–0 9.♗e2!? – see 7.♗e2 0–0 8.♘c3 c6 9.♘d4.

8.♕xd3 c6 9.♘d4 0–0

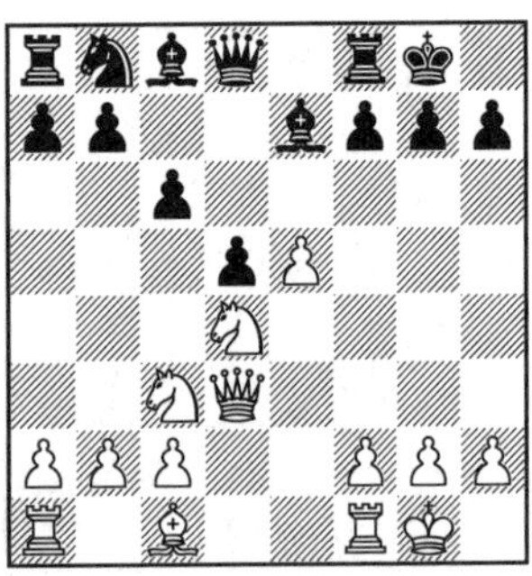

10.♕g3

10.♘f5 ♗xf5 11.♕xf5 ♕d7 12. ♕d3 ♘a6 13.♘e2 f6∓ Berndt – Ernst, Germany 2009.

10.♗f4 ♘a6 11.♘f5 ♘c5 12. ♘xe7 ♕xe7 13.♕d2 ♗f5∓; Black has every chance of advancing with d5-d4, while White has no promising ideas. Black's blockade on the f5- and e6- squares is quite secure, Parligras – Landa, Germany 2008.

10.f4 f5! White's kingside operations are completely blocked. Now, to accomplish anything, White would need to organize a blockade of the dark squares b6-c5-d4, but in the game he did not manage to achieve this: 11. ♘b3 ♘a6 12.♗e3 (After 12.♖d1

♘c7 13.♗e3, Black should play, not 13...♘e6?! 14.♘e2 ♔h8?! 15. c4± and Black has failed to solve the problem of his c8-bishop, Hracek – Motylev, Dresden 2007, but 13...b6! – Black should prepare the development of his bishop on b7 or a6, after which he should try to advance with c6-c5 – 14.♗f2 ♗b7 15.♘d4 ♕d7∓) 12... ♘c7 13.♘e2 b6 14.♘bd4 ♗a6 15. ♕d2 ♕e8 16.c3 c5 17.♘f3 ♖d8∓. Black's knight will occupy the excellent blockading square on e6 and he has a stable advantage, Navara – Kramnik, Prague 2008 (**game 8**).

10...♔h8

It is also good to play 10...♗h4 11.♕f3 ♘d7 (Black's pawn-barrier completely restricts the enemy knight on c3, so it would not be good to continue with 11...c5 12.♘f5 ♗xf5 13.♕xf5 ♘c6 14. ♗f4±, because White's knight on c3 would then become active.) 12.♗f4 ♖e8 13.♖ae1 ♘f8! 14.♗g3 ♘g6=. White's forces are tied up protecting his e5-pawn and Black has a very good position.

11.♖e1

11...♘a6

Here the move 11...c5!? looks good, because Black maintains firm control of the light squares e6 and f5. 12.♘f3 ♘c6 13.♘b5! (White achieves nothing with 13. ♗g5 ♗xg5 14.♘xg5 h6 15.♘f3 ♗e6∓) 13...♗f5 14.c3 ♗g6 15.♗g5 f6 16.exf6 gxf6 17.♗f4 ♖g8 18.♕h3 ♗e4 19.♖e3 ♕c8 (The game is sharp and very unclear after 19... ♖c8!? 20.♖d1 ♕b6 21.c4 ♘d4∞) 20.♕xc8 ♖axc8=, with an approximately equal endgame.

12.♗f4

Now it would be very interesting for Black to continue with

12...c5!?

Black's most solid line would be: 12...♘c5 13.♖ad1 a5, with the idea of ♗c8-d7, b7-b5-b4, etc. The game is about equal.

He has an alternative in 12... ♘c7 13.♖ad1, but now it is not good for Black to play 13...♗h4 14.♕f3 ♘e6?! He is ready to exchange knights, but this is not really necessary. 15.♘ce2 ♘xd4 16. ♘xd4± Predojevic – Mijailovic, Neum 2008. It is stronger for Black to play instead 13...♗d7!=, with the idea of b7-b5-b4, after which, having reduced the pressure against his d5-pawn, he should be able to advance c6-c5.

13.♘db5 ♘b4 14.♖e2

(diagram)

14...g5!?

There is a quieter option here in 14...♗h4 15.♕f3 ♗e6 16.♘d6 ♕d7=, with a complicated and approximately equal position.

15.♗c1 ♗e6!

Black's king is a bit open, so he should block the centre. It is bad to play 15...♗f5?! 16.♘d6 ♗g6 17. a3! ♘xc2 18.♖xc2 ♗xc2 19.♘xd5 h6 20.b4→ and White is attacking.

16.♘d6 f5!∞ – the position is very complicated but Black has excellent prospects.

B) 7.♗e2

7...0–0

7...♘e6?! It is too early for Black's knight to obstruct the diagonal of his light-squared bishop, since he has not yet completed his development. 8.♕d3!? (Black is able to carry out his idea after 8.♘c3?! c6 9.♘d4 ♘xd4 10.♕xd4 0–0 11.♗e3 f6!= Szabo – Giri, Rijeka 2010. It might also be interesting for White to try the set-up 8.c3!? 0–0 9.♕c2±. Then he can develop his rook on d1, or play ♗e2-d3, provoking g7-g6 and securing the h6-square for his dark-squared bishop.) 8...0–0 (after 8...♘c5 White has the promising move 9.♕e3±) 9.♖d1 c6 10.c4 dxc4 11.♕xc4 ♕c7 12.♘c3 ♘d7 13.♕e4 ♘dc5 14.♕e3± and White has a slight edge.

8.♗e3

White cannot achieve much with 8.♘c3, because this knight is restricted by the pawn-barrier c6-d5 and is thus misplaced, so his position is prospectless: 8...c6 9. ♘d4 (9.b4 ♘e6 10.♖b1, Skoberne – Srebrnic, Maribor 2011, and now with 10...b5!∓ Black can emphasize the bad position of the enemy knight on c3. He can continue with a7-a5 and White will have problems with the protection of his b4-pawn.)

Black has two reasonable possibilities here: the immediate 9... f6 and 9...♕c7!

After 9...f6 Black must play

very accurately to equalize. 10. f4 (Black need not fear 10.exf6 ♗xf6 11.♗e3 ♘e6!=, with equality, Dembo – Mamedyarova, Khanty-Mansyisk 2010) 10...fxe5 (10... ♕b6 11.♔h1 fxe5 12.fxe5 ♖xf1 13. ♕xf1 ♘bd7 14.♘f5 ♗f8 15.♕f4 ♘e6 16.♕g3 ♔h8 17.b3± and although Black might be able to hold this position White obviously has the initiative) 11.fxe5 ♘bd7 12.b4 (After 12.♗f4 Black should not play 12...♕b6 13.♔h1 g5? 14.♗e3! ♕xb2 15.♕d2→ and he comes under a dangerous attack, but, 12...♖xf4! 13.♖xf4 ♘xe5⩱∞ and his compensation for the exchange is quite sufficient.) 12...♖xf1 13.♗xf1 ♘e4 14. ♘xe4 dxe4 15.♘f5 (after 15.♗f4 Black solves his problems with the move 15...♘b6!=) 15...♘xe5 16.♘xe7 ♕xe7 17.♕d4 ♗f5 (17... ♘g4 18.♗c4 ♔h8 19.♗b2±) 18.♗b2 ♖e8 19.♕xa7 ♕c7 20.♗e2 (if 20. ♕c5 Black has the response 20... b6! 21.♕c3 ♘g4 22.g3 e3!⇄, with sufficient counterplay) 20...♗g4 21.♗a6 ♗c8 22.♗e2 ♗g4=, with a draw by repetition of moves.

9...♕c7! It is useful to provoke the move f4 before undermining the e5-pawn.

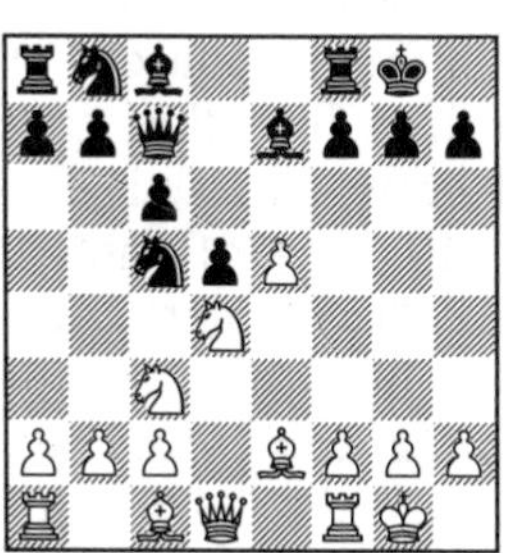

10.♗f4 (If 10.f4, then 10...f6 11.exf6 ♗xf6 12.♗e3 ♘e6 and here it is bad for White to play 13.♘b3 d4! 14.♘xd4 ♘xd4 15.♗xd4 ♖d8 16.♗c4 ♔h8 17.♖e1 ♗f5-+, because he loses his bishop on d4, while if 13.♘xe6 ♗xe6 14.f5 ♗f7= Black should not be afraid of the advance of White's g-pawn, because he has sufficient counterplay along the e-file.) 10...♘bd7 11.♘f3 (after 11.♖e1 ♘e6 12.♘xe6 fxe6 13.♗g3 a5 14.♗g4 ♘c5= a strategically very complicated position arises, with approximately equal chances) 11...♘e6!. Black's blockade on e6 is particularly effective when White cannot advance his f-pawn in the near future (It is less good, but possible, for Black to play 11...♘e4 12.♗d3 ♘dc5 13. ♖e1 ♕b6 14.♗xe4 dxe4 15.♘d2 ♕xb2 16.♘dxe4 ♘xe4 17. ♘xe4 ♗f5 18.♘d6 ♕xc2, draw, J.Polgar – Giri, Hoogeveen 2009.) 12.♗g3 ♘dc5∓. Black is ready to continue his queenside attack with b7-b5, a7-a5, ♗c8-a6 and b5-b4, while White's pieces are misplaced.

Now Black has a choice between the developing move **B1) 8...♘c6** and the radical solution **B2) 8...c6**.

B1) 8...♘c6

Black completes his development and will have a flexible pawn-structure, but his pawn on d5 will not be supported by its neighbour – the c-pawn. This is the reason why Black can only equalize in this variation and finds it difficult to seize the initiative.

9.♘c3 ♗e6

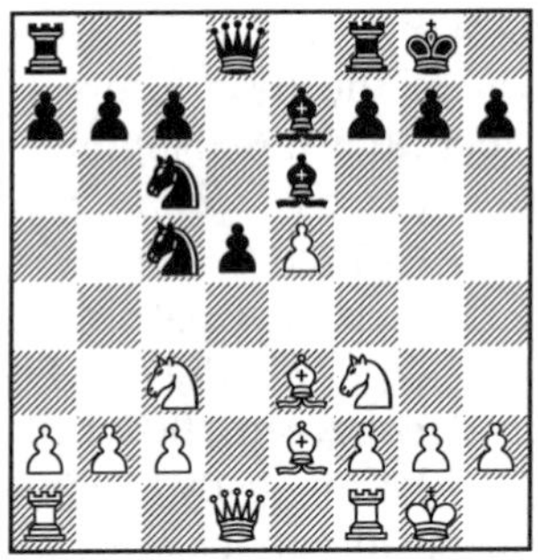

10.♗b5

We should analyze White's alternatives:

10.♕c1 ♘d7! (10...♕c8 11.♖d1 ♖d8 12.♗g5 h6 13.♗xe7 ♘xe7 14.♘d4 – 14.♕e3± – 14...♗g4 15.f3 ♗d7 16.f4 c6 17.♕e3 ♘e6 18.♘xe6 ♗xe6 19.♕c5 ♘g6 20.♕f2 ♗g4 21.h3 ♗xe2 22.♘xe2± – White can try to prepare f4-f5; having an extra pawn on the flank where the kings are placed gives him a slight advantage, Almasi – Landa, Reggio Emilia 2008) 11.♗f4 f6 12.exf6

Now:

Black cannot equalize with 12...♗xf6 because of 13.♘g5! and he must give up his dark-squared bishop, guaranteeing a slight edge for White: 13...♘c5 (13...♗xg5 14.♗xg5 ♘f6 15.♖e1 h6 16.♗h4 ♕d7 17.♕d2±) 14.♕e3 d4 (14...♘d4 15.♖ad1 h6 16.♘xe6 ♘cxe6 17.♗g3±) 15.♘xe6 dxe3 16.♘xd8 exf2 17.♖xf2 ♖axd8 18.♖ff1 g5 19.♗e3 ♗d4 20.♗xd4 ♘xd4 21.♗c4 ♔g7 22.♖xf8 ♖xf8 23.♖e1±;

it is correct for Black to play 12...♘xf6! 13.♘b5 (or 13.♖e1 ♗c5 14.a3 ♘h5 15.♗g5 ♕d7 16.b4 ♗d6 17.b5 ♘e5 18.♘d4 ♗g4 19.f3 ♕f7∓ and Black has the initiative) 13...♖c8 14.c4 ♕d7= – the position is quite complicated, but Black's prospects are no worse.

10.a3 – White brings the b4-square under control and awaits his opponent's reaction. Black's most natural response to White's prophylaxis on the queenside would be to play actively in the centre: 10...♘e4!? 11.♘b5 (11.♕d3 ♘xc3 12.♕xc3 f6=) 11...♗c5 (after 11...♕d7, Black must reckon with 12.c4!) 12.♗xc5 ♘xc5 13.♘bd4 ♘xd4 14.♕xd4 ♘d7= and he is close to equality. He can also try prophylaxis with 10...a6!? 11.♕e1 ♕e8 (It is also good for Black to play 11...♕c8 12.♖d1 ♖d8= Najer – Gelfand, Odessa (rapid) 2009) 12.♘d4 ♘xd4 (12...♘xe5!?) 13.♗xd4 ♘a4 14.b3 ♘xc3 15.♗xc3 f5 16.exf6 ♗xf6 17.♗d3 ♗f5= and further simplification is unavoidable, so the game should end in a draw, Kamsky – Akopian, Jermuk 2009.

10.♘b5 ♘d7 (10...♗g4 11.♘bd4 ♘xd4 12.♘xd4 ♗xe2 13.♕xe2±) 11.♗f4 a6 12.♘bd4 ♘xd4 13.♘xd4 c5 14.♘xe6 fxe6 15.♗g3 c4 16.♗g4, Shirov – Gelfand, Kallithea 2008. Here, after the game continuation 16...♘c5 17.b4! cxb3 18.axb3, White obtained some advantage. Instead, Black should have played 16...♕b6!=, with approximately equal chances.

10.♕e1 ♘e4

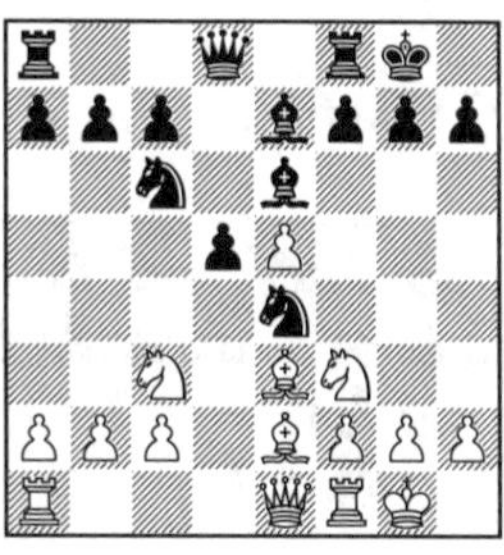

11.♘b5 (After 11.♖d1 Black has the rather unpleasant pin 11...♗b4∓. If 11.a3 it is possible for Black to continue with 11...f6 12.♘xe4 dxe4 13.♖d1 ♕e8 14.exf6 ♗xf6 15.♘d4 ♘xd4 16.♗xd4, but now not 16...♕g6 17. ♕c3± Salgado – Lovik, Kemer 2009, but 16...♕c6!= and Black holds the balance. However, it is even simpler for him to play 11...♘xc3! 12.♕xc3 f6=) 11...♕d7 12.♘bd4 ♗g4 (A very interesting position arises after 12...f6!? 13.exf6 ♗xf6 14.♘xe6 ♕xe6 15.c3 ♖ae8 16.♕d1∞ – Black's pieces are very active but his light squares are vulnerable. In addition, White has the bishop-pair, so the prospects are about equal.) 13.♘xc6 bxc6 14.♘d4 ♗xe2 15.♘xe2 f6 16. f3 ♘g5 17.♕d2

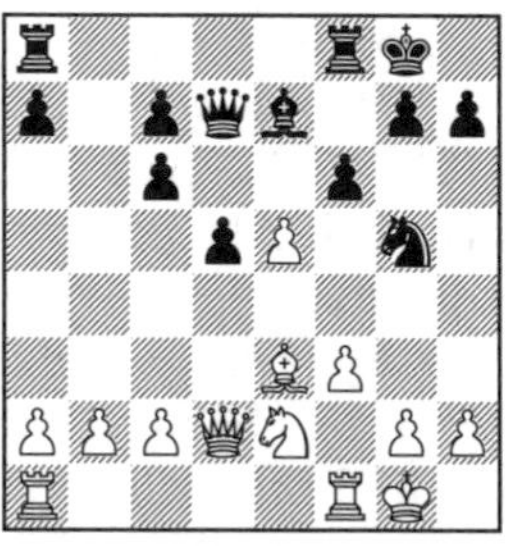

17...♘f7! (It is less precise for Black to continue with the natural line: 17...♘e6 18.exf6 ♗xf6 19.♘d4 ♘xd4 20.♗xd4 ♗xd4 21.♕xd4 ♕d6±; White maintains a slight edge, but his winning chances are only minimal, Balogh – Grabarczuk, Wroclaw 2009.) 18.exf6 ♗xf6 19.♗d4 ♗xd4 20.♘xd4 (20.♕xd4 ♕d6=; Black advances with c6-c5, after which he will have no problems whatsoever.) 20...c5 21.♘b3 c4! 22.♘c5 ♕d6 23.♕d4 ♘h6 24.♖fd1 (White must place this rook on d1, because if 24.♖ad1 Black plays 24...♘f5 25.♕xd5 ♕xd5 26.♖xd5 ♘e3 – a double attack!) 24...c6 25.♕xc4 ♖xf3!∓. With this tactical shot, Black not only solves all his problems but even obtains the advantage.

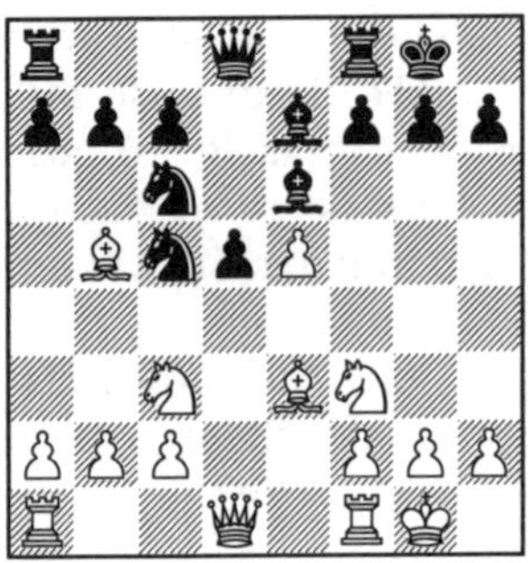

10...a6!?N

It is too passive to continue with 10...♘d7 11.♘xd5 and now Black is unable to achieve complete equality:

11...♗xd5 12.♕xd5 ♘dxe5 13. ♗xc6 ♘xc6 14.♕b5 (The move a7-a6, which Black will play later with tempo, is useful to Black, so maybe it would be better for White to play immediately 14. ♕b3!?) 14...♕c8 15.♖ad1 ♗f6 16. ♖fe1 ♖e8 17.♗f4 ♖xe1 18.♖xe1 a6 19.♕b3 h6 20.h3 ♖b8, Efimenko – Motylev, Wijk aan Zee 2009. Now White has the strong move 21.♖d1!±, depriving Black's queen of the d7-square;

11...♘dxe5 12.♘xe7 ♕xe7 13. ♘xe5 ♘xe5 14.♕d4 ♖fd8 (14...♘g4 15.♕c5 ♕f6 16.♗d4 ♕f4 17.g3 ♕h6 18.h4±) 15.♕xe5 ♖d5 16.♕e4 ♖xb5 17.b3 c6 18.c4 ♖h5 19.h3±; Black's rook on h5 will have problems returning to the centre, so he is doomed to a rather difficult defence, Kariakin – Gelfand, Jermuk 2009.

11.♗xc6 bxc6 12.♘d4 ♗d7 13.♘b3

Or 13.f4 f6 14.♕d2 fxe5 15.fxe5 ♖b8 16.b4 ♘e6 17.a3 a5∓ and White will be unable to maintain the blockade on the dark squares.

13...♘xb3 14.axb3 f6 15. exf6 ♗xf6 16.♗c5 ♖e8=

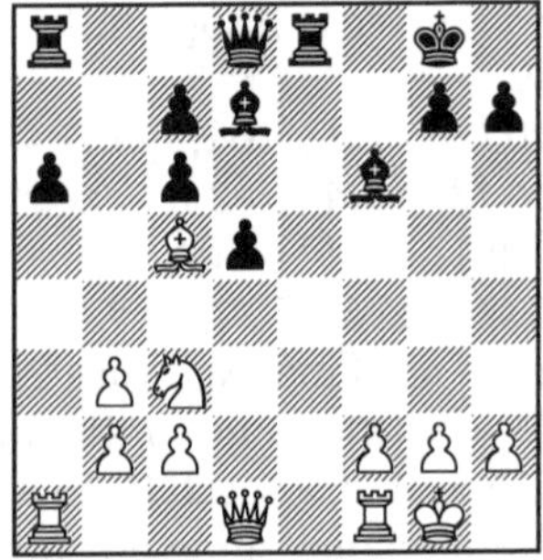

The defects in Black's pawn-structure are compensated for by his bishop-pair, so the game is approximately equal.

B2) 8...c6!

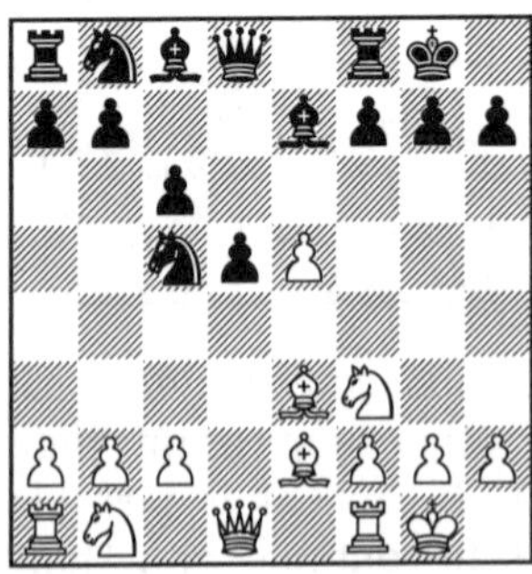

This is the most flexible move for Black. First of all he bolsters his d5-pawn. It is important that Black's undeveloped minor pieces on the queenside can be be deployed straight to very harmonious positions and will not require any additional manoeuvring , so that Black's minimal loss of time and slight lag in development should be of no consequence.

9.c4

Or 9.♘d4 ♕c7! 10.f4 f6 11.exf6 (11.♘f3 fxe5 12.♘xe5 ♘bd7∓ Balogh – Rustemov, Germany 2006) 11...♗xf6 12.♘c3 ♘e6!

13.♘xe6 (It is bad for White to play 13.f5? ♘xd4 14.♗xd4 ♗f5 15.♔h1 ♗xd4 16.♕xd4, Nisipeanu – Handke, Germany 2010; here Black can continue with 16...♕b6!, retaining his extra pawn without any compensation for White whatsoever. It is even more precise for Black to play 13...♕e5! 14.♘xe6 ♕xe3 15.♔h1 ♗xe6 16.fxe6 ♕xe6∓, also with an extra pawn. Or 13.♘b3 d4! 14.♘xd4 ♘xd4 15.♗xd4 ♖d8 16.♗c4 ♔h8 17.♖e1 ♗f5∓ and White has difficulties getting out of the pin along the d-file.) 13...♗xe6 14.f5 ♗f7∓. Black's operations in the centre are much more effective than White's pawn-offensive on the kingside.

After 9.♘bd2 ♘e6 10.♘b3 c5 11.c4!? (After 11.♖e1 b6 12.c4 ♗b7∓ Black's pieces are very harmoniously placed and his game is clearly preferable, Inarkiev – Kasimdzhanov, Jermuk 2009) 11...d4 12.♗c1

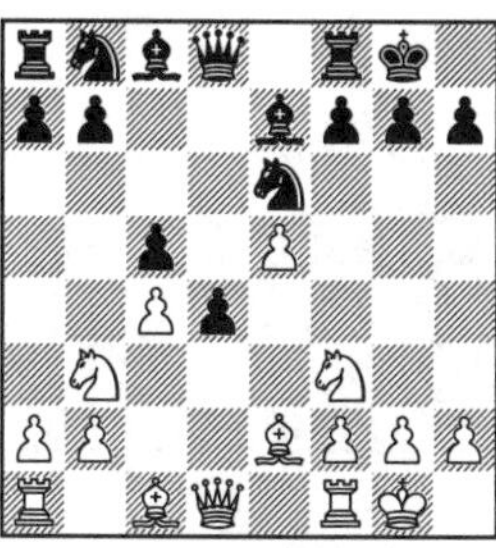

12...♘c6 (It might be interesting to try 12...f5!? 13.exf6, but here not 13...♗xf6 14.♗d3 ♘c6 15.♖e1↑ and White has the initiative, Palac – Kunin, Schwarzach 2010, but 13...♖xf6! – Black's bishop should go to d6, from where it will aim at White's kingside – 14.♗d3 ♘c6∞ and the position is rather unclear.) 13.♗d3 a5! Black should try to undermine the base of the enemy knight on b3. 14.a4 ♕c7! Black has various possible set-ups, but I prefer one which forces White to protect his e5-pawn. 15.♖e1 ♖e8!∓ and now Black can use the f8-square for manoeuvres with any of his minor pieces, while his knight on c6 will always be ready to go to the b4-square and his queen's rook may come into play via the a6-square. Black has an excellent position.

9...dxc4

It is weaker to play 9...♗e6 10.

cxd5 cxd5 11.♘c3 ♘c6 12.♖c1 ♖c8 13.♘b5 ♘d7 14.♗f4±, with a slight edge for White.

10.♗xc4

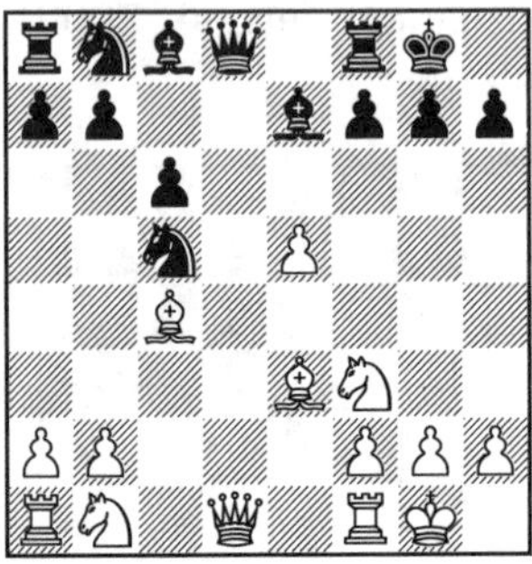

10...♘bd7!?

Black can afford to play this move in his fight for the initiative, exploiting the circumstance that White's e5-pawn lacks sufficient protection.

Black also has a simpler solution available: 10...♕xd1 11.♖xd1 ♘bd7 12.♖c1 (12.♘c3 ♘b6 13.♗e2 ♘ca4! 14.♘xa4 ♘xa4 15.♖d2 ♘b6 and thanks to the possible outpost on d5 for his knight, Black solves his problems, for example: 16.♗g5 ♗xg5 17.♘xg5 ♗f5 18.g4 ♗e6!=, with a very safe position.) 12...♘a4 13.b3 ♘ab6 14.e6 fxe6 15.♗xe6 ♔h8 16.♘bd2 ♘e5 17.♗xc8 ♘xf3 18.♘xf3 ♖fxc8 19.♗c5 ♖e8= and the endgame is completely equal, Gashimov – Gelfand, Bursa 2010.

11.b4!?

This is White's most principled option; otherwise, Black's game is easy and problem-free:

11.♘bd2 ♘b6 12.♗xc5 ♗xc5 13.♗b3 ♗f5 14.♗c2. This position was reached in the World Championship for computer programs in the game between "Rybka" and "Hiarcs", Leiden 2010. Black's most precise road to equality would now have been 14...♗d3 15.♗xd3 ♕xd3 16.♘b3 ♕xd1 17.♖fxd1 ♗e7=;

11.♕c2 ♕c7 12.♗e2 ♘e6 13.♗d3 ♘xe5 14.♘xe5 ♕xe5 15.♗xh7 ♔h8 16.♗d3 ♗d6 17.g3 ♘c5∓ – Black is slightly better, Bologan – Sakaev, Kragujevac 2009;

11.♗e2 ♕c7 12.♕c1 ♘e6 13.♕c3 ♘b6∓;

11.♘c3 ♕c7 (Black can simplify the position if he so wishes: 11...♘b6 12.♗e2 ♕xd1 13.♖fxd1 ♘ca4, reaching a position which usually arises after 10...♕xd1.) 12.♕d4 ♘b6! (It would be too risky for Black to weaken his pawn-structure; after 12...b5 13.♗e2 ♘e6 14.♕e4 f5 15.♕c2! f4 16.♗d2!↑, although White may lose his e5-pawn, he will gain excellent play on the weak light squares.) 13.♗e2 ♗f5! 14.♕f4 ♗g6∞ – the position offers chances to both sides.

11...♘e6

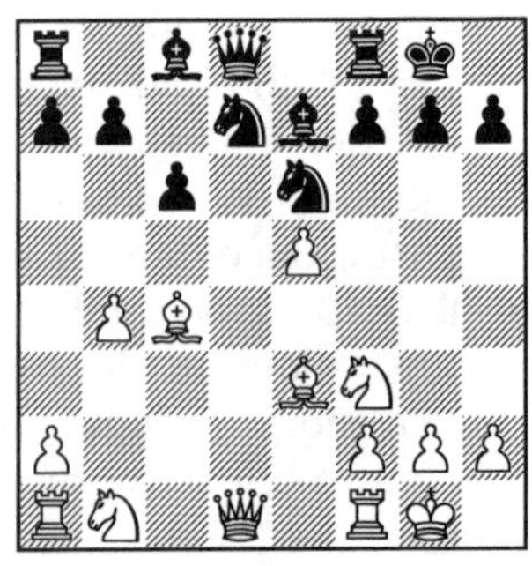

12.♕b3

12.♕c2 ♕c7 (It is weaker for Black to play 12...♘b6 13.♖d1. Now 13...♘xc4?! 14.♖xd8 ♖xd8 15.♗d2 ♘xd2 16.♘bxd2 ♗xb4 17.♘e4↑ is creative but unsound; White has excellent chances of organizing a strong kingside attack.) 13.♕b2 ♘b6 14.♗b3 (14.♘bd2 ♘xc4 15.♘xc4 b6∓ with an excellent game for Black) 14...♖d8 (It is inferior to continue with 14...♘d5 15.♗xd5 cxd5, since White should play here, not 16.♘c3, which Black can counter with 16...♕c4 17.♖fd1 ♖d8 18.♕b3 ♕xb3 19.axb3 d4 20.♘xd4 ♗xb4=, with equality, but 16.♖c1! ♕d7 17.♖d1!± and White maintains an edge.) 15.♘c3 (after 15.a3, Black has the excellent positional move 15...♘f8!∓, opening the diagonal for his light-squared bishop) 15...♗xb4 16.♗xe6 ♗xc3 17.♗xf7 ♕xf7 18.♕xc3 h6 19.♖fe1 ♘d5=, with a good game for Black.

12...a5!

After 12...♘b6 13.♖d1 ♕c7 14.♘bd2± White has protected all his pawns and completed his development, preserving the better prospects.

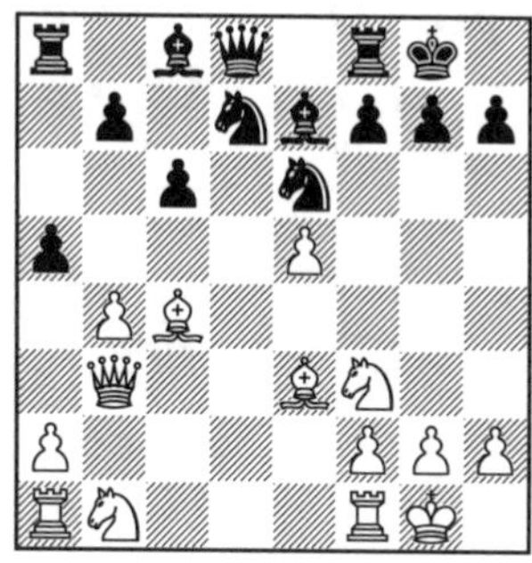

13.b5

The line 13.♗xe6?! fxe6 14.♕xe6 ♔h8 15.♘bd2 axb4 16.♕b3 ♕c7∞ leads to a sharp position with a slight edge for Black.

13...a4 14.♕b2 ♘b6 15.♘bd2 ♘d5 16.bxc6 bxc6 17.♘e4 ♗a6 18.♗xa6 ♘xe3 19.fxe3 ♖xa6 20.♖ad1 ♕b6 21.♕e2 ♖a5!= The chances for both sides are approximately equal, and after **22.♘d6** Black has the amazing, purely "computer" move **22...♗xd6!**, solving all his problems. After **23.exd6 ♖d5** it becomes clear that White will be unable to hold on to his d6-pawn, for example: **24.♕f2 ♕b8!∓** and White even has to start thinking about maintaining equality.

Conclusion

Just as in the previous chapter, in which we analyzed the variation 3.d4 ♘xe4 4.dxe5 d5 5.♘bd2, White's prematurely far-advanced e5-pawn enables Black's pieces to be deployed comfortably around it. In addition, Black can attack it or else undermine it with the move f7-f6, opening the f-file for his rook in the process. I like variation B2) very much, particularly the move 8...c6!, since it leads to a very complicated fight in which Black's prospects are not at all worse.

Chapter 11 1.e4 e5 2.♘f3 ♘f6 3.d4 ♘xe4 4.♗d3 d5 5.♘xe5

This is the main line of theory. The position is almost symmetrical, although White is slightly more active thanks to having the first move. Still, the placement of his bishop on d3 has a certain drawback. After the possible exchange on e5, White's pawn will be removed from d4 and his bishop is then often exposed to attack, or exchange, by Black's knight, which goes from e4 to c5.

5...♘d7

With this move Black exchanges the knights. His knight is just developed, while the enemy knight is well-placed in the centre. If White allows his opponent to exchange on the e5-square, then Black's knight on e4 will go to c5 and White's bishop on d3 will come under the threat of a rather unpleasant exchange.

There was a time when it was very popular for Black to develop his bishop symmetrically with 5...♗d6, but then it was established that the position which arises by force after 6.0–0 0–0 7.c4 ♗xe5 8.dxe5 ♘c6 9.cxd5 ♕xd5 10.♕c2 ♘b4 11.♗xe4 ♘xc2 12.♗xd5 ♗f5 (it is disastrous for Black to play 12...♘xa1 immediately, since after 13.♗e4 he soon loses his knight stranded on a1) 13.g4 ♗xg4 14.♗e4 ♘xa1 15.♗f4 f5 16.♗d5 ♔h8 17.♖c1, turns out to be in White's favour. Hence Black stopped playing this line.

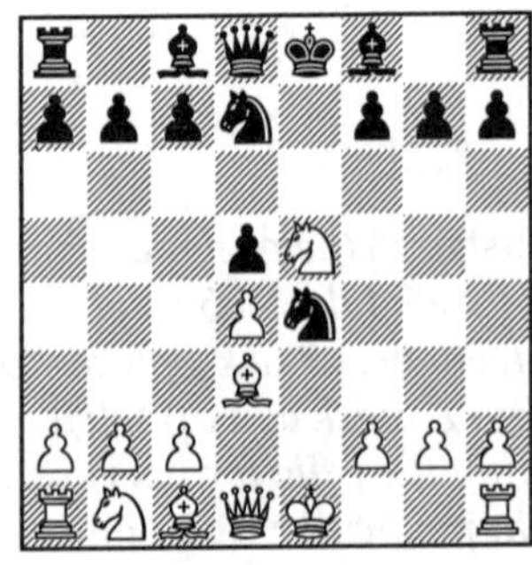

6.♘c3

The main theoretical line of this variation – the move 6.♘xd7 – will be analyzed in Chapters 13-15 and the move 6.0–0 – in Chapter 12.

Early development of White's queen in the centre is not at all promising: 6.♕e2 ♘xe5 7.♗xe4 dxe4 8.♕xe4 ♗e6 9.♕xe5 ♕d7 10. 0–0 (10.♗e3 ♗b4 11.c3 ♗d6 12. ♕xg7 0–0–0 13.♘d2, Oll – Khalifman, Sochi 1984; Black can continue here with 13...♕c6!↑, with a dangerous initiative) 10... 0–0–0 11.♗e3

11...♗b4! Black deprives the enemy queen of its possible retreat to the a5-square (another interesting try for Black is 11... ♗d6!? 12.♕a5 ♗d5) and now White can repel the enemy bishop but after 12.c3 ♗d6 his pawn on c3 deprives the knight of this square and also blocks the white queen's line of retreat back into its own camp. 13.♕h5 (after 13.♕a5 Black has the resource 13...♗d5!↑ and his threats such as ♕d7-c6 and ♗d5xg2 are very dangerous) 13... f5 14.f4 ♖he8⩱. Black's initiative more than compensates for the sacrificed pawn. White can ignore the enemy bishop on b4 and continue with his development: 12.♘c3, but Black can counter this with 12...f6 13.♕g3 ♗xc3 (I like the immediate 13...h5!? even more, keeping the possible exchange on c3 in reserve.) 14.bxc3 h5⩱. Black has good prospects of developing an initiative on the kingside, while White's extra queenside pawn is devalued and insignificant, Karpov – Larsen, Tilburg 1980 (**game 9**).

6...♘xe5

White's knight on e5 was solidly placed and an attempt by Black to force his opponent to exchange the knights himself does not work: 6...♘xc3 7.bxc3 ♗d6 8.0–0 0–0 9.♖e1±

7.dxe5 ♘xc3 8.bxc3

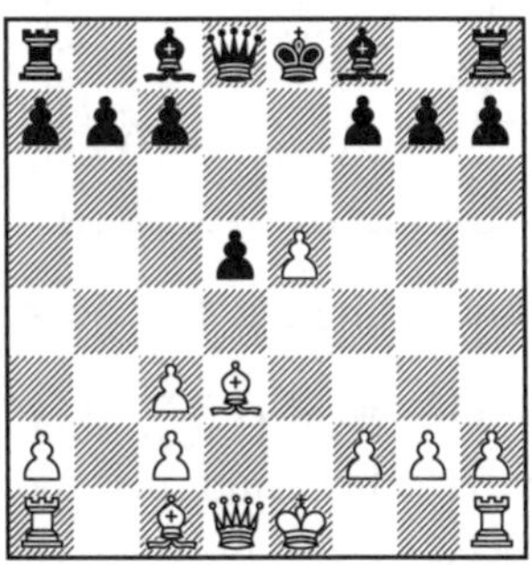

8...♗e7

The game is much more lively after 8...♗c5. Black's dark-squared bishop, if it is not exchanged, will retreat to b6 and then Black might even castle queenside under its protection. 9.♕h5 (After 9.0–0 0–0 10.♕h5 g6 11.♕h6 ♕e7 12.♗f4 f5 13.♖ab1 b6 14.♖fe1 ♗e6 15.♗g5 ♕f7 16.♕h4 c6 17.a4 ♖fe8=. Black is ready to exchange bishops via the e7-square and then organize some active play with the pawn-advance c6-c5, Gashimov – Kramnik, Baku 2009) 9...♗e6 (It is less precise for Black to opt for 9...g6 10.♕h6 ♗f8 11.♕e3± – White's queen is very well placed on e3, from where it can participate in the struggle for the dark squares. After 11...♗e7, White can choose between 12.0–0, 12.♕g3 and the surprising move 12.h4!?, and in all these lines Black must fight for equality.)

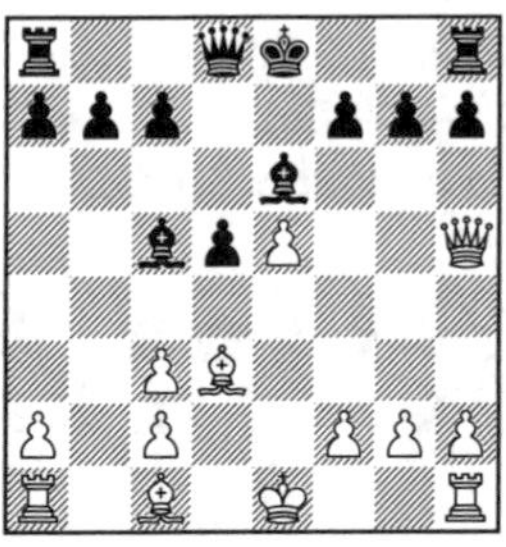

Now White has two possibilities:

10.♖b1 ♕d7 11.♗g5 (but not 11.♖xb7? ♗b6∓ and his rook is trapped) 11...h6 12.0–0 ♖g8 13.♗d2 0–0–0∞ Movsesian – Haba, Czech 2004;

10.0–0 ♕d7 11.♕h4 (11.♗g5 ♗f5 12.♖ab1, Movsesian – Navara, Czech Republic (blitz) 2005. Black's b7-pawn is not really hanging yet, since White's rook would be trapped on b7 after the move ♗c5-b6, so Black can simply castle and after 12...0–0= the position is approximately equal.) 11...♗e7 12.♗g5 (the game is double-edged after 12.♕g3 0–0–0∞) 12...♗xg5 13.♕xg5 0–0= Hracek – Z.Polgar, Pardubice 1994.

9.0–0

White sometimes tries to weaken Black's kingside with 9.♕h5 ♗e6 10.♖b1 ♕d7 11.h3 (the position is equal after 11.♗g5 c6 12.0–0 ♗xg5 13.♕xg5 0–0 14.f4 h6 15.♕g3 f5= Gashimov – Gelfand, Sochi 2008)

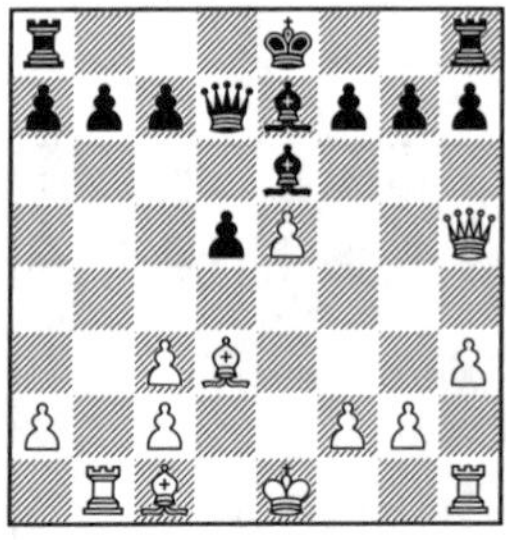

and here he can solve the problem of the protection of his b7-pawn in two equally good ways:

11...c6!? 12.0–0 b5. Black thus deprives his opponent of the possibility of c3-c4 and seizes space, which he might need later when he begins his queenside offensive. 13.♗e3 (after 13.a4 Black should play, not 13...a6, Diu – Frolyanov, Taganrog 2011, because of 14.♖a1!± and White exerts pressure on the a-file, but 13...bxa4!∞, with a very complicated struggle.) 13...g6 14.♕h6 ♗f8 15.♕f4 ♗e7=. If White does not repeat moves, Black castles with a very good position.

The move 11...b6 is less active than the plan with c7-c6 and b7-b5 but is very solid and quite safe. 12.0–0 g6 13.♕h6 ♗f8 14.♕h4 ♗e7 15.♗g5 ♗xg5 16.♕xg5 0–0 17.f4 ♕d8 18.♕g3 ♔h8 19.f5 gxf5 20.♖f4!? (20.♗xf5 ♖g8= Shirov – Gelfand, Moscow 2008) 20...♖g8 (Black should abstain from entering sharp complications with the line: 20...f6 21.♖e1 fxe5 22.♖xe5 ♕d6 23.♕e3 ♖ae8= Sutovsky – Shirov, Kemer 2007) 21.♕f3 ♕g5 22.♗xf5 ♕g3=. The ensuing rook and pawn ending looks equal and should end in a draw.

9...0–0

(diagram)

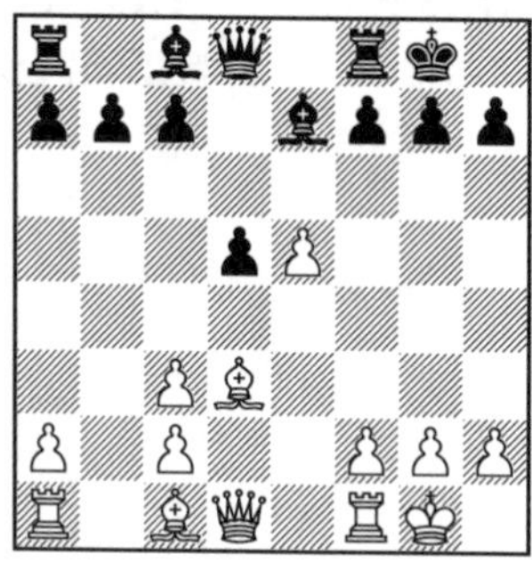

10.♖b1

10.f4 f5 11.♗e3 (after 11.♖b1, Korneev – Garcia Salamero, Madrid 2007, Black should take the opportunity to develop his dark-squared bishop to a more active position with 11...♗c5!? 12.♔h1 c6 13.c4 b6 14.cxd5 ♕xd5 15.♕e2 ♗e6=) 11...♗e6 12.♖b1 b6=

10...b6 11.♕h5 g6 12.♕e2 ♗e6 13.♗b5 ♗d7= Iordachescu – Smeets, Dresden 2008.

Conclusion

In the variation with 6.♘c3 White immediately exchanges all the knights, so Black is forced to block his opponent's far-advanced e5-pawn with his bishop. Black has no open files on the queenside and this is in White's favour, because Black cannot quickly attack White's doubled c-pawns. On the other hand, Black has neither weaknesses, nor bad pieces, so he can maintain the balance with accurate play. It is essential for him to be able to parry White's possible kingside initiative with the timely blocking pawn-advance f7-f5!. If White does not react to this, Black will gradually organize an offensive on the queenside, or, if one of the files on the kingside becomes open, several major pieces will be exchanged on it. As a rule, this all results in an equal position.

Chapter 12 1.e4 e5 2.♘f3 ♘f6 3.d4 ♘xe4 4.♗d3 d5 5.♘xe5 ♘d7 6.0–0

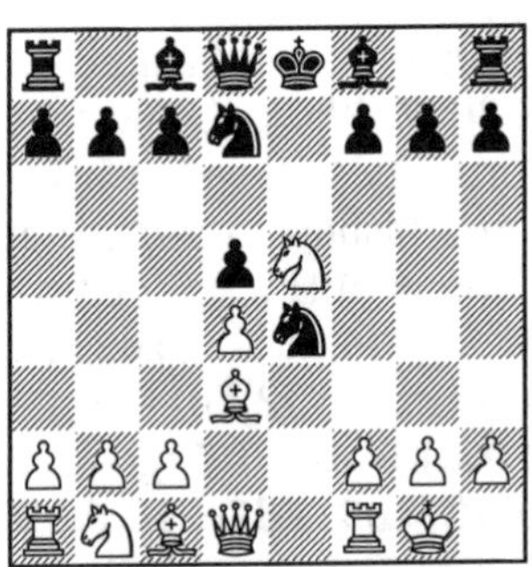

With this move White is trying not to assist Black's development and he continues to mobilize his own forces as quickly as possible. However, the subsequent alteration to the pawn-structure is advantageous to Black. He obtains the excellent c5-square for his knight and then White's bishop on d3 is threatened with exchange. In addition, Black can set up a secure blockade on the e6- and f5- squares.

6...♘xe5

We cannot recommend 6...♗d6?!, because after 7.c4 c6 8.cxd5 cxd5 9.♗f4 the loose black bishop on d6 is a tactical weakness.

7.dxe5 ♘c5 8.♗e3

After 8.♗e2 ♗e7 9.♗e3, the game transposes to the variation 8.♗e3 ♗e7 9.♗e2.

The move 8.f4 presents Black with a choice:

after 8...g6, White can change his mind and avoid the exchange of his light-squared bishop with. 9.♗e2. After 9...♗f5 10.♗e3 c6 11.♘d2 ♗e7 (it is not good for Black to play 11...d4 12.♗f2 d3 13.cxd3 ♘xd3 14.♗e3±) 12.♘f3 ♘e6 13.♗d3 ♗xd3 14.cxd3 d4 15.♗d2 ♕d5∞, a complex strategical battle arises, with chances for both sides, Karjakin – Topalov, Nice (rapid) 2009;

8...♘xd3!? I like this move best. 9.♕xd3 ♗c5 (9...g6 10.♗e3 ♗e7 11.♘c3 c6 12.♘e2 – see 8.♗e3 ♗e7 9.f4 ♘xd3 10.♕xd3 g6 11.♘c3 c6 12.♘e2) 10.♗e3 ♗xe3 11.♕xe3 ♗f5=. Black has obtained a good position.

After 8.♘c3, Black bolsters his d5-pawn with 8...c6

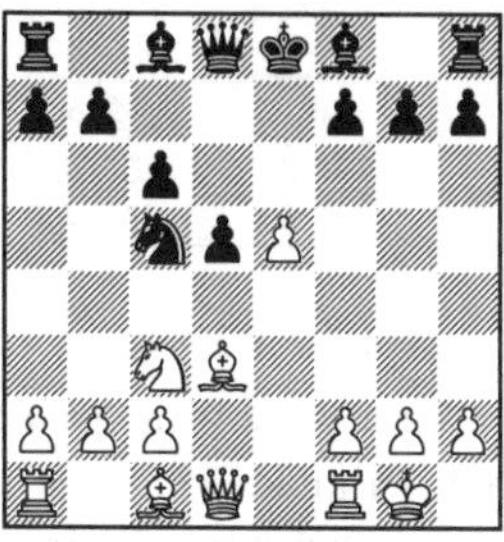

and then:

9.♕f3 ♗e6 10.♘e2 ♕d7 11.♘f4 ♘xd3 12.cxd3, Tiviakov – Deviatkin, Moscow 2009. After 12...♗f5 13.♗d2 ♗e7 (13...0–0–0!?) 14. ♘h5 0–0 15.♕g3 ♗g6 16.♘f4 ♗f5= there is a possible repetition of moves. However, the only reasonable possibility of avoiding this is for Black to castle queenside on his 13th move.

9.f4 g6 (9...♘xd3!? 10.♕xd3 ♗c5 11.♔h1 g6=) 10.♘e2, Inarkiev – Akopian, Jermuk 2009. This was the right time to capture the bishop: 10...♘xd3! 11.♕xd3 ♗f5=, with a fine position.

9.♘e2 – I believe that this is White's most logical move. His knight is restricted by the pawn-chain c6-d5 and he wants to redeploy it to a better location. 9...♗e7 10.f4 f6 (for 10...♘xd3 11.♕xd3 g6 12.♗e3 – see 8.♗e3 ♗e7 9.f4 ♘xd3 10.♕xd3 g6 11.♘c3 c6 12.♘e2) 11. ♗e3 ♘xd3 12.♕xd3 0–0 13.c4 fxe5 14.fxe5

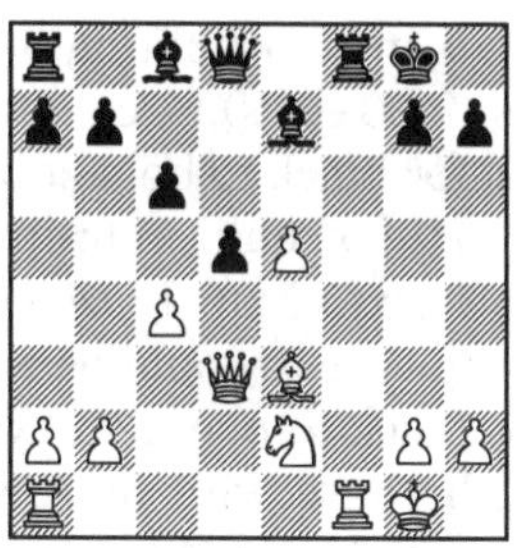

14...♗e6 (it was also good for Black to opt here for 14...♕c7!? 15.cxd5 ♕xe5 16.dxc6 bxc6=) 15. ♘f4 ♗f5 16.♕d4 ♗g5 17.cxd5 ♗xf4 18.♖xf4 ♕xd5 19.♕xd5 cxd5 20. ♖af1 (20.♖c1 ♗e6 21.♖xf8 ♖xf8 22. ♖c7 ♖f7 23.♖xf7 ♔xf7 24.♗xa7 d4=. Black is a pawn down, but with bishops of opposite colour Black should easily draw this position.) 20...g6 21.g4 ♗e6 22. ♖xf8 ♖xf8 23.♖xf8, draw, Mamedyarov – Kramnik, Wijk aan Zee 2008.

8...♗e7

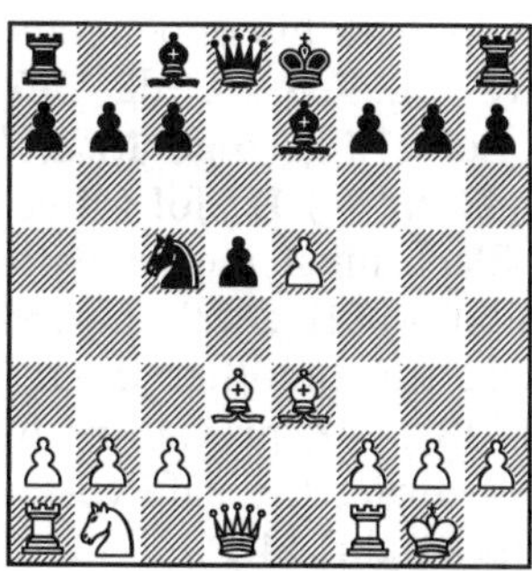

9.f4

9.♗e2. White avoids the exchange, but is forced to move his bishop to a less active post. He loses a valuable tempo in doing so, and in the meantime Black succeeds in coordinating his own pieces. 9...0–0 10.f4 c6! It is essential for Black to bolster his d5-pawn. (He should refrain from 10...f6 11.exf6 ♖xf6 12.c4 ♗e6 13. cxd5 and here it would be a disaster for Black to play 13...♗xd5 14. ♘c3±, because with queens present on the board White's advantage is overwhelming, thanks to his great piece-activity in the centre and on the kingside, Tkachiev – Giri, France 2010. The correct way for Black is to play 13...♕xd5 14.♘c3 ♕xd1 15.♖axd1± and White's position is only slightly more active.). 11.c3 (The reckless move 11.f5?! irrevocably weakens his e5-pawn and Black can exploit this immediately with 11...♘d7! 12.f6 gxf6 13.exf6 ♗xf6 14.♘c3. White cannot develop his knight to any other reasonable square, but here it is restricted by the pawn-chain c6-d5 and thus Black easily parries his opponent's initiative. 14...♖e8 15.♕d2 ♕e7 16. ♖f3 ♘e5 17.♖g3 ♘g6 18.♖f1 ♗e5 19.♖gf3 ♕d6∓) 11...f6! (after 11... ♗f5 Black must reckon with the possibility of 12.g4!?) 12.exf6 ♖xf6 13.♘d2 ♗f5 (another interesting try is 13...a5!?, preventing b2-b4 and securing the safe c5-square for his knight) 14.g4 ♗d3 15.♗xd3 ♘xd3 16.♕c2 ♘c5 17.♖ae1 ♖f8=. White's position is seemingly more active, but all Black's pieces are well placed and his c6- and d5- pawns solidify his position. The game is approximately equal.

9...d4!?

This is a very interesting possibility for Black.

It is too risky to continue with 9...0–0 10.f5 d4 11.♗f4!±; with his last move White bolsters his pawn-centre.

It is quite sound for Black to continue with the popular line: 9...♘xd3 10.♕xd3 g6 11.♘c3 c6 12.♘e2 0–0 (After routine play by Black, White maintains a slight edge: 12...♗f5 13.♕d2 ♕d7 14.♘g3 0–0 15.♖ae1±. It might be interesting for Black to try to secure the blockading square f5 for his bishop: 12...h5!? 13.♖ad1 h4 14.h3 ♗f5⇄; White has been deprived of the g3-square for his knight, while if he attacks the enemy bishop on f5 with his knight from d4, Black will play ♗f5-e4.)

13.♘g3 (it would be premature for White to play 13.f5?! ♗xf5 14.♖xf5 gxf5 15.♗h6 ♔h8 16.♗xf8 ♗xf8 17.♖f1 ♕b6 18.♔h1 ♕xb2 19.♘d4 ♖e8∓; White does not have enough pieces left to organize an effective attack, while Black has already gobbled up a couple of pawns, Polgar – Gelfand, Khanty-Mansyisk 2009) 13...♗h4 (Black cannot halt the enemy f-pawn without exchanging his dark-squared bishop. After 13... h5 14.f5 h4, White's knight joins in the attack with 15.♘h5!!+- and Black is in big trouble. It is not good either to continue with 13... f5 14.exf6 ♗xf6 15.f5 gxf5 16.c3↑ and White has the initiative; and if 13...♕c7 14.f5 ♕xe5 15.♗d4 ♕c7 16.♖ae1→ White's attack is tremendously dangerous.) 14.♗c5 ♖e8 15.♔h1

15...b6! (Black does not yet need to defend against f4-f5 in radical fashion by playing 15... ♗xg3. He would prefer to trade his dark-squared bishop for its white counterpart, or not exchange it at all. After 16.♕xg3 ♗f5 17.c3 h5 18.h3 ♔h7 19.♔h2 b6, Adams – Gelfand, Plovdiv 2010, White could maintain an edge with 20.♗d6!±, penetrating into the enemy camp with his bishop.) 16.♗d6 ♗e7! Black is reluctant to tolerate the enemy bishop on d6 for long, especially since after its exchange White will find it difficult to to advance with f4-f5. 17. ♗xe7 ♕xe7. Black has a good game, since f4-f5 is no longer a threat. For example, he can counter 18.♖ae1 with 18...a5! 19.♕d2 ♗a6 20.♖f3 f5∓. White's kingside play has been blocked, while Black is ready to gradually prepare to advance with c6-c5 and d5-d4, seizing the initiative.

10.♗f2 0–0

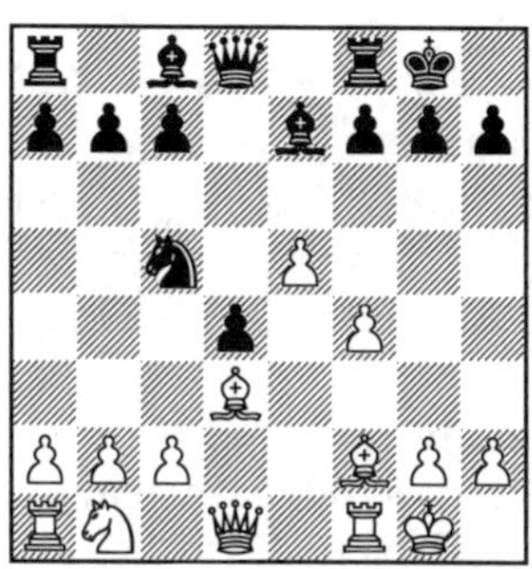

11.f5

White's pawns look beautiful, but they are not supported effectively by his pieces, so Black gains excellent counterplay.

An attempt by White to win the enemy d4-pawn by any means would not bring any benefit: 11. ♗c4 ♗f5 12.g4 ♗d7 (another interesting option is 12...♗e4!? 13.♘d2 b5 14.♗xb5 ♗b7≂ and Black has good compensation for the pawn, thanks to the weakened long diagonal in White's camp) 13.f5 ♘e4 14.♗xd4 ♗c6 15.c3 ♗h4↑; Black plans to use the g5-square for his queen or knight, and he also has the undermining move h7-h5 in reserve. Even though- White has an extra pawn his defence is very problematic.

11...♗g5!

Black's bishop is activated, evading the possible threat of f5-f6 in the process.

12.♘a3

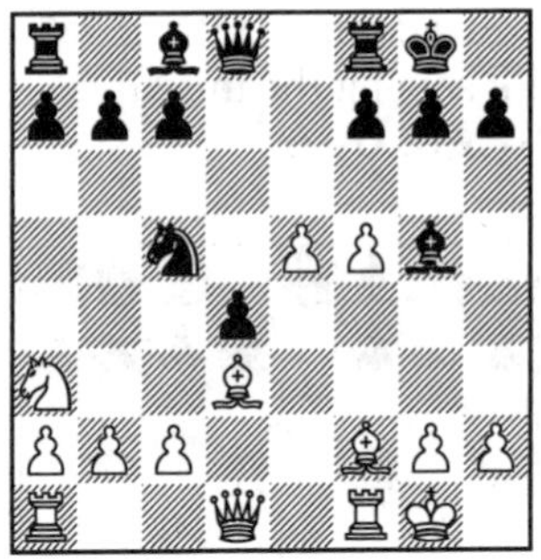

12...b6!?

Black could have played the even simpler 12...♕d5 13.♘b5 ♕xe5 14.♗g3 ♕e3 15.♔h1 ♘xd3 16.cxd3 ♗d7 17.♘xc7 ♖ad8 18.♘d5 ♕d2 19.♕xd2 ♗xd2 20.♗c7 ♖a8 (another interesting option is 20...♖de8!? 21.♗d6 ♖e2 22.♗xf8 ♔xf8≅ and in this position Black's domination compensates for the exchange) 21.f6 g5!=, and Black should be able to to hold the balance.

13.♕f3 ♗b7 14.♕g4 ♘xd3 15.cxd3 f6!? 16.h4 ♗h6 17.e6 c5∞

The position offers chances for both sides, since they both have their trumps for the coming struggle.

Conclusion

In this line, just as in the variations in which White captures on e5 with his pawn, preserving his knight on f3 from exchange, complicated, fighting positions arise in which Black has good prospects. The move 9...d4!?, which I believe is a very interesting possibility, deserves serious tests.

Chapter 13 1.e4 e5 2.♘f3 ♘f6 3.d4 ♘xe4 4.♗d3 d5 5.♘xe5 ♘d7 6.♘xd7 ♗xd7 7.0–0

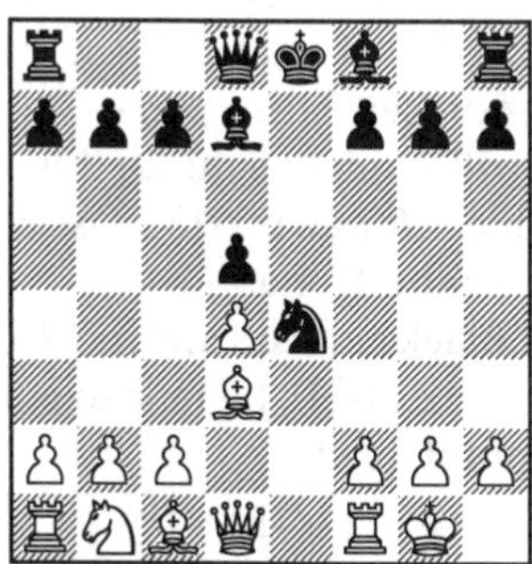

7...♗d6

This move is simple, natural and the best. Black only needs to castle to complete his development. White's task is to exploit the somewhat exposed position of his opponent's knight on e4 and to try to attack something, or to provoke some weakening move (such as f7-f5). We shall try to analyze all these possibilities, one by one.

I am not going to try to analyze all of Black's possibilities here, so I shall skip the famous theoretical line starting with 7...♕h4, followed by castling queenside, which is very risky for Black.

8.♕h5

The position becomes completely equal if White plays in primitive fashion with 8.♘d2 0–0 9.♘xe4 dxe4 10.♗xe4 ♗xh2 11.♔xh2 ♕h4 12.♔g1 ♕xe4 13.♖e1 ♕f5=

White's more popular options 8.♘c3 and 8.c4 will be analyzed in the next two chapters.

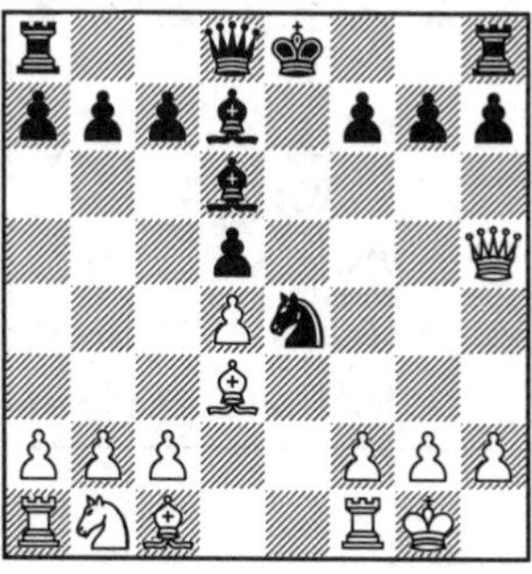

8...♕f6!

This is the most precise and forcing way for Black to equalize.

It is weaker for him to play 8...♘f6 9.♖e1 ♔f8± and his position is uncomfortable, since he has lost his castling rights.

9.♘c3

The alternatives lead to a draw:

9.♗e3 ♗f5 10.f3 g6 11.♕h6 ♗f8

12.♕f4 ♗d6= Iordachescu – Landa, Reggio Emilia 2006;

9.♕xd5 ♗c6 10.♕h5 (but not 10.♕c4?! 0–0–0↑ and Black's initiative is tremendously powerful) 10...♕xd4 11.♘d2 0–0 (capturing the pawn is too risky – after 11...♘xd2 12.♗xd2 ♕xb2?! 13.♖fe1 ♔f8 14.♕h4↑, although White has no direct threats, Black has lost his castling rights, and White's long-term initiative based on this is worth much more than a pawn) 12.♘xe4 ♗xe4 13.♗e3 ♕d5 14.♕xd5 ♗xd5=. There will hardly be any fight left in this position.

9...♕xd4

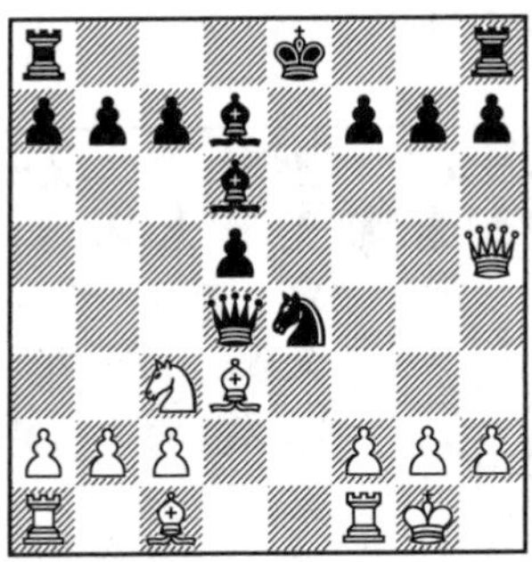

10.♗e3

10.♕xd5 ♕xd5 11.♘xd5 ♘c5=

10.♘xd5 ♗c6 11.♘e3 g6 12.♕h3

12...0–0! Whenever you don't know what to do, develop your pieces! This principle is quite appropriate in this position, because castling is Black's most reliable road to equality. 13.♘c4 ♘c5 (a good alternative is 13...♖fe8 14.♗e3 ♕f6 15.♘xd6 ♘xd6 16.c3 ♗e4=. Black's knight is headed for the f5-square) 14.♗e3 ♕f6 15.♘xd6 (15.♗e2 ♘e6 16.♘xd6 cxd6 17.c3 ♘f4 18.♗xf4 ♕xf4=. Black will soon seize the open e-file and this will compensate for his vulnerable d6-pawn.) 15...♘xd3 16.♘xb7 ♘xb2 17.♘a5 ♗e4=

If Black chooses any move other than 12...0–0, he fails to equalize completely:

12...♘g5 13.♕g4 ♕f4 (or 13...♕xg4 14.♘xg4 ♘e6 15.♖e1 0–0–0 16.♘e5± and White's bishop-pair will create long-term problems for Black) 14.♕xf4 ♗xf4 15.♘c4⩲ and White maintains some pressure, Deep Fritz – Kramnik, Bonn 2006;

12...♘c5 13.♖d1! (13.♗c4 ♗d7 14.♕f3 0–0–0 15.♖d1 ♕e5 16.g3 ♗e6=) 13...♘xd3 14.♖xd3 ♕e4 15.♗d2±.; White has a dangerous initiative on the dark squares.

10...♕e5 11.♕xe5 ♗xe5 12.♘xd5 ♘f6

(diagram)

13.♖ae1

This move is much trickier than 13.♖fe1 0–0=, when Black equalizes immediately, Tiviakov – Giri, Hoogeveen 2010.

13...♘xd5 14.♗d4

After 14.♗d2 f6 15.f4 ♘xf4

16.♗xf4 0–0 17.♗xe5 fxe5 18.♗c4 ♔h8 19.♖xf8 ♖xf8 20.♖xe5 ♖e8 21.♖xe8 ♗xe8 22.h4 h6 23.♔f2 g5 24.hxg5 hxg5 25.♔e3 ♔g7 26.♔d4 ♔f6=, although White's king is more active he cannot achieve much.

14...0–0–0 15.♗xe5

If 15.♖xe5 ♘f4 16.♖e7 ♘xd3 17.cxd3 ♗c6=

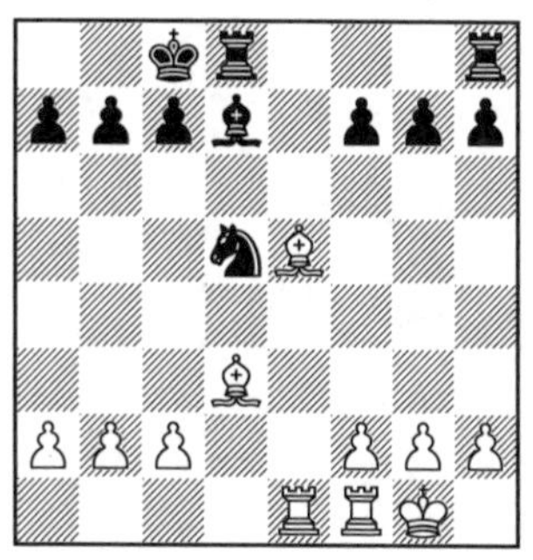

15...♘b4!

It is essential for Black to eliminate White's advantage of the bishop-pair quickly, and he can achieve this by means of some intricate tactics.

16.♗c4

Or 16.♗xg7 ♘xd3 17.cxd3 ♖hg8, followed by ♗d7-c6=

16...♘xc2 17.♖e2 f6 18.♗c3 ♗f5

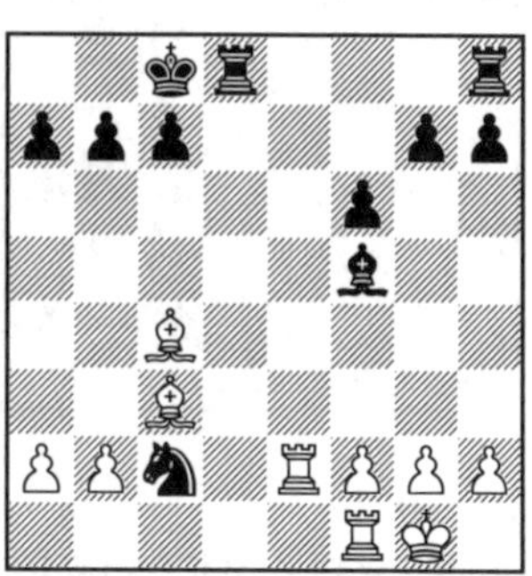

19.g4

Black also equalizes convincingly after White's other options:

19.♖e7 ♖d7 20.♖xd7 ♔xd7 21.♖d1 ♔e7 22.♖c1 c5 23.g4 ♗g6 24.♗b3 ♘d4 25.♗xd4 cxd4 26.♖c7 ♔d6 27.♖xb7 ♖e8∓. Black's d-pawn is so powerful that White must worry about maintaining equality.

19.♖c1 ♘d4 20.♖e7 g5!=; White has some compensation for the pawn, but only enough to keep the balance.

19...♗g6 20.f4

If 20.♖c1 ♘d4 21.♖e7 ♖he8 22.♖xg7 ♖e4 23.h3 ♘f3 24.♔g2 ♖xc4 25.♔xf3 ♖d3 26.♔g2 b5=

20...♘d4 21.♖e7 ♖he8 22.♖xg7 f5 23.g5

Or 23.♗xd4 ♖xd4 24.b3 a6 25.a4 ♖ee4=

23...♘e2 24.♔g2

24.♗xe2 ♖xe2 25.♖f2 ♖xf2 26.♔xf2 ♖d7 27.♖g8 ♖d8=

24...♘xc3 25.bxc3 ♖e4 26.♗g8 ♖d2 27.♖f2 ♖xf2 28.♔xf2 ♖xf4 29.♔g3 ♖g4 30.♔f3

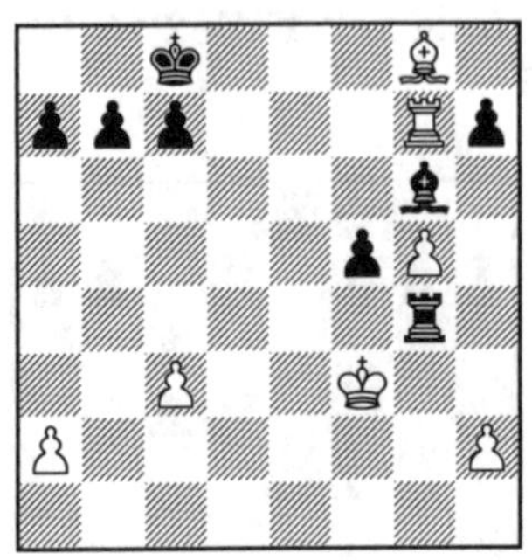

30...b5!

In this way Black plans to create a passed pawn on the queenside.

It is less precise for him to play 30...♖xg5 31.♗e6 ♔d8 32.♖d7 ♔e8 33.♖xc7±, and White has a slight edge, although the most probable result of the game is a draw.

31.♗xh7 ♗xh7 32.♖xh7 ♖xg5 33.h4 ♖g4 34.h5 ♖h4 35.♔g3 ♖g4 36.♔h3 ♖g1 37.h6 f4 38.♔h4 f3 39.♖f7 ♖h1 40.♔g5 ♖g1 41.♔h5 ♖h1 42.♔g6 ♖g1=. White is forced to repeat moves, because if he moves his king to h7 he might even lose.

Conclusion

The move 8.♕h5 leads to simplification and complete equality. Naturally, the most likely result will be a draw if both sides play correctly.

Chapter 14 1.e4 e5 2.♘f3 ♘f6 3.d4 ♘xe4 4.♗d3 d5 5.♘xe5 ♘d7 6.♘xd7 ♗xd7 7.0–0 ♗d6 8.♘c3

In this variation Black must play accurately to equalize.

8...♘xc3

It would be too risky for Black to play here 8...♕h4 9.g3 ♘xc3 10.bxc3 ♕h3 (after10..♕g4 11.♖e1± Black loses his castling rights and is thus faced with a long and rather unpleasant defence) 11.♖b1! 0–0–0 12.c4 dxc4 13.♕f3 c6 14.♗xc4↑ and White's initiative is very dangerous, Zhigalko – Li Chao, Puerto Madryn 2009.

9.bxc3 0–0 10.♕h5

This is the idea of the move 8.♘c3. White allows his c-pawns to be doubled, but provokes an important positional weakeness in the enemy camp. Black's f5-pawn will not only restrict his bishop but also weaken the e5-square, which might be very unpleasant for him if he is unable to prevent the disadvantageous exchange of the dark-squared bishops.

For 10.♖b1 b6 11.♕h5 f5 – see 10.♕h5.

10...f5

11.♖b1

11.♖e1 c6 (Black is close to equality after 11...♕f6 12.♕f3 ♕f7! 13.♗f4 ♖ae8, Korneev – Khenkin, Drezden 2007.) 12.♗g5 (White does not achieve much with 12.c4 ♕f6 13.c3 ♖fe8 14.♗g5 ♕f7 15.♕xf7 ♔xf7= Rozentalis – Harikrishna, Germany 2008.) 12...♕c7 13.c4 (it is a draw after 13.♗e7 ♖fe8 14.♗xf5 ♗xh2 15.♕xh2 ♕xh2

16.♔xh2 ♗xf5= Balogh – Yusupov, Bastia 2004) 13...♗e8

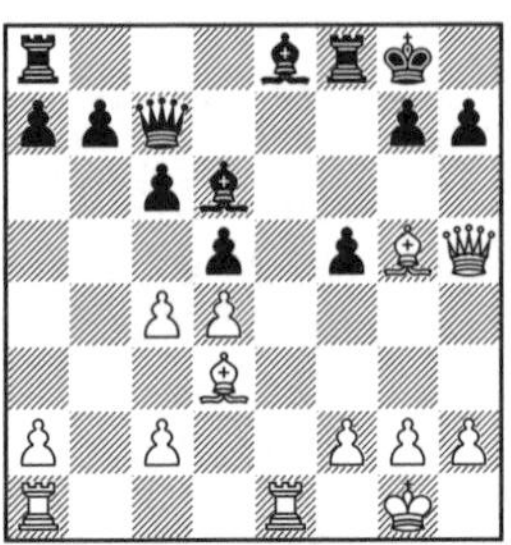

14.♕h4 dxc4 15.♗xc4 ♗f7 16.♗d3. Here it is imprecise for Black to play 16...♗g6, Dominguez – Gelfand, Bermuda 2005. White can continue with 17.c4!±, keeping a slight edge. It is much stronger for Black to bravely play 16...g6!, without being afraid of ghosts. His kingside pawn-structure is quite harmonious and after 17.♗f6 ♖fe8= White cannot exploit the slight weakening of the dark squares in Black's camp.

14.♕h3 dxc4 15.♗xc4 (The position is equal after 15.♗xf5 h6 16.♗e6 ♗f7 17.♗xh6 gxh6 18.♕xh6 ♗xh2 19.♕xh2 ♕xh2 20.♔xh2 ♗xe6 21.♖xe6 ♖xf2 22.♖e7, draw, Vachier Lagrave – Gelfand, Khanty-Mansyisk 2009.) 15...♗f7 16.♗e6

16...♗xe6 (Here 16...g6 is less precise. Even though it is harmless for Black if White now plays 17.♖e2 ♖fe8 18.♖ae1 ♖xe6 19.♖xe6 ♗xe6 20.♖xe6 ♕b6 21.g4 ♕xd4 22.gxf5 ♗c5= Mamedyarov – Gashimov, Kallithea 2008, after 17.c4!± instead, Black has to play very precisely to equalize, if indeed that is now possible.) 17.♖xe6 ♖ae8 18.♖ae1 ♖xe6 19.♖xe6. In the game Zhigalko – Stupak, Minsk 2010, after 19...♕d7 20.♕b3± White gained an edge, but Black could have equalized convincingly with the move 19...♕b6!=, exploiting the vulnerability of his opponent's back rank.

11...b6

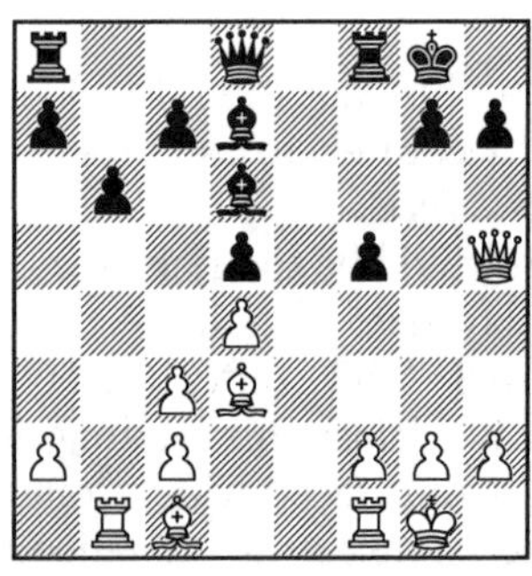

12.♖e1

If 12.♗g5 ♕e8 13.♕f3 ♕g6 14.♗f4 ♗xf4 15.♕xf4 ♕d6 16.♕xd6 cxd6 17.c4 ♗e6 18.cxd5 ♗xd5 19.c4 ♗e4= Korneev – Landa, Casablanca 2005.

12...c6 13.♗g5

If 13.c4 ♕f6=

13...♕c7 14.c4 ♗e8

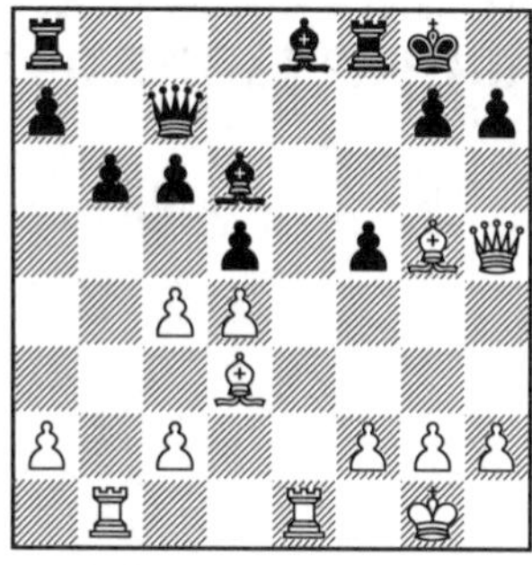

15.♕h3

Black can counter 15.♕f3 with 15...dxc4! (Unnecessary complications arise after 15...♗f7 16.♕xf5 g6 17.♕h3 dxc4 18.♗e4±) 16.♗xc4 ♗f7 17.♗xf7 ♖xf7 18.h3 ♕d7=, preparing to move his rook to e8, after which the position will be further simplified.

15...dxc4

Black can also repulse the enemy bishop first with 15...h6 16. ♗d2 dxc4 17.♗xc4 ♗f7, not fearing the line 18.♗d3 ♗xa2! 19.♖a1 ♗d5! 20.c4 ♗e4 21.♗xe4 fxe4 22.♖xe4 ♕f7=. Black's outside passed-pawns on the queenside are potentially very dangerous, so his prospects are not at all inferior.

16.♗xf5

After 16.♗xc4 ♗f7 17.♗e6 ♗xe6 18.♖xe6 ♖ae8 19.♕b3 (After 19. ♖be1 ♖xe6 20.♖xe6 ♕d7 21.♕b3 ♖f7= Black's plans will include the pawn-advance b6-b5, advantageously stabilizing the pawn-structure. This should fully compensate for White's piece-activity.) 19...♖xe6 20.♕xe6 ♖f7 21.♕e8 ♖f8 22.♕e6 ♖f7=, draw, Shirov – Kramnik, Casorla 1998.

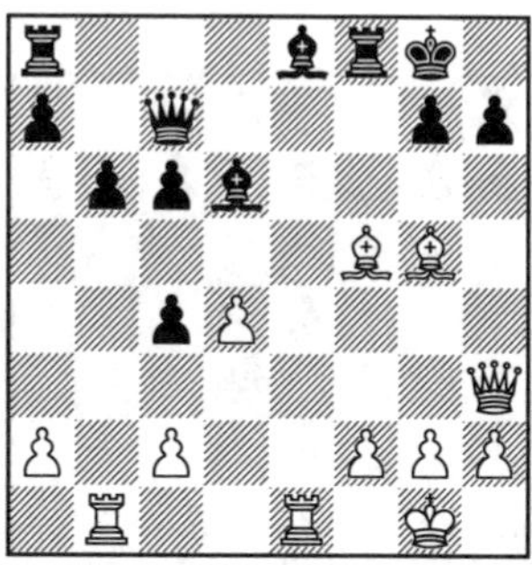

16...h6!

It is weaker for Black to play 16...g6 17.♗g4± when the position is rather complicated but White's chances are preferable, Vachier Lagrave – Gelfand, Khanty-Mansyisk.

17.♗e6 ♗f7 18.♗xh6 gxh6 19.♕xh6 ♗xh2 20.♕xh2 ♕xh2 21.♔xh2 ♗xe6 22.♖xe6 ♖xf2 23.♖xc6 ♖xc2 24.♖c7 ♖f8 25. ♖xa7 ♖f6=. The material on the board has been almost annihilated, so the position should be a draw.

Conclusion

There were times when the move 8.♘c3 was the cause of serious worries for devotees of the Petroff Defence. Nowadays I do not see any difficultes for Black in achieving equality, but you can scarcely hope for more than that, since most of the variations are quite drawish.

Chapter 15 1.e4 e5 2.♘f3 ♘f6 3.d4 ♘xe4 4.♗d3 d5 5.♘xe5 ♘d7 6.♘xd7 ♗xd7 7.0–0 ♗d6 8.c4

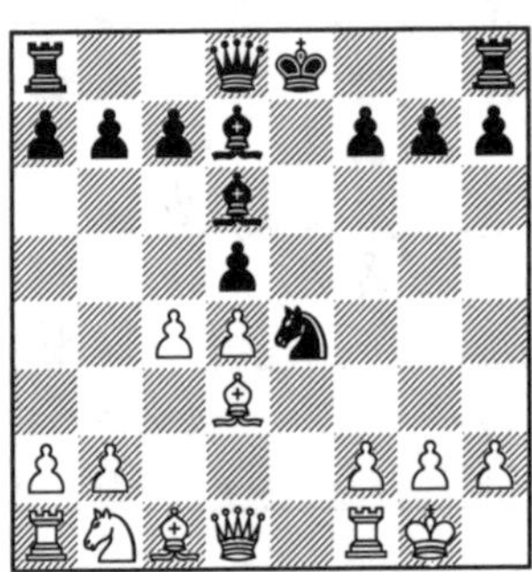

This is the most popular move for White in recent years and it creates the most problems for Black.

8...c6 9.cxd5

The variation 9.♘c3 0–0 10. cxd5 ♘xc3 11.bxc3 cxd5 transposes to the main line.

9...cxd5 10.♘c3

Previously White used to play 10.♕h5 0–0 11.♕xd5 ♗c6 12.♕h5 g6 13.♕h3 (The move 13.♕h6 is senseless, because the queen is misplaced there and after 13...♖e8 Black has the useful extra possibility of moving his bishop to f8.) 13...♘g5!

(diagram)

and Black has excellent compensation for the pawn, for example:

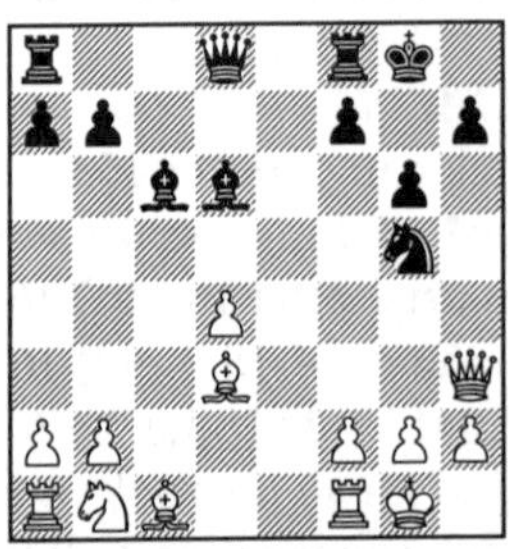

14.♗xg5 ♕xg5 15.♘c3 ♖fe8 (It is slightly less precise for Black to play 15...♖ae8 16.♖ad1 ♖e7 17.d5 ♗d7 18.♘e4 ♖xe4 19.♕xd7 ♕e7 20.♕xe7 ♖xe7= and White's edge is only symbolic, Wedberg – Pe. H.Nielsen, Sweden 2000.) 16.d5 ♗xd5 17.f4 ♕d8 18.♘xd5 ♗c5 19. ♔h1 ♕xd5 20.♖ac1, Shirov – Kramnik, Cazorla 1998. Black can continue here with 20...♖e3 21.♗c4 ♕d4=, solving all his problems.

After 14.♕g4 Black plays 14... ♘e6

and now:

15.♘c3 h5∓;

15.♗e3 h5 16.♕h3 ♘f4 17.♗xf4 ♗xf4 18.♘c3 ♕xd4 19.♘e2 ♕f6 20.♘xf4 ♕xf4∓;

the move 15.♗h6 can be countered with the spectacular shot 15...♗f4!! 16.♗xf8 (Or 16.♗xf4 ♕xd4 17.♘c3, Holzke – Schandorff, Germany 2001, and now after 17...h5! and White would have serious problems to solve, for example: 18.♕g3 ♘xf4 19.♖fd1 ♕f6 20.♗f1 ♖ad8∓ – Black's pieces are considerably more active.) 16...♕xd4∓; all White's pieces are hanging and although Black has a material deficit, he has the advantage.

15.d5! (This is the only move after which White may feel more or less confident.) 15...♗xd5 16.♘c3 ♗c6 (Here 16...h5!? is worth considering.) 17.♗h6 ♖e8 18.♖ad1 ♕b6 (after 18...♕c7, Black must reckon with 19.♘b5±) 19.♗xg6 ♗xh2 20.♔xh2 hxg6 21.♖d2 ♖ad8=

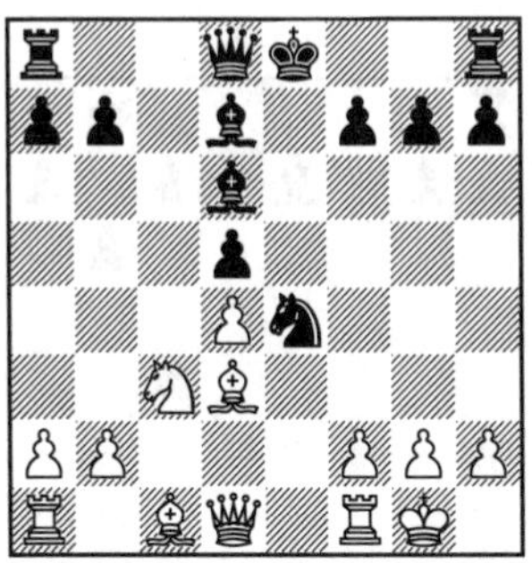

10...♘xc3 11.bxc3 0–0 12.♕h5 g6

The move 12...f5 weakens the e5-square and after 13.♕f3 ♔h8 14.♗f4± White maintains a stable advantage.

13.♕xd5 ♕c7

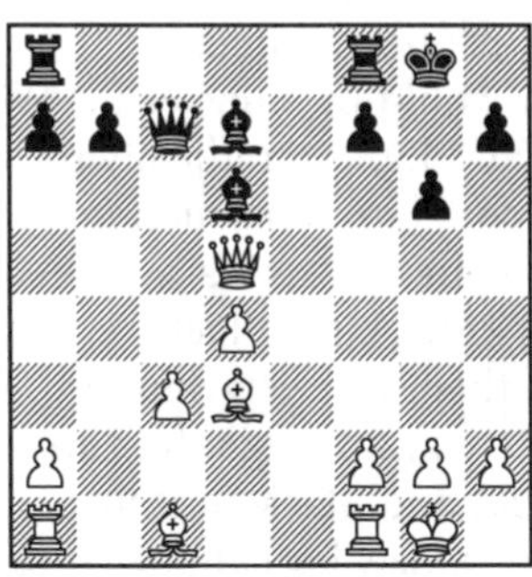

We shall analyze now **A) 14.c4** and **B) 14.♗h6**.

For 14.h4 ♗e6 15.♕f3 ♕xc3 16.♗h6 ♖fd8 – see 14.♗h6 ♖fd8 15.h4 ♗e6 16.♕f3 ♕xc3.

If 14.♕f3 ♕xc3 15.♗h6 (if 15.♕f6, then Black saves the day with 15...♕c6! 16.♗g5 ♖fe8 17.♖ac1 ♖e6 18.♖xc6 ♖xf6= Grigoriants – Motylev, Krasnojarsk 2007), Black can reply with 15...♖fd8 16.♕f6 ♗f8 17.♗xf8 ♖xf8 18.♗e4 ♗c6, as well as with 15...♖fe8 16.♕f6 ♗f8 17.♗xf8 ♖xf8 18.♗e4 ♗c6 and in both cases there is a transposition to the variation 14.♗h6 ♖fd8 15.♕g5 ♕xc3 16.♕f6 ♗f8 17.♗xf8 ♖xf8 18.♗e4 ♗c6.

White's kingside initiative after 14.h3 ♗e6 15.♕f3 ♕xc3 is unpromising. He will have to seek active play on the queenside, but this will only be sufficient for equality and no more. After 16.♖b1 ♗xa2 (it is a draw after 16...♕xd4

17.♗e4 ♕e5 18.g3 ♗xh3 19.♗b2 ♕g5 20.♕c3 f6 21.♖fd1 ♗e5 22.♕c4 ♔h8 23. ♗xe5 ♕xe5 24.♖xb7 ♖ac8 25.♕d5 ♕xd5 26.♖xd5=, but this is unnecessarily complicated) 17. ♖xb7 ♕xd4 18.♗b2 ♕f4=, and the draw is unavoidable.

It would be smarter for White to play 14.g3, to radically prevent the possible construction of his opponent's batteries ♗d6-♕e5, or ♗d6-♕f4, but Black equalizes even then. 14...♗e6 (here 14...♗h3 fails to 15.♖d1 ♗g4 16.♗h6 ♖fd8 17.♖dc1 and Black ends up a pawn down, since he cannot continue with 17...♗xg3 owing to 18.♕g5! – White is threatening ♕f6 and Black's bishop on g4 is hanging.) 15.♕f3 ♕xc3 16.♖b1 ♕xd4 17.♗e4 ♕c4

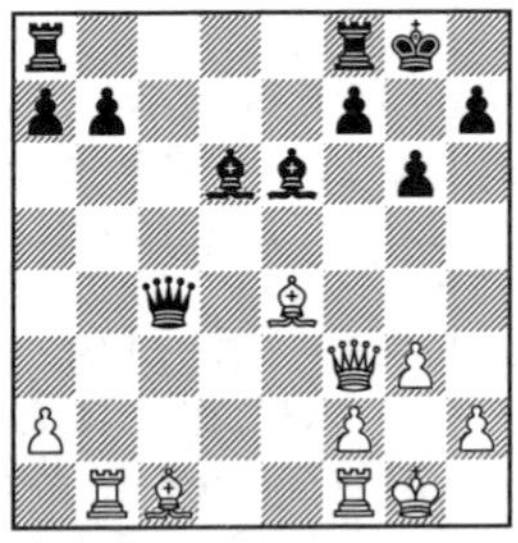

and now:

18.♖xb7 ♖ae8! (it is less precise for him to opt for 18...♖ab8 19.♕f6 ♗h3 20.♖e1 ♕e6 21.♕xe6 fxe6 22.♖e3 ♖xb7 23.♗xb7 a5± and here White is slightly better, but this will hardly provide him with any meaningful winning chances, Vallejo Pons – Gelfand, Leon (rapid) 2010). Now, after 19.♗h6 ♗c8 20.♗xf8 ♖xe4 21.♕xf7 ♕xf7 ♖xf7 ♗xf8 23.♖xa7, or 19. ♗b2 ♗h3 20.♗d3 ♕e6 21.♖a1 ♗e5, the drawish outcome of the game is unavoidable;

White has another insidious possibility here in 18.♗b2, when Black should parry his opponent's threats on the long diagonal, not with 18...♗e7, because of 19.♖fc1 ♕xa2 20.♖c7 ♗d8 21.♖xb7+– and the difference in activity of the pieces is so great that he is beyond salvation, Negi – So, New Delhi 2011, but with 18...f6! 19.♖fd1 ♗e5!=, equalizing;

The other possibility for White here is 18.♗xb7 ♖ad8 19.♗h6 ♖fe8 20.♖fc1 ♕g4 21.♕xg4 ♗xg4 22. ♗e3 ♗a3! – Black uses his bishops to force White's rook to leave the back rank and then he exploits this weakness – 23.♖c3 ♗f5 24. ♖b5 ♖d1+ 25.♔g2 ♗d6 26.♗xa7 ♗d3=; Black is ready to give perpetual check with his bishops from the f1- and e2- squares.

A) 14.c4

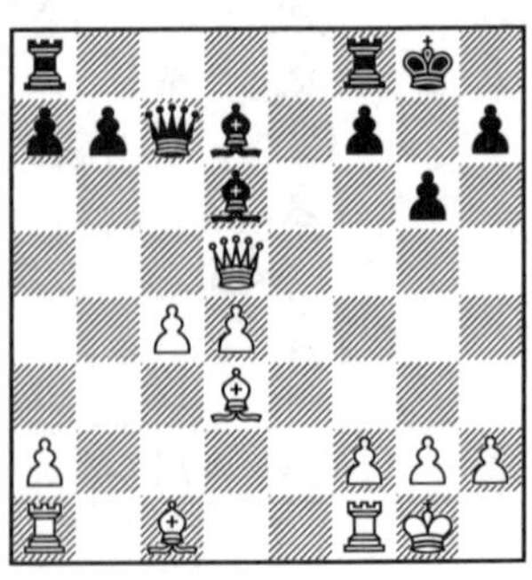

14...♗c6!

14...♗e6 15.♕f3 ♗xc4 16.♗h6 ♖fd8 (16...♖fc8 17.♖fc1 b5 18.a4±, Volokitin – Maslak, Rijeka 2010; 16...♖fe8 17.♖fc1 b5 18.g3± Anand – Ivanchuk, Calvia 2004) 17.♖fc1 b5, Anand – Shirov, Wijk aan Zee 2007. Here White could have continued with 18.g3!±, with the plan of a2-a4, and this would have increased his advantage (in the game he played 18.a4 ♕e7 19.♗xc4 bxc4 20.♖xc4 ♕h4 21.♕h3 ♕xh3 22.gxh3 ♖ac8 23.♖ac1 ♖xc4 24.♖xc4 f5± and Black managed to hold this rather unpleasant endgame).

15.♕g5 ♗xh2 16.♔h1 ♗d6 17.♗b2

17.♗d2 ♖fe8 18.♖ae1 ♗e7 19.♕f4 ♗d6 20.♕h4 ♗e7 21.♗g5 ♗xg5 22.♕xg5 ♕d6 23.d5 ♗d7=.

17.d5 ♖ae8 18.♗b2 ♗e5 19.♗xe5 (19.♕d2 ♗d7 20.♖fe1 b6=) 19...♖xe5 20.♕g3 ♗d7 21.♖ae1 ♖fe8=

17...♖ae8

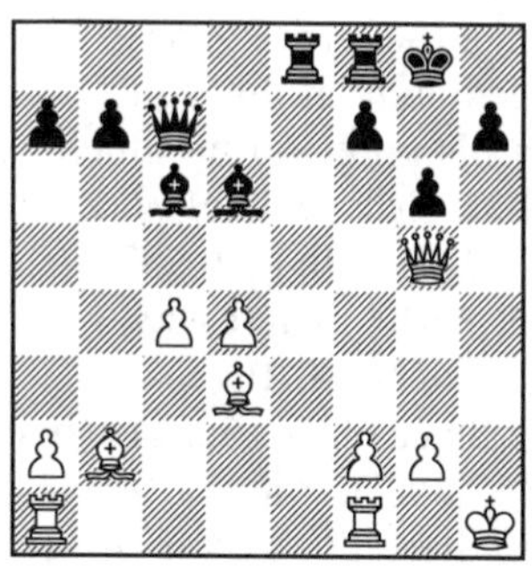

18.♖ae1!

This is the correct rook for White to place on e1; if the f1-rook goes there it will be hanging with check once Black's queen goes to the a5-square.Thus the line: 18.♖fe1 f6 19.♕h6 (or 19.♕h4 ♕a5∓) allows 19...♕a5! 20.♖xe8 ♖xe8 21.♔g1 ♖e1 22.♖xe1 ♕xe1 23.♗f1 ♗xg2 24.♔xg2 ♕e4= with a draw by a perpetual check.

18...f6!

White played less strongly in the game Yakovenko – Gelfand, Sochi 2009, which continued 18...♕d8 19.♕xd8 ♖xd8 20.d5±. White's bishop goes to f6 after which Black has some serious problems.

19.♕h6

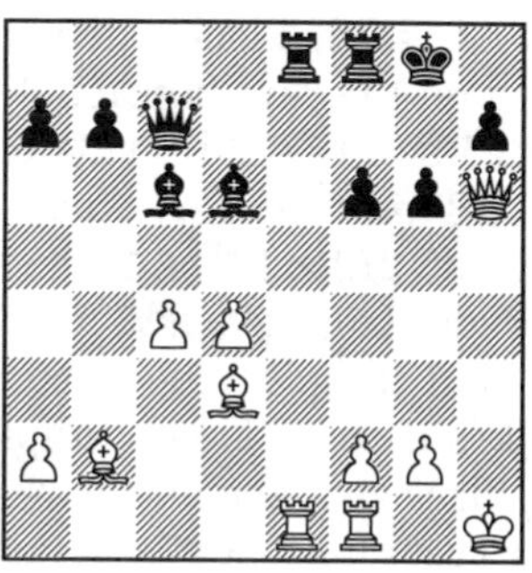

19...♖xe1!

It is essential for Black to exchange all the rooks and this is the point of his idea on move 18. In the game Korze – Helbich, ICCF 2008, Black tried to harass his opponent's queen but after 19...♗f4 20.♕h4 ♗g5 21.♕g4 ♗d7 22.♕f3± White gained an edge.

Black cannot solve his problems with the move 19...♕a5, because after 20.♖xe8 he is forced to recapture with 20...♗xe8, giving up the e-file (He cannot play 20...♖xe8 because of 21.d5; now you can see why White moved his a1-

rook rather than his f1-rook to e1.). Now after the simple move 21.a3± White keeps his powerful centre intact and thus retains a slight but very stable advantage.

20.♖xe1 ♖e8! 21.♖xe8 ♗xe8

Now, after the rooks have disappeared off the board, White's connected pawns are not at all dangerous and can be easily blockaded.

B) 14.♗h6 ♖fd8

It is less convincing, but still probably sufficient for a draw, to play 14...♖fe8. Black's defence is based on the variation 15.h4 ♗e6 16.♕g5 ♕xc3 17.♖fd1 (17.♕f6 ♗f8 18.♗xf8 ♖xf8 19.♗e4 ♖ad8 20.♖fd1 ♗d5 21.♖ac1 ♕b4 22.h5 ♕d6 23.♕xd6 ♖xd6 24.♗xd5 ♖xd5 25.h6, and despite the fact that White's h-pawn is very unpleasant, Black should manage to draw with accurate defence, Rausis – Studnicka, Decin 2009.) 17...♕xd4 18.♗xg6 ♕e5 19.♗e4 ♕xg5 20.♗xg5 ♗e5=. Black's king is rather exposed, but with so little material left on the board Black should be able to save the game.

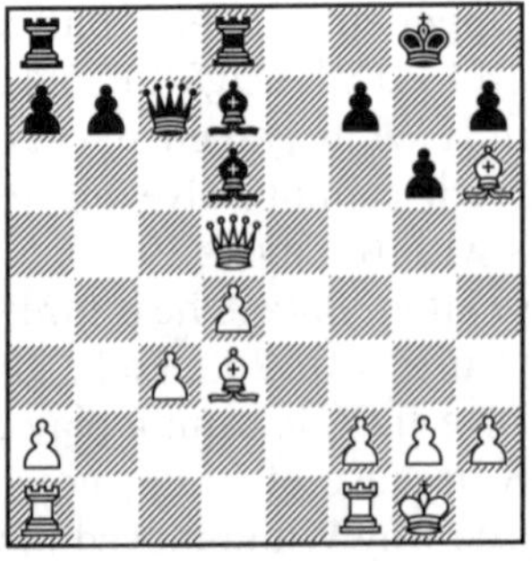

Here, White has a choice between **B1) 15.♕g5** and **B2) 15.h4.**

For 15.♕f3 ♕xc3 16.♕f6 ♗f8 – see 15.♕g5 ♕xc3 16.♕f6 ♗f8.

B1) 15.♕g5 ♕xc3

Black is quite close to equality after 15...♗xh2 16.♔h1 ♗d6 17.c4 ♗f8 18.♗xf8 ♖xf8= Guseinov – Kramnik, Baku 2009.

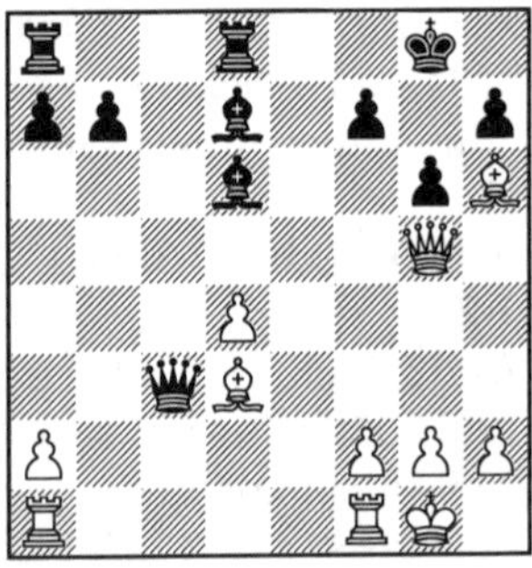

16.♕f6

After 16.♖fd1 Black has the resource 16...♗f8!; Black should exchange the dark-squared bishops immediately if he can, because then his king will be much safer. 17.♗xf8 ♖xf8 18.♖ac1 ♕b2 19.♗c4 ♖ac8 20.h4 ♕b4 21.♗b3 ♖xc1 22.♕xc1 ♕d6= Rublevsky – Wang Yue, Ningbo 2010.

If Black plays 16...♗a4 (instead of 16...♗f8!), then after 17.♖ac1 ♕a3? (here 17...♕b4 is better, but after 18.♖c4 ♗xd1 19.♖xb4 ♗xb4 20.♕b5± Black still has problems to worry about) 18.♖c7!±, and White has a clear advantage, Rublevsky – Volokitin, Poikovsky 2008.

16...♗f8 17.♗xf8 ♖xf8 18. ♗e4

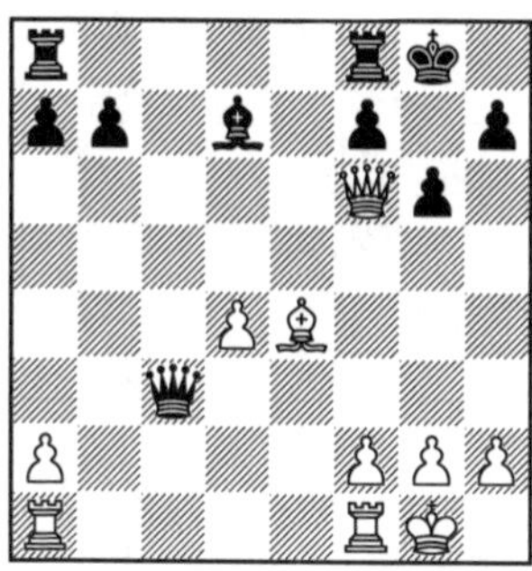

Here the easiest way for Black to save the draw is the move:

18...♗c6!

It is fair to say that Black should be able to hold the position even with the passive line: 18...♖ab8 19.♖ac1 (19.♖ab1 b6 20.♖bc1 ♕a5 21.♖c7 ♗e6=; 19.♖fc1 ♕a5 20.h4 ♖fe8 21.♕f4 ♗e6 22.♖ab1 ♖bd8 23.♗xb7 ♗xa2 24.♖a1 ♕b6 25.♖xa2 ♕xb7=) 19...♕a5 20.h4 ♖fe8 21.♖c5 ♕d2 22.♖c7 ♖e6 23.♕f3 ♕xd4 24.♖d1 ♕xe4 25.♕xe4 ♖xe4 26.♖dxd7=, draw.

19.♖ac1

White does not change anything with 19.♖fc1 ♕b2 20.♖cb1 ♕c3 21.♖c1=, draw, So – Gelfand, Amsterdam 2010.

(diagram)

19...♕b4

Here there is a more attractive way for Black to save the day: after 19...♕a5 20.♗xc6 bxc6 21.♕xc6 ♕xa2 22.d5, White's d-pawn looks very powerful, but Black's passed pawn can also advance: 22...a5! 23.d6 a4 24.♖fe1 (24.d7

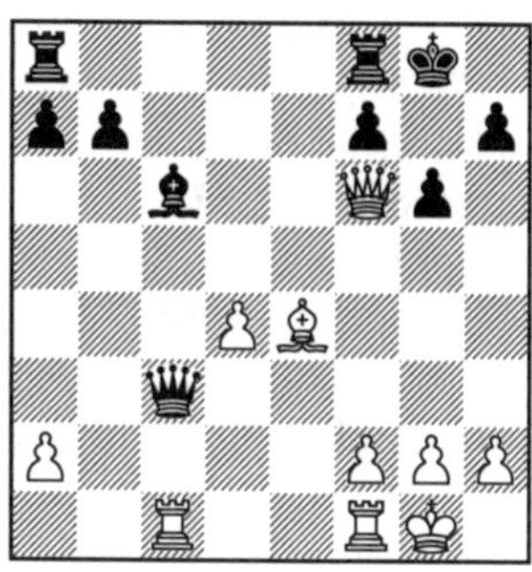

♕e6=) 24...a3 25.d7 ♕d2 26.♖cd1 ♕a5 27.♖e8 ♖d8 28.♕c8 a2=. It all ends with the exchange of the critical pawns on d7 and a2 and a draw.

20.♗xc6 bxc6 21.♖xc6 ♖ad8 22.♖a6 ♕xd4 23.♕xd4 ♖xd4 24.♖xa7 ♖c8=. Black's rook will go to the c2-square, after which White will not be able to hold on to his a-pawn, Tiviakov – Kramnik, Wijk aan Zee 2007.

B2) 15.h4 ♗e6

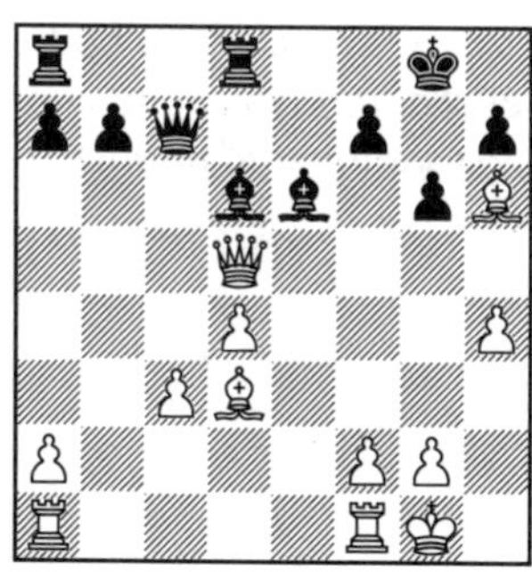

16.♕g5

Black has no problems after 16.♕f3 ♕xc3 17.♗g5 ♖d7, for example: 18.♗f6 ♗d5 19.♕e3 ♕c6

20.♕g5 ♗f8 21.♖ac1 ♗h6 22.♗b5 ♕xc1 23.♕xc1 ♗xc1 24.♗xd7 ♗h6=, followed by ♗g7.

16...♕xc3 17.♖fd1

It would be a blunder for White to continue with 17.♕f6? in view of 17...♕xd4! 18.♕xd4 ♗h2 19.♔xh2 ♖xd4∓ and he ends up a pawn down for nothing, Zakhartsov – Maslak, Irkutsk 2010.

17...♗f8

Black loses after 17...♗a3 18.♗xg6! hxg6 19.♕f6 ♗f8 20.♗xf8 ♔xf8 (20...♖xf8 21.h5 ♔h7 22.♖ac1+–) 21.♖ac1 ♕a5 22.d5 ♗xd5 23.h5! gxh5 (White was threatening 24.hxg6, as well as 24.h6!) 24.♖e1 ♔g8 25.♕g5 ♔f8 26.♕h6 ♔g8 27.♖e5+–

18.♗xf8

(diagram)

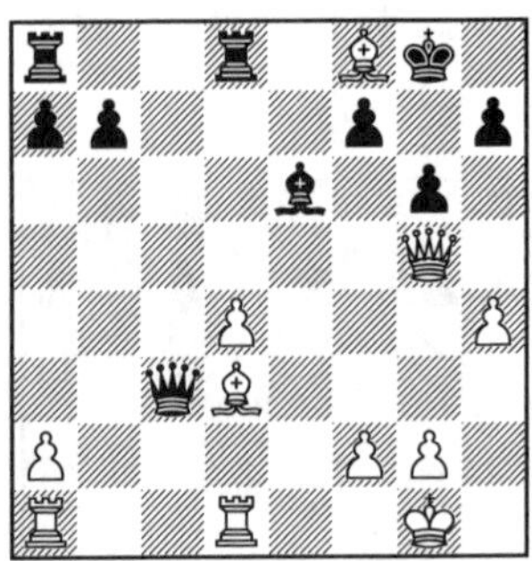

18...♔xf8!

Here it would be inaccurate for Black to play 18...♖d5 19.♕f6 ♖xf8 20.♗e4± since his rook comes under attack with tempo, Anand – Kramnik, Nice 2009.

19.♕h6 ♔g8 20.h5 ♖xd4 21.♖ac1 ♕b2 22.♖b1 ♕c3 23.♖bc1=. It ends in a draw by repetition (it would be senseless for White to try 23.hxg6 hxg6 24.♗xg6 ♖xd1 25.♖xd1 ♕g7∓ – the endgame is even slightly better for Black).

Conclusion

The variation beginning with the move 8.c4 is very tricky and requires very precise play by Black. If he is well-prepared however and has several improvements up his sleeve in various well-known variations, as shown and analyzed in this chapter, he has nothing to worry about.

Part 4

1.e4 e5 2.♘f3 ♘f6 3.♘xe5

The Petroff Defence 3.♘xe5

The move 3.♘xe5 is White's most popular choice. After that, White can try many different systems but the abundance of all kinds of rarely played options should not be a cause of worry for Black. Nevertheless, he must be very well prepared against one particular line, namely **3.♘xe5 d6 4.♘f3 ♘xe4 5.d4 d5 6.♗d3 ♗e7 7.0–0 0–0 8.c4 ♘b4 9.♗e2 0–0 10.♘c3 ♗f5 11.a3 ♘xc3 12.bxc3 ♘c6 13.♖e1 ♖e8 14.cxd5 ♕xd5 15.♗f4 ♖c8**

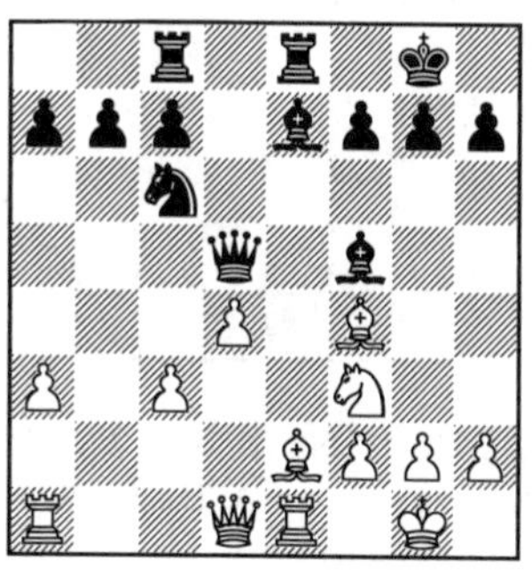

Here he must be ready to counter a multitude of alternatives for White.

White's other possible continuation, **5.♘c3 ♘xc3 6.dxc3 ♗e7 7.♗e3,**

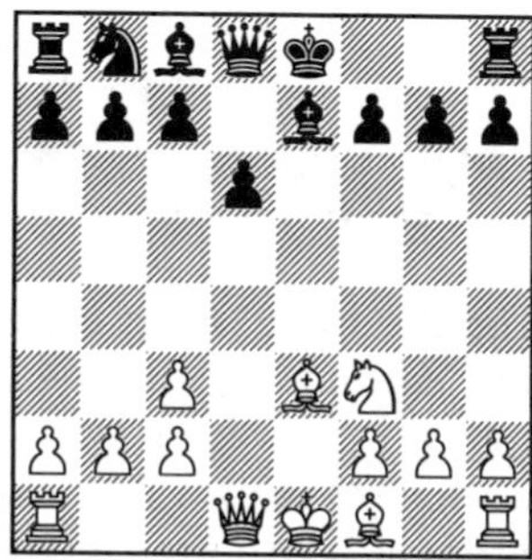

will no doubt continue its theoretical and practical development. Black has no reason to be afraid of playing 7...0–0, since the ensuing fight, with opposite sides castling, offers him rich and promising prospects.

Chapter 16 1.e4 e5 2.♘f3 ♘f6 3.♘xe5 d6 4.♘xf7?!

Cochrane Gambit

The Cochrane Gambit was invented as long ago as the 19th century. There were times when such attempts to provoke an early crisis on the board were terrifying to Black. Nowadays, in the computer age, professional chess players only smile condescendingly at such romantic experiments. In fact, the correct reaction in this case is for Black to play actively and avoid keeping his pieces on the last two ranks, since that might well end in disaster.

4...♔xf7 5.d4

The stupid move 5.♗c4 leads to a situation in which White is almost immediately lost! This is the truth – I am not joking! 5...d5! 6. exd5 (After 6.♗b3, Black's most precise reaction would be 6...c5!. He has a material advantage and seizes the initiative! 7.d3 ♘c6 8. ♘c3 c4! 9.dxc4 dxe4 10.c5 ♔g6–+ – White has no compensation for the piece and Black should win. It is no better for White to choose 7.exd5 ♕e8 8.♕e2 ♕xe2 9.♔xe2 ♗d6–+ – his pieces are discoordinated and he will lose his d5-pawn.)

6...♗d6 (Black has a good alternative here in 6...♕e8 7.♗e2 c6!. This is all done for the sake of the quickest possible development! 8.dxc6 ♘xc6 9.0–0 ♘d4 10.♗c4 ♗e6 11.♖e1 ♕c6 12.♗xe6 ♘xe6 13.d4 ♖e8–+) 7.0–0 ♖f8 8. h3 ♔g8–+; Black has extra material and good chances for a kingside attack.

5.♘c3. This is an insidious move, which White must play anyway. The idea is that he does not allow his pawn-centre to be immediately undermined.

5...c5! It is essential for Black to control the central squares, since under the cover of his pawns he can develop his pieces to active positions (The passive move 5...c6 enables White to advance his pawn-chain a long way in the centre: 6.d4 ♗e7 7.f4 ♖f8 8.e5 ♘d5 9.♕h5 ♔g8 10.♗d3 g6 11.♗xg6 hxg6 12.♕xg6=, with a draw by perpetual check, Heberla – Grabarczyk, Lublin 2008.). 6.♗c4 ♗e6 7.♗xe6 ♔xe6 8.d4 ♔f7 9.dxc5 ♘c6∓ and the game transposes to our main-line game – Topalov – Kramnik, Linares 1999.

5...c5!

(diagram)

6.dxc5

If 6.♗c4 d5 7.exd5 it is very good for Black to continue with 7...b5! 8.♗e2 (it is even worse for White to play here 8.♗xb5 ♕xd5 9.0–0 ♗b7 10.f3 ♕xd4 11.♕xd4 cxd4–+) 8...♗b7 9.dxc5 (9.0–0 ♕xd5 10.♗f3 ♕d7–+) 9...♗xc5

10.0–0 ♕xd5 11.♕xd5 ♗xd5 12.♗xb5 and White's drawing chances are absolutely minimal, for example: 12...a6 13.♗d3 ♘bd7 14.♘c3 ♗e6–+

6...♘c6 7.♗c4 ♗e6 8.♗xe6 ♔xe6

9.♘c3

9.0–0 ♔f7 10.♕e2 (White's queen can go to d3 and from there it may be transferred to b3 or to b5, but it will come under attack: 10.♕d3 ♕d7 11.♖d1 ♕e6 12.cxd6 ♘b4! 13.♕b5 ♗xd6 14.♘c3 ♖ad8 15.♗f4 ♗xf4 16.♕xb4 b6–+; Black wins beautifully in the variation 14.c3 ♘c2 15.♖xd6 ♖hd8!–+) 10...♕e8 11.♖e1

11...♕e6! (this is stronger than 11...d5 12.e5 ♘e4 13.♘c3 ♘xc3, Short – Shirov, Dubai 2002, **game 10**. White can continue here with 14.♕f3 ♔g8 15. ♕xc3 b6 16.♗e3⩱, obtaining sufficient compensation for the piece.) 12. ♘c3 ♖d8! (Black should refrain from 12...dxc5, since after 13.e5 ♘d4 14.♕d3⩱ White retains some compensation for the knight.) 13.♗g5 (If 13.♖d1 ♗e7! 14.cxd6 ♗xd6∓ Black is clearly better) 13... dxc5 14.e5 h6 15.♗xf6 (Black's position is preferable after 15.♗h4 g5 16.♗g3 ♘d4 17.♕d3 ♘h5–+) 15...gxf6 16.f4 (16.♕h5 ♔g7 17. exf6 ♕xf6 18.♖ad1 ♗e7–+ and Black parries the attack while retaining the extra piece) 16...f5!∓; Black's blockade is secure and the extra knight should tell.

9...♔f7!

The king is not the best fighting unit when the board is full of pieces, so this modest retreat is Black's best move.

10.♕e2 ♕d7

Black's queen on the d-file prevents White from castling queenside.

It is weaker for Black to opt for 10...♕e8 11.♗e3 dxc5 12.0–0–0 and White has compensation for the piece.

11.♗e3

11.cxd6 ♗xd6 12.0–0 ♖ad8 13.♗e3 ♗e5∓

After the pseudo-active move 11.♗g5, Black can force his opponent to enter an endgame: 11... ♕g4 (White's plans would be justified after 11...dxc5 12.♗xf6 gxf6 13.♘d5 ♖g8 14.0–0–0 ♕g4 15.f3 ♕e6 16.f4⩱) 12.♕xg4 (12.♕c4? d5! 13.♘xd5 ♕xe4–+) 12...♘xg4 13. 0–0–0

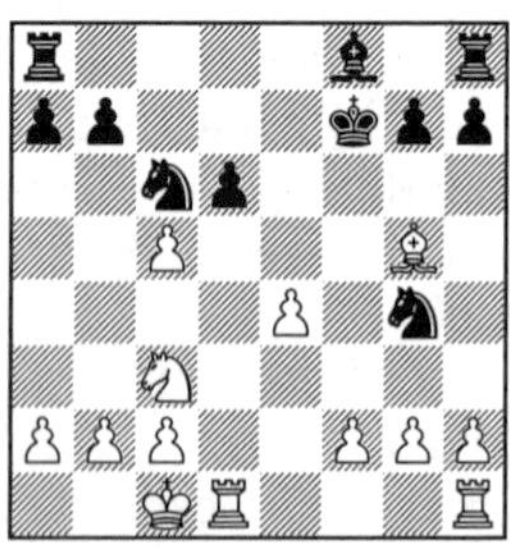

13...h6! Black plays actively and does not necessarily hold on to his material (after 13...♔g6 14. ♗h4 dxc5 15.h3 ♘f6 16.f4 ♗e7 17. e5 ♘d5 18.♖xd5 ♗xh4∞ a very unclear position arises, in which

Black's king is exposed to various rather unpleasant checks). 14.♗h4 g5 15.♗g3 dxc5 16.♖d7 ♔e6 17.♖xb7 ♗d6 18.♘d1 ♖ab8 19.♖xb8 ♗xb8 20.♗xb8 ♖xb8 21.h4 ♘ce5 22.hxg5 hxg5 23.f3 ♘f6∓. The material left on the board has been considerably reduced and the most likely outcome is a draw. However, only Black can play for a win here, since his piece-formation in the centre is very strong.

11...dxc5 12.f4

After 12.0–0 Black has the resource 12...♕e6, defending against the check from the c4-square and removing his queen from the d-file in the process.

12...♘d4!N

It is weaker for Black to opt for 12...♖e8, Topalov – Kramnik, Linares 1999 (**game 11**).

13.♗xd4 cxd4 14.0–0–0

White's position is even worse after 14.♕c4 ♕e6 15.♕xd4 ♖c8–+

14...♖c8 15.e5

After the prophylactic move 15.♔b1 Black has enough time to consolidate his forces: 15...♗c5 16.e5 ♖he8 17.♘e4 ♘xe4 18.♕xe4 ♔g8∓ and now 19.c3 fails to 19...♗b6 20.cxd4 ♖c4–+

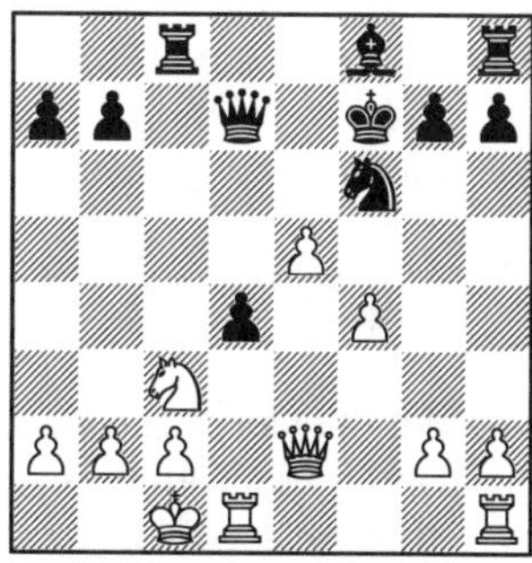

15...♖xc3 16.bxc3 ♗a3 17.♔b1 ♘d5 18.♔a1 ♕c6∓ – Black has an overwhelming advantage.

Conclusion

The Cochrane Gambit is not sound and if Black plays precisely White cannot obtain sufficient compensation for the sacrificed piece.

Chapter 17 1.e4 e5 2.♘f3 ♘f6 3.♘xe5 d6 4.♘c4

Paulsen Attack

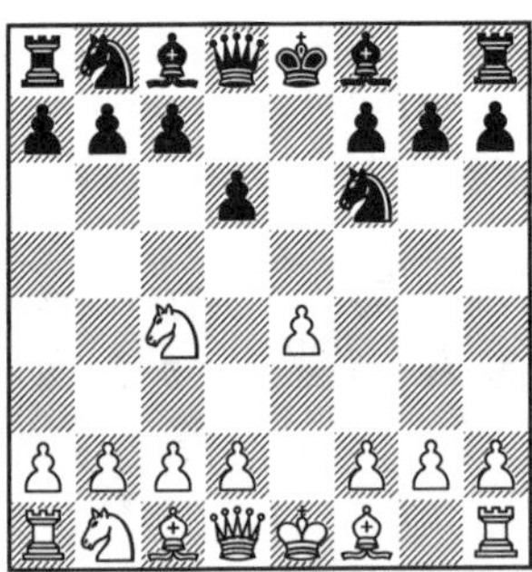

Just like the Cochrane Gambit which we analyzed in the previous chapter, this rather awkward retreat of the knight originated during the 19th century. It was invented by Louis Paulsen, one of the most famous players of the time. White's knight on c4 is restricted by Black's pawn on d6 and has no good prospects, so the entire variation can be evaluated as quite original but in fact completely harmless to Black.

4...♘xe4

White has three logical possibilities in this position: **A) 5.♘c3**, **B) 5.♕e2** and **C) 5.d4**.

A) 5.♘c3 ♘xc3 6.bxc3

After 6.dxc3, Black's simplest reaction is 6...d5 7.♘e3 (if 7.♘e5 Black can attack this knight with tempo: 7...♗d6) 7...♗e6 8.♗d3 ♗c5 9.0–0 0–0=

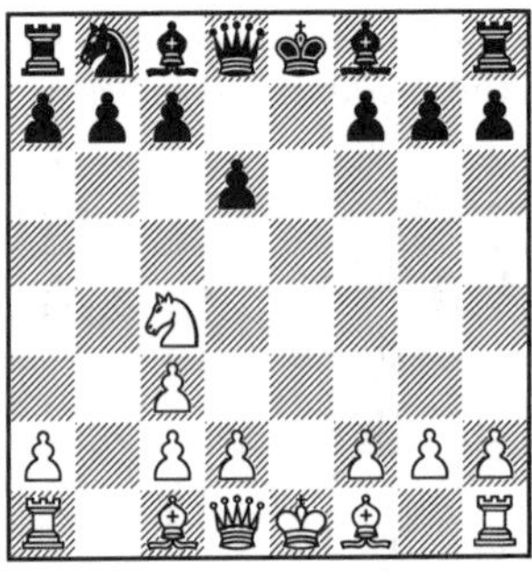

6...g6

Black is trying to create a complicated position. A line sufficient for equality is 6...d5 7.♘e3 c6 8.d4 ♘d7 9.c4 (for 9.♗d3 ♘f6 10.0–0 ♗d6 11.c4 0–0 – see 9.c4) 9...♘f6 (Black should refrain from 9...♗b4?! 10.♗d2 ♕a5 11.cxd5 cxd5, Khairullin – Andreikin, Serpukhov 2003, because White can continue with 12.♗d3 0–0 13.♖b1 ♗xd2 14.♕xd2 ♕xd2 15.♔xd2±, maintaining a great advantage) 10.c3 (if 10.cxd5 Black continues with 10...♘xd5!, preserving the flexibility of his pawn-structure) 10...♗d6 11.♗d3 0–0 12.0–0 ♗e6=. Both sides have completed the mobilization of their forces and have no pawn weaknesses. The position is approximately equal.

7.d4

An attack along the h-file would obviously be premature, so Black should not be afraid of 7.h4. He should continue calmly with his development: 7...♗g7 8.h5 0–0 9.♘e3 ♘d7∓. White's pieces are discoordinated and Black has easy and effective play in the centre and on the e-file, Bertok – Bajec, Sarajevo 1951.

7...♗g7 8.♗d3 0–0 9.0–0

It would be rather adventurous for White to try 9.h4 ♖e8 10.♔f1, Inarkiev – Chadaev, Olginka (rapid) 2011. Here Black can strike a powerful counter-blow with 10...d5! 11.♘e3 (11.♘e5 ♘d7 12.f4 h5∓) 11...c5 12.h5 ♘c6∓ and his action in the centre is much more effective than White's attack on the flank.

9...♘d7

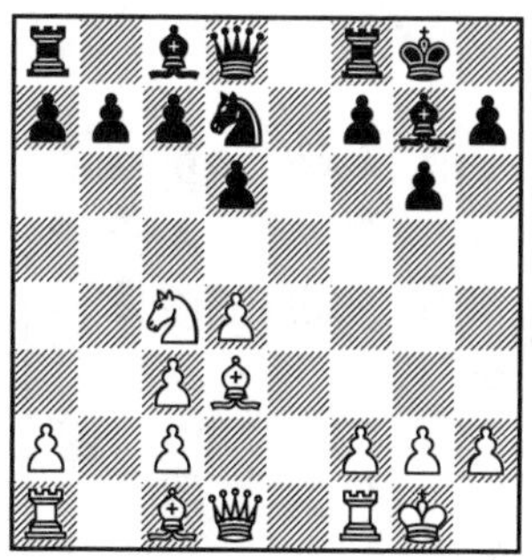

We should now examine the risky move **A1) 10.f4** as well as **A2) 10.♕f3**.

A1) 10.f4 ♘b6 11.♘e3 ♘a4! 12.♗d2 ♘b2

The move 12...c5 can lead to complications, but Black does not need to go in for them. 13.f5 cxd4 14.cxd4 ♗xd4 (after 14...♘b2 15.♕f3 ♘xd3 White has the intermediate move 16.f6!±) 15.♔h1 ♘b2 16.♕g4 ♗xe3 (after 16...♕f6 White can play 17.♘d5 ♕e5 18.♗e4 ♘c4 19.♖ad1→) 17.♗xe3 ♘xd3 18.cxd3 ♕a5 19.♗d4 ♗xf5 20.♕g5 f6 21.♗xf6 ♖f7∓. It looks as though White is unable to exploit the weakened long diagonal in his opponent's position, but there is still tension on the board and Black's defensive task is far from easy.

13.♕f3 ♘xd3 14.cxd3

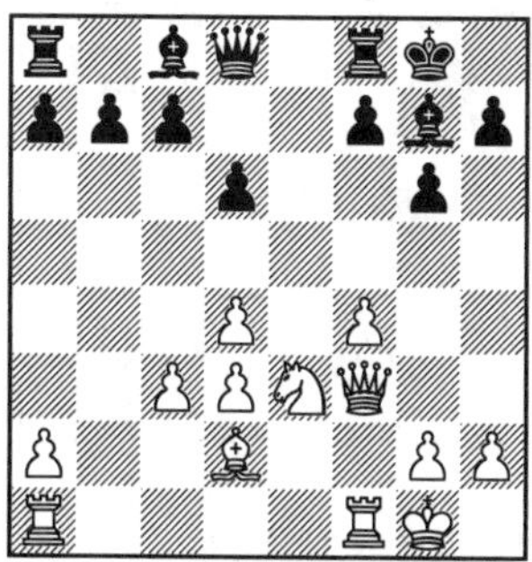

14...c5!

It is considerably weaker to play the immediate 14...f5, not because of 15.d5, which is obviously bad, since it reduces the scope of White's own queen: 15...♗d7 16.♖ab1 ♖b8∓ Ovetchkin – Motylev, Sochi 2004 (**game 12**), but because of 15.♕d5+ ♔h8 16.♖ae1 c6 17.♕b3=. White wants to play d4-d5 and c3-c4, after which he will have the rather unpleasant positional threat of exchanging the dark-squared bishops from the c3-square. Meanwhile, White also has good prospects of dominating the e-file.

15.d5 f5∓. Now White can only dream about the exchange of the dark-squared bishops on the long diagonal. Black plans to seize additional space on the queenside and after the preparatory move ♗c8-d7 he would like to continue with b7-b5. His slight but stable edge is not in doubt.

A2) 10.♕f3

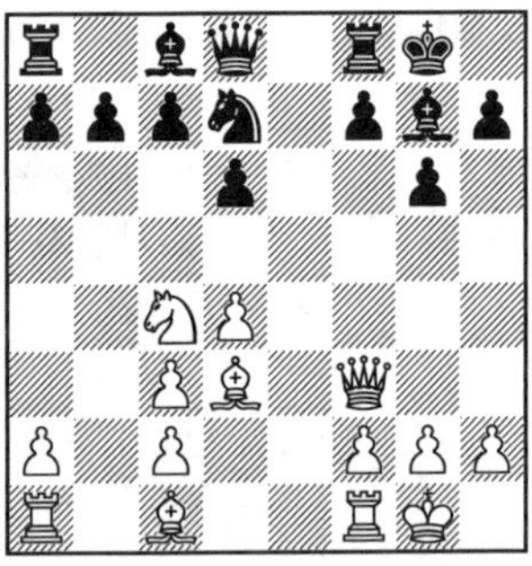

10...♘b6 11.♖e1

The move 11.♘e3 is a bit too slow and Black can immediately exploit this with 11...c5! 12.dxc5 dxc5 13.a4 ♗d7! (Computer programs recommend here 13...♗xc3 14.♖a3 ♗b4, but White's compensation, after 15.♖d1 for example, seems quite real from the human point of view.) 14.a5 ♘a4 15.♕xb7 ♘xc3 16.♗d2 ♗e6∓. Black's pieces are much more active, Carlsen – Kramnik, Nice 2008 **(game 13)**.

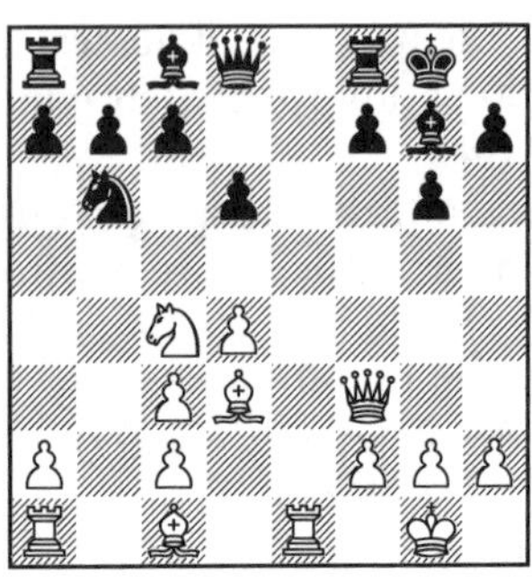

11...♗e6!

Black solves all his problems with this temporary pawn-sacrifice. Black's other moves do not develop pieces and enable White to preserve his piece-activity. This position was reached once in a game between computers and it continued with: 11...c5 12.♗f4! d5 13.♘d6! cxd4 14.cxd4 ♗xd4 15. ♖ab1, when White's compensation for the pawn was more than sufficient, "Rybka" – "The Baron", Leiden 2008.

12.♘xb6 axb6 13.♕xb7 ♖a5 14.♕f3 ♗xa2∓

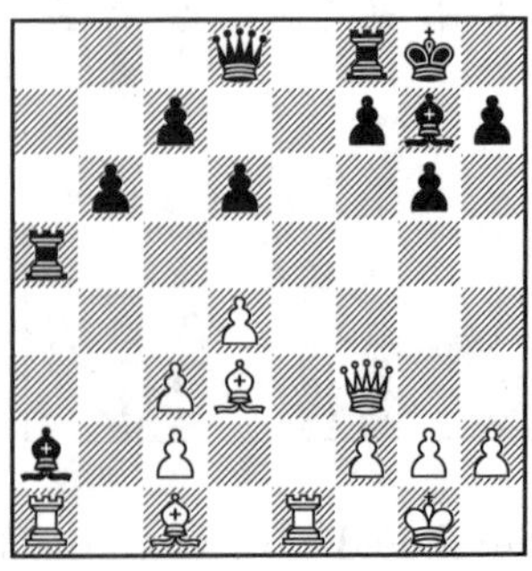

Black's position is slightly preferable, thanks to his superior pawn-structure.

B) 5.♕e2

5...♕e7 6.♘e3

It is harmless for White to play 6.d3 ♘f6 7.♗g5

and now:

after the timid line: 7...♕xe2 8.♗xe2 ♗e7± White has a slight edge;

Black has also tried 7...♗e6, which seems to me to be a bit artificial. It is a well-known principle in chess to try to develop first the knights and then the bishops. After 8.♘c3 ♘c6 9.0–0–0 h6 10. ♗xf6 (Black's idea can be best seen in the variation 10.♗h4 ♘d4 11.♕d2 g5 12.♗g3 ♗g7, with an excellent position.) 10...♕xf6 11. d4!? (in the game Ljubojevic – Hort, Bugojno 1980, White continued with 11.♘d5 ♕g5 12.♘ce3 and the opponents agreed a draw, in view of the sample variation 12...♘d4 13.♕e1 ♗xd5 14.h4 ♕e5 15.♘xd5 0–0–0=) 11...♘xd4 12. ♕e4 ♘c6 13.♘d5 ♕d8 14.♘ce3$\overline{\overline{\infty}}$ White has excellent compensation for the pawn;

7...♘c6! This is Black's best response. He should not be afraid of his pawns being doubled on the f-file, because then he seizes the initiative and obtains the advantage of the bishop-pair. 8.♘c3 (He has no need to fear 8.♗xf6 gxf6 9.♕xe7 ♘xe7 10.♘c3 ♗e6=, because then his bishop goes to h6 and Black begins to fight for the initiative.) 8...♘d4

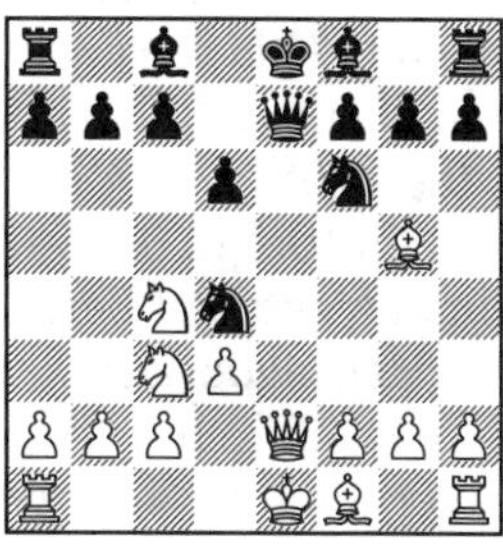

Black's knight is perfectly placed on d4 and he forces his opponent to exchange queens, gaining tempi for development in the process. 9.♗xf6 gxf6 10.♕xe7 ♗xe7 11.♘e3 c6=. The position is approximately equal. Black's main strategic task is to prevent by all means the exchange of the light-squared bishops, because then White would maintain a clear advantage thanks to the excellent f5-outpost for his knight.

6...c6

It is inferior for Black to play 6...♘f6. He should not move his knight away from the centre, since it is not under any attack. 7.♘c3!, V.Todorovic – Stefanova, Singapore 1990. White wishes to capture on d5 with his knight at some point. (Black can counter the creative move 7.b3 with activity in the centre: 7...♘c6 8.♗b2 ♗e6 9.g3 d5 10.♗g2 0–0–0∓ with a slight advantage, Berg – Pe. Nielsen Helsingor 2009, **game 14**) 7...♗e6 8.g3 ♘c6 9.♗g2, reaching a very interesting position which has not yet been thoroughly analyzed. It looks as though White's game is the more pleasant.

7.♘c3

The move 7.c4 weakens the d4-square and Black can highlight this immediately with 7... g6!. There might follow for example: 8.g3 ♗g7 9.♗g2 0–0 10.0–0 ♖e8 11.♘c3 ♘g5∓ Balogh – Gross, Austria 2009.

7...♘xc3 8.bxc3 ♘d7 9.g3 g6=. The prospects for both sides are approximately balanced, Stevic – Sakaev, Budva (blitz) 2009.

C) 5.d4 d5 6.♘e3 ♕f6

This move enables Black to create some disharmony in White's camp.

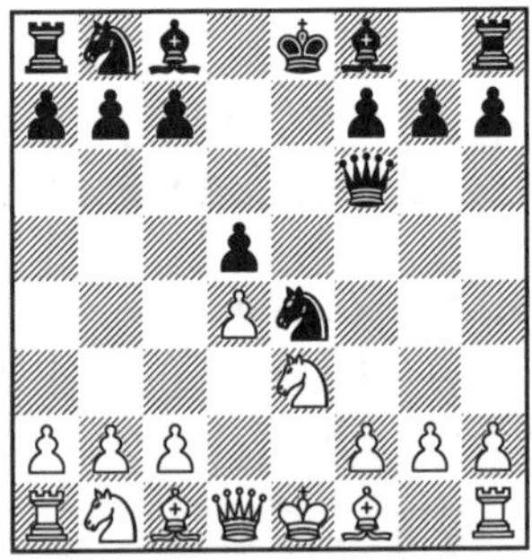

We shall now analyze **C1) 7.♗b5** and **C2) 7.♕e2**.

An amateur player might well continue here with 7.f3?!, but after 7...♕h4+ 8.♔e2 Black has the grandmasterly reply 8...♕f2+! (White would still have some counterplay after the "pseudo-masterly" response 8...♘g3 9. hxg3 ♕xh1 10.♘xd5 ♗d6 11.♔f2 0–0 12.♘bc3⇄) e.g. 9.♔d3 ♘c6! 10.fxe4 dxe4 11.♔c3 ♗e6∓ and Black's attack is tremendously dangerous.

C1) 7.♗b5+ c6 8.0–0

This idea looks interesting, but the concrete variations indicate that the complications should end in Black's favour.

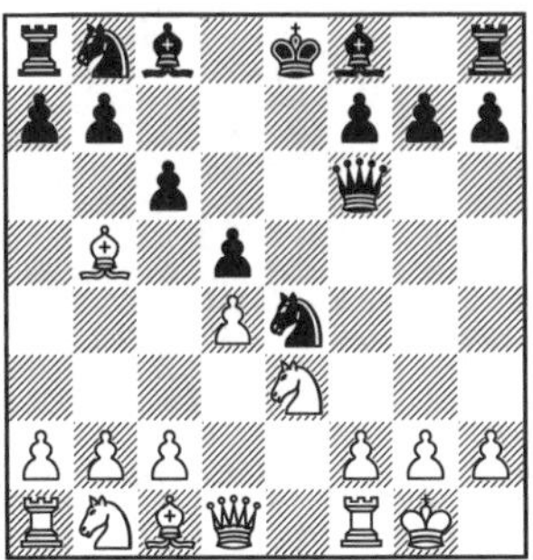

8...cxb5

Black should not be afraid to capture the piece, and in fact he must do so, since after the unprincipled move 8...♗d6 9.♘xd5, Black would end up a pawn down.

9.♘xd5 ♕d8 10.♖e1 ♕xd5 11.♘c3 ♕d8

12.♖xe4

After the spectacular move 12.♗g5, Black can react resolutely with 12...♕xg5! 13.♘xe4 ♕g6 14.♘f6 ♔d8 15.♖e8 ♔c7 16.♘d5 ♔d7 17.♕e2 ♕d6 18.♕g4 (White's attempt to complicate matters with the move 18.c4 fails to the cold-blooded response 18...bxc4–+) 18...f5 19.♕xf5 ♔xe8 20.♕xc8 ♔f7 21.♕xb7 ♘d7 22.♕xa8 ♕xh2 23.♔xh2 ♗d6–+, with a decisive advantage for Black in the endgame.

12...♗e7 13.♗g5

13.♕e2 0–0! (or 13...♗f5 14.♕xb5 ♕d7 15.♖xe7! ♔xe7 16.♘d5 ♔d8 17.♕a5 ♔c8 18.♗f4 ♘c6! 19.♘b6 ♔d8 20.♕a3 axb6 21.♕xa8 ♕c8 22.♕a3 ♕d7 23.♕a8 ♕c8= with a repetition of moves) 14.♖xe7 ♘c6 15.♖e3 ♘xd4 16.♕d3 ♗f5 17.♘e4 ♘e6∓, with advantage to Black.

13...♘c6!

It is much worse to play 13...f6 14.♗xf6 gxf6 15.♕h5 ♔f8 16.♖ae1 ♘c6 17.♘d5 h6 18.♘xe7 ♘xe7 19.♖xe7 ♕xe7 20.♖xe7 ♔xe7 21.♕xb5 b6± and although the most likely result would be a draw, Black will need to fight for it.

14.♕e2

After 14.♗e7 ♘xe7 15.♕e2 a6 16.♖e1 ♗e6 17.d5 ♘xd5 18.♖d1 0–0 19.♘xd5 ♗xd5 20.♖e5 ♕a5 21.♖exd5 ♕xa2∓ Black can play for a win without risking anything.

14...f6 15.d5

The move 15.♗xf6 would not lead to a draw by perpetual check: 15...gxf6 16.♕h5 ♔f8 17.♕h6 ♔f7 18.♕h5 ♔g7–+ and Black's king squeezes out the enemy queen.

15...♘e5 16.♖d1 0–0

Black has a good alternative here in 16...♗g4, for example: 17. f3 b4! 18.d6 bxc3 19.dxe7 ♕b6+ 20.♗e3 ♕c6∓ and he has the advantage, or 17.♖xg4 ♘xg4 18.d6 fxg5 19.♘xb5 ♘f6∓ and there arises a position in which White has some compensation, but he cannot really hope for more than a draw.

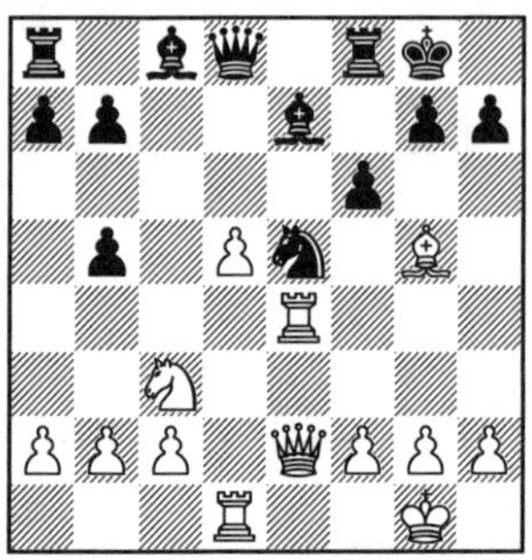

17.d6 ♗xd6 18.♘xb5 ♗f5 19.♖e3 ♘d3! 20.g4 ♗g6 21. ♖exd3 ♗xd3 22.♕e6 ♔h8 23. ♘xd6 ♗g6 24.♗e3 ♕c7∓ and Black maintains some advantage, mostly owing to the fact that White has weakened his position with the move g2-g4.

C2) 7.♕e2

(diagram)

7...♗e6 8.c3

If 8.♘d2, then after 8...♕xd4

9.♕b5 ♘d7 10.♕xb7 ♖b8 11.♕xc7 ♗d6 12.♕c6 0–0 13.♘xe4 dxe4 14.c3 ♕e5 15.♘c4 ♗xc4 16.♕xc4 ♘c5↑ Black has a very dangerous initiative.

8...♘d7

Or 8...c6 9.♘d2 (9.g3 ♘d7 10. ♗g2 0–0–0 – see 8...♘d7) 9... ♘xd2 10.♗xd2 ♘d7 11.g3 ♗d6 12. ♗g2 0–0 13.0–0=, with complete equality.

It is possible for Black to play here 8...♘c6 9.♘d2 0–0–0 10.g3 (White should not play 10.♘xd5? ♘xc3! 11.♘xc3 ♘xd4→ and Black's attack is decisive. And it would be over-optimistic for White to opt for 10.♘xe4?! dxe4 11.g3, B. Savchenko – Linchevski, St.Petersburg 2008, since Black can counter this with 11...♖xd4! 12.♗g2 ♖d8 13.♗xe4 ♕e5 14.♗xc6 bxc6 15.♕a6 ♔b8 16.♕xc6 ♗c8! 17.0–0 ♗b7 18.♕c4 ♗c5↑, with a dangerous initiative.)

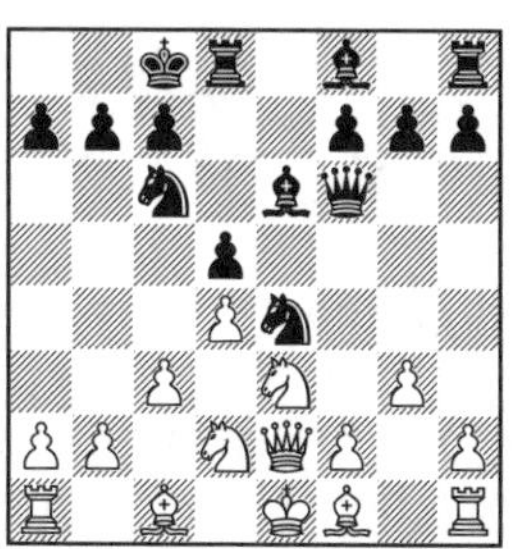

10...♘d6!N I particularly like this move. 11.♗g2 ♘e7!∓, leaving the c1-bishop obstructed by its own pieces and removing the knight from the c6-square, since it has already completed its mission there.

Black could also continue in direct fashion with 10...♘xd2 (instead of 10...♘d6) 11.♗xd2 h5=, reaching a position with a dynamic balance on the board, Smagin – Makarichev, Moscow 1990. Black has a slight lead in development, but he must keep in mind that his knight on c6 is restricted by White's pawn-chain c3 – d4 and is not very harmoniously placed.

9.g3

Black can counter 9.♘d2 with 9...0–0–0.

(diagram)

9...0–0–0

It is a bit slow for Black to play 9...c6 10.♗g2 ♕g6 11.♘d2 f5, which has been tested in practice

several times, including at grandmaster level in the game B. Savchenko – Frolyanov, Ulan-Ude 2009. Now White could have played 12.c4!, emphasizing the fact that Black has not castled. (In the game White played 12.♘f3 0–0–0 13.♗h3 ♗e7 14.♘g2 ♕f7 15.♘f4 g5 16.♘d3∞, with a complicated position offering excellent prospects for Black.) 12...♗d6 13.cxd5 cxd5 14.♕b5 0–0 (Black's compensation for the pawn after 14...♕f7 15.♘xe4 fxe4 16.0–0 0–0 17.♕xb7± is clearly insufficient.) 15.♘xd5 ♕f7 16.♘c3 ♘xd2 (16...a6 17.♕xb7 ♘xd2 18.♗xd2 ♖ab8 19.♕xa6 ♖b6 20.♕e2 ♘f6 21.b3 ♖e8 22.0–0±) 17.d5! (This is an important intermediate move, showing why 12.c4 was so strong.) 17...♘e4 (Black's compensation for the pawn is insufficient after 17...♘e5 18.dxe6 ♘df3 19.♔e2! ♘d4 20.♔f1 ♘xe6 21.♕xb7 ♗c7 22.♗d5±) 18.dxe6 ♕xe6 19.0–0±; White has a clear advantage, thanks to his powerful bishop-pair.

10.♗g2 c6 11.♘d2 ♘d6 12.a4

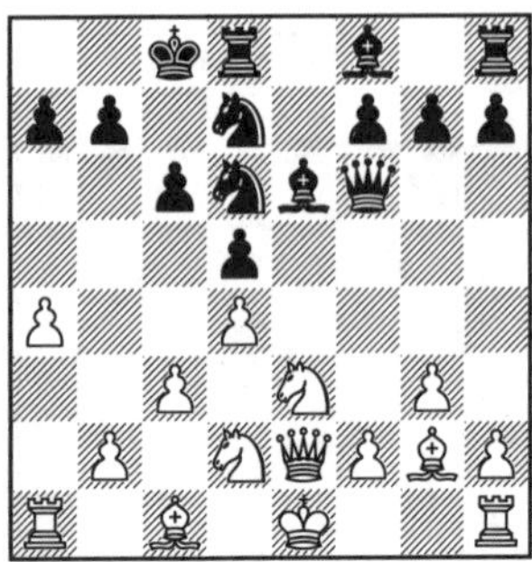

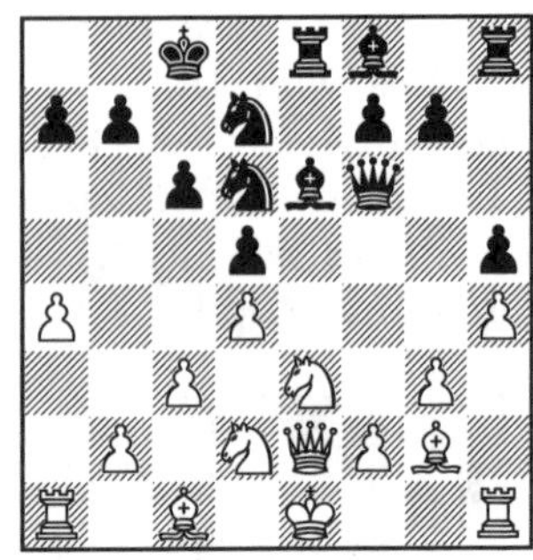

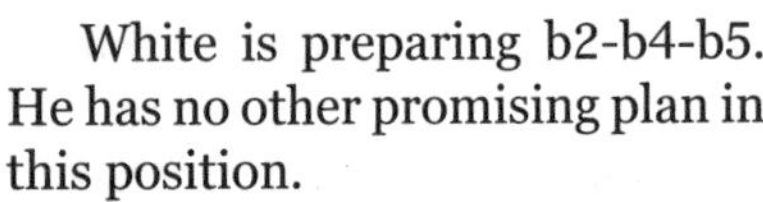

White is preparing b2-b4-b5. He has no other promising plan in this position.

12...h5

The comments to the previous move are applicable to Black as well. He must concentrate his actions on the kingside and the e-file.

13.h4 ♖e8∓

The position is very complicated, but Black's prospects are slightly better. Depending on how White continues, Black can move his bishop to g4 or else open up the game with g7-g5. The quite reasonable plan of g7-g6, followed by ♗f8-h6, exerting pressure against White's knight on e3, is also worth considering.

Conclusion

White's knight, which retreats to the c4-square on move 4, has only one possible prospect – to move eventually to the e3-square. But White loses another tempo in the process and obstructs his bishop on c1. It is clear that Black has nothing to fear in this variation.

Chapter 18 1.e4 e5 2.♘f3 ♘f6 3.♘xe5 d6 4.♘f3 ♘xe4

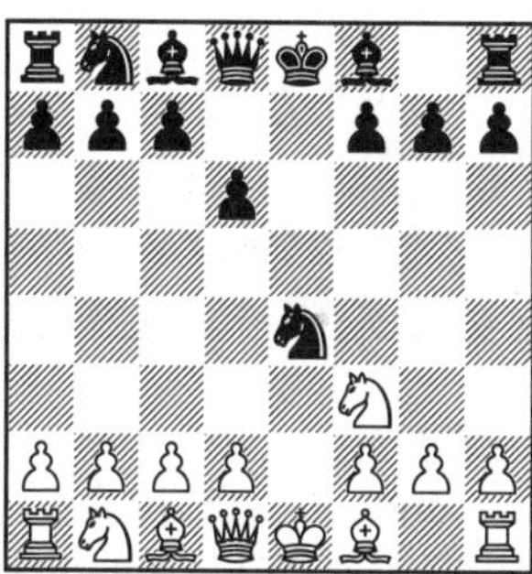

In this chapter we shall analyze some seldom played lines in which White plays neither the immediate 5.d4 nor the popular plan of castling queenside after 5.♘c3 ♘c3 6.dxc3. His options for avoiding the main lines are **A) 5.c4**, **B) 5.♕e2** and **C) 5.♗d3**.

A) 5.c4

This is an original move, but that's about the most positive thing that can be said about it.

White can show even less ambition with 5.d3, when after 5...♘f6 6.d4 Black can play 6...d5, if he so wishes, transposing to the exchange variation of the French Defence, but it is even better for him to continue with 6...♗e7 7.♗d3 0–0 8.0–0 ♘c6! (Black's knight is generally not very well placed on c6, but it is a developing move and creates the rather unpleasant threat of 9...♘b4 10.♗c4 ♗f5) 9.c3 ♗e6 (the other possibility here is 9...♗g4 10.h3 ♗h5 11.♖e1 d5= and Black has almost equalized) 10.♘g5 (otherwise Black would continue with ♕d8-d7 and ♗e6-f5) 10...♗d7 11.♘e4 ♖e8 12.♖e1 ♘xe4 13.♗xe4 ♗g5= and the position is equal.

5...♘c6!

This is the best move, discouraging d2-d4.

Naturally Black can also play 5...♗e7 6.d4 0–0 7.♗d3 ♘g5=, with something close to equality.

6.♘c3

After 6.d4?! d5, only White can have problems.

The line: 6.♗e2 ♗e7 7.0–0 0–0 8.d4 ♗f6= is harmless; Black has comfortable development and an easy game, Nisipeanu – Giri, Wijk aan Zee 2010.

6...♘xc3 7.dxc3

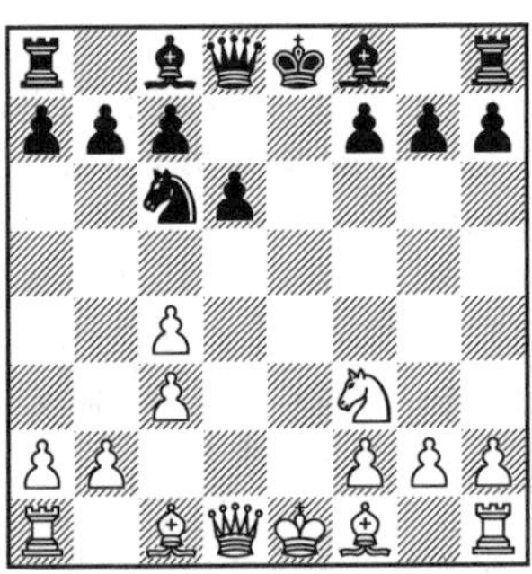

7...g6!

This is the most promising move, with which Black ensures the harmonious development of his kingside.

The move 7...♗e7 is also possible, but I like it less.

Black holds the position, but only just, after 7...♗f5 8.♗d3 ♕d7 (8...♗xd3 9.♕xd3 ♗e7 10.0–0 0–0 11.♖e1 ♗f6 12.♗f4±) 9.0–0 ♗e7 10.♗xf5 ♕xf5 11.♖e1! (11.♕d5 ♕xd5 12.cxd5 ♘e5 13.♘xe5 dxe5 14.♖e1 f6=, Miton – Gashimov, Havana 2007) 11...0–0 12.♕d5. Here the road to equality is rather complicated: 12...♕c2! 13.♗f4 ♖ab8! (13...♗f6 14.♕b5!±) 14.♖ab1 ♖fe8=

8.♗e2

After 8.♗d3 Black should play 8...♕e7!, creating disharmony in White's camp.

8...♗g7 9.♗g5

Otherwise Black will complete his development and have no problems whatsoever.

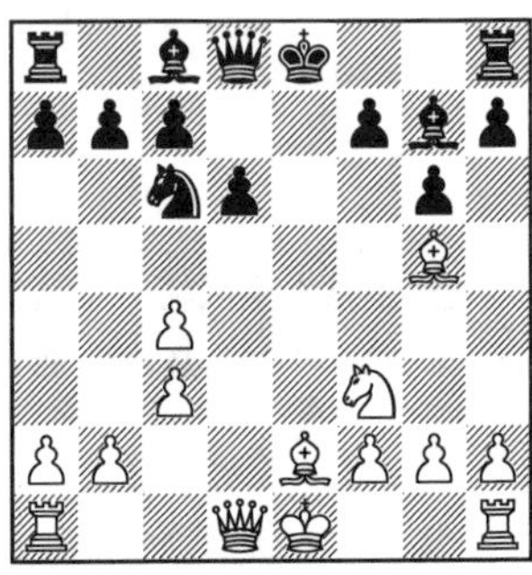

9...♕d7!

The line: 9...♗f6 10.♗h6 ♗f5 11.0–0 ♕d7∞, with the idea of continuing with 0–0–0, is also possible but rather risky for Black.

10.0–0 0–0 11.♖e1 ♖e8=. If the black queen remains on d7 for long, Black's light-squared bishop will be fianchettoed to b7. The position is equal.

B) 5.♕e2

5...♕e7 6.d3 ♘f6 7.♗g5

Black will have to exchange on e2, either now or on the next move, thus increasing White's lead in development. However, the position is closed and the premature development of White's bishop to g5 balances this advantage, so Black has no problems in the exchange variation.

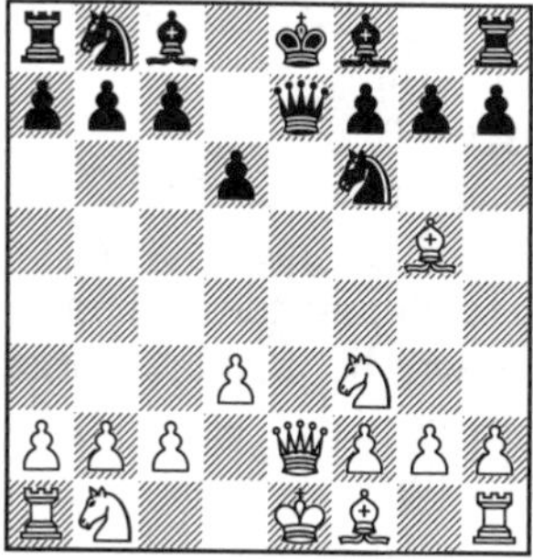

7...♘bd7

I like this move, because it is quite safe but also retains some chances of obtaining a fighting position rather than a dull and drawish one.

It is very solid to play: 7...♕xe2 8.♗xe2 ♗e7 9.♘c3 c6 10.0–0–0 (White cannot achieve much with 10.0–0 ♘a6 11.♖fe1 ♘c7 12.♘d4 ♘e6 13.♗e3 g6= Sadvakasov – Timman, Hoogoveen 1999.) 10...♘a6 11.♖he1 ♘c7 12.♘e4 ♘xe4 13. dxe4 ♗xg5 14.♘xg5 ♔e7=. White's edge is so minimal that if both sides play correctly the game should end in a draw, for example: 15.f4 ♘e6 16.♘h3 ♘c5 17.♘f2 ♖d8 18.♗f3 f6 19.h4 ♗e6 20.g4 a5 21.a3 h6 22.h5 ♖d7 23.♘h1 ♖e8 24.♘g3 ♔d8, draw, Spassky – Hort, Reykjavik 1977.

8.♘c3 ♕xe2 9.♗xe2 h6

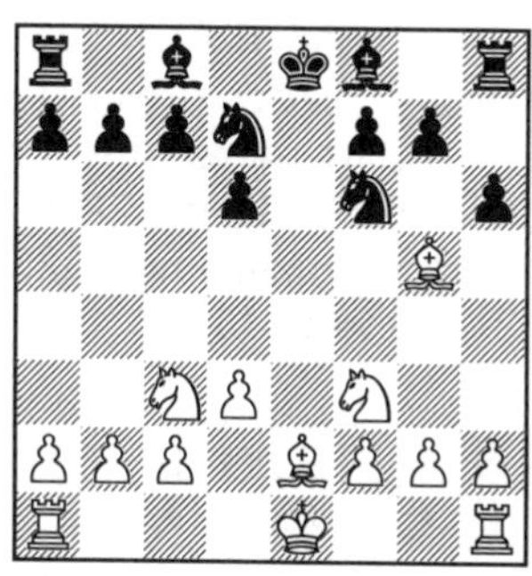

10.♗d2!

In practice, here White more often plays 10.♗h4 g5! 11.♗g3

and now Black has two possibilities:

it is calm and safe to play 11...♘b6 12.0–0–0 ♗d7 13.♘d2 (13.♘e4 ♗g7=; 13.♖he1 0–0–0 14.♗f1 ♗g7∓ Ermenkov – Makarychev, Lublin 1976) 13...0–0–0 (The move 13...h5 is useful, but is not worth a tempo at the moment and after 14.h4 g4 15.♘de4± White maintains a slight edge, Apicella – Motylev, Bucharest 2000) 14. h4 ♗g7=, and the position is approximately equal.

11...♘h5!? This combative move is quite natural and promising for Black. 12.♘d5 ♔d8 13.h4 (13.♘e5 ♘xe5 14.♗xh5 ♗e6=) 13...g4 14.♘d2 ♘b6 15.♘f4 ♘xg3 16.fxg3 ♗g7=. Black's prospects are not at all worse in this rather complicated endgame, Reinderman – Kasimdzhanov, Wijk aan Zee 1999 (**game 15**).

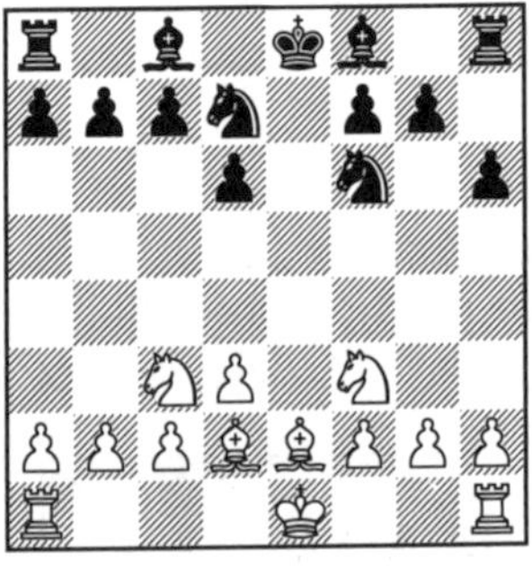

10...c6

This is Black's most reliable equalizing move.

It is also good, but not quite sufficient to equalize the position, to play 10...♘c5 11.0–0 ♘e6 12.d4 d5 (after 12...c6, Black must reckon with 13.d5!?) 13.♗e3 c6 14.♘e5 ♗d6 15.f4 0–0 16.♖ae1±, and White is slightly better. The play is much more interesting after 10...♘b6!? 11.0–0! (11.0–0–0 ♗d7 12.h3 g6 13.♘e4 ♘xe4 14.dxe4 ♗g7= Vogt – Kasimdzhanov, Germany 2006. Black should not be afraid of 11.♘b5 ♘bd5 12.c4, but here he should continue, not with 12...c6, Adams – Kramnik, Dos Hermanas 1999, because of 13.cxd5 cxb5 14.♘d4±, but with 12...a6! 13.♘c3 ♘xc3 14.♗xc3 ♗e7 15.0–0 0–0=, with equal chances) 11...♗d7 (11...♗e7 12.♖fe1 0–0 13.♘d4!± and White's bishop goes to f3, with powerful pressure on the long diagonal) 12.a4! 0–0–0 13.a5 ♘bd5 14.♘xd5 ♘xd5 15.a6 b6 16.c4 ♘f6 17.♖fe1±. White has a slight advantage, but Black has counter-chances. If White's initiative reaches a dead end, his a6-pawn might turn into a liability in the long run.

11.0–0

Black can counter 11.0–0–0 with 11...d5!= and later the knight goes to c5 and the bishop to d6; White will be unable to organize any active play.

11...d5!

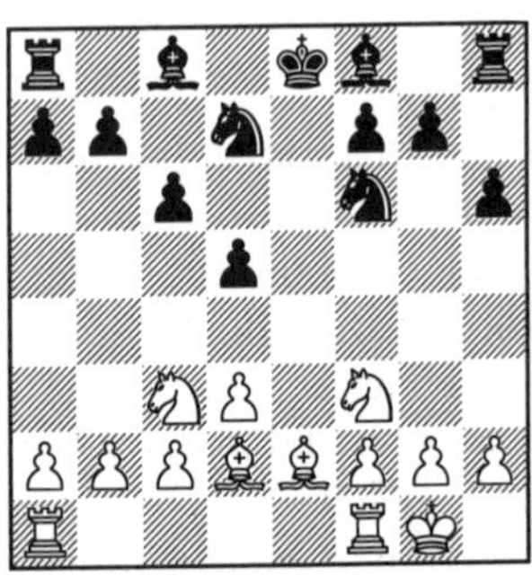

It is important for Black to develop his bishop on the d6-square (in practice, he usually puts it on e7), because it is very actively placed there and does not come under attack, as it would on the e-file.

12.♖fe1 ♗d6 13.d4

If 13.♘d4 g6=

13...♘f8 14.♗d3 ♘e6 15.

♘e2 0–0 16.♘g3 ♖e8 17.c3 ♘f8 18.♖xe8 ♘xe8 19.♘f5

After 19.♖e1, Black can play 19...♗e6 20.♘f5 ♗c7, freeing the d6-square for his knight.

19...♗xf5 20.♗xf5 g6 21.♗d3 ♔g7 22.♖e1 ♘f6 23.♔f1

Or 23.♘e5 ♖e8 24.♔f1 ♖e7=

23...♖e8 24.♖xe8 ♘xe8=

The position is closed, so White's bishop-pair is not so dangerous and the chances are balanced, Reshetnikov – Sakaev, Taganrog 2011.

C) 5.♗d3 ♘f6

It is less reliable for Black to play 5...d5 6.♕e2 ♕e7 7.0–0 ♘d6 8.♕d1 ♕d8 9.♖e1 ♗e7 10.♘c3 c6 11.♕e2 ♗g4 12.b3

Now he fails to equalize after the following possibilities:

12...♘d7, Morozevich – Kramnik, Sarajevo 2009. White has numerous attractive options here, for instance: 13.♗a3 ♘c8 14.♘a4 ♗xf3 15.♕xf3 0–0 16.♗xe7 ♘xe7 17.♖e2 b5 18.♖ae1 ♘g6 19.♘b2±, with advantage;

if 12...♗xf3 it is very promising for White to respond with 13.gxf3!?⩲, although he also maintains an edge after 13.♕xf3 0–0 14.♗a3⩲ Movsesian – Harikrishna, Sarajevo 2009.

6.0–0 ♗e7 7.h3

Otherwise Black's bishop will be developed to the comfortable g4-square: 7.c3 0–0 8.♗c2 ♗g4 9.d4 ♘bd7 10.♘bd2 d5 (The move 10...♖e8 allows White's knight to occupy the c4-square, but this is not very dangerous for Black either: 11.♘c4 ♗h5 12.♘e3 ♗f8 13.♘f5 c6 14.a4 d5= Ivanchuk – Gelfand, Bazna 2009.) 11.♖e1 ♗d6 12. ♘f1 ♖e8 13.♖xe8 ♕xe8 14.♘e3 ♗h5= Naiditsch – Jakovenko, Odessa (rapid) 2009.

7...0–0 8.c3

8...b6!

The deployment of Black's pieces will be quite harmonious after the fianchetto of his bishop to b7. In addition, he does not waste any tempi on for unnecessary pawn-moves such as d6-d5.

9.Bc2 Bb7 10.d4

Sometimes White begins with the move 10.Re1, but after 10...Nbd7 his next move would again be 11.d4 and the game transposes to positions which we shall analyze later.

10...Nbd7

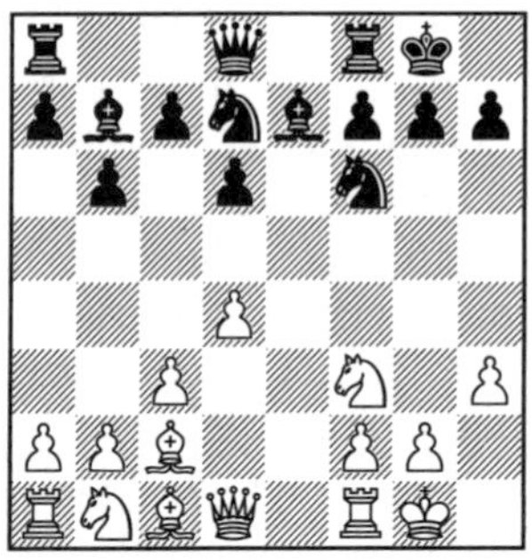

11.Nbd2

11.a4 a6 12.Re1 Re8 13.Bg5 h6 14.Bh4 Nh5 15.Qd3 Nf8 (15...g6=, with the idea of putting his d7-knight on the f6-square) 16.Bxe7 Rxe7= Movsesian – Kasimdzhanov, San Sebastian 2009.

11.Bg5 Re8 12.Re1 Nd5 13.Qd3 g6 14.Bd2 c5 15.c4 Nc7 16.Bc3 d5= Ni Hua – Motylev, Tiayuan 2005 (**game 16**).

For 11.Re1 Re8 12.Nbd2 (12.Bg5 Nd5 – see 11.Bg5 Re8 12.Re1 Nd5) 12...Bf8 – see 11.Nbd2 Re8 12.Re1 Bf8.

11...Re8 12.Nc4

12.Re1 Bf8 13.Rxe8 Qxe8 14.Nf1 g6 15.Bf4 Bg7 16.Ne3 Nd5 17.Nxd5 Bxd5= Tiviakov – Wang Yue, Khanty-Mansyisk 2007.

12...Bf8 13.Bg5

13...h6

It is also possible for Black to opt for the more prudent move 13...Qc8, evading the pin on the knight. After 14.Ne3 Be4 15.Bb3 (after 15.Nd2 Bxc2 16.Qxc2 Qb7 17.Rfe1 h6 18.Bh4 d5= Black is very close to equality) 15...Qb7 16.Nd2 Bg6 17.Re1 b5! 18.Ndf1 a5 19.a3 c5!=. Black obtained an excellent position in the game Najer – Lintchevski, Taganrog 2011.

14.Bh4 g5

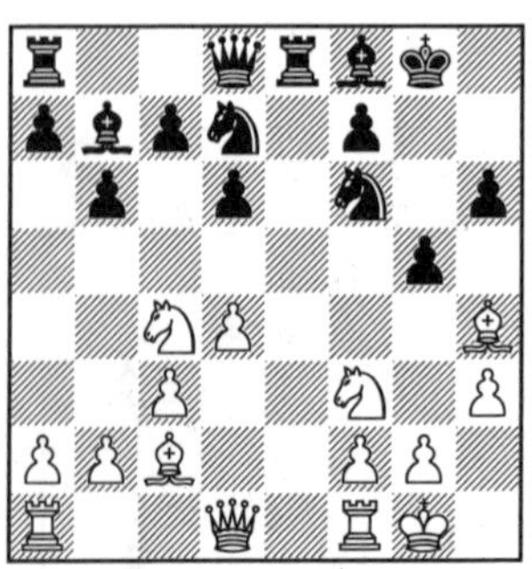

15.♗g3

It is interesting, but still insufficient for any white advantage, to play 15.♘xg5 hxg5 16.♗xg5 ♗a6 17.♘e3 ♗xf1 18.♕xf1∓. White has no real threats, while Black has a whole extra rook for two pawns.

15...♘e4 16.♘fd2 ♘xg3 17. fxg3 ♘f6=

(diagram)

Although Black's light squares on the kingside are vulnerable, there is no way for White to exploit this, so Black's prospects are not at all worse, Tiviakov – Giri, Germany 2010 (**game 17**).

Conclusion

Whenever White plays 5.c4, he is mostly relying on the effect of surprise. If Black reacts correctly, he will have no problems in the opening whatsoever.

If White chooses the variation with the exchange of queens after 5.♕e2, it almost always means that he is in the mood to make a draw. This is the usual result, but in some of the games that we have analyzed in this chapter, if there is a real fight, victory usually goes to the side that plays better in this practically equal endgame.

The variation with 5.♗d3 is quite original but leads to solid, classical positions in which the prospects are approximately equal.

Chapter 19 1.e4 e5 2.♘f3 ♘f6 3.♘xe5 d6 4.♘f3 ♘xe4 5.d4

5...d5

If Black voluntarily retreats his knight from e4, he ends up in a passive and cramped position, for example: 5...♗e7 6.♗d3 ♘f6 7.0-0 0-0 8.h3± with a slight edge for White.

6.♗d3 ♘c6

Black's other possibility is to abstain from exerting pressure against the centre with his pieces and to fortify his d5-pawn instead. For this purpose Black usually plays 6...♗d6 7.0–0 0–0 8.c4 c6. There is a lot of theory on this variation and I believe White has much more chance of fighting for an opening advantage here than in the variation we analyze in this chapter.

There is another possibility too – 6...♗e7 with the idea of answering 7.0–0 with 7...♘c6 and then transposing to the main line. In that case Black must also reckon with the move 7.c4, so it is much better for him to develop his knight first.

7.0–0

The other two possibilities for White require precise play from Black:

7.♕e2 ♗f5 8.♘bd2 ♕e7 9.0–0 ♘d6 10.♕d1 0–0–0! (It is weaker for Black to opt for 10...♗xd3?! 11.cxd3 ♕d7 12.♘e5 ♘xe5 13.dxe5 ♘f5 14.♘f3±, with a slight edge for White, Grischuk – Sakaev, Moscow 2007.) 11.♖e1 ♕f6 12.♘b3

Bg4 (12...Ne4 13.c4 dxc4 14.Bxe4 Bxe4 15.Rxe4 cxb3 16.Qxb3 Qg6 17.Re2 Qf5=) 13.Bg5 (13.c3 Be7 14.Be2 Ne4=) 13...Qxg5 14.Nxg5 Bxd1 15.Raxd1 Nb4 16.c3 Nxd3 17.Rxd3 c6 18.Rf3 f6 19.Ne6 Re8 20.Rfe3 b6 21.R3e2 g6=;

7.Nc3 Nxc3 (After 7...Bb4 8. 0–0 Bxc3 9.bxc3 0–0 10.c4 Bf5 11.cxd5 Qxd5 12.c4± White maintains a slight advantage.) 8. bxc3

8...Bd6! Black's bishop is more actively placed here than on e7. In addition, he can transfer his knight to the kingside via the e7-square (He should refrain from 8...Bg4 9.Rb1 Rb8 10.h3 Bh5 11. Bb5 Be7 12.g4 Bg6 13.Ne5 0–0 14.Bxc6 bxc6 15.Nxc6 Rxb1 16. Nxd8 Ba3 17.Bxa3 Rxd1+ 18.Kxd1 Rxd8 19.Kd2 Rb8 20.Re1± and White is closer to victory than Black is to the draw, Leko – Gelfand, Miskolc 2010.). 9.0–0 0–0 10.Ng5 g6 11.Qf3 Ne7 12.Re1 c6 13.Bf4 Nf5=

7...Be7

(diagram)

8.Re1

White has two popular alternatives here – 8.Nc3 and 8.c4 and we shall analyze these in the following chapters.

8.Nbd2 Nxd2 9.Bxd2 Bg4 10. c3 0–0= Vallejo Pons – Gelfand, Linares 2010.

8.c3 Bg4 9.Nbd2 (for 9.Re1 f5 – see 8.Re1 Bg4 9.c3 f5) 9...Nxd2 10.Bxd2 0–0 11.Re1 Bd6 12.h3 Bh5= Morozevich – Bu Xiangzhi, Yerevan 2008.

8...Bg4 9.c3

9.Bxe4 dxe4 10.Rxe4 Bxf3 11. Qxf3 (It is bad for White to play 11.gxf3 f5 12.Re1 Qxd4∓ and his pawn-structure has been weakened, so Black has the advantage.) 11...Nxd4 12.Qd3 Ne6= and the position is equal.

We shall deal with the move 9...c4 in the next chapter.

9...f5 10.Nbd2

Black also answers 10.Qb3 with 10...0–0, when White has nothing better than 11.Nbd2, transposing to the main line, since it is wrong for White to play 11.Qxb7 owing to 11...Rf6! and Black's rook is ready to join in the attack via the sixth rank. 12.Bf4 (It is even worse for White to play 12.Qb3 Bxf3! 13.gxf3 Rb8!, for example: 14.♕c2 ♖g6+ 15.♔f1 ♕d6∓; 14.♕d1 ♖g6+ 15.♔f1 ♕d6∓; or 14.♕a4 ♖g6+ 15.♔f1 ♗g5∓) 12...♗xf3! 13.♗xc7 ♖g6 14.♖xe4 fxe4 15.♗xd8 ♖b8 16.♕xc6 ♖xc6∓

10...0–0

11.♕b3

It is useless for White to play 11.♕c2, because in comparison with the main line: 11.♕b3 ♘a5 12.♕c2 ♘c6 he simply presents his opponent with an extra tempo.

The move 11.♘f1 even increases the effect of the pin on the f3-knight, so it cannot be dangerous to Black. Black now has numerous attractive possibilities, of which I shall show you just the ones which seem to me the most purposeful: 11...♗h4 (Black can also refrain from forcing the issue, by playing 11...♗d6, increasing his kingside pressure. There might follow: 12.♕b3 ♔h8 13.♕xb7 ♕f6↑ and Black has a very dangerous initiative as compensation for his minimal material deficit.) 12.♘g3 (After 12.♖e2, Black has many attacking ideas, but I like best the prophylactic move 12...♖b8!, defending against the possibility of ♕d1-b3. It is then hard to see how White can complete his development.) 12...♘xf2 (Black can maintain the tension here with the move 12...♕d6!?) 13.♔xf2 f4 14.♕c2 ♗xf3 15.gxf3 ♕f6 16.♗xh7+ ♔h8 17.♗xf4 ♕xf4 18.♕d3 ♕h6 19.♗f5 ♗xg3+ 20.hxg3 (It would be too risky for White to opt for 20.♔xg3 ♘e7! 21.♗g4 ♘g6↑ and Black's knight penetrates to the f4-outpost with great effect.) 20...♕h2 21.♔f1=. If Black so wishes, he can now draw by perpetual check: 21...♕h1 22.♔f2 ♕h2, but he can also play for a win without too much risk.

11...♘a5

11...♔h8?! – This pawn-sacrifice is incorrect under these circumstances. 12.♕xb7 ♖f6 13.♕b3 ♖g6 14.♗b5 ♘xd2 (14...♗d6 15.♗xc6 ♘xd2 16.♗xd2 ♗xf3 17.g3+-) 15.♘xd2 ♗d6 16.g3 ♘e7 17.♗d3! (It is less impressive for White to choose 17.♗f1 f4 18.♗g2 ♖b8 19.♕c2= and thanks to his pawn-wedge on f4, Black can be optimistic about the future, Smeets – Bayram, Antalya 2004.) 17...♖f6 18.c4 c6 19.c5 ♗c7 20.f4±; White has a solid extra pawn and Black's compensation is obviously insufficient.

(diagram)

12.♕c2

12.♕a4 ♘c6 13.♗b5. Bearing in mind what follows in this variation, it would be more prudent for

White to retreat his queen to b3 now. 13...♗h4! (Black provokes, with tempo, an important weakening of the white king's shelter.) 14.g3 (but not 14.♘xh4 ♕xh4 15.♖f1 ♖f6→ and White will come under direct attack) 14...♗f6 15. ♗xc6 bxc6 16.♕xc6

16...♖b8!. This is a very powerful attacking move (it is much weaker for Black to play 16...♖e8 since after17.♘e5± he will need to worry about maintaining the balance, Anand – Kramnik, Wijk aan Zee 1999). 17.c4 (After 17.♕e6+ ♖f7 18.♘xe4 dxe4 19.♘e5 ♗xe5 20.♕xe5 ♗f3∓ Black's queen will be continually trying to get to the h3-square and White's position is very dangerous.) 17...f4 18.♘xe4 dxe4

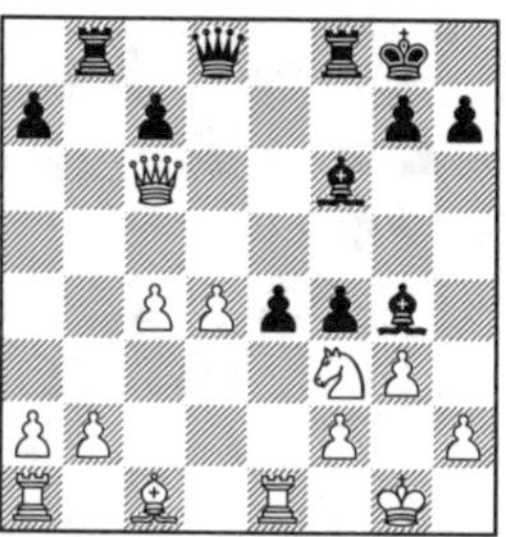

and now:

19.♕xe4 ♗xf3 20.♕xf3 fxg3 21.hxg3 ♗xd4 22.♗f4 ♖xb2 23.♖f1 ♖xf2 (here it might be stronger for Black to continue with 23...♕d7!?, increasing the pressure) 24.♖xf2 ♗xa1∓. Black has an extra pawn, but realising it will not be at all easy, Cheparinov – Gelfand, Sochi 2008;

19.♘e5 ♗xe5 20.dxe5 fxg3 21. hxg3 ♖b6 22.♕xe4 (It is even worse for White to choose 22. ♕d5+ ♕xd5 23.cxd5 ♗f3 24.g4. He has no other defence against his opponent's manoeuvre ♖f5-h5. 24...♗xg4 25.♖xe4 ♗f3 26.♖f4 ♖xf4 27.♗xf4 g5 28.♗g3 ♖xb2∓ and Black has excellent chances of winning this position.) 22...♗f3 23.♕h4 ♕xh4 24.gxh4 ♖g6+ 25. ♔h2 ♖g2+ 26.♔h3 ♖xf2 27.♗e3 ♖xb2∓ and only Black has winning prospects.

12...♘c6 13.b4 a6

(diagram)

White has two logical possibilities now: **A) 14.♖b1** and **B) 14.a4**.

A) 14.♖b1 b5!

Black exploits the circumstance that White's rook has

abandoned the a-file and blocks the advance of his b4-pawn indefinitely.

15.a4 ♖b8 16.axb5 axb5

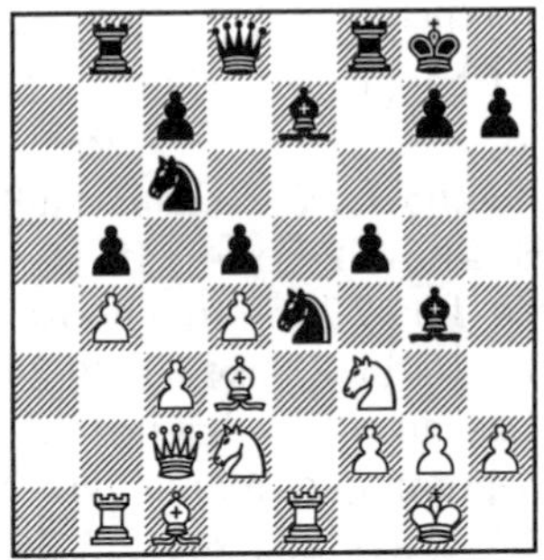

17.♖a1

17.♘e5 ♘xe5 18.dxe5 c5! (The ex-World Champion played too riskily here: 18...♘xf2 19.♔xf2 ♗h4+. Here, instead of 20.♔f1 ♗xe1 21.♔xe1 ♕h4+ 22.g3 ♕xh2 23.♘f1 ♕xc2 24.♗xc2∞ Howell – Kramnik, London 2009, which led to a very complicated endgame, it would be much stronger for White to play 20.g3 f4 21.♔g2 fxg3 22.hxg3 ♗h3+ 23.♔xh3 ♗xg3 24.♘f3 ♖xf3 25.♔g2 ♖f2+ 26.♔xg3 ♖xc2 27.♗xc2± and Black should be happy if he manages to save the game with a perpetual check against White's exposed king.) 19.f3 ♕b6 20.♗xe4 fxe4 21.fxg4 cxb4+ 22.♔h1 ♕f2 23.♖g1 (the game Amonatov – Kunin, Moscow 2009, continued with 23.♕d1? bxc3–+ and Black won) 23...♗c5 24.♗b2 e3 25.cxb4 ♗xb4 26.♕b3 ♗xd2 27.♕xd5+ ♕f7 28.e6 ♕e7 29.♖a1 b4 30.♗d4 ♖bd8 31.♕e5 ♖xd4 32.♕xd4 ♕xe6∓. White will be hard pressed to save the game.

17...♖b6 18.♘e5 ♘xe5 19.dxe5

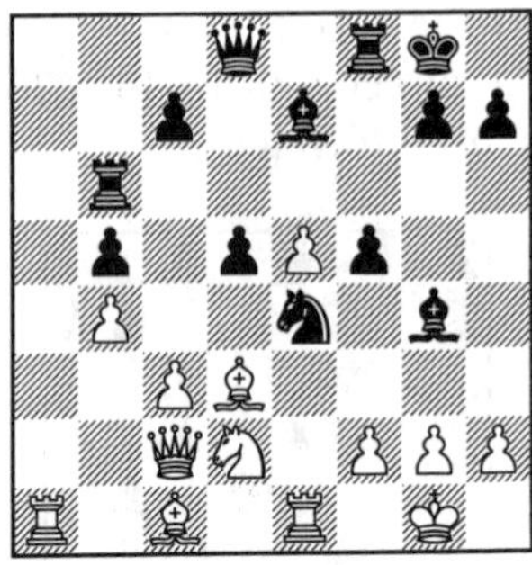

19...c5!?N

Now some very interesting complications arise. Black has also tried 19...♘xf2 20.♔xf2 ♗h4+ 21.♔f1 (21.g3 f4 22.♔g2 fxg3 23.hxg3 ♗xg3 24.♗xh7+ ♔h8 25.♖h1 ♗xe5= and, strangely enough, White has nothing better than perpetual check) 21...♗xe1 22.♔xe1 ♕h4+ 23.g3 ♕xh2 24.♘f1∞, and the position is very unclear, Stellwagen – Fridman, Netherlands 2007.

20.f3 cxb4 21.♘b3!

After 21.cxb4, Black should

continue with the far-from-obvious move 21...♖g6!→, with a crushing attack.

In the variation 21.fxe4 fxe4 22.♘xe4 (White cannot keep his extra piece: 22.♗e2 ♗c5+ 23.♔h1 ♕h4–+, or 22.♗f1 ♗c5+ 23.♔h1 ♕h4–+) dxe4 23.♗xe4 bxc3 24.♕c3 b4∓ White's e5-pawn is safely blockaded by Black's bishop, while Black's outside passed b4-pawn is tremendously dangerous, so he has the advantage.

21...♗h5!

White is clearly better after 21...♗h4 22.♖f1 ♖c6 23.fxg4 ♖xc3 24.♕b1 fxg4 25.♖xf8+ ♕xf8 26.♗e3 ♗f2+ 27.♗xf2 ♕xf2+ 28.♔h1±

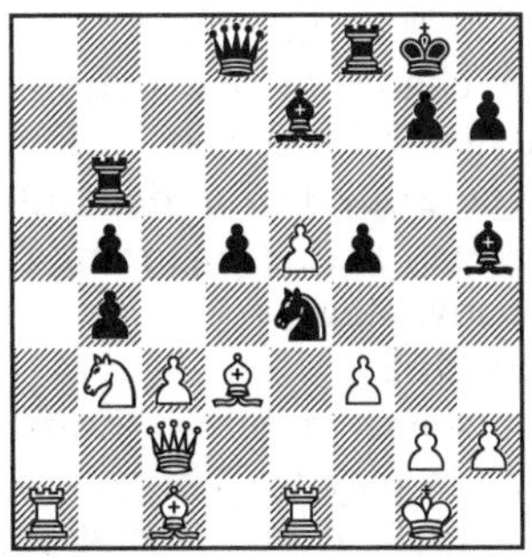

22.cxb4

Black has a very good position after 22.fxe4 fxe4 23.♗e2 ♗xe2 24.♖xe2 ♖c6=, obtaining several passed pawns for the piece.

22...♗xb4 23.♖f1 ♖b8

There is a transposition of moves after 23...♖b7 24.fxe4 dxe4 25.♗e2 ♖c7 26.♕a2 ♗f7 27.♖b1! (it is weaker for White to opt for 27.♖d1 ♕e7 28.♗xb5 ♖c3 29.♗a4 ♕xe5 30.♕b2 ♗h5 31.♖d4 ♗d6 32.♗f4 ♕xf4 33.♖xd6 ♖h3! 34.gxh3 ♕xd6= with a probable draw) 27...♖c3 28.♔h1.

24.fxe4 dxe4

It is not good for Black to continue with 24...♕b6+ 25.♕f2 ♕xf2+ 26.♖xf2 fxe4 27.♗e2.

White also maintains a clear advantage after 24...fxe4 25.♖xf8+ ♕xf8 26.♗f1 ♖c8 27.♕a2±

25.♗e2 ♖c8 26.♕a2 ♗f7

26...♗xe2 27.♕xe2 ♕d5 28.♖b1 ♕xe5 29.♗f4±

27.♖b1! ♖c3 28.♔h1!

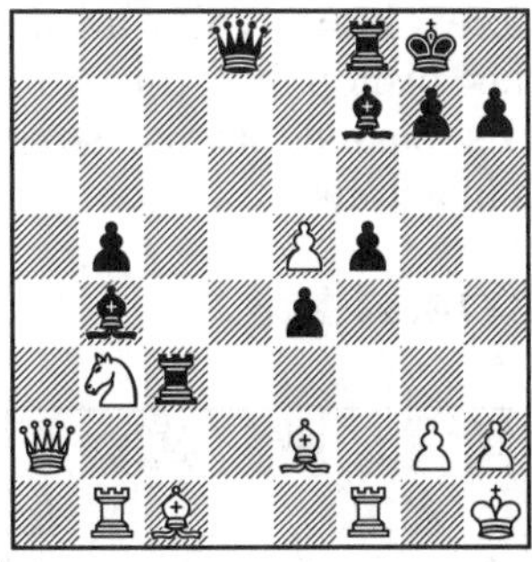

28...♕b6

There are numerous tactical nuances in this position and I would evaluate it as approximately equal from the dynamic point of view.

White is better after 28...e3 29.e6! ♗xe6 30.♕a6 ♗c4 31.♗xc4+ bxc4 32.♘d4 ♕xd4 33.♕e6+ ♔h8 34.♖xb4± and the fact that Black's king has no escape square is decisive.

29.♖xf5

Or 29.♗f4 ♖fc8 30.♖b2 h6!⩱∞ with excellent compensation for the pawn.

29.♗g5!? e3 (29...h6!? 30.♗h4 ♔h7!?) 30.♗h4 ♕c6 31.♖b2 ♖c4! 32.♗g3 (32.♗g5 ♗d5 33.♔g1 ♖a8 34.♕b1 ♗c3 35.♖c2 ♖b4 36.♗f3 ♗xf3 37.♖xf3 ♕e4 38.♖f4 ♕d3 39.♖xb4 e2 40.♖c1 ♕xb1 41.♖xb1 ♗xb4∓) 32...♗d5 33.♗xc4 (33.♔g1 f4∓) 33...♗xc4 34.♖f3 ♗c3 35.♖b1 ♕e4 36.♗e1 ♗xe5∓ and despite the absence of a whole rook, Black is on top in this position.

29...♗xb3 30.♖xf8+ ♗xf8 31.♕b2 ♗c2 32.♕xc3 ♗xb1 33.♕b3+ ♔h8 34.♕xb1 ♕f2 35.♗g5 ♕xe2 36.e6 b4 37.e7 ♗xe7 38.♗xe7 b3=. White must give up his bishop in order to stop Black's passed pawns, so it all ends in a draw.

B) 14.a4 ♗d6

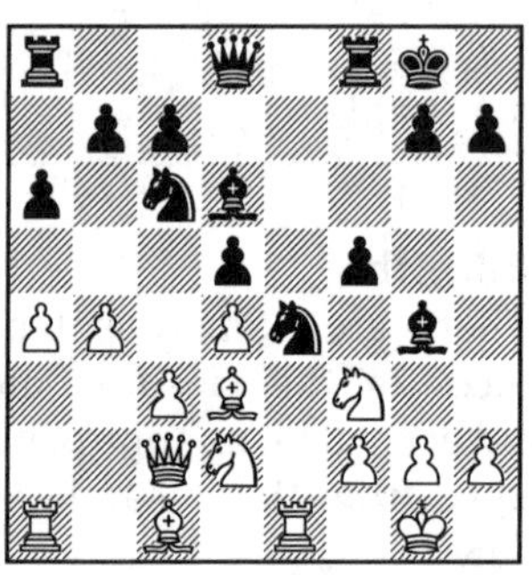

15.♗a3

15.♖b1 ♔h8 16.b5 axb5 17.axb5 ♘a5 18.♘e5 ♗xe5 19.dxe5 ♗h5 20.f3 ♕h4! (In the game Sulypa – Turov, Latschach 2009, Black played the overly cautious move 20...♘xd2?, when White could have played 21.♕xd2! ♘c4 22.♕f4±, obtaining an overwhelming advantage.) Now, after 21.♖e2 or 21.♖f1, Black can play 21...♕e7∞, with a complicated position. and

15...♔h8

Black cannot obtain much with straightforward play: 15...♖f6 16.b5 (After 16.h3 Black's correct reaction would be, not 16...♘xd2? 17.♘xd2 ♗xh3 18.gxh3 ♖g6+ 19.♔f1+– and White parried his opponent's attack and won the game, Lastin – Slugin, Voronezh 2005, but 16...♗h5 17.b5 axb5 18.♗xd6 cxd6 19.axb5 ♘a5=, with an acceptable position.) 16...axb5 (After 16...♘xd2, White has the rather elegant variation 17.♕xd2! ♗xf3 18.bxc6 ♖g6 19.g3 bxc6 20.♗xd6 cxd6 21.♗xf5 ♖f6 22.♕d3 g6 23.♕xf3±, with every chance of realising his advantage, Morozevich – Karpov, Prague 2002.) 17.♗xd6 cxd6 18.axb5 ♘a5 19.♖a3! planning ♕a2!, with advantage.

16.♕b2

It seems a bit awkward for White to play 16.♖eb1 ♕e7 (After 16...♘xd2?! 17.♘xd2 ♕h4 18.♘f1 ♘e7 19.f3 ♗h5 20.b5± Black's attacking potential was neutralized, while his bad bishop and the weakness of the e5-square would later tell, Morozevich – Gelfand, Yerevan (rapid) 2008. However, a fairly reliable continuation for Black is 16...b6 17.b5 ♗xa3 18.♖xa3 axb5 19.♗xb5 ♕d6 20.♖aa1 ♘xd2 21.♘xd2 f4!=,with approximate equality.) 17.♕b2 ♘d8! (Black's knight is headed for the f4-square.) 18.b5 axb5 19.♗xd6 cxd6 20.♗xb5 ♘e6∓ and Black's position is at least equal.

After 16.b5 axb5

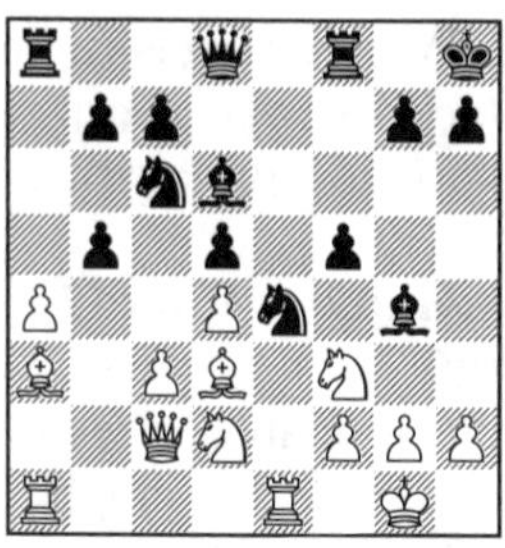

we shall analyze two possibilities: 17.♗xd6 and 17.♗xb5.

17.♗xd6 cxd6 18.axb5 (18.♗xb5 ♘a5 – see 17.♗b5 ♘a5 18.♗xd6 cxd6) 18...♘a5 19.h3 ♗h5 20.♘h2 ♖c8 21.♖a3 b6 22.♘df1 f4 23.f3 ♕h4 24.♖e2. Here it is very promising for Black to play 24...♖fe8!, increasing the pressure (in the game Ponomariov – Adams, Wijk aan Zee 2005, there followed 24...♘g3 25.♘xg3 fxg3 26.♘f1 ♗xf3! 27.gxf3 ♖xf3∞ and Black had sufficient compensation for the piece). After 25.♕c1 ♘g3 26.♖xe8+ ♖xe8 27.♘g4 ♘xf1 28.♗xf1 ♕g3=, only White might have difficulties in the final position.

17.♗xb5 ♘a5 (It would be too risky for Black, from the point of view of strategy, to play 17...♗h5 18.♗xc6 bxc6 19.♘e5 ♕g5 – 19...c5 20.f3± – 20.♘df3 ♗xf3 21.♘xf3 ♕e7 22.♗xd6 cxd6 23.♘d2 ♕h4 24.♘f1± Amonatov – Iljin, Sochi 2007.) 18.♗b4 (18.♗xd6!? cxd6 19.♖ac1 ♖c8 20.♕b2 ♗h5= Cheparinov – Korneev, Coria del Rio 2005).

Now Black's most promising move seems to be 18...♖f6! (Naturally, he can also play a calm prophylactic move, such as 18...b6 or 18...♗h5.), with the standard idea of ♗d6-f4, and also preserving the possibility of transferring the rook to g6 or h6 to organize an attack against White's king. 19.♘e5 (after 19.h3 Black does not need to sacrifice material or exchange pieces; he can simply play 19...♗h5) 19...♗xe5 20.dxe5 ♖h6∓; White's king is seriously endangered.

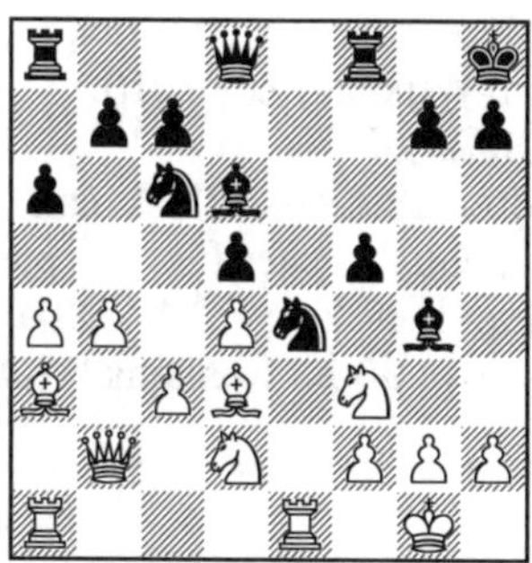

16...♘e7!

This move has a very bad reputation, but in fact it is very good. Black's knight is transferred to the kingside, adding to his already excellent piece formation there.

The alternatives are inferior:

16...♕e7 17.b5 ♗xa3 18.♖xa3 axb5 19.♗xb5 ♗xf3 20.♘xf3 ♘d8 21.♗d3 ♘f7 22.c4 dxc4 23.♗xc4 ♘fd6 24.♗a2± Andreikin – Rakhmanov, Dagomys 2009;

16...♖e8 17.b5 axb5 and here White would not achieve much with 18.♗xb5 ♕f6 (here 18...♗f4!? is also very good, isolating the enemy bishop on a3) 19.♗xd6 cxd6 20.a5 (after 20.h3, Black can play calmly 20...♗h5∞, maintaining the tension) 20...♖eb8∓; White has lost his a5-pawn and must fight for equality, Svidler – Pe.H.Nielsen, Dortmund 2005. Instead, it would be correct for him to continue with 18.axb5! ♘a5 19.♗xd6 cxd6 20.b6±, retaining a slight edge.

17.♘e5 ♘g6!

It is bad for Black to play 17... ♗xe5 18.dxe5 ♘g6 19.f3 ♘xe5 20. ♗f1± when his compensation for the piece is clearly insufficient, So – Giri, Wijk aan Zee 2010.

18.♘xg4

After 18.♗xe4, Black can advantageously sacrifice a piece: 18...fxe4! 19.♘xg4 ♕h4 20.♘e5 (the move 20.h3 weakens White's kingside and after Black's simple reaction 20...h5∓ White is clearly worse) 20...♕xf2+ 21.♔h1 ♘xe5 22.dxe5 ♗xe5 23.b5 ♖f5 24.bxa6 bxa6!∓. White's king is vulnerable and Black's powerful centralized pieces provide him with an advantage.

18...♘xd2 19.♕xd2 fxg4 20.♗xg6

White is unable to restrict the mobility of Black's knight; after 20.g3, Black has the reply 20... ♘h4!

20...hxg6 21.♖e6 ♖f6=

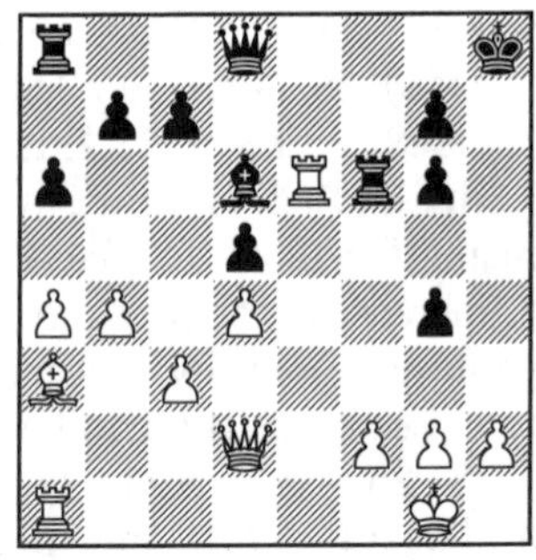

Black has no problems at all. His bishop is much more powerful than its white counterpart and his tripled (!) pawns are quite safe.

Conclusion

White usually castles on move 7, but the moves 7.♕e2 and 7.♘c3 require very precise play from Black in order to maintain equality. In the main line, White has the possibility of repeating the position on his thirteenth move by playing 13.♕b3. If he does not do so, however, Black obtains very active play and his prospects seem to be at least equal.

Chapter 20 1.e4 e5 2.♘f3 ♘f6 3.♘xe5 d6 4.♘f3 ♘xe4 5.d4 d5 6.♗d3 ♘c6 7.0–0 ♗e7 8.♖e1 ♗g4 9.c4

After this move the character of the game is entirely different from the one arising after 9.c3, when White intends to go to b3 with his queen and attacks on the dark squares. Now, there is an immediate sharp conflict in the centre and the play is mainly tactical, without any clear positional guidelines.

9...♘f6

As a result of the move 9.c4, the base of the black knight on e4 is undermined, so it must retreat. White now has two possibilities: to force a clarification of the situation in the centre with **A) 10.cxd5**, or to increase the pressure with **B) 10.♘c3.**

A) 10.cxd5 ♗xf3

A well-known theoretical position arises after 10...♘xd5 11.♘c3 0–0 12.h3 ♗e6 13.a3±. White has an isolated pawn, but his pieces are so active that it is very difficult for Black to equalize.

11.♕xf3 ♕xd5

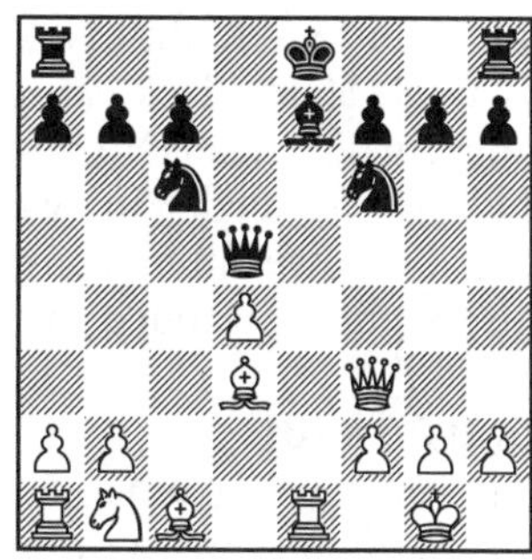

White must choose now between sharp lines, based on the sacrifice of his d4-pawn – **A1) 12.♕g3?!** and **A2) 12.♕h3**, and allowing simplification into an endgame with **A3) 12.♕xd5**.

A1) 12.♕g3?!

This is one of two possibilities for White to keep the queens on the board and try to exert pressure in the centre, but it turns out to be futile.

12...♕xd4 13.♘c3 0–0 14.♘b5

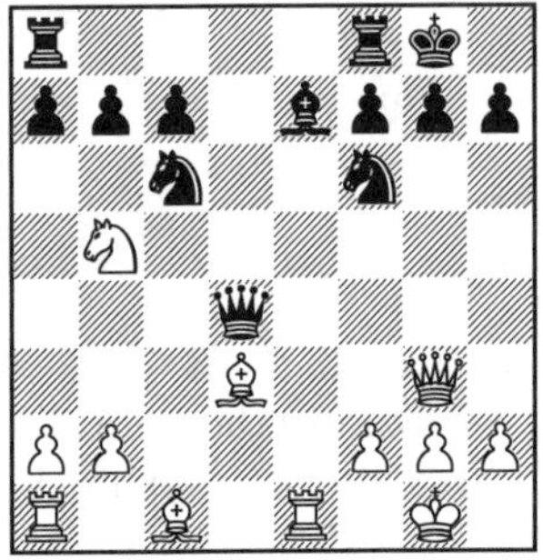

14...♕b4!

It is playable but inferior for Black to opt for 14...♕g4 15.♕xg4 ♘xg4 16.♗f5 ♘f6 17.♘xc7 ♖ad8 18.♗e3, Kamsky – Khalifman, Las Vegas 1999. Here Black can play 18...a6!∞, which leads to a very complicated struggle in which White has a powerful bishop-pair but his knight is stranded in enemy territory.

15.♗g5 ♖ad8!

This centralising move is the best, as is often the case in open positions, and it even allows Black to fight for the advantage! In many variations White's bishop on d3 is hanging and his lack of an escape hole for the king is bound to tell as well.

Black only equalizes with the line: 15...♘h5 16.♗xe7 ♘xg3 17.♗xb4 ♘xb4 18.♖ad1, Shaplyko – T.Balogh, Zagan 1995. Here he should continue with 18...♖ad8!=

16.♖ad1

White fails to trap the enemy queen with 16.a3 ♕xb2 17.♖ab1 ♕a2∓ and here he is stuck for a continuation.

16...a6! 17.♘xc7

After 17.♘c3 it is very good for Black to continue simply with 17...♖fe8∓, with a solid extra pawn.

17...♗d6 18.♕h3 ♗xc7 19.♗xf6 ♖xd3 20.♕xd3 gxf6 21.♖e4 ♕a5 22.♖g4+ ♔h8 23.♖h4 f5 24.♕h3 ♔g8 25.♖xh7 ♗e5∓. Black has parried his opponent's attempt to mate him and has preserved the extra material, so he maintains an advantage.

A2) 12.♕h3!?

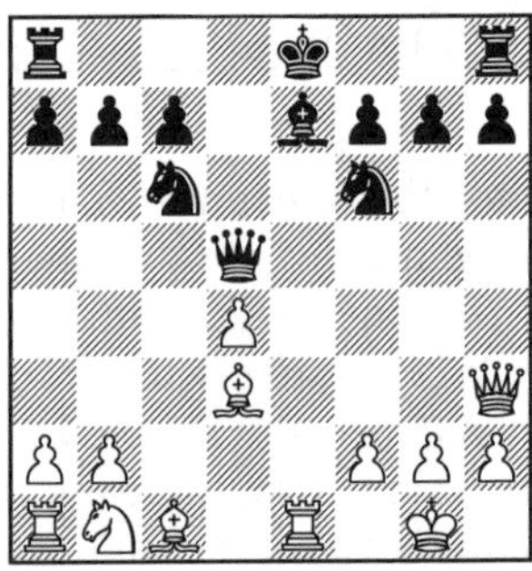

This queen-sortie is much more interesting, but Black can still seize the initiative with precise play.

12...♕xd4!

Black can only struggle to reach equality with 12...♘xd4 13.♘c3 ♕d7 14.♕xd7+ ♔xd7 15.♗e3 ♘e6 16.♖ad1 ♗d6 17.♗f5 (Another good white option is 17.f4!? ♖he8 18.♘e4 ♘xe4 19.♗xe4 g6 20.f5

♘d8 21.♗d4 ♘c6 22.♗c3±; Black's forces are all squashed into the last few ranks, but he has an extra pawn and should not lose.) 17...♔e7 18.♘b5 ♖hd8 19.♘xd6 cxd6⩱; White has at least enough compensation for the pawn, Kasparov – Karpov, Moscow (m/28) 1984.

13.♘c3

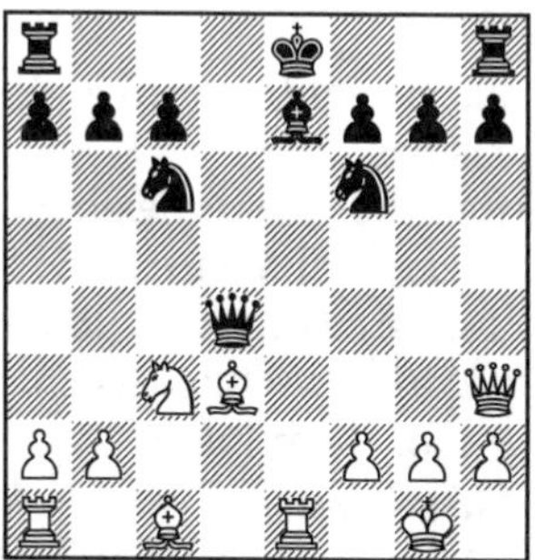

13...♘g4!

Black's knight is perfectly placed on g4 and White is forced to protect his f2-pawn.Having blocked the h3-c8 diagonal, Black often has the possibility of castling queenside.

Here Black usually plays 13...♖d8, but then he must reckon with the possibility of 14.♗c2!? (it is useless for White to try 14.♗b5 in view of 14...0–0∓, when the bishop on e7 is not hanging, owing to the vulnerability of White's back rank; and it is hard to see how White can continue his attack after 14.♗f5 0–0 15.♗e3 ♕b4 16.a3 ♕b3!∓) 14...0–0 15.♗e3 ♕b4 16.♗g5↑, or even 16.♖ab1!?↑

14.♖f1

We should glance at the alternatives for White here:

14.♖e2 0–0–0 15.♗e3 ♕xd3 16.♕xg4+ ♔b8 17.♕xg7 ♕f5 18.♕h6 ♖hg8∓; Black has a more active position;

14.♗e3 ♕xd3 15.♕xg4 ♕g6∓, and White must play precisely to equalize.

14...h5! 15.♗e4 ♕e5 16.g3

After 16.♗e3 a good continuation for Black would be 16...0–0 17.♖ae1 ♗d6 18.g3 ♖fe8∓

16...♕e6 17.♗f4 0–0–0∓, with an excellent position for Black.

A3) 12.♕xd5 ♘xd5 13.♘c3

For 13.♗e4 0–0–0 14.♘c3 – see 13.♘c3 0–0–0 14.♗e4.

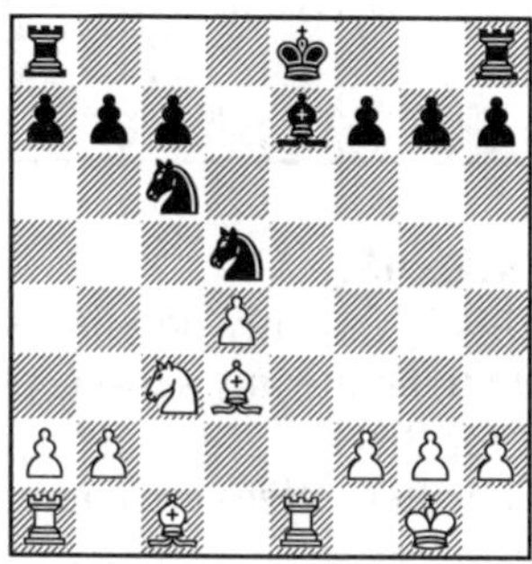

13...0–0–0

We should point out that Black has a very interesting alternative at his disposal here: 13...♘db4!? 14.♗e4 ♘xd4 15.♗e3 ♘dc2! (but not 15...c5? in view of 16.♗xd4! cxd4 17.♘b5±, with a stable advantage to White) 16.a3 ♘xe1 (it is also quite safe for Black to opt for 16...♘xa1 17.axb4 ♗xb4 18.♖xa1 c6=, when his pawn-chain b7-c6 considerably restricts the activity of White's bishop on e4) 17.axb4 (in the variation 17.♖xe1 0–0–0 18.♗xa7 b6 19.♗f5+ ♔b7 20.♖xe7 ♖he8 21.♖xe8 ♖xe8 22.♗e4+ ♘c6∓, White's bishop stranded on a7 is in much greater trouble than Black's knight pinned on c6.) 17... ♗xb4 18.♖xe1 0–0–0=. Black's rook and two pawns do not seem to be any weaker than White's two minor pieces.

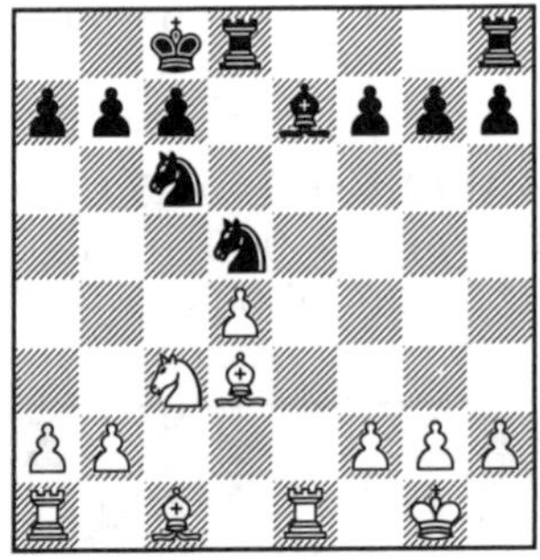

14.♘xd5!

This is the only possibility for White to create any serious problems for Black.

The alternatives are completely harmless:

14.♗c4 ♗b4 15.♗d2 ♘xd4 16. ♘xd5 ♗xd2 17.♖ed1 c6 18.♖xd2 cxd5 19.♖xd4 dxc4 20.♖xc4+ ♔b8= Aseev – Razuvaev, Tashkent 1984;

14.♗e4 ♗b4 15.♗d2 (15.♗xd5 ♖xd5 16.a3 ♗xc3 17.bxc3 ♔d7=) 15...♘f6 16.♗xc6 bxc6 17.♗e3= Kamsky – Karpov, Linares 1994.

14...♖xd5 15.♗e3!

(diagram)

15...♘xd4!

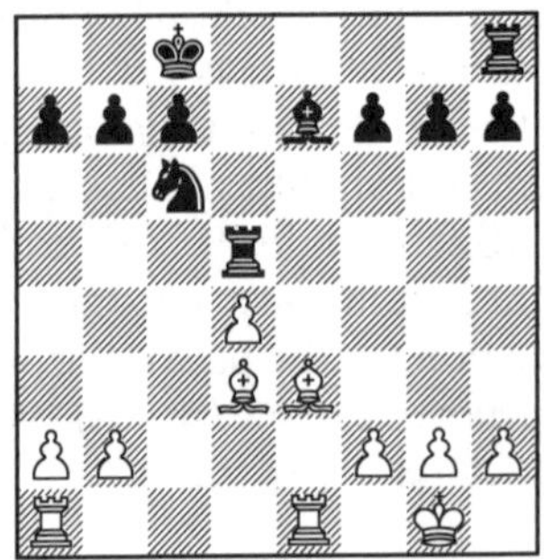

This straightforward and solid move is best here.

After the "more flexible" 15... ♗f6 16.♗e4 ♖b5 (16...♖a5 17.d5 ♘e7 18.b4!) 17.d5 ♘e7 18.♖ad1↑, or 18.♗xa7!?↑, White has chances to fight for the initiative.

16.♗e4 ♖d7 17.♗xd4 ♖xd4 18.♗xb7+ ♔xb7 19.♖xe7 ♖hd8 20.♔f1 ♖8d7=. The rook and pawn ending is equal and a draw is very likely.

B) 10.♘c3

10...♗xf3

There is another theoretical line here: 10...♘xd4 11.cxd5 ♗xf3 12.gxf3 c5±, but I do not consider it to be completely safe for Black.

There is also a well-known variation: 10...0–0 11.cxd5 ♘xd5 12.h3 ♗e6 13.a3±, which can also arise after 10.cxd5 ♘xd5 11.♘c3 0–0 12.h3 ♗e6 13.a3±

11.♕xf3 ♘xd4 12.♕d1

A completely equal endgame is reached after 12.♕h3 dxc4 13.♗xc4 ♘c2 14.♖d1 ♕c8 15.♕g3 0–0 16.♖b1 ♗d6 17.♕h4 ♕g4= Caruana – Gelfand, Biel 2009.

There is a transposition of moves after 12.♕g3 dxc4 13.♗xc4 0–0 14.♖d1 (14.♗g5 ♗d6 15.♕h4 h6 16.♗xf6 ♕xf6 17.♕xf6 gxf6∓ Lobron – Karpov, Hanover 1983) 14...c5 15.♗h6 ♘h5 16.♕h3 (16.♕g4 ♕d6) 16...♘f6 (16...♕d6 17.♗e3=) 17.♕g3=

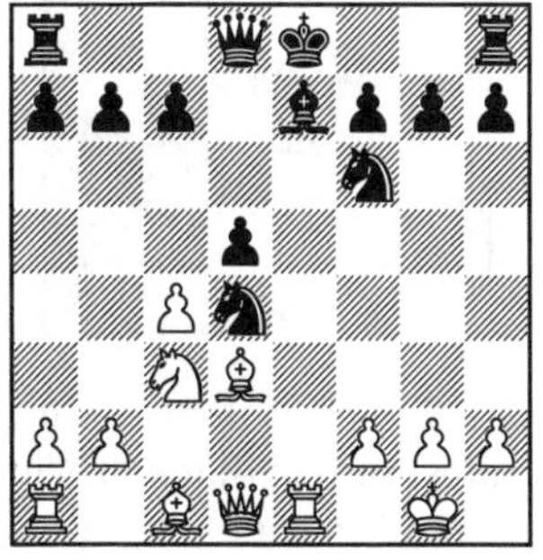

After 12.♕d1 Black can equalize in two ways. The move **B1) 12...♘e6** has been played numerous times, but there is also the simpler and more precise move **B2) 12...dxc4!**

We shall deal with them both, in order to make the situation completely clear.

B1) 12...♘e6

This move has been extensively analyzed in theory and tested many times in practice. Black can hold the position, but he must memorize a lot of variations and know them thoroughly. He plugs the all-important e-file, which White can open only by giving up his light-squared bishop, a tremendously important attacking piece.

White can now continue opening files with **B1a) 13.cxd5**, or else try to increase the pressure with **B1b) 13.♗f5**.

B1a) 13.cxd5 ♘xd5 14.♗b5+ c6 15.♘xd5 cxb5

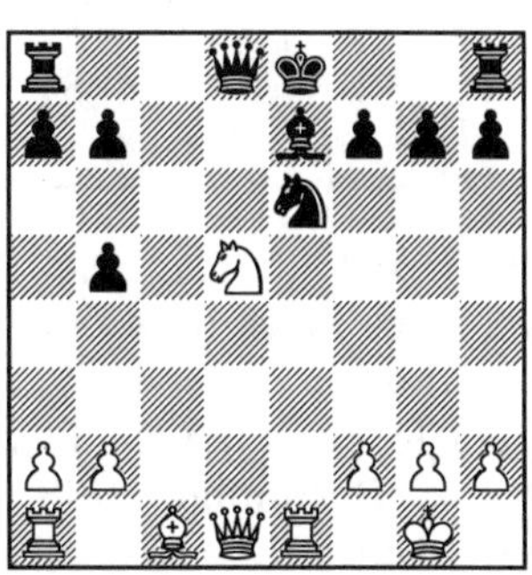

16.♕b3

White has also tried some other moves here:

16.a4 0–0 17.axb5 ♗c5 18.♗e3 ♗xe3 19.♖xe3 ♕g5 20.g3 ♖fd8 21.♖d3 ♔h8=, and White's edge is merely symbolic, Gashimov – Gelfand, Linares 2010;

16.♕h5 0–0 17.♘xe7+ ♕xe7 18.♕xb5 ♖fd8 19.♗e3 a6 20.♕b3 ♖ac8 21.♖ad1=, draw, Vachier Lagrave – Gelfand, Biel 2009;

16.♕d3 0–0 17.♗e3 ♘c7!N This is Black's most precise response (the position is less clear after 17...♗c5 18.♖ad1 ♗xe3 19.♖xe3±). 18.♘xe7+ ♕xe7 19.♗xa7 ♕d8!. Black has nothing to be afraid of with the queens off the board. His doubled pawns on the b-file are not really a liability. 20.♕xd8 ♖fxd8 21.♗b6 ♖dc8 22.a3 ♘d5 23.♗d4 f6=, with ideas of 24...♖c2 or 24...b4;

16.♗f4 ♘xf4 17.♖xe7+ ♔f8 18.♖e5 ♕d6 19.♕d2

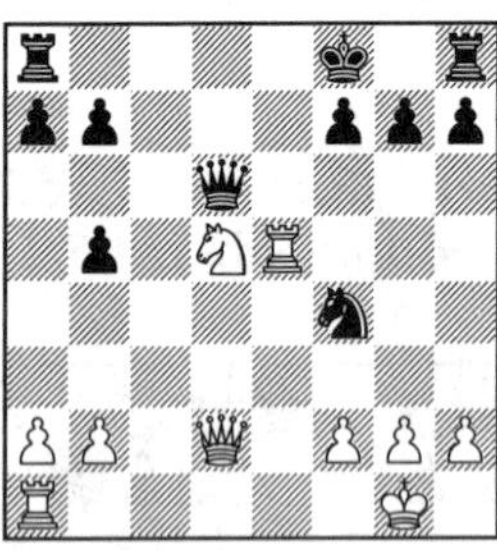

16...♕xe5! This is the right move, since Black does not need to be afraid of ghosts! (19...♘g6 20.♖ee1 f6 21.♖ad1± Naiditsch – Kramnik, Dortmund 2008) 20.♕b4+ ♔e8 21.♕xb5+ (White achieves nothing much with 21.♖e1 ♘e2+ 22.♔f1 ♖c8 23.f4 ♕xd5 24.♖xe2+ ♔d7 25.♖d2 ♕xd2 26.♕xd2 ♔c7 27.♕c3+ and now Black can choose between 27...♔b8 28.♕xg7 with an approximately equal but double-edged fight on both sides of the board, and the immediate draw after 27...♔b6 28.♕e3+ ♔a6 29.♕a3+) 21...♔d8 22.♖d1 ♘e2+ 23. ♔h1 (White loses immediately following 23.♔f1 ♘d4 24.♕a4 ♘c6–+ – and he remains a whole rook down, without having any dangerous discovered checks.) 23...♘d4 24.♕xb7 ♖c8 25.h3

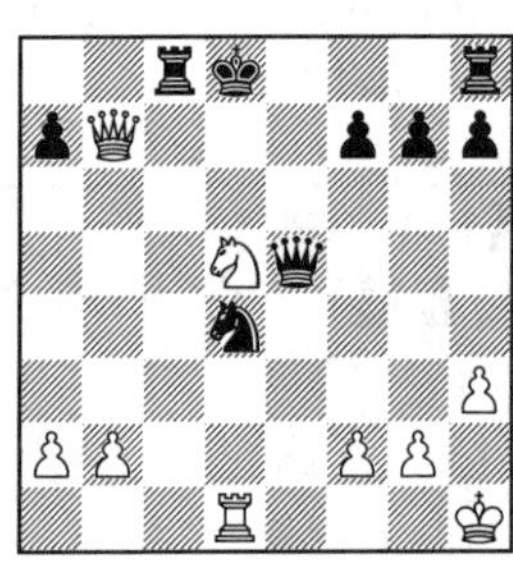

25...g5! This is the simplest and safest move; Black prevents a possible f2-f4 and at the same time protects his rook on h8 with his queen. Now White captures the knight on d4 in various lines, but in the meantime Black brings his king to safety and activates his h8-rook (instead, after 25...♖c5∞ the position becomes very sharp) 26.♕xa7 (26.♘c3 ♖c7 27.♕b8+ ♔d7 28.♕b4 ♔c8 29.♖xd4 ♖d8∓) 26...♔e8 27.♕xd4 ♕xd4 28.♖xd4 ♖c2 29.♖b4 ♔d7∓ and only White can lose this position.

16...0–0

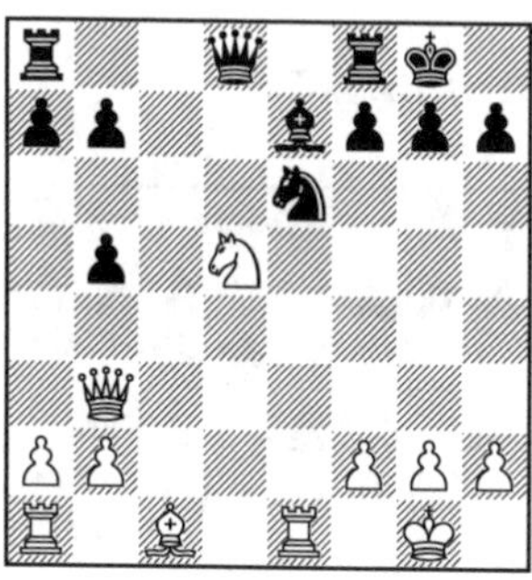

17.♗e3

17.♘xe7+ ♕xe7 18.♕xb5 ♖fd8 19.♗e3 a6 20.♕b3 ♖ac8 21.♖ad1=, draw, Vachier Lagrave – Gelfand, Biel 2009, and despite the fact that the bishop is usually stronger than the knight when there is play on both flanks, in this particular situation Black is safely holding the position. There are queens present on the board, and queen and knight work together at least as well as queen and bishop. It is also very good for Black that on the queenside his pawn-base on b7 is very securely protected.

17...♗c5 18.♖ad1 ♗xe3 19. ♖xe3 ♕a5

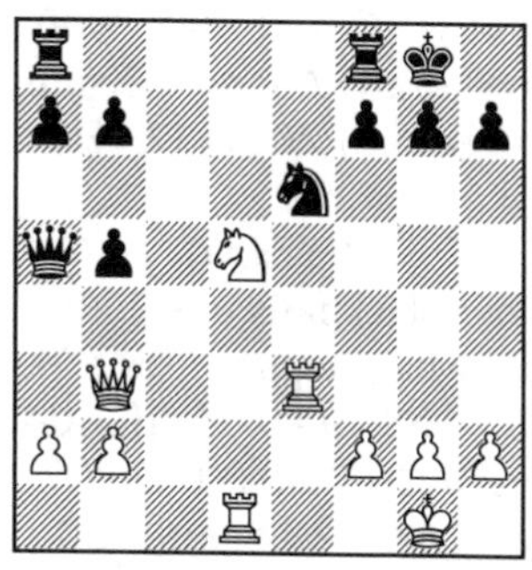

20.♕c2

In order to develop his initiative, White must somehow combat the enemy knight on e6, so it seems very logical for him to opt for the immediate 20.f4.

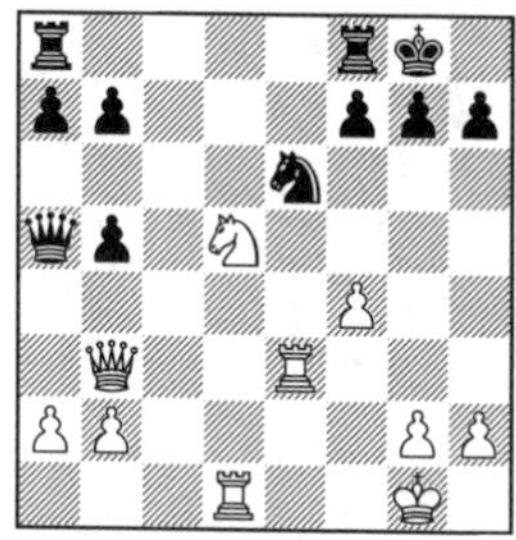

and now:

if Black retreats his knight immediately, before it has even been attacked, with 20...♘c7, then after 21.♕c3 ♕xc3 22.♘e7+ ♔h8 23. ♖xc3 ♘e6 (or 23...♘a6 24.♖d7 b4 25.♖c2 b6 26.♘c6 ♘c5 27.♖xa7 ♖xa7 28.♘xa7 ♖a8 29.♘c6 ♖xa2 30.♘xb4± and Black has no problems at all) 24.f5 ♖ad8 25.♖xd8 ♘xd8 26.♖c7± there arises an endgame in which Black's pieces are stuck on the back rank and his defence will be difficult;

it is more accurate for him to continue with 20...♖fd8 21.f5 ♘c7 22.♘e7+ ♔h8 23.♖de1 ♕b6 24. ♕xf7 ♖d1 25.♖xd1 ♕xe3+ 26.♔f1 (26.♔h1 ♕e2 27.♖b1 ♖d8=) 26... ♕f4+ 27.♔g1 ♕e3=, with a draw by perpetual check.

20...♖fe8 21.f4 b4 22.f5 ♘f8 23.♖ed3

23.♘e7+ ♔h8 24.♕c4 ♘e6 25. ♘d5 ♖ad8 26.♖ee1 ♕c5+ 27.♕xc5 ♘xc5 28.♖xe8+ ♖xe8 29. ♘xb4 g6

30.fxg6=, draw, Svidler – Gelfand, Moscow 2009.

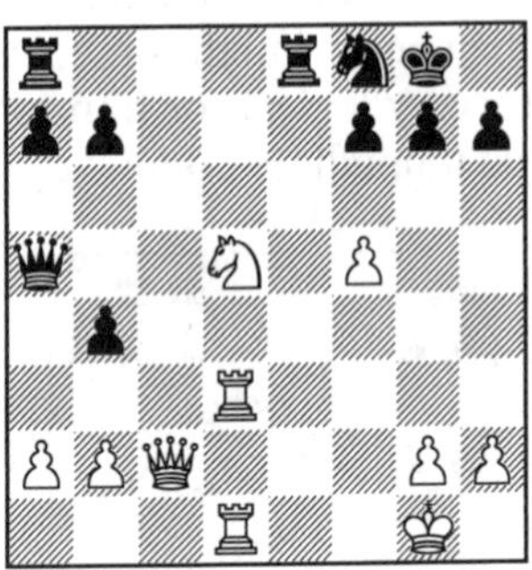

23...♖e5!

In the game Leko – Gelfand, Nalchik 2009, Black went wrong with: 23...♘d7?! and after 24.♕c7 ♕c5+ 25.♔f1 ♕b5 26.♕g3± he came under positional pressure.

24.f6 ♖ae8 25.fxg7

Or 25.♘e7+ ♔h8 26.♕f2 ♘e6 27.♖d7 g5=, and Black creates active counterplay, while preserving the extra material.

25...♔xg7 26.♕f2 ♘g6=

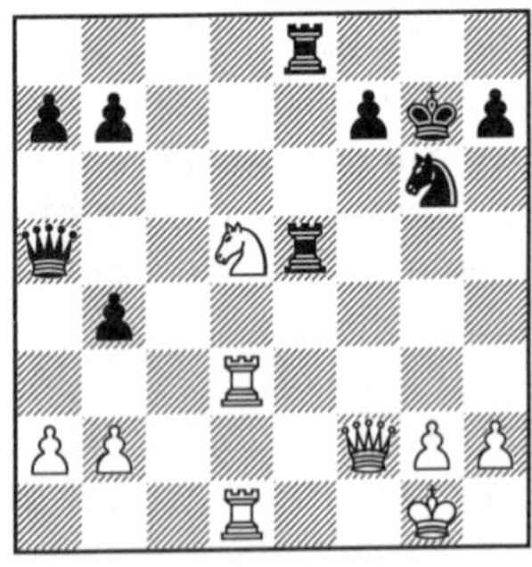

The position is so open that White must worry about his opponent's numerous unpleasant checks, so he is unable to exploit the fact that Black's king lacks safe shelter.

B1b) 13.♗f5

13...c6!

With this move Black protects his light squares as best he can.

The alternatives would not solve his problems:

13...d4 14.♘e2 d3 15.♘f4 ♘xf4 16.♗xf4 0–0 17.♕f3↑; Black's d-pawn is lost and White maintains the initiative;

13...dxc4 14.♕a4+ c6 15.♗xe6! (after 15.♕xc4, besides a transposition to the main line with: 15...0–0, White must reckon with 15...♘d4 16.♖d1 ♕a5 17.♗h3 c5∞, with a rather unclear position.) 15...fxe6 16.♕xc4 0–0 17.♖xe6! (17.♕xe6+ ♖f7 18.♗e3 ♕d6 19.♕xd6=, draw, Anand – Kramnik, Mainz (rapid) 2001) 17...♘d5 18.♗e3.

(diagram)

Now Black fails to equalize, no matter what he plays:

18...♔h8 19.♘xd5 (19.♗d4!?±) 19...cxd5 20.♕a4 (20.♕d3!? ♗f6 21.♗d4 ♕d7 22.♖ae1±) 20...♗f6

21.♖d1 ♗xb2 22.♕b5 ♗f6 23.♖xd5 ♕c8 24.♖ed6±, and White maintains a slight edge, thanks to his command of the centre.

18...♗f6! 19.♗c5 (19.♖d1 ♕d7 20.♖e4 ♗xc3 21.bxc3 ♖ae8 22.♖xe8 ♖xe8 23.♗xa7 b5 24.♕d4 ♕e7 25.h3 ♕a3 26.♗c5 ♕xa2=) 19...♕d7! (In the blitz game Morozevich – Ivanchuk, Moscow 2007, there followed 19...♖e8?! 20.♖xe8+ ♕xe8 21.♘xd5 cxd5 22.♕xd5+ ♕f7. Now White could have continued with 23.♕xf7+ ♔xf7 24.♗e3±, preserving his extra pawn and all his winning chances.)

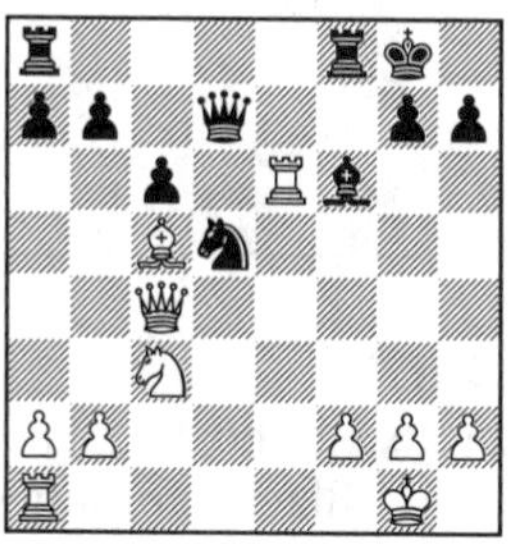

20.♖d6 (20.♖ae1 b5 21. ♕d3 ♗xc3 22.bxc3 ♖fe8=) 20...♕f7 21.♘xd5 cxd5 22.♖xd5 (22.♕xd5 ♖fd8 23.♕xf7+ ♔xf7 24.♖ad1 ♖xd6 25.♖xd6 b6 26.♗a3 ♖c8 27.g3 ♖c2 28.♖d7+ ♔g6 29. ♖xa7 ♗xb2=, and in this rook and pawn ending, Black only needs to exchange the queenside pawns to draw the game.) 22...♖fd8 23.♖ad1 ♖xd5 24.♖xd5 (in the variation 24.♕xd5 ♕xd5 25.♖xd5 ♗xb2 26. ♖d7 ♖c8 27.♗e3 a5 28.♖xb7, Black holds the balance thanks to the elegant move 28...♗d4!=) 24...♖e8 25.♗e3 ♗xb2 26.♕d3 ♗f6 27.h3±. White is better but Black should be able to draw with accurate defence.

14.cxd5 ♘xd5 15.♕g4

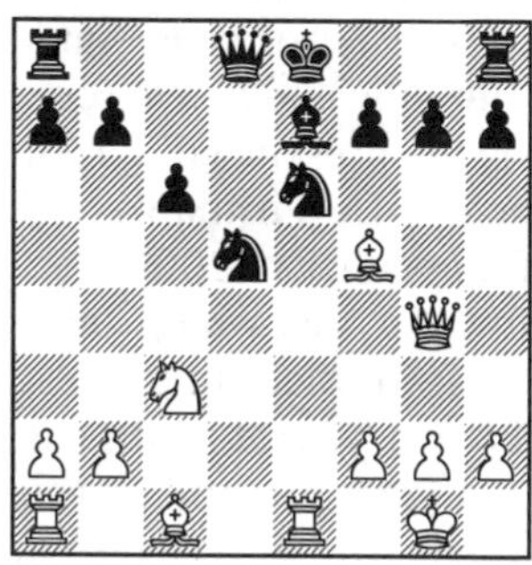

15...0–0

The move 15...♘xc3 opens additional files for White's attack and in the game Radjabov – Gelfand, Medias 2010, he exploited this brilliantly with 16.bxc3 0–0 17.♖b1! ♕c7 18.♗h6! ♗d6 19.♕h3! ♖fe8 20.♗xg7!+–, winning.

16.♘xd5

16.♗xe6 ♘xc3 17.bxc3 fxe6=

16.♕h3 g6 17.♗xe6 fxe6 18. ♕xe6+ ♖f7=

16...cxd5 17.♗xe6 fxe6 18. ♕xe6+ ♖f7 19.♗e3

19.♗f4 ♗c5=

19...♗f6 20.♖ad1

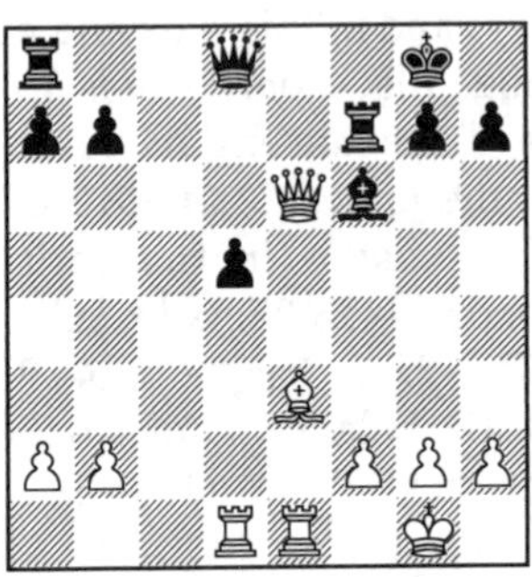

20...♕d7!

Here it would be imprecise for Black to opt for 20...♗xb2 21.♖xd5 ♕e7 22.♕g4±, and White maintains some advantage thanks to his safer king and active rooks, as well as the presence of queens on the board, De Firmian – Schandorff, Copenhagen 2000.

However, it would also be quite safe for Black to play 20...d4 21.♕b3 ♕d7 22.♗f4 ♖d8 23.♗e5 ♗xe5 24.♖xe5 g6=,and he will not part easily with his key d4-pawn.

21.♕xd5 ♕xd5 22.♖xd5 ♗xb2=; Black should draw effortlessly.

B2) 12...dxc4! 13.♗xc4 c5

14.♕a4+

White should enter an endgame in order to prevent his opponent from comfortably completing his development after castling. White keeps his two bishops and restores the material balance in the process, but falls behind in development.

14.♘b5 0–0 15.♘xd4 cxd4 16.♗f4 ♖c8 17.♕d3=; White has sufficient compensation for the pawn, but no more.

The line 14.♗g5 0–0 15.♖xe7 ♕xe7 16.♘d5 ♕d6 17.♘xf6+ gxf6 18.♗h6, Lawitsch – Halasz, Austria 1995, fails to 18...f5 19.♗xf8 ♖xf8∓, and Black ends up with a solid extra pawn.

14...♕d7 15.♕xd7+ ♔xd7

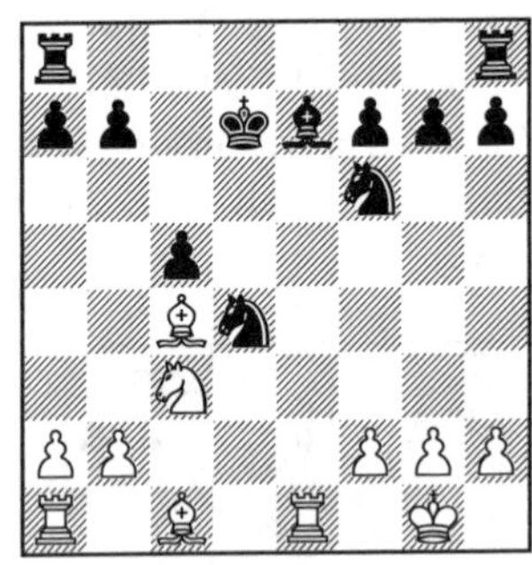

16.♗xf7N

After 16.♗g5 h6 17.♗h4 g5 18. ♗g3 ♗d6=, Black simplifies the position advantageously.

16.♗e3 ♖hd8! This is the right rook to place here, so that he can bring his king to safety on the e8-square. 17.♗xd4 (17.♗xf7 ♘c2∓; 17. ♖ac1 ♔e8!∓) 17...cxd4 18.♗b5+ ♔d6 19.♖ad1 ♔c5 (Black also equalizes with 19...♗f8 20.♖xd4+ ♔c7 21.♖f4 ♖ac8 22.♗c4 ♖d7=) 20.♖e5+ ♔d6 21.♖ee1 (White would not achieve much with 21. f4 ♗f8 22.♖xd4+ ♔c7 23.♖c4+ ♔b8 24.♗a4 a6 25.♗b3 ♖a7 26.a4 b6=) 21...♔c5 22.♖e5=, draw, Smirin – Giri, Khanty-Mansyisk 2010.

16...♗d6!

This is an important multi-purpose move. Black preserves the possibility of going to f8 with either of his rooks, depending on circumstances, and his bishop goes simultaneously to a very active position, creating the threat of ♘d4-c2.

Black cannot solve his problems with the natural line: 16...♖hf8 17.♗c4 ♗d6 18.♘b5! ♘xb5 (it is rather dubious for Black to opt for 18...♘c2 19.♖d1 ♘xa1 20.♘xd6 ♔c6 21.♗b5+ ♔b6 22.b4!± and White has a dangerous attack, despite the transition into an endgame) 19.♗xb5+ ♔c7 20.♗d2± and White has a slight edge, thanks to his bishop-pair.

17.♗c4

Black can counter 17.♖d1 with 17...♖af8!. This move is not easy to find, but it solves all his problems. His other rook remains on h8 as an attacking piece! 18.♗c4 ♘g4 19.f4 (if 19.f3 ♗xh2+ 20.♔h1 h5 21.♘e4 ♔c6∓ – see how useful the rook on the h8-square is!; or 19.h3 ♗h2+ 20.♔h1 ♘xf2+ 21.♔xh2 ♘xd1 22.♘xd1 b5∓ and Black's prospects are preferable) 19...♗xf4 20.♗xf4 ♖xf4 21.♘e2 ♖e4 22.♘xd4 ♖xd4 23.♖xd4+ cxd4 24.♖d1 ♘e5 25.♖xd4+ ♔c6=; Black maintains equality, thanks to his active pieces.

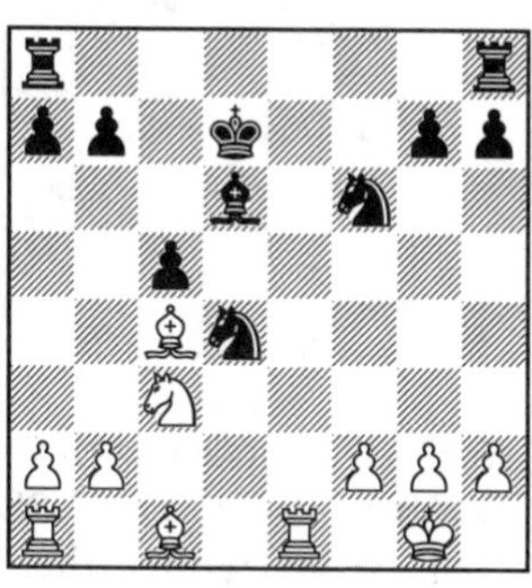

17...♘c2!

This is a concrete decision by Black; he cannot solve his problems just by playing positionally: 17...♔c6 18.♗d3! (Black is better after 18.♗g5 ♘c2 19.♗xf6 gxf6 20.♖e6 ♘xa1 21.♗b5+ ♔c7 22.♘d5+ ♔c8 23.♖xd6 ♖d8∓; the position is equal after 18.♖d1 ♖ad8 19.♗g5 h6 20.♗xf6 gxf6=) 18...♖ae8 (if 18...c4 19.♘e2! cxd3 20.♘xd4+ ♔d5 21.♘f3±, Black's d3-pawn will soon be lost) 19.♗d2± and although Black's pieces are centralized, White has the advantage thanks to his two powerful bishops.

18.♖d1 ♘xa1 19.♗f4

(diagram)

19...♘e8!

This is the most precise way to draw; the alternatives are not completely convincing:

If 19...♘c2 20.♖xd6+ ♔e7 21.♘d5+ ♘xd5 22.♖xd5± White's position is possibly preferable.

After 19...♖ad8 20.♖xd6+ ♔e7

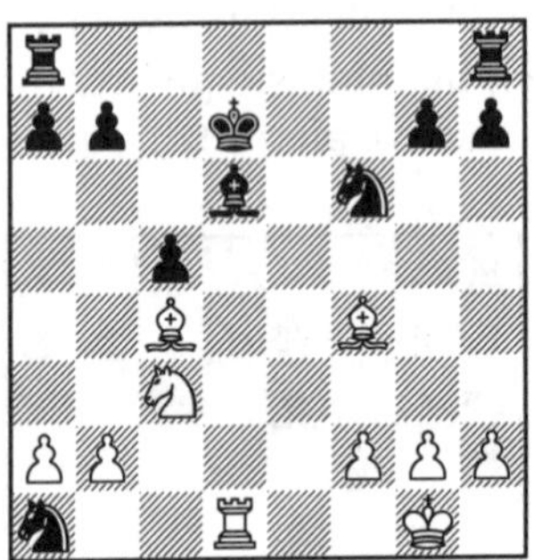

21.♖e6+ ♔d7, White has the rather risky try: 22.♖e5!? a6! 23.♗f1 ♖he8 24.♖xc5∞, with rather unclear consequences.

20.♘e4

It is again a draw after the transposition of moves 20.♘b5 ♖d8 21.♘xd6 ♘xd6 22.♖xd6+ ♔e7 23.♖e6+ ♔d7=

20...♖d8 21.♘xd6

After 21.♗g5 ♖a8 22.♖xa1 ♔c7∓ White's compensation for the exchange is insufficient.

21...♘xd6 22.♖xd6+ ♔e7 23.♖e6+ ♔d7=

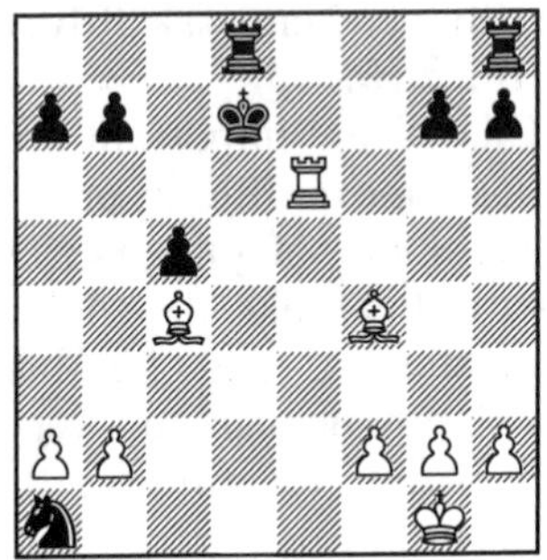

White must take the draw by perpetual check.

Conclusion

The variation with 9.c4 which we have analysed in this chapter does not present a serious danger to Black, as long as he is well prepared and understands the main ideas. I believe that in the key variation 9...♘f6 10.♘c3 ♗xf3 11.♕xf3 ♘xd4 12.♕d1, after 12...dxc4! Black equalizes even more convincingly than with the the more popular move 12...♘e6, especially since there are fewer lines to memorize.

Chapter 21 1.e4 e5 2.♘f3 ♘f6 3.♘xe5 d6 4.♘f3 ♘xe4 5.d4 d5 6.♗d3 ♘c6 7.0–0 ♗e7 8.♘c3

This variation was the cause of serious worries for Black for a long period of time. It is still quite popular, but the situation is different now, because Black has found reliable ways of obtaining an acceptable position. White is willing to slightly weaken his pawn-structure, but in return he gains a lead in development, which can even be increased in the future, because Black will have to redeploy his knight from the c6-square. It turns out to be misplaced there, since White's pawn-chain c3-d4 hampers its mobility and Black will need time to improve its position.

8...♘xc3

The other popular theoretical line here is: 8...♗f5 9.♖e1 ♘xc3 10. bxc3 ♗xd3 11.♕xd3 0–0±, but this seems to me to be much riskier for Black.

9.bxc3 ♗g4

If 9...0–0, then 10.h3!± and Black's light-squared bishop is deprived of any active squares to go to.

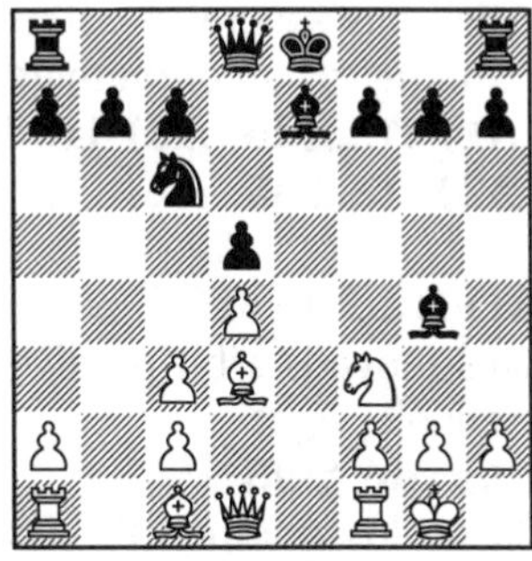

Now White's most popular alternative is the natural developing move **A) 10.♖e1**, but lately he has been playing more and more often **B) 10.♖b1**, intending to follow another scheme of development.

For 10.♗f4 0–0 11.♖e1 – see 10.♖e1.

For 10.h3 ♗h5 11.♖b1 ♖b8 – see 10.♖b1 ♖b8 11.h3 ♗h5.

A) 10.♖e1 0–0 11.♗f4

Here, after 11.♖b1, Black should play, not 11...♖b8, which transposes to the variation 10.♖b1 ♖b8 11.♖e1 0–0, but 11...b6! – reinforcing his entire queenside formation, while White's rook on b1 turns out to be useless.

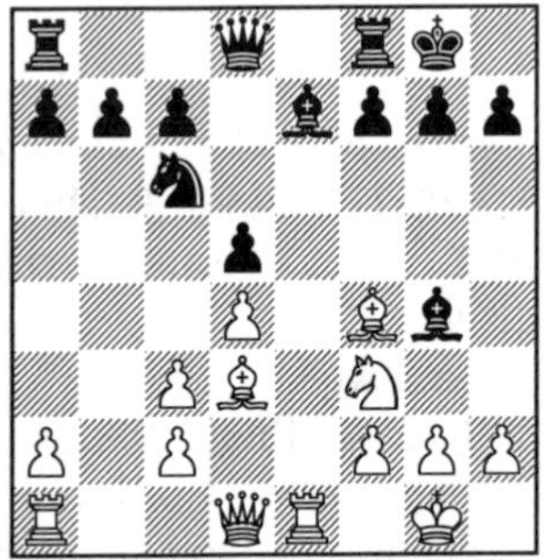

Black has several possibilities now and nearly all of them equalize: **A1) 11...♗d6**, **A2) 11...♖b8** and **A3) 11...♗h5**.

A1) 11...♗d6

This move is a bit passive but still reliable.

12.♗xd6 ♗xf3

Black loses after 12...♕xd6? 13.♗xh7+ ♔xh7 14.♘g5+ ♔g6 15.♕xg4 f5 16.♕h4 ♖h8 17.♖e6+ ♕xe6 18.♕xh8 ♖xh8 19.♘xe6+–

After 12...cxd6, White has the strong reply 13.h3! (It is weaker to play 13.♖e3 ♕d7 14.h3 ♗h5 15.♕d2. In the game Topalov – Gelfand, Wijk aan Zee 2008, Black now played 15...♖ae8 16.♘h4↑, when White had a rather unpleasant initiative, so it was much better to continue with 15...f5!N. It seems that this move solves all Black's problems. A possible continuation is: 16.♘g5 ♖f6 17.f4 h6 18.♘f3 ♗xf3 19.♖xf3 ♖e8 20.♖e3 ♖xe3 21.♕xe3 ♖e6 22.♕f3 ♘e7 23.c4 ♕a4 24.♗xf5 ♘xf5 25.♕xd5 ♘xd4 and here if 26.f5 ♘e2+ 27.♔h1 ♘f4∓ White is even slightly worse, while after 26.♕xd4 ♕c2 27.♕d5 ♕e4= it all ends in a draw.) 13...♗h5 14.♖b1 ♕d7 15.g4! ♗g6 16.♘h4!± – White has the initiative.

13.♕xf3

The endgame is about equal after 13.♗xc7 ♗xd1 14.♗xd8 ♗xc2 15.♗xc2 ♖fxd8=

13...♕xd6

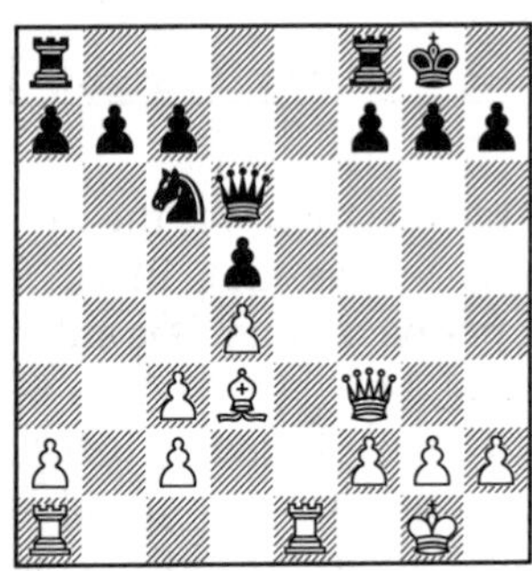

14.♖e3

14.h4 ♖ae8 15.h5 ♖e6 16.g3 ♖fe8 17.♖xe6 ♖xe6 18.♔g2 ♘e7= Ivanchuk – Huzman, Ohrid 2009.

White has tried 14.♖b1 here, but it does not seem sensible to provoke b7-b6. After 14...b6 15.♖e3 ♖ae8 16.♖be1, Svetushkin – Haba, Germany 2009, Black can opt for 16...♖e7!, as in the game Grischuk – Kramnik from the main line, except for the inclusion of the useful move b7-b6.

14...♖ae8 15.♖ae1

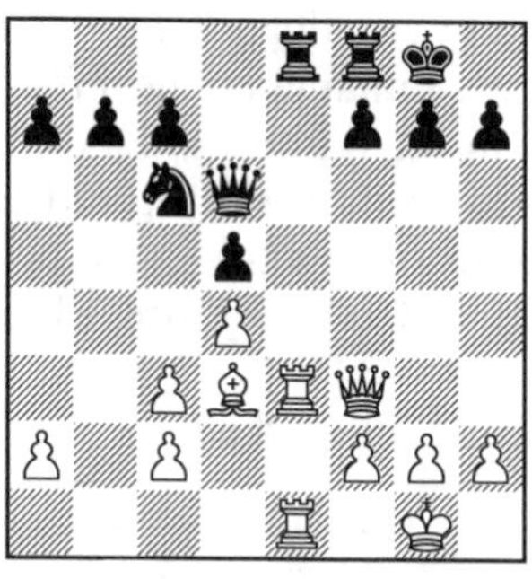

15...♖e7!

This excellent idea comes from Vladimir Kramnik and it practically equalizes the game.

If 15...♖xe3 16.♖xe3 g6 17.h4 ♘b8 18.h5 ♘d7, then after19.g4!± Leko – Kasimdzhanov, Nalchik 2009, White has the e-file and extra space on the kingside, so Black's defence will not be at all easy.

16.♖xe7 ♘xe7 17.h4 ♖d8!

Black plans to regroup his forces with h7-h6, ♔g8-f8 and ♘e7-g8-f6.

18.c4 b6 19.c3

The variation 19.♕e2 dxc4 20. ♗xc4 ♘f5 21.c3 g6= leads to equality.

19...h6 20.cxd5

Black replies to the prophylactic move 20.g3 with the consolidating move 20...c6, after which it is hard to see how White can improve his position.

20...♘xd5 21.♗c4 c6 22. ♖e5, Grischuk – Kramnik, Kazan 2011.

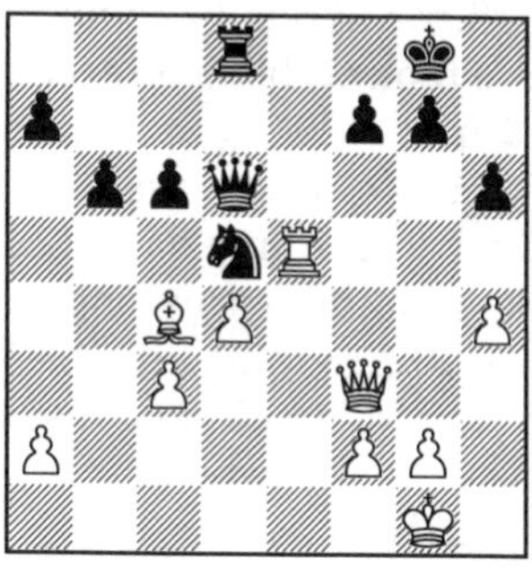

Here Black can equalize by force with **22...b5 23.♗b3 a5 24.g3 a4 25.♗xd5** (after 25.♗c2, Black continues with 25...♕a3 26.♕d3 g6∓ and White cannot hold on to his c3-pawn) **25... cxd5**=. The position has been simplified and a draw is very likely.

A2) 11...♖b8

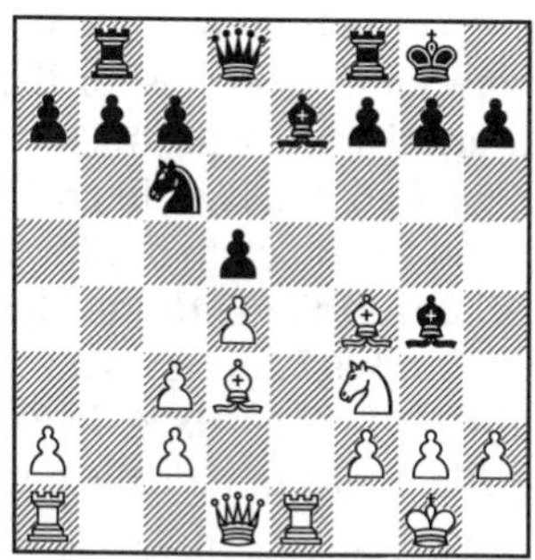

This amusing move was found by GM Alexander Motylev and it is not a bad one. The idea is for Black to play (say after 12.♖b1) 12...♗d6 13.♗xd6 ♕xd6 and now White does not have the move 14.♗xh7+ because after 14...♔xh7 15.♘g5 ♔g6 16.♕xg4 f5 17.♕h4

♖h8 18.♖e6 ♕xe6 19.♕xh8 ♔xg5 Black's rook on b8 is protected!

12.h3

For 12.♖b1 ♗d6 – see 10.♖b1.

After the immediate 12.♖e3, Black has the surprising reply 12...g5! 13.♗g3 f5 14.♗e5 ♘xe5 15.♖xe5 ♗d6 16.♖e1 c6∓ and his position is in no way worse.

12...♗h5

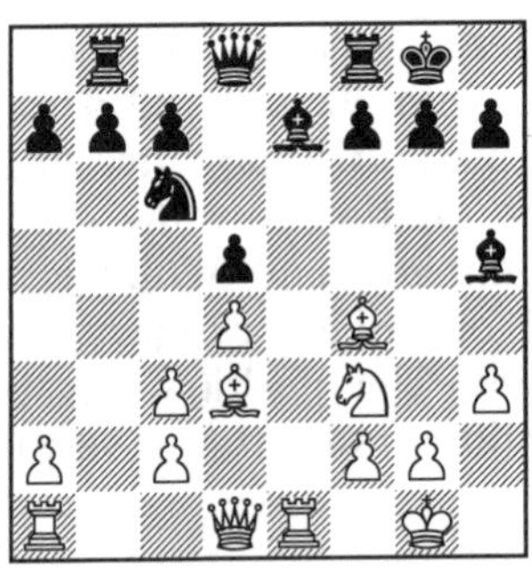

13.♕e2!N

This is the only way for White to create some problems for Black; the alternatives are harmless:

13.g4 ♗g6 14.♗xg6 hxg6 (it is also good for Black to opt for 14...fxg6 15.♗g3 ♕d7= with the idea of ♗e7-d6 and h7-h5) 15.♕d3 ♖e8 16.♖ab1 ♕d7 17.c4 dxc4 18.♕xc4 ♗d6= Black has practically equalized, Bologan – Motylev, Poikovsky 2010;

13.♖e3 ♗d6 14.♗xd6 ♕xd6 15.♖b1, Svidler – Motylev, Ohrid 2009. Here, Black played the rather tentative move 15...f6 and after 16.c4 dxc4 17.♗xc4+ ♔h8 18.c3 he ended up in a very unpleasant position. As is often the case in similar pawn-structures, with a white rook on e3 it would have been very good for Black to continue with 15...f5!. This pawn is ready to advance one square further, enhancing the effect of the pin on White's knight on f3. We analyzed the same position by transposition after 10.♖b1 ♖b8 11.♖e1 0–0 12.♗f4 ♗d6 13.♗xd6 ♕xd6 14.♖e3 f5! 15.h3 ♗h5.

13...♗d6 14.♕e3

14...♖e8

After Black's other options White maintains a slight advantage, which is quite typical for this variation. He dominates the e-file and his bishop is much better than Black's knight: 14...♕d7 15.♗xd6 ♕xd6 16.♘h4 ♗g6 17.♘xg6 hxg6 18.♖ab1±; 14...♗xf4 15.♕xf4 ♗xf3 16.♕xf3 ♕d6±

15.♕xe8+ ♕xe8 16.♖xe8+ ♖xe8 17.♗xd6 cxd6 18.♘h4 ♗g6 19.♘xg6

(diagram)

19...fxg6!

This is not a very obvious move; the idea is to be able to bring the king closer to the doubled central pawns.

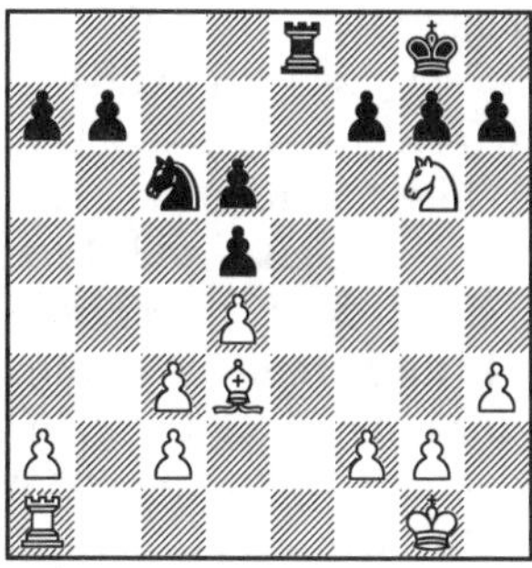

After the natural line: 19...hxg6 20.♖b1 b6 21.♔f1± White maintains the pressure.

20.♔f1 ♔f7 21.♖b1 b6 22.♗b5

It is essential for White to force the enemy rook away from the e8-square, in order to be able to bring his king closer to the centre.

22...♖c8 23.♔e2 ♘a5 24.♔d3 ♖c7 25.f4 ♖e7 26.g4 ♔f6=

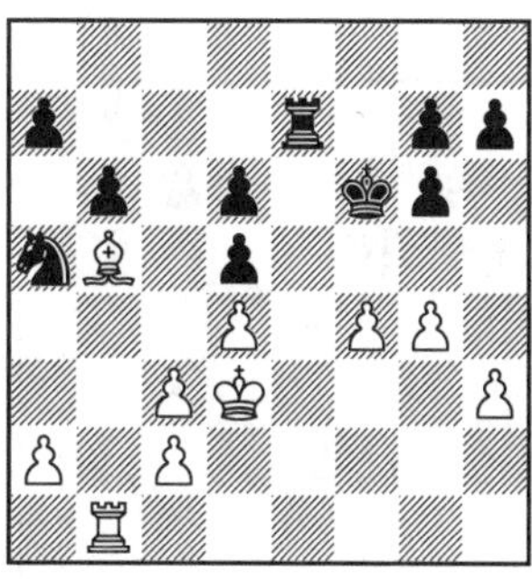

Black is simply waiting. White's position is slightly more pleasant, but he has practically no chances of achieving anything meaningful from his tiny edge.

A3) 11...♗h5

12.♖b1

It is bad for White to play 12.♖e3, Karjakin – Macieja, ACP Blitz 2004, in view of 12...g5! 13.♗g3 f5 14.♗e5 g4 15.♘d2 ♘xe5 16.♖xe5 ♗d6∓

12...♖b8

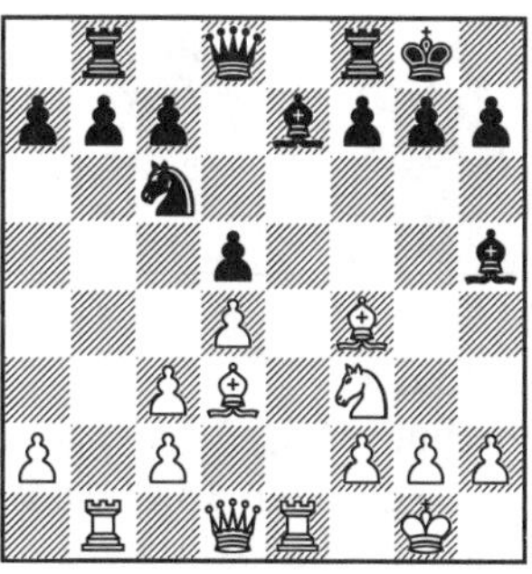

13.♕e2

Just as before, it is unfavourable for White to try to get rid of the pin on the knight with the help of the rook, because after 13.♖e3 Black has the powerful riposte 13...g5! 14.♗g3 f5 15.♗e5 g4 16.♘d2 ♘xe5 17.♖xe5 ♗d6∓

If 13.h3 ♗d6 14.♗xd6 ♕xd6 15.♖e3 f5!= and by transposition of moves we have again reached the position arising from the variation 10.♖b1 ♖b8 11.♖e1 0–0 12. ♗f4 ♗d6 13.♗xd6 ♕xd6 14.♖e3 f5 15.h3 ♗h5.

13...♗d6 14.♕e3 ♕d7

It is rather dubious for Black to play 14...f6 15.♗xd6 ♕xd6 16. ♘h4 ♖fe8 17.♕h3±

White obtains a normal slight edge, which is just what he is striving for in this variation, after 14...♗xf4 15.♕xf4 ♗xf3 16.♕xf3 ♕d6 17.♖e3 g6 18.h4± Sasikiran – Wang Yue, Visakhapatnam 2008.

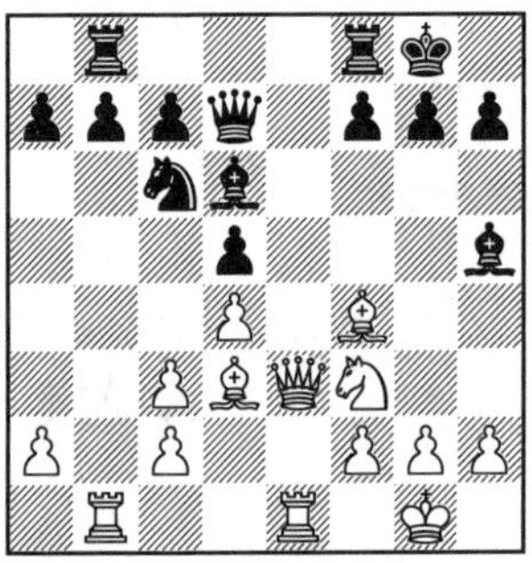

15.♗xd6

The line: 15.♘e5 ♗xe5 16.dxe5 ♗g6 17.♗xg6 hxg6 18.♖bd1 ♕e6= leads to an approximately equal position, Smeets – Gelfand, Nice 2010.

15.♘g5 h6 16.♘h3 ♗g6!N (It is weaker for Black to play here 16... ♗g4 17.♕g3 ♗xh3 18.♗xd6 cxd6 19.♕xh3 ♕xh3 20.gxh3 ♖fd8 21. ♖b5 ♔f8 22.♖eb1 b6 23.♖xd5 ♖bc8 24.c4 ♔e7, Bacrot – Wang Yue, Nanjing 2010. White now avoided a fight with 25.♖e1+ ♔f8 26.♖b1=, but he could have tried 25.♔g2⩲, since the immediate attack on the c4-pawn would not solve Black's problems after 25...♘a5 26.♖e1+ ♔f8 27.c5 dxc5 28.♖xd8+ ♖xd8 29.dxc5 bxc5 30.♖e5 ♖c8 31.♗b5± and White maintains a clear advantage.) 17.♕g3 ♗xd3 18.♗xd6 ♕xd6 19.♕xd6 cxd6 20.cxd3 b5 21.♘f4 (there remains nothing to fight for after 21.a3 a5 22.♘f4 b4 23.axb4 axb4=) 21...b4 22.♘xd5 bxc3 23.♘xc3 ♘xd4 24.♘e4 d5 25.♘c3 ♖xb1 26.♖xb1 ♖c8 27. ♘xd5 ♖c2 28.a4 ♖a2= with an imminent draw in sight.

15...♕xd6 16.♘h4 ♗g6 17. ♘xg6 hxg6 18.h4

The move 18.♕g3= leads to an equal endgame, draw, Bologan – Gelfand, Khanty-Mansiysk 2010.

18...a6!

Black's idea is to continue with b7-b5.

19.a4 ♘a5 20.g3 ♕c6 21. ♕g5, Fressinet – Li Chao, Wijk aan Zee 2011.

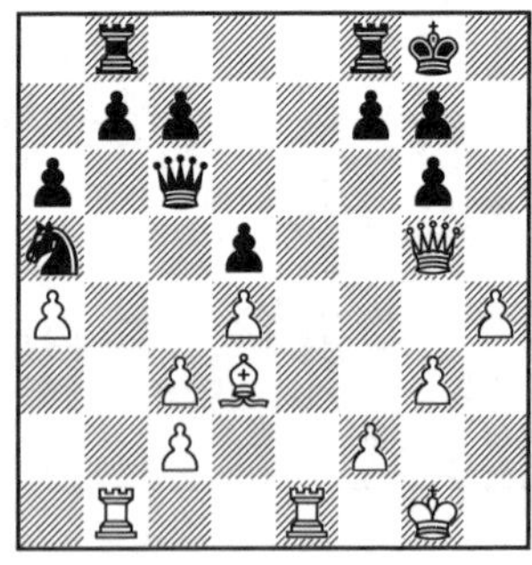

Here, in order to maintain the balance, Black needed to play **21...♖fe8!**, for example: **22.♔g2** (The idea of this move is after h4-h5 to redeploy the rook to the h-file for an attack) **22...♖xe1**

23.♖xe1 ♕xc3 24.♖e7 ♕xd4 25. ♖xc7 ♘c6 26.f4 ♕c5 27.♖d7 (27.♕g4 ♖d8 28.f5 – 28.♖xb7 ♘b4∓ – 28...♕d6 29.♖xb7 ♘e5=) **27...♘b4 28.♕e5 ♘xd3 29. ♕xb8+ ♔h7 30.cxd3 ♕c2+ 31.♔h3 ♕xd3**= White cannot avoid the perpetual check.

B) 10.♖b1

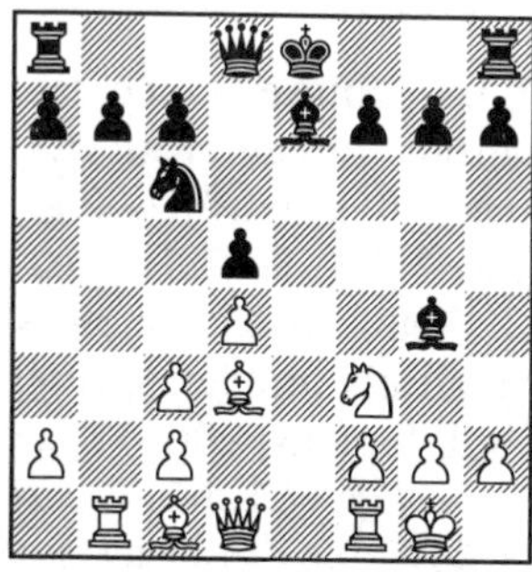

It is considered useful to attack the b7-pawn, forcing Black to make an awkward move with his rook. Later, White can transfer his own rook to the kingside, via the b3- or b5- squares (naturally, after clearing the third rank by advancing c3-c4).

10...♖b8 11.♖e1

Black is in no danger after 11.h3 ♗h5 12.g4 (12.♖e1 – see 11. ♖e1 0–0 12.h3 ♗h5; 12.♗f5 0–0 13.♕d3 ♗g6 14.♖e1 – see 10.♖b1 ♖b8 11.♖e1 0–0 12.h3 ♗h5 13.♗f5 ♗g6 14.♕d3; after 12.c4, Black's simplest reaction would be 12... ♘xd4 13.g4 ♘xf3 14.♕xf3 ♗g6=) 13.♘e5 ♗xd3 14.♘xd3 0–0 15.♕f3 ♘a5 16.♗f4, Kamsky – Inarkiev, Jermuk 2009. Black's simplest and most natural way to equalize would be 16...♘c4. After 17.♖fe1, Black can play 17...♗d6!, equalizing, because the d5-pawn would be taboo; if 18.♕xd5, Black has the tactical shot 18...♘d2!∓

11...0–0

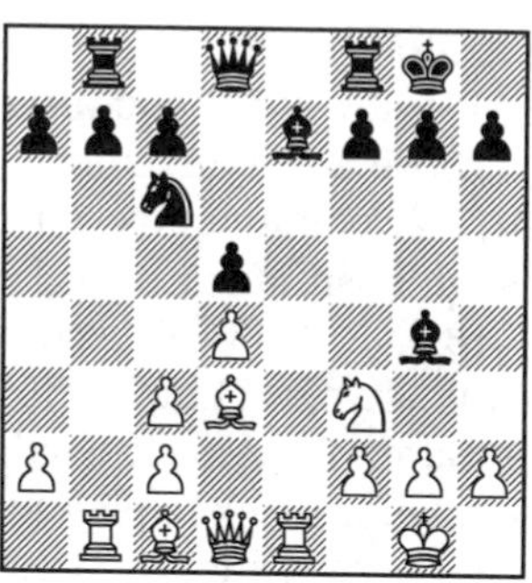

12.h3

White has also tried developing his bishop to f4 in this position:12.♗f4 ♗d6 13.♗xd6 ♕xd6 14. ♖e3 (for 14.h3 ♗h5 15.♖e3 f5! – see 14.♖e3 f5! 15.h3 ♗h5)

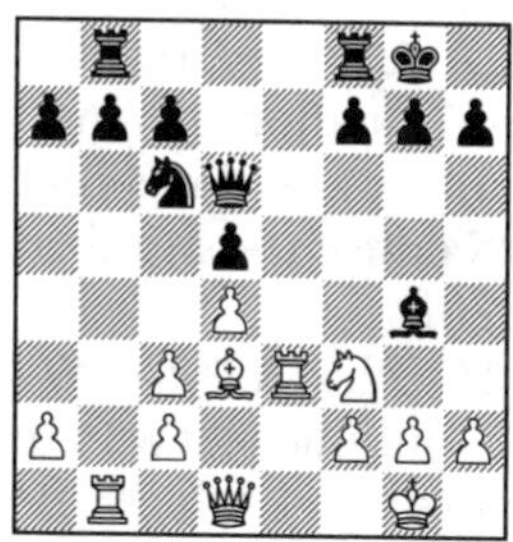

14...f5! The idea of this move is very simple. After f5-f4, the pin on the knight will be very unpleasant. 15.h3 (It is also possible for White to play 15.♖e1, with the idea of continuing with ♗d3-e2, in order to get rid of the pin and later exploit the vulnerability of the e5 and e6-squares, caused by the move f7-f5. In that particular case, Black can solve all his problems with 15...b6!=, freeing the rook from the defence of the b7-pawn and planning to continue with ♖be8) 15...♗h5 16.♕e1 (16. ♕e2?! ♖f6 17.♖ae1, Brkic – Huzman, Plovdiv 2008 and after the all-purpose fortifying move 17... ♖bf8!, Black obtains an even more pleasant position) 16...f4 17.♖e6 ♕d7 18.♗b5 ♗xf3 19.♗xc6 bxc6 20.♖xb8 ♖xb8 21.♖e7 ♕f5 22. ♖e8+ (after 22.gxf3, it would be quite safe for Black to play simply 22...h6=, securing an escape square for the king on h7) 22... ♖xe8 23.♕xe8+ ♕f8 24.♕e6+ ♕f7 25.♕c8+ ♕f8 26.♕e6= with a draw by perpetual check.

Black's other possible responses to 14.♖e3 fail to solve his problems:

14...♕d7 15.h3 ♗f5 16.♗xf5 ♕xf5 17.♕e2± and thanks to his total domination of the d-file, White maintains dangerous pressure, Naiditsch – Murdzia, Germany 2011;

if 14...♗h5 15.♕d2 f6 White should continue, not with the routine move 16.c4, which after 16... dxc4 17.♗xc4+ ♔h8 18.c3 ♗xf3 19.gxf3 ♘e5= leads to approximate equality, but with 16.♘h4!↑ and White maintains a dangerous initiative, which will require very precise play from Black to neutralize.

14...f6 15.h3 (15.c4 dxc4 16. ♗xc4+ ♔h8 17.c3 ♘e7 18.h3 ♗f5=) 15...♗h5

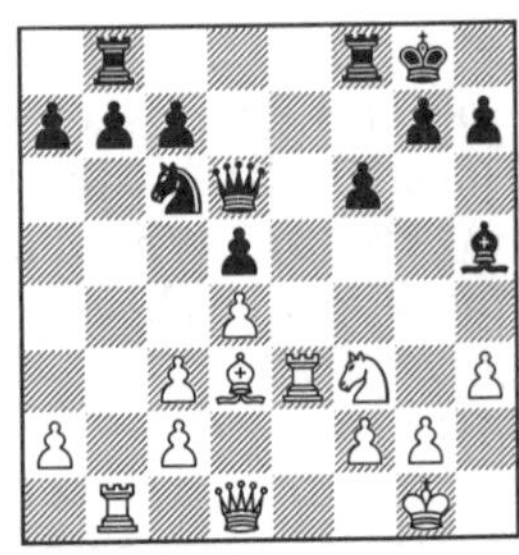

16.c4 (White cannot create any dangerous threats with 16.♕e2, because after 16...♕d7 17.g4 ♗f7 18.♘h4 ♖fe8 19.♘f5 ♖xe3 20. ♕xe3 ♖e8= Black successfully solves all his problems, Anand – Gelfand, Monaco 2006) 16...dxc4 (if 16...♘xd4 17.♗xh7+ ♔xh7 18. ♕xd4 ♗f7 19.c5↑ Black's king is very weak, thanks to which White initiative develops effortlessly) 17.♗xc4+ ♔h8 18.c3± with a better position for White, Svidler – Motylev, Ohrid 2009.

12...♗h5

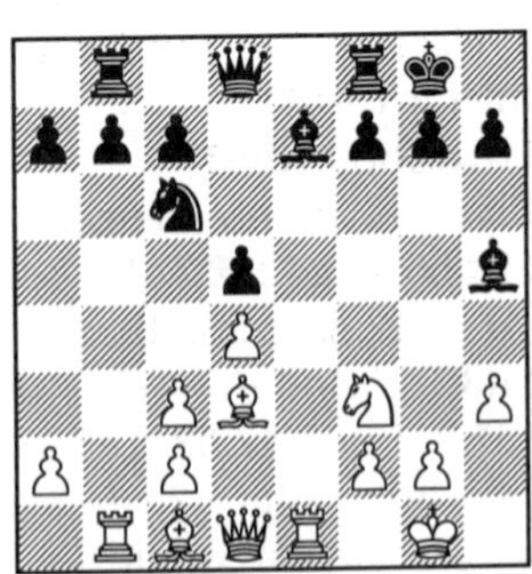

13.♗f5

The move 13.g4 only creates additional weaknesses, so it is not at all dangerous. After 13...♗g6 14.♗f4 ♗d6 15.♕d2 ♘e7 (15...♕d7=) 16.♘e5 ♗xd3 17.♘d3 ♘c8 (17...♘g6 18.♗xd6 ♕xd6 19.f4 f5 20.g5 c5=) 18.♘e5?! (it would be more prudent for White to continue with 18.♖e2=) 18...♘b6∓ Black's position was even more pleasant in the game Gashimov – Illescas Cordoba, Barcelona 2007.

In Solak – Istratescu, Dresden 2008, White played 13.c4!? dxc4 (An endgame a pawn down arises after 13...♘xd4 14.♗xh7+ ♔xh7 15.♕xd4 ♗f6 16.♕xd5 ♕xd5 17.cxd5 ♗xf3 18.gxf3 ♖fd8 19.c4 b5 20.♖e4± and it would be far from easy for Black to save the game.) 14.♗xc4 ♗d6 (if 14...♗xf3 15.♕xf3 ♘xd4 16.♕e4 ♗c5 17.♖xb7 ♖xb7 18.♗d3 g6 19.♕xb7 ♘e6 20.♕e4± White maintains a slight edge, and the same is true of the variation 14...b5 15.♖xb5 ♖xb5 16.♗xb5 ♗xf3 17.♕xf3 ♘xd4 18.♕e4 ♘xb5 19.♕xe7 ♘d4 20.♕e4± – White's bishop is better than his opponent's knight in a position with play on both wings, so Black cannot equalize) 15.c3

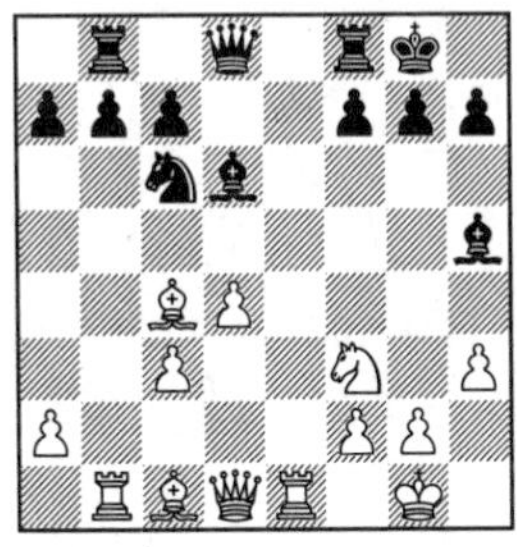

Now Black's most precise move seems to be the developing 15...♖e8 (In the above-mentioned game there followed 15...a6 16.♗d3 b5; Here White can play 17.a4! b4 18.♗d2!± creating definite problems for his opponent, because in many variations Black's knight on c6 has no comfortable squares to go to) 16.♗e3 (16.♖xe8+ ♕xe8 17.♗e3 ♘e7=; 16.♖e3!? h6 17.♗d3 ♖xe3 18.♗xe3 ♘e7 19.c4 c6=) 16...h6 17.♗d3 ♕f6= with equality.

13...♗g6 14.♕d3

14...♗xf5!N

The alternatives for Black are less convincing.

It is bad for him to opt for 14...♕d6 15.♗xg6 hxg6 16.c4 dxc4 17.♕xc4 and his queen on d6 is misplaced in many different variations, for example: 17...♗f6, Sutovsky – Zhou Weiqi, Khanty-Mansiysk 2009, 18.d5! ♘e5 19.♘xe5 ♗xe5 20.♖b3 ♖fe8 21.♖be3±

Black holds his position by a miracle after 14...a6 15.♗xg6 hxg6 16.c4 (otherwise Black plays b7-b5) 16...dxc4 17.♕xc4 ♗f6

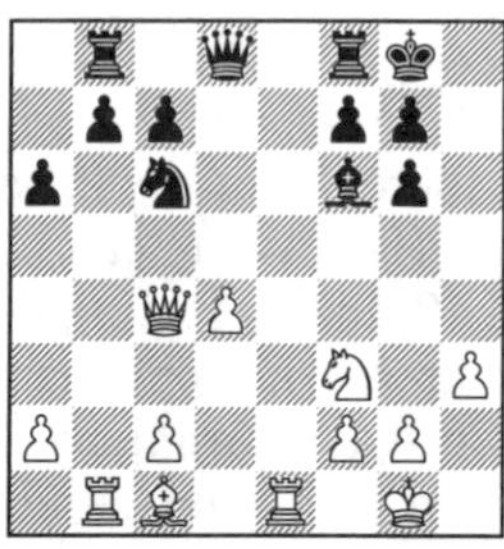

18.♗f4 (18.d5 ♘a5 19.♕d3 b5=; if 18.c3, then not 18...♖e8, because of 19.♗f4± and he must reckon with the threat d4-d5, but 18...♕d7 19.♗g5 b5 20.♕c5 ♕d6 21.♕xd6 cxd6 22.♗f4 ♖fd8=) 18... ♘xd4 19.♘xd4 ♕xd4 20.♕xd4 ♗xd4 21.♗xc7 ♖be8 22.♖ed1 ♗c5 23.♖d5 b6, Efimenko – Li Chao, Wijk aan Zee 2011. White can continue here with 24.a4! (the above-mentioned game continued 24.♗xb6 ♗xb6 25.♖xb6 ♖e1+ 26.♔h2 ♖e2= and it ended immediately in a draw) 24...♖c8 25.♗xb6 ♗xb6 26.♖xb6 ♖xc2 27. ♖xa6 ♖e8 28.♖d4 g5 29.♖g4±, White maintained some winning chances, but with correct defence Black should be able to draw.

It is quite possible to play 14... ♘a5.

Now White would not achieve much with 15.♘e5 ♗d6 16.♗f4 (16. ♘d7 ♖e8 17.♗d2 ♖xe1+ 18.♖xe1 ♖a8=) 16...c6 (With this move Black secures the c7-square for his queen) 17.♗xg6 fxg6! (after 17...hxg6 it would be problematic for him to advance f7-f6) 18.♗g3 ♕c7 19.♖e2 ♖be8 20.♖be1 ♗xe5 21.♖xe5 ♕f7=. A continuation presenting more danger to Black is 15.♗f4 ♘c4 16.♘e5! (After 16. ♖e2 Black can play 16...♗f6 and the position simplifies to equality after both 17.♘d2 ♘xd2 18.♗xd2 ♖e8= and 17.♘h2 ♗g5! 18.♗xg6 fxg6 19.♗xg5 ♕xg5=) 16...♗d6 17. ♗xg6 hxg6 18.♗g3! White is able to maintain the tension with this move (18.♘xc4 dxc4 19.♕f3 b5 20. ♗xd6 cxd6 21.♕d5 ♕a5=) but after 18...♗xe5 19.dxe5 ♖e8 20.♖ed1 ♘b6± Black plans to transfer his queen to the blockading square e6. White has only a minimal advantage in this complicated position, thanks to his extra space.

15.♕xf5 b5!

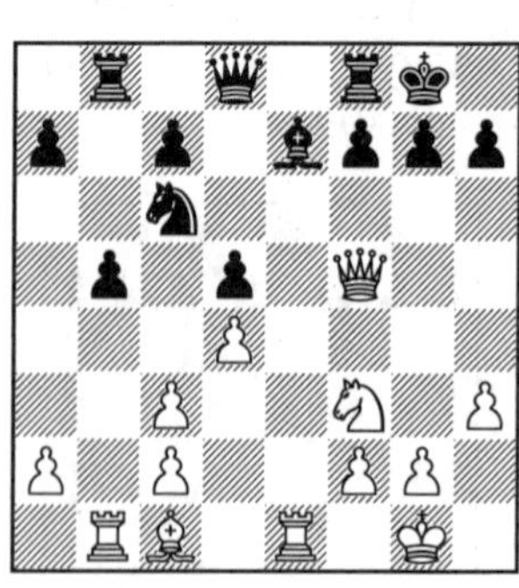

It is essential for Black to deprive his opponent of the possibility of c3-c4. As well as controlling the c4-square, Black has the possibility of preparing the breakthrough b5-b4, activating his forces on the queenside.

16.♗f4 g6 17.♕g4 ♗d6 18.♖e2 ♗xf4 19.♕xf4

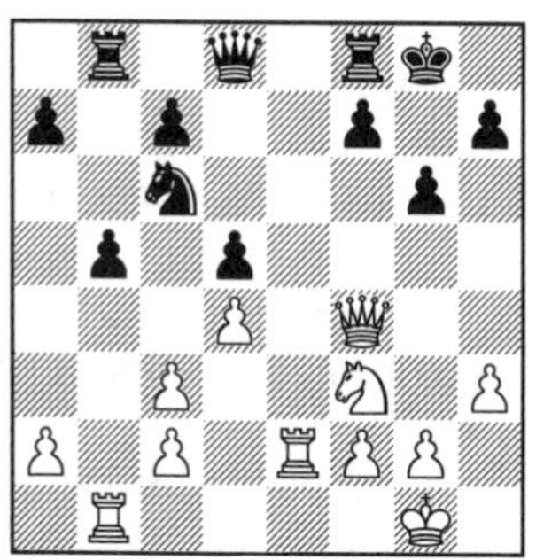

19...♔g7!

It is very important not to let White's queen go to the h6-square, because in that case Black will have to weaken his pawn-structure.

After 19...♕d6 20.♕h6 f6 21.♖be1 ♕d7 22.♕f4, Black still has problems to worry about.

20.♖be1 ♕d6=

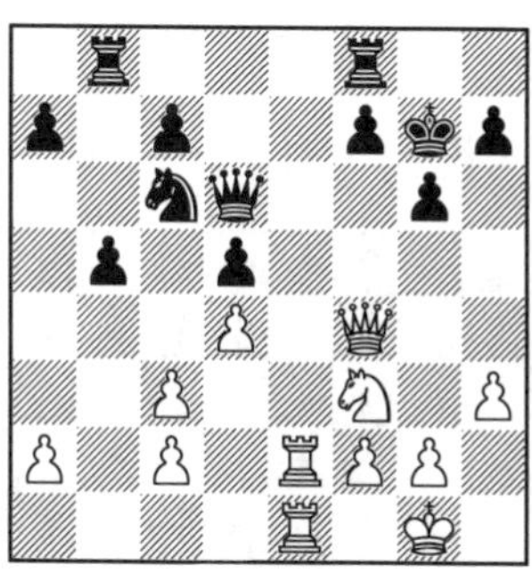

Black equalizes, because after **21.♕g4** he has the strong reply **21...♖b6!**, with the idea of continuing with ♖b6-a6, reminding White that he has numerous weaknesses on the queenside.

Conclusion

The variation beginning with 8.♘c3 is very problematic for Black and requires very precise play from him to maintain equality. It is essential to remember that if White tries to get rid of the pin on his f3-knight with the help of the move ♖e1-e3, then it is almost always good for Black to play f7-f5!, seizing the initiative on the kingside. Strangely enough, this resource, even under the most favourable circumstances, has been generally ignored by Black.

Chapter 22 1.e4 e5 2.♘f3 ♘f6 3.♘xe5 d6 4.♘f3 ♘xe4 5.d4 d5 6.♗d3 ♘c6 7.0–0 ♗e7 8.c4

8...♘b4

The move 8...♘f6 is also quite well regarded by theory; Black is trying to gain secure control over the d5-square.

Black sometimes plays 8...♗g4, but White can continue with the following unpleasant variation: 9.cxd5 ♕xd5 10.♘c3 ♘xc3 11.bxc3 0–0 12.♖b1 ♗xf3 (12...♗d6 13.♗e4 ♕h5 14.h3±) 13.♕xf3 ♕xf3 14.gxf3± and thanks to his two powerful bishops, White maintains a slight but stable advantage.

In this chapter we shall analyse **A) 9.cxd5** and **B) 9.♖e1**.

If White allows his bishop to be exchanged without creating any immediate threats, Black has every reason to be happy with the position after for example 9.♘c3 ♘xc3 10.bxc3 ♘xd3 11.♕xd3 dxc4 12.♕xc4 0–0∓. White's central pawns are harmless, while Black's bishop-pair might become a powerful force.

It is not sensible for White to exchange his bishop for the centralized enemy knight: 9.♗xe4 dxe4 10.♘e5 0–0 11.a3 (it is even worse for him to opt for 11.♘c3 f6 12.♘g4 ♘d3∓) 11...♘c6 12.♘xc6 bxc6 13.♘c3 f5∓ and Black's prospects are again preferable, owing to his powerful bishop-pair.

In the next chapter we shall deal with the retreat of White's bishop 9.♗e2, which is a very solid move and the main line of this variation.

A) 9.cxd5

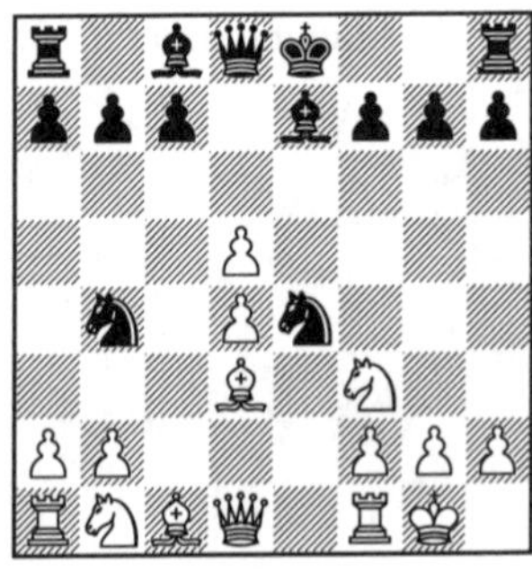

This is a very sharp and concrete move which leads to a long forcing line. White is willing to part with his light-squared bishop and he allows its possible exchange. In return he gains the e-file, on which he plans to organize an attack against the enemy king, which has not yet castled.

9...♘xd3 10.♕xd3 ♕xd5

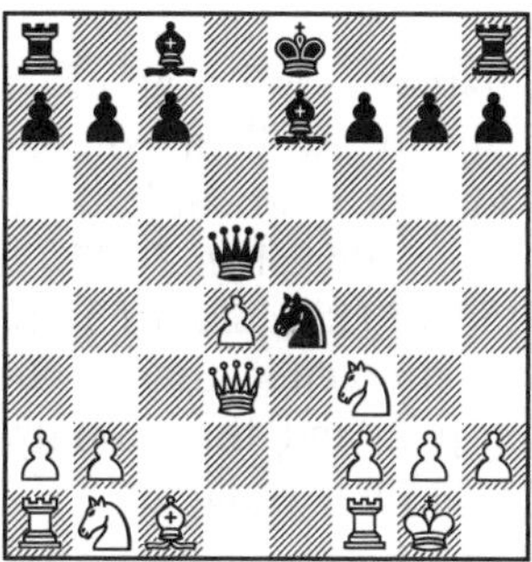

11.♖e1

White exerts pressure along the e-file and attacks the knight on e4; this is the only way for him to justify his positional concession on move nine.

If he plays less ambitiously, then after 11.♘c3 ♘xc3 12.bxc3 0–0 13.c4 ♕f5∓, Black's prospects are slightly better.

11...♗f5

(diagram)

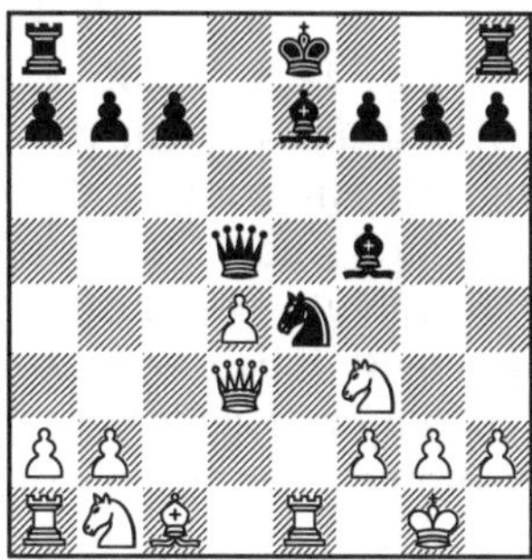

12.g4

The idea of this move is to force the enemy bishop to go to g6, so that Black cannot plug the open e-file with ♗f5-e6.

White's alternatives here cannot provide him with anything more than equality:

12.♘e5 0–0–0! (this move is much more promising for Black than the more popular 12...g6) 13.♕f3 g6 14.g4 (It would be more prudent for White to play here 14.♘c3 ♘xc3 15.bxc3 ♕xf3 16. gxf3 ♗e6 17.♘xf7 ♗xf7 18.♖xe7 ♖d7= with simplification and a draw.).

Here, Black can choose between two attractive possibilities:

14...♗b4 15.♖e3 (In the game Adams – Smeets, London 2009 White made a terrible blunder, which is hardly surprising in such a sharp and complicated position: 15.♖e2? ♗xg4 16.♘xg4 ♘c3 17.♕xd5 ♘xe2+ 18.♔f1 ♖xd5 19.♔xe2 ♖xd4 20.♘e3 ♖h4 21.♘f1 ♗d6–+ – and after the further loss of his h2-pawn White went on to lose the game.) 15...♕xd4 16.gxf5 ♘g5 17.♕e2 ♗d6 18.♔f1 ♕f4 19.♘d3 ♕xf5∞ – The position arising is tremendously difficult to evaluate, since there are so many possibilities to consider.

14...♖hg8! I believe this is a very good move for Black; it indirectly protects the bishop on f5. 15.gxf5 (If White does not capture the bishop, he will simply be left with too many kingside weaknesses to worry about: 15.♘c3 ♘xc3 16.♕xc3 ♗d7 17.♗f4 ♗d6∓) 15...♗b4N 16.♖e3 gxf5+ 17.♔f1 (17.♔h1?? ♘xf2#) 17...♕e6 18.♘d3 (18.a3 ♗d6→) 18...♖xd4 19.♘xb4 ♖xb4 20.♘c3 ♖d4 21.♖e1 ♕g6 (Black has an alternative here in 21...♕c4+ 22.♘e2 ♖d6→, with numerous threats.) 22.♘xe4 ♖xe4 23.♖xe4 fxe4∓ – Black's attack is extremely dangerous and there are too many annoying checks lurking on all sides.

12.♘c3 ♘xc3 13.♕xc3 ♗e6

14.♖e5 (After White's routine developing move 14.♗f4 Black can simply complete his development with 14...0–0∓, or else play 14...♗d6 15.♗xd6 cxd6∓ and in both cases he has no problems whatsoever. If White becomes greedy and gobbles up the pawn, then he will end up in a very passive position with "bad" pieces. 14.♕xc7 ♗d6 15.♕c3. White will not change anything by retreating the queen to c2, because Black can simply castle and then bring his rooks into action. 15...0–0⩱ – Black has two powerful bishops and a perfect blockade on d5, and he also dominates the c-file, all of which adds up to excellent compensation for the pawn, Mihalcisin – Pavasovic, Portoroz 2005.) 14...♕c6 15.♕a5 (15.♕xc6 bxc6= Black has no problems, thanks to his bishop-pair and the d5-outpost. The position is equal after 15.♕e1 0–0–0 16.♗g5 ♗xg5 17.♘xg5 ♖xd4 18.♘xe6 fxe6 19.♖xe6 ♕b5=) 15...♖d8 16.♗f4 (16.♗g5 ♗xg5 17.♘xg5 0–0 18.♘xe6 fxe6 19.♕c3=, draw, Vallejo Pons – Kasimdzhanov, San Sebastian 2009) 16...0–0 17.♖c1 ♕b6 18.♖b5 ♕xa5 19.♖xa5 ♖a8 20.d5 ♗d7 21.♘e5 ♗d6 (21...♗e8 22.♖xc7 ♗b4 23.♘c4 ♗xa5 24.♘xa5∞) 22.♗g3 ♗xe5 23.♗xe5 c6= Naiditsch – Kramnik, Dresden 2008.

12...♗g6 13.♘c3

It is bad for White to play 13.♘e5, for example: 13...♘xf2 14.♕g3 ♘e4 15.♘c3 ♕xd4 16.♗e3 ♕d6 17.♘xe4 ♗xe4 18.♖ad1 ♗d5 19.b4 b6 20.♗f4 0–0∓ – He cannot create any real threats, while the variation 21.♘f3 ♕d7 22.♖xd5 ♕xd5 23.♖xe7 a5∓ leads to an advantage for Black.

13...♘xc3 14.♕xc3 f6!

This is the most reliable move. Black secures the f7-square for his king and simultaneously deprives his opponent's pieces of the e5-square.

15.♗f4

We must examine White's alternatives here:

15.b3 ♔f7 16.♕xc7 ♖he8 17.♕c4 ♕xc4 18.bxc4 b6∓ – White's pawn-centre is so unstable that Black's position is preferable, despite the absence of a pawn, Zhang Penqxiang – Motylev, Shanghai 2001 (**game 18**).

15.♘h4 ♔f7 16.♕xc7 ♖he8 17.♘xg6 hxg6 18.♗f4 ♖ad8 19.♖ad1 ♖d7 20.♕c3 g5 21.♗g3 ♗d8 22.♖xe8 ♔xe8= Black transferred his bishop to the b6-square and drew effortlessly, Adams – Smeets, Wijk aan Zee 2009;

15.♕xc7 0–0 16.♖xe7 ♕xf3 17.♖xg7+ ♔h8 18.♗h6 ♕xg4+ 19.♕g3 ♕xd4 20.♖xg6 hxg6= Anand – I. Sokolov, Dortmund 1999.

15...♔f7 16.h4

16.♖e3 ♖he8 17.♖ae1 c6∓ White's attack reaches a dead end, while the chronic pawn-weaknesses in his camp remain.

16.♕xc7 ♖he8 17.♘h4 ♗e4 18.♘f5 ♗xf5 19.gxf5 ♖ad8=

16...h5

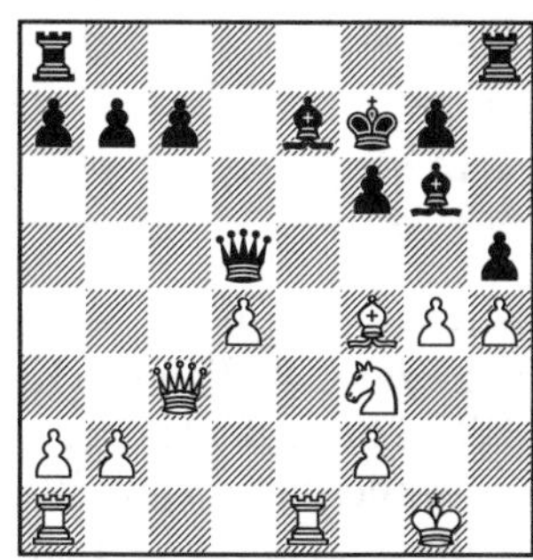

17.♕xc7

After 17.gxh5, Black's best move is 17...♗f5! (or 17...♗xh5 and 18.♕xc7 ♖he8 19.♘g5+ fxg5 20.♗xg5 – White wins a pawn, but his chances of realising it are only minimal) 18.♕xc7 ♖he8 19.♕c3 (This move is necessary, because White's knight is hanging and Black is also threatening ♖a8-c8.) 19...♖ac8 20.♕b3 ♗e6∓ and in the ensuing endgame Black will deploy his bishop on d5, dominating the entire board.

White fails to achieve much with 17.♖e5 fxe5 (Black can also retreat with 17...♕d7=, intending to continue with ♗e7-d6) 18.♘xe5 ♔g8 19.♘xg6 ♕e4 20.♕b3+ ♔h7 21.gxh5 ♖he8 22.♗e5 ♕f5∓ – Black can continue playing without any risk, because he has at least a perpetual check at any moment.

17...♖he8 18.♘g5+ fxg5 19.♗xg5

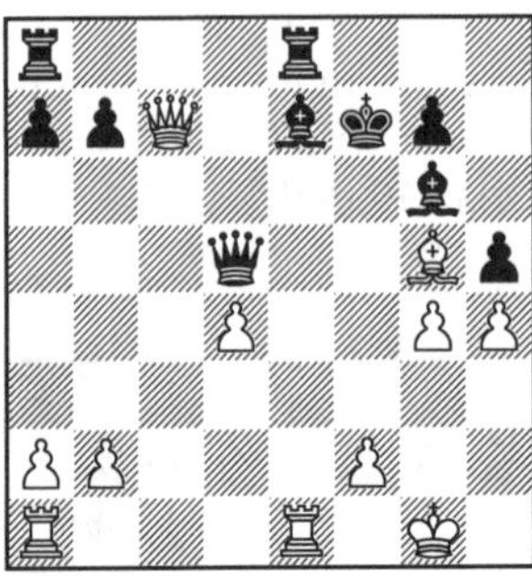

19...♕f3

In the game Radjabov – Kramnik, Nice 2009, Black chose 19...♔g8±, acquiescing to a position a pawn down. However, that did not prevent the ex-world champion from drawing easily.

Black has another interesting alternative here in 19...♗e4 20.♖ac1 ♗h1 (after 20...b6, White has the cold-blooded reply 21.♖c3!±, with the very powerful threat of ♖ce3) 21.♖xe7+ ♖xe7 22.♕xe7+ ♔g8 23.f3 ♗xf3 24.♕e5 hxg4 25.♖c7 ♕xe5 26.dxe5 ♖e8= and this should also lead to a draw.

20.♖xe7+

20.♗xe7 ♗xe4 21.♗g5+ ♔g8 22.♕h2 ♕xg4+ 23.♕g3 ♕d7= Black has very active play on the light squares and, despite White's extra pawn, the draw seems inevitable.

20...♖xe7 21.♕xe7+ ♔g8 22.♕e6+ ♔h7 23.♖e1 ♖e8 24.♗e7 ♖xe7 25.♕xe7 ♕xg4= Black has perpetual check.

B) 9.♖e1

This move is played with the same idea of exerting pressure along the e-file, just as in variation **A**, but here the game is much quieter.

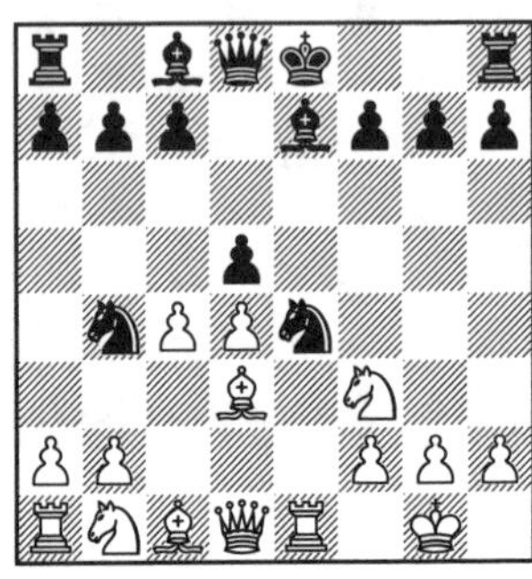

9...♘xd3 10.♕xd3 c6 11.cxd5 cxd5

12.♕b5+

Before placing his queen on b3, from where it attacks Black's pawns on b7 and d5, White wishes to force the enemy queen to occupy the d7-square, hampering the development of his light-squared bishop.

12...♕d7 13.♕b3 0–0

(diagram)

14.♘c3

The alternatives are not at all dangerous for Black:

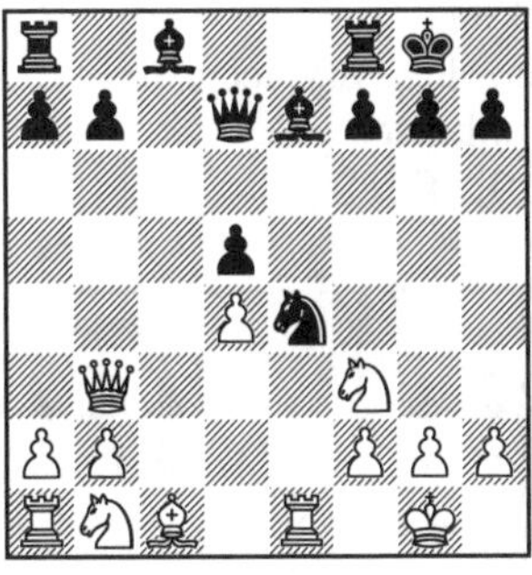

14.♘e5 ♕d8 15.f3 ♘d6! This knight is much better deployed here than on f6. 16.♘c3 ♗e6 17. ♗f4 ♖e8 18.♖ad1 ♕b6 19.♘xd5 ♕xb3 20.♘xe7+ ♖xe7 21.axb3 ♗xb3=, draw, Anand – Kramnik, Linares 1999;

14.♘bd2 ♗f6 15.♘xe4 dxe4 16. ♖xe4 ♕f5 17.♖f4 ♕h5 18.♗e3 b6 19.d5 (in the game Ponomariov – Motylev, Ohrid 2001, White continued with 19.♘e5= and the opponents agreed to a draw) 19... ♗b7 20.♖d1 ♖ad8 21.d6 ♖d7 22. ♗d4 ♕h6 23.♗e3 ♕h5=;

14.♗f4 b6 15.♘e5 ♕b7 16.♘c3 ♗e6= Peng Xiaomin – Motylev, Shanghai 2001.

14...♘xc3 15.bxc3

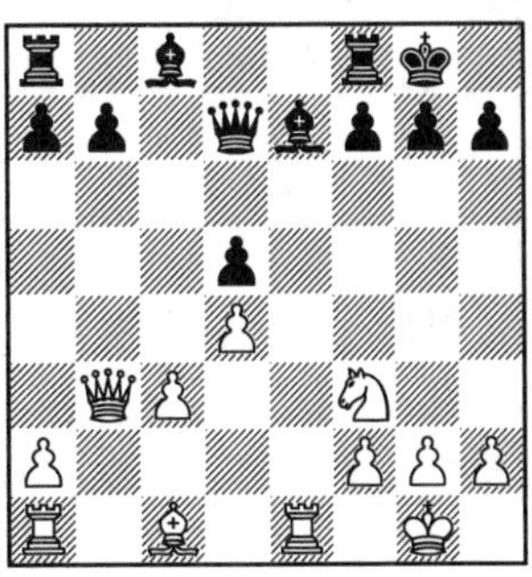

Black can play here either **B1) 15...♖d8**, which involves an absolutely correct positional pawn-sacrifice, or he can allow the exchange of his dark-squared bishop with **B2) 15...♖e8;** in principle this exchange is undesirable, although nothing serious to worry about. In both cases the position remains about equal and the choice is just a matter of taste and style.

B1) 15...♖d8 16.♗a3

White must try to exchange the dark-squared bishops, otherwise Black's defence will be very simple: 16.♘e5 ♕d6 17.a4 ♕a6 18.h3 ♗e6=

16...♗f6 17.♖e3

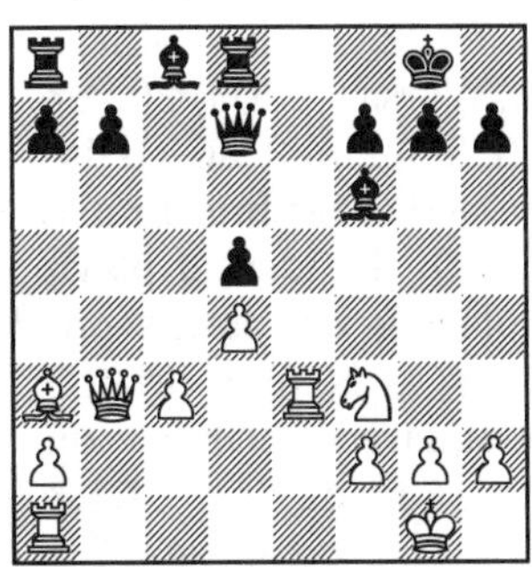

17...♕c7!

This is an excellent positional move. Black gives up his d5-pawn, but preserves his bishop-pair and blockades his opponent's isolated pawn-couple. In addition, White is left with a "bad" bishop on a3.

The move 17...♕c6 is sufficient for Black to hold the draw, despite the fact that his position looks a bit ugly, since his light-squared bishop is restricted by the pawn on d5. 18.♗e7 ♖e8

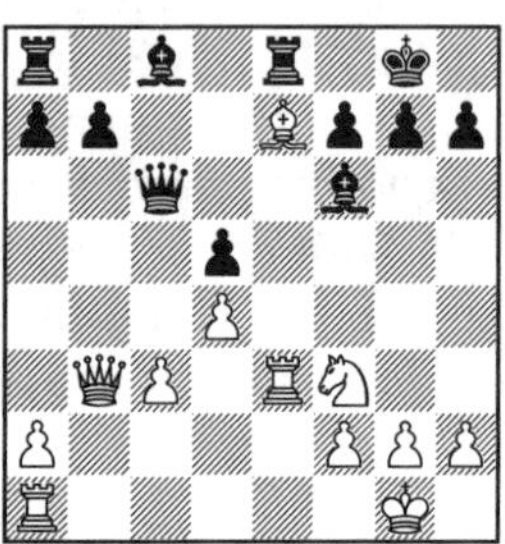

19.♖ae1 (19.♗xf6 ♖xe3 20.fxe3 gxf6= Black has doubled pawns but his counterplay, mostly based on the pressure on the c-file against the backward enemy pawn, is quite adequate.) 19... ♗xe7 (19...♖xe7 20.♖xe7 ♗xe7 21. ♖xe7 f6 22.♘e1 b6= Kritz – Macieja, Warsaw 2005) 20.♖xe7 ♗d7 21.h3 f6 22.♕a3 a6 (It is much more active for him to play 22... b6!, with the idea of playing a7-a5, placing his pawns on dark-squares, as is appropriate with a light-squared bishop on the board.) 23.♘d2 ♖xe7 24.♖xe7 ♖e8 25.♘f1 ♖xe7 26.♕xe7 ♕e6 27. ♕d8+ ♕e8 28.♕b6 ♗c6=. Black's g7- and f6- pawns cover the dark squares perfectly and he maintained the balance in the game Topalov – Kramnik, Las Vegas 1999.

18.♕xd5 ♗e6 19.♕b5

In the endgame arising after 19.♕c5 ♕xc5 20.♗xc5 b6 21.♗b4 ♖ac8= Black has no problems at all; moreover White has so many weaknesses in his camp that he must play very accurately to hold the balance.

19...♖ac8

Black's compensation for the pawn is sufficient, as tournament practice has confirmed.

20.h3 h6 21.♕e2

21.♕b2 b6 22.♖ae1 ♕c4 23. ♖1e2 ♕a4 24.♔h2 ♖d5 25.♗b4=, draw, Topalov – Adams, Dortmund 2001.

21...♕c4 22.♕e1 ♕a6 23. ♗c1 ♕c6 24.♗d2=, draw, Leko – Gelfand, Moscow 2008.

B2) 15...♖e8

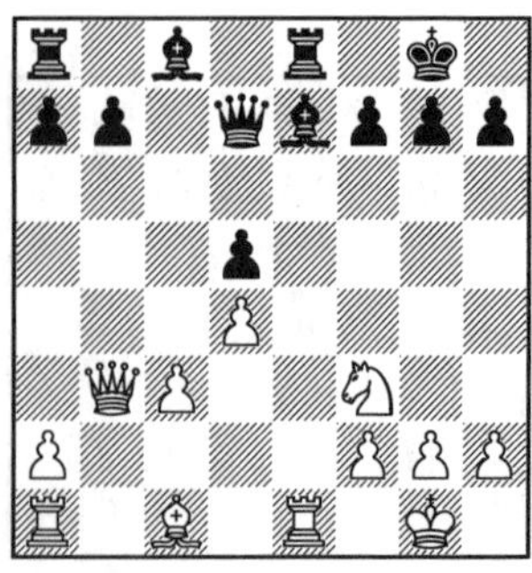

16.♗a3

After 16.♘e5, Black can retreat with his queen to c7, obtaining adequate compensation for the d5-pawn, or to the d8-square, not forcing the issue for the moment. His simplest move however is 16...♗f6, aiming for an equal position with bishops of opposite colours on the board.

16...♗xa3 17.♕xa3 b6

Black's light-squared bishop is restricted by the d5-pawn, so Black should try to deploy his pawns on dark squares.

It is almost equally good for him to continue with 17...f6 18.♖xe8+ ♕xe8 19.♖e1 ♕c6=

18.h3

18.♖ab1 ♖xe1+ (It would be a blunder for Black to play 18...♕d8? 19.♖xe8+ ♕xe8 20.♖xb6 ♗g4 21.♖b7 ♗xf3 22.gxf3± and White realised his extra pawn in the game Anand – Giri, Monaco 2011.) 19.♖xe1 ♕c6 (with 19...f6 20.♖e7 ♕c6= Black also maintains equality, despite his position not looking completely safe.) 20.♘e5 (20.♖e7 f6 21.h3 a5=) 20...♕c7 21.c4 ♗e6 22.c5 bxc5 23.dxc5 d4=. Black's passed d4-pawn is sufficient to counter-balance White's passed c5-pawn.

18...h6

Or 18...f6 19.♖xe8+ ♕xe8 20.♖e1 ♕c6 21.♖e7 a5=

19.♖ab1 ♕c6 20.♖xe8+ ♕xe8 21.♖e1 ♕f8=

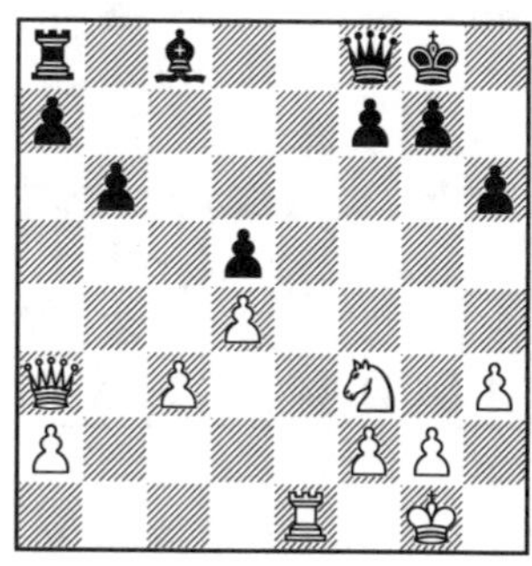

Dominguez – Kramnik, Wijk aan Zee 2010.

Conclusion

The variation with 9.cxd5 is rather drawish and if both sides play correctly a draw becomes the most likely result. As for the move 9.♖e1, Black has several quite reliable ways of equalizing against it. White's attempts to exert pressure on the e-file are not dangerous and Black is able to solve his problems convincingly in all variations.

Chapter 23 1.e4 e5 2.♘f3 ♘f6 3.♘xe5 d6 4.♘f3 ♘xe4 5.d4 d5 6.♗d3 ♘c6 7.0–0 ♗e7 8.c4 ♘b4 9.♗e2

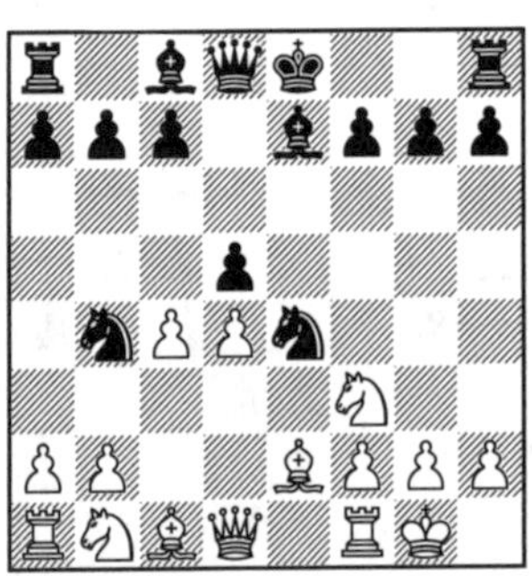

We have already seen in the previous chapter that White's attempts to create immediate pressure along the e-file fail and give him no chances of obtaining an advantage in the opening, so he should avoid the exchange of his bishop.

9...0–0 10.a3

This is an attractive move and it was very popular at the dawn of the development of this variation. White immediately reduces the tension in the centre and defines the pawn-structure.

Nowadays White almost automatically chooses the more precise move 10.♘c3, maintaining the tension and preserving more options. We shall analyze this move in the following chapters.

10...♘c6 11.cxd5

If 11.♘c3, then after 11...♘xc3 12.bxc3 Black brings another piece into the fight for the central squares: 12...♗e6! 13.cxd5 ♗xd5=. Black's bishop is perfectly placed on d5 and he obtains a very good position without any problems whatsoever.

11...♕xd5 12.♘c3 ♘xc3 13. bxc3 ♗f5

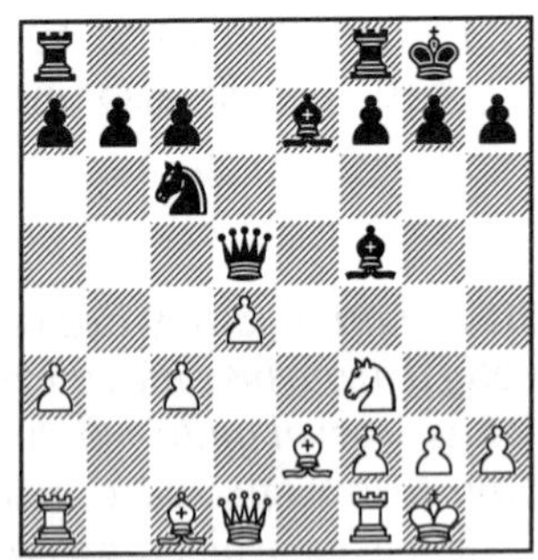

14.♗f4

White can bolster his centre with 14.♗e3, but his bishop is not so active on e3 and Black can effortlessly develop his pieces to active positions: 14...♘a5 (it is also good for him to play here 14...♗f6)

15.♘d2 (if 15.♘e5, then Black can dislodge the knight with 15...f6!) 15...♖fe8 16.♗f3 ♕d7=

White would not achieve much with 14.♘d2. He wants to transfer his knight to e3 via the c4-square, so it would be logical for Black to prevent this: 14...♘a5 15.♗f3 ♕d7 16.♘b3 ♘xb3 17.♕xb3 c6=

White has tried advancing his connected pawns immediately, when Black should organize a blockade on the dark squares: 14.c4 ♕d6 15.d5 ♘e5 16.♘d4 ♗d7 17.a4

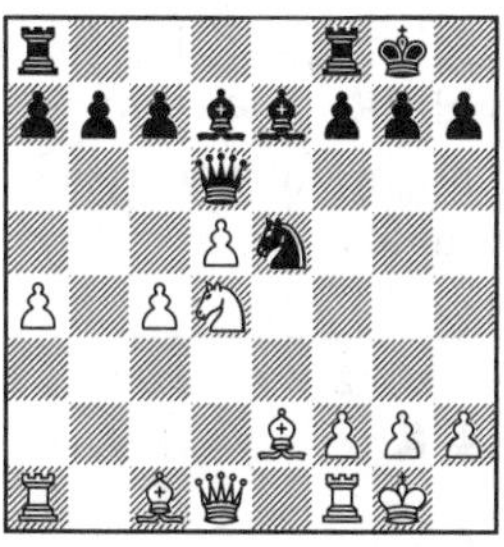

17...♖fe8 (it is less reliable to play 17...♕g6 18.♗f4 ♗d6 19.c5 ♘f3+ 20.♘xf3 ♗xf4 21.g3± Black has the bishop-pair, but White's connected pawns are more important) 18.♘b5 (It is inferior to opt for 18.♗e3?! ♕g6 19.♘b5 ♗h3 20.♗f3 ♗d6 21.♗d4 ♘xf3+ 22.♕xf3 ♗g4 23.♕c3 ♗f4∓ and White is forced to fight for equality, Ivanchuk – Kramnik, Nice 2008.) 18...♗xb5 19.axb5 ♘d7 20.♖a2 ♘c5 21.g3 a5 22.bxa6 ♖xa6= Black's blockade on the d6- and c5- squares seems quite harmonious and he has equalized completely, Radjabov – Jakovenko, Elista 2008.

It seems to me that the quiet move 14.♖e1 is White's best and after 14...♖e8 15.♗f4,

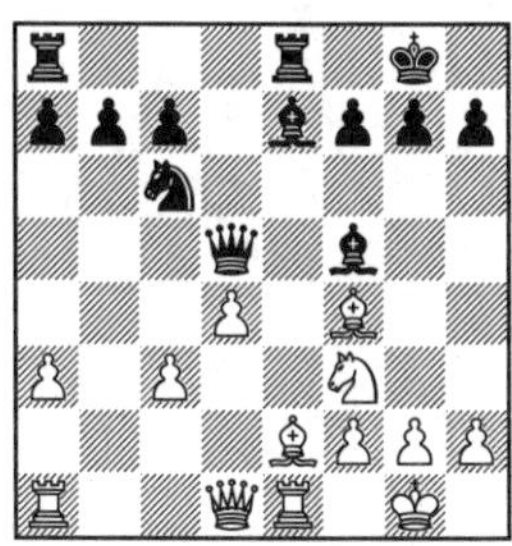

it is not good for Black to sacrifice the c7-pawn: after 15...♘a5 16.♗xc7 ♖ac8 17.♕a4 b6 18.♗b5 ♗c2 19.♕xc2 ♕xb5 20.♗f4± his compensation for the pawn is insufficient, so he should continue with 15...♖ac8 – see 10.♘c3 ♗f5 11.a3 ♘xc3 12.bxc3 ♘c6 13.♖e1 ♖e8 14.cxd5 ♕xd5 15.♗f4 ♖ac8.

14...♘a5!?

Black sacrifices a pawn with this move, trying to reach a positional draw. He can accomplish this by establishing a blockade on the dark squares in a few moves.

If he wants to enter a much more complicated struggle, he can transpose to the main line arising after 10.♘c3 by playing 14...♖ac8 15.♖e1 ♖fe8.

15.♗xc7

If 15.♖e1, then 15...♗d6 16.♘e5 ♕b3 – see 15.♘e5 ♗d6 16.♖e1 ♕b3.

After 15.♘e5, Black can equalize in several different ways:

(diagram)

15...c5 16.♕a4 (16.♗f3 ♕b3=)

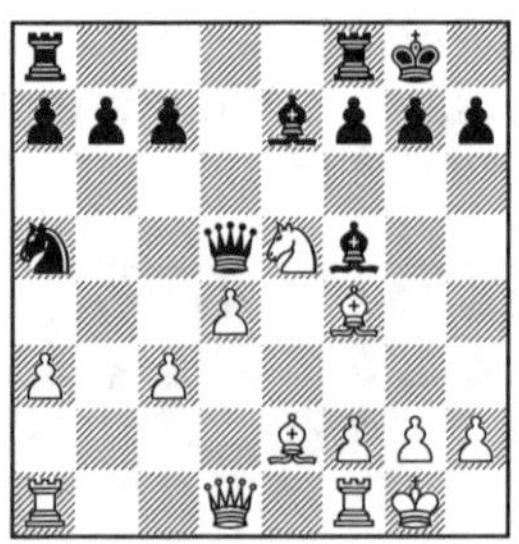

16...cxd4 17.♗f3 ♕c5 18.g4 ♗g6 19.cxd4 ♗c2 20.♕d7 ♕d6=;

15...♕b3 16.♕xb3 ♘xb3 17.♖ae1 ♘a5 18.♗f3 ♗d6 19.♗d5 ♖ac8=;

15...♗d6 16.c4 (16.♖e1 ♕b3 17.♕d2 ♕c2 18.♕xc2 ♗xc2=; 16.g4 ♗e4 17.f3 ♗g6 18.♕a4 b6=, with a very complicated struggle and approximately equal chances) 16...♕e4 17.♗g3 ♕c2 18.c5 ♗xe5 19.♗xe5 ♘c6 20.♗xc7 ♘xd4 21.♕xd4 ♕xe2=

15...♖ac8 16.♗xa5 ♕xa5 17.c4 ♗f6 18.♗d3

After 18.♕b3 ♕b6 (Black can also practically equalize with 18...♖fe8=) 19.♕xb6 axb6 20.♖a2 (after 20.♖fd1 Black can increase his pressure against the enemy centre with 20...♖fd8⩱, obtaining sufficient compensation for the pawn, Wedberg – Nielsen, Munkebo 1998) 20...♖fd8 (it is less precise for him to opt for 20...♗g4 21.d5 ♗xf3 22.gxf3 ♗d4± when White still preserves some, albeit minimal, winning chances, Karjakin – Andreikin, Oropesa 2000) 21.♖b2 ♗xd4 (21...♖d6⩱) 22.♘xd4 ♖xd4 23.♖xb6 ♖d2 24.♗f3 ♖xc4 25.♖xb7 g6= Black saves the draw thanks to his active rooks, since White will be unable to hold on to his a-pawn.

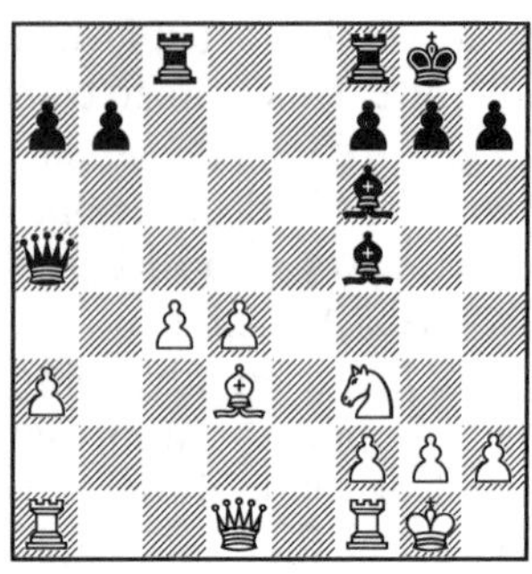

18...♗e6!

If 18...♖fd8 19.♖b1±

Black cannot solve his problems with 18...♗g4 19.h3 ♗xf3 20.♕xf3 and he fails to reach complete equality:

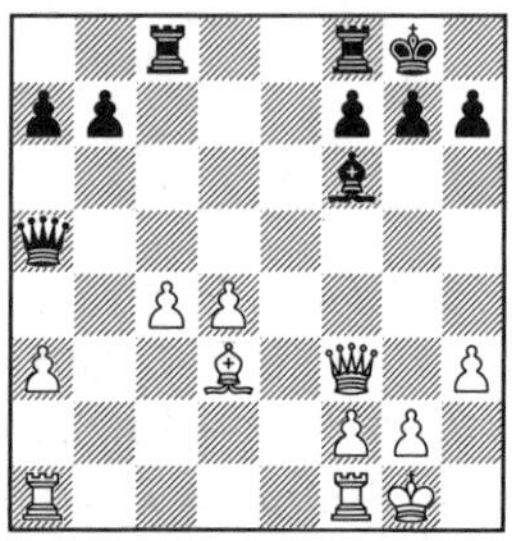

20...♖cd8 21.♖ab1 ♗xd4 22.♖xb7 g6 23.♗e4 ♖d6, Zhang Zhong – Karpov, Cap d'Agde 2000, 24.♗d5 ♖f6 25.♕d1 ♗b6 26.a4 ♖e8 27.♔h1±, with the idea of advancing his f-pawn;

20...♕d8, Kramnik – Anand, Sofia 2005, 21.♖ab1 b6 22.♖fd1 g6 23.c5 ♗xd4 24.cxb6 (24.c6±) 24...axb6 25.♕f4 ♕f6 26.♕xf6 ♗xf6 27.♖xb6± and White still has some minute winning prospects.

19.♕b3 ♖fd8 20.♖fd1

20.♖ae1 ♗xd4 21.♘xd4 ♖xd4 22.♗xh7+ ♔xh7 23.♖xe6 ♖dxc4 24.♖e7 ♖c1=

20...g6 21.♗f1

21.♗e2 ♗g4 22.♕xb7 ♗xf3 23.♕xf3 ♗xd4 24.♖ab1 ♗c5 25.♖xd8+ ♖xd8 26.♖b7 ♕e1+ 27.♗f1 f5 28.♕e2 ♕xe2 29.♗xe2 ♖d2=

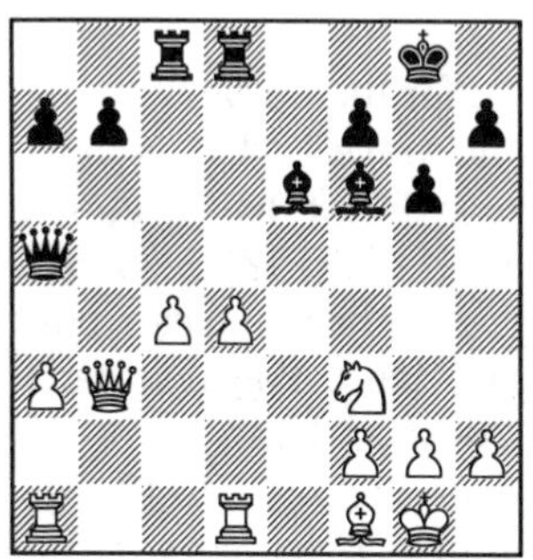

21...b6

It is also interesting for Black to try here 21...♗g4!? 22.♕xb7 ♖b8 23.♕e4 ♗xf3 24.gxf3!? (24.♕xf3 ♗xd4 25.♖ab1 ♖xb1 26.♖xb1 ♖d6=) 24...♖b2⩱ – his pieces are so active that he should be able to regain one of his opponent's connected pawns and save the game.

22.♖ac1 ♗g4 23.d5 ♗e7 24.♖a1

24.h3 ♕xa3! 25.♕xa3 ♗xa3 26.♖a1 ♗xf3 27.gxf3 ♗c5 28.♖xa7 b5 29.♖b7 bxc4 30.♗xc4 ♗xf2+ 31.♔xf2 ♖xc4=

24...♗f6

24...♗d6 25.h3 ♗xf3 26.♕xf3 ♖e8±

25.♖a2 ♕c3 26.♕xc3 ♗xc3=

Black will exchange his light-squared bishop for the enemy knight and his dark-squared bishop will be transferred to the c5-square, building a rock-solid, drawish set-up.

Conclusion

In the variation we have analyzed, beginning with the move 10.a3, White reduces the tension in the central pawn-structure too early. The straightforward move 14.♗f4 (it is more flexible for him to continue with 14.♖e1, transposing to the main line after 10.♘c3) provides Black with the additional possibility of 14...♘a5!?, sacrificing the c7-pawn and later, with precise play, he can equalize completely.

Chapter 24 1.e4 e5 2.♘f3 ♘f6 3.♘xe5 d6 4.♘f3 ♘xe4 5.d4 d5 6.♗d3 ♘c6 7.0–0 ♗e7 8.c4 ♘b4 9.♗e2 0–0 10.♘c3

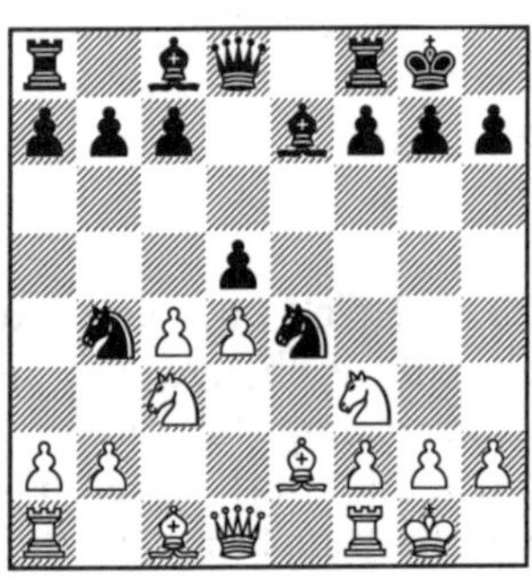

White exerts additional pressure against the centre before expelling the enemy knight from the b4-square and clarifying the pawn-structure. Now, Black is faced with a choice of where to develop his light-squared bishop.

10...♗f5

The variation 10...♗e6 11.♘e5 f6 12.♘f3± was popular for a while, but later on it lost its good reputation. The move f7-f6 weakens Black's position and this is likely to tell in the future.

11.a3

On the f4-square White's bishop can come under attack by the enemy knight and after 11.♗f4 dxc4 12.♗xc4 ♘xc3 13.bxc3 ♘d5= White must lose an important tempo for its retreat.

The move 11.♕b3 is harmless, because Black has a choice between 11...♘f6 12.c5 a5 13.♘e1∞ with a rather unclear position, Morozevich – Polgar, Buenos Aires 2000 and the more reliable 11...dxc4 12.♗xc4 ♘f6 13.♘g5 (the position is repeated after 13.♘e5 ♕xd4 14.♗xf7+ ♔h8 15.♘f3 ♕d7 16.♘e5 ♕d4= Bologan – Zarnicki, Buenos Aires 2000) 13...♗g6 14. a3 ♘c2 15.♘xf7 ♗xf7 16.♗xf7+ ♖xf7 17.♕xc2 ♕xd4=

11...♘xc3 12.bxc3 ♘c6

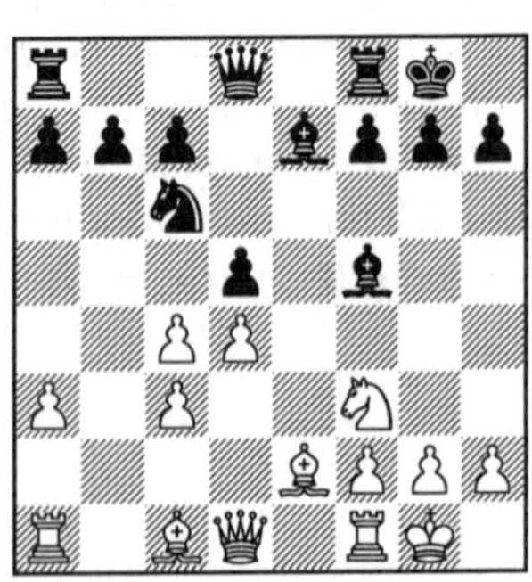

13.♖e1

For 13.cxd5 ♕xd5 – see. 10.a3.

After 13.♗e3 Black can equalize in various ways, for example with 13...♘a5=, or 13...dxc4 14.♗xc4 ♗d6 15.♖e1 h6= and White's bishop on e3 has no good prospects.

White's bishop will be exchanged on f4 and after 13.♗f4 dxc4 14.♗xc4 ♗d6= the position is equal.

13...♖e8

14.♗f4

White's pawn-centre looks powerful, but he cannot achieve anything with it. His attempt to advance it with the help of the bishop on e3 is not dangerous for Black at all, since on e3 his bishop is not active. 14.♗e3 ♗f6 15.♘d2 ♘a5 16.cxd5 ♕xd5 17.♕a4 ♗d7 18.♕b4 ♗e7 19.♕b2 ♗c6 20.♗f3 ♕d7= Topalov – Anand, Wijk aan Zee 2005.

The move 14.♖a2 is rather crafty. The b1-square is attacked by Black's light-squared bishop, so White wants to occupy the b-file using the b2-square. After that, his rook can be redeployed to e2 to fight for the e-file.

(diagram)

Now after 14...♗e6 White can establish a stable positional advantage with the simple move 15.c5±

It is possible for Black to play the thematic move 14...♘a5, but after 15.cxd5 ♕xd5 16.♖b2 c6, White has the interesting resource 17.♘e5!? (in the game Kasimdzhanov – Gelfand, Elista 2007, White tried 17.♕a4 ♕d8 18.c4 ♗f6 19.♗e3 ♗e4 20.♖d2 b6 21.♘e5 ♕e7 22.♘g4 ♗g5= and the position remained approximately equal) 17...♗xa3 18.♗f3 ♕d6 19.♖be2 ♗xc1 20.♕xc1 ♗e6, but here not 21.♗h5, Melia – Nebolsina, Rijeka 2010, but 21.♕b1!=∞ and White has good compensation for the pawn; in particular he wishes to provoke the move g7-g6 with ♗f3-e4 and then begin an attack on the kingside with the help of the pawn-advance h2-h4-h5.

Black's most precise response is 14...♗f6! 15.♖b2 b6 16.♗f4 ♘a5 17.cxd5 ♕xd5 18.♘e5 ♗xe5 19.♗f3 ♕d7 20.♗xe5 ♘c4 21.♖be2 c6 22.d5 ♘xe5 23.♖xe5 cxd5 24.♕xd5 ♖ad8 25.♖xe8+ ♖xe8 26.♖xe8+ ♕xe8 27.g4 ♗e6 28.♕b7 ♕c8 29.♕xa7 ♗xg4 30.♗d5 ♗h5 31.♕xb6= with a draw by perpetual check, Alekseev – Kramnik, Dortmund 2007.

The most logical and popular line for White is first to exchange pawns with: 14.cxd5 ♕xd5 and only then play 15.♗f4, and we shall analyze this variation in the following chapters of the book.

14...dxc4

After 14...♖c8, White has the powerful riposte 15.c5 ♗f6 16.♕a4 (It might be even more promising to continue with 16.♕b3 ♖b8 17.♗b5 ♖e4 18.♖xe4 ♗xe4 19.♘d2±) 16...a6 17.♗f1 ♕d7 18.♕b3 ♖xe1 19.♖xe1 ♖b8 20.♗g5 ♗xg5 21.♘xg5± and Black has a light-squared bishop and numerous pawns on the same colour, so his position is rather unpleasant to defend, Motylev – Gashimov, Poikovsky 2009.

15.♗xc4 ♗d6 16.♖xe8+

16.♕d2 ♕d7 (it is also good for Black to play here 16...h6, depriving White's knight of the g5-square) 17.♗xd6 cxd6 18.♘h4 ♘a5 19.♗a2 ♗e6 20.d5, Morozevich – Gelfand, Sochi 2007. Black can obtain a reliable position without any problems with the move 20...♗f5=

16...♕xe8

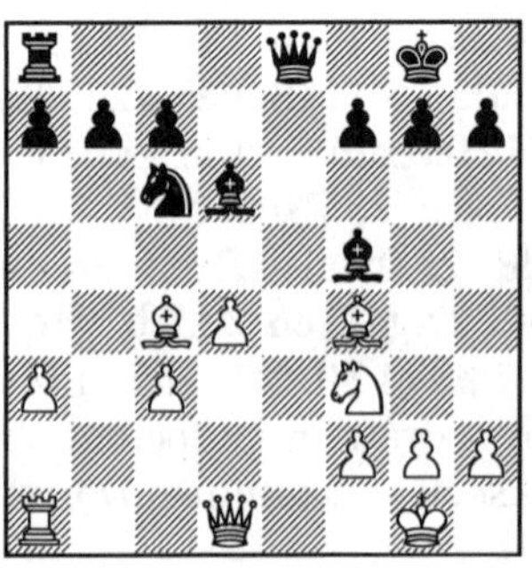

17.♘g5

For 17.♗xd6 cxd6 18.♘g5 ♗g6 – see 17.♘g5.

White does not achieve much with 17.♕d2 ♕d7 18.♗xd6 cxd6 19.♖e1 ♖e8= Svidler – Topalov, Wijk aan Zee 2005.

After 17.♘h4, Black cannot achieve full equality with 17...♘a5 18.♘xf5 ♘xc4 19.♕f3 ♖b8 20.♗h6 g6, in view of 21.♘xd6 (21.♘e3 ♘xe3 22.fxe3 ♕e7 23.h3 ♕h4 24.♗f4 ♗xf4 25.exf4= Jakovenko – Gelfand, Khanty-Mansyisk 2009) 21...♘xd6 22.♕f6 ♘f5 23.♗f4± with a slight edge for White.

It is more precise for Black to play here 17...♗d7!18.♕f3 ♕e7 19.♗xd6 cxd6 20.♘f5 ♗xf5 21.♕xf5 g6 22.♕f3 ♖c8 23.♗d5 ♔g7= and his knight coordinates perfectly with his queen, so it is not inferior to White's bishop, Volokitin – Smeets, Germany 2009.

17...♗g6 18.♗xd6 cxd6

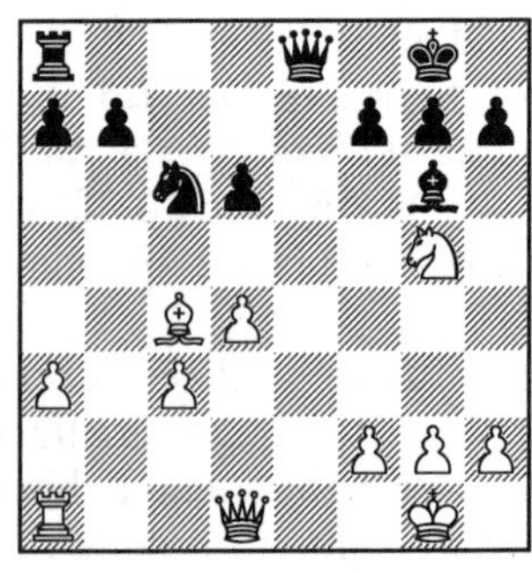

19.h4

If White does not attack the enemy bishop on g6, Black will easily improve the coordination of his pieces. In addition, White does not have an escape-hole for his king and this is likely to tell at some point: 19.♕g4 h6 20.♘f3 ♕e4 21.♕g3 ♕c2 22.♘h4 ♗e4 23.♖e1 d5 24.♗f1, Karjakin – Topalov, Leon 2003. Here it is very good for Black to play the all-purpose defensive move 24...♖f8! and after 25.♖e3 ♕c1!∓ he pins the bishop on f1 and at the same time attacks the pawn on a3.

19...♕e7 20.♕g4

White can simplify the position with the line: 20.h5 ♕xg5 21.hxg6 ♕xg6 22.♗d3 ♕g5 23.♕b1 b6 24.♗xh7+ ♔f8 25.♗e4 ♖c8= Belov – Bu Xiangzhi, Moscow 2010.

20...h6

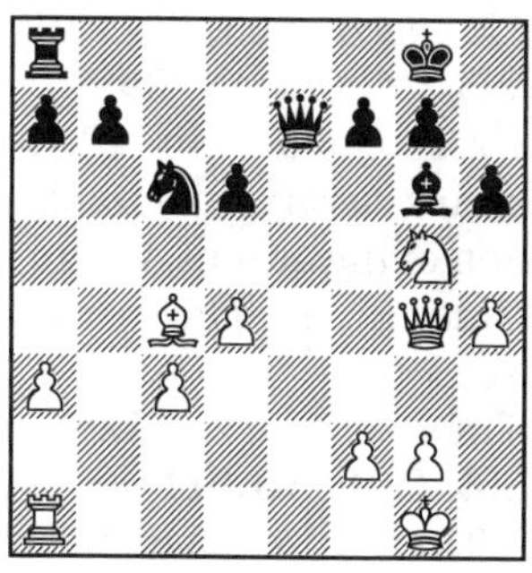

21.♘h3

It is a forced draw after 21.h5 ♗xh5 22.♕xh5 hxg5 23.♖d1 ♖f8 24.♖d3 ♕e1+ 25.♔h2 ♕xf2 26.♕xg5 ♕f6 27.♕xf6 gxf6 28.♖g3+ ♔h8 29.♖h3+ ♔g7 30.♖g3= Radjabov – Wang Yue, Medias 2010.

21...♕e4 22.♕g3

Only Black can be better if White plays in simple fashion – 22.♕xe4 ♗xe4 23.♖e1 ♗f5 24.♘f4 ♖c8=

An equal endgame arises after 22.♕d7 ♘a5 23.♗a2 ♕c6 24.♕xc6 ♘xc6= Bologan – Shirov, Poikovsky 2009.

If White puts his knight voluntarily in a pin with 22.♘f4, then Black can exploit this with the variation 22...♘e5! 23.dxe5 ♕xc4 24.exd6 (24.e6 fxe6 25.♕xg6 ♕xf4 26.♕xe6+ ♔h8=) 24...♕xc3 (24...♖d8 25.♖d1 ♗c2 26.♖d5 ♕xc3 27.♔h2±) 25.♖d1 (after 25.♖f1, Black continues with 25...♗e4 and White cannot support his d6-pawn with his pieces) 25...♗c2 26.♖d5 ♗e4 27.♖d1 ♗c2= and a draw by repetition of moves.

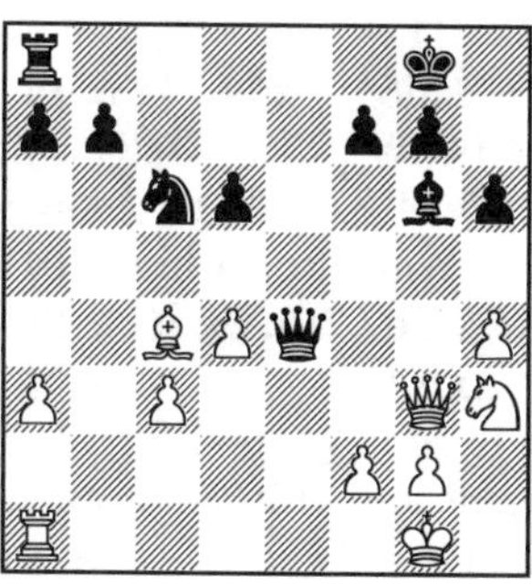

22...♖c8!

This is a developing move and it definitely solves all Black's problems, so I prefer it.

It is less convincing for Black to choose the more concrete approach 22...♘a5 23.♗a2 ♕c2 (after 23...♕d3, White has the problem-like reply 24.♖f1!± and Black will have some difficulties to contend with, Grischuk – Adams, Halkidiki 2002) due to 24.♗d5! (White cannot achieve much with

24.h5, because Black has the strong response 24...♗f5=. It is also possible for him to opt for 24...♗e4 25.♕xd6 ♕xc3 26.♖f1 ♕d2, Hou Yifan – Bu Xiangzhi, China 2009. Now, White must force a draw by a perpetual check with 27.♗xf7+ ♔xf7 28.♕d7+ ♔f8 29.♕d6=) 24...♖c8 (after 24...♖e8, White has the quiet move 25. ♔h2!± and it is difficult for Black to improve his position) 25.♖e1 ♕xc3 26.♖e8+ ♔h7 27.♖xc8 ♕xc8 28.♕xd6 ♕e8 29.♘f4 ♗e4, Nijboer – Li Chao, Wijk aan Zee 2011. After 30.♗a2! ♘c6 31.♕c5!± Black must be prepared for a long and patient defence.

23.♗f1

23.♕xd6 ♘xd4 (23...♕c2!?) 24.♗d5 ♘b5 25.♕d7 ♕e8 26.♕xe8 ♖xe8 27.c4 ♘d6 28.c5 ♗e4= Hou Yifan – Wang Yue, China 2011.

23...♘e7 24.♕xd6 ♘f5 25. ♕b4 ♘xh4

It is equally good for Black to continue here with 25...b6 and then if 26.g3 ♕c6 (There is no need to enter the sharp complications arising after 26...♘xg3 27.fxg3 ♕e3+ 28.♘f2 ♕xg3+ 29.♗g2 ♖xc3 30.♕e7∞ with a very unclear position.) 27.♘f4 (but not 27.♖c1, because of 27...a5∓ and White's d4-pawn is hanging) 27...♕xc3 28.♖d1=

26.d5

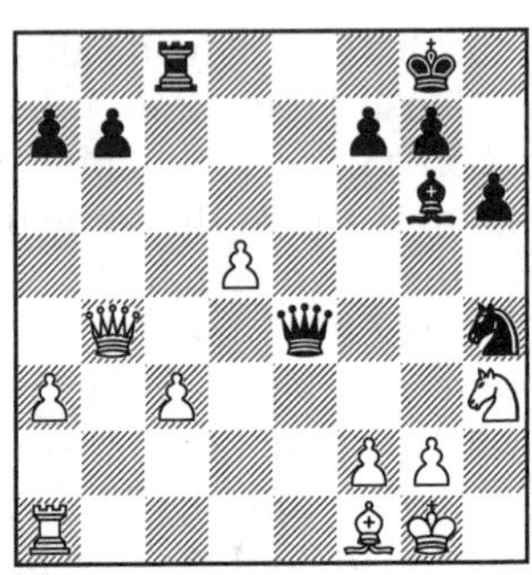

26...a5!

In the game Topalov – Gelfand, Monaco 2003, Black played 26...♗f5, to which White could have responded with 27.♘f4!±, preserving a very favourable opposition of the queens, where neither side can exchange advantageously.

27.♕xe4 ♗xe4 28.c4 ♘f5 29.♘f4 ♘d6 30.♖c1 b6 31.f3 ♗h7= There arises an unbalanced endgame in which Black's prospects are by no means worse.

Conclusion

The variation beginning with the move 14.♗f4 leads to simplification and results either in a draw or an unbalanced position with approximately equal chances.

Chapter 25 **1.e4 e5 2.♘f3 ♘f6 3.♘xe5 d6 4.♘f3 ♘xe4 5.d4 d5 6.♗d3 ♘c6 7.0–0 ♗e7 8.c4 ♘b4 9.♗e2 0–0 10.♘c3 ♗f5 11.a3 ♘xc3 12.bxc3 ♘c6 13.♖e1 ♖e8 14.cxd5 ♕xd5**

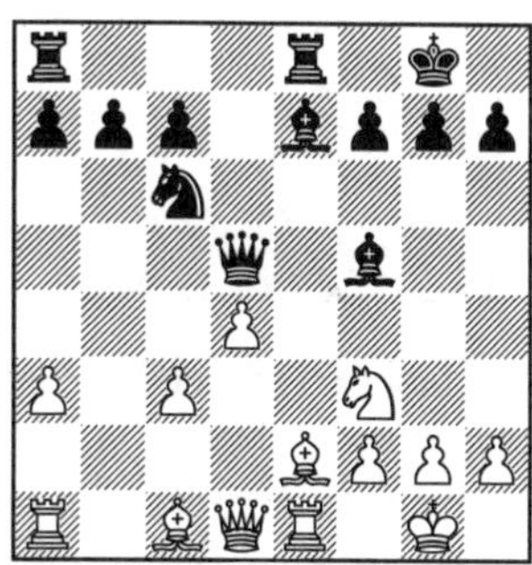

15.♗f4

As is often the case in similar positions, on e3 White's bishop is passive and limited in its scope: 15.♗e3 ♗f6 16.♘d2 ♖ad8 17.♗f3 ♕d7 18.♘b3 b6= Movsesian – Haba, Czech Republic 2003.

It is not good for White to play 15.c4 under these circumstances, because of 15...♕d6 16.d5 (Here, practically no matter what White plays, Black's bishop comes to the f6-square with great effect.) 16...♗f6! and White does not have the move 17.c5? (which would have been possible without the inclusion of the moves ♖f1-e1 and ♖f8-e8) in view of 17...♕xc5 18. dxc6 ♗xa1 19.cxb7 ♖ab8 20.♗e3 ♖xe3!–+ and Black wins. So White has to continue with 17.♖a2, but after the simple move 17...♘e5∓, Black's position is preferable.

15...♖ac8

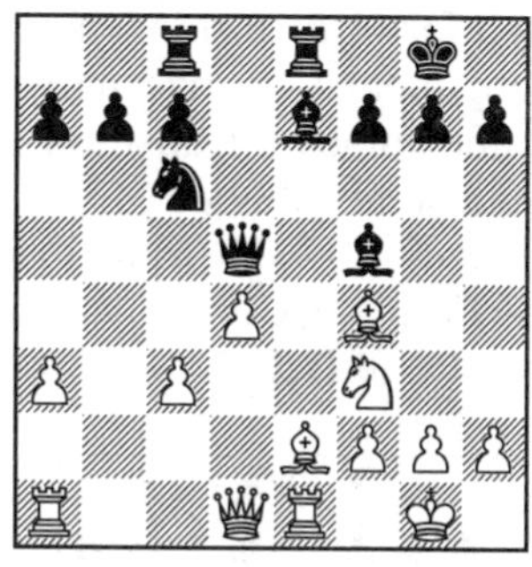

This is one of the tabias of the Petroff Defence. It would appear that Black's knight is misplaced on c6, because it hampers the pawn-advance c7-c5, but extensive tournament practice of this variation has shown that it is very difficult for White to deploy his pieces to active positions in order to advance his c and d-pawns effectively. Black's forces remain very active. One of his main ideas is to play ♘a5 and follow that with the undermining move c7-c5. It is worth mentioning that all the possible exchanges are favourable for Black, because his pawn-structure is without any defects and this would be very useful in an eventual endgame.

The prophylactic move **16.h3** is one of White's trickiest options and it will be analyzed in the following chapters.

Now, we shall analyze thoroughly: **A) 16.♕a4**, **B) 16.g3** and **C) 16.♗d3**.

Black's defensive task is much simpler after White's alternatives.

16.♘d2 ♘a5 17.♘f1 ♕b3! As often happens, Black reacts in straightforward fashion against his opponent's strange manoeuvres and forces a transition into an endgame. 18.♘e3 ♕xd1 19.♖axd1 ♗d7 20.♘d5 ♗d6= Pruijssers – Fridman, Germany 2008.

16.c4 ♕e4 17.♗e3

17...♕c2! The exchange of queens again solves all Black's problems. (After 17...♗f6, White can fight for the initiative with the move 18.♖a2!±, depriving Black's queen of the c2-square.) 18.d5 ♘a5 19.♘d4 ♕xd1 20.♖exd1 (White would not change much with 20.♖axd1 ♗d7 21.♘b5 b6 22.♘xa7 ♖a8 23.♘b5 ♗xb5 24.cxb5 ♗xa3=; 22.♘xc7 ♖xc7 23.d6 ♗xd6 24.♖xd6 ♗e6 25.c5 bxc5 26.♗b5 ♖f8=) 20...♗d7 21.♗d2 ♗f6 22.♗xa5 ♗xd4 23.♖xd4 ♖xe2=, draw, Leko – Kramnik, Brissago 2004.

16.♗g3

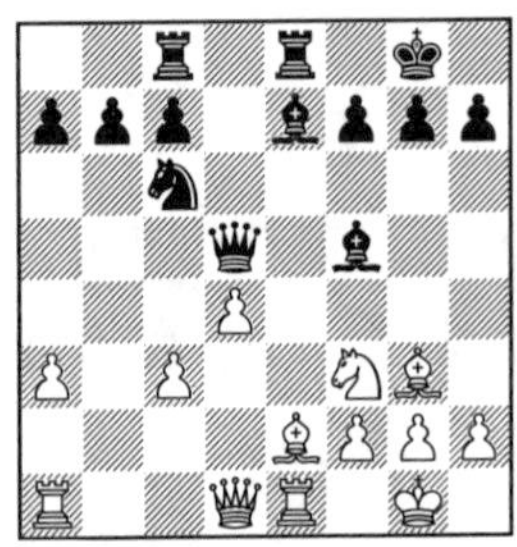

This bishop is placed on a protected square, but Black has enough time to simplify the position. 16...♗d6! 17.♘d2 (17.♕a4 ♗d7 18.♕c2 ♗f5 19.♕b2 ♘a5 20.♘d2 ♗xg3 21.hxg3 c5 – it is even more solid for him to opt for 21...b6 22.♘f1 ♕b3= – 22.♕b5 b6 23.♗g4 ♔f8 24.♗xf5 ♕xf5 25.♘f3= Carlsen – Pe.Nielsen, Faaborg 2007) 17...♗xg3 18.hxg3 ♘a5 19.♕a4 ♗d7 20.♕c2 b6 (20...♗f5 21.♕a4=) 21.♗d3 h6 22.♗h7+ ♔h8 23. ♗e4 ♕d6 24.♘f3 ♗e6= – the position is equal, Adams – Anand, Sofia 2005.

16.♕c1

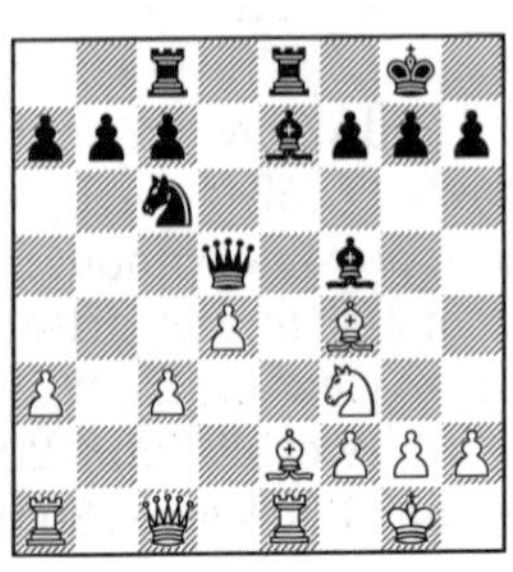

16...♗f6! This is a typical move in this pawn-structure. Black improves the placement of his pieces as much as he can, before making the move ♘a5. (The alternatives would not solve his problems: 16...♘a5? 17.c4! ♕e4?? 18.♗d1 ♕d3 19.♖e3 ♕xc4 20.♖e5, 1-0 Anand – Kramnik, Sofia 2005. Black has not yet tested the move 16...♕d7 at high level. It seems to me that after 17.♕b2 ♗d6 18.♗e3 ♘a5 19.c4⩲ White maintains a slight edge.) 17.♕b2 ♘a5 18.♘e5 ♕b3 19.♕d2 ♗xe5 20.♗xe5 ♘c4 21.♕g5 ♗g6 22.♗g4 ♖a8 (The other possible route to equality for Black here is 22...h6 23.♕h4 f5 24.♗h5 ♘xe5 25.dxe5 ♗xh5 26.♕xh5 ♕e6=) 23.♗d7 f6 24.♗xf6 ♖xe1+ 25.♖xe1 gxf6 26.♕xf6 ♗f7 27.♗e6 ♗xe6 28.♕xe6+ ♔h8 29.♕f6+ ♔g8 30.♕g5+ ♔h8 31.h4 ♖f8 32.♖e7 ♕b1+ 33.♔h2 ♕g6 34.♕xg6 hxg6 35.♖xc7 ♘xa3 36.♖xb7 ♖xf2= and it all ends in a draw.

16.♗f1 ♗d6

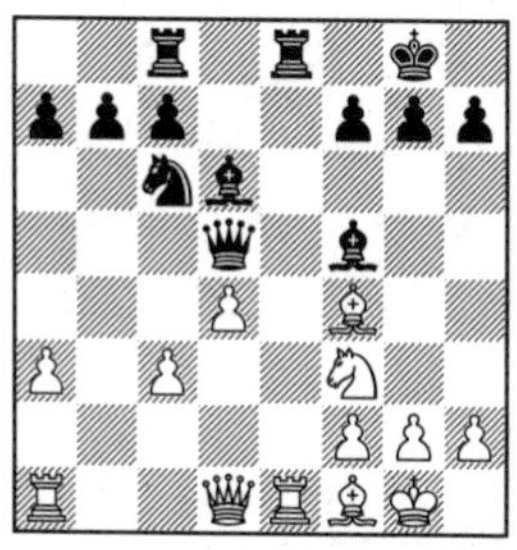

17.♖xe8+ (17.c4 ♖xe1 18.♕xe1 ♕e4 19.♗xd6 ♕xe1 20.♖xe1 cxd6 21.d5 ♘a5 22.♘d4 ♗d7 23.♖e7 ♖d8∓) 17...♖xe8 18.c4 ♕e4 19.♗xd6 cxd6 20.♕d2 ♕c2! This move is typical in such positions. We have already mentioned that any simplification is advantageous for Black. (It is weaker for him to play passively with 20...♕e7?! 21.♖e1 ♕d7 22.♖xe8+ ♕xe8 23.♕f4 ♕d7 24.d5 ♘e7 25.♘d4± since Black's position is cramped, his d6-pawn requires protection and White is threatening to break through with c4-c5, Akopian – Dominguez, Turin 2006.) 21.♕f4 h6! This is an excellent prophylactic move. (It is also possible for Black to play 21...g6, but he should try to deploy his pawns on dark squares, having a light-squared bishop.) 22.h3 (The pawn is poisoned, because after 22.♕xd6?! ♕b2 23.♖d1 ♗g4 24.d5 ♗xf3 25.♕d7 ♔f8 26.♕d6+ ♖e7! 27.gxf3 ♘e5→ Black's initiative is very dangerous.) 22...♕c3 23.♖d1 ♕c2 24.♖d2 ♕b1 25.♕xd6 ♘a5 26.♘e5 ♘b3 27.♖e2 f6 28.♕d5+ ♔h7 29.♘d3 ♗xd3 30.♖xe8 ♕xf1+ 31.♔h2 ♕xf2 32.♕g8+ ♔g6 33.♖e7 ♕f4+ 34.♔h1 ♕f1= and a draw by a perpetual check.

A) 16.♕a4

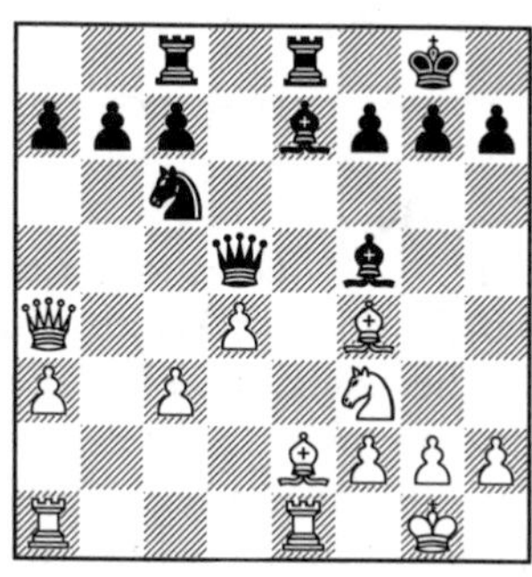

16...♗d7!

It is useful to repulse the enemy queen. It is less precise for Black to continue with the seemingly active move 16...♗e4 17.♗g3 ♕f5, owing to 18.♕b5! (18.♘d2?! ♗c2 19.♕b5 ♕xb5 20.♗xb5 a6 21.♗xc6 bxc6= Negi – Fridman, Germany 2008) 18...♕xb5 19.♗xb5 ♗d5 20.♘e5 a6 21.♘xc6 ♗xc6 22.♗xc6 bxc6 23.♔f1± – Black's queenside pawn-structure has been weakened, therefore White has the edge in this simple-looking position.

17.♕c2

After 17.♖ab1, Black can equalize with this long variation: 17...♗d6 18.♗xd6 cxd6 19.♖b5 ♘e7 20.♖xd5 ♗xa4 21.♖a5 ♗c6 22.♖xa7 ♗xf3 23.gxf3 ♘f5 24.♖xb7 ♖xc3 25.♗f1 ♖ec8 26.♗h3 ♖xf3 27.♖e3 ♖f4 28.♖c7 ♖b8=

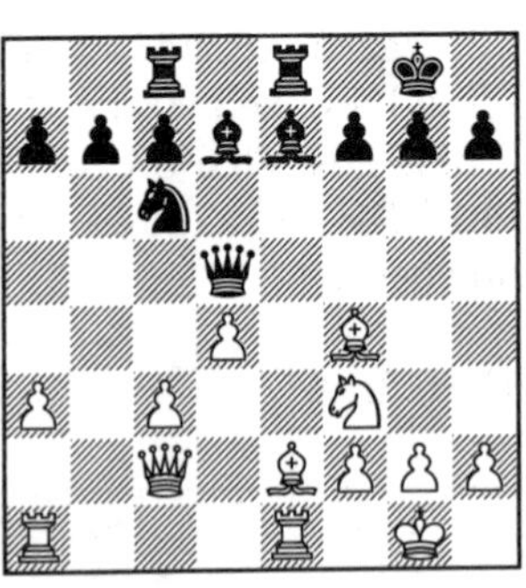

17...♕f5

If 17...♗d6 (The move ♗e7-d6 is usually good if White cannot avoid the exchange of bishops.) White can play 18.♗e3! ♗f5 19.♕c1!± – and his central pawns are ready to advance, while Black's bishop on d6 turns out to be misplaced in this case, because it might come under attack with tempo after c3-c4 followed by c4-c5.

However, it would be good for Black to play 17...♗f5 18.♕b2 ♘a5 19.♘e5 ♕b3= and he would be very close to equality.

18.♕xf5

It is useless for White to continue to roam all over the board with his queen, because after 18.♕d2 ♗d6 19.♗xd6 cxd6= Black has no problems at all.

18...♗xf5 19.♗b5

White weakens his opponent's pawn-structure with this move, but presents him with the advantage of the bishop-pair.

He would not achieve much with 19.d5 ♘a5 20.♘d4 ♗d7=

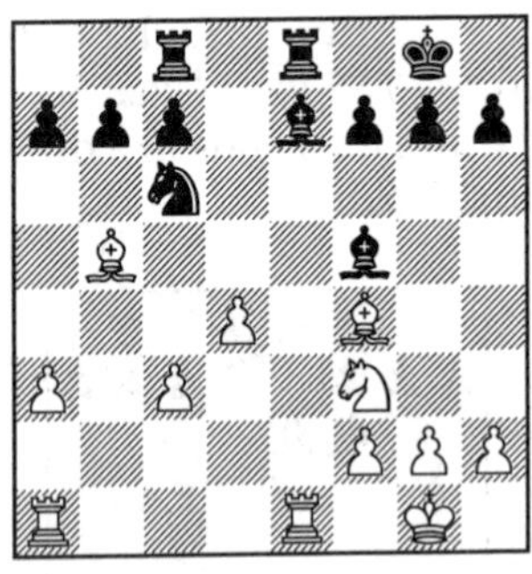

19...a6!

It is less precise for Black to play 19...♗d7 20.d5 (20.♘d2 a6 21.♗d3 ♘a5=) 20...♘e5 21.♘d4! (White will be in trouble after 21.♗xd7 ♘xd7 22.♗xc7 ♖xc7 23.d6 ♖xc3 and here, after 24.♖xe7 ♖xe7 25.dxe7 ♘f6 26.♘d4 a6∓, with the plan of ♘f6-e8, f7-f6 and ♔g8-f7, White's e7-pawn remains without the support of the rest of his pieces and is doomed; while after 24.dxe7 f6 25.♖ad1 ♖c7 26.♘d4 ♘e5 27.f4 ♘c6 28.♘xc6 bxc6∓ White must play accurately to make a draw, Anand – Kramnik, Mexico 2007) 21...c6 (The other possibility for Black here is 21... ♗xb5 22.♘xb5 ♗d6 23.♘xa7 ♖a8 24.♘b5 ♘f3+ 25.gxf3 ♗xf4± – he should be able to draw, but playing a pawn down might be rather unpleasant.) 22.♗f1 ♘g6 23.dxc6 bxc6 (Black fails to solve his problems with 23...♗xc6 24.♘xc6 ♖xc6 25.♗e3± and White exerts pressure thanks to his powerful bishop-pair, while Black cannot exchange all the pawns on the queenside: after 25...a6 26.♖eb1 ♖xc3 27.♖xb7 ♖xa3? White wins with the simple response 28. ♖xe7+–) 24.♗g3 ♗c5 25.a4± and White maintains a slight advantage thanks to his more active pieces.

20.♗xc6 bxc6 21.♖e5 ♗d3 22.♖ae1 ♔f8 23.♖a5 ♗d6 24. ♘e5 ♗xe5=

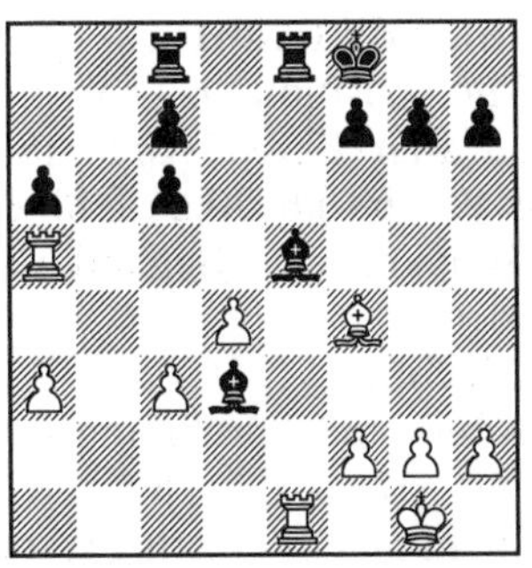

White's edge is merely symbolic and Black should manage to draw without too much effort.

B) 16.g3

This is an original move, but it does not create any serious problems for Black.

16...♗f6

It is too risky for him to opt for 16...b5?! 17.♘d2 ♘a5?! Karjakin – Smeets, Wijk aan Zee 2010. White can continue with 18.a4! b4 19.♗a6±, obtaining a material advantage.

17.♘d2

17.♖c1 h6 18.c4 ♕a5 (Black equalizes even more simply with the standard move 18...♕d7=) 19. d5 ♘e5 20.♗xe5 ♗xe5 21.♗d3 ♗g4 22.♗h7+ (It is overly ambitious for White to choose 22.♖e4?! Ivanchuk – Gelfand, Monaco 2011, because after 22...f5! 23.♖xg4 fxg4 24.♘xe5 ♖xe5 25.♕xg4 ♖f8 26.♕d4 ♖e1+ 27.♖xe1 ♕xe1+ 28. ♔g2 b6∓ he can only struggle to draw.) 22...♔xh7 23.♕d3+ ♔g8 24.♘xe5 f6 25.♕g6 ♗h3 26.♕f7+ ♔h7 27.♕g6+ ♔g8= and a draw by perpetual check.

17...♕d7 18.♘c4 ♗h3!

This move emphasizes the weakening of the light squares in White's camp, caused by his sixteenth move.

19.♕d3

19...g5!

Black weakens his king's shelter a little, but this is not important here, because it causes disharmony in the set-up of White's pieces. His bishop must retreat to e3, thus depriving his own knight of this square.

20.♗e3 ♕d5 21.♗f1 ♗xf1 22.♕xf1

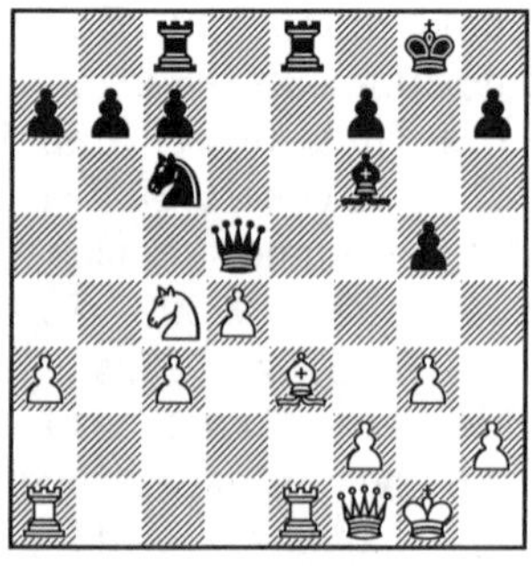

22...b5!

After 22...♘e7 White can activate his forces with 23.f4! (23.♖ab1 ♘f5 24.a4 a6 25.♕d3 b5 26.♘a3 c6 27.♘c2 ♕f3 28.♕d1 ♕xd1 29.♖exd1 ♘d6∓ Gashimov – Wang Yue, Nanjing 2010) 23...gxf4 (it would be too risky for Black to opt for 23...g4 24.♘e5± and White's centre is very powerful) 24.♗xf4⩲ with a slight edge for White.

23.♘d2 h6!= This is a useful prophylactic move, protecting the g5-pawn. The position is approximately equal and 24.f4 is not dangerous in view of 24...♖e6!∓ and Black exerts pressure along the e-file.

C) 16.♗d3

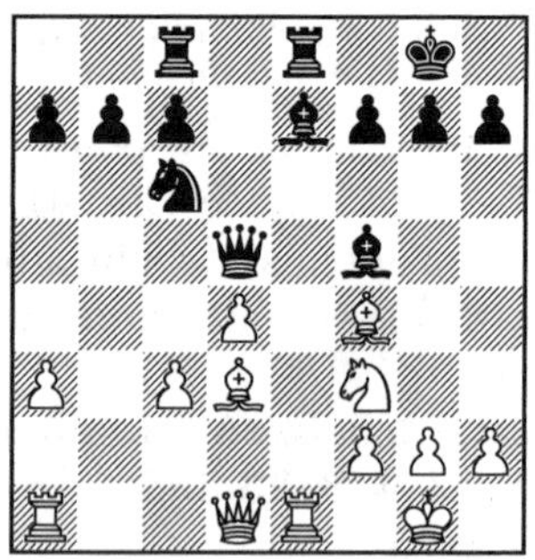

16...♕d7 17.♖b1

The position is completely equal after 17.♗xf5 ♕xf5 18.♗g3 ♗d6 19.♕b3 b6 20.c4 ♕f6 21.d5 ♘d4= Ivanchuk – Gelfand, Calvia 2004.

17...b6!

After the preliminary exchange 17...♗xd3 18.♕xd3 b6, White has an interesting resource at his disposal – 19.♖e3!? (the move 19.d5 transposes to the main line of the variation) 19...♗xa3 20.♘g5 g6 21.♘e4 (It is not very dangerous for Black if White tries 21.♖h3 h5 22.♖xh5 ♘e5 23. ♕c2 ♕g4 24.♖h8+ ♔xh8 25.♗xe5+ ♔g8 26.♘xf7 ♔xf7 27. ♕b3+ ♕e6 28.♕xa3 a5 29.♖e1 c5∞ – the position remains very complicated, but Black's defensive resources seem to be sufficient for equality) 21...♗e7 22.♖be1⩲ White has numerous possibilities for developing his initiative in return for his minimal material deficit, so Black must defend super-precisely to keep the balance, Grischuk – Gelfand, Moscow 2006.

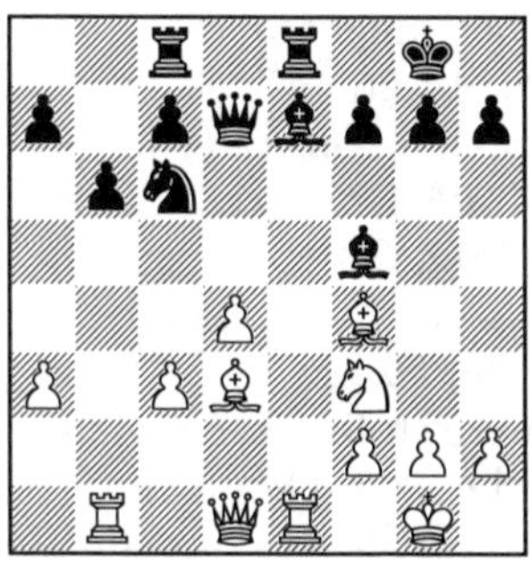

Now White can sharpen the game with the move **C1) 18.♗b5**, or he can continue playing in a purely positional manner **C2) 18.d5**.

C1) 18.♗b5 ♗xb1 19.♕xb1

19.♘e5 ♕f5 20.♗xc6 ♕xf4=

19.d5 ♖cd8 20.♕xb1 ♕xd5 21. c4 ♕c5 22.♗e3 ♕d6 23.♕e4 ♘a5 24.♗xe8 ♖xe8∓ White is unable to exploit the pin on the e-file.

19...♗f6 20.♖d1

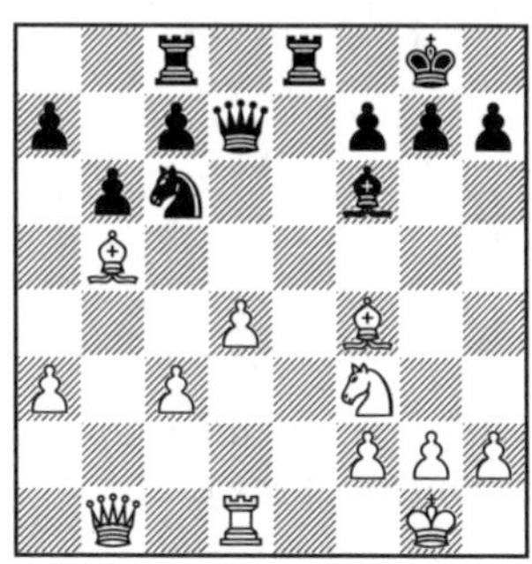

Here, Black has two queen-sorties: **C1a) 20...♕g4** and **C1b) 20...♕d5!**

C1a) 20...♕g4 21.♗g3

Black maintains a slight edge following 21.♗xc6 ♕xf4 22.♗xe8 ♖xe8∓, because his bishop is stronger than the enemy knight when the fight continues on both sides of the board.

21...♘e7 22.♗xe8 ♖xe8 23. ♖e1 ♕d7 24.♕e4

24...c6!

Black could have evaded the

pin even earlier with 24...♖c8.

White cannot take advantage of his control of the e-file:

25.♕b7 ♕c6 26.♕a6 (26.♕xc6 ♘xc6 27.♗xc7 h6 (27...♗e7 28.♗f4 ♗xa3 29.d5 ♘a5 30.♘d4 ♗f8 31.d6 ♖d8=) 28.♗f4 ♘a5=) 26...♖f8=;

25.♗e5 ♗xe5 26.♘xe5 ♕e6 27.♕b7 f6 28.♘d3 (28.♘f3 ♕c6 29.♕a6 ♖e8 30.c4 ♘c8 31.♖xe8+ ♕xe8 32.♕b7 ♕d7=) 28...♕c6 29.♕xc6=, draw, Nisipeanu – Fridman, Turin 2006;

The move 25.h4 has several drawbacks; in some variations this pawn is hanging; White no longer has the h4-square available, which he uses as a base for his pieces in some variations; and he no longer has the possibility of g2-g4, in order to dislodge Black's knight from the f5-square, which it may occupy in some lines. 25...h6 (Also worth considering is 25...b5!? 26.♗e5 ♘d5 27.♗xf6 gxf6⇄ – if White's pawn had been on h3 here instead of h4, he could have transferred his knight to f5, via the h4-square, while now he is unable to do this and Black has sufficient counterplay. Black has yet another interesting possibility – 25...♘f5 26.♗xc7 h5 27.♗e5 ♖xc3 28.♗xf6 gxf6 29.d5 ♖c5 30.♖d1 ♘d6 31.♕f4 ♔g7= and he maintains equality here as well.) 26.♗e5 ♗xe5 27.♘xe5 ♕e6 28.♕b7 f6 29.♘d3 ♕c6= Jakovenko – Wang Yue, Nizhny Novgorod 2007.

White can improve his position with the move 25.h3!

There might follow:

25...b5 26.♗e5±;

25...h6 26.♗e5 (26.♗h4 ♘d5 27.c4 ♗xh4 28.♕xh4 ♘f6 29.♘e5 ♕d6 30.♖e3 ♖e8 31.♖g3 ♔f8 32.♖e3 ♔g8=) 26...♗xe5 27.♘xe5 ♕e6 28.♕b7 f6 29.♘f3 ♕c6 30.♕xc6 ♘xc6 31.d5 ♘a5 32.♖e7 c6 33.♘d4 cxd5 34.♘f5± and White has some chances of maintaining a slight edge;

25...c6 26.♘e5 ♗xe5 27.♕xe5 ♘d5 28.c4 ♘f6 29.♕e3 ♖e8 30.♗e5 ♕f5 31.♕g3 g6 32.♕c3± with a minimal advantage for White.

25.a4

This move is aimed at preventing b6-b5 and, in addition, White's pawn is removed from a square on which it might sometimes come under attack.

He cannot achieve much with the straightforward line: 25.♘e5 ♗xe5 26.♕xe5 ♔f8= with the plan of continuing with ♘e7-f5.

If 25.c4, then not 25...♖c8, even though after 26.♗h4 ♗xh4 (It would be a huge positional concession for Black to play 26...♘g6? 27.♗xf6 gxf6± Timofeev – Wang Yue, Ningbo 2010.) 27.♘xh4 ♖e8± Black has excellent chances of neutralizing White's initiative, but simply 25...h6!= with ideas of ♖e8-d8 and b6-b5.

After 25.h3, besides the prophylactic move 25...h6, it is possible for Black to continue with 25...b5! 26.♘h2 ♕e6 27.♕xe6 fxe6 28.♖xe6 ♔f7 29.♖d6 ♘d5= and the activity of his pieces compensates for the sacrificed pawn.

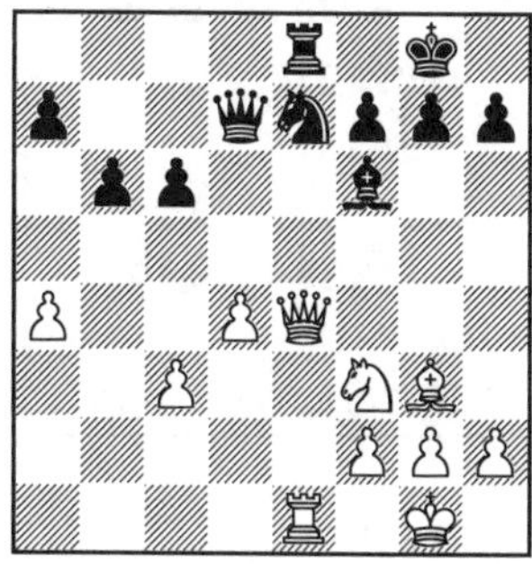

25...b5!

It is high time Black played actively!

He still has some problems in the variation 25...h6 26.h3 a6 27.♘e5 (White has an interesting resource here in 27.♘h2!? and Black loses after 27...♔f8 28.♘g4 ♘d5 29.♗d6+ ♗e7 30.♕h7 f6, in view of 31.♗g3!+–. He can maintain equality only after very precise defence: 27...h5! 28.♘f3 b5 and now it would be bad for White to continue with 29.axb5 cxb5 30.♗h4 ♗xh4 31.♘xh4 a5 32.♕e5 ♕e6 33.♕xe6 fxe6 34.♖xe6 a4∓ and Black's outside passed pawn is so powerful that White must play very accurately to make a draw. Instead, it is stronger for White to opt for 29.♘e5 ♕e6! 30.♕c2 g6!± when Black's position is still acceptable, but from a purely practical point of view White's game is easier.) 27...♕e6 28.♕b1 ♘c8 29.c4 (It is also attractive for him to try 29.a5!? bxa5 30.♘d3 ♕d7 31.♖xe8+ ♕xe8 32.♕b7 ♘e7 33.♕xa6 ♘f5 34.♗e5 ♗xe5 35.♘xe5 c5 36.♕xa5 cxd4 37.cxd4 ♘xd4 38.♘xf7 ♘f3+ 39.gxf3 ♕xf7± and Black must play precisely to save the game.) 29...♗xe5 30.♖xe5 ♕d7± Black's position here is solid but passive, Timofeev – Wang Yue, Ningbo (rapid) 2010.

26.axb5 cxb5

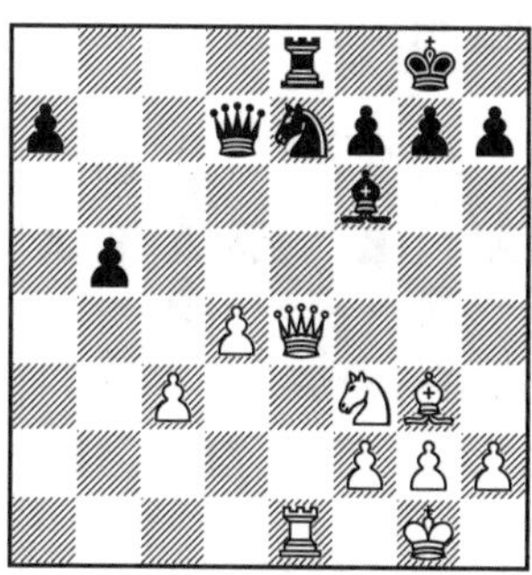

27.♘e5 (But not 27.d5?, because of 27...♖d8! 28.d6 ♘f5∓) **27...♗xe5 28.♕xe5 f6 29.♕c5 ♘f5 30.♖xe8+ ♕xe8 31.h3 ♘xg3 32.fxg3 ♕d7=**

C1b) 20...♕d5!

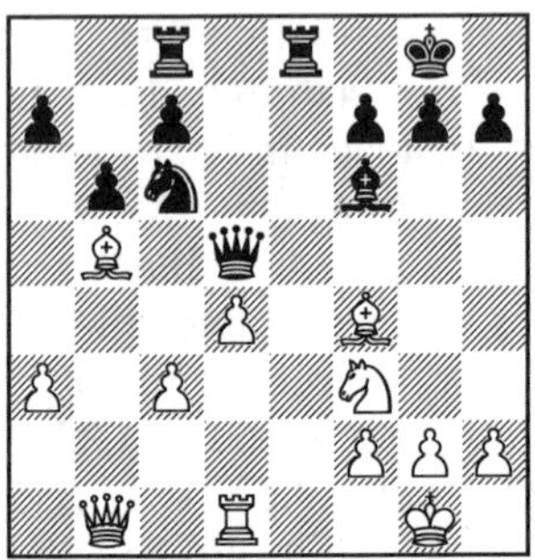

21.♗g3 ♘e7 22.♘e5

22.c4 ♕f5 23.♗xe8 ♖xe8 24.d5 (24.♕b3 ♕d7=) 24...♕xb1 25.♖xb1 c6!=

22.♗xe8 ♖xe8 23.♗xc7 ♕c4 24.♗e5 ♘d5= After an exchange on f6, Black should recapture with the pawn, making use of the circumstance that White's pieces are too passive to exploit effectively the defects of Black's king shelter.

22...♖f8

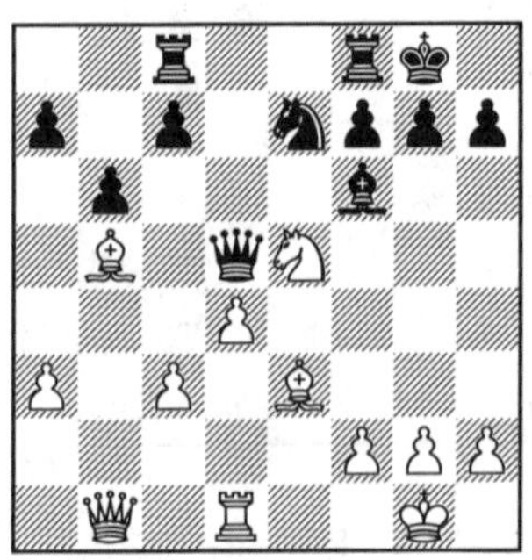

23.c4

Black is better after 23.♘d7 c6 24.♘xf8 cxb5 (24...♕xb5 25.♘xh7 ♗xd4 26.♕e4∞) 25.♘xh7 ♖xc3 26.♘xf6+ gxf6∓

23...♕b7 24.♘d7 c6 25.♘xf8

After 25.♘xf6+ gxf6 26.♗a4 ♕a6∓ White's compensation for the exchange is insufficient.

25...cxb5 26.♘xh7 bxc4 27.♘xf6+ gxf6 28.d5 c3 29.♕c2 ♘xd5 30.♗d6 ♕c6 31.♕f5 c2 32.♕g4+ ♔h7 33.♕h5= and the game ends in a draw by perpetual check.

C2) 18.d5 ♗xd3 19.♕xd3

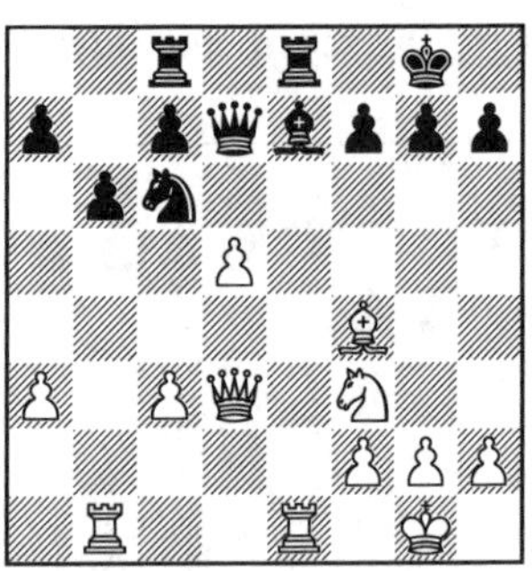

19...♗xa3!

This is Black's most direct route to equality.

The quieter move 19...♗f6 leads to a safe position, but fails to equalize completely in view of White's simple reply 20.c4

(diagram)

and now:

20...h6 21.h3 ♘e7 22.♘e5 ♗xe5 23.♖xe5 (or 23.♗xe5 ♘f5±

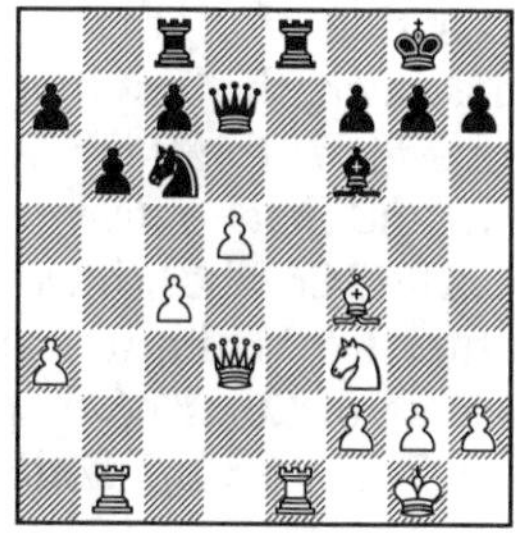

and White again has a slight edge) 23...♘g6 24.♖xe8+ ♖xe8 25.♗g3± with a pleasanter position for White, Anand – Shirov, Monaco (blindfold) 2005;

20...♘e7 21.♖bd1! (Black has nothing to fear after 21.♗e5 ♗xe5 22.♘xe5 ♕d6=. White can simplify the position rather quickly with 21.♘e5 ♗xe5 22.♗xe5 f6 23.♗f4 ♘f5. In the game Svidler – Kramnik, Dortmund 2006, further exchanges followed: 24.c5 bxc5 25.♕c4 g5 26.♗d2 ♘d6 27.♕xc5 ♘e4 28.♕a5 c6 29.♗e3 cxd5 30.♕xa7 ♕xa7 31.♗xa7 ♘c3 32.♖xe8+ ♖xe8 33.♖b8 ♖xb8 34.♗xb8 d4 35.♔f1 ♔f7 36.♗a7 d3 37.♔e1 d2+ 38.♔xd2 ♘b1+ 39.♔d3= and a draw.) 21...♖cd8 22.h3 ♘g6 23.♗g3 h6 24.♕b3 ♖e7 25.a4 ♖de8 26.♖xe7 ♘xe7 27.♖e1 c6 28.♗e5 cxd5 29.♗xf6 dxc4 30.♕xc4 gxf6 31.♘h4± White's initiative more than compensates for the sacrifices pawn, but with precise defence Black should manage to hold, Leko – Kramnik, Dortmund 2007.

20.♘g5

20.♖xe8+ ♖xe8 21.♕b5 ♘b8 22.♕xd7 ♘xd7=

20...g6 21.♘e4 ♕f5

The move 21...♗e7 cannot be refuted directly but seems quite risky:

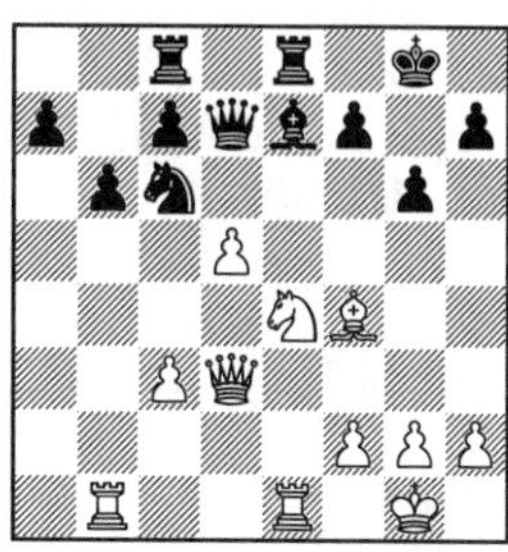

22.♕b5 ♕f5 23.♗xc7 ♖xc7 24.♘d6 ♗xd6 25.♖xe8+ ♔g7 26.dxc6 ♗c5=;

22.♖bd1 f5 23.d6 (White should have preferred here 23.♘g5 ♗xg5 24.♗xg5⩱, with some compensation for the pawn.) 23...cxd6 24.♕d5+ ♔h8 25.♘xd6 ♗xd6 26.♗xd6 ♖xe1+ 27.♖xe1 ♖e8 28.♖xe8+ ♕xe8 29.h3 h6 30.c4 ♔h7=, draw, Jakovenko – Kramnik, Moscow 2007. Black's position is slightly pleasanter, but his chances of winning are just negligible, since his king is quite exposed;

22.♕d1!? ♘a5 23.♗h6 ♕f5 24.♖e3± Black might succeed in holding this position with very precise play, but the defence would be arduous;

The most dangerous variation for him is 22.♕d2 ♘a5 23.♗h6 ♕f5 24.♕d4 f6 25.♕a4 (25.♘g3 ♕d7 26.♘e4=) 25...♘b7 (25...g5 26.d6 cxd6 27.♘xd6 ♗xd6 28.♖xe8+ ♔f7 29.♖be1 ♔g6 30.g4!+–) 26.♖bd1→ and White's initiative is very powerful.

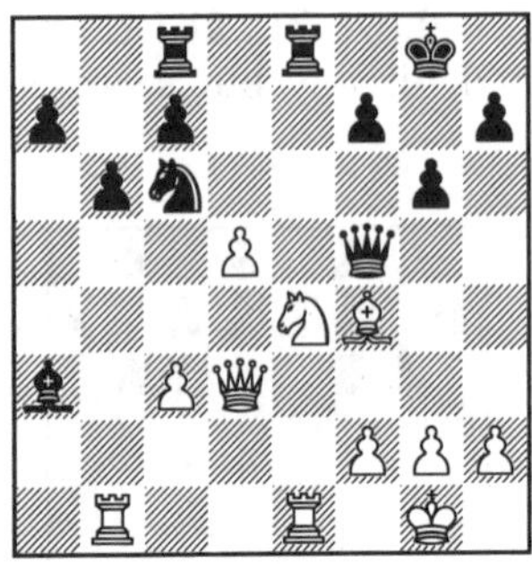

22.♗xc7

Or 22.♕f3 ♘e5 23.♗xe5 ♕xf3! (23...♖xe5 24.♕xf5 ♖xf5 25.♖a1=) 24.gxf3 ♖xe5 25.♘f6+ ♔g7 26.♖xe5 ♔xf6 27.♖e4 ♗d6∓ and only White might have problems here.

22...♖xc7

It is interesting but very risky for Black to opt for 22...♘e5!? 23.♗xe5 ♖xe5 24.c4 ♖ce8 25.f3

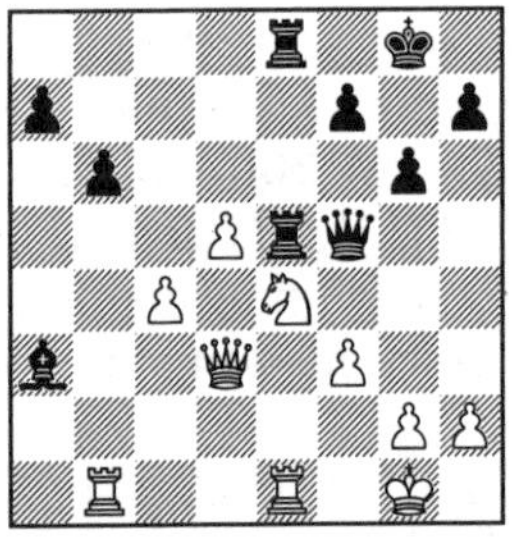

and now:

25...♗c5+ 26.♔h1 a5. Black's a-pawn boldly advances, exploiting the fact that White cannot capture it comfortably, since his king is vulnerable. 27.♖f1! a4 28.♖a1! (28.♕c3 a3 29.♖a1 ♕f4 30.♘xc5? ♖h5 31.h3 ♖xh3+ 32.gxh3 ♖e2–+; 28.♘xc5 bxc5 29.♕xf5 ♖xf5 30.♖b5 a3=) 28...♖a8±. A series of manoeuvres will follow, but, as compensation for the outside passed a-pawn, the best that Black can hope for is to attack White's c4-pawn and make a draw;

25...♗f8!? 26.♖bd1 (it would be premature for White to play 26.d6 because of 26...♕e6, with the threat of f7-f5) 26...♗g7 27.d6 ♖d8±

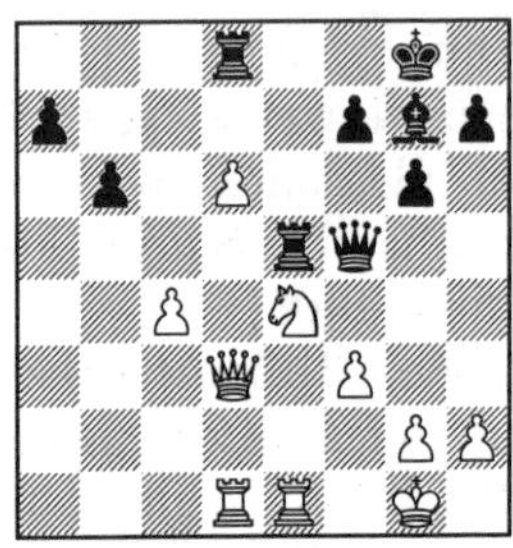

White's d6-pawn looks dangerous, but Black also has his trumps. His bishop is stronger than the enemy knight and if he manages to advantageously retreat his queen and oust White's knight 0 the initiative and his opponent's d-pawn will become a target.

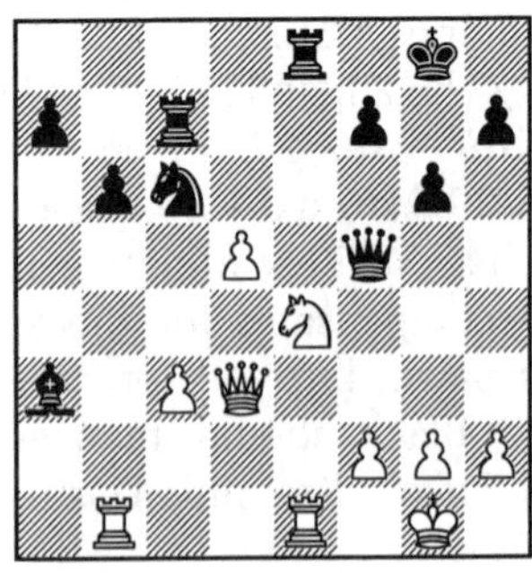

23.♘f6+ ♕xf6 24.♖xe8+ ♔g7 25.dxc6 ♗c5 26.♖b2 ♖xc6 27.♕d8 ♕xd8 28.♖xd8 a5=

11.a3 ♘xc3 12.bxc3 ♘c6 13.♖e1 ♖e8 14.cxd5 ♕xd5 15.♗f4 ♖ac8

Leko – Gelfand, Moscow 2009.

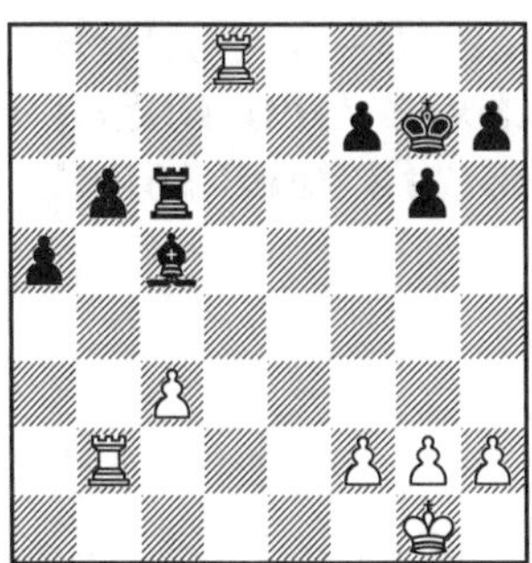

Black's bishop on c5 is completely stable and it supports the a-pawn, which will soon be advanced to the a3-square. It also attacks the f2-pawn and White will be tied down to its defence. Meanwhile, Black's rook is free to roam all over the board, attacking the enemy pawns. Having all this in mind, Black would not have any problems and the game should end in a draw.

Conclusion

We have examined how White can attempt lively piece-play, but Black has no serious problems anywhere. Black's main strategic ideas are as follows:

1) He must exert pressure against White's pawn-chain c3-d4, preventing its advance, since that might cramp Black's position. It is usually beneficial for him to place his bishop on f6. If White succeeds in advancing his c-pawn to c4, then Black must try to force White to push d4-d5 too, so that he can then organize a blockade on the c5-square.

2) He must constantly consider the possibility of playing ♘a5, followed by the undermining move c7-c5.

3) Exchanges are almost always useful for Black. It is particularly advantageous for him to exchange the queens, as well as the bishops. In order to simplify, he has the following resources up his sleeve:

– with a knight on a5, Black can play ♕d5-b3, exchanging queens, which might be rather unpleasant for White;

– with a bishop on f5 and a queen on e4, Black can often play ♕e4-c2!;

– it is sometimes useful for him to play ♗e7-d6, if this forces the exchange of the dark-squared bishops. Furthermore he can also exchange the rooks along the e-file.

Chapter 26 **1.e4 e5 2.♘f3 ♘f6 3.♘xe5 d6 4.♘f3 ♘xe4 5.d4 d5 6.♗d3 ♘c6 7.0–0 ♗e7 8.c4 ♘b4 9.♗e2 0–0 10.♘c3 ♗f5 11.a3 ♘xc3 12.bxc3 ♘c6 13.♖e1 ♖e8 14.cxd5 ♕xd5 15.♗f4 ♖ac8 16.h3**

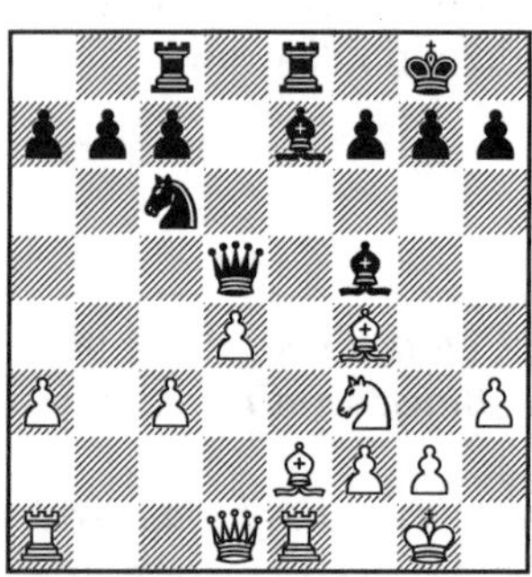

This is White's most popular move here. He opens an escape hole for his king and creates the possibility of playing g2-g4 at some point, ousting the enemy bishop from f5 and opening the long diagonal for his own bishop. Black has two reasonable responses and both of them are sufficient for him to face the future with optimism: with **16...♗e4**, he puts direct pressure on the knight on f3 and "x-rays" the pawn on g2; alternatively he can reply in similar fashion with the prophylactic move **16...h6** (which we shall analyze in the next chapter), letting his opponent clarify his intentions first.

16...♗e4

White has a rich choice of possibilities here. He can begin forcing play with the move **A) 17.♘d2**, strengthen his centre with **B) 17.♗e3**, remove his pawn from attack with **C) 17.a4**, or start to transfer his queen to a more active position with the moves **D) 17.♕a4** or **E) 17.♕c1**.

A) 17.♘d2

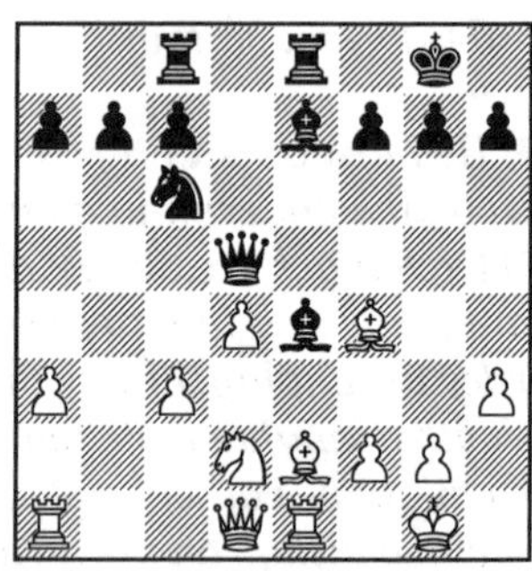

White invites the enemy bishop into his camp, hoping that it might become trapped. However, the concrete variations show that White cannot trap it and can only exchange it.

17...♗xg2 18.♗g4 ♗h1 19.f3 ♗h4

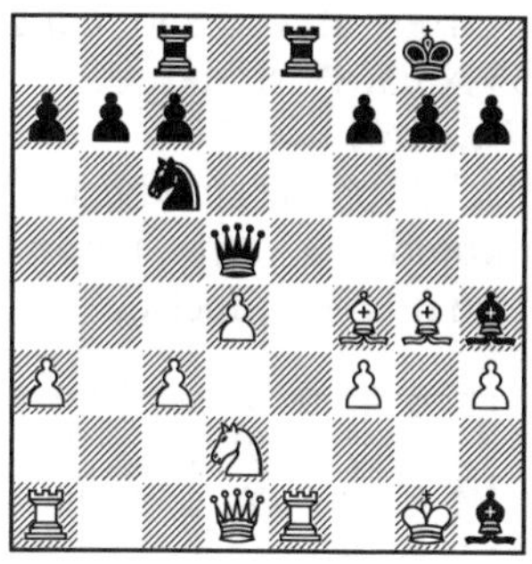

20.♖e4

After 20.♖f1 f5 21.♗h5 g6 22.♔xh1 gxh5 23.♖g1+ ♔h8∓ Black has a pawn, which is doubled but still extra, Leko – Anand, San Luis 2005.

20.♖xe8+ ♖xe8 21.♔xh1 f5! (21...♖e1+ 22.♕xe1 ♗xe1 23.♖xe1 f5 24.♖e8+ ♔f7 25.♖c8 fxg4 26.♖xc7+ ♔g8 27.♖c8+ ♔f7 28.♖c7=) 22.♕g1 ♕f7!∓ White's pawn-structure has been weakened and Black's prospects are better.

20...f5 21.♔xh1 fxg4 22.hxg4

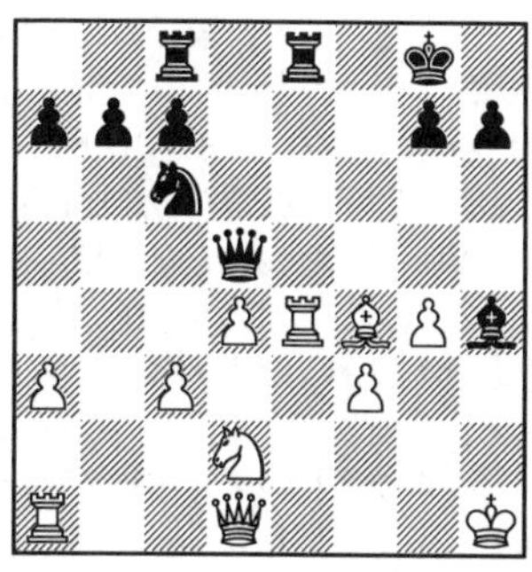

22...♕f7

It seems very good to play 22...♘e7 immediately here. After 23.♗h2 ♕f7, White has nothing better than to repeat moves with 24.♖f4 ♕e6 25.♖e4=

23.♕b3 ♘e7 24.♕xf7+ ♔xf7 25.c4 ♘g6 26.♗h2 ♗f6= The endgame is approximately equal, Shirov – Kramnik, Wijk aan Zee 2010.

B) 17.♗e3 ♘a5

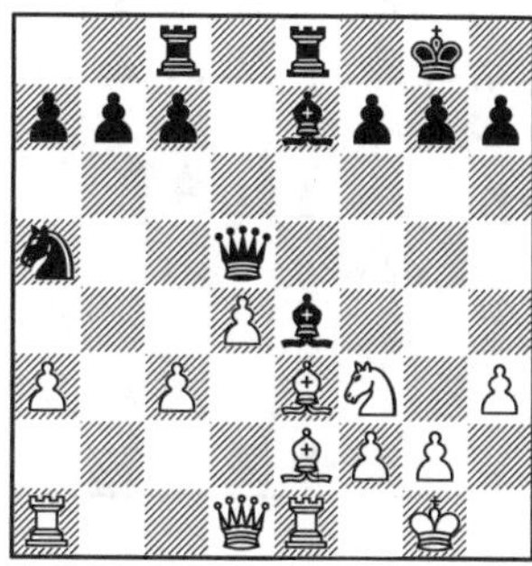

18.♘d2

18.♘e5 ♗f6 19.♘g4 (19.♗g4 ♖cd8 20.♕a4 ♘c6 21.f3 ♗g6 22.♘xg6 hxg6= White's bishop on g4 is restricted by its own pawns and thus Black has a very comfortable position. He has nothing to fear after 19.c4 ♕d6 20.♘g4 ♗h4= since White's pieces lacks harmony) 19...♗e7 20.♘e5=, draw, Timman – Erenburg, Goteborg 2005.

18.c4 ♘xc4 19.♗xc4 ♕xc4 20.♘d2 ♕d5 21.♘xe4 ♕xe4 22.♗g5 ♕xe1+ 23.♕xe1 ♗xg5 24.♕a5 ♗f6 25.♕xa7 c5= Black has sufficient compensation for the queen with a rook, a bishop and a passed c-pawn supported by the bishop, Leko – Kramnik, Brissago 2004 (**game 19**).

18...♗f5 19.c4

White cannot create any problems for his opponent with the line: 19.♗f3 ♕d7 20.♘e4, Laznicka – Stopa, Legnica 2004. Black's most solid move here would be 20...b6!=, cementing the queenside and depriving White's knight of the c5-square.

19...♕d7 20.♘f3 ♗f6 21.♖c1 c5 22.dxc5 ♕xd1 23.♖cxd1 ♘b3 24.c6 ♖xc6 25.♗xa7 ♗c3 26.♖f1 ♖a6 27.♗e3 h6= Ivanchuk – Kramnik, Wijk aan Zee 2008.

C) 17.a4

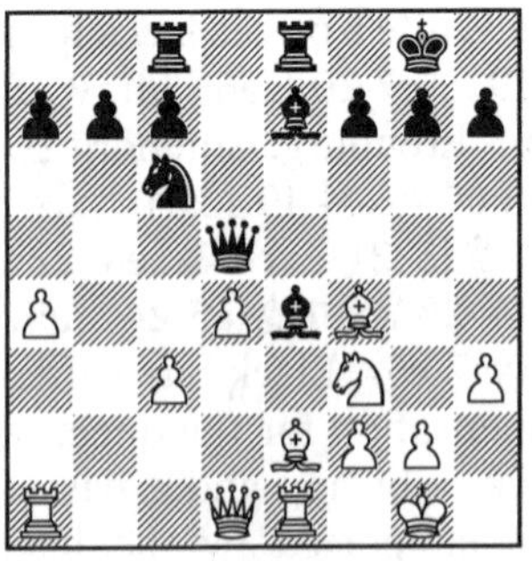

This move is typical for similar positions. White removes his pawn from attack and controls the b5-square just in case.

17...♗d6!

Black's other standard reply here would be 17...♗f6, but in this position it is less precise.

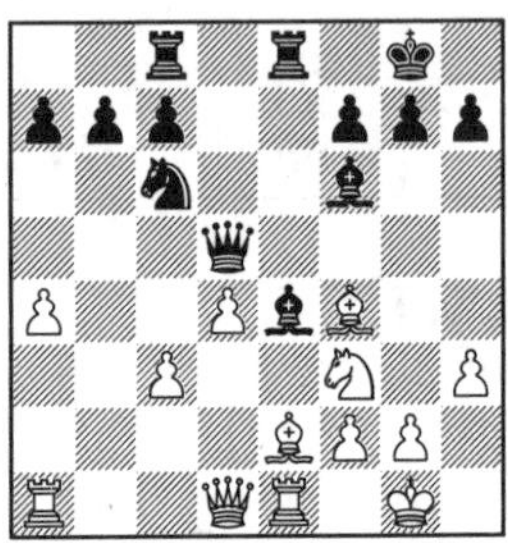

Having played a3-a4, White is not planning to advance with c3-c4 any time soon. Black usually places his bishop on f6 in order to prevent the advance of his opponent's central pawns.

Now White would not achieve anything by trying to sharpen the game: 18.♘d2 ♗xg2 19.♗g4 ♗h1 (19...♖xe1+ 20.♕xe1 ♖f8 21.♖b1 h5 22.♖b5 ♕d8 23.♖xh5 g6 24.♖b5 ♗d5 25.♗xc7 ♖e8 26.♕d1 ♕xc7 27.♖xd5± Ivanchuk – Gelfand, Sochi 2008) 20.♘f3 (20.f3 ♗h4 21.♖xe8+ ♖xe8 22.♕b3, Asrian – Wang Yue, Taiyuan 2007, 22...♕xb3 23.♘xb3 f5⩱) 20...♖xe1+! (20...♗xf3 21.♕xf3 ♕xf3 22.♗xf3⩲) 21.♕xe1 ♗xf3 22.♗xc8 ♘e7 23.♗g4 ♗xg4 24.hxg4 ♕f3 25.♗xc7 ♕xg4+ 26.♗g3 h5=∞ and Black's counterplay is sufficient for equality.

It is stronger for White to choose the positional move 18.♗d3! Any simplification is usually in Black's favour, but in this particular case he has problems, because with a bishop on f6 his c7-pawn is hanging.

He has several possibilities to choose from but none of them equalize:

18...♗xf3 19.♖xe8+ ♖xe8 20.♕xf3 ♕xf3 21.gxf3± White is better, thanks to his bishop-pair;

18...g6 19.♖e3 ♗xd3 20.♕xd3 ♖xe3 21.fxe3±;

18...♗xd3 19.♖xe8+ ♖xe8 20.♕xd3± Black has difficulties protecting his c7-pawn;

18...♖e7 19.♖xe4 ♖xe4 20.c4 ♕f5 (it would be too risky for him to opt for 20...♕e6 21.d5 ♕e8 22.dxc6 ♖xf4 23.cxb7 ♖b8 24.♖b1 ♕c6 25.♕e2 ♗d4 26.♘xd4 ♖xd4 27.♕e3±. White's bishop will come to the long diagonal and after that Black's position will become difficult) 21.♗e3 ♘b4 22.♗xe4 ♕xe4 23.♕b1 ♕e7 24.♕f5± and White maintains a slight edge.

18.♗e3

(diagram)

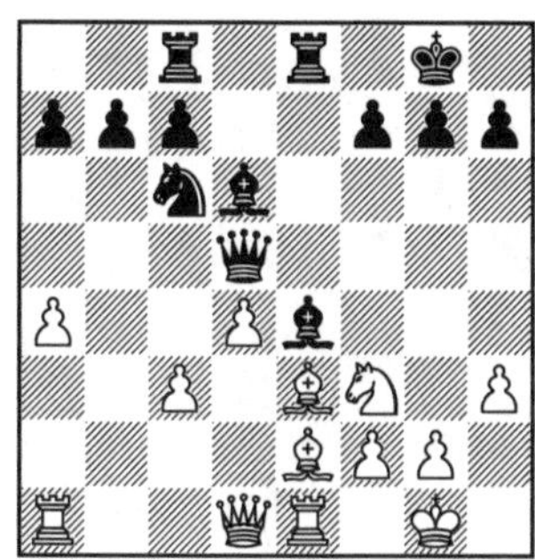

18...♘a5

In the game Smirin – Volokitin, Crete 2007, Black tried 18...♕a5?!. In this variation, that can hardly be the right square for Black's queen. 19.♕b3 ♕f5 20.♘d2 ♘a5. By playing 21.♕a2!±, White could have obtained the advantage of the two bishops, since Black would not have the move 21...♗c6, in view of 22.♗g4 ♕g6 23.d5+–

19.♘d2 ♗f5 20.c4 ♕e6 21.c5

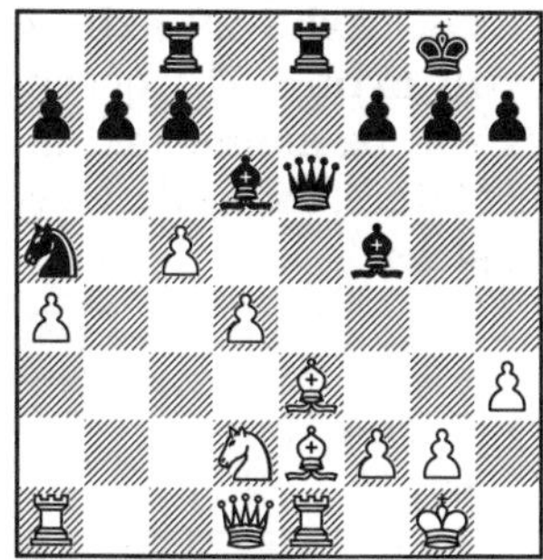

21...♗f8

Here Black has a good alternative in 21...♗e7=, planning the transfer of his bishop to the f6-square.

22.♖c1 b6 23.♘f3 ♕b3 24.♕xb3 ♘xb3 25.♖c3 ♘a5 26.d5

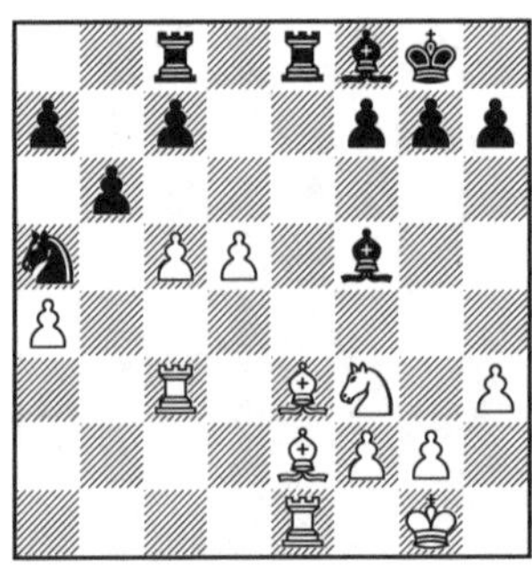

26...♗d7

It would be a mistake for Black to play 26...bxc5 27.♗xc5 ♗d7, Radjabov – Wang Yue, Baku 2008. Here, White can maintain the advantage with the far-from-obvious line: 28.♗xf8 ♔xf8 29.♔h2!±, threatening 30.♗a6 ♖xe1 31.♗xc8.

27.♗a6 ♖a8!

But not 27...♖d8, because of 28.d6! ♗xd6 29.cxb6±

28.♗b5 ♗xb5 29.axb5 ♘b7 30.cxb6 cxb6= The queenside pawns will be annihilated in the nearest future, so the draw seems inevitable.

D) 17.♕a4

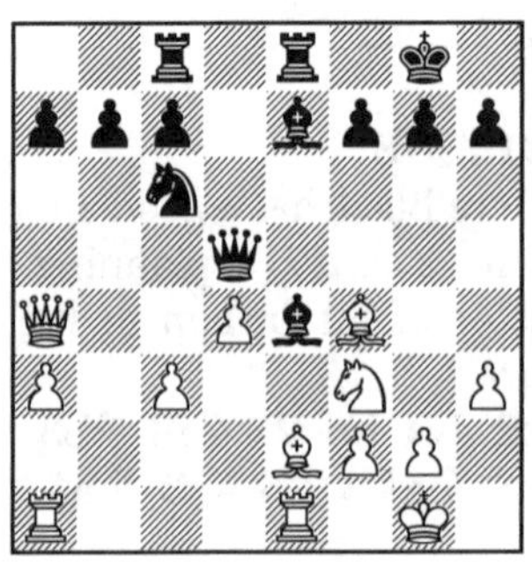

17...♕f5

Here Black could consider 17...a6!?, depriving his opponent of the important b5-square. 18.♘d2 (after quieter play Black's game will be even easier: 18.♗g3 ♗d6=; 18.♗e3 ♕f5 19.♘d2 ♗c2 20.♕c4 ♘a5 21.♕a2 ♕g6=) 18...♗xg2 19.♗g4 ♗h1 20.f3 f5 21.♗h5 g6 22.♔xh1 gxh5 23.♕c4 ♕xc4 24.♘xc4 ♗f6 25.♖xe8+ ♖xe8 26.♗xc7, Kulaots – Nouro, Finland 2006; now with 26...b5! 27.♘b6 ♔f7 28.♘d5 ♘e7= Black equalizes effortlessly.

18.♗g3 ♗c2

18...♗d6 19.♘e5 ♗xe5 20.♗g4 ♕g6 21.dxe5 ♗f5 22.♗f3± Grischuk – Pe.Nielsen, Monaco 2006.

19.♕b5 ♕xb5 20.♗xb5 a6 21.♗xc6 bxc6 22.♖e5

If 22.♖a2 ♗a4 23.c4, then 23...c5! (it is weaker for Black to opt for 23...♗b3 24.♖ae2 ♔f8 25.c5 ♗d5 26.♘e5 ♖cd8 27.♖e3± since his position is terribly cramped, so White's prospects are preferable, Grischuk – Volokitin, Foros 2006) 24.d5 ♗f6 25.♖ae2 ♔f8=

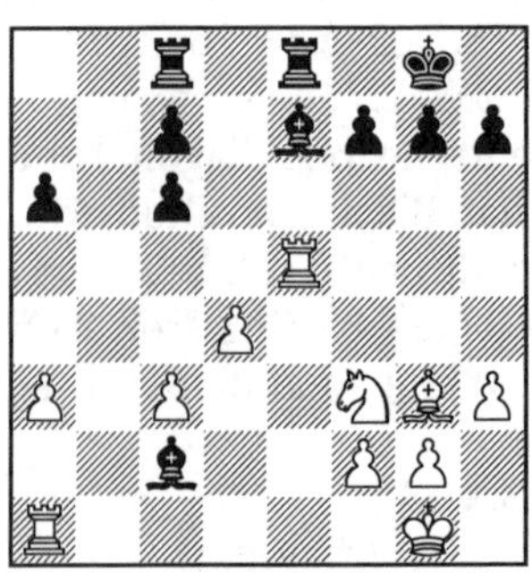

22...c5!=

It is essential for Black to accomplish this pawn-break at this precise moment, while White's rook has not yet occupied the excellent a5-square. If instead Black plays 22...f6 23.♖a5 ♗d3 24.♘e1± he still has some difficulties to worry about, Svidler – Anand, Morelia/Linares 2007.

23.♖ae1 ♔f8 24.dxc5 f6 25.♖d5 ♗b3 26.♖d7 ♗a4 27.♖d4 ♗c6= Shirov – Gelfand, Moscow 2007.

E) 17.♕c1

White's queen is free to manoeuvre from this square and his bishop on f4 is protected, which is also useful.

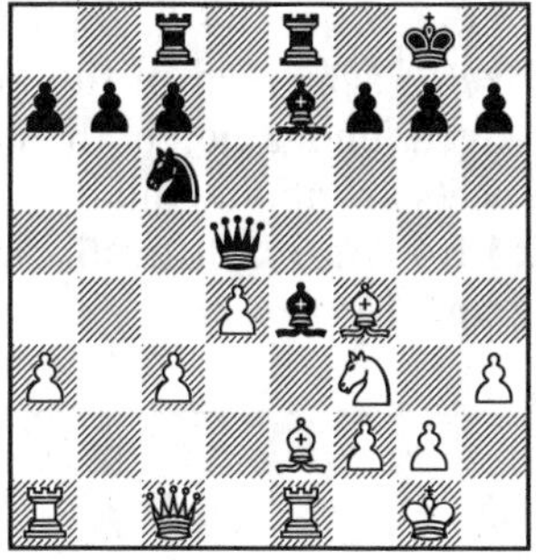

17...♗f6!N

As is often the case in such positions, this is the most favourable square for the bishop. It is good for Black to place it on d6 only if White cannot avoid the exchange of the dark-squared bishops.

It is rather dubious for Black to play 17...♘a5?! 18.♕e3! ♗f8?! (It is slightly preferable to continue with 18...♗f5, but after 19.♘e5 c5 20.♗h5 cxd4 21.cxd4 ♗e6 22.♗f3± White is clearly better.) 19.c4 ♕d8 20.♘e5 ♗f5 21.♕c3± and White is dominating the entire board, Anand – Kramnik, Wijk aan Zee 2010.

After 17...♗d6, White has the reply 18.♗e3±; now Black's bishop is misplaced on d6, since it does not prevent the advance of White's central pawns.

18.♕b2 ♘a5

Black wishes to play ♕d5-b3, bringing about advantageous simplification.

19.♘d2!?

This is the only move for White to fight for the advantage.

19...♗xg2 20.♗g4

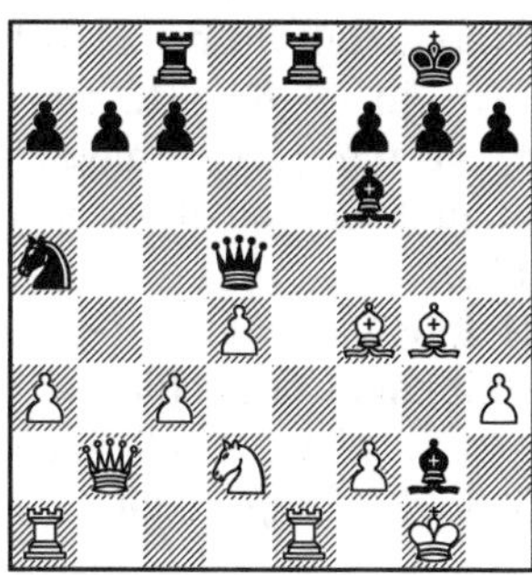

Now Black can equalize with precise play:

20...♖cd8!

This is the best move.

It is less convincing to opt for 20...h5 21.♗xc8 ♖xc8 22.♖e3 c5 23.♖ae1!± when White mobilizes his last undeveloped forces and begins a counter-offensive.

The move 20...♖a8 also equalizes for Black, but in a much more difficult way. Furthermore, it is psychologically unpleasant for him to return the rook to its initial square. 21.f3 h5! (in the variation 21...♗h4 22.♖e5 ♖xe5 23.♗xe5 h5 24.♔xg2 hxg4 25.hxg4 ♗g5 26.♖h1 f6 27.♕c2! ♗xd2 28.♗xf6! ♕f7 29.♗xg7! ♕xg7 30.♕a2+ ♔f8 31.♕xd2→ White has a very dangerous attack) 22.♔xg2 hxg4 23.hxg4 ♘c4 (Black can hold the balance in another long variation too: 23...♗g5 24.♗xg5 ♕xg5 25. ♘e4 ♕d5 26.♕f2 f5 27.♘g5 fxg4 28.♕h4 gxf3+ 29.♔g3 ♖xe1 30.♖xe1 f2 31.♖h1 ♕d6+ 32.♔xf2 ♖f8+ 33.♔e1 ♖e8+ 34.♔d1 ♕h6 35.♕xh6 gxh6 36.♖xh6= with a draw) 24.♘xc4 ♕xc4 25.g5 ♗e7 26.♕xb7 ♕xc3 27.♖ac1 ♕xd4 28.♖e4 ♕b6 29.♕xb6 axb6 30.♖ce1 ♔f8 31.♗xc7 (31.♖h1 ♔g8=) 31...♗c5= Almost all the pieces have been eliminated, so the draw is unavoidable.

21.♗xc7

White does not achieves much with 21.f3 ♗h4 22.♖e5 ♖xe5 23.♗xe5 h5 24.♔xg2 hxg4 25.hxg4 ♗g5=

21...h5 22.♗xd8 ♖xd8

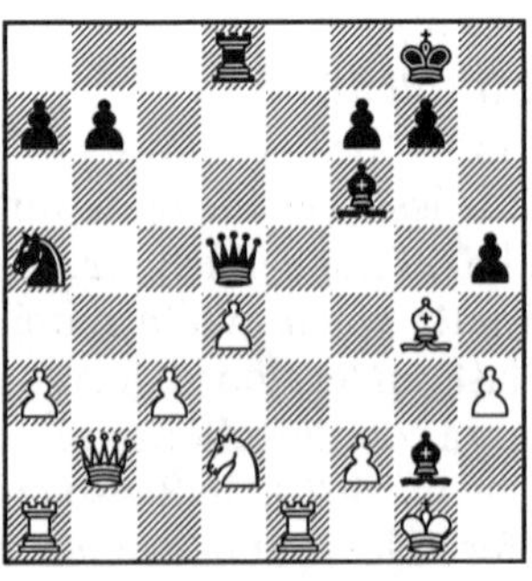

23.♗d1

After the alternatives for White, perpetual checks are lurking on all sides:

23.♗f5 ♕xf5 24.♔xg2 ♕g6+ 25.♔h2 (25.♔h1 ♕f5=; 25.♔f1 ♕d3=) 25...♗g5 26.♘e4 ♗f4+ 27.♔h1 ♕f5 28.♔g2 ♕g6+ 29.♔f1 ♕f5=;

23.♗xh5 ♗h1 24.f3 ♕xh5 25.♔xh1 ♕xh3+ 26.♔g1 ♕g3+ 27.♔f1 ♕h3=;

23.f3 hxg4 24.♔xg2 gxh3+ 25.♔xh3 (if White does not capture this pawn, his position can only be worse) 25...♕h5+ 26.♔g2 ♕g6+ 27.♔f1 ♕d3+ 28.♔g2 ♕g6= with a draw.

23...♕g5

It is interesting for Black to try here 23...♗xh3!? 24.♘e4 ♗e7 25.♗f3 ♕f5 26.♕e2 h4 27.♘g3 ♕e6 28.♕xe6 ♗xe6= and in this double-edged endgame, both sides' prospects are about equal.

24.h4 ♕g6 25.♗xh5 ♕xh5 26.♔xg2 ♕g4+

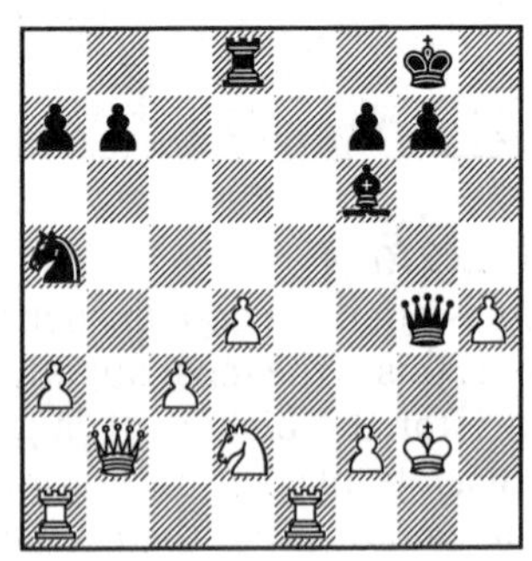

27.♔h2

It is too risky for White to play 27.♔f1 ♕h3+ 28.♔e2 ♗xh4⩱ – his king will be very unsafe and

Black's initiative more than compensates for the sacrificed exchange.

27...♕xh4+ 28.♔g2 ♕g4= and the game ends in perpetual check.

Conclusion

The move 16...♗e4 objectively equalizes. However, as often happens when Black's bishop captures the g2-pawn, the resulting lines require concrete and precise calculation. Every mistake becomes crucial. We have analyzed numerous forcing variations and it is very easy for a player to go astray in them. Accordingly, the quieter lines arising after 16...h6, a move we shall deal with in the next chapter, are much more popular at grandmaster level.

Chapter 27 **1.e4 e5 2.♘f3 ♘f6 3.♘xe5 d6 4.♘f3 ♘xe4 5.d4 d5 6.♗d3 ♘c6 7.0–0 ♗e7 8.c4 ♘b4 9.♗e2 0–0 10.♘c3 ♗f5 11.a3 ♘xc3 12.bxc3 ♘c6 13.♖e1 ♖e8 14.cxd5 ♕xd5 15.♗f4 ♖ac8 16.h3 h6**

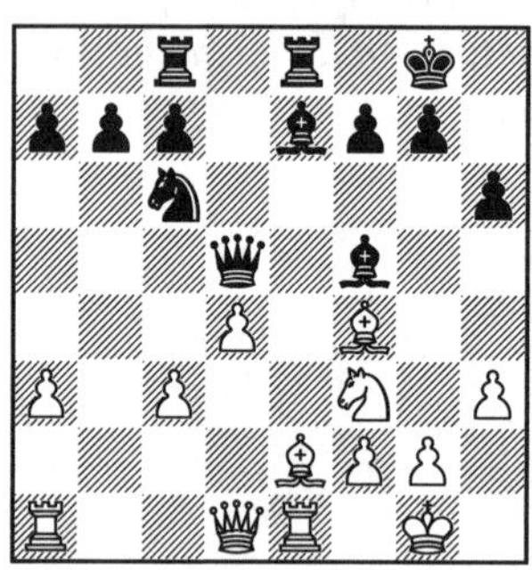

The position is of a non-forcing nature and White has numerous possibilities. We shall analyze them thoroughly: **A) 17.♕a4, B) 17.♗f1, C) 17.c4, D) 17.g4, E) 17.♘d2** and **F) 17.♕c1.**

White has also tried:

17.a4. White removes his pawn away from a square on which it might come under attack, but Black can use this tempo to simplify the position: 17...♗d6 18.♗e3 ♘a5= Hracek – Dydyshko, Czech Republic 2010;

17.♘h2. The transfer of this knight to the e3-square takes too much time for White, so that he cannot expect to obtain any advantage. 17...♗d6 18.♗xd6 ♕xd6 (it is also good for Black to play here 18...cxd6 19.♘f1 ♗d7 20.♘e3 ♕g5=) 19.♘f1 ♘a5 20.♘e3 ♗g6 21.♕a4 b6 22.♗a6 ♖cd8 23.♘c4 ♖xe1+ 24.♖xe1 ♘xc4 25.♗xc4 a5, followed by the exchanging manoeuvre ♖d8-d7-e7, and Black equalized convincingly in the game Lutz – Landa, Germany 2007.

A) 17.♕a4

With the help of this move, White hopes to bring his light-squared bishop into action via c4 or b5.

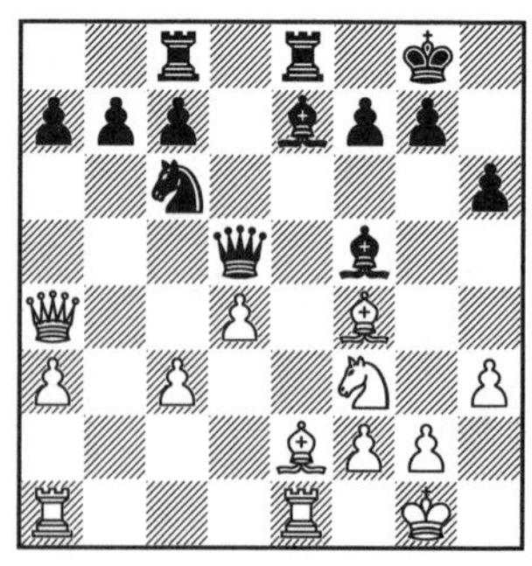

17...♗d7

It would be rather dubious for Black to opt for 17...♕a5?! 18.♕b3 ♕b6, Fedorov – Stupak, Minsk

2010. Here White could have played 19.♕xb6! axb6 20.♗b5± with an advantage.

18.♖ab1

18.♕c2 ♕f5 19.♕xf5 ♗xf5 20.♗b5 (20.d5 ♘a5 21.♘d4 ♗d7 22.♘b5, Svidler – Dominguez, Poikovsky 2005. By replying with 22...♗f6!= Black could have solved all his problems.) 20...a6 21.♗xc6 bxc6 22.♖e5 ♗d3 23.♖ae1 ♔f8 24.♖a5 ♗d6 25.♘e5 ♗xe5= and the draw is imminent.

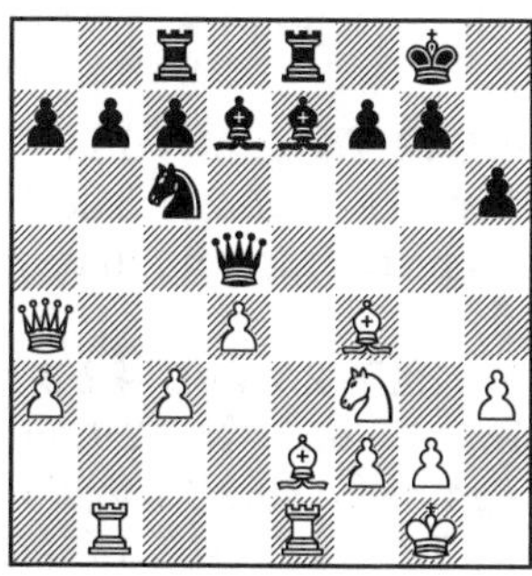

18...♗d6

It is a mistake for Black to try 18...a6, in view of 19.♕d1! (19.♘d2 ♘a5 20.♕c2 ♕f5= Quezada – Bu Xiangzhi, Khanty-Mansyisk 2010) 19...b5 20.a4 ♗f5 21.axb5! ♗xb1 22.♕xb1± – the light squares in Black's camp are terribly weak.

However, he has a good option in 18...♕f5 19.♗e3 ♖b8= with approximately equal prospects.

19.♗xd6

After 19.♗e3 Black has the simple reply 19...b6=

19...♕xd6 20.♘d2 b6 21.♗b5 ♖cd8= – The position has been simplified a little; Black has no weaknesses and his pieces are harmoniously deployed.

B) 17.♗f1 ♗d6

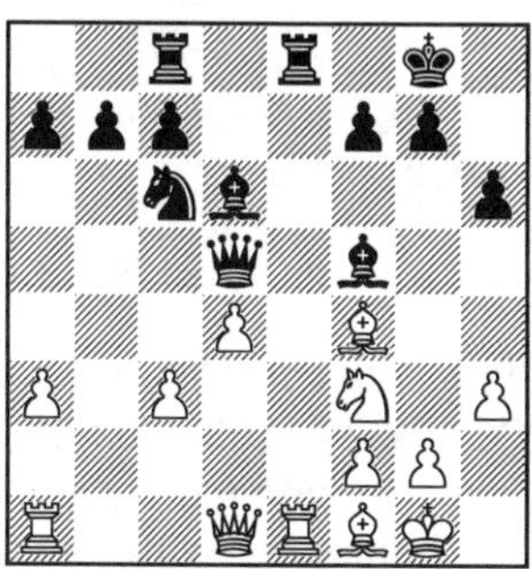

18.♖xe8+

18.c4 ♖xe1 19.♕xe1 ♕e4 20.♗e3 b6= Firman – Giri, Germany 2010.

18.♗e3 ♘a5 19.♘d2 b6 20.c4, Al-Modiahki – Dao Thien Hai, Doha 2006. It is most precise for Black to retreat now with 20...♕c6!=. White's pieces are tied to the protection of his c4-pawn, while Black's queen can retreat to the comfortable d7-square. Black has no problems whatsoever.

18...♖xe8 19.c4 ♕e4 20.♗xd6 cxd6 21.♕d2

21.♖a2 ♖e7 22.♖e2 ♕b1=

21...♕c2 22.♕f4

Or 22.♕xc2 ♗xc2 23.d5 ♘a5 24.♘d4 ♗a4 25.♘f5 ♘b3 26.♖b1 ♖d8∓ with a slight edge for Black.

22...♕b2 23.♖d1

(diagram)

23...♕b3!

This is Black's most precise response.

The alternatives do not pro-

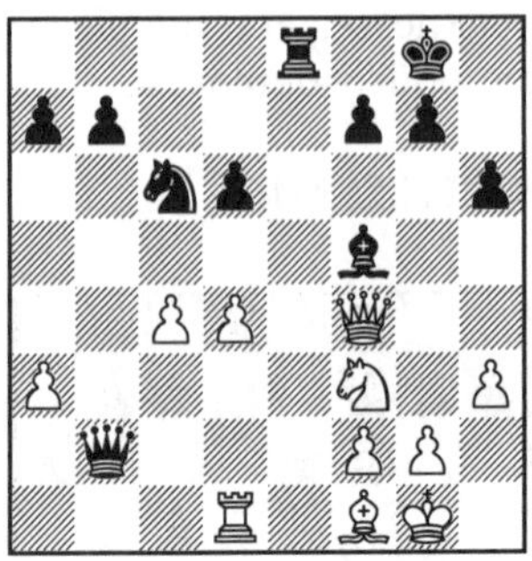

vide him with complete equality:

23...♗c2 24.♕d2 ♕b3 25.♖c1 (White can create more problems for his opponent with 25.♖e1! ♖xe1 26.♕xe1 ♕b1 27.♕e8+ ♔h7 28.♕xf7 ♗d3 29.♘d2 ♕c1 30.♕f3 ♗xf1 31.♘xf1 ♕xc4 32.♕f5+ ♔h8 33.♕c8+ ♔h7 34.♕xb7 ♘xd4 35.♔h2± and thanks to his much safer king White's position is preferable, although Black should manage to make a draw with accurate defence.) 25...♗e4 26.♖e1 ♖e7 27.♖e3 (27.♕f4 d5=) 27...♕b1 28.♖e1=, draw, Belov – Bu Xiangzhi, Moscow 2010;

23...♗g6 24.♕xd6 ♗e4 25.♖e1! (If 25.♕f4, then 25...♗xf3 and after 26.♕xf3 ♘xd4= the position is equal, Akopian – Gashimov, Elista 2008. The move 26.gxf3, with the idea of preserving the d4-pawn, seems to be too risky. Black can immediately exploit White's weakened king-position by playing 16...♖e6. White cannot avoid the variation 27.d5 ♖g6+ 28.♗g2 ♕e2 – 28...♘e5!? – 29.♖d2 ♕e1+ 30.♔h2 ♘e5 31.♖a2 ♘xf3+ 32.♕xf3 ♕e5+ 33.♔g1 ♕e1= and Black draws by perpetual check.) 25...♖d8 26.♕c7 ♗xf3 27.d5! ♕d2 28.♖b1 ♗xd5 (Black cannot preserve the extra piece under favourable circumstances: 28...♕g5 29.♖xb7 ♘e5 30.h4 ♕f6 31.♕e7 ♕xe7 32.♖xe7 ♘g6 33.♖xa7 ♗e4 34.a4± and White has excellent chances of promoting his pawns.) 29.cxd5 (it is bad for White to play 29.♖xb7? ♗e6 30.♕xc6 ♕e1∓) 29...♖xd5 30.♖xb7 ♖f5 31.♕c8+ ♘d8 32.♕xf5 ♘xb7± Black must work hard here to make a draw, because with play on both flanks his knight is inferior to White's bishop.

24.♖d2 ♕b1 25.♕xd6

After 25.g4 ♗g6 26.♕xd6 ♕c1⩱ White's pieces turn out to be misplaced.

25...♘a5 26.♘e5 ♘b3 27.♖e2 f6 28.♕d5+ ♔h7 29.♘d3

29.g4 fxe5 30.gxf5 ♘xd4 31.♖e3 ♘xf5 32.♖xe5 ♖xe5 33.♕xe5=

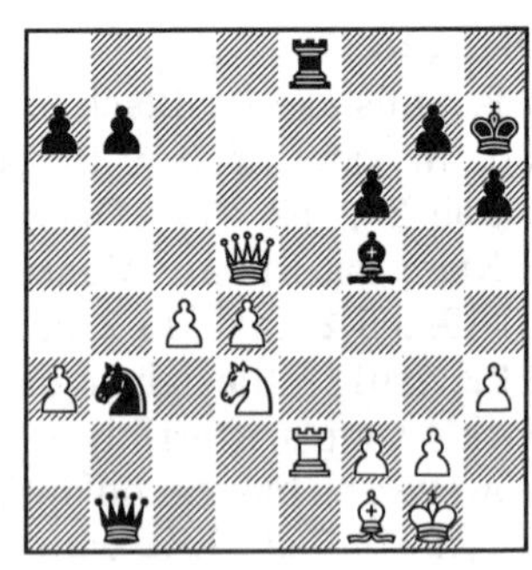

29...♕xf1+

29...♗xd3 30.♖xe8 ♕xf1+ 31.♔h2 ♕xf2 32.♕g8+ ♔g6 33.♖e7 ♕f4+ 34.♔h1 ♕f1=

30.♔xf1 ♗xd3 31.♔g1 ♖xe2 32.♕xb7 ♘d2 33.c5 ♖e1+ 34.

♔h2 ♗e4 35.♕xa7 ♘f1+ 36. ♔g1= Black is unable to weave any mating nets against his opponent, so he must take the draw by perpetual check.

C) 17.c4 ♕e4

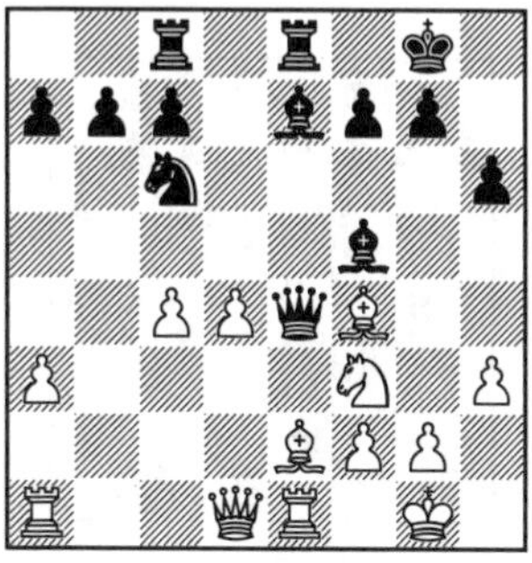

18.♗g3

After 18.♗e3 Black replies with the standard move 18...♕c2! (If he does not exchange queens and plays for example 18...♗f6, then White can immediately protect the c2-square with the move 19. ♖a2!. The position after 19...♘a5 20.♗f1 ♕c6 21.d5 ♕d6 was tested in the game Sengupta – Suvrajit, New Delhi 2010. By playing 22. ♗d3! ♗e4 23.♗xe4 ♖xe4 24.♕d3, White could have maintained an advantage: 24...♖xc4 25.♘d2 ♖c3 26.♕f5± or 24...♖ce8 25.♖ae2±) 19.d5 (19.♕xc2 ♗xc2 20.d5 ♘a5 21.♘d4 ♗a4=) 19...♘a5 20.♘d4 ♕xd1 21.♖axd1 (21.♖exd1 ♗d7 22. ♗d2 ♗f6=) 21...♗d7 22.♘b5 b6 23.♘xa7 ♖a8 24.♘b5 ♗xb5 25. cxb5 ♗xa3=

18...♗f6 19.♗f1 ♕c2 20. ♕xc2 ♗xc2 21.♖xe8+ ♖xe8 22.♖c1

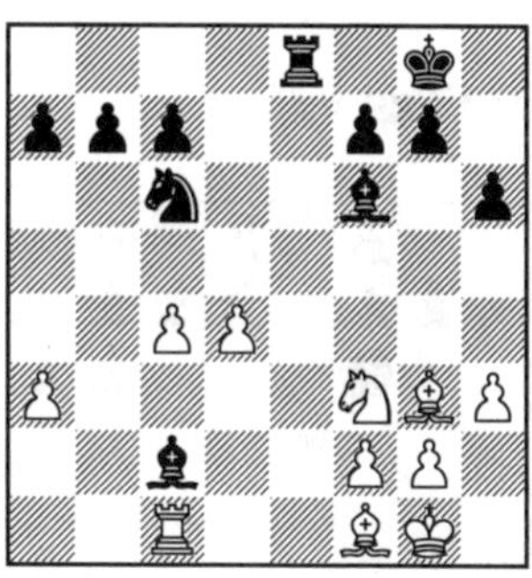

22...♗g6!

It is quite reliable, but less convincing, for Black to continue with 22...♗a4 23.d5 ♘e5 24.♘d2= Shomoev – Landa, Sochi 2006.

23.d5 ♘e5 24.♘xe5

24.♘d4 ♘d3∓

24...♗xe5

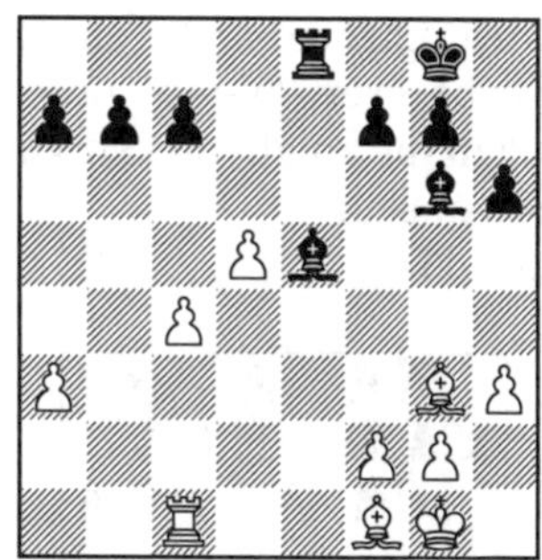

25.♗xe5

The bishop ending arising after 25.♖e1 f6 26.♗xe5 ♖xe5 27. ♖xe5 fxe5 could even be losing for White, since his opponent's king would march to the c5-square.

25...♖xe5 26.f3 ♔f8

If 26...♖e3?! White has the

rather unpleasant response 27.c5. **27.♔f2 ♔e7 28.f4 ♖e4 29. g3 ♖d4 30.♔e3 ♖e4+ 31.♔f2**=

D) 17.g4 ♗g6

D1) 18.♗f1
D2) 18.♗d3

D1) 18.♗f1

This move is played with the idea of transferring the bishop to the long diagonal and from there it will be exert "x-ray" pressure (through the knight on f3) against Black's queen.

18.♗d3

The fact that White has played g2-g4 means that Black is now forced to exchange on d3, which he is usually reluctant to do when his bishop is on f5. 18...♗xd3 19.♕xd3 ♕d7! (It is less precise for him to play 19...♗d6 20.c4 ♕a5, Ivanchuk – Kramnik, Nice 2010, 21.♖xe8+! ♖xe8 22.♗d2± White's centre is securely protected and he has the idea of g4-g5 in reserve, so he has the better prospects) 20.d5 ♗f6

21.♖ab1 (21.♖xe8+ ♖xe8 22. ♕b5 ♘e5 23.♕xd7 ♘xd7 24.♗xc7 ♗xc3=; 22.♖b1 ♘e7 23.c4 ♘g6 24.♗g3 b6= Howell – Gelfand, Amsterdam 2010) 21...♖xe1+ 22. ♖xe1 ♘e7 23.c4, Karjakin – Gelfand, Nice (rapid) 2010. The game is equal after 23...h5! 24.g5 ♘g6 25. ♗g3 ♗e7 26.♔g2 ♗d6=

18...♗d6

18...♗f6?! 19.♖xe8+ ♖xe8 20. ♗xc7 ♖c8, Jakovenko – Fridman, Dresden 2008, 21.♗f4 ♘a5 22. ♖c1±

19.♖xe8+ ♖xe8 20.c4 ♕e4 21.♗e3

(diagram)

21...♗f8!N

White hopes to advance d4-d5 and c4-c5 with tempo, so Black's prophylactic retreat with the bishop is his simplest and most reliable way to equalize.

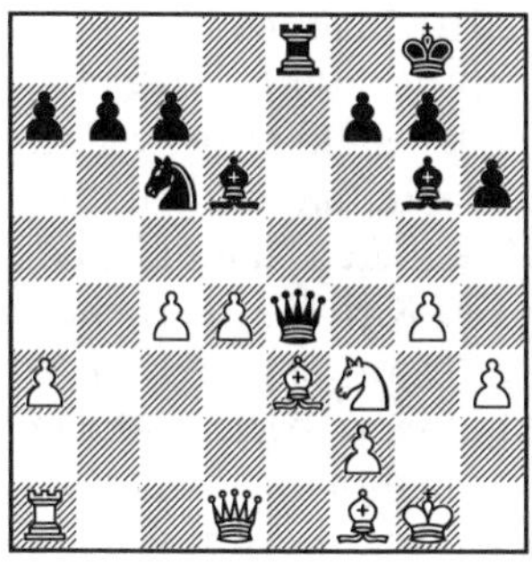

It might be interesting for him to try the double-edged move 21.. ♖d8!? 22.♗g2 (if 22.♘d2, Black has the resource 22...♕e7 23.c5 ♗g3!) 22...♕e7! (22...♕c2 23.d5 ♘a5 24.c5± Yemelin – Polak, Czech Republic 2010)

and now:

23.g5 ♗c5 24.♖a2 (24.gxh6 ♗h5∓) 24...♗h5 (24...hxg5∓) 25. ♖d2 ♗xa3 26.gxh6 ♗b4∓ This position is very rich in possibilities, but Black's chances are a bit better, Grischuk – Ivanchuk, Linares 2009 (**game 20**);

23.♕c1 ♕d7 24.♕c3 ♗e7=;

White's best option here might be 23.♕b3! ♗e4 (23...♕f6 24. ♖d1±) 24.c5 (24.♘d2 ♗xg2 25. ♔xg2 b6=) 24...♗xc5 25.dxc5 ♗xf3 26.♗xf3 ♕f6 27.♔g2 ♕xa1 28.♕xb7 ♘e5 29.♕xc7 ♖e8 30. ♗d5. Black might objectively be able to hold this position, but fighting against White's far-advanced passed pawn, supported by his bishop-pair, is likely to be rather an unpleasant task. 30... ♕xa3 31.♗f4 ♕d3 32.♕d6 ♕e2 33.c6 ♘d3 34.♗g3 ♘e1+ 35.♔h2 ♘f3+ 36.♔g2 ♘e1=

22.♗g2

22.d5 ♘e5 23.♘d2 ♕c2 24. ♕xc2 ♗xc2=

22...♕d3=

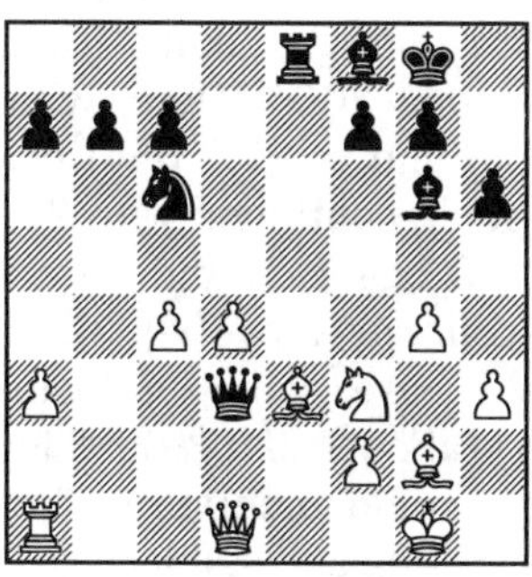

The prospects of both sides are about equal in the ensuing endgame.

E) 17.♘d2

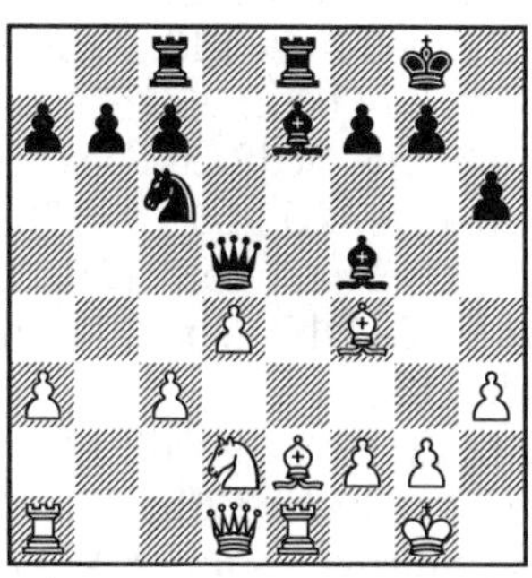

17...♘a5

Black has also tried a few other moves here:

17...♕d7 18.♘c4 ♗d6 19.♗xd6 (19.♕d2 ♗xf4 20.♕xf4 ♖e4 21.♕g3 ♖ce8 22.♘e3 ♖4e7 23.♗b5 a6 24.♗c4 ♘a5 25.♗a2 ♗e6 26.d5 ♗f5= Kasparov – Motylev, Moscow 2004. The idea of avoiding all the possible exchanges with the move 19.♗e3!? deserves attention; after, for example, 19...♘e7 20.♕b3 b6 21.♘xd6 ♕xd6 22.c4 ♗e4 23.f3± White's position is preferable.) 19...cxd6 20.♘e3 ♖a8 21. ♕a4 a6, Karjakin – Gelfand, Pamplona 2004. Here, with the simple move 22.♘xf5 (instead, the game continued with 22.♕b3 ♗e4 23.♗g4 ♕c7 and here after the concrete move 24.f3!? Black would have some problems to worry about) 22...♕xf5 23.♕b3± White would maintain a slight but long-lasting and stable edge.

As usual, if White can avoid the exchange of the bishops, he should do so, thus after 17...♗d6, White has the possibility of 18. ♗e3! (18.♗f3 ♕a5 19.♗xd6 cxd6= Wan Yunguo – Bu Xiangzhi, Beijing 2010, 20.♘c4 ♖xe1+ 21.♕xe1 ♕c7 22.♘e3 ♖e8=) 18...♘a5 19.c4 ♕e6 20.♕a4 b6 21.c5 ♗e7 22.♖ac1 ♗f6 23.♗a6 ♖cd8 24.♘c4 ♘xc4 25.♗xc4 ♕e7 26.♗b5 ♗d7 27.♗xd7 ♕xd7 28.♕xa7 ♖a8 (28...♗xd4 29.c6!±) 29.♕b7 ♖eb8 30.♕e4±

18.♗f3

18.♘f1 ♕b3 19.♕d2 ♘c4 20. ♗xc4 ♕xc4 21.♘e3 ♕b5 22.c4 ♕d7 23.c5, Shirov – Smeets, Wijk aan Zee 2010. Black could have played actively here with 23...♗e4!∓, after which he could have even tried to seize the initiative.

18.♗g4 ♗g5 (It is quite possible that GM Kiril Georgiev chose this move from a purely aesthetic point of view, because the rectangle formed by the bishops is very unusual and beautiful. However, Black could have equalized immediately with the simple move 18... ♗d6=.) 19.♗f3 ♖xe1+ 20.♕xe1 ♕d8 21.♗xg5 ♕xg5 22.♕e5 (22.h4 ♕f6= Akopian – Kir.Georgiev, Vrnjacka Banja 2010) 22...♗g6 23.♕xg5 hxg5 24.♖e1 f6=

18...♕d7

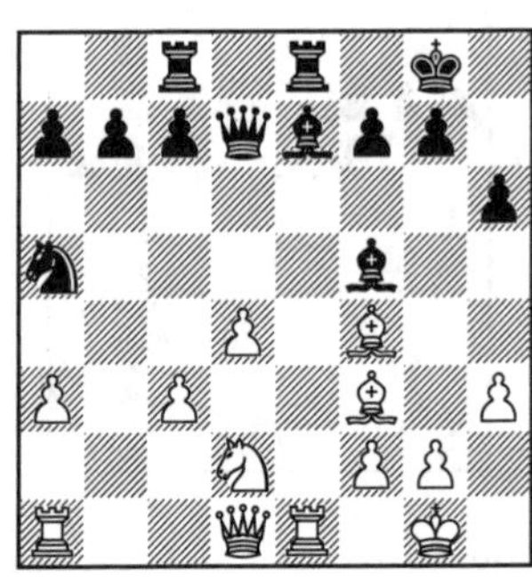

19.♘b3

After 19.♘e4, Black has several possibilities.

19...♗f8?! 20.♖a2! b6 (it is possibly preferable for him to choose 20...♘c4±). Now it is rather dubious for White to continue with 21.g4?! ♗g6 22.a4 f5 23.♘g3 fxg4 24.♗xg4 ♖xe1+ 25.♕xe1 ♖e8∓ Shirov – Gashimov, Sestao 2010. The correct reaction is 21.♖ae2! and having set up a battery on the e-file, White seizes the initiative.

Black has a good alternative in 19...♗e6!?=, taking control over the light squares in the centre and preventing the transfer of White's rook to e2 via the a2-square.

It is also good for Black to play 19...♖cd8, exerting powerful pressure against the central squares with the plan of advancing later with c7-c5. The game Akopian – Kasimdzhanov, Nalchuk 2009, continued 20.♘g3 ♗g6 21.♗h5 ♗d6 22.♗xd6 ♖xe1+ 23.♕xe1 cxd6 24.♗xg6 fxg6∓ and Black had no problems, in fact his position was even preferable. After 20.♖a2 instead, Black has the response 20... ♗e6 21.♖ae2 ♘c4. The logical continuation of the game might be 22.♘d2 (What else? White must try to clear the e-file.) 22...♘b6! 23.♕c2 (after 23.♗xb7, Black equalizes with 23...c5!) 23...♗f5 24.♕b3 c5=

19...♘xb3 20.♕xb3 b6 21.g4

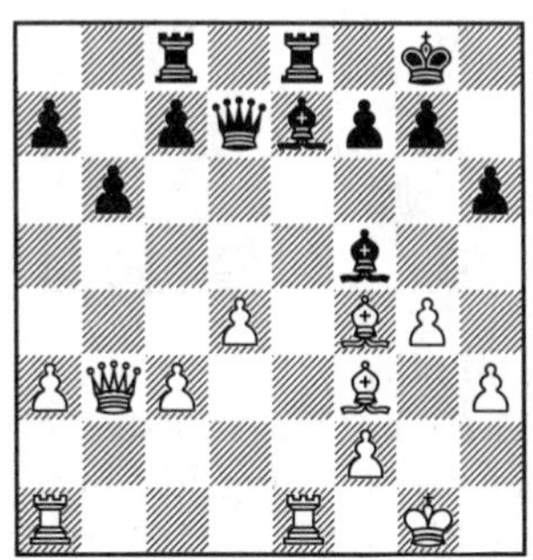

21...♗d3!N

It is less precise to play 21... ♗g6 22.♗b7 ♖b8 23.♕d5 ♕xd5 24. ♗xd5 ♗d6 25.♗xd6 cxd6±, because with the help of the manoeuvre ♗d5-c6 and d4-d5, White will gain control of the e-file and obtain a slight edge, although Black should be able to draw with accurate defence, Shirov – So, Khanty-Mansyisk 2010.

22.♖e3

22.♗b7 ♖b8 23.♕d5 ♗b5 24.a4 (24.c4 ♗a4 25.♕xd7 ♗xd7=) 24... ♖xb7! 25.♕xb5 c6=

22...c5 23.♕d5

23.♖ae1 c4!∓

23...♕b5! 24.♕b7

24.♖ae1 ♗f8=

24...♗h4!

25.♖d1

But not 25.♗d5, in view of 25... ♔h7! Black indirectly protects his f7-pawn in spectacular fashion: 26.♗e5 ♗xf2+! 27.♔xf2 ♕b2+ 28. ♔g3 ♕xa1 29.♖xd3 ♕e1+ 30.♔f4 cxd4 31.♗e4+ ♔h8 32.♗xd4 ♖c7 33.♕d5 ♖ce7–+ – Black's attack is decisive.

25...♕b2 26.♖exd3 ♕xf2+ 27.♔h1 ♖e1+ 28.♖xe1 ♕xe1+ 29.♔h2 ♕f2+ 30.♔h1 ♕f1= Black draws by perpetual check.

F) 17.♕c1

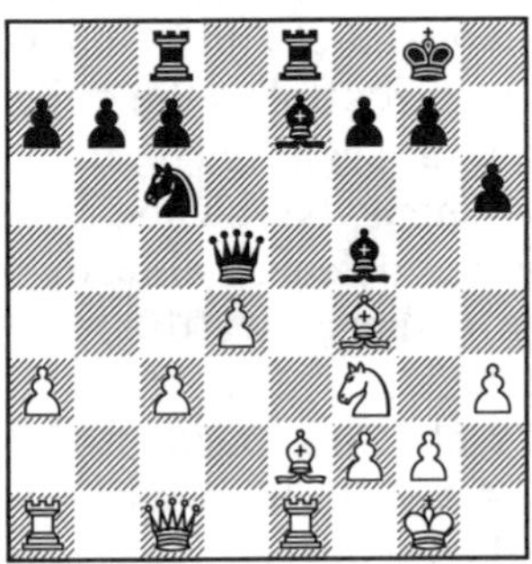

17...♕d7

It is also quite reliable for Black to continue with 17...♗f6 18.♕b2 ♘a5 19.♗e5 (19.♘e5 ♕b3=; or 19.♖ad1 ♕b3 20.♕xb3 ♘xb3 21.♗c4 ♘a5 22.♗a2, Al-Modiahki – Wang Yue, Ha Long City 2009. Here, his most solid move would be 22...b6!=) 19...♗xe5 20.♘xe5 c5 21.♗f3 ♕d6 22.♖ad1 b6 23.♕a2 ♗e6 24.d5 ♗xh3 25.♘xf7 ♖xe1+ 26.♖xe1 ♔xf7 27.gxh3 ♖e8 28.♖xe8 (if 28.♗e4, with the idea of preserving the rooks in order to organize an attack, then 28...♖e7! 29.♖e3 ♔e8!=, removing the king to a safer area) 28...♔xe8 29.♕e2+ ♔d8 30.♕a6 ♕g6+ 31.♗g2 ♕b1+ 32.♔h2 ♕f5 33.♕xa7 ♕f4+ 34.♔g1 ♕c1+ 35.♔h2 ♕f4=, draw, Ponomariov – Gelfand, Khanty-Mansyisk 2009.

18.♕b2 ♗d6 19.♗xd6

After 19.♗e3, Black has at his disposal a tactical shot: 19...♗xh3! 20.gxh3 ♕xh3 21.♕xb7 ♕g4+ 22.♔f1 ♕h3=, ending the game with a perpetual check.

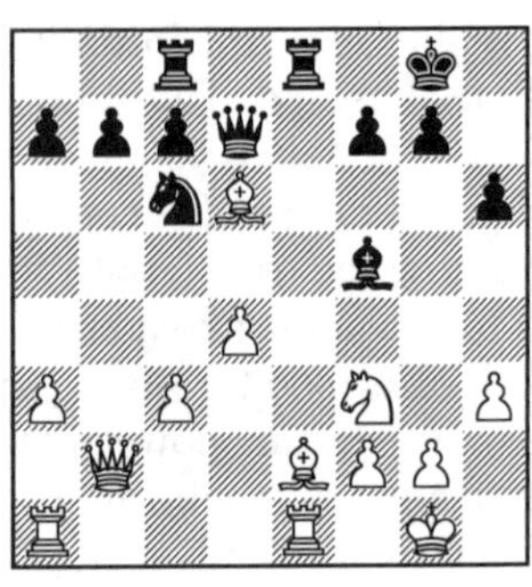

19...cxd6

I believe it is less precise for him to choose 19...♕xd6 20.♗c4 (if 20.♘d2 b6 21.♗b5 ♖xe1+ 22.♖xe1 ♘a5=, Black advances with c7-c5 and solve all his problems; or 20.♕xb7 ♖xe2 21.♖xe2 ♖b8 22.♕xb8+ ♘xb8 23.♖e8+ ♔h7 24.♖xb8 ♕c6 25.♖e1 ♕xc3 26.♖e3 ♕c1+ 27.♔h2 ♕c2 28.♔g3 ♗e6= when White's pieces are not sufficiently coordinated and so Black equalizes easily) 20...b6

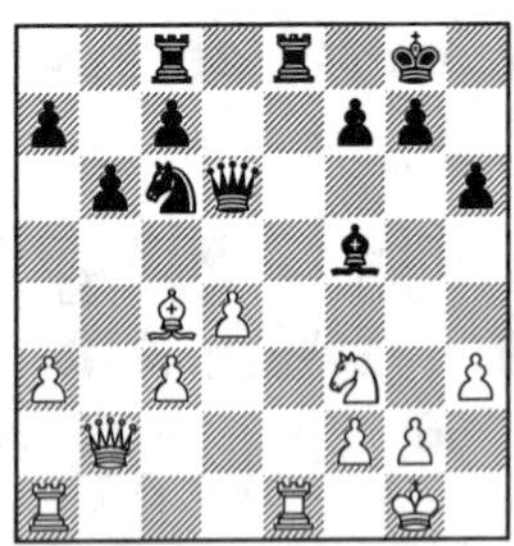

and now:

21.♕b5. This transfer of the queen to the kingside need not worry Black. 21...♗d7 22.♕h5 ♕f4 (it would be even simpler for Black to respond with 22...♖xe1+! 23.♖xe1 ♖f8=) 23.♗b5 ♖cd8 24.a4 and the most direct road to equality for Black now is to quickly simplify the position on the e-file with 24...♖xe1. (it is less precise to play 24...♔f8 25.g3 ♕f6, Akopian – Gelfand, Astrakhan 2010, 26.♔g2 ♖xe1 27.♖xe1 ♖e8 28.♖xe8+ ♗xe8 29.♕d5±). 25.♖xe1 g6 26.♕d5 (26.♕h4 ♕xh4 27.♘xh4 ♔f8=) 26...♗e6!=. Now White cannot play 27.♕xc6? owing to 27...♗d5 28.♖e8+ ♔g7 29.♖xd8 ♗xc6 30.♗xc6 ♕f6 31.♖d7 ♕xc6 32.♖xf7+ ♔g8–+ and Black wins;

it is reasonable for White to continue with 21.♕a2 ♕f6 22.♗b5 ♗d7 23.a4± and his position is a little better.

20.♘h4 ♗e6 21.♖ad1 d5 22.♗d3

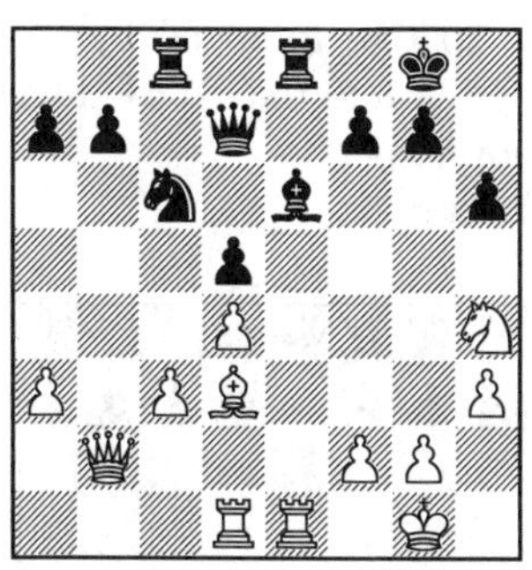

22...♕c7!N

This is the most concrete plan for Black. He wants to exchange all the rooks, considerably reducing the attacking potential of his opponent's pieces.

In the game Akopian – Wang Yue, Astrakhan 2010, Black chose another line: 22...b6 23.♗b1 (it is better for White to play here 23.♖e3±, preparing to double his rooks along the e-file) 23...♕d8 24.♘f3 ♕f6= Black's light-squared bishop has acquired freedom of movement and the game is equal.

23.♖e3 ♗d7 24.♖de1 ♖xe3 25.♖xe3 ♖e8 26.♖xe8+ ♗xe8=

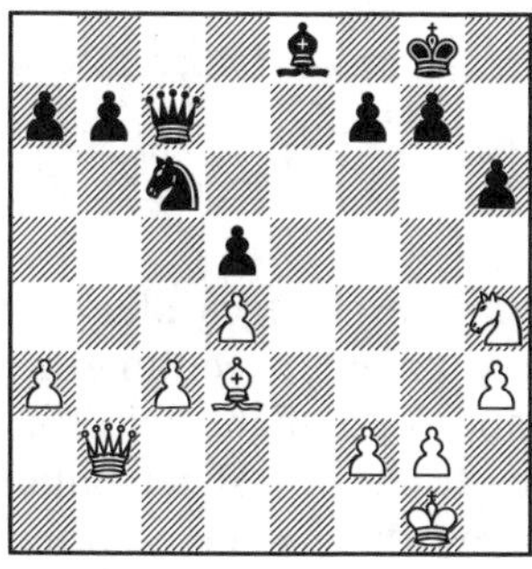

Black's bishop is not very good, but White has a backward c3-pawn, so these two defects balance each other out.

Conclusion

You should be convinced by now that 16...h6 is Black's calmest and most reliable move. If, during a tense competitive game, a player with Black fails to remember some of the variations provided in this chapter, he still has excellent chances of finding the right path over the board by himself. It is essential, not so much to memorize the long forcing lines, but to understand the main ideas of the variation. These have all been explained quite thoroughly in the conclusion of Chapter 25, which is very similar to this chapter, with respect to both the lines and the ideas.

Chapter 28 1.e4 e5 2.♘f3 ♘f6 3.♘xe5 d6 4.♘f3 ♘xe4 5.♘c3

White exchanges Black's centralized knight, accepting the appearance of a slight defect in his pawn-structure. Meanwhile, he prepares queenside castling. In the last few years this line has become tremendously popular, which is not surprising, because Black often faces difficulties.

5...♘xc3

If Black retreats his knight with 5...♘f6, White obtains an advantage thanks to his extra tempo for development.

6.dxc3

After 6.bxc3, White's pawn-structure is seriously weakened and he has no chance of gaining an advantage. Black can obtain a very good position is several ways:

6...d5 7.d4 ♗d6! Black has already played d6-d5, so it is appropriate to develop his bishop to an active position. 8.♗d3 0–0 9.0–0 h6=;

6...♗e7 7.d4 0–0 8.♗d3 d5 9. 0–0 c5 10.dxc5 (otherwise Black will deploy his knight on c6, while after 10.♘e5, Black has the strong reply 10...c4, followed by f7-f6∓) 10...♘d7 11.c6 dxc6 12.♘d4 ♗d6! 13.♘f5 ♗e5=

6...♗e7

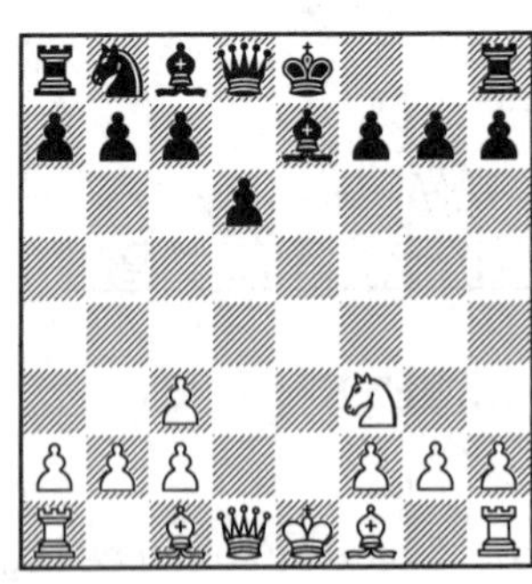

7.♗f4

White's other possibility here is 7.♗e3, with the same idea of preparing queenside castling; we shall analyze this in the next chapter, in a somewhat different version.

If White castles kingside here, Black has no problems at all. After 7.♗d3 0–0 8.0–0 ♘c6 (it is also good for him to opt for 8...♘d7 with the idea of 9...♘c5) 9.♖e1 ♗e6= followed by ♕d7, the position is equal.

The transfer of White's queen to f4 is not dangerous for Black, since after 7.♕d4 0–0 8.♗e3 ♘c6 9.♕f4, he has a safe route to equality: 9...♕d7 10.h3 (preventing 10...♕g4) 10...♕f5 11.♕a4 ♕a5=, entering an equal endgame, D.Schneider – Ilincic, Torokbalint 2004.

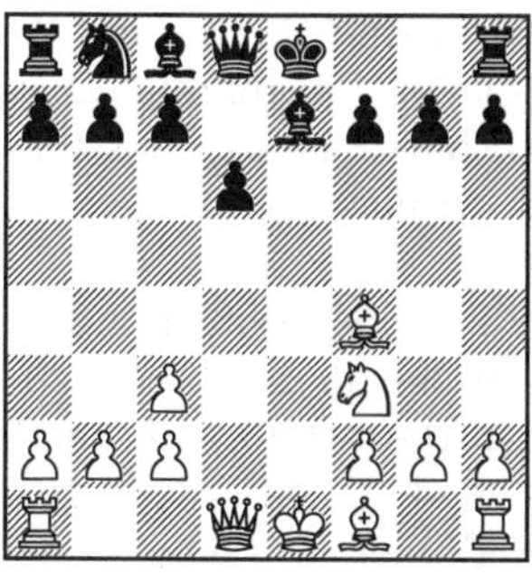

After **7.♗f4**, one possibility for Black is **A) 7...♘c6**. He prepares to castle on the same side as White, to prevent his opponent from organizing an attack. This scheme of development is very safe, but somewhat passive, and it leaves Black with almost no chance of seizing the initiative. Black's other possible development scheme is based on the double-edged move **B) 7...0–0** and in that case there arises a very complicated position, which sometimes becomes very sharp, with opposite-sides castling.

A) 7...♘c6

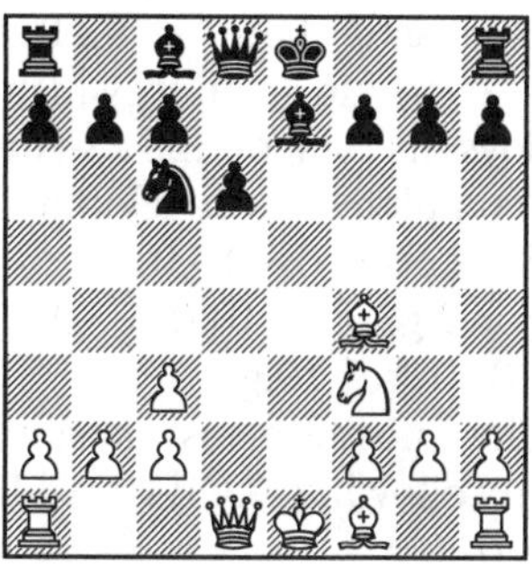

8.♕d2

If 8.♗b5, Black's simplest way to equalize is with 8...0–0 (The position remains very unclear after 8...a6 9.♗xc6+ bxc6 10.♕d3 0–0 11.0–0–0∞ Jobava – Motylev, Poikovsky 2010. White's plan is quite standard; he wants to push h2-h4 and use the g5-square as a springboard for his minor pieces.) 9.♕d3 ♕d7 10.0–0–0 ♕f5 11.♕xf5 ♗xf5 12.♖he1 ♗f6 13.♘d4 ♘xd4 14.cxd4 a6 15.♗a4 g5 16.♗g3 h5 17.f3 h4 18.♗f2 d5=, draw, Kuzubov – Andreikin, Lubbock 2009.

Black should not be afraid of the move 8.♗d3 – the white bishop will come under attack from Black's minor pieces, since he will prepare the development of his bishop to f5, or his knight to the e5-square. This will tend to lead to exchanges, which should suit Black, since his position is a bit cramped. 8...♗e6 9.♕e2 (White cannot achieve much with 9.♕d2 ♕d7 10.0–0–0 0–0–0=). It will be very good for Black to develop his rook to the e-file in order to attack the enemy queen, so he can boldly castle here – 9...0–0!N 10.0–0–0 ♗f6=, after which he deploys his rook on the e8-square and completes his development.

8...♗e6 9.0–0–0

For 9.g3 ♕d7 10.0–0–0 – see 9.0–0–0 ♕d7 10.g3.

The position is absolutely equal following 9.♘d4 ♘xd4 10. cxd4 0–0=

If 9.♘g5, besides the transposition to the main line with 9... ♗xg5 10.♗xg5 ♕d7 11.0–0–0 f6 12.♗e3 0–0–0, Black has the interesting move 9...♗f5!?, preserving both bishops.

9...♕d7

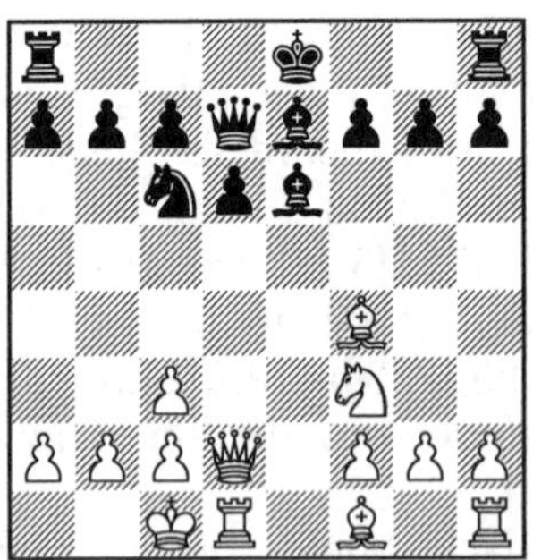

The position of White's bishop on f4, rather than e3 (the same position, with a bishop on e3, arises after 7.♗e3 ♘c6 8.♕d2 ♗e6), has some nuances that are worth mentioning. Here White does not have one of the ideas of ♗e3, which is to play ♘f3-d4 and after the trade of the knights his dark-squared bishop attacks the enemy queenside. Neither can he achieve anything much with the move h2-h4, preparing a knight-sortie to the g5-square. On the other hand, White has the possibility of exchanging his knight for his opponent's dark-squared bishop, which Black can avoid when White's bishop is on e3.

10.♘g5

The position would be very similar to the main line after 10.♗e2 0–0–0 11.♘g5 ♗g5 12. ♗xg5 f6=

If 10.g3, a complicated struggle arises after 10...0–0∞ J.Polgar – Ghaem Maghami, Dresden 2008, but it is also possible for Black to play 10...0–0–0 11.♗g2 ♔b8=

White does not obtain much with 10.h4 h6 11.♗b5 (11.g3 ♗f6 12.♗g2 0–0–0 13.♔b1 ♖he8 14. ♖he1 ♗g4 15.♕d5 ♖xe1 16.♖xe1 ♖e8= Efimenko – Zhou Jinchao, Al Ain 2008) 11...a6 12.♗a4 b5 13.♗b3 ♗xb3 14.axb3 ♕f5 15.♖he1 0–0= Volokitin – Erenburg, Sochi 2006.

10.♔b1 0–0–0

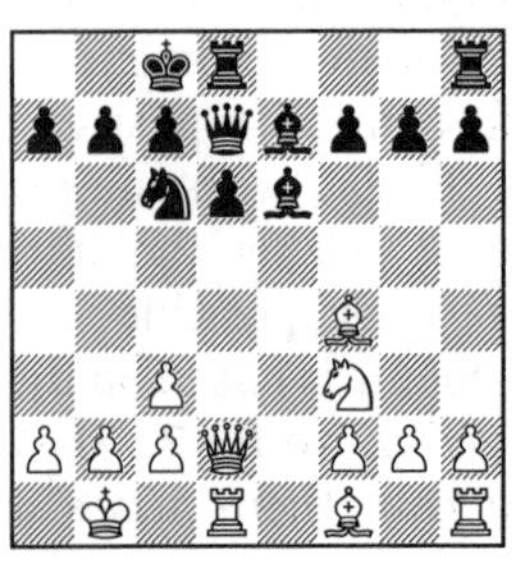

11.♘g5 ♗xg5 12.♗xg5 f6 13.♗e3 – see 10.♘g5 ♗xg5 11.♗xg5 f6 12.♗e3 0–0–0 13.♔b1.

The position is equal after 11.♘d4 ♘xd4 and here, following 12.cxd4, it is good for Black to play 12...♗f6 13.d5 ♗f5, preparing to free the e-file, while he can counter 12.♕xd4 with the move 12...c5= equalizing, since after 13.♕xg7 ♖dg8 14.♕h6 Black has not only the line: 14...♖g6 15.♕h5 ♗g4 16.♕d5 ♗xd1 17.♕xd1∞ but also the possibility of 14...♗g4 15.♗d3 ♗f8 16.♕f6 ♗e7 17.♕xf7 ♖f8 18.♕g7 ♖dg8 19.♕h6 ♗f8= with an unavoidable repetition of moves.

11.♗b5 a6 12.♗a4 ♗f6 13.♗g5 (13.♖he1 h6 14.♘d4 ♗d5 15.f3 ♖he8 16.♘e2 ♗c4= Karjakin – Ivanchuk, Sochi 2008) 13...♗xg5 14.♕xg5 b5 15.♗b3 f6 16.♗xe6 ♕xe6 17.♕f4 h5 18.h3 g5 19.♘d4 ♕d5 20.♘xc6 ♕xd1+ 21.♖xd1 gxf4 22.♘xd8 ♔xd8 23.♔c1 ♖g8 24.♖g1 f3 25.g3 ♖e8 26.♖d1 ♖e2 27.♖d2 ♖e1+ 28.♖d1 ♖e2=, draw, Ivanchuk – Kramnik, Moscow 2008.

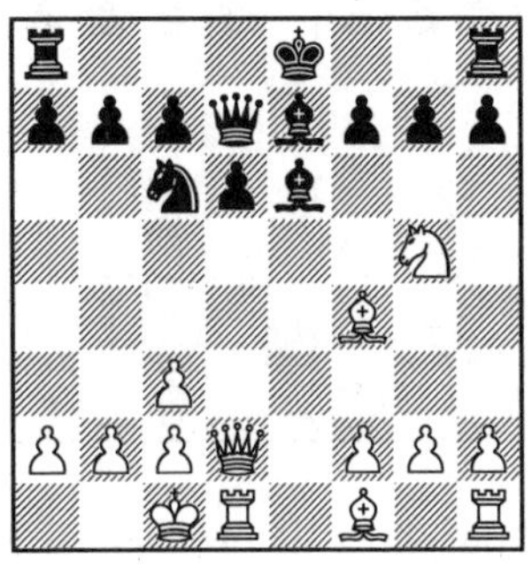

10...♗xg5

It would be interesting, although a bit risky, for Black to try the move 10...♗f5!? 11.♗c4 (White achieves nothing with 11.h3 h6 12.♘f3 0–0–0=) 11...h6 12.♘f3 0–0∞ and the position is double-edged.

11.♗xg5 f6 12.♗e3 0–0–0

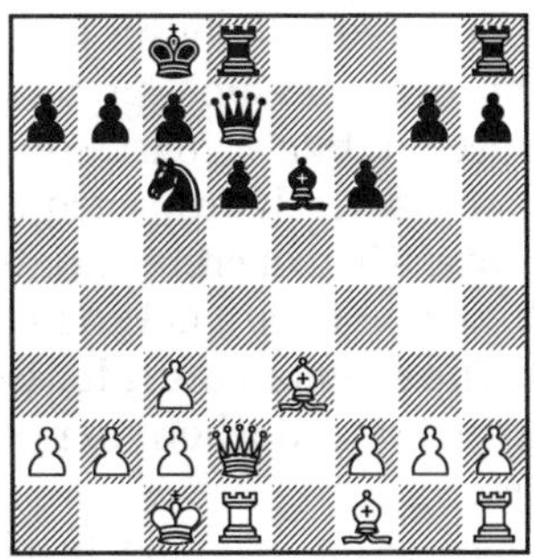

A similar, but less advantageous for Black, position arises after 7.♗e3 ♘c6 8.♕d2 ♗e6 9.0–0–0 ♕d7 10.♔b1 a6 11.♘g5 ♗xg5 12.♗xg5 f6 13.♗e3 0–0–0

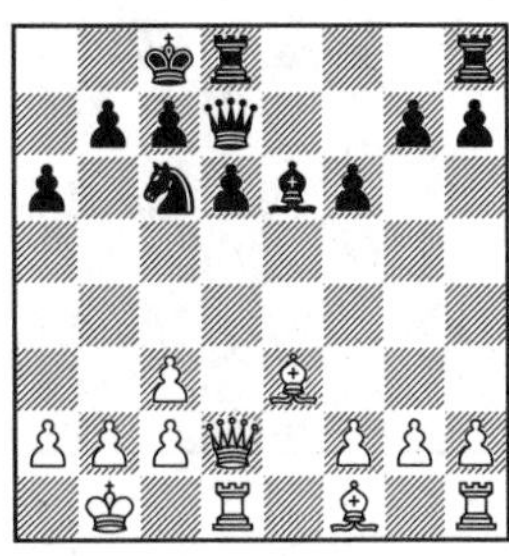

The difference is that White's king is on c1 rather than b1, which is not very important, and Black's pawn is on a7 rather than a6, which is definitely preferable for him. With the black pawn on a6 White has the possibility of advancing with a2-a4, followed by a march of the b-pawn to b5, while with the pawn on a7 this idea would not work.

Black's plan is now very simple. He should not touch the pawn-chain c7-d6-f6-g7 but should strive to exchange pieces. If he manages to exchange the light-squared bishops his position might even become preferable, because White's dark-squared bishop is severely restricted in its mobility. The concrete variations in this situation are not so important. The essential thing for Black is to understand where to put his pieces.

Here is an example to show how the struggle might develop:

13.b3 ♔b8 14.♗e2 ♖he8 15. ♖he1 ♗g4

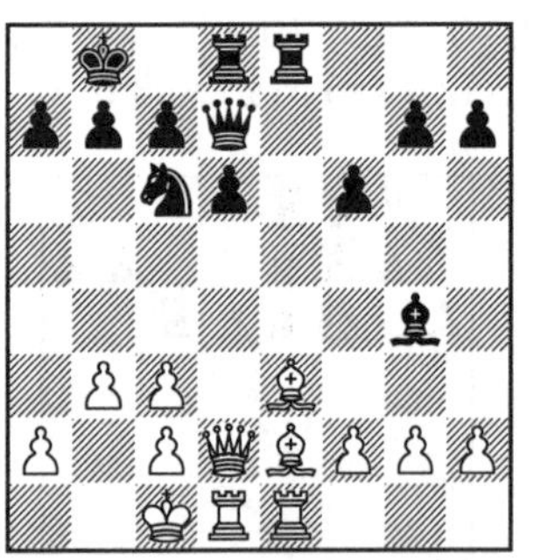

Black provokes the advance of the enemy pawn, since the weakening might prove helpful. **16.f3 ♗h5 17.♗f2 ♗f7 18.♔b2 ♖e7 19.♗f1 ♖xe1 20.♖xe1 ♖e8 21. ♖d1 ♗g6 22.a4 ♕f5 23. ♗g3 ♕e6 24.♗c4 ♕e3 25.♕xe3 ♖xe3 26.♗f2 ♖e7**= Black drew without any problems in the game Rasmussen – Fridman, Novi Sad 2009.

B) 7...0–0

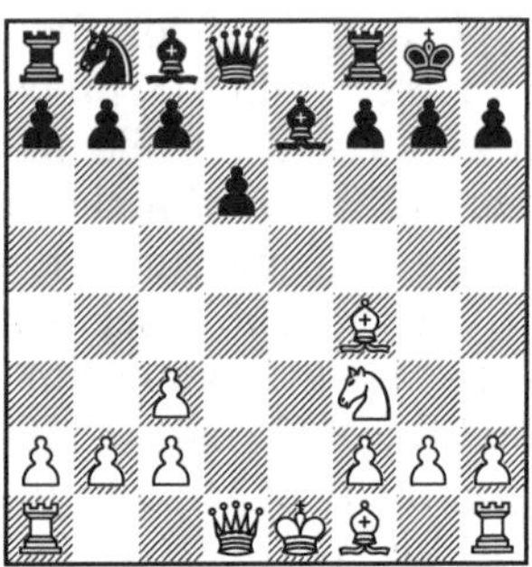

With the white bishop on f4, kingside castling is a good choice for Black.

8.♕d2

It is weaker for White to play 8.♗d3, owing to 8...♘d7 followed by ♘d7-c5 – White's bishop on d3 will come under the threat of being exchanged.

8...♘d7 9.0–0–0 ♘c5

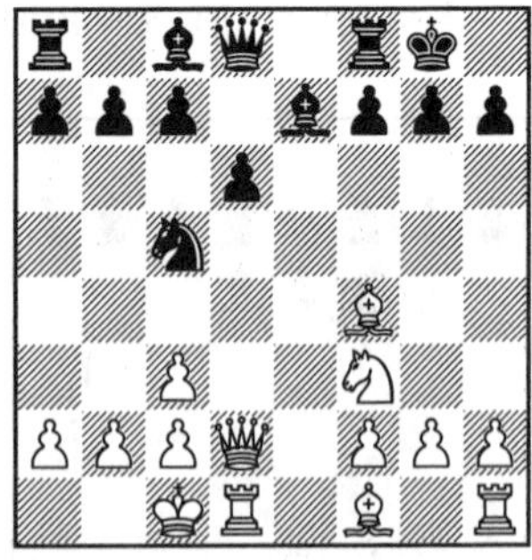

The plans of both sides have become clear. White has good prospects on the kingside, while Black has chances both on the queenside and in the centre, exploiting the e-file.

White must regroup his forces in order to begin an effective kingside attack. He must eventually play f2-f3 in order to cover the e4-square against possible invasion by Black's knight, and to do that he must first move his own knight from f3. White's bishop on f4 is not helpful in the development of his initiative either; it is restricted by Black's pawns at the moment.

Now we shall analyze all White's reasonable options here: **B1) 10.♗c4**, **B2) 10.♘d4**, **B3) 10.h4** and **B4) 10.♗e3**.

It would obviously be a bad idea for him to try 10.h3?! ♖e8 11.g4, since after 11...♘e4 12.♕e1 ♗f6∓ Black seized the initiative in the game Tseshkovsky – I.Zaitsev, USSR 1975.

The move 10.♔b1 looks rather indifferent and Black should respond with 10...♖e8. The inclusion of these moves is advantageous for Black, because White's king is only slightly better on b1 than on c1, while Black's rook is very useful on e8, where it is very active and stands ready to support the knight if it goes to e4.

B1) 10.♗c4

(diagram)

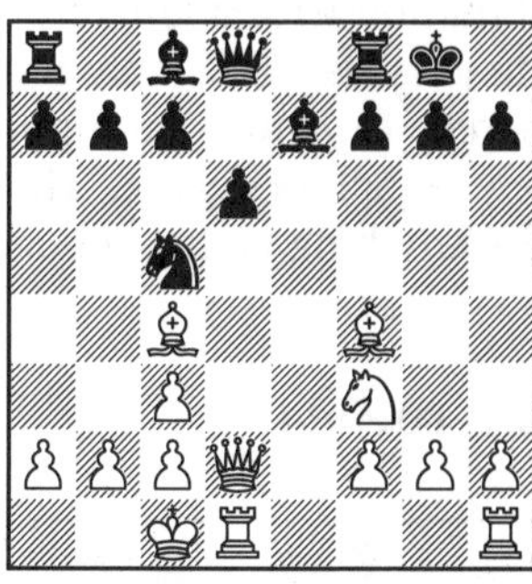

With this move White just provokes an exchange which is in Black's favour, since his position is a bit cramped.

10...♗e6 11.♗xe6 ♘xe6

It is rather dubious to play 11...fxe6?! 12.♗e3 and Black will have to play d6-d5 at some point, after which his e6-pawn will become backward.

12.♗e3 ♕d7

It might be interesting for him to opt for 12...c6!? 13.h4 d5 14.♘g5 h6 15.♘xe6 fxe6 16.h5 e5=. White's rook can penetrate into the enemy camp along the route h1-h3-g3-g6, but Black's centre is very powerful, so the position offers chances to both sides.

13.h4 ♕b5! Val.Popov – Khenkin, Sochi 2005.

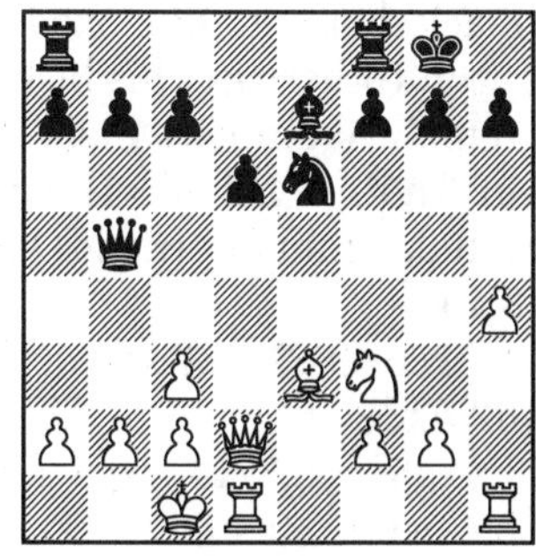

Black deprives the enemy queen of the all-important d3-square, from where it can create threats against Black's king in combination with a knight on g5. White can play ♕d3 only if he is prepared to enter an approximately equal endgame. He has hardly anything better, though...

B2) 10.♘d4

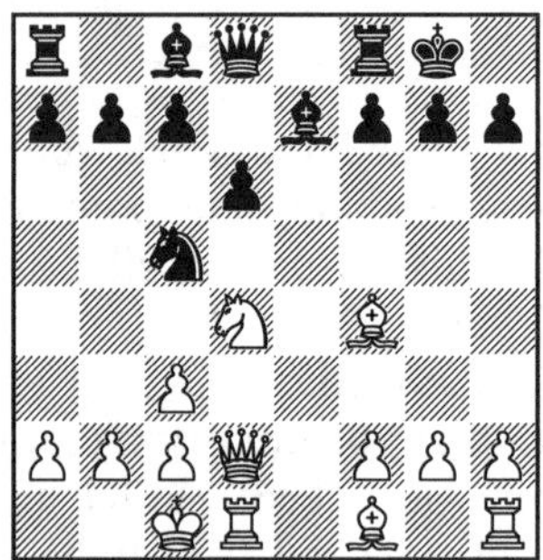

White is preparing f2-f3, to deprive Black's knight of the e4-square and to prepare the advance of his g-pawn.

10...♖e8 11.f3 ♘e6 12.♗e3 ♗g5

The other reliable possibility for Black here is 12...♘xd4 13. cxd4 ♗f5! (otherwise, his bishops will remain cramped) 14.g4 ♗g6 15.♔b1 ♗h4! 16.♗f2 h6= Huebner – Kramnik, Frankfurt (rapid) 1996.

13.f4

13.♘xe6 ♗xe3 14.♘xd8 ♗xd2+ 15.♔d2 ♖xd8=

13.♗xg5 ♕xg5 14.♕xg5 ♘xg5 15.♘b5 ♘e6 16.♗c4 ♗d7= Yemelin – Kochyev, St.Petersburg 1997.

(diagram)

13...♘xd4!

13...♗f6 14.♘f3±

14.fxg5 ♘c6 15.h4 ♗g4 16.

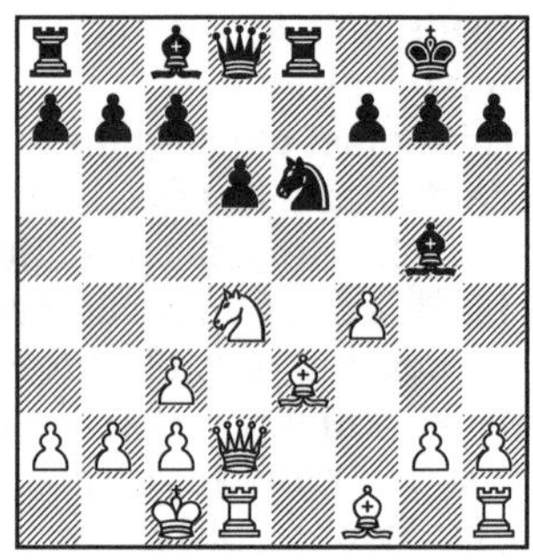

♖e1 ♕d7= Adams – Kramnik, Wijk aan Zee 2008.

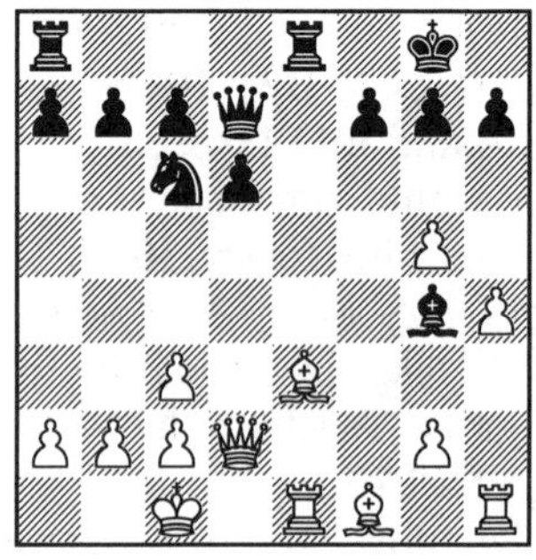

Black plans to follow up with ♖e8-e5, preparing to double his rooks on the e-file. He also has active possibilities on the light squares and all this provides him with good chances of equalizing.

B3) 10.h4

With this move White secures the g5-square as a springboard for his knight and sometimes even a black pawn on h6 does not preclude this manoeuvre. It would be very dangerous for Black to capture the knight, since White's mating attack along the h-file could prove fatal.

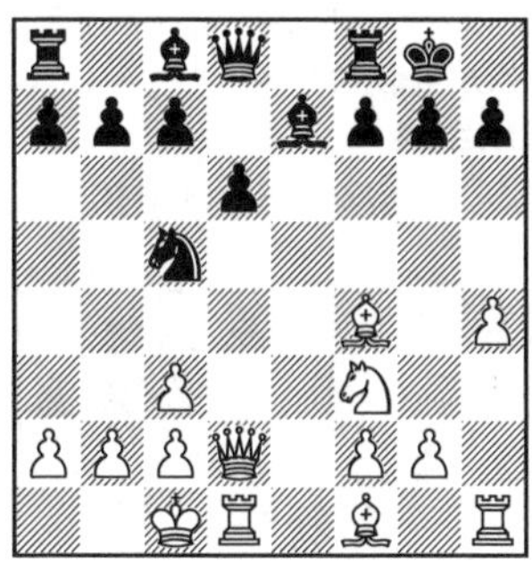

10...c6

This is the safest road to equality for Black. He prepares d6-d5 in order to acquire some space and he also opens the way to the a5-square for his queen.

Black's other popular options here: 10...♖e8, 10...♗f6 and 10...♗g4 all lead to a complicated struggle, but with more possibilities for White to seize the initiative.

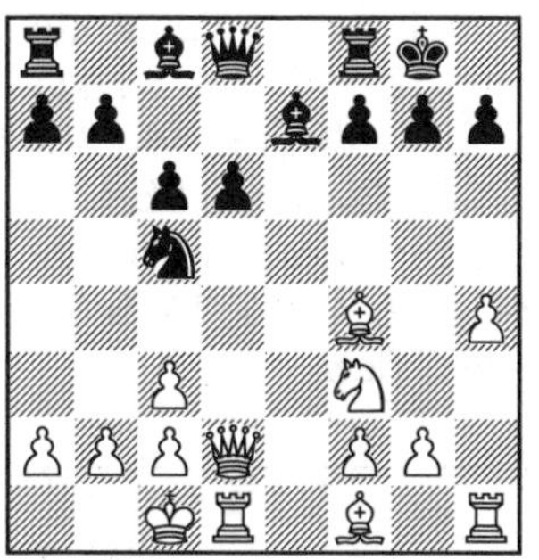

11.♗xd6

After 11.h5, it is good for Black to play 11...h6=, or 11...d5 12.h6 g6= Andrews – Haessel, Chikago 2007.

White cannot achieve much with 11.♗g5, in view of 11...d5 12.♗xe7 ♕xe7 13.♘d4 ♘e4 14.♕e1 ♕f6 15.f3 ♘d6= Rozentalis – Arencibia, Elista 1998.

11...♗xd6 12.♕xd6 ♕xd6 13.♖xd6 ♘e4 14.♖d4 ♘xf2 15.♖g1 ♘g4

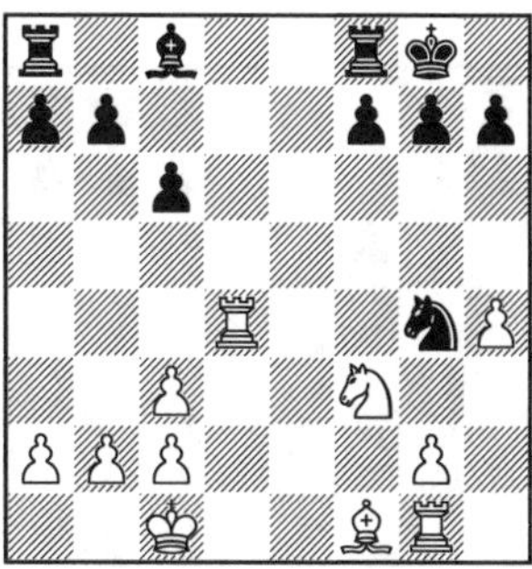

This endgame looks simple, but in fact it is quite insidious and Black must find several accurate moves in order to equalize. If he plays imprecisely, the vulnerability of his queenside pawns is bound to tell.

16.♗c4

Black need not fear the line: 16.♗d3 ♖e8 17.♔d2 ♘f6= Almasi – Gashimov, Lugo 2007.

If White seizes additional space on the queenside with 16.a4, Black should reply, not with 16...♗e6, which would enable White to improve his pawn-structure with 17.♘g5 ♗f5 18.♗d3 ♗xd3 19.cxd3 ♘f6 20.♖e1 ♖fe8 21.♖xe8+ ♖xe8 22.♔d2 ♔f8 23.b4± and Black will have to work hard to make a draw, Efimenko – Khalifman, Sochi 2006, but with 16...♖e8 17.♗d3 h6 18.a5 ♗e6 19.♖e1 ♘f6= Topalov – Gelfand, Monaco (rapid) 2006.

16...♗f5 17.♗d3 ♗xd3 18. cxd3 ♘f6 19.♔d2

19.♖e1 ♖fe8 20.♖xe8+ ♖xe8 21.♔d2 ♔f8 22.a4, Topalov – Gelfand, Wijk aan Zee 2006. Here Black could have equalized convincingly with 22...c5 23.♖f4 b6=

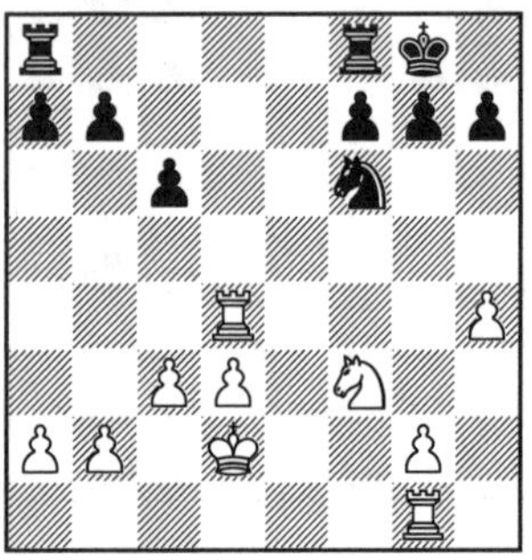

19...♖fe8!N

It is too passive to play 19...♖fd8 20.a4 ♘e8 21.♖e1 ♖xd4 22.♘xd4 ♔f8 23.a5 ♘c7 24.b4± Cheparinov – Dominguez, Cuernavaca 2006.

20.g4 c5 21.♖c4

The move 21.♖d6? loses the exchange without compensation: 21...♔f8 22.g5 ♔e7 23.gxf6+ ♔xd6 24.fxg7 ♖g8 25.♘g5 ♔e7 26.♘xh7 ♖ac8! (Black's rook is ready to join in the action along the 6th rank) 27.♖e1+ ♔d8 28.♖g1 ♖c6 29.♘g5 ♔e7 30.♘e4 ♖g6 31.♖e1 ♖g2+ 32.♔c1 ♔d8 33.♘xc5 b6 34.♘e4 ♖8xg7 35.♘g5 ♖h2∓ and Black has excellent winning chances.

21.♖a4 ♘d5 22.♖e1 ♖xe1 23.♘xe1 f6=

21...b6 22.g5 ♘d5

It is also safe to defend with 22...♘d7!? 23.♖e4 ♖xe4 24.dxe4 ♔f8 25.♔e3 ♔e7=

23.♖e4

23.♖e1 ♖xe1 24.♘xe1 f6=

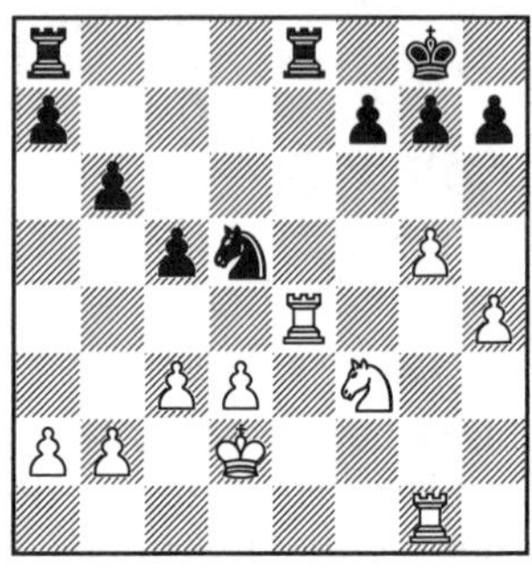

23...f5!

It is less convincing for Black to continue with 23...♖xe4 24.dxe4 ♘e7 25.♔e3 ♖d8 26.b4! c4!?. This pawn is now separated from the rest of his forces, but this is the only way for Black to prevent the opening of files, which White's rook might use to penetrate into his camp. 27.♘d4 ♖e8 28.♔f3 ♘g6 29.h5 ♘e5+ 30.♔e3 ♖d8 31.a4 g6 32.h6 ♔f8 33.a5± and Black still has some difficulties to worry about.

24.gxf6 ♘xf6 25.♖e5 ♖xe5 26.♘xe5 ♖e8=

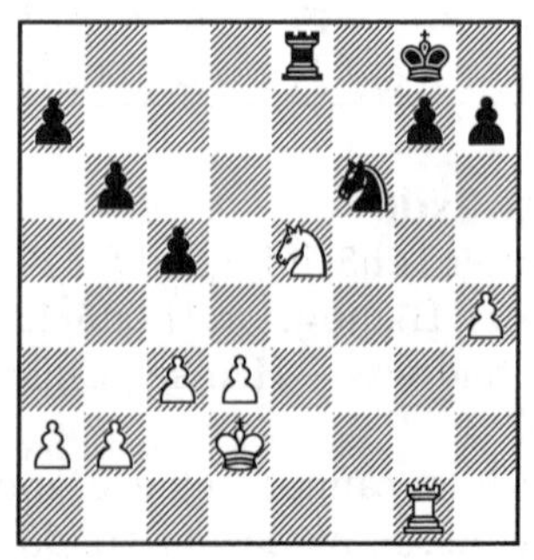

White has been unable to attack his opponent's vulnerable queenside pawns, while Black has the possibility of creating his own passed pawn on the kingside in the future.

B4) 10.♗e3

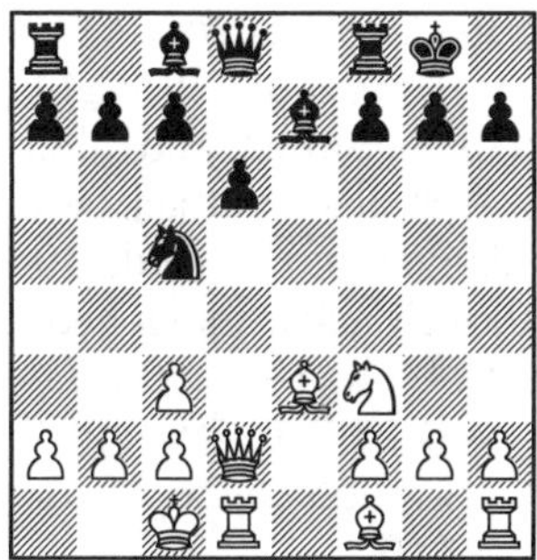

10...c6!

It seems very reasonable for Black to fortify his knight on c5 with the move 10...b6, but after 11.♘d4 ♗b7 12.f3 ♗f6 13.♔b1 a6 14.h4 ♖e8 15.♕f2→ White is ready to seize the initiative on the kingside and the advance of his g-pawn might be particularly dangerous for Black.

Here Black's most popular line is: 10...♖e8 11.♗c4 ♗e6 12.♗xe6 ♘xe6 13.h4 ♕d7 14.♕d5 ♕c6 15.♕f5 ♕c4 16.♔b1 (strangely enough, the following variation has been tested only once at top level: 16.♘g5 ♗xg5 17.hxg5 ♘f8 18.♔b1± and White's position is slightly better, Karjakin – Kramnik, Wijk aan Zee 2007.) 16...g6 17.♕h3 h5 18.♘d2 ♕e2 19.♖de1 ♕g4 20.♕h2 d5 21.f3 ♕a4 22.g4 ♗d6 23.♕f2↑. The theory of this line goes even further, but I think that from Black's point of view we should stop the analysis here. His defence is difficult and he must find some "only moves" in order to survive, Szabo – Huzman, Budva 2009.

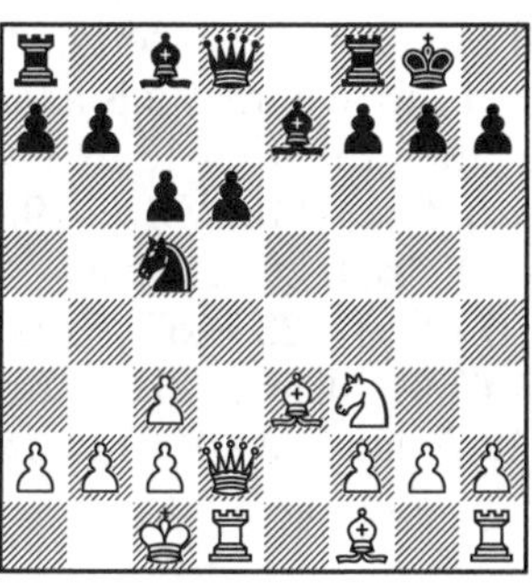

11.♗xc5

This is the only way for White to justify the retreat of his bishop on the previous move.

Black wins a tempo for active operations after 11.♔b1 and following 11...♖e8 (it is also good for him to play the immediate 11...♘e4) 12.♘d4 ♘e4 13.♕c1 d5 14.f3 ♘d6∓ his position is preferable, Val.Popov – Frolyanov, Sochi 2006.

It is more or less the same after 11.♘d4 ♘e4 12.♕e1 ♖e8 13.f3 ♘f6∓ Sebag – Koneru, Ekaterinburg 2006.

If 11.h4, it is very good for Black to continue with 11...♕a5 12.♔b1 ♗e6 13.a3 ♘e4 14.♕e1 ♗f6= and his prospects are not at all worse, Deepan – Koneru, Visakhapatnam 2006.

After 11.c4, Black's best line would be 11...♘e4! 12.♕d3 ♗f5 13.g4 ♗g6 14.♕b3 ♕c8! and if 15.♖g1 then 15...f5!↑ and he seizes the initiative.

11...dxc5 12.♕f4 ♕a5 13.♗d3 ♗e6 14.a3 ♖ad8

It is less precise for Black to opt for 14...♗f6, in view of 15.♘g5! (for 15.♖he1 ♖ad8 – see 14...♖ad8 15.♖he1 ♗f6, whereas it is a forced draw after 15.h4 c4 16.♗e4 ♗xc3 17.bxc3 ♕xa3+ 18.♔b1 f5 19.♘g5 fxe4 20.♕xe4 ♗f5 21.♕xc4+ ♔h8 22.♘f7+ ♖xf7 23.♕xf7 ♕xc3 24.♕xf5 ♕b4+, draw, Leko – Kramnik, Wijk aan Zee 2008) 15...♗xg5 16.♕xg5 ♖ad8 17.♖he1±

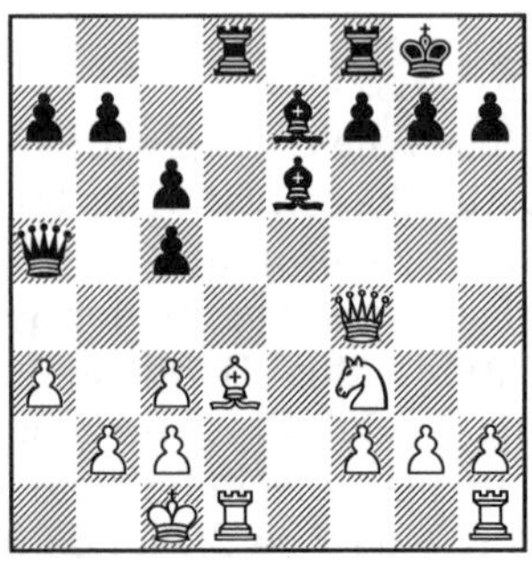

15.♖he1

15.h4 c4 16.♗xc4 ♕a4 17.♕c7 ♕xc4 18.♕xe7 ♖de8 19.♕b4 ♕a2 20.♘d4 ♖c8 21.♘xe6 fxe6 22.♕b3 ♕xb3 23.cxb3 ♖xf2= Sjugirov – Frolyanov, St.Petersburg 2009.

White can deprive his opponent of the advantage of the bishop pair with 15.♕e4 g6 16.♗c4 and here the seemingly attractive pin of White's bishop turns out to be the wrong decision for Black. After 16...♕a4 17.♖he1 ♖xd1+ (17...♗xc4 18.♕xe7 ♗d5 19.g3±) 18.♔xd1 ♗xc4 19.♕xe7 ♗d5 20.♘e5 ♗e6 21.♕xc5 ♗f5 22.b3 ♕f4 23.♕e3 ♕xh2 24.g3± his light-squared bishop is restricted by his own pawns and so White maintains a slight edge. It is correct for Black to play the straightforward 16...♗xc4! 17.♕xe7 (17.♕xc4 ♕c7=) 17...♖de8! 18.♕h4 (the pawn is poisoned and after 18.♕xb7 ♖b8! Black's attack becomes very dangerous) 18...♗d5 19.♘g5 h5 20.c4 (Black is much better after 20.g4? ♕a4–+) 20...♕a4 21.♖he1 ♖xe1 22.♖xe1 ♕xc4 23.♕xc4 ♗xc4 24.♖e7 b6 25.♖xa7 ♖e8=

15...♗f6

But not 15...g6 16.h4↑ with a powerful initiative for White.

16.♖e3

Black is clearly better after 16.♘g5?! c4 17.♗xh7+ (17.♘xh7 ♗xc3 18.♘xf8 cxd3 19.♖xe6 fxe6 20.♘g6 ♗f6∓) 17...♔h8 18.♘xe6 fxe6 19.♖xd8 ♖xd8 20.♕e4. White is unable to parry the threat of ♗f6-g5 and cannot protect his bishop in any other way. 20...♗xc3 21.♖e2 ♕g5+ 22.♕e3 ♕xe3+ 23.fxe3 ♗xb2+ 24.♔xb2 ♔xh7 25.♔c3 b5∓

It is possible for White to continue with the standard move 16.h4, when Black has a choice between a move which leads to an unclear position and a move which equalizes.

16...♗xc3!? 17.♖xe6 fxe6 18.♕e4 ♗f6 19.♕xh7+ ♔f7 20.♘g5+ ♔e7 21.♘xe6 ♕b6 22.c3 ♔xe6

23.♕f5+ ♔d6 (23...♔f7? 24.♗c4+ ♖d5 25.♖xd5 cxd5 26.♕d7+ ♗e7 27.♗xd5+ ♔f6 28.♕g4 ♔e5 29.♕e4+ ♔f6 30.♕e3 ♔g6 31.♕xe7 ♕f6 32.♕xc5±) 24.♗c4+ (24.♕f4+ ♔e7 25.♕e3+ ♔f7 26.♗c4+ ♖d5 27.♖xd5 cxd5 28.♗xd5+ ♔g6 29.♗e4+ ♔f7 30.♗d5=) 24...♗d4 25.♕g6+ ♔c7 26.♕g3+ ♖d6 27.cxd4 ♖fd8 28.♕xg7+ ♔b8∞ This position is non-standard and completely unclear;

16...c4 17.♖xe6 (If 17.♗xc4 ♖xd1+, and after 18.♖xd1 ♕a4∓ or 18.♔xd1 ♗xc4 19.♕xc4 ♕b6 20.♕b4 ♕xf2 21.♕xb7 ♕xg2 22.♕xc6 ♗xh4∓ Black is clearly better.) 17...cxd3 (17...fxe6 18.♕xc4≂ White has excellent compensation for the exchange) 18.♖xf6 gxf6! (18...d2+ 19.♘xd2 gxf6 20.♖e1 ♕d5 21.♘e4 ♕a2 22.♘d6 ♕d5 23.♘f5 ♔h8 24.b3 ♕xg2 25.♘g3) 19.cxd3 ♕c5 20.♕xf6 ♕xf2 21.♕g5+ ♔h8 22.♕f6+ (after 22.♖d2, Black has the intermediate move 22...f6!) 22...♔g8=

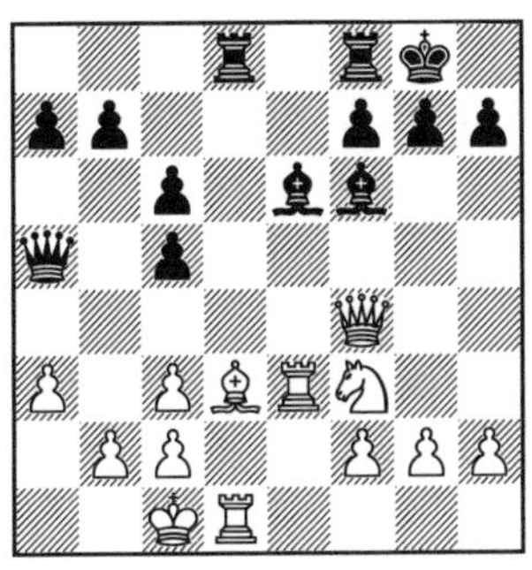

16...b5N 17.♖de1

17.♕e4 g6 18.♕xc6 b4 19.♕a6 ♕xa6 20.♗xa6 bxa3 21.bxa3 ♖xd1+ 22.♔xd1 ♖d8≂ White's pawns are vulnerable and Black has excellent compensation for his minimal material deficit.

17...c4

If 17...♕b6 18.♘g5 (after 18.g4, Black has the strong move 18...b4!) 18...♗xg5 19.♕xg5 ♖d5 20.♕g3±

18.♗e4

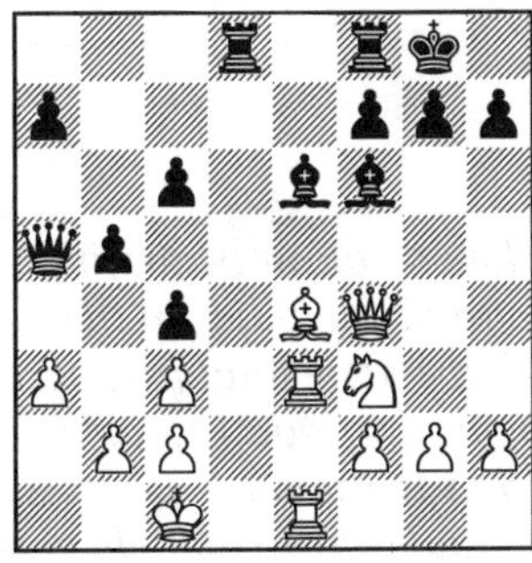

18...h6!

This is a very important prophylactic move, which is not at all obvious. It has become possible, because White is unable to open the kingside by advancing his g-pawn.

If 18...♕b6 19.g4! (19.♘g5 ♗xg5 20.♕xg5 c5=; 19.h4 c5 20.♘g5 b4→ Black's attack against the enemy king is faster) 19...c5 (19...a5 20.g5 ♗e7 21.♘d4 ♕c5 22.♕h4 h6 23.f4 ♖d6± Black's defence is nearly collapsing and his position is very precarious; 19...♗e7 20.♘e5 ♖d6 21.g5 c5 22.♗f5↑) 20.g5 ♗e7 21.♗f5±

19.♔b1

Black is clearly better after 19.g4 ♗e7 20.g5 (20.♗f5 ♗xa3 21.

♔b1 ♗xb2 22.♔xb2 b4∓; 20.♔b1 ♗d6 21.♘e5 f6–+) 20...♗xa3 21. gxh6 ♗d6 22.♗h7+ ♔xh7 23.♕e4+ g6 24.♘g5+ ♔h8 25.♔b1 ♗xh2∓

19...c5 20.♗f5 ♗d5 21.♗e4

(diagram)

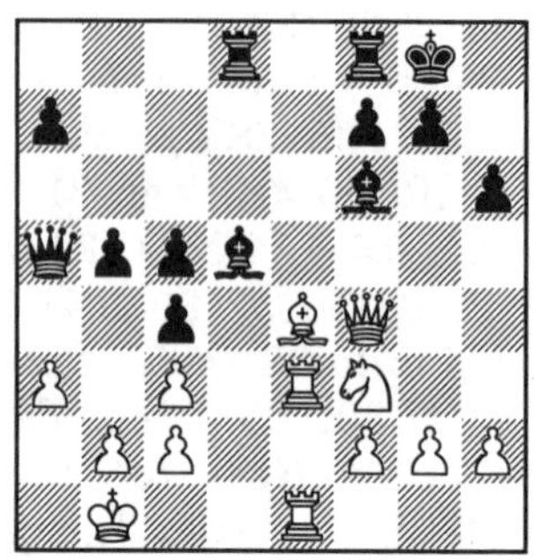

21...♗xe4

The move 21...♗e6= leads to a repetition of moves.

22.♕xe4 b4 23.♘e5 bxc3 24.♖xc3 ♖fe8 25.f4 ♖d4∓ Black's position is even slightly preferable.

Conclusion

The variation beginning with the move 5.♘c3 is one of the most dangerous for Black in the Petroff Defence. As for the line with 7.♗f4 which we have analyzed in this chapter, we can recommend to players who are ready to defend a minimally worse but quiet and safe position the move 7...♘c6. Players who are not afraid of a complicated and approximately equal struggle with opposite-sides castling can choose the move 7...0–0.

Chapter 29 1.e4 e5 2.♘f3 ♘f6 3.♘xe5 d6 4.♘f3 ♘xe4 5.♘c3 ♘xc3 6.dxc3 ♗e7 7.♗e3

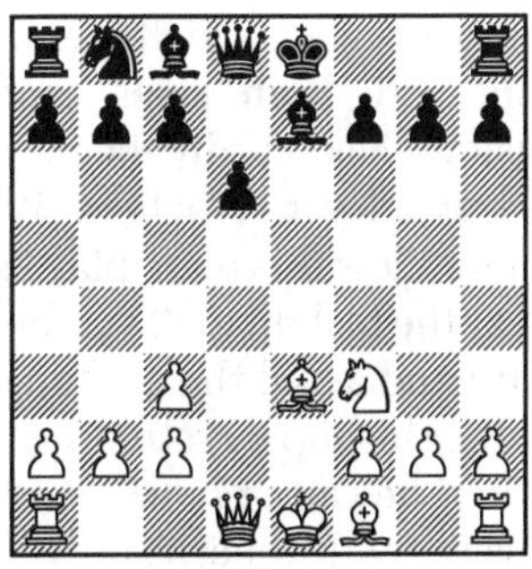

I think this is the most dangerous move for Black to face. The only advantage of putting the white bishop on f4, rather than e3, is that the e-file remains open, but White has no plans to use the e-file anyway! On e3 the bishop is eyeing the queenside, which might prove useful if Black castles on that side. If the black king seeks shelter on the kingside, then the bishop deprives Black's knight of the c5-square, and is also more harmoniously placed on e3 for the development of White's kingside initiative.

Now, just as after ♗f4, Black has two plans at his disposal: the cautious **A) 7...♘c6**, with the idea of preparing queenside castling, and the double-edged **B) 7...0–0**.

A) 7...♘c6

With this move Black is trying to equalize and wants to avoid getting into sharp positions with opposite-sides castling. He is preparing to castle queenside himself.

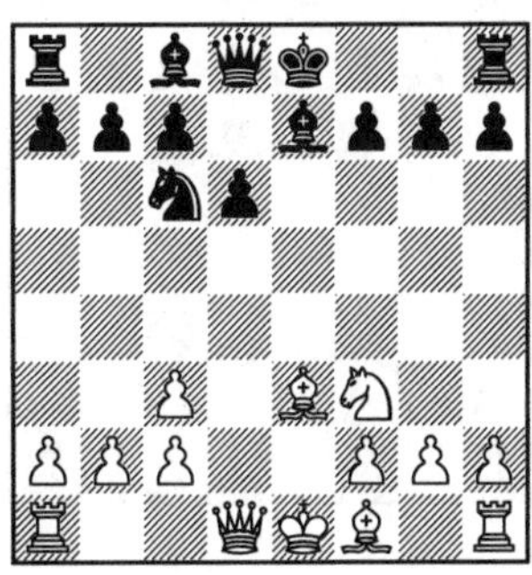

8.♕d2

White's far-flung queen-manoeuvres should not trouble Black in the least: 8.♕d5 ♗e6 9.♕b5 ♕c8 10.0–0–0 a6 11.♕a4 0–0 12.♕f4 ♗f6 13.♗d3 ♘e5= and the game is equal, Karjakin – Erenburg, Sochi 2006.

It is not worth White losing a

tempo for the prophylactic move 8.h3, because the development of the bishop to g4 is not part of Black's plan. It is pointless to pin the knight, since White can simply ignore it. If Black exchanges his bishop on f3, doubling his opponent's pawns, then White will develop his initiative along the open g-file. The game Leko – Adams, Miscolc (rapid) 2005, continued with 8...♗e6 9.♕d2 ♕d7 10.0–0–0 a6 11.♘g5 ♗xg5 12.♗xg5 f6 13.♗e3 0–0–0 and there arose a typical pawn-structure for this variation. However, it seems much more sensible for Black to follow the plan of castling kingside: 8...0–0! followed by ♘c6-e5.

8...♗e6

9.0–0–0

After 9.♘g5 Black is not obliged to exchange his dark-squared bishop. He can play instead 9...♗f5!N (after 9...♗xg5 10.♗xg5 ♕d7, White has the possibility of castling kingside: 11.♗e2!? 0–0 12.0–0 ♖fe8 13.♖fe1 ♗f5± Landa – Wang Yue, Nakhchivan 2011.

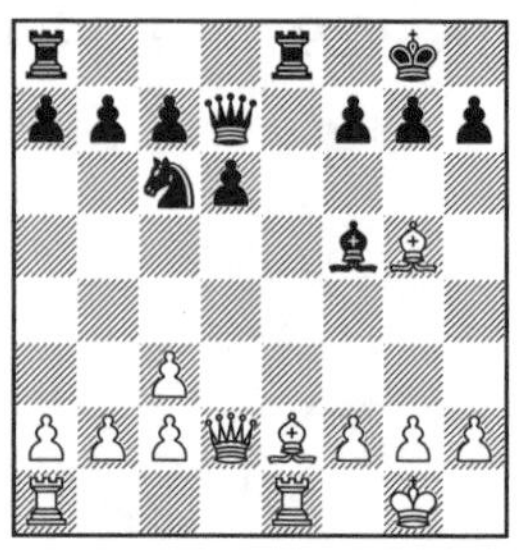

Now White played imprecisely with 14.♗f3= and his bishop was soon exchanged. This type of position, with both sides castling kingside, has hardly been analyzed at all yet. I believe White should follow this plan: play f2-f3, retreat the bishop to f2 via the h4-square and avoid the exchange of his other bishop by retreating it to f1. Then he can organize a pawn-offensive on the queenside. Black's defence is rather unpleasant, while White's edge is minimal but stable.) 10. 0–0–0 (or 10.♗c4 ♘e5 11.♗b3 0–0= and his bishop on b3 is not doing much) 10...♕d7=

9...♕d7

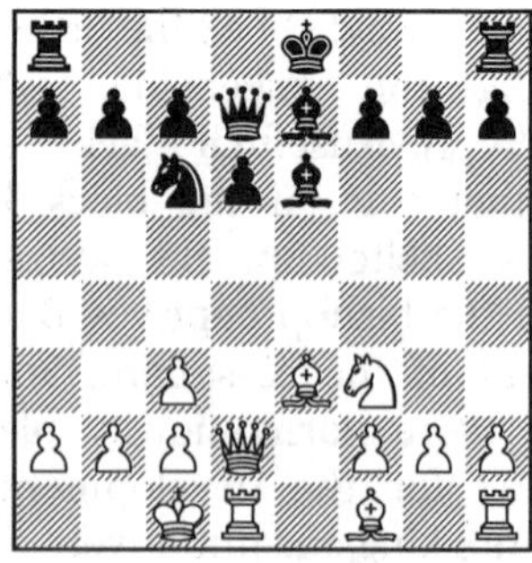

Now we shall analyze in detail the moves **A1) 10.h4** and **A2) 10.♔b1**.

The position is equal after 10.♗b5 a6 11.♗a4 b5 12.♗b3 0–0 13.♗xe6 ♕xe6=

The immediate 10.♘g5 seems pointless.

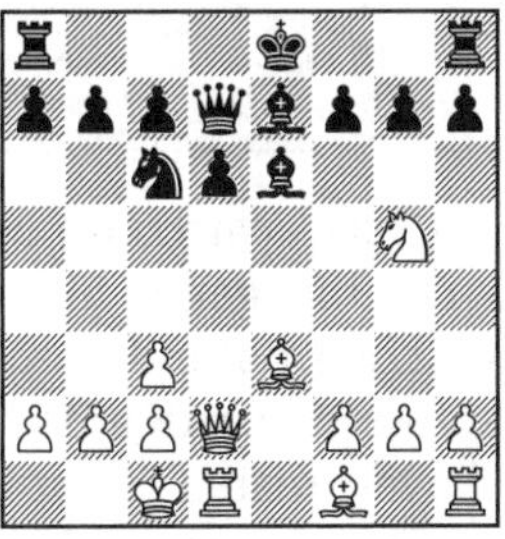

Naturally, Black can continue with the simple line: 10...♗xg5 11.♗xg5. After 11...f6 12.♗e3 0–0–0± there arises a standard position – Black has completed the mobilization of his forces without losing any tempi with moves such as a7-a6 or ♗e7-f6. Mevertheless, White's position is slightly.preferable.

Going in for a position with opposite-sides castling is unnecessarily risky for Black and after 11...0–0, White can play 12.b3! With this strong move White prevents the possible exchange of his important light-squared bishop via the c4-square. 12...♖fe8 (if 12...a5, White plays 13.a4!±, blocking the queenside) 13.h4 ♘e5 14.♗f4 ♕c6 15.♔b2± and thanks to his control of the e-file, Black will always have counterplay, but White's king is safer and he has the advantage of the bishop-pair, so his position is preferable, Sjugirov – Sakaev, Dagomys 2010.

However, it is very good for Black instead to choose 10...♗f5!? (analogously to the variation 10.♔b1 a6 11.♘g5 ♗f5, but under even more favourable circumstances) 11.♗c4 h6 12.♘f3 ♗e6 13.♗b5 a6 14.♗a4 b5 15.♗b3 ♗f6= Sjugirov – O.Ivanov, Plovdiv 2010.

It is possible for White to play 10.h3, in order after 10...a6 11.♘g5 to force the opponent to give up his dark-squared bishop for the knight. After 11...♗xg5 12.♗xg5 f6 13.♗e3 0–0–0, we again reach a standard position with a minimal edge for White. Therefore it would be sensible for Black to opt for 11...h6 followed by ♗e7-f6 and 0–0–0, with an approximately equal game.

A1) 10.h4

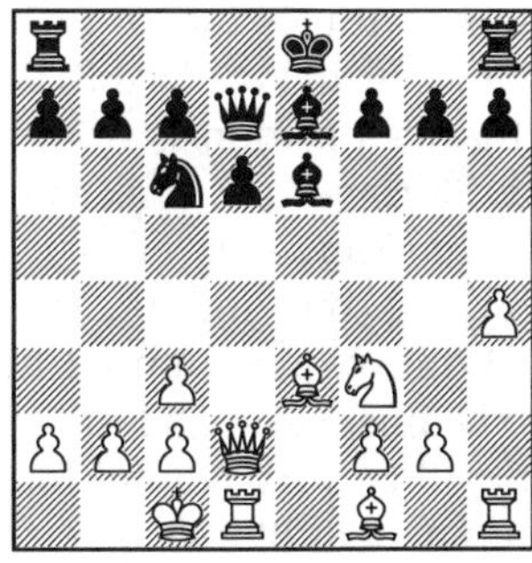

The idea of this move is to play ♘f3-g5 and after an exchange on g5 to recapture with the pawn, improving White's pawn-structure. Naturally, Black should not allow this.

10...h6!

Black not only prevents the appearance of his opponent's knight on g5, but keeps in mind the possibility of castling kingside. This does not happen very often with his knight already developed to c6, but.Black is still prepared to castle queenside, after all...

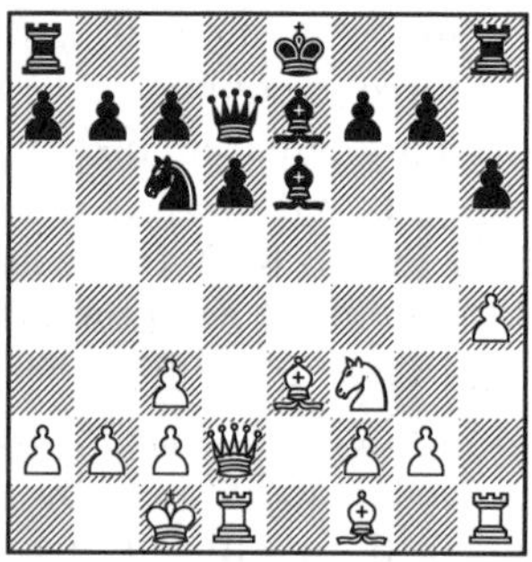

11.♘d4

If 11.♗b5 a6 12.♗a4 b5 13.♗b3 ♗f6 14.♕e2, then it is quite safe to continue with 14...0–0–0 15.c4 ♘a5 16.c5 ♘xb3+ 17.axb3 ♕c6= and Black's position is not at all worse, Shirov – Giri, Wijk aan Zee 2011. However, it is even better for him to opt for 14...0–0!?∓ since White's queen on e2 turns out to be misplaced and the move b7-b5 will be very helpful for the development of Black's queenside initiative.

After the prophylactic move 11.♔b1,

(diagram)

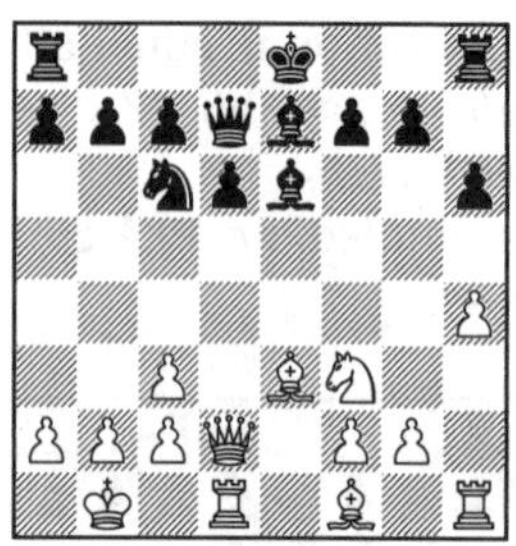

Black has a choice:

11...♗f6 12.♘d4 ♘xd4 13.♗xd4 ♗xd4 14.♕xd4 0–0 15.♗e2 ♖ae8 16.♗f3, Ni Hua – Giri, Wijk aan Zee 2010. Black can continue with 16...b6 (in the game he played 16...♕b5 17.g4 b6 and here, with the resolute move 18.g5!± White could have created great problems for his opponent) 17.g4 f6±, building a defensive line which White will find difficult to break, although he still maintains a slight edge;

I much prefer the move 11...a6!? for Black, with which he prepares to castle queenside, while preserving the option to castle kingside. After 12.♘d4 ♘xd4 13.♗xd4, Black should continue, not with the passive line: 13...♖g8?! 14.c4 0–0–0 15.♕c3 g6 16.♗e2± with considerable pressure for White, Bologan – Motylev, Poikovsky 2009, but with 13...0–0!⇄ - the move a7-a6 turns out to be useful, since Black can counter c3-c4, to lengthen the diagonal of White's bishop, with the move b7-b5!

11...♘xd4 12.♗xd4

(diagram)

12...0–0!?N∞

I like this move very much. White will try to prepare the advance of his g-pawn and in the meantime Black combines active

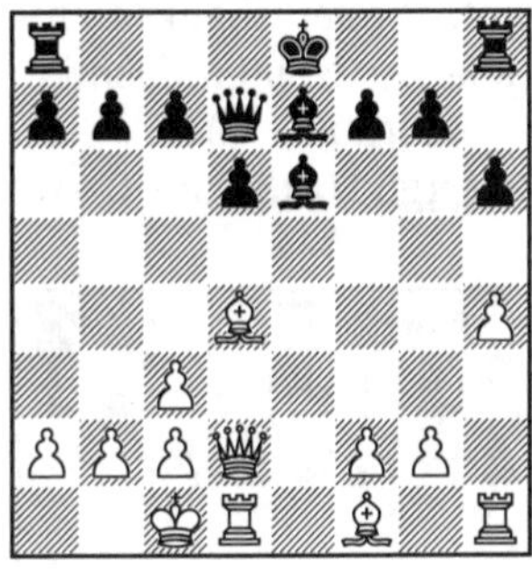

queenside play with an offensive using his c- and d- pawns, obtaining completely sufficient counterplay.

Black has also tried 12...♖g8 13.c4 c5 14.♗c3 0–0–0 15.♕e3 ♖de8 16.♔b1 ♗f6 17.♕g3 ♗xc3 18.♕xc3 ♕c6± when White's game is slightly pleasanter, but nevertheless the position seems quite drawish, Nisipeanu – Wang Yue, Medias 2010.

A2) 10.♔b1

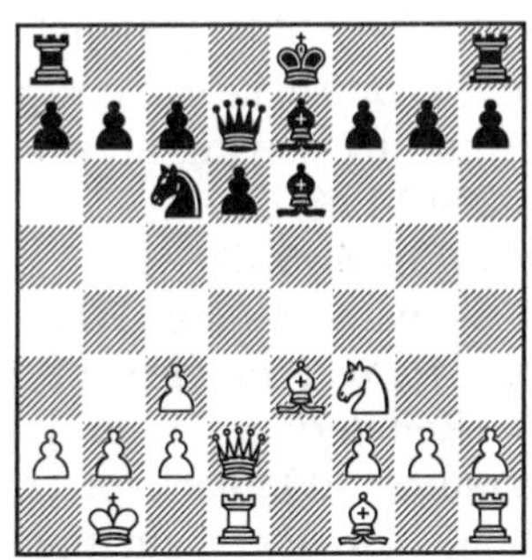

This is a useful prophylactic move and Black must now make up his mind about how to complete his development. In response, he can choose between the standard move **A2a) 10...a6** and **A2b) 10...♗f6!**

It would be bad for him to opt for 10...0–0–0 11.♘d4 ♘xd4 12.♕xd4± losing a pawn.

A2a) 10...a6

Black's position is very solid after this move, but he fails to equalize completely.

11.♘g5

It would be senseless for White to choose 11.h3, since Black can respond simply with 11...0–0–0, reaching a typical position after 12.♘g5 ♗xg5 13.♗xg5 f6.

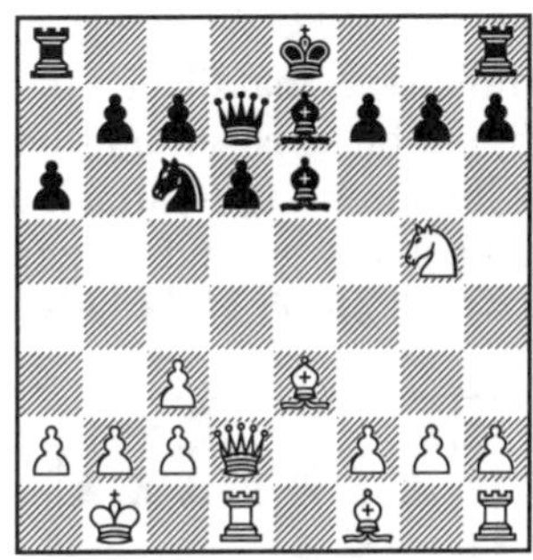

11...♗xg5

GM Vasily Ivanchuk had an interesting but not completely convincing idea here: 11...♗f5!?

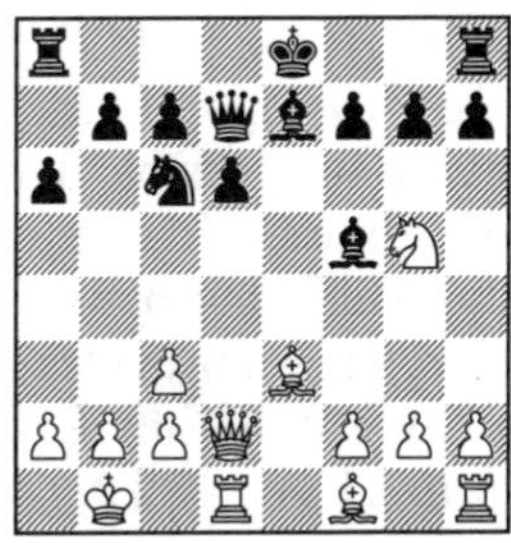

Black is trying to avoid the exchange of White's knight for one of his bishops. If White continues routinely there will be exchanges, which will be in Black's favour: 12.♗c4 h6! 13.♘f3 (White can expect no advantage from the risky line: 13.♘xf7 ♖f8 14.♕d5 ♗g6 15.♘xh6 gxh6 16.♗xh6 ♗f7 17.♕e4 ♖h8 18.♗xf7+ ♔xf7=) 13...♗e6! 14.♗e2 ♗f6! Black has deployed his forces harmoniously and White is forced to simplify the position. 15.♘d4 ♘xd4 16.♗xd4 ♗xd4 17.♕xd4 0–0 18.♗f3 ♖ae8= White's edge is purely symbolic, Alekseev – Ivanchuk, Astrakhan 2010.

It is much trickier if White chooses 12.h3!?. With this move he emphasizes that Black's bishop on f5 is a bit exposed and he reveals his intention to attack it by advancing his g- and f- pawns. 12...0–0 13.♗e2 (13.♘f3 ♗f6=)

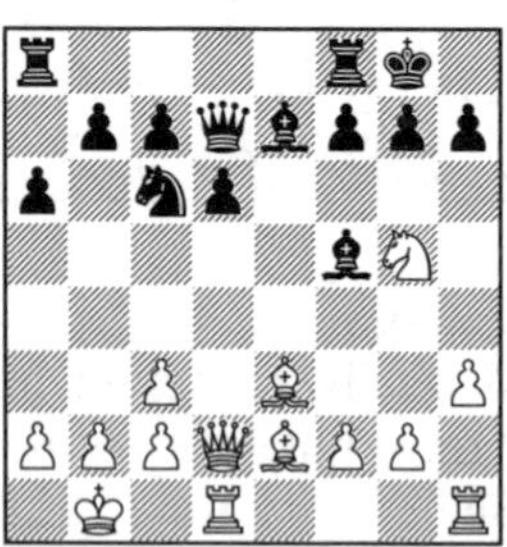

13...♘e5 (If 13...h6 14.♘f3 ♖fe8 15.g4 ♗e4 16.♖hg1± Black must reckon with the possible development of White's initiative on the kingside, which his pawn on h6 only helps, since it provides White with a target.) 14.♘f3 ♘xf3 15.♗xf3 c6 16.g4 ♗e6 17.♗g2± White is slightly better, thanks to his extra space, Nepomniachtchi – Alekseev, Irkutsk 2010.

12.♗xg5 f6 13.♗e3 0–0–0

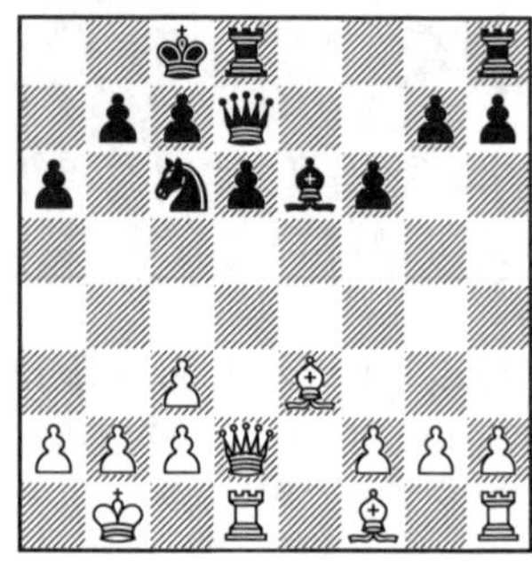

It is very difficult now for White to break Black's defensive line. His only real plan would be to trade a pair of rooks and then advance his queenside pawns. This plan is not easy to implement, however.

14.b3

Bearing in mind that Black intends to go with his queen to the f7-square, attacking the a2-pawn, White needs this prophylactic move. Of course, he can postpone it a while by playing here 14.f3, 14.♗e2 or 14.h3.

14...♖he8 15.f3

It is harmless for White to choose 15.♗e2, in view of 15...♗g4= Reinderman – Fridman, Hilversum 2009. Black forces the exchange of the light-squared bishops, because if 16.f3 ♕e7∓ his position would be preferable.

15.h3 ♕f7! He transfers his bishop to b7, after which his queenside will be much more secure. 16.♗e2 ♔b8 17.♖he1 ♗c8 18. c4 b6 19.♕d5 ♘e5 20.♕xf7 ♘xf7 21.♗h5 ♖d7 22.♗d2 ♖e5= Inarkiev – Adams, Baku (rapid) 2008.

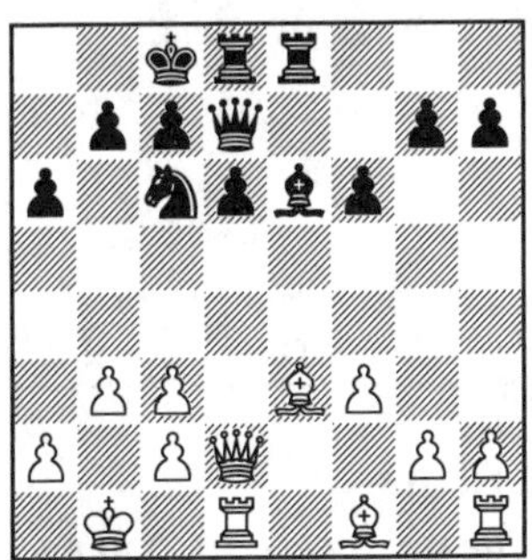

15...♕f7!N

Black's queen is comfortably placed on the f7- and g6- squares, while it would be reasonable for him to retreat his bishop to c8 in order to later prepare the thematic move b7-b6, restricting White's dark-squared bishop.

Black has also tried 15...h5 16.♗f2 ♗f5 17.♗e2 ♖e7 18.♖he1 ♖de8 19.♗f1 ♖xe1 20.♗xe1 ♖e7 21. ♗f2 ♕e8 22.c4 a5 23.a3 b6 24.♕c3 (24.b4 axb4 25.axb4 ♘e5=) 24... ♘b8 25.♔b2 (After this indifferent move White cannot achieve anything. He could have created some problems for his opponent with the energetic 25.b4!±) 25... ♕c6 26.♕d2 ♘d7 27.♕d5 ♘e5 28. ♖e1 ♗e6 29.♕d2 ♕e8 30.f4 ♘c6 31.♗d3 ♗f7 32.♖xe7 ♕xe7 33.♕d1 ♔b8 34.♕f3 ♘d8 35.♗e4 f5 36. ♗d3 g6 37.g3 ♗e8 38.♕e3 ♕xe3 39.♗xe3 ♘e6 40.b4 axb4 41.axb4 c5=, draw, Kramnik – Adams, Dortmund 2006.

16.♗f2 ♔b8 17.♗e2 ♕g6!= – White has no convenient way to protect his g2-pawn, but even if he were able to play ♖he1 and ♗e2-f1, Black would have nothing to worry about, since White's edge is minimal.

A2b) 10...♗f6!

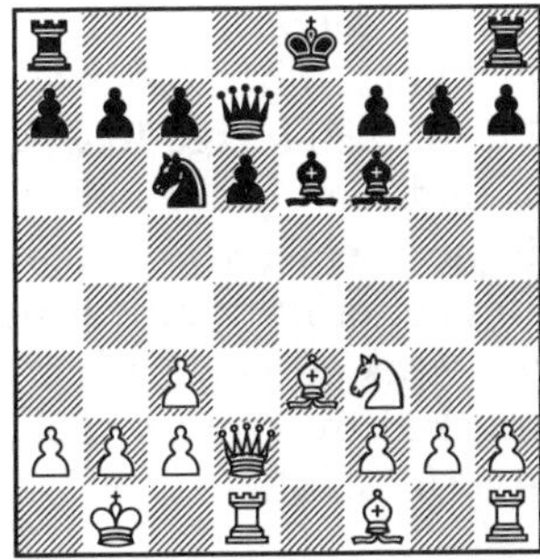

This is the contemporary treatment of this variation. Black does not agree to the exchange of his dark-squared bishop for the enemy knight.

11.h4

After 11.♘g5, he should play 11...♗f5= of course, and White achieves nothing.

11.♗e2 0–0–0 12.♘d4, Dominguez – Wang Yue, Sofia 2009. Here, the simplest way for Black to equalize is 12...♘xd4! (in the game he played 12...♗xd4 13. cxd4±) 13.♗xd4 ♗xd4 14.♕xd4 ♔b8=. Now, after 15.♕xg7, the position would be simplified even more with the line: 15...♗xa2+ 16.♔xa2 ♕e6+ 17.♔b1 ♕xe2=

11.♗g5 ♕e7 (it is less precise for Black to continue with 11...

♗xg5 12.♘xg5 0–0–0 13.♘xe6 fxe6 14.♗d3± and his knight on c6 is misplaced) 12.♗b5 (12.♕f4 ♗xg5 13.♘xg5 0–0–0 14.♘xe6 fxe6 15.♕a4 ♔b8 16.♗b5 ♘e5 17. f4 ♘d7 18.♖he1 c6 19.♗f1 ♖he8 20. g3 e5= Black's pieces are well centralized and his e5-square is well protected.) 12...0–0 (It is less accurate to play 12...a6, Ivanchuk – Gashimov, Monaco 2011. There might follow 13.♗xc6+! bxc6 14. ♖he1 0–0 15.♕f4 ♗xg5 16.♘xg5 c5 17.f3± and there will soon arise a multi-piece endgame which will be a bit better for White owing to Black's weak a6-pawn, which can be attacked by White's rook, via e1-e4-a4.) 13.♗d3

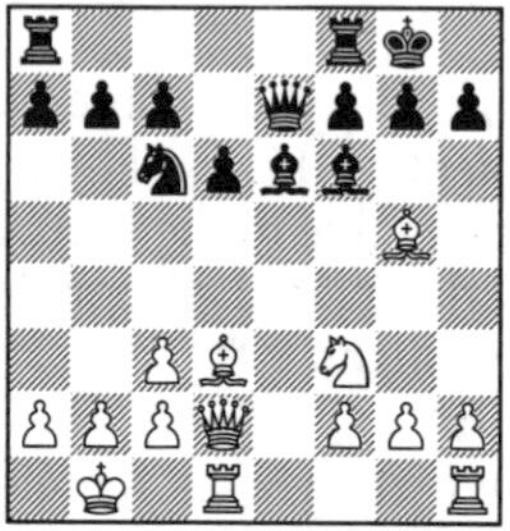

White's attempt to attack on the kingside looks dangerous, but Black's defence seems adequate: 13...♘e5! (not 13...h6?! 14.♗xh6! gxh6 15.♕xh6→) 14.h4 ♘xd3! After the exchange of White's light-squared bishop, he has no more threats on the kingside. 15.cxd3 ♖ae8 16.♕f4 c5 17.♗xf6 ♕xf6 18.♕xf6 gxf6= Black's doubled pawns are not a problem at all and the endgame is approximately equal.

11...0–0–0

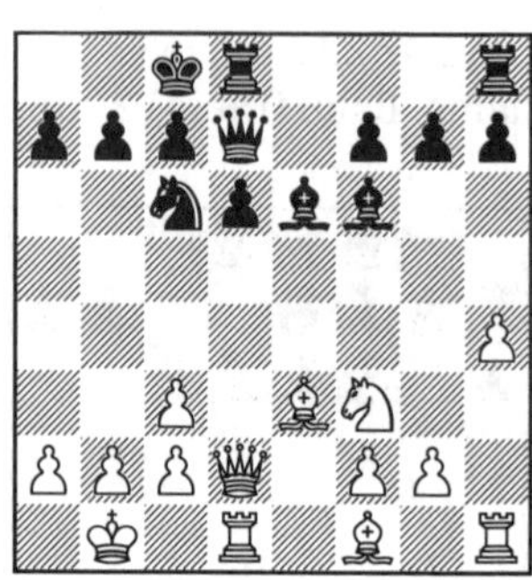

12.♘d4

The prospects are balanced after 12.♗g5 ♕e7 13.♕f4 h6 14.♗xf6 ♕xf6 15.♕xf6 gxf6 16.♘d4 ♗d7=. Black places his rooks on the g- and e- files and White's move h2-h4 turns out to have been a weakening..

The knight-sortie 12.♘g5 is not dangerous here: 12...♗f5 13. ♗d3 (13.♗c4 ♘e5 14.♗b3 h6 15. ♘h3 ♗g4 16.f3, draw, Karjakin – Li Chao, Khanty-Mansyisk 2010. If we continue this variation a bit further, then after 16...♘xf3! 17. gxf3 ♗xh3 18.♗xa7 ♗e6∓ Black's chances are superior.) 13...♗xd3 14.♕xd3, Inarkiev – Wang Yue, Astrakhan 2010. Black can solve all his problems now with 14...h6! 15.♘e4 ♕e6!=. Black's next move will be ♖de8, forcing White to exchange on f6, after which the position is equal.

12...♘xd4

If 12...♗xd4 13.cxd4 (after 13. ♗xd4 f6= we reach a standard position, except for an extra weakening move by White – h2-h4)

13...d5 14.h5 h6 15.f3⩲ White maintains a slight but stable advantage, thanks to the bishop pair.

13.♗xd4 ♗e5 14.♗e2!

White would not gain any advantage with 14.♕e3 ♕a4 15.c4 ♕a5= since Black's queen on a5 protects the e5- and c7- squares and is perfectly placed.

After 14.f4, Anand – Gashimov, Monaco 2011, Black equalizes with the counter-attacking line: 14...c5! 15.♗e3 ♗f6=

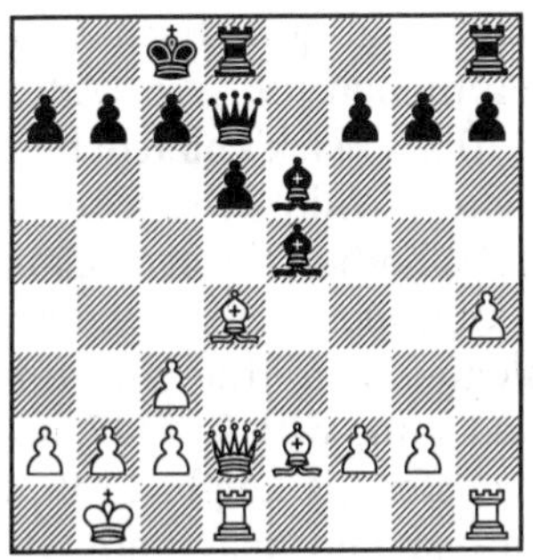

14...♗xd4!

Black should exchange on d4 now, despite the loss of a tempo, because White's bishop has been developed on e2 and thus his g2-pawn is hanging in some variations.

The move 14...f6 is double-edged, since it deprives Black's bishop of a square to retreat to. 15.♗e3 ♕a4 16.b3 (It is also possible for White to play simply 16.a3 d5 17.♖he1⩲) 16...♕a5 17.♔b2 d5 18.h5!? c6 19.♖h4 a6 20.♖a4 ♕c7 21.♗c5⩲

Black fails to solve his problems with 14...♕a4 15.b3 ♕a5 16.f4 ♗xd4 17.♕xd4 f6 (White has almost the same minimal edge after 17...g6 18.h5 ♕c5 19.♗f3⩲) 18.♖he1 ♖he8 19.♗f3 ♗f7 20.g4⩲ and of course it should end in a draw, but White has acquired much more space, so he has chances of torturing Black for a bit longer.

15.♕xd4 ♔b8

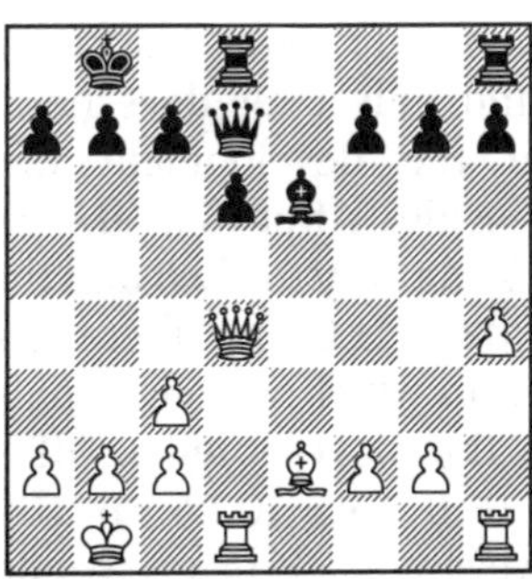

16.h5

16.♗f3 f6=

16.♕xg7 ♗xa2+ 17.♔c1 (17.♔xa2 ♕e6=) 17...♗e6 18.♕d4 ♖hg8 19.g3 ♗g4= In this major-piece endgame White cannot exploit his slightly better pawn-structure, because Black's isolated f-pawn is ready to advance with f7-f5-f4, and White will be unable to blockade.it successfully.

16...h6 17.♗f3 f6= McShane – Giri, Wolvega 2010.

B) 7...0–0

(diagram)

8.♕d2

GM Alexander Motylev had an interesting, but not very good, idea here of playing 8.h4. White

immediately sends his knight to g5 and only later does he complete the development of his queenside. After 8...♘d7 9.♘g5 Black can play 9...♘e5 and then if 10.♕d2 c6 11.0–0–0 there arises a position which we have analyzed with the move-order 8.♕d2 ♘d7 9.0–0–0 ♘e5 10.h4 c6 11.♘g5. However, Black has a wonderful alternative here – 9...♘f6!N. His knight perfectly protects the h7-square and controls the central squares. After 10.♕d3 c5 11. 0–0–0 d5∓ Black has excellent prospects.

8...♘d7

It is interesting, but strategically risky, for Black to opt for 8... c5. This move is aimed at preventing the opponent from castling queenside, because then Black plans to advance with b5-b4, opening up the queenside. At the same time his opponent's knight is deprived of the d4-square.

(diagram)

Nevertheless, White's most promising move is still 9.0–0–0 (White can also try to begin an all-out assault with 9.h4. He is preparing a kingside attack, but his own king is not securely protected. In the game Mamedyarov – Nabaty, Ningbo 2011, there followed 9...♘d7 10.♘g5 ♘f6 11.f3 d5 12.g4 ♕a5∞ with a double-edged struggle, but quite favourable for Black though.) 9...♗e6 (After 9... ♕a5 10.a3, Black's plan of b5-b4 is too slow. White is first to create threats, both in the centre and on the kingside. If Black continues analogously to the above-mentioned game with 9...♘d7, hoping to transfer his knight to f6, then White should play, not 10.♗f4 ♘f6 11.♗c4 b5 12.♗xb5 ♖b8∞ with a completely unclear position, but 10.♗g5! ♗xg5 11.♘xg5 ♘f6 12. ♗c4 b5 13.♗xf7+ ♖xf7 14.♘xf7 ♔xf7 15.♕xd6 ♕xd6 16.♖xd6 ♗b7 17.f3± Black's minor pieces lack secure squares and White's prospects are preferable.) 10.a3 ♘c6 11.♘g5 ♗f5∞ The position is double-edged and needs practical tests. I have to say that this does not seem to be a safe line for Black. His d6-pawn is backward and the bishop on f5 might come under attack by White's pawns.

9.0–0–0

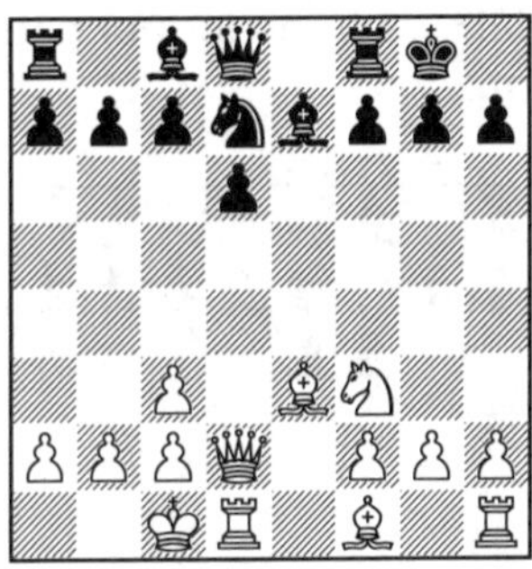

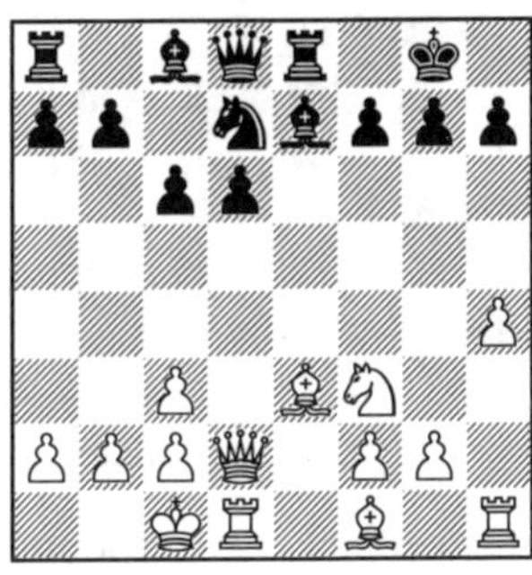

Black can choose here the cautious move **B1) 9...♖e8**, which has not yet been tested much in practice, or he can try the more concrete line: **B2) 9...♘e5**.

B1) 9...♖e8

The idea of this move is to postpone the decision about where to move the knight – to e5, f6 or c5.

10.h4

After 10.♗d3, Black can continue with 10...♘c5 11.♗xc5 dxc5 12.♖he1 g6=, or 10...c6 11.♖he1 ♕a5 12.♔b1 ♘e5 13.♘xe5 dxe5= and in both cases the position remains approximately balanced.

If 10.♔b1, then 10...c6 and after White's most logical move 11.h4 – see 10.h4 c6 11.♔b1.

10...c6

(diagram)

11.♔b1

The inclusion of the moves 11.h5 h6 has some drawbacks for White too. It will be difficult for White to open the g-file now and he loses the g5-square as a springboard for his knight. 12.♔b1 ♘f6 13.♗d3 ♗f8 14.♖dg1 ♘g4 (It is not good for Black to opt for 14...♗g4, in view of 15.♘h2! and he will have to allow his bishop to be exchanged, since if it retreats White's g-pawn will advance, joining in the attack. Black can accept the challenge, though: 14...d5!? 15.g4 ♘xg4∞ with a very unclear position, because White has no real concrete threats.) 15.♗f4 ♕f6 16.♘h2, Topalov – Gelfand, Linares 2010. 16...♘e5 17.g4 ♘xd3 18.cxd3 ♕e7. Black's position looks unpleasant, but he can obtain sufficient counter chances with precise play: 19.♗e3 (19.g5 hxg5 20.♗xg5 ♕e2 21.♕xe2 ♖xe2 22.♗e3 ♗f5 23.♖d1 ♖e8 24.♘f1 ♗g4 25.♖c1 d5∓ White is the only one taking a risk here, because after 26.♘g3, Black continues with 26...♖8xe3 27.fxe3 ♖xe3 and he picks up the d3-pawn too as compensation for the exchange.) 19...f6 20.♖g3 ♗e6 21.f4 f5! 22.g5 hxg5 23.fxg5 ♕f7∞ The position is completely unclear and both sides have their trumps in the ensuing contest.

White can continue with the quiet developing move 11.♗d3, to

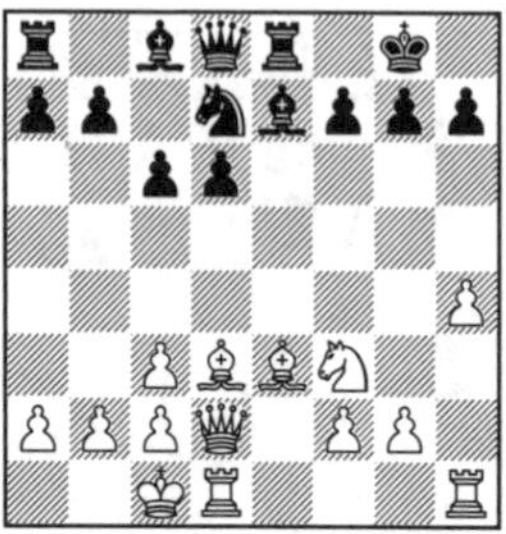

which Black can respond in various ways:

after 11...♕a5, Black must bear in mind that if his queen's access to the kingside becomes blocked by the pawn capture d6xe5, the position of the queen on a5 might turn out to be unfavourable. 12. ♔b1 ♘e5 (12...♘f6!?) 13.♘xe5 dxe5 14.♕e2 ♗e6 15.c4! (15.♗c4?! ♗xc4 16.♕xc4 ♖ad8 17.h5 ♖xd1+ 18.♖xd1 ♖d8 19.♖d3 a6 20.♕g4 ♕c7= Caruana – Kramnik, Wijk aan Zee 2010) 15...♖ad8 16.♕f3±;

11...♘f6 12.♖de1 (It might be interesting for White to try here 12.h5 h6 13.♔b1 d5 14.♗xh6 gxh6 15.♕xh6 ♗f8 16.♕g5+ ♔h8∞ and although it appears that Black's defences might hold, some players might find it all a bit too scary.) 12...d5 13.♗d4 c5 14.♗xf6 ♗xf6 15.♕f4, Nakamura – Kramnik, Moscow 2010. Here Black should have played 15...♗d7! 16. ♖xe8+ (16.g4 ♖xe1+ 17.♖xe1 ♕b8 18.♘e5 ♗xe5 19.♕xe5 ♕xe5 20. ♖xe5 ♗xg4 21.♖xd5 b6=) 16... ♗xe8⇄, obtaining sufficient counterplay thanks to his powerful bishop-pair.

I believe a very good decision for Black here would be to play 11...d5!?, with the idea of putting the knight on c5.

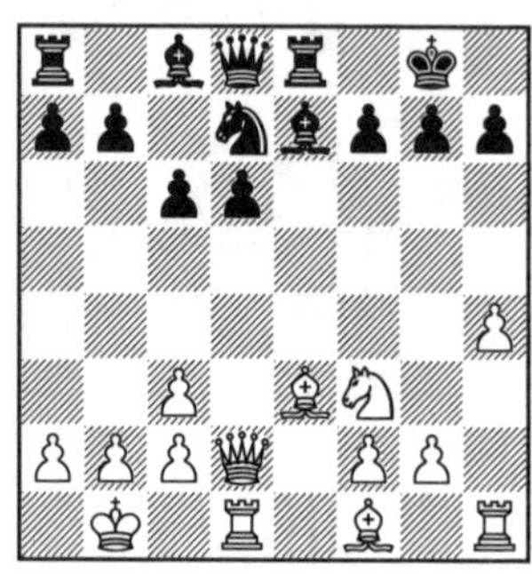

11...d5N

It mighty be too risky to play 11...♕a5, because there the queen can often turn out to be cut off from the main field of action. 12. h5 (12.♗d3 – see 11.♗d3 ♕a5 12. ♔b1) 12...h6 13.♗d3 ♘e5 (13...♘f6 14.♗xh6! gxh6 15.♕xh6+-; 13... ♗f8 14.g4→ and Black comes under a dangerous attack, Ivanchuk – Gelfand, Nice (rapid) 2010) 14.♘xe5 dxe5 15.♕e2 ♗e6 16.♗c4 ♗xc4 17.♕xc4 ♖ad8 18.♕g4 ♔f8 19.♖d7 (White's position remains slightly pleasanter after 19.♕f5 f6± since Black's kingside pawns are fixed on the same colour as his own bishop.) 19...♖xd7 20.♕xd7 ♕b5 (It would be too hazardous to opt for the line: 20...♕d5 21.♕xd5 cxd5 22.♗xa7 ♖a8 23.♗e3 b5± when Black has some active prospects, but not enough to compensate for the lost pawn, Dominguez – Gelfand, Nice 2010) 21.b3± White maintains a slight advantage.

It is interesting for Black to continue with 11...♘f6 12.♗d3 d5

13.h5 ♘e4 14.♕c1 (14.♗xe4 dxe4 15.♕e2 ♕a5 16.♘d2 h6⇄ and he has sufficient counterplay, while after 17.♘xe4 ♗e6 18.b3 he has the resource 18...f5!) 14...♗f6 15. h6 g6= Both sides' prospects are approximately equal.

12.♗d3

12.c4 ♘f6=; 12.h5 h6 13.♗d3 ♘c5=

12...♘c5 13.♘g5 ♘xd3 14. ♕xd3 g6 15.c4

Black has no problems after 15.♕d2 f6 16.♘f3 ♗g4=

15...♗f5 16.♕b3 ♕c7∞

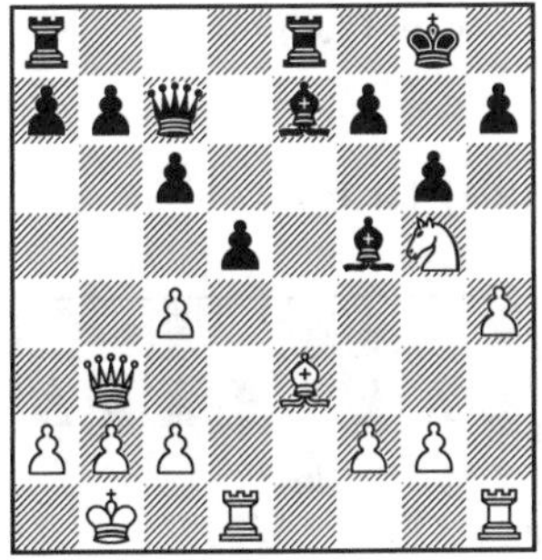

A complicated position has arisen on the board, offering chances for both sides.

B2) 9...♘e5

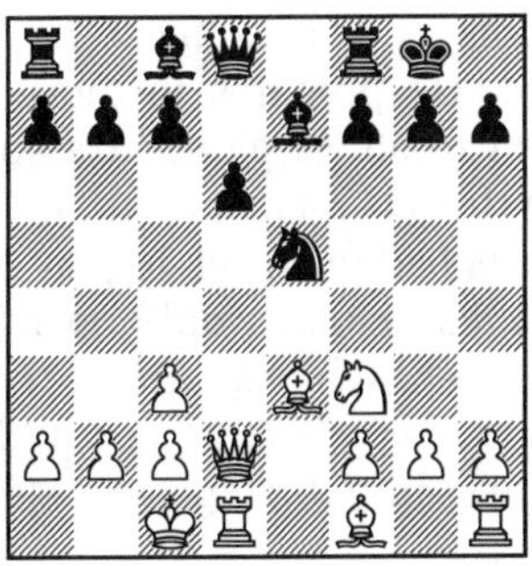

Now White can choose between **B2a) 10.♔b1** and **B2b) 10.h4**.

It is inferior to opt for 10.♘d4, owing to 10...c5! 11.♘b5 ♗e6 12.♘xd6 ♕b6 13.f4 ♘g4 14.♘c4 (14.f5? ♗xa2 15.♗f4 ♖ad8 16.b3 ♘f6 17.♔b2 ♗xd6 18.♗xd6 ♗xb3 19.cxb3 ♘e4∓ and Black ends up with an extra pawn) 14...♕a6 15. ♘a3 ♕a5 (15...c4 16.f5 ♗xf5 17. ♗xc4 ♕g6 18.♗f4 ♗xa3 19.bxa3∞) 16.c4 ♕xd2+ 17.♔xd2 ♗f6↑ Black has seized the initiative and it is White who must think about equalizing.

B2a) 10.♔b1 c6 11.♗e2

For 11.h4 ♕a5 – see 10.h4 c6 11.♔b1 ♕a5.

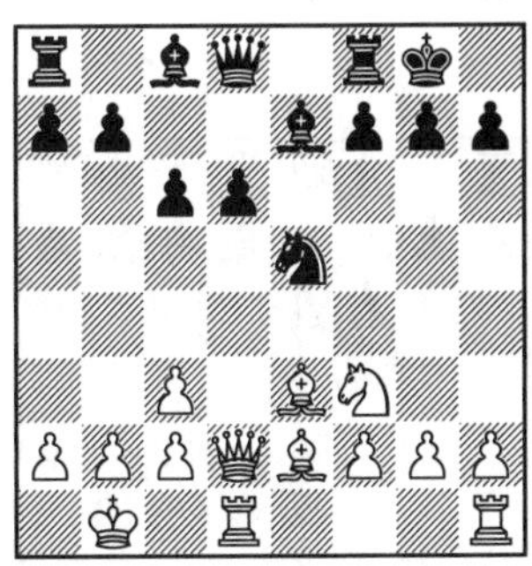

11...♖e8!

This move is always useful for Black. Now White must clarify his intentions: is he going to play in the centre or organize an attack on the kingside?

It is less precise for Black to play the immediate 11...♘g4, because of 12.♗d4! (After 12.♗d3 Black should play, not 12...d5 13.

♗f4 ♗d6 14.h3! ♗xf4 15.♗xh7+! ♔h8 16.♕xf4 ♘xf2 17.♘g5 f6 18.♘f7+ ♖xf7 19.♗g6 ♘xd1 20. ♕h4+ ♔g8 21.♖e1+– Anand – Kasimdzhanov, Tashkent 2011, but 12...♘xe3!. The powerful bishop should be exchanged at the first opportune moment!. 13.♕xe3 ♖e8 and now after 14.♖he1 ♗e6 15. ♘d4 ♗d7= the position is equal, while for 14.h4 d5 – see 11...♖e8 12.h4 ♘g4) 12...c5 13.h3 cxd4 14. hxg4 dxc3 15.♕f4! h6 16.♗d3 ♕b6 17.b3 d5 18.g5 ♕b4 19.♕xb4 ♗xb4 20.gxh6± and the endgame is slightly better for White.

12.h4

The prospects are balanced after 12.♖he1 ♘g4 13.♗d3 ♘xe3 14. ♕xe3 ♗e6 15.♘d4 ♗d7=

12...♘g4 13.♗d3 ♘xe3 14. ♕xe3

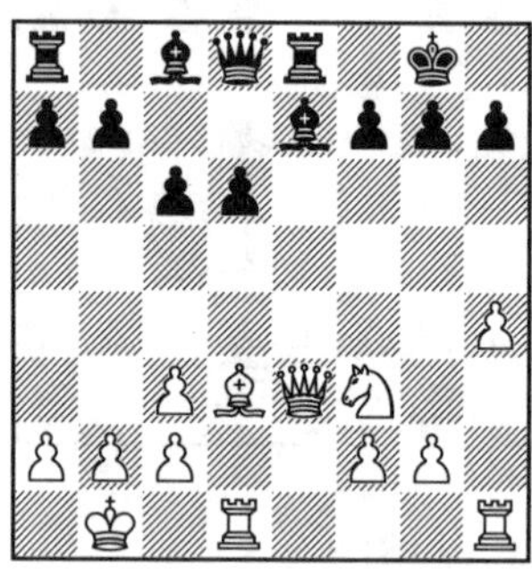

14...d5!

Black wants to develop his bishop on d6, from where it will deprive White's queen of the wonderful f4-square.

It is inferior for Black to play the seemingly attractive line 14... ♗f6 15.♕f4 ♕b6 (15...h6 16.g4 ♕b6 17.♘d4↑), because of 16.♘g5! (16.♕xd6 ♗g4 17.♕b4 ♕xb4 18. cxb4 g6 19.c3 ♗xf3 20.gxf3 ♖e5 21.♗e4 ♖d8= White's h4-pawn is hanging, thanks to which Black convincingly holds the balance.) 16...h6 17.♗h7+ ♔h8 18.♔a1! ♕c7 19.♗d3 ♔g8 20.♖he1 ♖e7 (20... ♖e5 21.♘f3 ♖xe1 22.♖xe1 ♗e6 23. a3±) 21.♕g3 ♖xe1 22.♖xe1 ♗d7 23.♘e4 ♗e7 24.♕f4± White maintains the initiative and Black must play accurately to equalize.

15.♕f4 h6 16.♖de1 ♗e6 17. ♘d4 ♗d6= The prospects for both sides are equal.

B2b) 10.h4

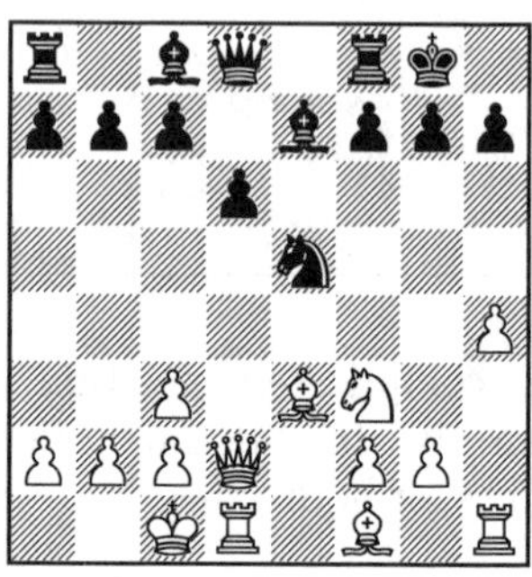

10...c6

This is Black's most flexible move. He prepares to move his queen to a5, or gain extra space with the pawn-advance d6-d5.

It is bad for Black to play 10... ♘xf3, since that would open the g-file for White's attack. After 11.gxf3 ♗e6 12.♖g1↑, or 12.h5↑ White's initiative grows effortlessly.

It is considered old-fashioned and inflexible for Black to continue with 10...♗g4 11.♗e2 ♕c8. Now the most dangerous way for White to develop his initiative seems to be: 12.h5 (it is weaker to opt for 12.♘xe5 ♗xe2 13.♘g6 fxg6 14.♕xe2 ♕e6 15.♔b1 ♖ae8= and Black is close to equality) 12...h6 13.♘xe5!? (13.♔b1!?±) 13...♗xe2 14.♕xe2 dxe5 15.♕b5 (after 15.♕c4 c6 16.a4± White has only a slight edge, Caruana – Gashimov, Khanty-Mansyisk 2009) 15...♗d6 16.g4↑

It is not advisable for Black to continue here with 10...♖e8, which was frequently tested in the early days of the development of this variation.

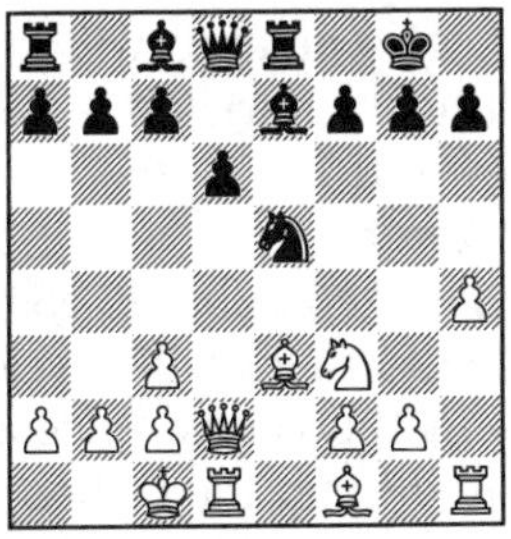

White can counter this in two promising ways:

11.♘xe5!? dxe5 12.♗d3 ♗d6 (it is preferable for Black to play 12...c6 here, but after 13.♕e2 ♕a5 14.♔b1 ♗e6 15.c4 ♖ad8 16.♕f3± White's position is better, since he can proceed with active play on the light squares on the kingside) 13.♗e4 f5, Caruana – Gashimov, Khanty-Mansyisk 2009. Here it would be very strong for White to play 14.♗g5!, forcing Black to block in his bishop on c8. After 14...♕d7 15.♗d5+ ♔h8 16.♔b1± Black has problems completing the development of his pieces.

White has a good alternative in the quiet move 11.h5. Now after 11...♗g4 12.♗e2 ♕c8 13.h6 g6 14.♘xe5 dxe5 (14...♗xe2 15.♘xg6+– Ponomariov – Gelfand, Odessa 2008) 15.♗xg4 ♕xg4 16.♕d5± he maintains a stable advantage, while after 11...♗f6, Anand – Gelfand, Mexico 2007, it is very promising to play simply 12.♘xe5 (Black also has problems after 12.♔b1±.) 12...♗xe5 13.h6 g6 14.♗e2± Black lacks space and the dark squares on his kingside are vulnerable.

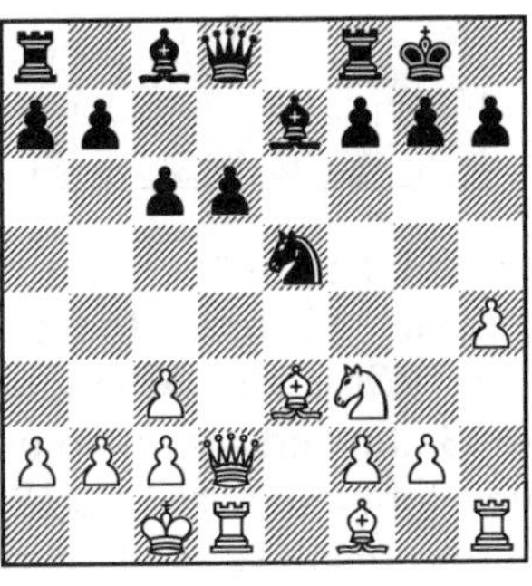

11.♔b1

We should examine White's alternatives here:

11.♘g5 ♕a5 12.a3, Motylev – Kramnik, Wijk aan Zee 2007. Now with 12...♗f5 13.♗e2 ♕a4! 14.f3 ♘c4 15.♗xc4 ♕xc4∓, Black could have obtained an excellent position;

11.c4 ♗e6 12.♘g5 ♗f5 13.f3 (If

13.♔b1 ♖e8 14.f3, then it is not good for Black to play 14...h6, after which in the game Karjakin – Kramnik, Moscow 2010, White coolly replied 15.♗e2!↑. It would then be very risky for Black to accept the piece-sacrifice but otherwise White will advance his g- and f-pawns, opening the position on the kingside. Instead, the correct reaction for Black is 14...f6! 15.♘e4 ♕c7 16.h5 h6⇄ and he is ready to continue with ♖ad8 and d6-d5, obtaining sufficient counterplay.)

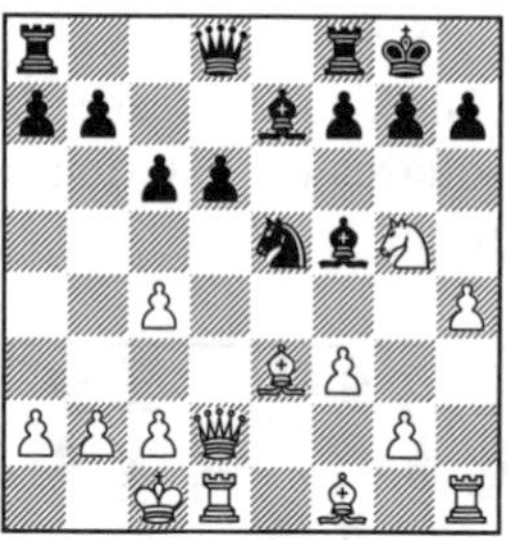

13...f6! This is the right pawn with which to repel the enemy knight. (White should ignore the move 13...h6 and simply complete his development with 14. ♗e2! – if Black accepts the knight-sacrifice, he is very likely to get mated along the h-file.) 14.♘h3 (After 14.♘e4, Black should continue with 14...♖e8=, indirectly protecting his d6-pawn. His plans include playing ♕d8-c7, ♖ad8 and then advancing d6-d5.) 14...♗e6 15.b3 a6 16.♘f4 ♗f7∓ White's kingside operations have reached a dead end, while Black is ready to continue his queenside initiative with the move b7-b5, Karjakin – Gelfand, Monaco (blindfold) 2011 (**game 21**).

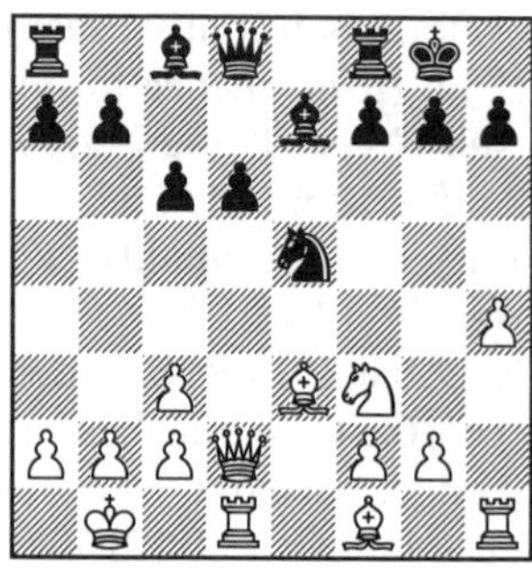

11...♕a5!

Black cannot solve his problems with 11...♗g4 12.♗e2 ♘xf3 13.gxf3 ♗h5 14.f4 ♗xe2 15.♕xe2 ♗f6 16.♖hg1± since White exerts powerful pressure on the g-file and Black's defence will be long and difficult, Karjakin – Gelfand, Moscow 2010.

12.♘xe5

12.♗e2 ♗e6 13.b3 (13.a3 ♕d5=) 13...♖fe8!=. Black will develop his forces in the centre, placing the rook on d8 and the bishop on f6, with a very good position. The more straightforward line: 13...♘xf3 14.♗xf3 ♗f6 was tried in the game Kokarev – Maslak, Dagomys 2010. Now by playing 15. c4!±, White could have maintained a slight but stable advantage.

12...dxe5 13.♗c4 b5 14.♗b3 ♕c7 15.♗g5 a5

(diagram)

16.♗xe7

After 16.a4, Black plays 16...

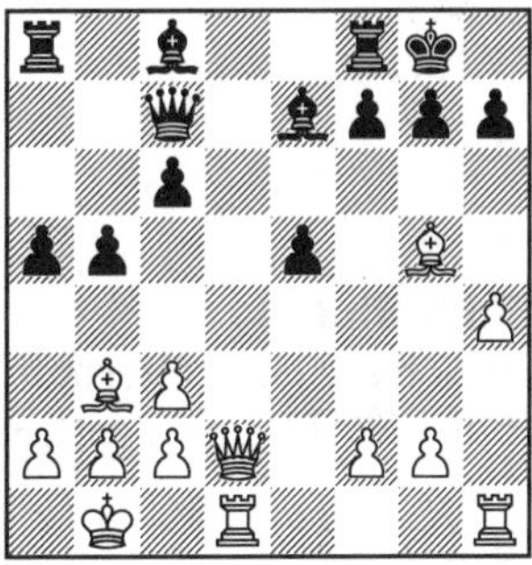

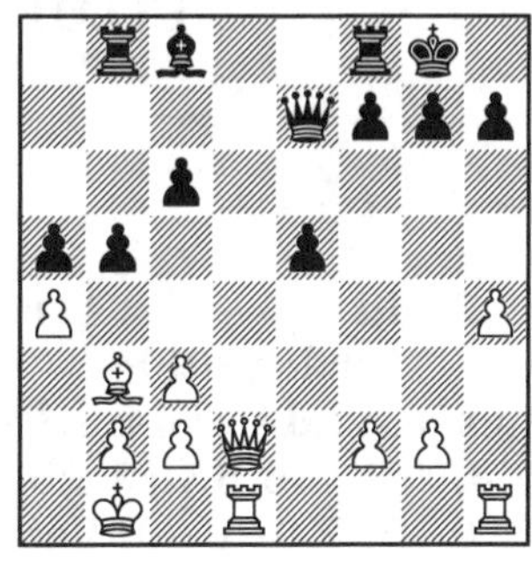

bxa4! and after 17.♗xa4 f6 18.♗e3 ♗e6∓ he obtains good prospects for active play on the b-file, while if 17.♗xe7, Pavlovic – Savic, Kragujevac 2010, he has the intermediate move 17...axb3! 18.♗xf8 ♗f5∓ and only White will have problems in this position.

16...♕xe7 17.a4 ♖b8

18.♕d6

After 18.axb5 a4! 19.♗c4 (if 19.♗xa4? ♕a7–+ and he either loses his bishop or is mated on the a-file) 19...cxb5∓ followed by b5-b4.

18...♕b7 19.axb5 ♕xb5 20. c4 ♕b7 21.♕xe5 a4 22.♗a2 ♗e6⩱ Black's compensation for the pawn is quite sufficient.

Conclusion

Nowadays, the variation 5.♘c3 ♘c3 6.dxc3 ♗e7 7.♗e3 seems to be one of the most dangerous for Black in the Petroff Defence. The plan of castling queenside after 7...♘c6 seems reliable enough, but he has practically no chances of winning the game. White obtains the advantage of the bishop-pair in some lines, enabling him to torture his opponent for a long time. Black might find this rather unpleasant from the purely practical point of view. The variation with 7...0–0 is much more interesting for Black and leads to a complicated struggle with chances for both sides, but one in which Black can face the future with optimism. There are still some positions which have not been well analyzed yet and players can improve their analytical capabilities by studying these variations. There are plenty of possibilities for realizing your creative potential over the board as well.

COMPLETE GAMES

1 Rudd – Avrukh
London 2010

1.e4 e5 2.d4 exd4 3.♕xd4 ♘c6 4.♕e3 ♘f6 5.♘c3 ♗b4 6.♗d2 0–0 7.0–0–0 ♖e8 8.♕g3 ♘xe4 9.♘xe4 ♖xe4 10.c3 ♗e7 11.f4 d5 12.♘f3 ♗f5 13.♗d3 ♕d7

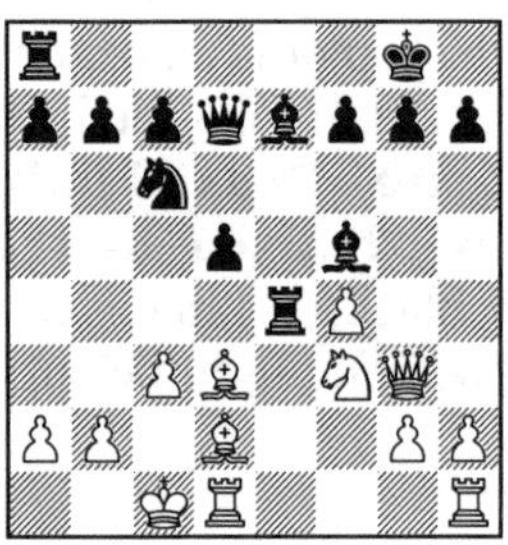

14.♗xe4

If White does not take the exchange, then Black's rook will go to the a4-square and White will end up a pawn down.

14...♗xe4 15.♗e3

After 15.♖he1, Black again plays 15...♘a5, opening the route for his queen to a4.

15...♘a5 16.♗d4

If 16.b3, Black has the powerful riposte 16...♕b5, threatening ♗e7-a3, ♘a5xb3 and eventually ♘a5-c4.

16...♗f8

Another very good move is 16...f6, restricting the bishop on d4 and depriving White's knight of the e5-square.

17.b3 ♕b5

Black has a good alternative in 17...♕d6 18.♕f2 ♕a6∓ with similar ideas.

18.♔b2 c5

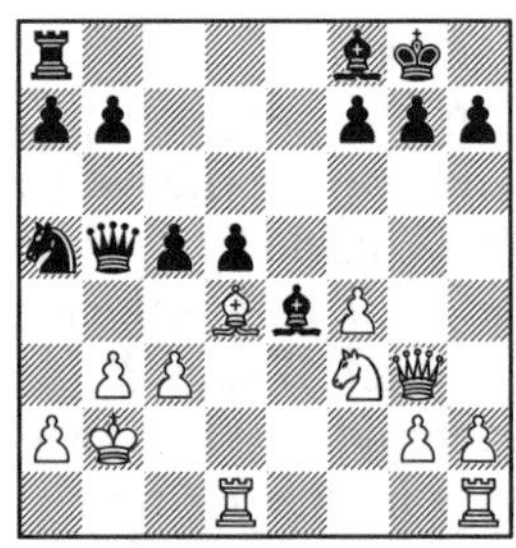

19.♗e5

It is more resilient for White to defend with 19.♗f2, although after 19...♘c4 20.♔a1 ♘a3 21.♖c1 (or 21.♘d2 c4 22.♘xe4 dxe4–+ and Black's attack is decisive; after 21.♖d2, he plays 21...a5!–+, with the unpreventable threat of a5-a4) 21...♕a6 22.♘e1 c4! 23.bxc4 (after 23.b4 the most precise move for Black is 23...♘b5–+, followed by ♕a6-a3 and a7-a5) 23...♕xc4–+. White's position is completely squashed and he has no moves, even though the board is full of pieces. Black's plan includes bringing his rook on a8 into action and this will be decisive.

19...♘c4 20.♔a1

After 20.♔c1 Black again wins with 20...♘e3.

20...♘e3 21.♘g5

White cannot change much with 21.♖c1 ♕e2 and Black is threatening ♘e3-c2.

21...♕e2 22.♖c1 ♘c2 23.♖xc2 ♗xc2 24.♖e1 ♕d3 25.♕g4 ♕f5. White resigned

2 McShane – Kramnik
London 2009

1.e4 e5 2.♗c4 ♘f6 3.d3 ♗c5 4.♘f3 0–0 5.♘c3 d6 6.♘a4 ♗b6 7.c3 ♗e6

Black carries out an important and advantageous exchange. White is prevented from gaining the advantage of the bishop pair, and loses the services of his bishop which is very active on c4.

8.♗b3

White could also have exchanged on e6. It is understandable that White was reluctant to present his opponent with the semi-open f-file. The position remains equal in either case.

8...♗xb3 9.axb3 ♘bd7 10.b4

(diagram)

10...♗xf2!

This move can be described as

a “justified risk”. Objectively speaking, the position remains balanced, possibly even slightly worse for Black, but White is very likely to make a mistake. If Vladimir Kramnik had been playing against Vishy Anand, for example, he would not have played this move, which sharpens the position tremendously, and instead he would have preferred some quieter continuation which might lead to a draw. In this game Kramnik complicates the issue, but he stays within a limited margin of risk, without coming close to a loss.

11.♔xf2 b5

12.♗d2?!

Black must carry out a pawn-break on the light squares if he wishes to seize the initiative, so White should fortify his light squares immediately. The d2-square is hardly any better for his bishop than the c1-square, so White practically wastes an important tempo.

It was necessary to deprive Black's knight of the g4-square with the move 12.h3. Then after, for example: 12...a5 (It would be too risky for Black to leave himself with a pawn-island on the a-file: 12...bxa4 13.♕xa4 c5 14.♗e3 and White maintains the advantage.) 13.bxa5 ♖xa5 14.b4± and his position is slightly preferable, but still quite close to equality.

You can say more or less the same about the position arising after 12.♖e1 a5 (here 12...bxa4 13. ♕xa4 c5 is very dubious for Black, in view of 14.b5 and the presence of White's rook on e1 prevents Black from advancing c5-c4 or d6-d5) 13.bxa5 ♖xa5 14.b4⩲

12...bxa4

Or 12...a5 13.bxa5 ♖xa5 14.b4 ♖xa4 15.♖xa4 bxa4 16.♕xa4= and the position is approximately equal.

13.♕xa4 c5

14.b5?!

White does not sense the danger and ignores his opponent's possible pawn-breaks on the light squares.

He had to strengthen his position with 14.♖he1 cxb4 15.cxb4. He has doubled pawns but all his pieces are very active and he has nothing to be afraid of.

14...d5! 15.exd5?!

Just as before, it was best for White to bring his inactive rook into play with the move 15.♖he1. After 15...c4 (He should not be afraid of 15...♘b6 16.♕c2 c4, because of 17.♗g5.) 16.exd5 ♘b6 17. ♕b4 ♘fxd5 18.♕a5 cxd3 19.♖xe5∞ the position would remain double-edged.

15...♘b6

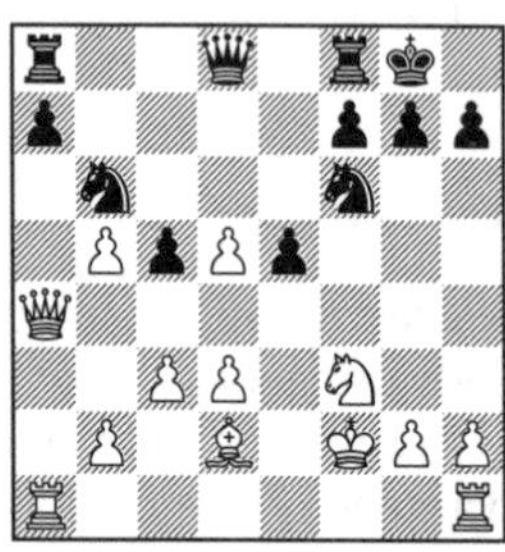

16.♕c2?!

White continues his series of mistakes. In fact, he is under the false impression that his position is quite acceptable.

Meanwhile, it was high time for resolute action and he had to play actively – 16.♕h4! ♕xd5 17. ♖hd1 (It is no better for White to play 17.♗g5 ♘fd7 18.♖hd1 ♕b3 19. c4 f6 20.♗e3 a6! 21.bxa6 ♖xa6∓ and one of his pawns will fall soon.) 17...♕xd3 18.♗g5 ♕c2 19.

♔g1∓. Black has an extra pawn and the advantage, but White has counterplay.

16...c4! 17.♘xe5

It is more resilient for White to defend with 17.♖he1 ♕xd5 18.d4, although after 18...e4 19.♘e5 ♕xb5 20.♔g1 h6 Black ends up with a solid extra pawn.

17...♕xd5 18.d4

This is positional capitulation, but White is already beyond salvation. For example, in the variation 18.♖he1 cxd3 19.♕xd3 ♕xd3 20.♘xd3 ♖ad8, he ends up a piece down.

18...♘e4 19.♔g1 ♖fe8

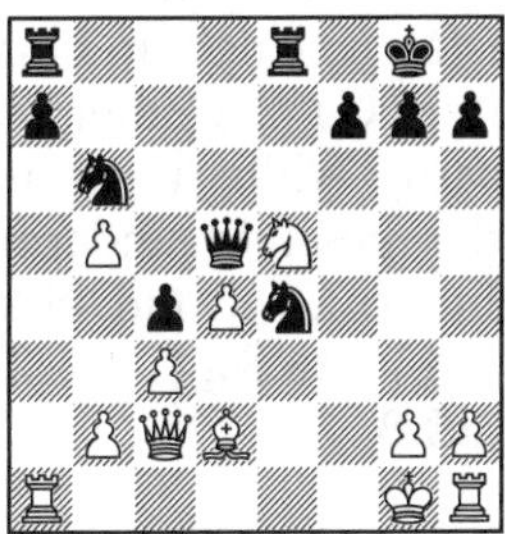

The game is practically over from the point of view of strategy. White is helpless against the combined pressure of all Black's pieces.

20.♘f3 ♕xb5 21.h4 ♕b3 22.♕b1 ♘d5 23.♖h3 h6

Black was winning easily with the straightforward move 23...♖ab8, but he could equally afford to play more patiently.

24.♕c1 ♕b6 25.♖a4 ♖ab8 26.♖a2 ♕b3 27.♕a1 ♖b6 28.♔h2 ♘df6 29.♗e1 ♘g4 30.♔g1 ♘ef6 31.d5 ♘xd5 32.♖g3 ♘df6 33.♗d2 ♖d6 34.♖a3 ♕b6 35.♔h1 ♘f2 36.♔h2 ♘6g4. White resigned

3 Movsesian – Bu Xiangzhi

Nanjing 2008

1.e4 e5 2.♗c4 ♘f6 3.d3 c6 4.♘f3 d5 5.♗b3 ♗d6 6.♘c3 dxe4 7.♘g5 0–0 8.♘cxe4 ♘xe4 9.♘xe4 ♗f5 10.♕f3 ♗xe4 11.dxe4 ♘d7

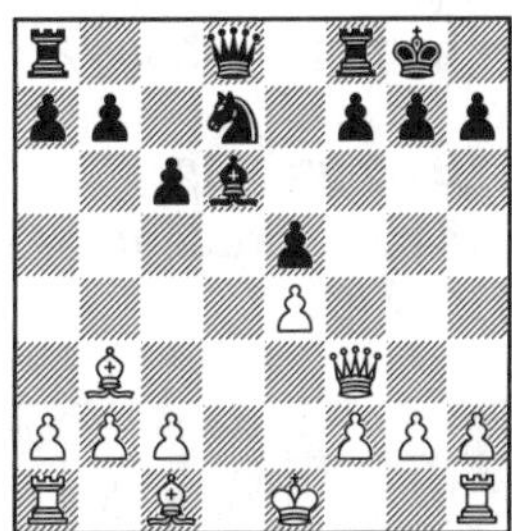

12.c3 a5 13.0–0 a4 14.♗c2 ♕e7 15.♖d1 ♖fd8 16. h4 h6 17.g3 b5 18.♗d2 ♘f8

Another good move here is 18...♘f6, planning to transfer his bishop to c5 and his knight eventually to the g4-square.

19.♕g4

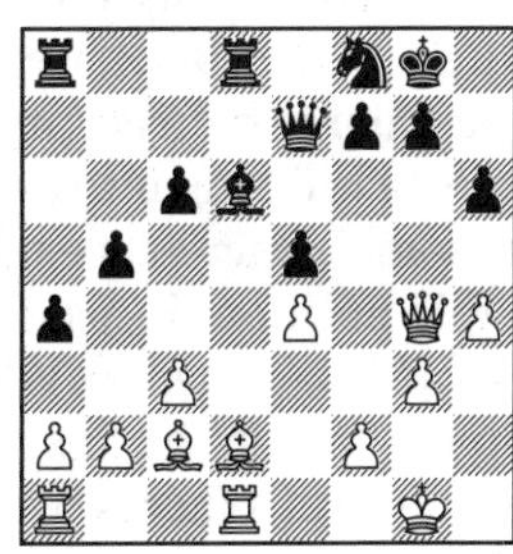

19...♕e6!

He could also have played a

middle game by opting for either 19...♔h8 and 19...♕f6, but he does not need to be afraid of anything in an endgame!

20.♕xe6 ♘xe6 21.♔f1 ♔f8 22.♗e1

White retreats his bishop to a square where it cannot be exchanged, so insisting by all means on maintaining his advantage of the bishop pair. It would all be perfect for White but for the fact that, the position is not sufficiently open and his bishops are very passive.

22...♔e7 23.♖d2

It was more prudent for White to play 23.♔e2.

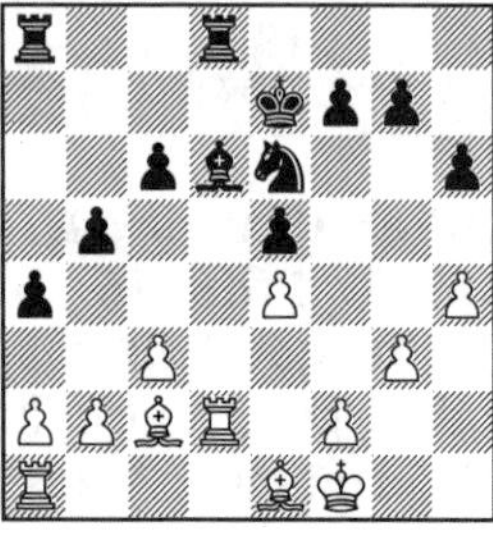

23...g5!

This move is not at all obvious and it is tremendously powerful! It might seem that Black weakens the light squares in his camp, but Bu Xiangzhi is taking into consideration some concrete peculiarities of this position, in particular the awkward placement of White's rook on d2, and he begins active play on the dark squares over the entire board!

The position would be equal after 23...c5, with the idea of c5-c4. There might follow, for example: 24.f3 c4 25.♖ad1 ♗c5 26.♖d5 ♖xd5 27.♖xd5 f6 28.f4 exf4 29. gxf4 ♖d8 30.♖xd8 ♔xd8 31.♗d2 ♗d6 and White is unable to support the pawn on f4.

After the routine move 23... ♖d7, White's idea would be justified, since after for example: 24. ♖ad1 ♖ad8 25.f3 ♗c5 26.♖xd7 ♖xd7 27.♖xd7 ♔xd7 28.♔e2, White obtains winning chances, thanks to his possible undermining moves f3-f4 and b2-b3, activating his bishops.

24.hxg5 hxg5 25.♗d1

Black can counter 25.♖ad1 or 25.♔e2 with 25...g4!, threatening to transfer his knight to f3 via the g5-square. On the other side of the board, White must reckon with the possible undermining pawn-breaks a4-a3 and b5-b4.

25...b4 26.♗g4 bxc3 27. bxc3 ♖ab8

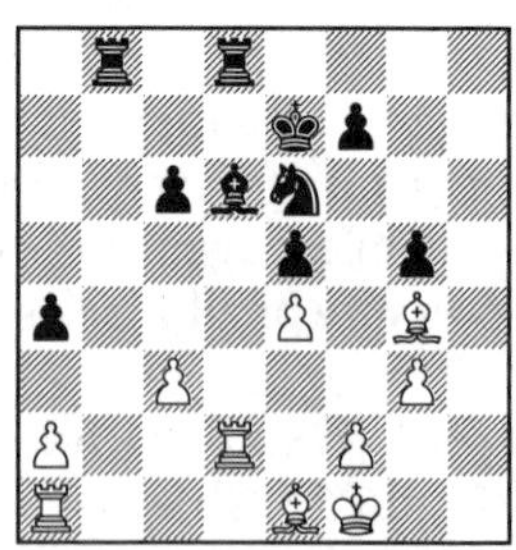

Black has occupied the b-file and prepared the penetration of his knight into his opponent's camp; White is practically helpless against this.

28.♖ad1

White's defensive task would

not be any easier after simplifications. In the variation 28.♗xe6 ♔xe6 29.♔e2 ♖h8 30.♖ad1 ♗c5∓ Black maintains the advantage, thanks to his extra space and more active pieces.

28...♘c5 29.f3 a3 30.♗f2 ♘a4 31.♗e3 f6 32.c4 ♘b2 33. ♖c1 ♗b4 34.♖h2 ♖h8

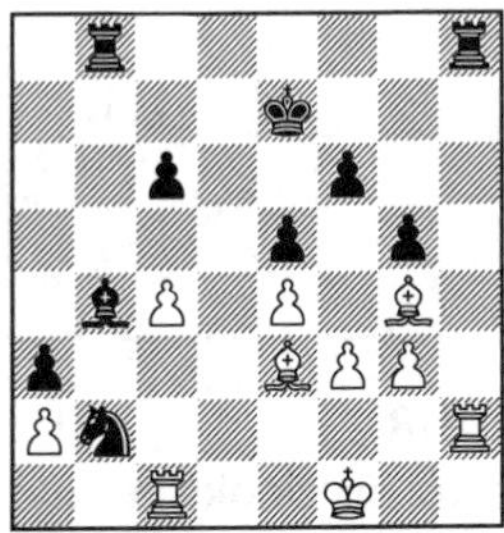

35.♖xh8

White loses valuable tempi, but in a practical game it would be almost impossible for him to find the very narrow path giving him some chances of saving the game. He had to play 35.♖cc2!, after which Black should not try to force the issue but should increase the tension with 35...♖bd8! (If Black captures the pawn with 35... ♘xc4 then 36.♗g1 leads to a draw: 36...♘d2 37.♖cxd2 ♗xd2 38.♗c5 ♔f7 39.♖xd2 ♖b1 40.♔e2 ♖h2 41. ♔d3 ♖xd2 42.♔xd2 ♖b2 43.♔c3 ♖xa2 44.♔b3 ♖g2 45.♗xa3 ♖xg3= and a mutual fortress position has arisen on the board; or 36...♖xh2 37.♖xh2 and White activates his forces, so that, for example, after 37...♖d8 38.♖h7 ♔d6 39.♖f7 c5 40.♔g2 ♔c6 41.♗e6 ♔b5 42.♗d7 ♔a5 43.♗e6 ♘d2 44.♗e3 ♖d6 45. ♗d5= it should all end in a draw.). Now White should continue to play in the same active way: 36. ♖xh8 ♖xh8 37.c5! (White is completely paralysed after 37.♗c1 ♘a4 38.♔g2 ♘c5!∓ and, to add to White's worries, Black's knight penetrates to the d3-outpost.) 37...♘a4 38.f4! (after 38.♔g2, it is very good for Black to play 38... ♖b8∓, threatening ♗b4-c3 and ♖b8-b2 and White's bishop on c1 is helpless to prevent this idea.) 38...exf4 39.gxf4 gxf4 40.♗d4!∓ and White still preserves good drawing chances.

35...♖xh8 36.♔g2 ♖d8 37. ♖h1

White can try passive defence but that would not help, because after 37.♖c2, Black penetrates inside his opponent's camp: 37... ♖d3 38.♗c1 ♘a4 39.f4 gxf4 40. gxf4 ♔d6∓ and White's pawns on a2 and c4 will soon fall.

37...♘xc4 38.♖h7 ♔d6 39. ♗a7 c5 40.♗h5

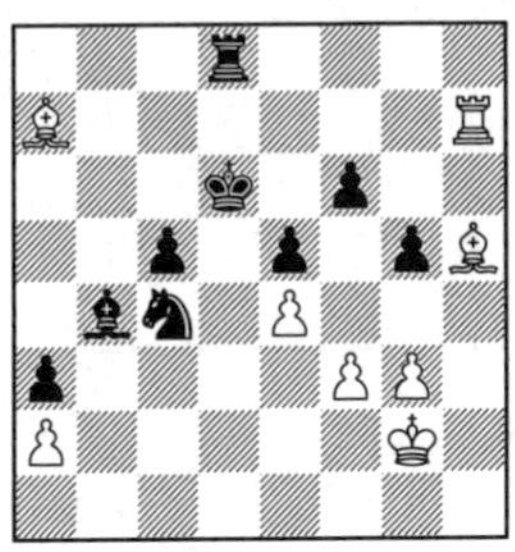

40...♗a5

This move complicates Black's win slightly, instead, he could have won easily with 40...♔c6−+, clearing the d-file for his rook.

41.♖f7 ♔c6 42.♖xf6 ♔b5 43.♔h3 ♖h8

Black provokes the move g3-g4, so that White's king cannot occupy that square, but it was much stronger for Black to play 43...♘e3 with the same idea. Then his rook penetrates to d1 or d2 (according to circumstances) and he wins easily.

44.g4 ♖a8

Black bases his hopes on White's stranded bishop on a7, but this provides his opponent with tactical chances.

His most reliable route to victory was to prevent all attempts at counterplay by playing 44...♘b2!, followed by the transfer of this knight to the d3-outpost.

45.♖f7 ♘d6 46.♖d7 ♔c6 47.♖h7 ♗b4 48.f4!

This is White's only practical chance.

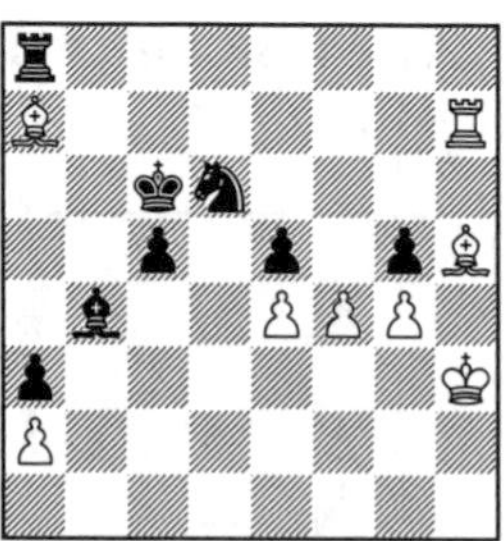

48...exf4

Black's win here was by no means easy to find. It seems at first sight that after 48...gxf4! 49.g5, White's passed g-pawn may be very dangerous, but in the line: 49...♖g8! 50.g6 ♘xe4! 51.♗f3 ♔d5–+ Black easily prevents its further advance.

49.e5 ♘c8

Things are not so clear in the variation 49...♘b5 50.e6 c4 51.♗f2∓

50.e6 ♔d6

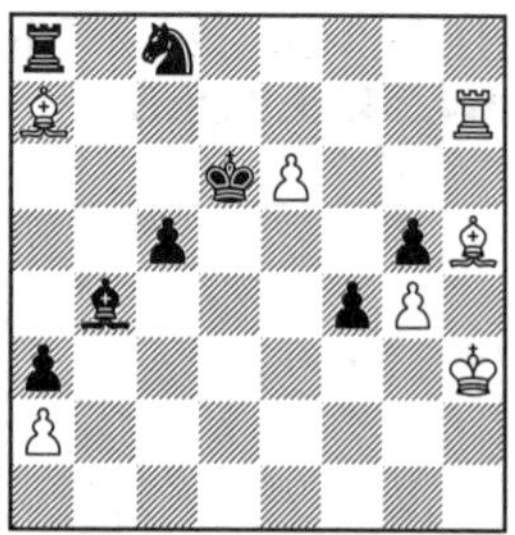

51.♖h8

White overlooks a chance of saving the game: 51.♗b6! ♘e7 (or 51...♔xe6 52.♗d8 ♖a7 53.♖h6 ♔e5 54.♗xg5 c4 55.♗f6 ♔e4 56.g5∞ and his g-pawn is as powerful as Black's passed pawns) 52.♗c7 ♔xc7 (52...♔xe6 53.♗f7 ♔d7 and now, in the variation 54.♗e5 c4 55.♗xc4 ♖c8 56.♗b3 ♗c3 57.♗a4 ♔e6 58.♗b3 ♔xe5 59.♖xe7 ♔d4∓, as well as after 54.♗c4 ♔xc7 55.♖xe7 ♔b6 56.♖e6 ♔a5 57.♖e5 ♖d8 58.♖xg5 ♖d4 59.♗e6, White has chances for a draw thanks to the presence of bishops of opposite colour) 53.♖xe7 ♔d6

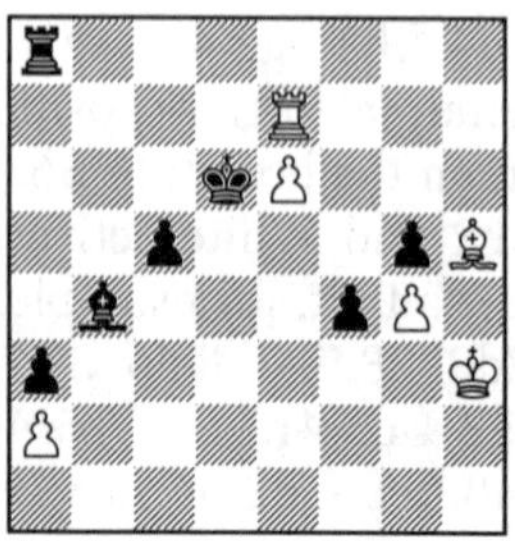

54.♖e8! Here, it looks as though the endgame with opposite coloured bishops after 54...♖xe8 55.♗xe8 ♔xe6 56.♔g2 is a draw after all: 56...♔e5 57.♔f3 ♔d4 58.♔e2 (but not 58.♗g6 ♔c3 59.♔e2 c4 60.♗f7 f3 61.♔xf3 ♔d3–+ and the c-pawn promotes) 58...c4 59.♔f3 ♗d6 60. ♗d7 ♔c3 61.♗b5! ♔d3 62.♗a6 and Black cannot make any progress. If 62...♔d4, then 63.♗c8= and if he advances his c-pawn, White's bishop goes to the b1-h7 diagonal.

It is correct for Black to play 54...♖a7!, keeping the rooks on the board. 55.♗g6 (If White advances his pawn further, Black will capture it, still keeping the rooks on the board. In the variation 55.e7 ♗c3 56.♔g2 ♗f6 57.♖a8 ♖xe7 58.♖a6 ♔e5 59.♖xa3 ♔d5-+ his passed pawns on c5 and f4 will settle the issue.) 55...♖c7 56.♔g2 ♔e5∓ and there is still some fight left.

51...♔xe6 52.♗g6 ♔d5 53. ♖d8 ♔c4 54.♗f5 ♖xa7 55.♖xc8 ♔c3 56.♖c6 ♔b2 57.♗e6 ♖e7 58.♔g2 ♖xe6. White resigned.

4 Sutovsky – Sakaev
Serbia 2009

1.e4 e5 2.♘f3 ♘f6 3.♘c3 ♗b4 4.♘xe5 0–0 5.♗e2 ♖e8 6.♘d3 ♗xc3 7.dxc3 ♘xe4 8. ♘f4 d6 9.0–0 ♘c6 10.a4!?

This is a very interesting and non-standard idea. White prepares to transfer his rook to the third rank.

10...h6

This is a useful multi-purpose move. Black can use the h7-square not only as an escape-hole for his king, but also as a retreat for his bishop on f5. It is also important that the h6-pawn restricts White's dark-squared bishop, depriving it of the g5-square.

11.a5

White radically prevents Black's plan of deploying his pawns on the dark squares. This is very reasonable from the strategic point of view, because White's dark-squared bishop obtains good prospects in the future.

11...a6

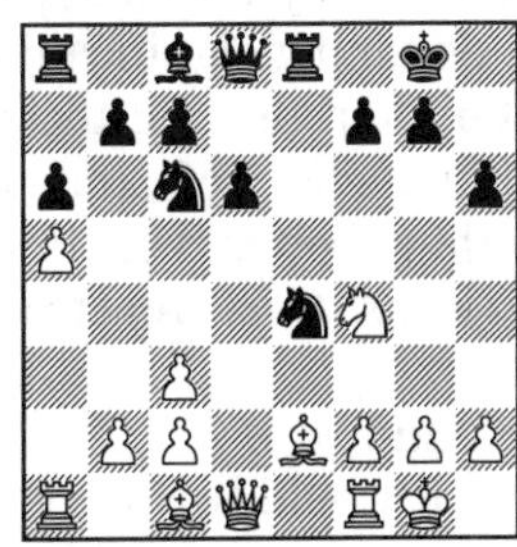

Black is obviously reluctant to play this move, but White was threatening to advance his a-pawn further, undermining the base of the enemy knight on c6.

Black's last move has some pluses too, because now White's a5-pawn will be permanently under attack by Black's knight.

12.c4 ♗f5 13.♖a3 ♘f6

Black's knight clears the e-file for future active operations.

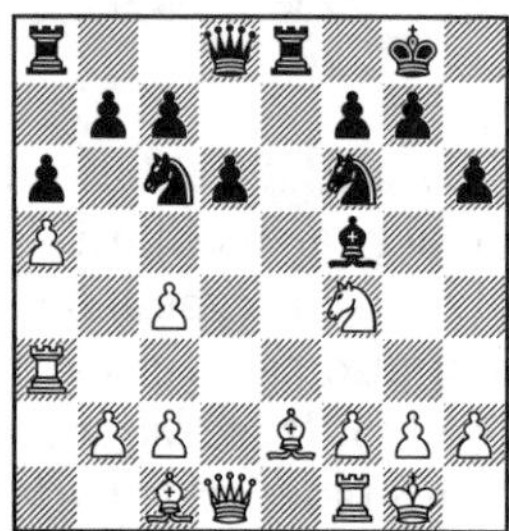

14.♖g3

White must play very precisely, because after the careless move 14.♘d5, Black has the resource 14...♗xc2!, winning a pawn.

After 14.♖e1, Black's most reliable move seems to be 14...♘b4 (14...♖e5 15.♖g3 ♘e4 16.♖e3 ♘f6 is also playable, but here White does not need to repeat moves and he can play for example: 17.♘d5⩱, obtaining significant compensation for the sacrificed a5-pawn.) 15.♘d3 ♘c6 and White has nothing better than 16.♘f4=, which leads to a repetition of moves.

14...♘e4

Here it would be too risky for Black to play 14...♘xa5. White has no immediately decisive continuation, but he has several attractive possibilities at his disposal:

15.b4 ♘c6 16.♗b2 ♘e5 17.♘h5± and Black will have serious problems on the a1-h8 diagonal, as well as on the g-file;

15.♘h5 ♗g6 (here 15...♘xh5 16.♗xh5 is bad, since the dark squares on Black's kingside are disastrously weak) 16.♘xg7!? (16.♘f4 ♗f5=) 16...♔xg7 17.♕d2 ♖xe2 18.♕xe2 ♘c6 19.♕d2⩱ and White has very good compensation for his minimal material deficit.

15.♖e3 ♘f6 16.♖g3 ♘e4 17.♖e3 ♘f6

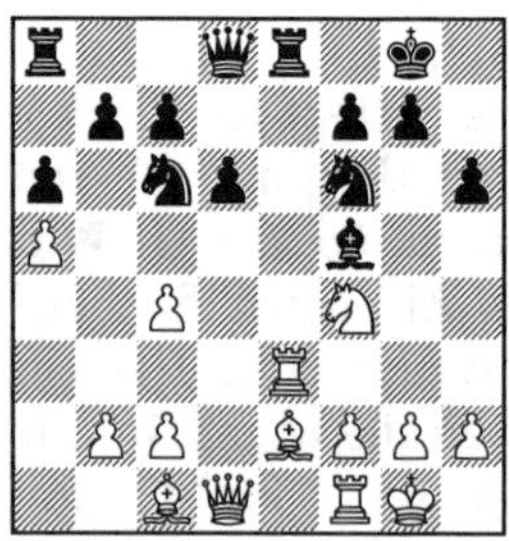

18.♖xe8

White is eager to continue the fight, although it would have been more prudent to repeat moves.

18...♕xe8 19.♖e1 ♘xa5

20.♘d5?!

This is a mistake. The correct move for White here is 20.g4!, and only after 20...♗h7 playing 21.♘d5, for example: 21...♘xd5

22.cxd5 b5 (Black cannot continue here analogously to the game with 22...♕e4 because of 23.♗d3 and White's d5-pawn is taboo.) 23.b4 ♘b7 24.c4 ♕d7 25.cxb5 axb5 26.♗f1 ♖e8 27.♖xe8 ♕xe8 28.f3 ♘d8=. White's initiative compensates for the sacrificed pawn, but no more than that and a draw seems to be the most likely outcome.

20...♘xd5 21.cxd5 ♕e4!

Emil obviously overlooked this move.

22.♗d2

Here, after long deliberation, White chose a very risky line in the hope of mating the opponent. Of course, not 22.♗d3 ♕xd5 and the bishop on f5 is protected.

White's objectively best move here was 22.♗xh6! and now:

after 22...gxh6, he continues with 23.♗d3 ♕f4 (if 23...♕xd5 24.♕h5⩱ with sufficient compensation) 24.g3 ♕g4 (after 24...♕g5 White plays 25.b4, comfortably regaining his piece) 25.♕xg4 ♗xg4 26.b4 ♗f3 27.bxa5 ♗xd5 28.♖e7 ♖c8 29.♗f5 ♔f8 30.♖xf7 ♔xf7 31.♗xc8= and this bishop and pawn ending is very sharp but should end in a draw;

Black's best line seems to be: 22...♕xc2 23.♕xc2 ♗xc2 24.♖c1 gxh6 25.♖xc2 c5 26.dxc6 ♘xc6 27.♗f3 ♖c8 (after 27...♘d4, White has the resource 28.♗xb7! ♖e8 29.♖c8!) 28.g3∓ and Black's pawn-structure is in ruins, so White has great drawing chances.

22...♕xd5 23.♗f3 ♕b5 24.♗c3 ♘c6 25.♗d5 ♖f8!∓

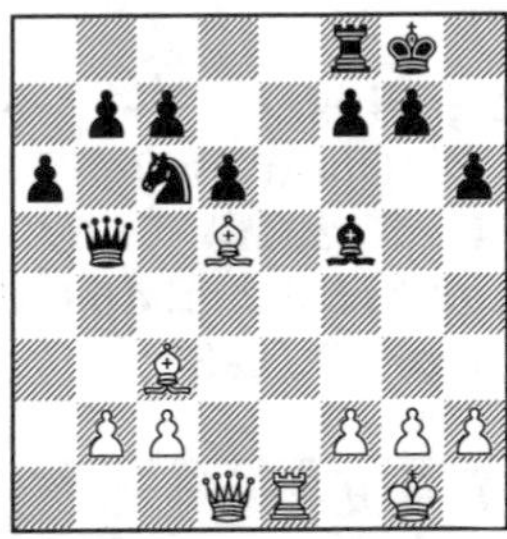

Black has consolidated his position. White's initiative can compensate for one of the sacrificed pawns, but not both, so Black has the advantage.

26.h3

White admits that his strategy was wrong. He could have rekindled his fading initiative with the not-so-obvious move 26.h4!, with the idea of advancing g2-g4-g5 with tempo. After, for example, 26...♗d7 27.♖e3 ♔h8 28.♖f3, he would have maintained some compensation, although not quite enough.

26...♔h7 27.h4 f6 28.f4 ♕c5 29.♔f1 ♘b4 30.♗b3 d5

Black begins his final offensive and his position is winning.

31.♕h5 ♗g6 32.♕g4 d4 33.

♗xb4 ♕xb4 34.♔f2 d3 35.h5 ♕c5 36.♔g3 ♗f5 37.♕d1 dxc2 38.♕d2 ♔h8 39.♔h4 ♕b6 40.♖e3 a5 41.g4 ♗h7 42.♖c3 c6 43.f5 a4 44.♗xa4 ♕xb2 45.♖xc2 ♕b1 46.♖c1 ♕b6 47.♗c2 ♖d8 48.♕f4 ♗g8 49.♖b1 ♕c5 50.♗e4 ♕e7 51.♖e1 ♖d4 52.♖e2 ♔h7 53.♕f3 ♕d6 54.♕g3 ♕b4 55.♗f3 ♖d3 56.♕c7 ♖xf3 57.♖e3 ♖f4. White resigned.

5 Zvjaginsev – Najer
Ohrid 2009

1.e4 e5 2.♘f3 ♘c6 3.♘c3 ♘f6 4.g3 ♗c5 5.♗g2 d6 6.d3 a6 7.♗e3 ♗xe3 8.fxe3

8...♘e7 9.♘h4 c6 10.♕d2 ♘g6 11.♘f5 ♗xf5 12.exf5 ♘f8 13.0–0–0 d5

14.♖hg1

This move prepares g3-g4, but is possibly imprecise, because White's rook is removed from the h-file, which will be opened.

It seems more logical to prepare the advance of the g-pawn with the help of the line: 14.♕e2!? h5 15.h3 ♕e7 16.g4

Now, Black is faced with a choice:

16...0–0–0 17.g5 ♘e8 18.h4 ♘d6 19.♕f2 ♕c7 (after 19...g6, White dominates the f-file, while if 19...f6 20.g6, Black's h5-pawn is isolated and might soon be lost) 20.f6 g6 21.d4∞ with a very complicated fight ahead;

16...g5!? (Black is trying to prevent his opponent from seizing additional space on the kingside.) 17.fxg6 fxg6 18.g5 ♘6d7 19.h4 0–0–0 20.♗h3 ♘e6 21.♖hf1 ♖hf8=. Black's pawns are placed on light squares and they perfectly restrict White's bishop. The game is equal.

14...h5 15.h3 ♕e7
(diagram)

16.e4?!

Now White's light-squared bishop remains in exile.

In fact, from the point of view

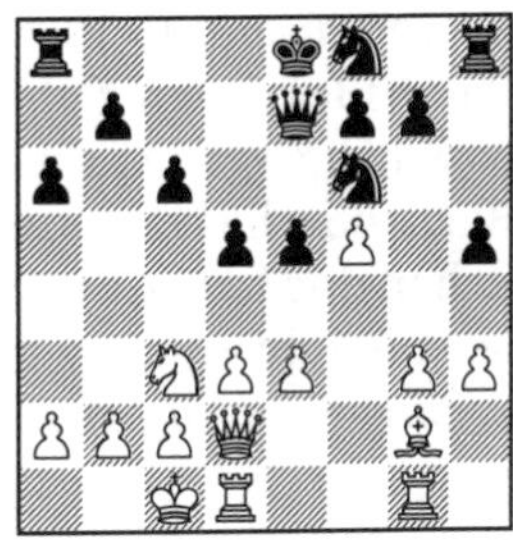

of correct pawn-strategy, White should try to advance d3-d4 and not e3-e4. It seems more logical for White to play 16.♗f3 ♘8d7 17.g4 hxg4 18.hxg4 0–0–0∞, with a complicated battle.

16...d4 17.♘e2 0–0–0 18.♗f3 ♘8d7 19.g4 hxg4 20.hxg4 ♘h7 21.g5 f6 22.g6 ♘g5∓

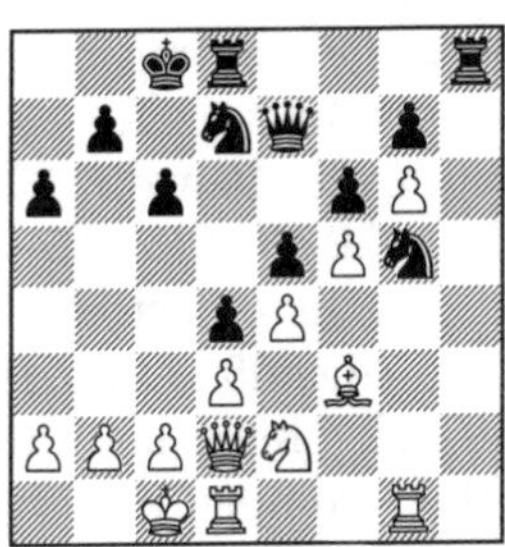

Black already has a slight but stable edge.

23.♗g2 ♖h2 24.♕e1 ♘b6 25.♘g3 ♕c5

Here 25...♔b8!? deserved consideration, preparing the advance of his c-pawn.

26.♘f1 ♖hh8 27.♘d2 ♕a5 28.a3 ♕b5 29.♕e2 ♘a4 30.♘b3

After 30.♘c4 Black would have possibly continued with 30...♕c5, followed by b7-b5.

30...a5 31.♖h1 ♘xb2 32.♔xb2 a4 33.♕d2 axb3 34.cxb3 ♔d7 35.♕c2 ♖a8 36.b4

Now the a2-g8 diagonal is open and White is able to organize sufficient counterplay along it.

36...♖xh1 37.♖xh1

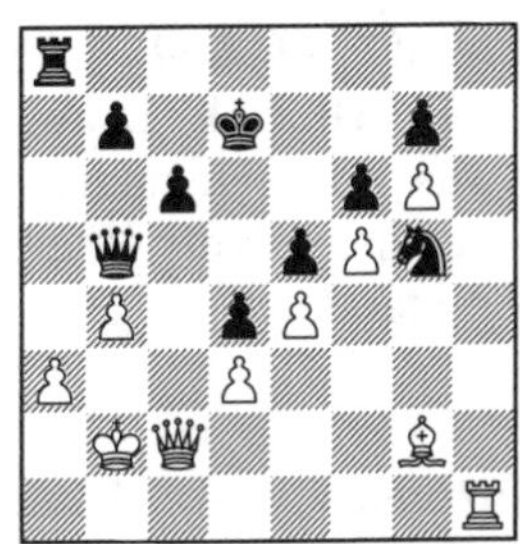

37...c5?!

Black should have kept the position closed.

He should have continued with 37...♔c7 38.♕b3 ♔b6, securely defending against White's only dangerous idea, based on playing ♖h1-h7. Neither side has any real chances of improving his position, so a positional draw appears on the board.

38.♕xc5 ♕xc5 39.bxc5 ♔c6 40.♗f1 ♔xc5 41.♗e2 ♔d6 42.♗d1 ♖c8 43.♗b3 ♔d7 44.♗c4 ♔d6

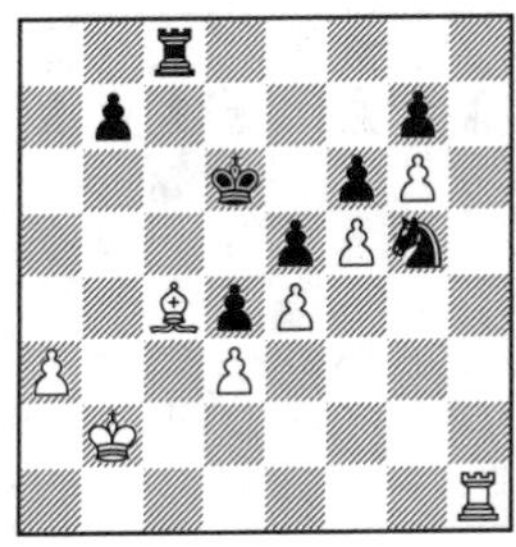

45.♗b3?!

White refuses to fight and this is not easy to understand. He had the opportunity to play 45.♔b3!, with the idea of penetrating with his king. After 45...♔c5 White plays 46.a4, followed by ♔a3, gradually squeezing Black's king.

45...♔d7 46.♗c4 ♔d6 47.♗b3 ♔d7 48.♗c4. Draw. This game was unspectacular; but it was nevertheless very interesting and non-standard.

6 Sutovsky – Kramnik
Baku (rapid) 2010

1.e4 e5 2.♘f3 ♘c6 3.♗b5 ♘f6 4.♘c3 ♘d4 5.♗c4 ♗c5 6.♘xe5 ♕e7 7.♘f3

7...d5 8.♗xd5 ♗g4 9.d3 0–0–0 10.♗g5 ♗h5!?

This is a common-sense move which is very useful to Black. He frees the g-file, clearing the way for a possible g7-g5. At the same time, Black now has the possibility of exchanging knights on f3, after which his light-squared bishop will no longer be attacked with tempo.

Besides this sharp move, it is good for Black to play here 10...h6!?, as we pointed out in the theoretical section of Chapter 8.

11.♔f1

After 11.0–0 Black can play 11...h6 12.♗e3 (it would be too risky for White to continue with 12.♗h4 g5 13.♗g3 ♗xf3 14.gxf3 h5 15.h3 g4→ and Black has a crushing attack) 12...♘xf3 13.gxf3 ♘xd5 and now the natural move 14.♘xd5 loses to 14...♕h4 15.♔g2 (15.♗xc5 ♖xd5 16.exd5 ♕h3–+) 15...♗d6 16.h3 c6 17.♘c3 f5–+ and Black's attack is decisive, while following 14.exd5 ♗xe3 15.fxe3 ♕xe3 16.♖f2 ♖he8↑ his initiative more than compensates for the sacrificed pawn.

White's best move here is 11.♗b3!, removing the bishop from possible attacks by the enemy rooks or knight. Black has no concrete operations in sight, so his best idea would be to protect the d5-square from invasion by the enemy knight with the move 11...c6! (11...♖he8 12.h3 h6 13.♗e3 ♘xf3 14.gxf3 ♗xe3 15.fxe3 ♘xe4 16.♘xe4 ♕h4 17.♔d2 ♖xe4 18.♕e1 ♗xf3 19.♕xh4 ♖xh4 20.♖hg1 g5 21.♗xf7±; 11...h6 12.♗e3 ♘xf3 13.gxf3 ♗xe3 14.fxe3 ♘d7 15.♔d2

♘e5 16.♖f1±).

It becomes clear now that Black has an excellent position in all variations: 12.♗h4 (12.0–0 ♗d6⩱; 12.♗e3 ♘d7 13.♗xd4 ♗xd4 14.♘e2 ♗xb2 15.♖b1 ♗a3⩱ and he has wonderful compensation for the pawn) 12...g5! 13.♗g3 (13. ♗xg5 ♖hg8 14.h4 h6–+) 13...♗xf3 14.gxf3 h5 15.h4 g4∓

11...c6 12.♗c4

Now Black has an additional resource, based on the advance of his b-pawn.

It was better for White to retreat his bishop a bit further with 12.♗b3, although after 12...♘xf3 (if 12...h6 White can retreat with 13.♗e3, where his bishop is very active in the fight for the central squares) 13.gxf3 h6 14.♗h4 ♗d4⩱ with the plan of g7-g5 followed by the transfer of the knight to e5, via the d7-square, Black obtains more than sufficient compensation for the pawn.

12...h6 13.♗h4

Here White should have played 13.♗e3, after which Black can choose between several promising possibilities for maintaining his initiative:

13...♘d7 14.♗xd4 ♗xd4 15. ♘e2∞;

13...♘xf3 14.gxf3 (but not 14. ♗xc5 ♕xc5 15.gxf3 ♘d7↑ and Black's knight will go to the e5-square with decisive effect) 14... ♗xe3 15.fxe3 b5 16.♗b3 b4 17.♘b1 ♘xe4 18.♘d2 ♘xd2 19.♕xd2 ♗xf3 20.♖g1 g5 21.a3∞;

it looks as though Black's best line here is: 13...♘g4 14.♗xd4 ♗xd4 15.♕d2 ♗xf2 16.h3 ♘e3 17. ♔xf2 ♘xc4 18.♕f4 ♕c5 19.♔e2 ♘xb2 20.♕f5 ♕xf5 21.exf5 ♖he8∓ and Black maintains a slight advantage, while after 22.♔f2 ♗xf3 23.gxf3 ♖e5 24.♖ab1 ♘xd3!? (24... ♖c5 25.♖xb2 ♖xc3 26.♖g1 ♖d5=) 25.cxd3 ♖xd3∓ he obtains three pawns for the piece and his pieces remain very active.

13...g5 14.♗g3 b5! 15.♗b3 b4 16.♘a4

Black is clearly better after 16.e5 bxc3 17.exf6 ♕xf6 18.♗e5 ♕f5 19.♗xd4 ♖xd4∓

16...♘xe4 17.♕e1 ♗xf3

Black would have a great advantage after 17...♘xf3 18.gxf3 ♗xf3 19.dxe4 ♗xh1 20.♘xc5 ♕xc5 21.♕e2 ♔b7 22.♔g1 f5∓ when Black has an extra exchange. The line he chooses in the game is even stronger.

18.dxe4 ♗e2 19.♔g1 ♗b5 20.c4

Or 20.h3 h5 21.♘xc5 ♕xc5 22.h4 ♘e2 23.♔h2 ♘xg3 24.fxg3 gxh4 25.c4 ♖hg8 26.cxb5 hxg3 27.♔h3 ♖g4!–+, with the unpreventable threat of ♕c5-e7.

20...♗xa4

It was much more practical, from the point of view of preventing future mistakes, to begin gaining material here with: 20...♘xb3 21.axb3 ♗xa4 22.bxa4 ♖he8–+ and Black would be totally dominant on the central files, with a very easy game.

21.♗xa4 h5

Black could maintain an overwhelming and easily realisable advantage with 21...♖he8, threatening to capture on e4, but Black obviously wants more than that.

22.h4 ♖hg8

After the immediate 22...f5! 23.hxg5 ♕xg5 24.♖h3 ♘f3! 25. gxf3 h4–+ his attack is decisive.

23.♗d1!

(diagram)

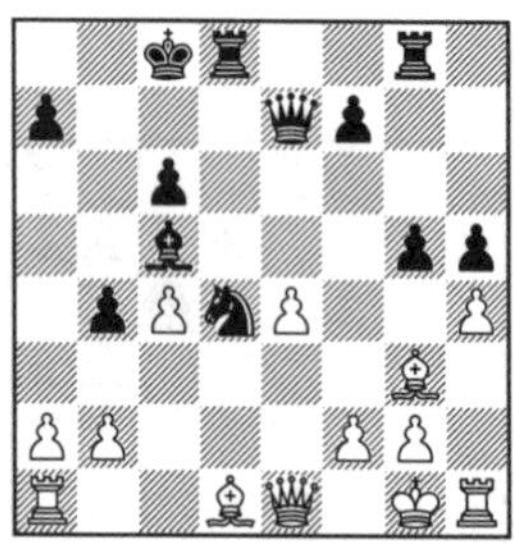

This is an excellent defensive resource for White. His bishop protects the f3-square against Black's knight-sorties and at the same time eyes the h5-square..

23...f5!

If Black had tried to play positionally, then after 23...g4 24.♔h2 ♖ge8 25.a3⇄ White would have organized counterplay.

24.hxg5

24...♖xg5

Black has played perfectly until now, but the position is still very sharp. He was evidently short of time (this was a rapid game) and inevitably mistakes start to appear...

It is very likely that in a game with a classical time-control Vladimir Kramnik would have found the line: 24...♕xg5! 25. ♖xh5 ♘e2! 26.♗xe2 ♕xg3 27.♕f1 ♖d2 28.♖e1 ♖g4!–+ with a decisive attack for Black.

25.♗h4 ♖dg8 26.♔f1

White could have gained some material here with 26.♗xg5 ♕xg5 27.♖h2 when continuation of Black's attack is far from easy.

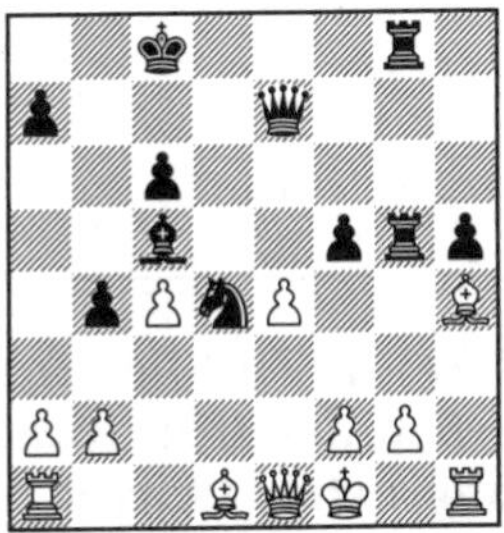

26...f4

Now White's f2-pawn, which is the main source of his worries, is reliably protected.

It was stronger for Black to play 26...fxe4 27.♗xg5 ♖xg5$\overline{\overline{\infty}}$, with sufficient compensation.

27.♗f3 ♕e5

This is an attempt to seek complications by all means. Black was not tempted to try to regain the exchange, because after 27...♘c2 28.♕d1 ♘xa1 29.♕xa1± he would end up a pawn down without any compensation.

28.♗xg5 ♖xg5 29.♕d1

It was stronger for White to play simply 29.♖d1±, with a clear advantage.

29...♔b7

Black should have assured himself of a queenside pawn-majority by playing 29...♘xf3 30.♕xf3 ♕xb2⇄ with excellent counterplay.

30.♖xh5

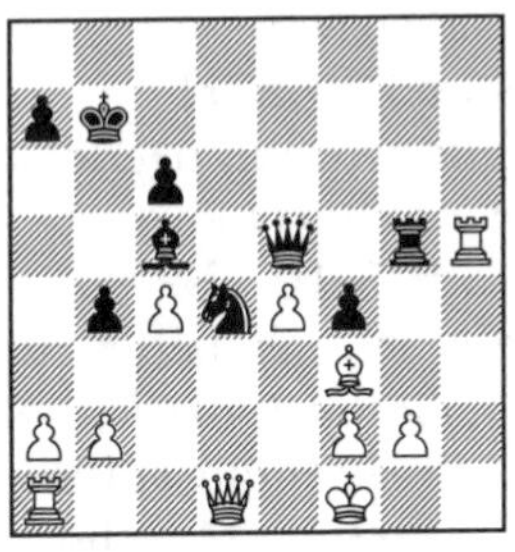

30...♖xh5

It is possible that in the heat of battle Black had overlooked that after 30...♘xf3 White has the intermediate check 31.♖h7+–

31.♗xh5 ♔b6 32.♕g4 ♕xe4 33.♖e1

It is stronger to play 33.♗g6!, not letting the enemy queen enter his camp. After 33...♕e5 34.♖e1 ♕h8 35.♕h5 ♕f6 36.♗e4+– White should gradually realise his advantage.

33...♕d3 34.♔g1 ♕d2 35.♖d1 ♕xb2 36.♕xf4 ♘e6 37.♕d2 ♕f6

38.♖b1?!

The correct plan here would be 38.♗g4! ♘d4 39.♖e1!±, freeing the d1-square for the bishop, from where it protects f3 and blocks the possible advance of Black's queenside pawns.

38...a5 39.a3?!

White probably overlooked his opponent's next move.

39...♕f5 40.♖b2

Here it was better to play 40.♖e1, although Black's counterplay is already quite sufficient.

40...♕xh5 41.axb4 axb4 42.♖xb4 ♔c7 43.♖b1 ♘d4

44.♕f4?

This is a blunder. After the natural move 44.♖e1± a complicated position arises, but White would still be slightly better.

44...♗d6 45.♕xd4 ♕h2 46.♔f1 ♕h1 47.♔e2 ♕xb1–+

Now it is all over and Black easily realises his extra bishop.

48.♕g7 ♔c8 49.♕g8 ♔b7 50.♕g7 ♗c7 51.♕f7 ♕e4 52.♔f1 ♕d3 53.♔e1 ♔b6 54.c5 ♔b7 55.♕e7 ♕d4 56.♔e2 ♕g4 57.♔e3 ♕xg2 58.♕h7. White resigned.

7 Nepomniachtchi–BuXiangzhi

Sochi 2009

1.e4 e5 2.♘f3 ♘f6 3.d4 ♘xe4 4.dxe5 d5 5.♘bd2 ♘xd2 6.♗xd2 c5 7.♗g5 ♕a5 8.c3 ♗e6 9.♗d3 ♘c6 10.0–0 h6 11.♗d2 ♕c7

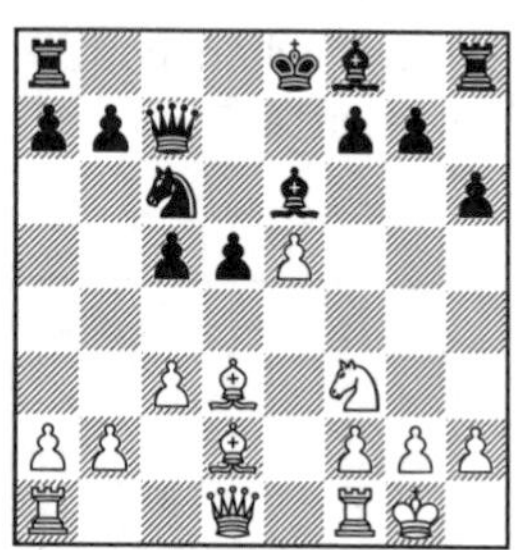

12.♖e1 ♗e7 13.♖c1 ♕d7 14.a3 0–0 15.b4 ♖fd8 16.♗e3 d4 17.cxd4 cxb4 18.axb4 ♘xb4 19.♗b1 ♖ac8 20.♕e2 ♖xc1 21.♗xc1 ♗d5∓ 22.♘d2

This knight is headed for the e4-square and the queen can go to h5, but White's actions on the kingside are too slow.

22...♖c8

It is high time that Black advanced his passed pawns, especially since after 22...b5! he would soon take control of the important e4-square. He exploits this in the variation 23.♘e4 ♗c4 24.♕h5 ♕xd4 25.♗e3 ♕b2 26.♘d6 ♗xd6 27.exd6 ♘d3 28.♗xd3 ♗xd3∓, ending up with an extra pawn.

23.♘e4

After 23.♘f1 Black can play 23...a5 24.♘e3 ♗e6 25.♗b2 ♘d5∓, securely blockading his opponent's centre pawns.

23...♕c6 24.♗a3! ♘c2 25. ♗xc2

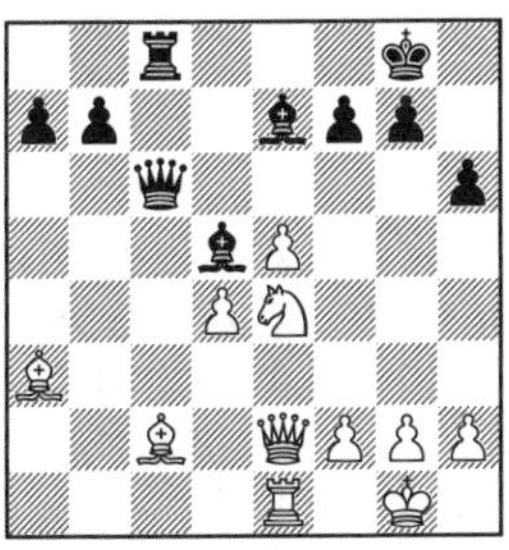

25...♕xc2

Black does not wish to risk anything. Although with 25...♗xa3 26.♗d3 a5∓ he could have maintained the advantage, he would need to precisely calculate various tactical complications, connected for example with a knight sacrifice on f6. Furthermore it would help White to exchange his dark-squared bishop, restricted by his pawns on d4 and e5.

26.♕xc2 ♖xc2 27.♗xe7 ♗xe4 28.f3 ♗c6 29.♖d1 ♗d5 30.♖a1

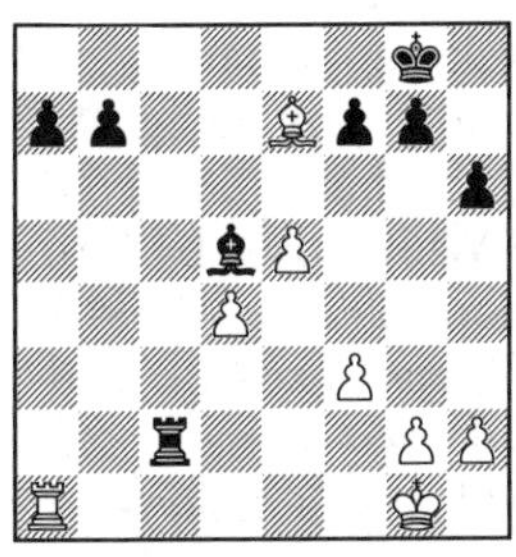

Black cannot keep his connected pawns and at the same time maintain the blockade on d5, so the draw is unavoidable.

30...♖c7 31.♗d6 ♖c4 32. ♖xa7 ♖xd4

The rest of the game is quite simple and of no interest..

33.♖a1 b5 34.♖b1 ♗c4 35. ♖b2 h5 36.♔f2 ♔h7 37.♔e3 ♖d3 38.♔e4 ♖d1 39.f4 ♖e1 40.♔f3 ♔g6 41.h3 ♖f1 42.♔e4 h4 43.♗c5 f5 44.♔e3 ♖e1 45. ♔f3 ♗d5 46.♔f2 ♖e4 47.g3 ♖c4 48.♗e3 b4 49.♗d2 ♖d4 50.♗xb4 ♖d3 51.gxh4 ♖f3. Draw.

8 Navara – Kramnik

Prague (rapid) 2008

1.e4 e5 2.♘f3 ♘f6 3.d4 ♘xe4 4.♗d3 d5 5.dxe5 ♘c5 6. ♘c3 c6 7.♘d4 ♗e7 8.0–0 0–0

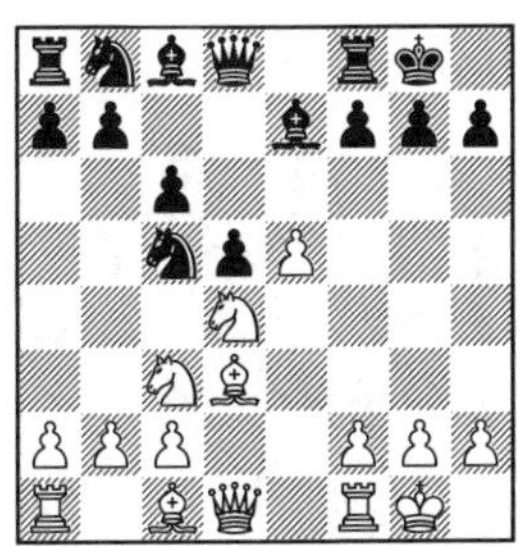

9.f4 ♘xd3 10.♕xd3 f5 11. ♘b3 ♘a6 12.♗e3 ♘c7 13.♘e2 b6 14.♘bd4 ♗a6 15.♕d2 ♕e8 16.c3 c5 17.♘f3 ♖d8∓ 18.♖fd1 ♘e6

(diagram)

19.a4

White does not have any active plan of his own, so all he can do is

prevent the development of Black's initiative. His last move is aimed at thwarting the advance of Black's queenside pawns.

19...h6

Black reminds his opponent that besides the queenside, there is a kingside where Black has excellent prospects based on the pawn-advance g7-g5.

20.a5

This move only helps Black. Instead, White should remain passive, playing for example: 20.b3.

20...♕b5 21.♘g3

21...bxa5

Here Black could have launched a decisive operation right away – 21...d4 22.cxd4 cxd4 23.♗f2 ♗b7∓ with an overwhelming advantage.

22.♕c2 g6

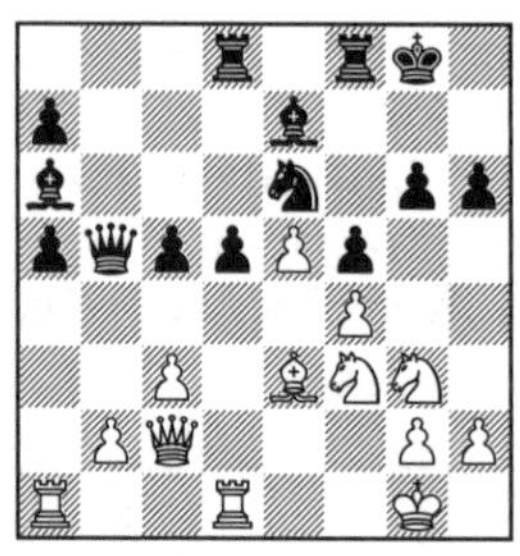

23.♕a4

Now White loses by force, but even after his relatively best line, 23.♖d2 ♕b6, Black cannot be prevented from advancing d5-d4, with decisive effect.

23...♕xa4 24.♖xa4 d4 25.cxd4 cxd4 26.♘xd4

It is hardly any better for White to play 26.♗d2 ♖d5–+ and Black dominates the entire board.

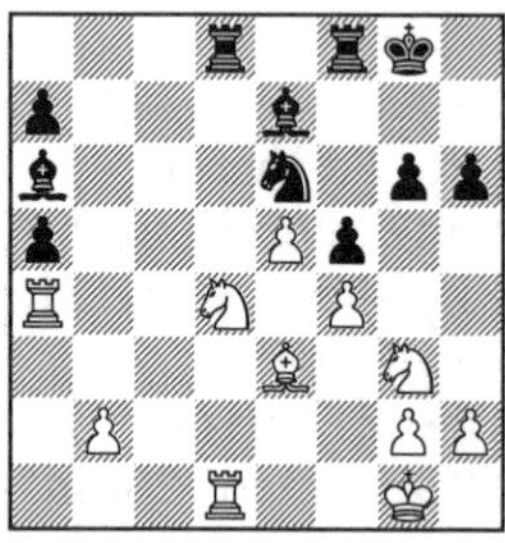

26...♗c5

Black could have maintained the deadly pin along the d-file with the move 26...♗b4!, after which White loses by force in all variations: 27.♖aa1 ♘xd4 28.♖xd4 ♗c5 29.♖xa5 ♗xd4 30.♗xd4 ♖xd4 31.♖xa6 ♔g7–+, or 27.♔f2 ♘xd4 28.♗xd4 ♗c4–+ followed by ♗c4-b3.

27.♖xa5 ♘xd4 28.♖xa6 ♘f3

29.♔f2 ♗xe3 30.♔xf3 ♖xd1 31.♔xe3

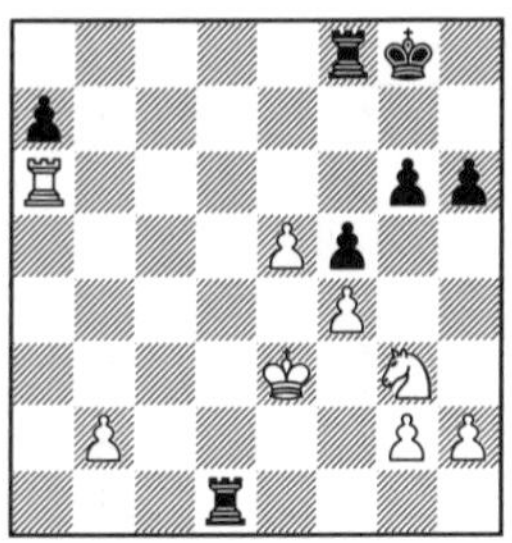

31...♖fd8

This was a rapid game, so it was quite natural that the opponents had practically no time left after move 30, so there were plenty of mistakes towards the end of the game.

It was stronger for Black to play 31...♔g7, maintaining the compactness of his pawn-chain on the kingside. White would need to play very precisely then in order to save the game.

32.♖xg6 ♔h7 33.♖a6 ♖8d3 34.♔f2 ♖1d2 35.♘e2 ♖d7 36. e6 ♖b7

After 36...♖c7, White can reply with 37.♔e3 ♖xb2 38.g4⇄ obtaining good counterplay.

37.♔e3 ♖dxb2 38.♘d4 ♖2b6

It is again a draw after 38... ♔g6 39.e7 ♔f7 40.♘xf5 ♖7b3 41.♔e4 ♖xg2=

39.♖xb6

The evaluation of the position would remain the same after 39.♖a5 ♔g6 40.♖e5 ♖e7=

39...♖xb6 40.e7 ♖b8 41. ♘xf5 a5

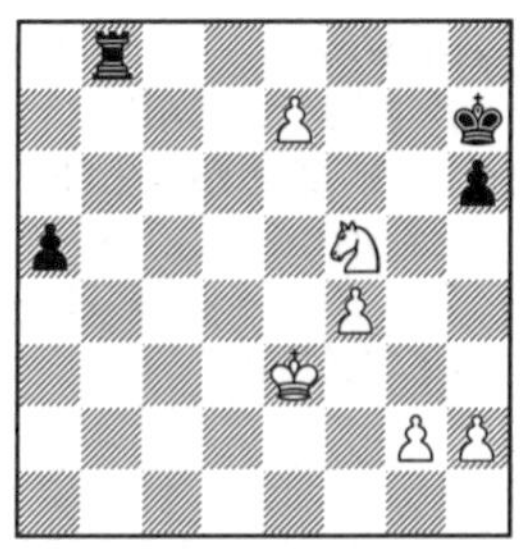

42.♘d4

This last move was imprecise. After 42.♔d4 a4 43.♔e5 a3 44. ♘d4 a2 45.♘c2 ♔g7 46.♔e6 ♖b6 47.♔d7 ♖b7 48.♔e6= there is an easy draw.

42...a4 43.♘c6 ♖e8 44.♔d4 ♔g7 45.♔c4 ♔f7 46.♔b4 ♖a8 47.♔a3 ♖a6 48.♘b4 ♖d6 49. ♔xa4 ♔xe7 50.♔b5 ♖d2 51.g4 ♖xh2 52.♔c5 ♔e6

53.♔d4?

This is White's decisive mistake. The move 53.♘d3= would have still drawn.

53...♖h4–+

Now it is all over, because White loses his most important pawn.

54.f5 ♔f7 55.♔e5 ♖xg4 56. ♘d5 ♖a4 57.♘c3 ♖b4 58.♘e4 h5 59.♘g5 ♔g8 60.f6 h4 61. ♔f5 ♖b5 62.♔g6 ♖xg5. White resigned.

9 Karpov – Larsen
Tilburg 1980

1.e4 e5 2.♘f3 ♘f6 3.d4 ♘xe4 4.♗d3 d5 5.♘xe5 ♘d7 6.♕e2 ♘xe5 7.♗xe4 dxe4 8.♕xe4 ♗e6 9.♕xe5

9...♕d7 10.0–0 0–0–0 11.♗e3 ♗b4 12.♘c3 f6 13.♕g3 ♗xc3 14.bxc3 h5=∞ 15.h4

This is an attempt by White to stop the development of his opponent's kingside attack. Black is ready to continue with g7-g5, followed by h5-h4, developing his offensive, after almost any move by White.

15...g5!

It would be sufficient for Black to equalize with the move 15...♖he8= followed by simplifying the position by exchanging the rooks along the e-file, but he wants to fight for more than a draw in this position.

16.f3

White hopes to restrict the enemy light-squared bishop with this move, but Black opens up the light squares anyway.

16...♖dg8 17.♖f2 ♕c6

The queen controls the long diagonal from this square, as well as restraining White's doubled pawns on the c-file.

18.♗d2 g4 19.f4 ♗c4!

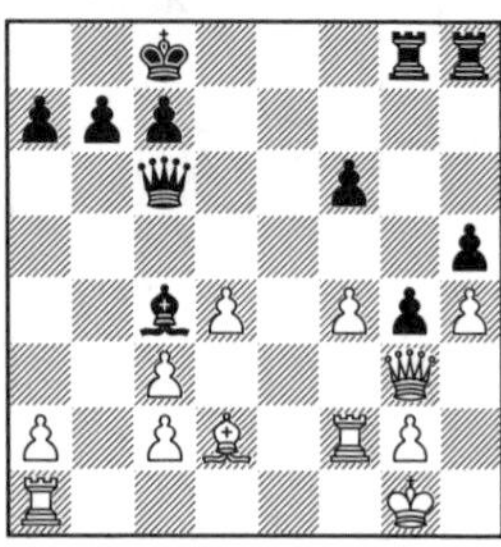

Black exerts powerful pressure on the light squares; meanwhile, White's queen and f2-rook are out of the game.

20.d5

This is a desperate attempt to free himself from the positional bind.

20...♗xd5 21.f5 ♖e8 22.a3 ♖e4 23.♖e1 ♖he8 24.♖xe4 ♖xe4 25.♔h2 ♕c5 26.♗f4 ♖e1 27.♗d2 ♖a1 28.♕e3 ♕d6 29.♖f4 b6 30.c4 ♗xc4 31.♕d4 ♕xd4 32.♖xd4 ♗b5

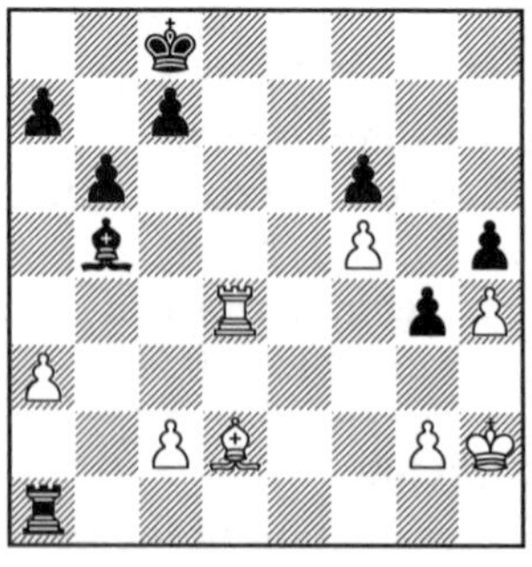

Now White also loses his a3-pawn.

33.♗h6 ♖xa3 34.♗g7 ♗d7

35.♖f4 ♖a5 36.♗xf6 ♗xf5 37.c3 ♗e6 38.♔g3 ♖d5 39.♖e4 ♔d7 40.♗e5 ♖d2 41.♔f4 ♖xg2 42.♔g5 ♖c2 43.♔xh5 g3 44.♗xg3 ♖xc3 45.♗e5 ♖c4 46.♖e3 ♗d5 47.♖a3 ♔e6 48.♗g3 ♔f5 49.♔h6 a5 50.♔g7 ♔g4 51.♔f6 a4 52.♖e3 ♗f3 53.♗e1 ♖c1 54.♖e7 ♔h3 55.♗d2 ♖c4 56.♖e3 ♔g2 57.♗e1 ♖c1 58.♗d2 ♖d1 59.♗c3 c5 60.♖e7 b5 61.♗e5 a3 62.♖h7 b4 63.h5 b3 64.h6 b2 65.♖g7 ♔f2 66.♗g3 ♔e3. White resigned.

10 Short – Shirov
Dubai (rapid) 2002

The following game was played with a fast time-control, so we should not be too critical towards the grandmasters. Even though they made many mistakes, the game was still tremendously interesting and creative, in the spirit of the old masters.

1.e4 e5 2.♘f3 ♘f6 3.♘xe5 d6 4.♘xf7 ♔xf7 5.d4 c5 6.dxc5 ♘c6 7.♗c4 ♗e6 8.♗xe6 ♔xe6 9.0–0

9...♔f7 10.♕e2 ♕e8 11.♖e1 d5

It is even stronger for Black to play 11...♕e6!, as was pointed out in the theoretical section of Chapter 16.

12.e5 ♘e4 13.♘c3 ♘xc3

14.bxc3

The defects of White's pawn-structure are more important than any initiative he can develop on the b-file.

It was preferable to continue with 14.♕f3 ♔g8 15.♕xc3 b6 16.♗e3⩱ Black is unable to castle artificially, while White's pawn-formation is really impressive and very effective.

14...♕e6 15.♖b1 ♖b8 16.♗e3 ♗e7

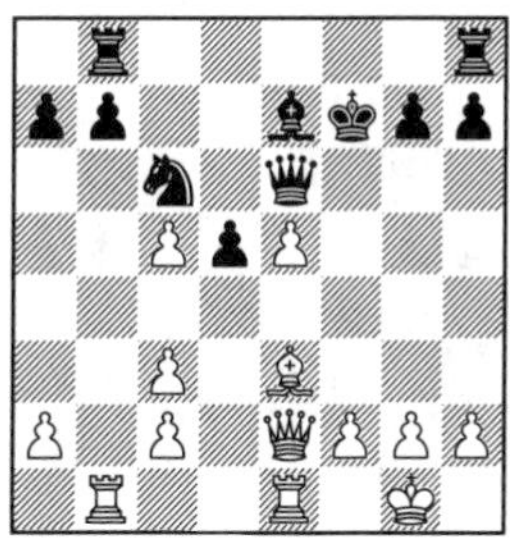

17.f4

Black has time now to bring his rook on h8 into play.

It would be much harder for

Black to prove any advantage after 17.♕f3 ♔g8 18.♖ed1 and here he could maintain an edge only after the not–so-obvious move 18...♕f7! (The endgame after 18...♘xe5 19.♕xd5 ♕xd5 20.♖xd5 ♘c6 21.♗f4 ♖d8 22.c4 ♔f7 23.♖xb7= seems to be approximately equal; White has too many pawns and his pieces are very active.) 19.♕h3 (After 19.♕xd5 ♕xd5 20.♖xd5 ♔f7∓ Black's king will occupy the e6-square and White's pawn-chain e5-f4 will soon be undermined with the move g7-g5.) 19...♘xe5 20.f4 ♘c6 (After the attractive variation: 20...♘c4 21.c6 ♘xe3 22.♖xb7 ♘xd1 23.♖xb8 ♗f8 24.♖xf8 ♔xf8 25.♕c8 ♔e7 26.♕c7= White draws by perpetual check.) 21.♕d7 h5! Black secures the h6- and h7-squares for his rooks and his king, as appropriate. 22.♖xb7 ♖xb7 23.♕xb7 ♕e6 24.♗f2 ♖h6 25.♖e1 ♕f7∓ Black has consolidated his forces and his extra piece (ignoring the tripled pawns) will surely tell.

17...♖hf8 18.♗d4 ♔g8 19.♖f1

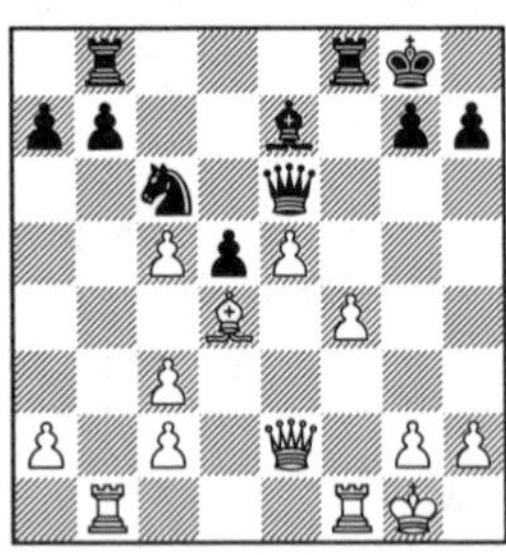

19...g5

This is a very risky move! It would be much more solid for Black to opt here for 19...♖f7, bringing his other rook to the f8-square and carrying out the undermining move g7-g5 only later.

20.fxg5 ♗xg5

After 20...♖xf1 21.♖xf1 ♗xg5 Black's king would be much more comfortable.

21.♖xf8 ♔xf8 22.♕h5

If 22.♕d3 Black would play 22...♔g8 23.♕g3 ♕g6 24.e6 ♗h6∓, parrying White's attack.

22...♕g6 23.♕f3 ♔g7 24.♕xd5

There will be no repetition of moves, because after 24.♖f1 ♖d8 25.♖b1 Black will play 25...b6! 26.cxb6 ♘xd4 27.cxd4 axb6∓

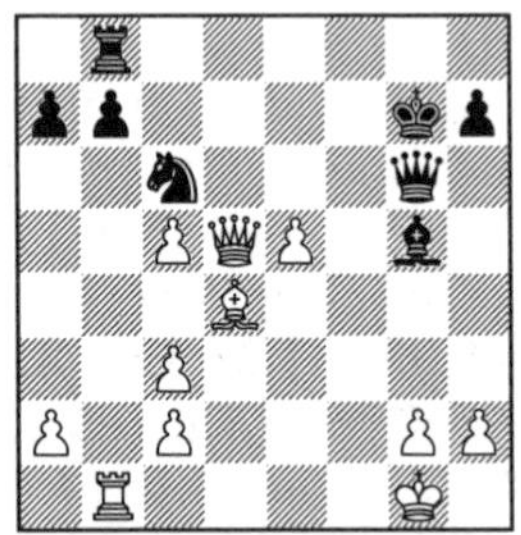

24...♕xc2!

This is a very important move and the best for Black in this position! Now, his king remains completely exposed, but with the help of his queen he succeeds in creating dangerous counter-threats.

25.e6

It was correct for White to play here 25.♖f1! ♘xd4 26.cxd4 ♕d3 27.♖f7 ♔h8 28.g3 ♗e3 29.♔g2 ♗xd4 30.♔h3!∓ and there would be plenty of fight left, but Black would still be much better.

25...♔g6

Black was winning with 25...♔h6! 26.♖e1 ♘xd4 27.♕xd4 ♖d8 28.♕e5 ♖f8 29.♕d4 (after 29.♖e2, Black's simplest solution would be the counter-attacking move 29...♖f5!–+) 29...♕d2–+ and after the exchange of queens his road to victory would be quite easy.

26.♖f1

It was more tenacious for White to defend with 26.♖e1, although the position arising after 26...♘xd4 27.cxd4 ♖f8 28.♕e4 ♕xe4 29.♖xe4 ♖f4 30.♖xf4 ♗xf4 31.♔f2 ♔f6–+ seems to be winning for Black in any case.

26...♕d3?

Black overlooks the possibility of concluding the fight in spectacular fashion with 26...♘xd4! 27.cxd4 ♖f8!–+

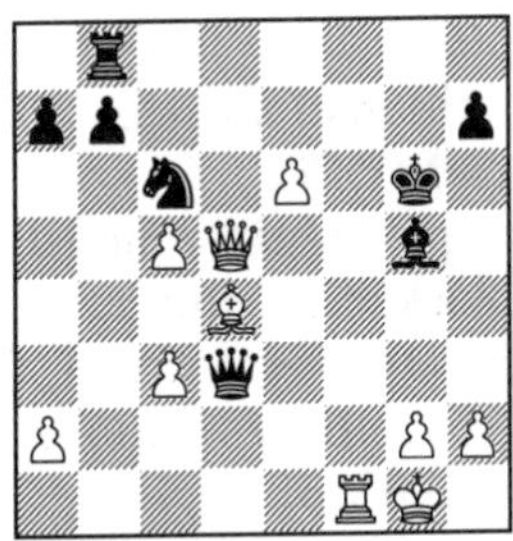

27.♕d7?

White misses a win in turn, although it is a rather complicated one: 27.h4! ♗e3 (or 27...♗xh4 28.e7! ♘xd4 29.♕d6 ♔h5 30.♕e5 ♗g5 31.♕xb8+– and Black has no dangerous checks) 28.♔h2 ♕xf1 (after 28...♘xd4 29.h5 ♔h6 30.♖f6 ♔g7 31.♕e5+– there is no defence against White's deadly discovered check) 29.h5 ♔h6 30.♗xe3 ♔g7 31.♕g5 ♔f8 32.♗f4+– and Black is helpless.

27...♗e3

It all ends in a draw in the variation 27...♘xd4 28.♕f7 ♔h6 29.cxd4 ♕xd4 30.♔h1 ♕e4 31.♖f3 ♖d8 32.h4! ♗xh4 33.♖f6 ♗xf6 34.♕xf6 ♔h5 35.♕xd8=

28.♗xe3 ♕xe3 29.♔h1 ♖f8

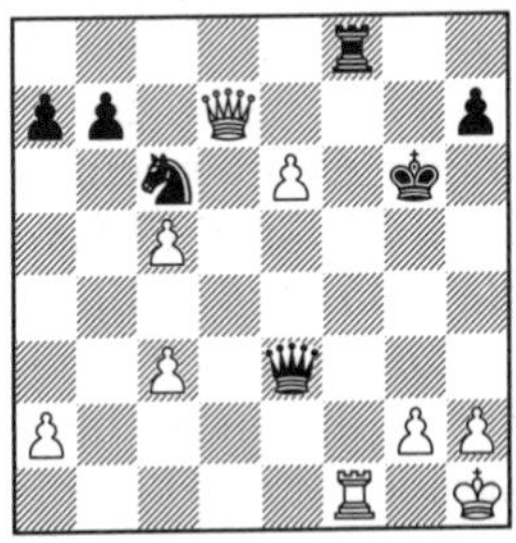

30.♖g1

Most probably, both players were blitzing and they overlooked the simple but very beautiful variation 30.♕f7! ♖xf7 31.exf7+–

30...♘e5 31.♕d6 ♖f6

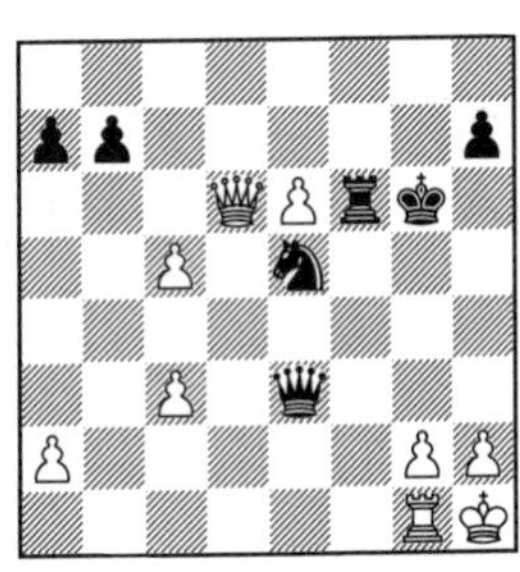

32.h3

If the opponents had had enough time, the game might have ended in brilliant and rather unusual fashion after 32.e7! ♘g4 33.♕g3 ♕xg3 34.e8=♕ ♔g5

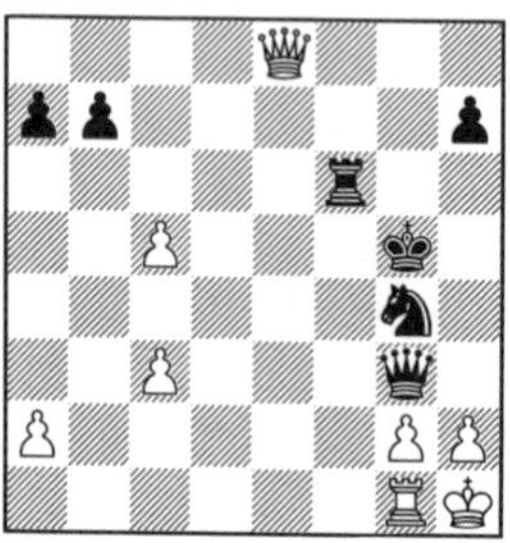

35.♕g8 (or 35.hxg3 ♖h6 mate!) 35...♖g6 36.♕xg6 hxg6 37.hxg3 ♘f2 38.♔h2 ♘g4= and Black's lone knight gives perpetual check.

32...♘d3 33.♕d5 ♘xc5 34. e7 ♕xe7 35.♕g8 ♔h6 36.♖d1 ♘e4. White resigned. This game was full of mistakes, but it was very impressive and beautiful!

11 Topalov – Kramnik
Linares 1999

1.e4 e5 2.♘f3 ♘f6 3.♘xe5 d6 4.♘xf7 ♔xf7 5.♘c3 c5 6. ♗c4 ♗e6 7.♗xe6 ♔xe6 8.d4 ♔f7

9.dxc5 ♘c6 10.♕e2 ♕d7 11.♗e3 dxc5 12.f4 ♖e8

We mentioned in the theoretical part that it is preferable for Black to continue here with 12...♘d4! 13.♗xd4 cxd4 14.0–0–0 ♖c8 15.e5 ♖xc3 16.bxc3 ♗a3 17.♔b1 ♘d5 18.♔a1 ♕c6∓

13.e5

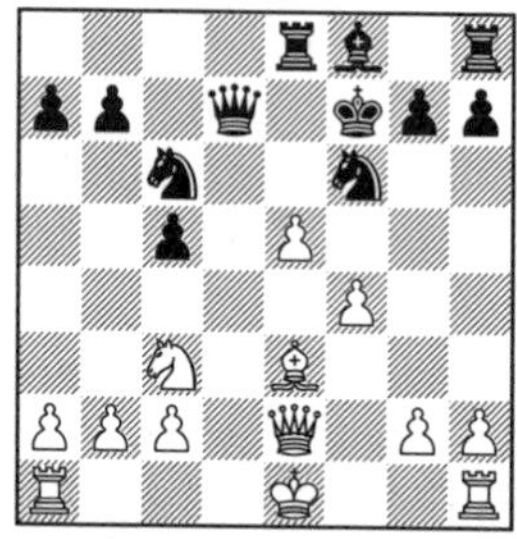

13...♘g4

He should answer an attack with a counter-attack, by playing 13...♘d4. The almost unbelievable variation 14.♗xd4 (Black is better after 14.♕c4 ♕e6 15.♕xe6 ♔xe6 16.♗xd4 cxd4 17.♘b5 ♘d5 18.♘xd4 ♔f7∓) 14...♕xd4 15.♕f3 g5 16.♘e2 ♕b4 17.♔f2 ♘e4 18. ♔e3 ♘f6 19.♔f2= leads to a draw by repetition of moves.

14.♖d1 ♕f5

The queen has occupied a very good blockading square.

Here 14...♕e6 would fail to 15.f5! ♕xe5 16.♕c4 ♔f6 17.♘d5±

15.0–0 h5!

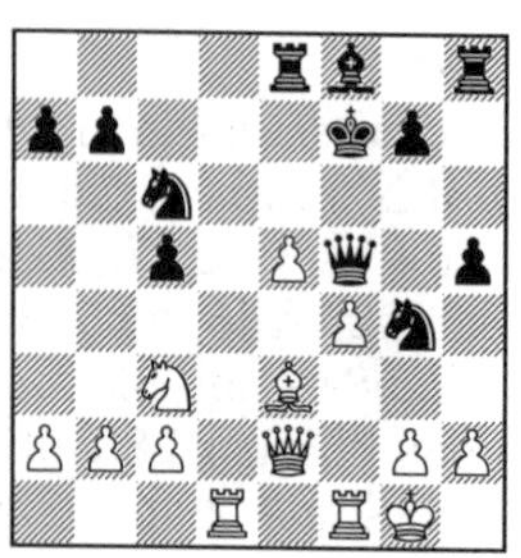

He continues with his blockading strategy and radically prevents the possibility g2-g4. Meanwhile, Black's rook might enter the game at some point via the h6-square.

16.♗c1

White avoids exchanges, but pays a hefty price for this, since his bishop goes back to its initial position.

It was better for him to choose 16.h3 ♘xe3 17.♕xe3 ♖h6 18.♘e4 ♔g8 19.c3⩱, maintaining good compensation for the piece.

16...♘d4 17.♕c4

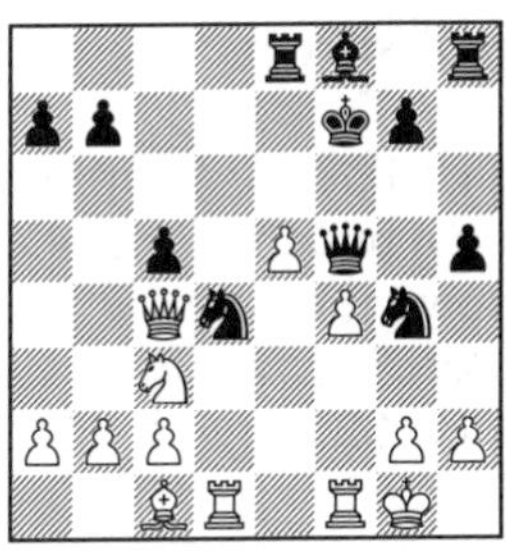

17...♔g6

Black overlooks the possibility of exchanging queens: 17...♕e6! 18.♕d3 ♕a6!∓. It is easy to miss a move like this, particularly when calculating several moves ahead. 19.♕e4 ♕c6 20.♕xc6 (White cannot really avoid the exchange of queens, because after 20.♕d3 Black has the resource 20...c4!–+) 20...bxc6 21.h3 ♘h6–+ and he is very close to victory.

18.h3 ♘h6 19.♘b5

It is no better for White to opt here for 19.♗e3 ♘xc2 20.♗f2 ♘d4∓, because Black's pieces come into play, while White's two pawns are insufficient to compensate for the sacrificed piece.

19...a6!

This is an excellent move for Black. His c5-pawn considerably restricts his own bishop and it is very useful for him to have it removed.

20.♘xd4 cxd4 21.♕xd4 ♖c8

Now White has not two, but three pawns for the piece.

It is stronger for Black to continue with 21...♕xc2! 22.♖f2 (it is no use for White to play 22.f5 ♘xf5 23.♕f4 ♗c5 24.♔h2 ♖hf8 25.♖d2 ♘e3!–+) 22...♕c6 (Black also maintains his advantage with the move 22...♕f5∓) 23.♕d3 ♘f5 24.♗e3 ♗e7 25.♖c2 ♕b5 26.♕e4 h4∓ Black has set up a secure blockade on the kingside and White's position is terrible.

22.♕b6 ♔h7 23.♕xb7 ♖xc2 24.♗e3

Gobbling pawns cannot end well for White: 24.♕xa6 ♗c5 25.♔h1 ♘g4!–+ and he is helpless against ♘g4-f2.

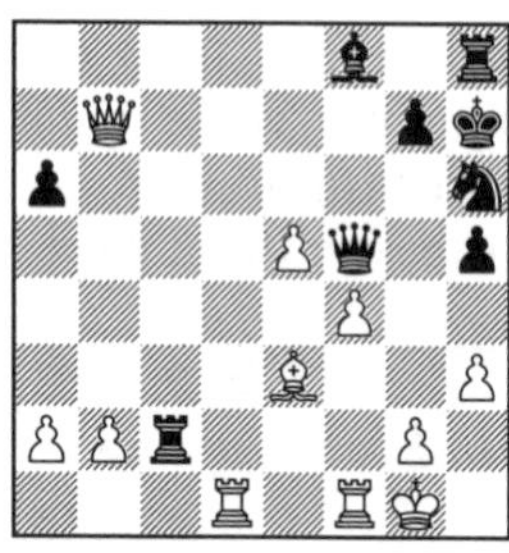

24...♕g6

This was played instantly but, as is often the case in open positions, there was a stronger continuation: 24...♖e2! 25.♗a7 ♕e4 26.♕xe4 ♖xe4∓ and Black would have still maintained a slight edge.

25.♖c1 ♖xc1

After 25...♖e2, the bishop does not need to flee: 26.♕f3! (or 26. ♖fe1 ♖xe1 27.♖xe1 ♘f5 28.♗f2 ♗e7 29.e6∞) 26...♖xb2 27.f5 ♘xf5 28. ♕xf5 ♖xg2 29.♔h1 ♖g3 30.♕xg6 ♔xg6 31.♖c6 ♔h7 32.♗c1 ♗b4=, with a draw.

26.♖xc1 ♘f5 27.♗f2 h4

Black frees the h5-square for his queen.

After 27...♗e7 28.♖c6 ♕f7 29. ♕xa6 ♖d8 30.♕e2± White is even better, because he already has four pawns for the piece and his connected pawns on the queenside are particularly dangerous.

28.♖c7

The game should end in a draw after 28.♖c6 ♕h5 29.♕xa6 ♗e7 30.♔h2 ♖d8 31.♖c8 ♕d1 32.♕e6 ♘g3 33.♗xg3 hxg3 34.♔xg3 ♕d3 35.♔g4 ♕e2 36.♔g3=

(diagram)

28...♘g3!

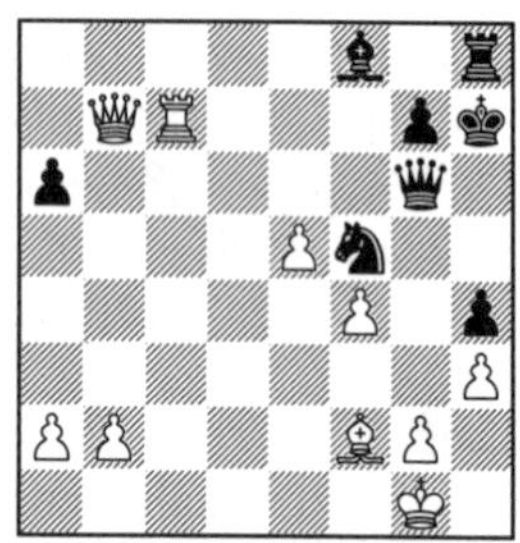

This is a prudent decision for Black, because after 28...♕h5 29. ♕e4± White is totally dominant and Black's pieces might never come into play.

29.♔h2 ♘f1 30.♔g1 ♕b1 31.♗xh4 ♗c5

This is not a stupid move. It is the simplest route to a draw for Black.

After 31...♘g3, White has the additional possibility of 32.♔f2!?, sharpening the game.

32.♖xc5. Drawn, in view of the line: 32...♘g3 33.♔h2 (or 33.♔f2? ♘e4–+ and White loses his rook) 33...♘f1.

12 Ovetchkin – Motylev

Sochi 2004

1.e4 e5 2.♘f3 ♘f6 3.♘xe5 d6 4.♘c4 ♘xe4 5.♘c3 ♘xc3 6.bxc3 g6 7.d4 ♗g7 8.♗d3 0–0 9.0–0

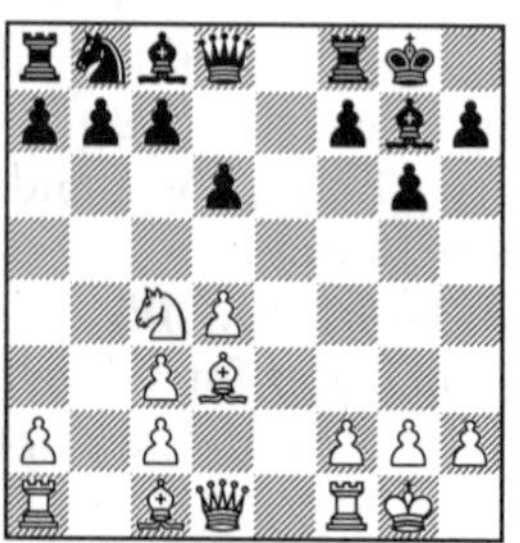

9...♘d7 10.f4 ♘b6 11.♘e3 ♘a4 12.♗d2 ♘b2 13.♕f3 ♘xd3 14.cxd3 f5 15.d5 ♗d7 16.♖ab1 ♖b8∓

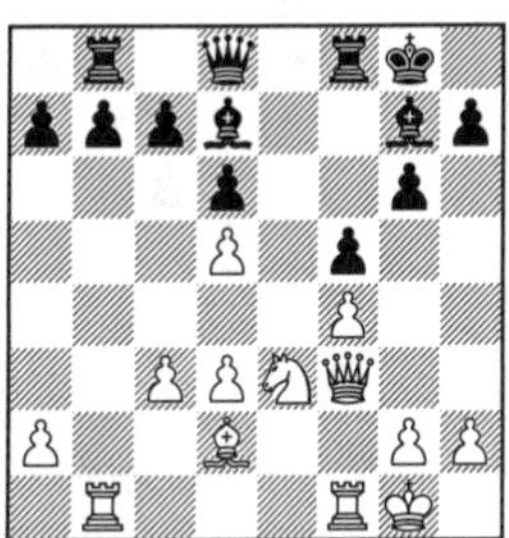

There will inevitably be a clash of pawns on the queenside and the position will then be opened up. Black has the bishop-pair, which will give him some advantage.

17.♕f2 c5

It is more or less the same after 17...c6, since White can hardly maintain the tension in the centre.

18.dxc6 bxc6 19.♘c4 ♕c7 20.♗e3 c5 21.♕d2 ♗c6 22.♗f2 ♖fe8 23.♖fe1 ♖xb1 24.♖xb1 ♗a8!

Black is already threatening ♕c7-c6!

25.♖e1 ♖xe1 26.♗xe1 ♗f6!

Black cannot create any direct threats yet, so he simply improves his position. His bishop on f6 continues to exert pressure along the long diagonal, forcing White to protect his c3-pawn. In addition, it has some new functions now, depriving White's bishop of the h4-square and his queen of e7, a possible invasion-square on the e-file.

27.♕e2 ♔f7

Black's king is brought closer to the centre in anticipation of the forthcoming endgame. He is already planning to exchange the strongest pieces on the board.

His other chances of realising his advantage would require him to keep the queens on the board and in that case it would be more natural for Black to play 27...♔g7.

28.♔f1 ♗e7

Black's bishop protects the d6-pawn in order to release the queen, which has been carrying out that task until now.

29.♕b2 ♕b7 30.♕xb7 ♗xb7

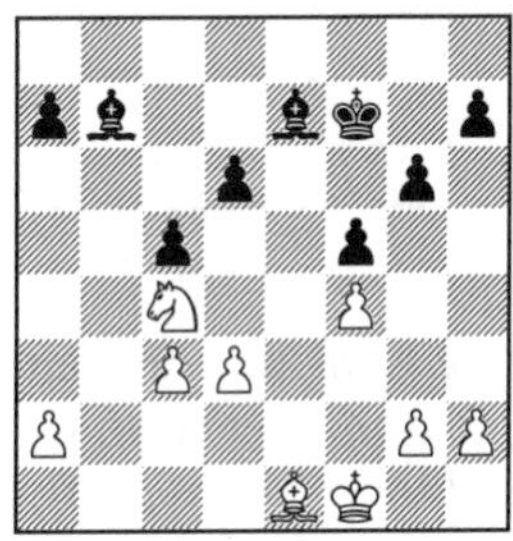

There are three pawn-islands each on the board: on the a-file, on the c- and d- files and on the f-, g- and h- files. This type of game, particularly since there is play on both flanks, is clearly in Black's favour, because he has a powerful bishop-pair. In addition, White's f4-pawn is terribly misplaced. If it had been on f3, he would have considerably more chances of a successful defence.

31.♘a5 ♗a8 32.c4 ♗f6 33.♗d2 ♔e6 34.♘b3 ♔d7 35.♔f2 ♔c6

Black makes several non-committal moves with his king before the time-control, following the endgame rule "don't hurry if you don't have to...".

It looks much more purposeful for him to transfer his bishop somewhere, for example to e6, or to play h7-h6, followed by g6-g5.

36.♗e3 ♗e7 37.d4 cxd4 38.♗xd4 a6 39.g3 ♗d8 40.♔e3 ♔d7

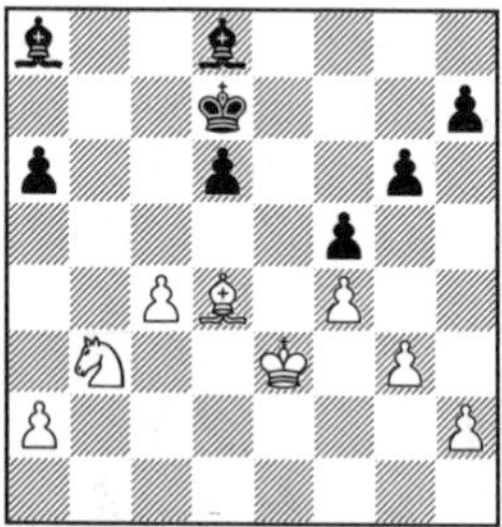

41.h4?

White loses patience and that is the reason why so many endgames of this type are lost!

The move g6-g5 is not a threat yet and it will be much easier for Black to attack the g3-pawn than the h2-pawn, so White's last move is a decisive mistake. He should have played the waiting move 41.♘d2, depriving Black's bishop of the e4-square in the process.

41...♗e4 42.♘d2

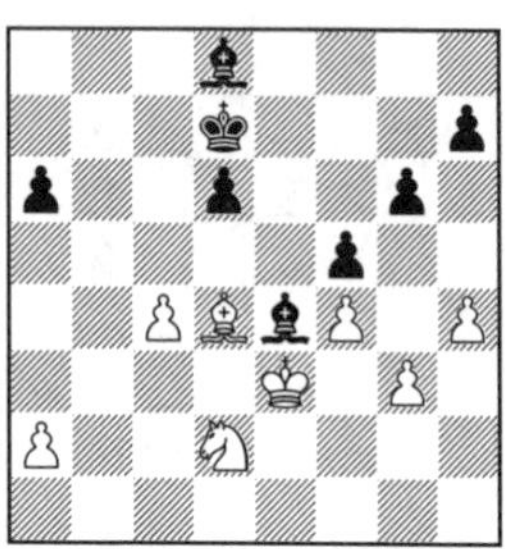

42...♗c2

Black could have created great problems for his opponent with the straightforward move 42...d5, opening the route for his king into the enemy camp via the light squares. On the other hand, from the practical point of view, the rule "don't hurry" is quite applicable here as well. White cannot do anything meaningful at the moment, so Black always has the pawn-break d6-d5 in reserve. Accordingly, Alexander Motylev's decision at this point can only be applauded!

43.♘f3 ♗a5 44.a3 ♗d1 45.♘g5 h6 46.♘f3

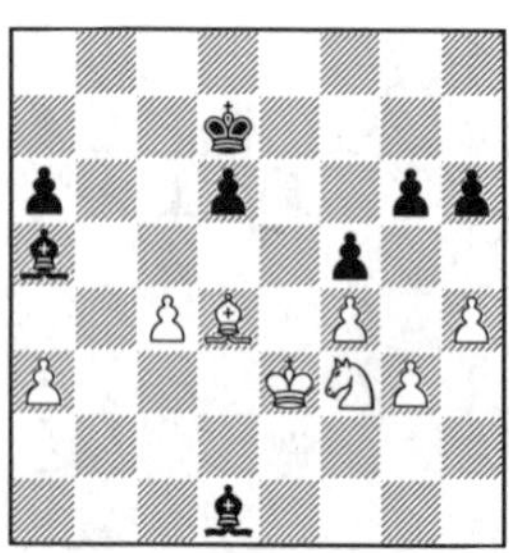

46...♗xf3!

Do you see the consequences of the move 41.h4? The bishop and pawn ending would have been a draw with a white pawn on h2 and Black would need to try to break with the move d6-d5.

47.♔xf3 ♗e1

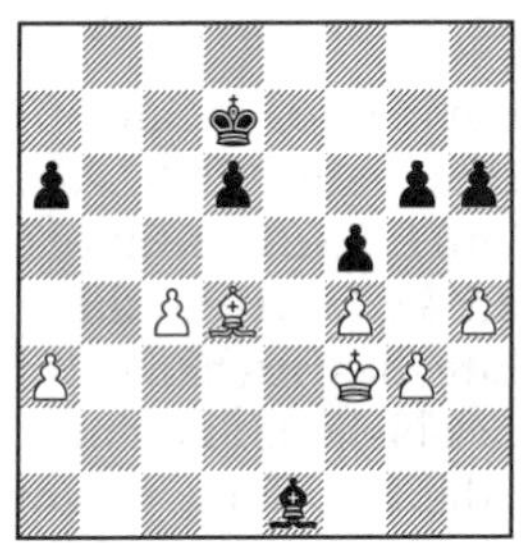

48.h5

White is in agony, because he is helpless against ♔d7-c6, followed by d6-d5. His king is stuck with the protection of his g3-pawn and in the king and pawn ending after 48.♗f2 ♗xf2 49.♔xf2 ♔c6 50.♔e3 ♔c5 51.♔d3 d5 52.cxd5 ♔xd5–+ Black is victorious, since his king gains the opposition – one of the most typical resources in all king and pawn endings.

48...gxh5 49.♗g7 ♔c6 50.♗xh6 ♔c5 51.♗f8 a5 52.♗e7 a4 53.♔g2 ♔xc4

Black wins even faster after 53...♗c3 54.♔h3 ♗b2 55.♔h4 ♗xa3 56.♗f6 ♗c1 57.♔xh5 a3–+ followed by ♗c1-b2 and the a-pawn promotes.

54.♗xd6 ♗c3 55.♔h3 ♗f6 56.♗f8 ♔b3 57.♗d6 ♗b2 58.♔h4 ♗xa3 59.♗e5 ♗b4 60.♔xh5 a3 61.g4 ♗c3 62.gxf5 a2. White resigned.

13 Carlsen – Kramnik

Nice (rapid) 2008

1.e4 e5 2.♘f3 ♘f6 3.♘xe5 d6 4.♘c4 ♘xe4 5.♘c3 ♘xc3 6.bxc3 g6 7.d4 ♗g7 8.♗d3 0–0 9.0–0

9...♘d7 10.♕f3 ♘b6 11.♘e3 c5 12.dxc5 dxc5 13.a4 ♗d7 14.a5 ♘a4 15.♕xb7 ♘xc3 16.♗d2 ♗e6∓ 17.♗xc3 ♗xc3 18.♖a4

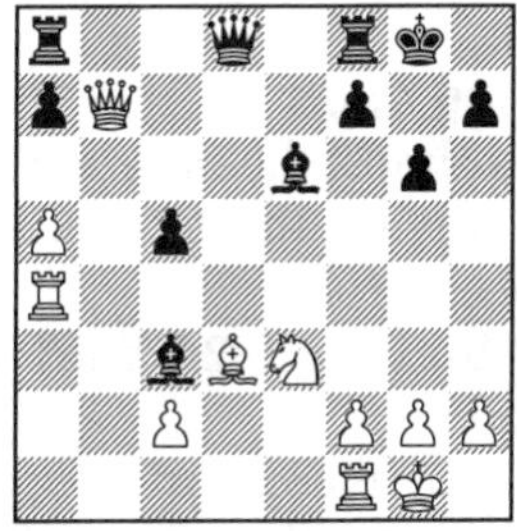

18...♕d7

Black wishes to play a slightly better endgame without any, even minimal, risk.

Another good option was 18...♗d4 (with the threat 19...♖b8 20.♕xa7 c4) and here:

White loses after 19.♗e4 ♖b8 20.♕xa7, in view of 20...♕d6! (Black is threatening 21...c5-c4) 21.♘c4 (or 21.c3 ♗xe3 22.fxe3 f5 23.♗f3 ♖f7–+ and he traps the enemy queen) 21...♗xf2 22.♔h1 ♗xc4 23.♖xc4 ♖fd8 followed by 24...♖d7–+;

Or 19.♗c4 ♗xc4 20.♘xc4 ♕f6∓ with a clear advantage for Black.

19.♕xd7 ♗xd7 20.♖a3 ♗b4 21.♖aa1 ♗c6

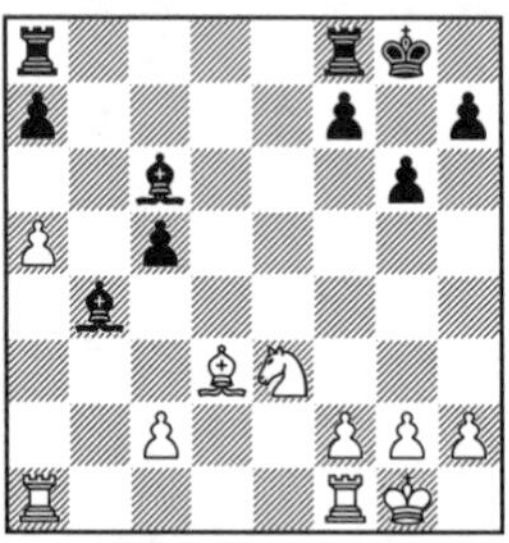

This situation is quite typical, because in a fight on both sides of the board, Black has the advantage, thanks to his powerful bishop-pair.

22.a6 ♖ad8

It is almost the same after 22...♖fd8, leaving the b8-square for his queen's rook.

23.♖fc1 ♗c3 24.♖ab1 ♖fe8 25.♗b5

Black's pieces are active all over the entire board, so White is trying to free himself from the positional bind. He will need to acquiesce to the eventual loss of his a6-pawn, which is likely after the exchange of the light-squared bishops.

25...♖e6 26.♗c4

(diagram)

26...♖e4

It is stronger for Black to play here 26...♖ed6! 27.♖d1 ♗d4∓, controlling the board and preventing

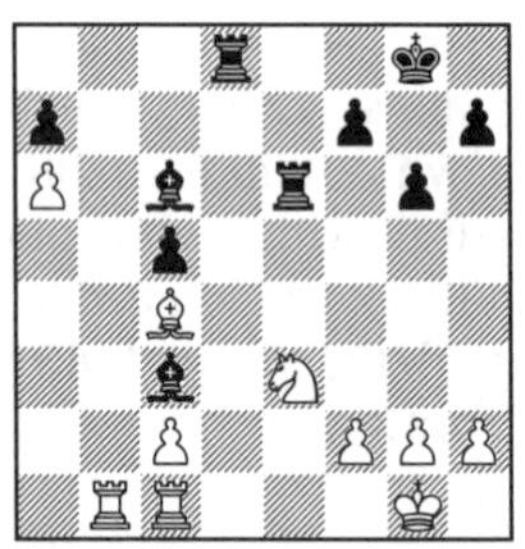

the exchange of a pair of rooks, which facilitates White's defence.

27.♖d1 ♖xd1 28.♖xd1 ♗d4 29.♗d5 ♗xd5 30.♘xd5

White has exchanged one of the black bishops and thus diminished the attacking potential of Black's pieces, but White's a6-pawn is defenceless now and Black could have exploited this.

30...♖e2

Black could have created great problems for his opponent with some delicate manoeuvres of his rook: 30...♖e5! 31.♘f4 ♖f5 32.g3 ♖f6 33.c3 ♗e5 34.♘d5 ♖xa6∓, winning a pawn and preserving excellent winning chances.

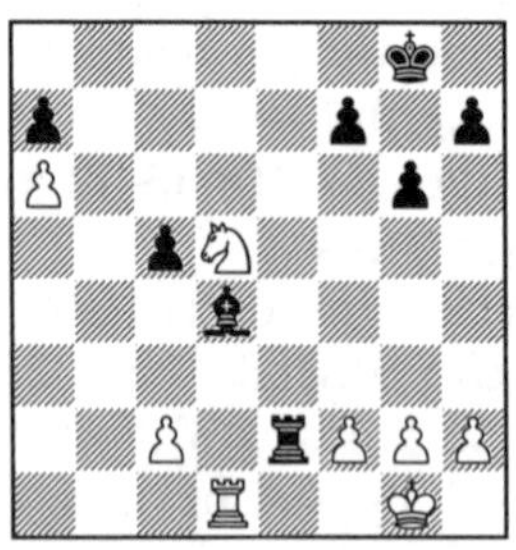

31.c3?

Now, the fight becomes very tense again.

It was an easy draw after 31.♘e3! ♗xe3 32.fxe3 ♖xc2 33.♖d7=

31...♗xf2 32.♔f1 ♖a2 33. ♖b1 ♗h4

Black is unable to keep his bishop on the a7-g1 diagonal: 33... c4 34.♖b8 ♔g7 35.♖c8. The c5-square is under attack by White's rook and the rook and pawn ending after 35...♗b6 36.♘xb6 axb6 37.♖xc4= is a draw.

34.g3

It is more precise for White to play 34.♖b8 ♔g7 35.♘c7, activating his pieces and attacking the enemy a7-pawn.

34...♗g5 35.h4 ♗d2 36.♘f6 ♔g7 37.♘e4 ♗h6 38.♖b7 ♖xa6 39.♘xc5 ♖c6 40.♘e4 ♖e6 41. ♘c5 ♖e5 42.♘d7 ♖e3 43.♖xa7 ♖xg3 44.♘e5 ♔f6

After 44...♖e3 45.♖xf7 ♔g8 46.♖e7 ♗f4 47.♘c6 ♖xc3 48.♘d4 ♖c4 49.♘f3 ♗g3 50.h5 gxh5∓ a very unusual position with doubled black h-pawns arises and here Black can continue to torture his opponent for a long time.

45.♘xf7 ♗e3 46.♖b7

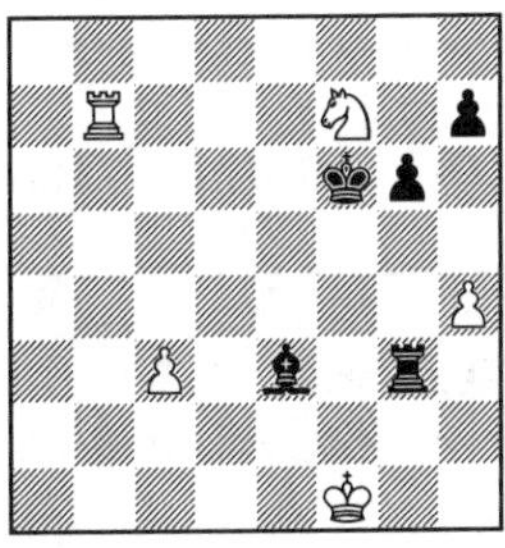

46...h5

White's pawn is fixed on the h4-square and is likely to be captured soon. From the strategic point of view, this move is strong, but it has a definite drawback. Suddenly, White succeeds in exploiting the vulnerability of the g6-pawn.

Black would have preserved decent winning chances with the line: 46...♖h3 47.♖b4 ♗c1 48.♘d6 ♔e5∓

47.♔e2 ♗f4

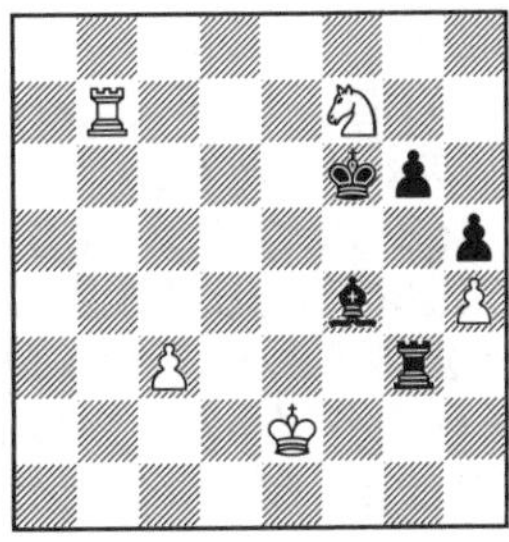

48.c4

White could have drawn immediately with 48.♘h8! ♗e5 49. ♖b6 ♔f5 50.♖xg6 ♖xg6 51.♘xg6 ♔xg6 52.♔f3= and later the white king goes into the corner and there, as is well-known, Black can only stalemate it!

48...♖e3

Black would have more practical winning chances after 48... ♔f5 49.♖b6 ♖e3 50.♔f1 ♖c3 51. ♘h8 g5 52.hxg5 ♔xg5 53.♖g6 (White loses after the careless move 53.♘f7 ♔g4–+ and Black's h-pawn becomes unstoppable.) 53...♔f5 54.♖c6 ♖c2 and there will soon arise an endgame of rook and bishop against rook, in which the defending side must play precisely to draw.

49.♔f1 ♖c3

50.♘h8!

Finally, a bit late but not too late, Magnus Carlsen demonstrates the correct idea to save the game.

50...♖xc4 51.♖b6 ♔f5 52.♘xg6 ♗g3 53.♔g2 ♔g4 54.♖b2 ♖e4 55.♖a2 ♗d6 56.♖a5 ♖e2 57.♔f1 ♖e6 58.♖g5 ♔f3 59.♖f5 ♔g4 60.♖g5 ♔h3 61.♔f2 ♖f6 62.♔e2 ♗g3 63.♔e3 ♖e6 64.♔f3 ♖f6 65.♔e3 ♖e6 66.♔f3. Draw.

14 Berg – Pe.Nielsen
Helsingor 2009

1.e4 e5 2.♘f3 ♘f6 3.♘xe5 d6 4.♘c4 ♘xe4 5.♕e2 ♕e7 6.♘e3 ♘f6

7.b3?!

We have shown in the theoretical section that White should prefer 7.♘c3 here.

7...♘c6 8.♗b2 ♗e6 9.g3 d5!

White has developed his pieces a bit awkwardly on the flank and Black counters this with straightforward play in the centre. Only nine moves have been played, but Black already has the advantage.

10.♗g2 0–0–0 11.d4

Look at White's bishop on b2 – a sorry sight!

11...h5!

This is a very useful move, because Black keeps the option of gaining additional space on the kingside with the move h5-h4, as well as using the g4-square as a base for his minor pieces.

12.♘d2 g6

The move 12...h4 would not create any concrete threats, so Black prefers to complete his development.

13.0–0–0 ♗h6 14.♖he1

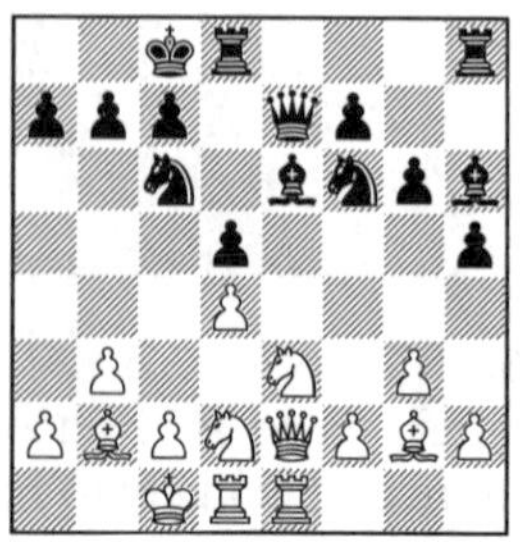

14...♕b4

Black attacks the d4-pawn and at the same time frees the e-file for his rook. However, in most variations White's d4-pawn is taboo, therefore instead of this move, bringing his last piece into action with 14...♖he8 was worth considering.

From a human point of view, the position is rather unclear after 14...♗xe3 15.♕xe3 (it would be anti-positional for White to play 15.fxe3 ♗g4∓ when Black would have very easy play on the light squares) 15...♘g4 16.♕e2 ♘xh2 17.f3 h4 18.g4 h3 19.♗h1 ♕d6 and in many variations Black must sacrifice a piece (in fact, he has no alternative, since his knight on h2 is trapped...). A possible continuation is 20.♕f2 ♖de8 21.♖e2 ♘xg4 22.fxg4 ♗xg4∓ and Black's three connected passed pawns are stronger than White's piece, mostly because the bishop on b2 is rather isolated from the real action.

15.a3

After 15.c3 ♕a5 16.♔b1 ♖he8∓ Black maintains some piece-pressure.

15...♕b6

16.♔b1

This is a useful prophylactic move, because White's king retreats to a safe place, away from the c1-h6 diagonal.

The d4-pawn is not hanging yet, so he does not need to protect it with the move 16.♕d3. Furthermore, after 16...♘g4 17.♘xg4 ♗xg4 18.♗f3 ♗f5 19.♕c3 ♗g7, the d4-pawn really would be defenceless and after 20.♘f1, Black wins with 20...♘xd4! 21.♖xd4 c5–+

16...♖he8

The pawn is taboo: 16...♘xd4? 17.♕d3 c5 18.b4!+– and White wins a piece.

17.♕d3?!

It was much more resilient to play 17.f4!, neutralizing the enemy bishop on h6. It would be rather difficult for Black to exploit the vulnerability of the light squares in the centre – e4-f5-g4 – and after, for example, 17...♗g4 18.♘f3 ♘e4 19.♕f1 ♗xf3 20.♗xf3 f5∓, Black's advantage would be only minimal.

17...♘g4

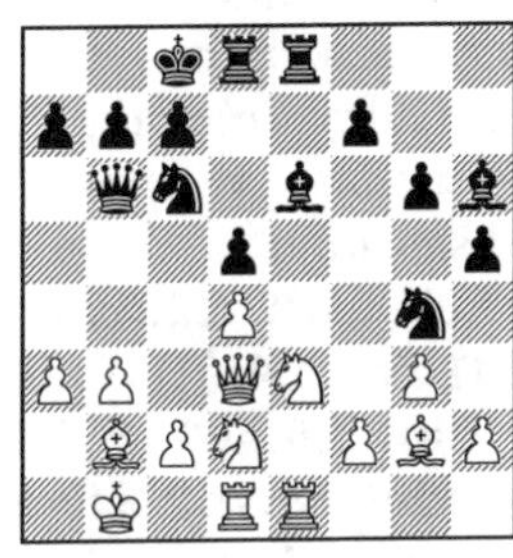

18.♘xg4

White could have tried to complicate matters a little with the line: 18.♘xd5!? ♗xd5 19.♖xe8 ♗xg2 20.♘c4 ♕a6 21.♕e2 ♗d5 22. f3 ♘f6 23.♖xd8 ♘xd8 24.♖e1∓ and although Black would have the edge, White would have counterplay.

18...hxg4

Black's g4-pawn restricts White's possibilities considerably, because now he does not even have the f3-square for his knight.

19.b4

White wants to place his knight on b3, but proves unable to do this.

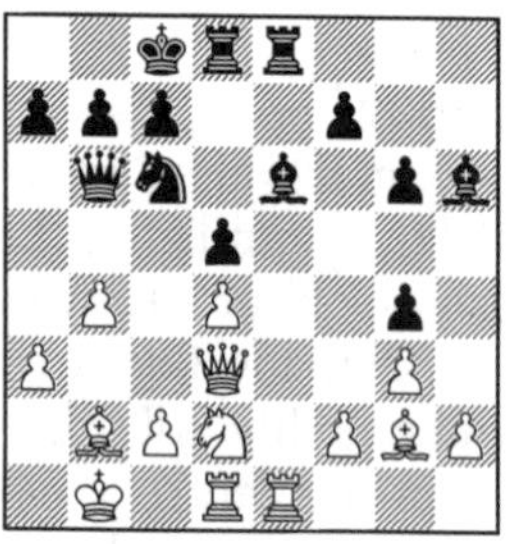

19...a5!

With his last move Black provokes new weaknesses in his opponent's camp.

20.bxa5 ♘xa5–+

White has numerous weak squares, bad pieces and a terrible pawn-structure, so he is already beyond salvation.

21.♕c3 ♗xd2 22.♖xd2 ♘c4 23.♖dd1 ♖d6 24.♗f1 ♘xb2 25. ♕xb2 ♖h8 26.♖e3 ♕xb2 27. ♔xb2 ♖xh2 28.♖d2 ♗f5 29.c4 ♗e4 30.♗e2 f5 31.c5 ♖d8 32. ♗d1 ♖dh8 33.♔c3 ♖h1 34.♗c2 ♖c1 35.♔b2 ♖hh1 36.♗xe4 fxe4 37.♔b3 ♖b1 38.♖b2 ♖xb2 39. ♔xb2 ♖d1 40.♔c3 ♔b8 41.a4. White resigned.

15 Reinderman–Kasimdzhanov

Wijk aan Zee 1999

1.e4 e5 2.♘f3 ♘f6 3.♘xe5 d6 4.♘f3 ♘xe4 5.♕e2 ♕e7 6.d3 ♘f6 7.♗g5 ♘bd7 8.♘c3 ♕xe2 9.♗xe2

9...h6 10.♗h4 g5 11.♗g3 ♘h5 12.♘d5 ♔d8 13.h4 g4 14.♘d2 ♘b6 15.♘f4 ♘xg3 16. fxg3 ♗g7 17.0–0–0

Or 17.c3 ♖e8 18.d4 ♗d7 19.♖f1 ♗h8∞, followed by c7-c6 and ♔d8-c7. The endgame is double-edged, but Black has a powerful bishop-pair and is not worse at all.

17...♖e8 18.♖de1

18...♗d4!?

Black seeks complications by

penetrating with his bishop into White's camp. The position would have been approximately equal after 18...♗d7 19.♖hf1 ♗e5 20.c3 c5 21.♘c4 ♔c7=

19.♖hf1 ♗e3 20.♘h5 f5 21.♘g7

Black will counter 21.c3 with 21...c5, not allowing his opponent to advance d3-d4.

21...♖e5 22.c3 c5 23.♔c2 d5!

This surprising move is also very strong. White wanted to play ♘d2-b3 and then d3-d4, in order to oust the enemy rook from the e5-square.

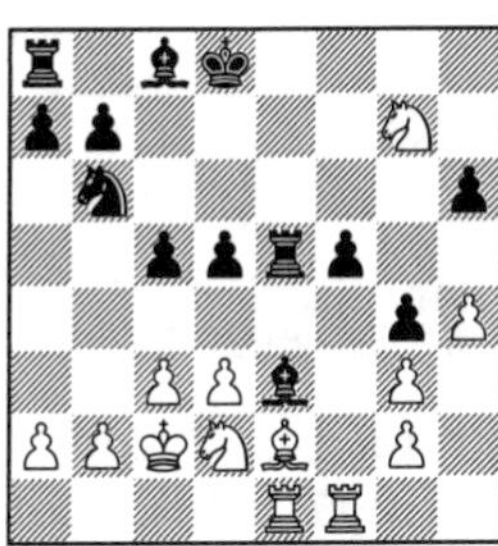

24.d4

After 24.♘b3, Black has the resource 24...d4!∓, securing reliable bases for his bishop on e3 and rook on e5 and maintaining a clear advantage.

White had here a very interesting move at his disposal in 24.b4!, with the idea of eliminating by all means the enemy pawn on c5. I have failed to find any advantage for Black:

24...cxb4 25.♘b3 bxc3 (25...♗d7 26.d4 ♖e4 27.♘c5 bxc3 28.♗d3 ♗d2 29.♗xe4 dxe4 30.♘xd7 ♔xd7 31.♖e2=) 26.d4 ♖e4 27.♗d3=;

24...d4 25.bxc5 ♖xc5 26.♘c4 ♘d5 27.♘xf5 ♗xf5 28.♖xf5 ♘b4 29.cxb4 ♖xf5 30.♗xg4 ♖f2 31.♔b3 ♖xg2 32.♘xe3 dxe3 33.♖xe3= and a draw is the most likely outcome.

24...cxd4 25.♗d3 dxc3 26.bxc3 d4

Black would not achieve much with 26...f4 27.gxf4 ♗xf4 28.♖d1 ♗g3 29.♖f8 ♔c7 30.♖f7= and White maintains the balance thanks to his piece-activity.

27.♘xf5 ♖c5 28.♘xe3 ♖xc3 29.♔b2

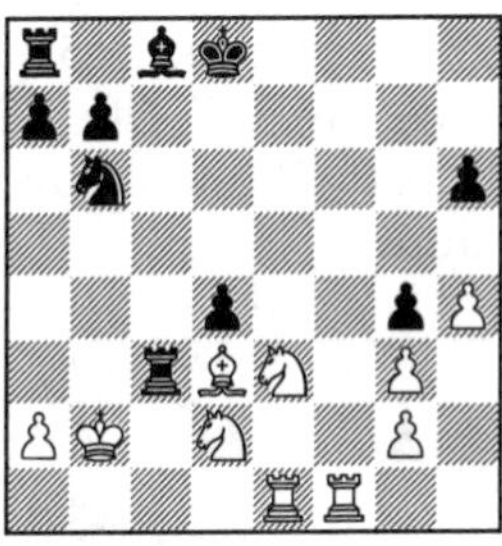

29...♘a4!

Here it would be bad for Black to play 29...♖xd3 30.♘ec4 ♘xc4 31.♘xc4 ♖xg3 32.♖f7↑. White seizes the initiative and with a tremendously powerful rook on the seventh rank he will at least manage to draw by perpetual check.

30.♔a1 dxe3 31.♖xe3 ♘c5 32.♖d1 ♖xd3 33.♖xd3 ♘xd3 34.♘e4 ♗f5 35.♖xd3

(diagram)

35...♔e7

It was much better for Black to advance his king to the queenside, because he could eventually cre-

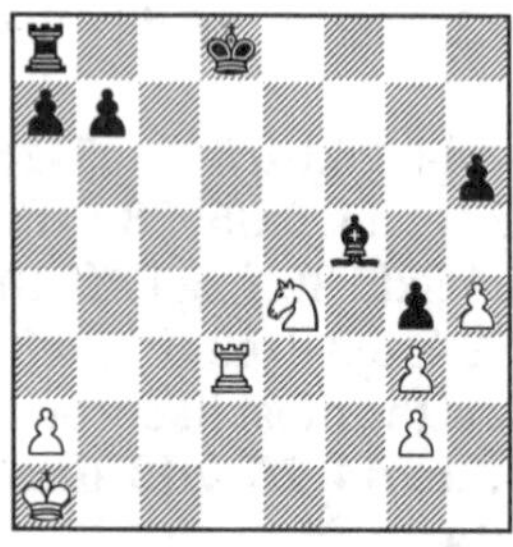

ate a passed pawn there: 35...♔c7 36.♖c3 ♔d7 37.♘c5 ♔c6∓, with excellent winning chances.

36.♖e3 ♖d8 37.♔b2 ♔f7 38. ♔c3 ♖d1 39.a3 ♔g6

Or 39...b6 40.♔c4 ♗xe4 (after 40...h5, White plays 41.♘c3= and his knight will go to the f4-square via e2) 41.♖xe4 h5 42.♖e5 ♖d2 43. ♖xh5 ♖xg2 44.♖h7 ♔f6 45.♖xa7 ♖xg3 46.♖a8= White should manage to draw.

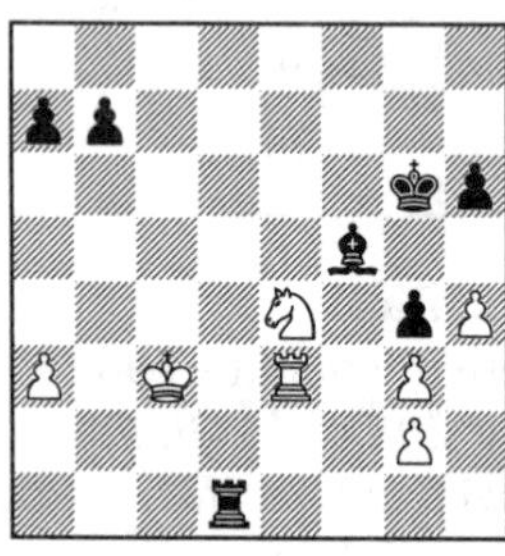

40.♔c4

This move is imprecise. It was better for White to opt for 40.♘c5 b6 41.♘e6= and he should not lose after transferring his knight to the f4-square.

40...b6

Black in turn makes a mistake. After 40...♗e6! 41.♔b4 ♔f5!∓ he would still have good chances of winning this game.

41.♘c3

White redeploys his knight to an active position and Black's edge evaporates.

41...♖d2 42.♘d5 ♔f7 43. ♖e7 ♔f8 44.♖e5 ♗g6 45.♘f4 ♗f7. Draw.

16 Ni Hua – Motylev

Tiayuan 2005

1.e4 e5 2.♘f3 ♘f6 3.♘xe5 d6 4.♘f3 ♘xe4 5.♗d3 ♘f6 6.h3 ♗e7 7.0–0 0–0

8.c3 b6 9.♗c2 ♗b7 10.d4 ♘bd7 11.♗g5 ♖e8 12.♖e1 ♘d5 13.♕d3 g6 14.♗d2 c5 15.c4 ♘c7 16.♗c3 d5=

17.♘bd2

This natural move is imprecise and enables Black to fight for the initiative.

It was correct for White to play 17.♘a3, with the following sample continuation: 17...♘e6 18.♖ad1 dxc4 19.♘xc4 ♘f4 20.♕e3 ♘d5 21. ♕d3 ♘f4= and a draw by repetition of moves.

17...b5! 18.cxb5

If 18.b3, then after 18...dxc4 19.bxc4 b4 20.♗b2 cxd4 21.♘xd4 ♘c5 22.♕g3 ♗f6∓ Black is slightly better, because his pawn-structure is superior and his pieces are more harmoniously deployed.

18...c4 19.♕e3 ♘xb5 20. ♗a4 a6∓

Black has seized more space and maintains an edge.

21.♗xb5 axb5 22.a3 ♗d6 23.♕h6 ♕f6 24.♘g5 ♕g7

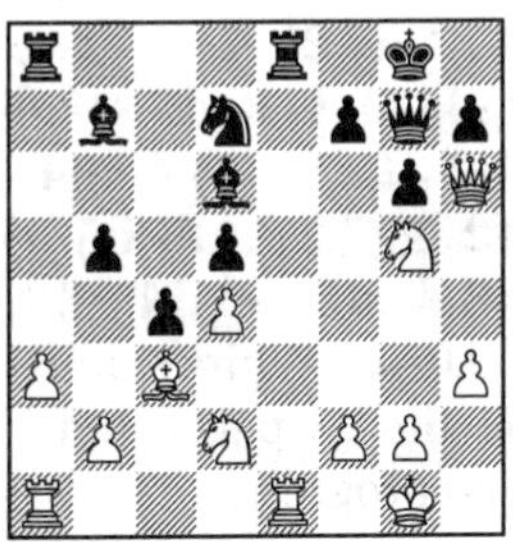

25.♖xe8

Black's position is preferable with queens present on the board and he can counter 25.♕h4 with 25...♘b6∓, with the idea of ♘b6-a4.

25...♖xe8 26.♕xg7 ♔xg7 27.♗b4 ♗f4 28.♘gf3 ♘b6 29. g3 ♗b8 30.♖e1 ♖xe1 31.♘xe1 ♗c8∓

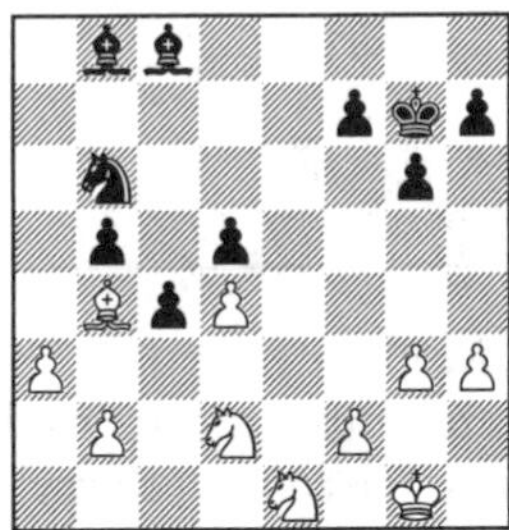

At this point the opponents agreed to a draw, which seems rather premature, because Black could have captured on a4 with his knight, creating serious problems for White.

17 Tiviakov – Giri

Germany 2010

1.e4 e5 2.♘f3 ♘f6 3.♘xe5 d6 4.♘f3 ♘xe4 5.♗d3 ♘f6 6. 0–0 ♗e7 7.h3 0–0

8.c3 ♖e8 9.♗c2 b6 10.d4 ♗b7 11.♘bd2 ♗f8 12.♘c4 ♘bd7

13.♗g5 h6 14.♗h4 g5 15.♗g3 ♘e4 16.♘fd2 ♘xg3 17.fxg3 ♘f6=

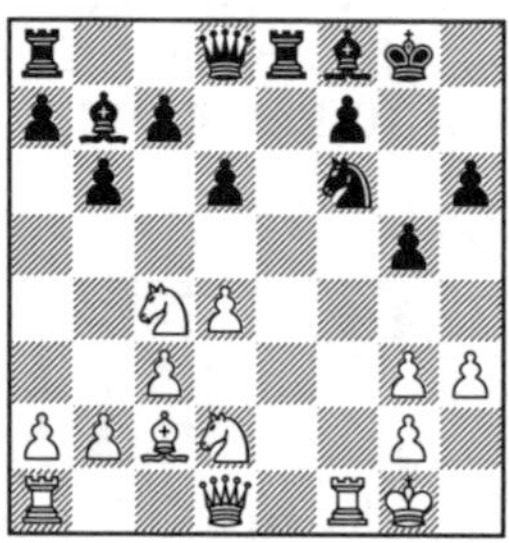

18.♖e1

White must try to exchange the rooks, because otherwise his queen cannot come into play, since it has no squares.

18...♖xe1

The position would be much more complex after 18...♕d7 19. ♘e3 ♖e7∞

19.♕xe1 ♕e7 20.♕xe7

If 20.♕f2, then Black continues with 20...♖e8, occupying the e-file and not allowing White's knight to go to the f5-square via e3.

20...♗xe7 21.♘e3 ♗f8 22. ♘f5 ♖e8 23.♗d3

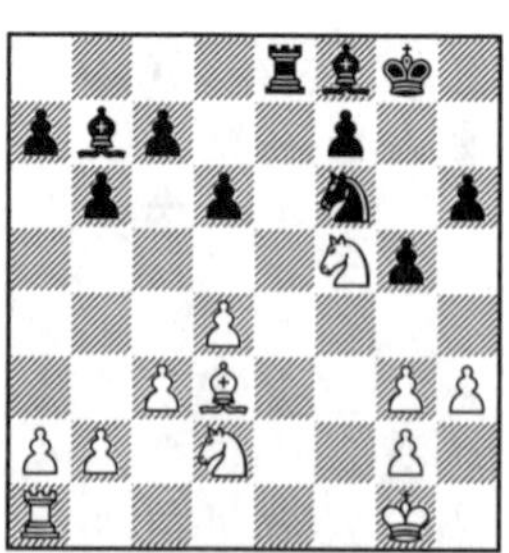

The f5-square is very weak; otherwise, Black would have the edge. Now the position is equal.

23...g4 24.♔f2 ♗c8

Black could have maintained the tension by playing 24...h5, but he decided to rely on simplification.

25.♖e1 ♖xe1 26.♔xe1 gxh3 27.gxh3 ♘d5

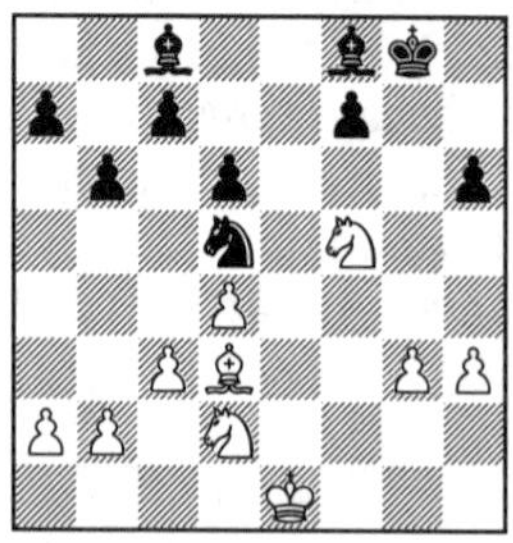

28.♔e2

It is slightly more precise for White to play 28.♘c4 ♘e7 29. ♘ce3 ♘xf5 30.♗xf5 ♗b7=, but even then the draw is certain. It is essential for Black to prevent the exchange of the light-squared bishops, since in that case he would end up with a "bad" dark-squared bishop. If he keeps both bishops, he has no problems whatsoever.

28...♘e7 29.♘xe7 ♗xe7 30. h4 ♗g4 31.♔e3 d5 32.♘f1 f5 33.♘h2 ♗d6 34.♘xg4 fxg4 35.♔f2 ♔g7 36.♗f5 h5 37.♗e6 c5 38.♗xd5 cxd4 39.cxd4 ♔h6. Draw. White's king must protect the g3-pawn and he can make no progress.

18 ZhangPengxiang–Motylev

Shanghai 2001

1.e4 e5 2.♘f3 ♘f6 3.♘xe5

d6 4.♘f3 ♘xe4 5.d4 d5 6.♗d3 ♘c6 7.0–0 ♗e7 8.c4 ♘b4

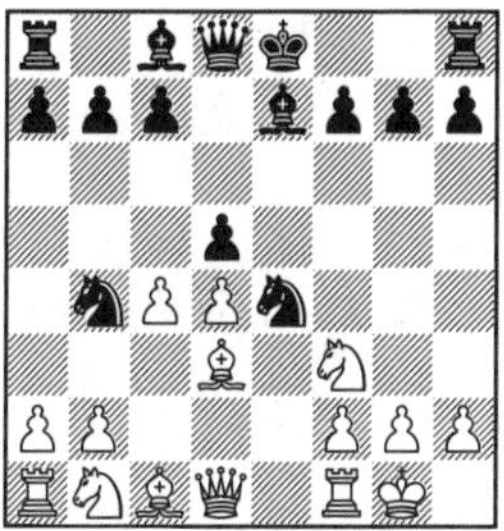

9.cxd5 ♘xd3 10.♕xd3 ♕xd5 11.♖e1 ♗f5 12.g4 ♗g6 13.♘c3 ♘xc3 14.♕xc3 f6 15.b3 ♔f7 16.♕xc7 ♖he8 17.♕c4 ♕xc4 18.bxc4 b6∓

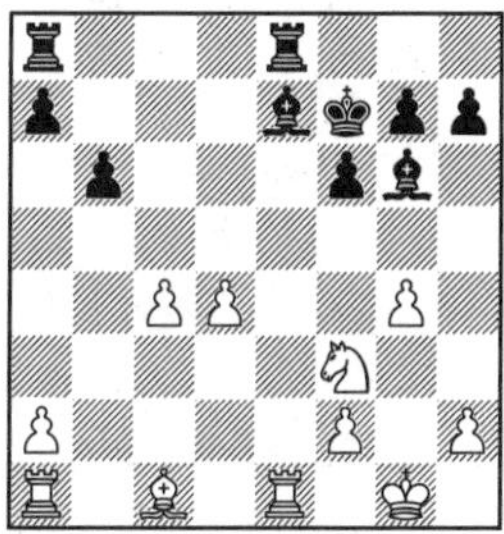

Black is a pawn down, but he has no problems at all. In fact, it is White who must play precisely, because his c4-pawn is not protected and the g4-pawn does not embellish his position either. If White had a light-squared bishop, instead of any other minor piece, his position would have been preferable.

19.♗b2

After this move White's kingside becomes even more vulnerable, in particular his f4-square.

Following 19.♗e3 ♖ac8 20.c5 (or 20.♘d2 ♗b4∓ and White is totally pinned, while after 20.♖ac1 ♗a3∓ he loses material) 20...bxc5 21.dxc5 ♗xc5 22.♗xc5 ♖xe1+ 23.♖xe1 ♖xc5∓ Black will be able to torture his opponent for a long time. His bishop is superior to the enemy knight and his rook is more active.

White needed imagination in order to reach equality. He could have solved his problems only after the not-so-obvious line: 19.♖e3! ♖ac8 20.♗a3!, exchanging the dark-squared bishops and maintaining the activity of his pieces. After 20...♗xa3 21.♖xa3 ♖xc4 22.♖xa7+ ♔f8 23.♖d1= Black has full compensation for the pawn, but no more than that. The game should end in a draw.

19...♖ac8 20.♖ac1 ♗d6 21.♖xe8

For 21.c5 ♗f4 22.♖xe8 ♖xe8 – see 21.♖xe8.

21...♖xe8 22.c5 ♗f4 23.♖c3 ♗e4

This bishop is ready to go to the d5-square, since this is the perfect place for it.

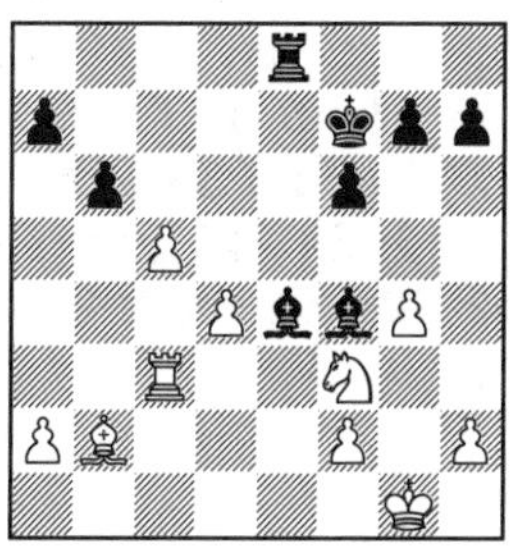

24.♘h4

White makes a mistake in a

difficult position. He wants to transfer his knight to the f5-square, but this proves to be impossible. After 24.♖a3, Black has the strong response 24...♗b8, keeping his queenside pawn-formation intact.

24...bxc5! 25.♖a3

It turns out that the c5-pawn is taboo, owing to the vulnerability of White's back rank.

After 25.♖xc5, Black wins with 25...♖b8–+, while if 25.dxc5 then 25...♖d8 wins.

25...♖b8 26.♖b3 c4–+

This is the simplest road to victory. Black's king goes to the d5-square after the trade of the rooks. The rest is very simple.

27.♖xb8 ♗xb8 28.♘g2 ♗xg2 29.♔xg2 ♔e6 30.h3 ♔d5 31.♔f3 g6 32.♔e3 ♗c7 33.♗c3 ♗b6 34.a4 a6 35.f3 f5 36.h4 fxg4 37.fxg4 h5 38.gxh5 gxh5 39.♔f4 ♗xd4 40.♗e1 c3 41.♔f5 c2 42.♗d2 ♔c4. White resigned.

19 Leko – Kramnik

Brissago (m/1) 2004

1.e4 e5 2.♘f3 ♘f6 3.♘xe5 d6 4.♘f3 ♘xe4 5.d4 d5 6.♗d3 ♘c6 7.0–0 ♗e7 8.c4 ♘b4

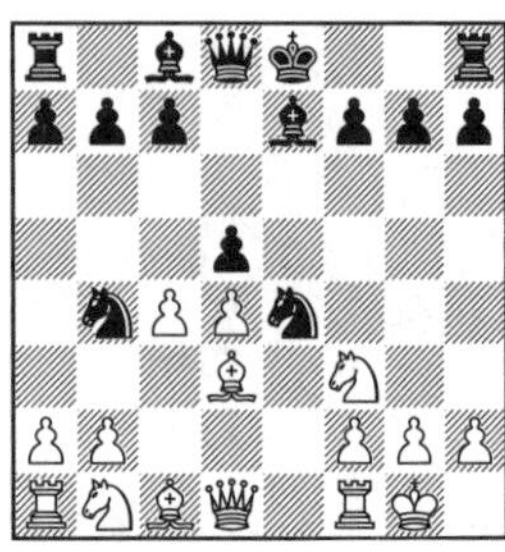

9.♗e2 0–0 10.♘c3 ♗f5 11.a3 ♘xc3 12.bxc3 ♘c6 13.♖e1 ♖e8 14.cxd5 ♕xd5 15.♗f4 ♖ac8 16.h3 ♗e4!

17.♗e3 ♘a5 18.c4 ♘xc4 19.♗xc4 ♕xc4 20.♘d2 ♕d5 21.♘xe4 ♕xe4 22.♗g5 ♕xe1+ 23.♕xe1 ♗xg5 24.♕a5 ♗f6 25.♕xa7 c5=

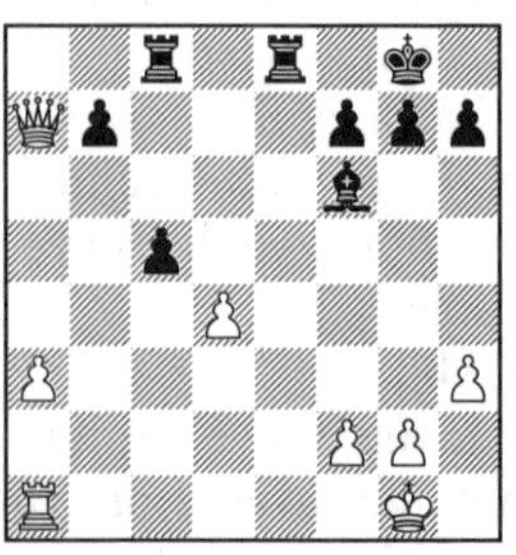

26.♕xb7

If White's rook escapes from the "X-ray" pressure of the enemy bishop with 26.♖b1, then Black plays 26...♗xd4 and after 27.♖xb7 ♖a8 28.♕b6 ♖xa3= White loses his only queenside pawn and, with it, any remaining illusions of being able to play for a win.

26...♗xd4 27.♖a2 c4

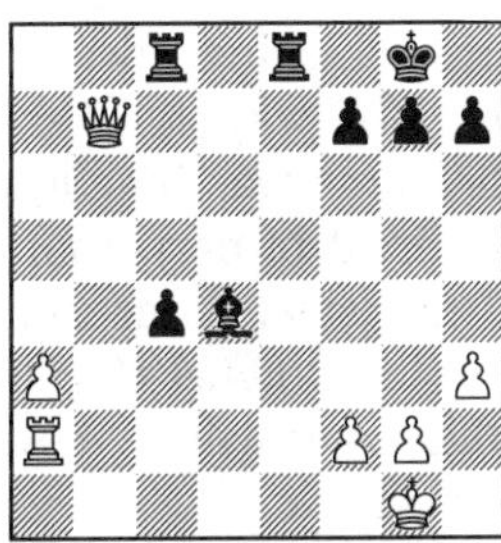

For the side having a queen against a rook and a bishop, it is usually advantageous to have an outside passed pawn. In this case however, White's a-pawn is not very dangerous, since Black's c-pawn has been advanced much further and is well supported by his pieces.

28.♖e2

Black can counter 28.♖c2 with 28...c3= and White's rook will remain passive.

28...♖ed8

After 28...c3?, the vulnerability of Black's back rank becomes the decisive factor and following 29.♖xe8+ ♖xe8 30.♕d7 ♖e1+ (30...♖b8 31.♕xd4 c2 32.♕d2+–) 31.♔h2 ♗e5+ 32.f4 ♗xf4+ 33.g3 ♖e2+ 34.♔g1+– White wins.

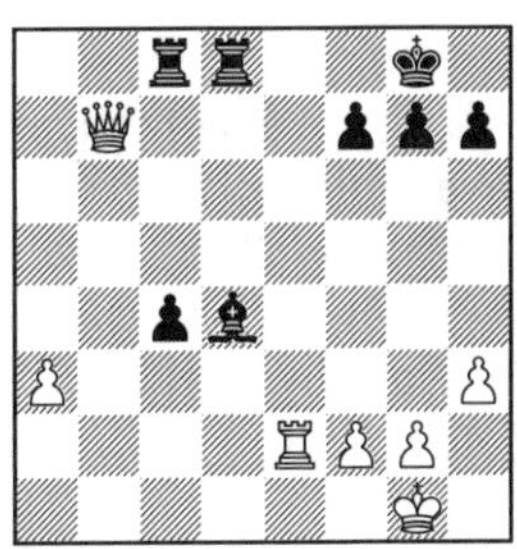

29.a4

If 29.♖d2, Black plays 29...♗f6 30.♖xd8+ ♖xd8= and he has everything protected and his c-pawn is ready to advance. After that he will use this pawn to deflect the enemy queen and will then pick up White's a-pawn. With pawns left on only one side of the board, the draw will become inevitable.

29...c3 30.♕e4

After 30.♕b3 ♖b8 31.♕c4 ♖dc8 32.♕d3 g6 33.♕xd4 (if White does not capture the bishop, Black plays ♖b8-b2!) 33...c2 34.♖xc2 ♖xc2∓. White's a-pawn will inevitably be lost, so Black is in no danger. In fact, it is White who will have to try to make a draw by a perpetual check on the kingside.

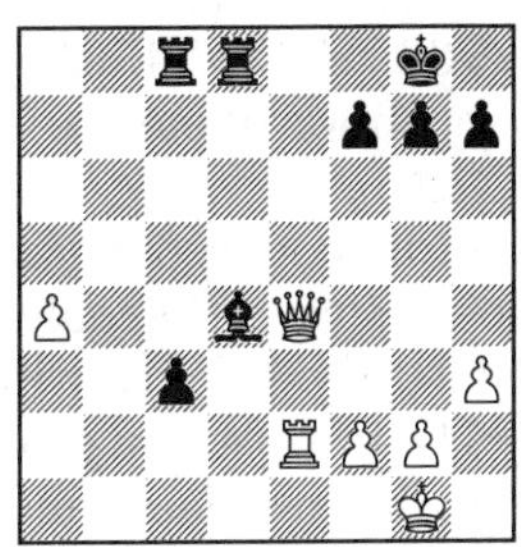

30...♗b6

This is a quiet positional reply. The advance of White's a-pawn has been stopped.

Black also had a tactical solution available: 30...g6!? 31.a5 ♗e5! 32.♕xe5 c2 33.♖xc2 ♖xc2 34.h4= when White should be able to draw by perpetual check after advancing his kingside pawns.

31.♕c2

White can also block the enemy c-pawn with his rook: 31.♖c2 ♗a5 32.♕f5 ♖a8= with a probable positional draw.

31...g6

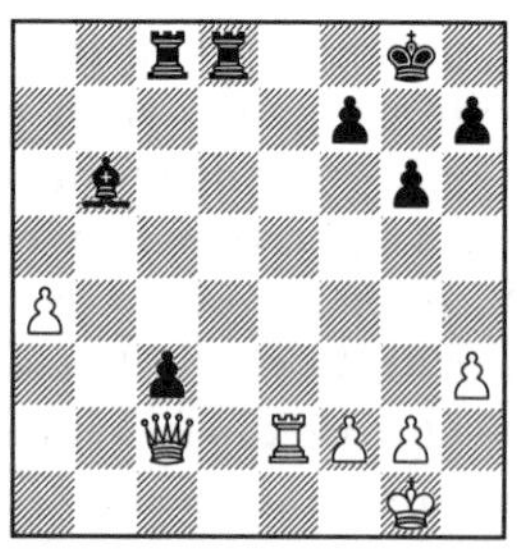

White's pawn is not threatening to advance, so Black has enough time to make a generally useful move.

32.♕b3 ♖d6

Here Black could have played 32...♗a5 33.♖e7 ♖f8 34.♖e2 ♖fd8= with a repetition of moves.

33.♖c2

White did not need to place his rook so passively. He could have maintained the balance with the move 33.g4=, planning to advance his h-pawn later and also securing the g2-square for his king.

33...♗a5 34.g4 ♖d2 35.♔g2 ♖cd8

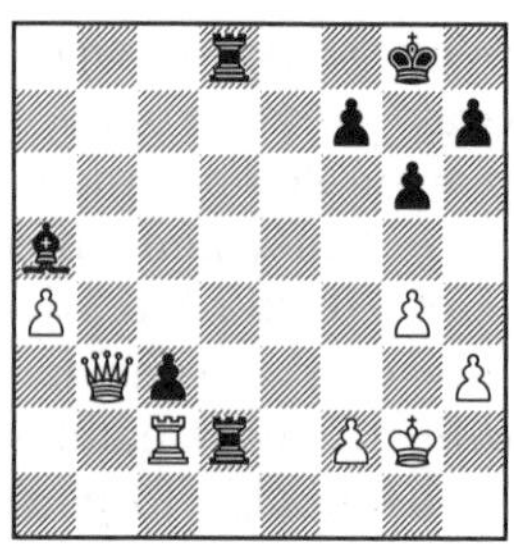

36.♖xc3?!

Now White will have great problems achieving a draw.

The right way for White to save the game was 36.g5!, creating the threat of perpetual check on the kingside. After 36...♖xc2 37.♕xc2 ♖d2 38.♕e4 c2 39.♕e8+ ♔g7 40.♕e5= it will be a draw by perpetual check.

36...♗xc3 37.♕xc3 ♖2d5

Black redeploys his rook to be able to capture the enemy a-pawn.

38.♕c6 ♖a5 39.♔g3 ♖da8 40.h4!

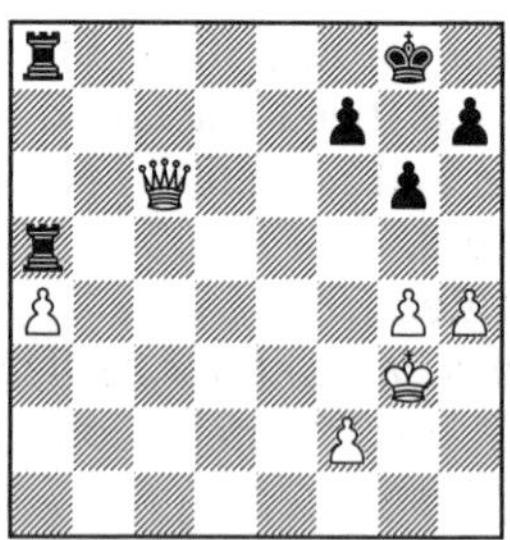

40...♖5a6

It would be imprecise for Black to play 40...♖xa4 41.h5=, intending h5-h6.

Black could have stopped the advance of White's h-pawn with 40...h6 41.h5 g5, although after 42.f4 (42.♕xh6? ♖8a6–+) 42...

gxf4+ 43.♔xf4 ♖xa4+ 44.♔g3 ♖4a6 45.♕d5∓ Black could have still tortured his opponent for a long time, transferring his rooks to attack the g4-pawn.

41.♕c1 ♖a5

Black continues to thwart the advance of the enemy h-pawn.

After the immediate 41...♖xa4, White can continue with 42.h5=

42.♕h6 ♖xa4 43.h5 ♖4a5

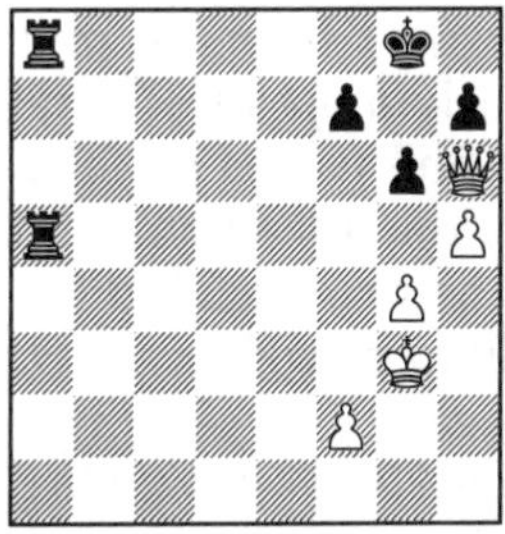

44.♕f4?

This is the decisive mistake. Now Black can keep the position closed, preventing the threat of perpetual check. Later he can redeploy his rooks for an attack against White's backward f-pawn.

Instead, White could have tried to open the position a little with the line: 44.hxg6 hxg6∓. There would still be plenty of fight left, but a draw would be the most likely result.

44...g5!–+ 45.♕f6 h6!

(diagram)

Thanks to this possibility, Black is able to cement his kingside pawn-structure.

46.f3

46.♕xh6 ♖8a6–+

An attempt to play actively

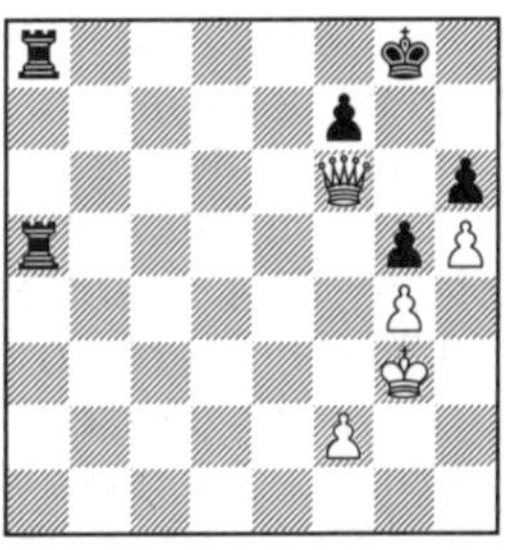

would fail; after 46.f4, Black wins for example with 46...♖a2 47.♔f3 ♖8a3+ 48.♔e4 ♖a4+ 49.♔e3 ♖2a3+ 50.♔e2 ♖b3–+, combining his threats to capture White's pawns with mating threats with his rooks.

46...♖5a6 47.♕c3 ♖a4 48.♕c6 ♖8a6 49.♕e8+ ♔g7 50.♕b5 ♖4a5 51.♕b4 ♖d5 52.♕b3 ♖ad6 53.♕c4 ♖d3!

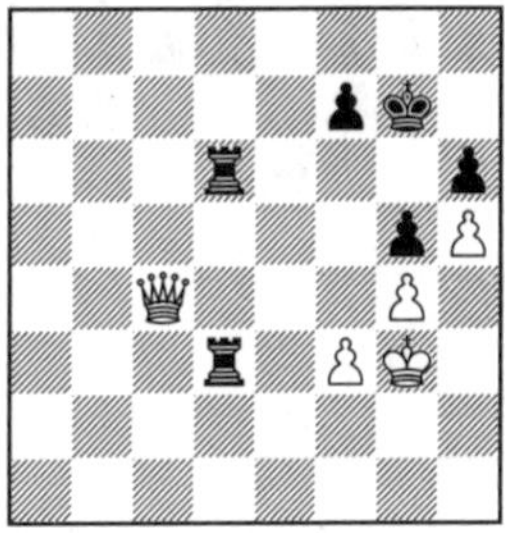

White is in zugzwang. If his queen retreats, Black redeploys his rooks for an attack against the f3-pawn, while if White's king retreats to the second rank, Black is able to avoid his rook being attacked with check and he wins a tempo for the transfer of his other rook to the f6-square.

54.♔f2 ♖a3 55.♕c5

After 55.f4 Black continues with 55...♖d2+ 56.♔e1 ♖h2! 57.

♕d4+ ♔g8 58.fxg5 ♖a1+ 59.♕xa1 ♖h1−+, winning the queen.

55...♖a2+ 56.♔g3 ♖f6. White's f3-pawn falls and the rest is simple. **57.♕b4 ♖aa6 58.♔g2 ♖f4 59.♕b2+ ♖af6 60.♕e5 ♖xf3 61.♕a1 ♖f1 62.♕c3 ♖1f2+ 63.♔g3 ♖2f3+ 64.♕xf3 ♖xf3+ 65.♔xf3 ♔f6**. White resigned.

20 Grischuk – Ivanchuk
Linares 2009

1.e4 e5 2.♘f3 ♘f6 3.♘xe5 d6 4.♘f3 ♘xe4 5.d4 d5 6.♗d3 ♘c6 7.0–0 ♗e7 8.c4 ♘b4 9. ♗e2 0–0 10.♘c3 ♗f5 11.a3 ♘xc3 12.bxc3 ♘c6 13.♖e1 ♖e8 14.cxd5 ♕xd5 15.♗f4 ♖ac8 16. h3 h6 17.g4 ♗g6

18.♗f1 ♗d6 19.♖xe8+ ♖xe8 20.c4 ♕e4 21. ♗e3 ♖d8 22.♗g2 ♕e7 23.g5 ♗c5 24.♖a2 ♗h5 25.♖d2 ♗xa3 26.gxh6 ♗b4∓

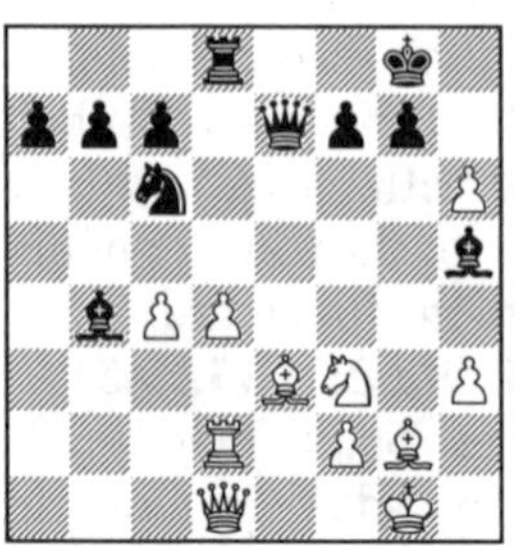

White has a pawn-centre, but Black's prospects are better thanks to his powerful pressure against it.

27.♖d3 ♖d6

This rook is going to the g6-square, from where it will exert pressure along the g-file and protect Black's king.

He cannot achieve much with the concrete variation 27...♗g6 28.♖b3 ♘a5 29.♗g5 f6 30.♖e3∞

It would be more promising for Black to opt for 27...a5!?, advancing his passed pawn and bolstering the bishop on b4. All this might be very useful in the eventual sharp struggle.

28.c5

After 28.♗f4 ♖g6 29.hxg7 ♗d6 30.♗xd6 cxd6∓, the material is equal, but Black retains the initiative.

28...♖g6 29.♗f4

29...♕f6

It would be more precise to continue with the immediate 29... gxh6 30.♗g3 a5∓ since Black's queen would not be forced to go from e7 to f6 as happened in the game. After 31.♔h2 b6 32.cxb6 (32.d5? ♘e5−+) 32...cxb6 33.

♕b3, White still preserves some compensation for the exchange, but only enough for equality at best.

30.♗g3 gxh6 31.♔h2 a5 32.♕a4

White wants to put his queen on b5, or advance d4-d5.

Instead, 32.♕b3∞ was worth considering, with the rather unpleasant threat of ♕b3-d5; the position would then have remained unclear.

32...♗xf3

After 32...♕f5 White continues with 33.♕b5±, with somewhat better chances. Thus Black's exchanging operation is completely justified.

33.♗xf3

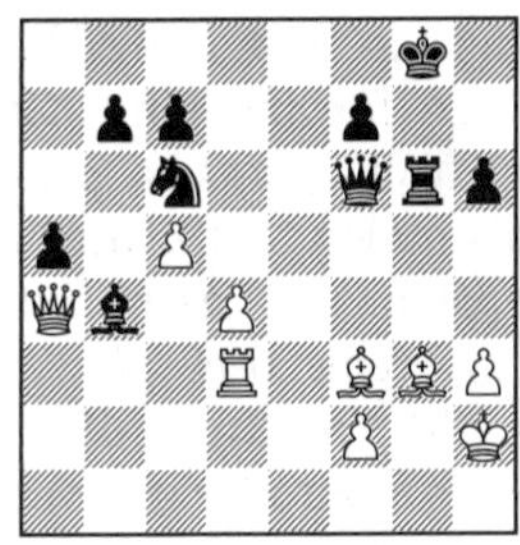

33...♖xg3! 34.fxg3 ♘xd4 35.♗g2 c6 36.♕d1 ♗xc5 37. ♕g4+ ♔f8

After 37...♔h7, White can play 38.h4=, depriving his opponent of the g5-square, after which Black cannot avoid perpetual check.

38.♕c8+ ♔g7 39.♕g4+ ♔f8 40.♕c8+ ♔g7 41.♕g4+. Draw

21 Karjakin – Gelfand

Monaco (blindfold) 2011

1.e4 e5 2.♘f3 ♘f6 3.♘xe5 d6 4.♘f3 ♘xe4 5.♘c3 ♘xc3 6. dxc3 ♗e7 7.♗e3 0–0 8.♕d2 ♘d7 9.0–0–0 ♘e5 10.h4 c6 11. c4 ♗e6 12.♘g5 ♗f5 13.f3 f6 14. ♘h3 ♗e6 15.b3 a6 16.♘f4 ♗f7∓

17.♕f2

Here White should have preferred 17.♘d3 b5 18.♘xe5∓, reducing the attacking potential of his opponent's pieces. After 18... fxe5 or 18...dxe5 Black would retain the initiative, but White would have considerable chances of equalizing.

17...b5 18.c5 ♕c7

It was also very good for Black to play the immediate 18...a5!?↑, when his threat of a5-a4 would be very serious, while White would have no chances of effectively exploiting the pin along the d-file.

19.♘d3

If White continues with the positional pawn-sacrifice 19.g3 dxc5 20.♗h3, with the idea ♘f4-e6, then Black responds with 20... c4 21.♘e6 ♕a5∓, preserving his extra pawn and the initiative.

19...a5 20.cxd6

It is no improvement for White to opt for 20.♘xe5 dxe5↑ – Black's initiative is dangerous and he can combine the threat of a5-a4 with the advance of his f- and e- pawns.

20...♗xd6 21.♗b6 ♕b8 22. ♗c5

White is trying to ease his defence by exchanging pieces.

22...♖d8

Here it was even stronger for Black to choose the straightforward move 22...a4↑ when White would come under a dangerous attack.

23.♘xe5 ♗xe5 24.♖xd8+ ♕xd8 25.f4 ♗d6 26.♗d3 a4 27. ♖d1 axb3 28.cxb3 ♗xc5 29. ♕xc5 ♕c7 30.♔b1 ♖d8 31.♕c2

31.♗c2 ♖xd1+ 32.♗xd1 ♕xf4 33.♕xc6=

31...♔h8 32.g3

Or 32.♕e2 ♖d4 33.g3 followed by moving the bishop out of the pin on the d-file.

32...♕d7

33.f5

White blocks the b1-h7 diagonal in this way to prevent Black's bishop from occupying it later.

However, White's pawn is rather misplaced on f5, since it restricts the movements of his own bishop. His only chance of saving the game was 33.♕e2! ♗g6 34. ♔c2 ♕a7 35.♗xg6 ♕xa2+ 36.♔c1 ♖xd1+ 37.♔xd1 ♕a1+ (The king and pawn ending arising after 37...♕xe2+ 38.♔xe2 hxg6 39.♔e3 c5 40.♔e4= is a draw.) 38.♔c2 hxg6 39.♕e4∓ and having regained his pawn, White should be able to save the game.

33...♕d6!

Black's queen exerts pressure across the whole board from this square.

34.♕f2 ♗d5!

Black's bishop has occupied a solid outpost in the centre. Black is ready to continue with h7-h6 on the kingside, obtaining the safe h7-square for his king. On the queenside he plans to penetrate with his queen to a3, after which his c-pawn will carry out the crushing break c6-c5-c4!

35.♕f4 ♕a3 36.♗e4?

This is a blunder in a very difficult position, most probably due to the fact that the game was played blindfold.

But even after the natural line: 36.♕d4 c5 37.♕b2 ♕a5 38.♗c2 h5!∓ White would be faced with a very difficult defence, because Black's king is safely sheltered, while its white counterpart is exposed.

36...♗xe4+ 37.♕xe4 ♖xd1+. White resigned.